PUBLICATIONS

OF THE

NAVY RECORDS SOCIETY

VOL. 149

SEA POWER AND THE CONTROL OF TRADE

The NAVY RECORDS SOCIETY was established in 1893 for the purpose of printing unpublished manuscripts and rare works of naval interest. The Society is open to all who are interested in naval history, and any person wishing to become a member should apply to the Hon. Secretary, Department of War Studies, King's College London, Strand, London WC2R 3LS. The annual subscription is £30, which entitles the member to receive one free copy of each work issued by the Society in that year, and to buy earlier issues at much reduced prices.

SUBSCRIPTIONS and orders for back volumes should be sent to the Membership Secretary, 1 Avon Close, Petersfield, Hants GU31 4LG.

THE COUNCIL OF THE NAVY RECORDS SOCIETY wish it to be clearly understood that they are not answerable for any opinions and observations which may appear in the Society's publications. For these the editors of the several works are entirely responsible.

SEA POWER AND THE CONTROL OF TRADE

Belligerent Rights from the Russian War to the
Beira Patrol, 1854–1970

Edited by

NICHOLAS TRACY

PUBLISHED BY ROUTLEDGE
FOR THE NAVY RECORDS SOCIETY

First published 2005 by Ashgate Publishing Limited

Published 2018 by Routledge
2 Park Square, Milton Park, Abingdon, Oxon OX14 4RN
52 Vanderbilt Avenue, New York, NY 10017

Routledge is an imprint of the Taylor & Francis Group, an informa business

© The Navy Records Society, 2005

Crown copyright material is reproduced by permission of The Stationery Office.

British Library Cataloguing in Publication Data

Sea power and the control of trade : belligerent rights from the Russian War to the Beira Patrol, 1854–1970. – (Publications of the Navy Records Society ; v. 149)
1.War, Maritime (International law) – History – 20th century – Sources 2.War, Maritime (International law) – History – 19th century – Sources 3.Sea-power – History – 20th century – Sources 4.Sea-power – History – 19th century – Sources 5.Great Britain – History, Naval – 20th century – Sources 6. Great Britain – History – 19th century – Sources I.Tracy, Nicholas, 1944– II.Navy Records Society (Great Britain)
341.4'5'09

Library of Congress Cataloging-in-Publication Data

Tracy, Nicholas, 1944–
    Sea power and the control of trade : belligerent rights from the Russian War to the Beira patrol : 1854–1970 / Nicholas Tracy.
        p. cm. — (Navy Records Society Publications; vol. 149)
    Includes index.
    ISBN 0-7546-5367-6
    1. War, Maritime (International law) – History. 2. Belligerency – History. 3. Sea control – History. 4. Capture at sea – History. 5. Freedom of the seas – History. 6. Shipping – History. I. Title. II. Publications of the Navy Records Society; vol. 149.

KZ6563.T73 2005
343.09'6–dc22
                                                                                            2004060796
ISBN 13: 978-0-7546-5367-7 (hbk) 978-1-911-42378-2 (pbk)

Typeset in Times by Manton Typesetters, Louth, Lincolnshire, UK.

CONTENTS

CHRONOLOGY

Some dates of Treaties, Acts, and Orders Respecting Belligerent Rights

2 March 1853– 27 April 1856	Russian War	
16 April 1856	Declaration of Paris	First revision of the laws of naval warfare.
23 June 1864	An Act for Regulating Naval Prize of War	Implementing the Declaration of Paris.
12 April 1861– 9–12 April 1865	US Civil War	
8 May 1871	Treaty of Washington	Treaty between Her Majesty and the United States of America for the amicable settlement of all causes of difference between the two countries.
29 July 1899	Hague (1), Convention III	Adaptation to maritime warfare of principles of Geneva Convention of 1864.
18 October 1907	Hague (2), Convention II	Limitation of employment of force for recovery of contract debts.
	Hague (3), Convention VI	Status of enemy merchant ships at the outbreak of hostilities.
	Hague (4), Convention VII	Conversion of merchant ships into war ships.
	Hague (5), Convention VIII	Laying of automatic submarine contact mines.

	Hague (6), Convention IX	Bombardment by naval forces in time of war.
	Hague (7), Convention X	Adaptation to maritime war of the principles of the Geneva Convention.
	Hague (8), Convention XI	Restrictions with regard to the exercise of the right of capture in naval war.
	Hague (9), Convention XIII	Rights and duties of neutral powers in naval war.
4 December 1908– 26 February 1909	London Naval Conference	Drafting the Declaration of London concerning the laws of naval war.
28 June 1911	Introduction of Naval Prize Bill into Parliament	Intended to implement the Declaration of London – not passed
1 August 1914– 11 November 1918	The Great War	
29 October 1914	Order in Council	Authorising rationing of neutral states – the first of a long series of such orders.
7 July 1916	Order in Council	Declaring the Declaration of London not part of British policy.
8 January 1918	President Woodrow Wilson's Fourteen Points	Proposing terms for a negotiated peace treaty.
28 June 1919	Treaty of Versailles	Peace treaty between Central Powers, the Entente and the United States. Includes the Covenant establishing the League of Nations.
6 February 1922	Washington Treaty	Five-power naval limitation treaty, placing limitations of capital ships and aircraft carriers.

16 October 1925	The Locarno Pact	Treaty of mutual guarantee between Germany, Belgium, France, Great Britain and Italy.
20 June 20– 4 August 1927	Geneva Conference	
5 December 1927	Formation of Sub-Committee of the Committee of Imperial Defence to consider the problem of Belligerent Rights	
27 August 1928	Kellogg–Briand Pact	Treaty between the United States and other Powers providing for the renunciation of war as an instrument of national policy.
22 January 22– 22 April 1930	Second London Naval Conference	Drafts Treaty of London of 22 April 1930 extending naval arms limitations to cruisers and smaller vessels.
2 February 1932	Geneva Disarmament Conference	
December 1935	Third London Naval Conference	Japan withdraws from naval controls and Germany agrees to reduced limitations.
3 September 1939– 2 September 1945	The Second World War	
26 June 1945	Charter of the United Nations	
8 August 1945	Nuremberg Trial Proceedings	Charter of the International Military Tribunal.
4 April 1949	North Atlantic Treaty	Creating a defensive alliance between Canada, the United States and the states of Western Europe.

12 August 1949	Additional protocols to the Geneva Convention	Deliberate starvation of civilians banned as a means of warfare.
25 June 1950–27 July 1953	Korean War	
22 October–21 November 1962	Cuban Missile Crisis	
20 November 1965–25 June 1975	Beira Blockade	

GENERAL INTRODUCTION

The capacity of navies to influence world events through control of seaborne trade was profoundly affected by nineteenth-century developments in economic theory, commercial organization, and naval technology. In turn, these changing circumstances led, from the outbreak of the Russian war in 1854, to repeated attempts to rewrite the international law of belligerent rights at sea. This collection of departmental files and treaties is intended to review the changing perceptions in the British government of the utility of naval control of trade, providing at once historical documentation, and material for analysis of the conflicting influences on policy and naval strategy.

The number of documents in the nineteenth century which bring light on British attitudes to belligerent rights at sea are relatively few, and consist largely of letters between government leaders, with some diplomatic communications. The apparatus for study of naval strategy was significantly improved by the formation of the Committee of Imperial Defence (CID) in 1904. From then, until the Second World War, the question of belligerent rights at sea was almost continuously under scrutiny, after 1927, by a Sub-Committee of CID. From the time of the Napoleonic war, questions about belligerent rights were the most divisive issue in Anglo-American relations, and the degree of attention the British government had to devote to the legal restraints on naval strategy kept pace with the growing naval and economic potential of the United States which was the only country in a position to pose a serious threat to British sea power.

The focus of this collection is on the work during the years of peace in preparation for war. This work was marked by a series of milestones: the need to find a modus vivendi with France at the eve of the Russian War; and the first effort at recodification of prize law in the post-war Declaration of Paris, 1856; the need to deal with the consequences of the American Civil War; the Peace Conferences at the Hague, which led to the London Conference which drafted the Declaration of London, 1909; the apparent effect of the economic blockade on the outcome of the First World War; the need to assess the significance for naval law of the formation of the League of Nations in 1919; and of the Kellogg-Briand Pact, 1927.

The First World War was the great experiment in the use of economic controls to deny enemy access to supply. There are masses of documents relating to the practicalities of enforcement, and of the consequential international complications. It has only been possible to include a few samples, of orders-in-council, and naval instructions. These are put in perspective by two extensive reviews of the wartime experience prepared for the Imperial War Cabinet, and for the Committee of Imperial Defence. These papers also serve as the launching point for the interwar discussion of belligerent rights, which is the most extensive part of the collection. The First World War vastly enhanced the prestige of naval blockade, and the systematic manipulation of prize law to circumvent the limitations imposed during the prior decades of peace contributed substantially to the post-war discussion. Circumstances during the Second World War no less greatly deflated the value accorded to economic blockade. Following the latter war, there were a number of occasions on which the British government had to respond to the exercise of belligerent rights by other states, but in the nuclear age there no longer was any expectation that naval control of commerce would again prove a decisive means of protecting British interests. In any event, the formation of the United Nations had largely put an end to the context in which hitherto Britain had exercised belligerent rights. The concept of neutrality all but disappeared, and resolutions of the United Nations Security Council became all the law of belligerency which was required, although states continued to be subject to the conditions of the 1949 Geneva Convention and the Cold War imposed a high degree of circumspection. Due to the impossibility of obtaining clearance to publish official documents concerning events less than thirty years ago, the last to appear in this collection relate to the role of the Royal Navy in the United Nations mandated Beira patrol.

* * *

In the age of sail practicalities had ensured that the focus of maritime trade war was on the seizure of valuable cargoes, both to deny them to the enemy, and to ensure that they could be pressed into use by the belligerent. Raiding enemy shipping also served to promote the trade of the belligerent by undermining the ability of the enemy to bring his goods to market at a competitive price. The marine insurance market played a role in that the more successful naval power could insure its shipping for smaller premiums. In the eighteenth century the British marine insurance business was extended to selling war-risk insurance to enemy ship owners, who thereby subsidised the British war economy through their payment of premiums. Captured ships might be sold back to their original owners. The strategies of peacetime protectionism and wartime trade control differed only in degree. Wartime mercantilist trade war was unquestionably, in Clausewitz's well-known phrase, the 'continuation by other means' of the protectionist economic policies of nations in peace time.

Mercantilist objectives were operationally coherent with the strategic calculus of states which were able to control relatively small financial resources. Wealth gained by seizing enemy shipping, and by taking monopolistic control of markets, was a strategic means of underwriting the cost of conducting naval and military operations. Naval warfare was carried out by the co-operation of public and private investment, both of which depended upon prize taking – to reward underpaid naval officers and unpaid privateersmen, and to pay dividends to investors in private warships. In the larger view, the monopolisation of markets was of greater national importance because the enhanced trade provided the tax base on which not only naval warfare, but also operations ashore, depended.

Attacks on very high-value targets, such as treasure ships, served both the mercantilist strategy, and to impoverish the enemy. Spain was most vulnerable to such attacks. Because of the very limited number of treasure ships sailing in any year, with well-established ports of departure and arrival and well-established times of sailing, there were some dramatic successes. Attempts to employ naval forces to deny an enemy access to bulk resources, on the other hand, were usually defeated by the limitations of contemporary naval technology. The most notable exception was the interception of naval stores needed for the mobilisation of war fleets. These cargoes were so bulky and so heavy that they had to be delivered by sea to the dockyards where they would be used, and naval powers had every incentive to focus their blockade effort to intercept the flow of naval stores to their enemy.

Mercantilist strategy began to fall into disrepute in the middle of the eighteenth century when Dean Tucker and Adam Smith began to argue that a monopoly of wealth was a logical absurdity, because nations could only become rich if their trading partners were also rich. This new thinking led Britain and France to an agreement to reduce tariffs. This first tentative step towards what is now referred to as the globalisation of trade was unpopular amongst the French bourgeoisie, and was one of the complaints which led to the French Revolution. The naval wars with the French republic and empire were fought with the old mercantilist strategic tools. Napoleon established military control over most of continental Europe partly in order to control access to its markets. In turn Britain employed the Royal Navy to control neutral trade as a means of forcing British commerce on Napoleon's vassal states, thus generating the wealth which was used to defeat Bonapartism by subsidising the armies of Austria, Prussia and Russia. Following the war, however, commercial lobbies succeeded in putting an end to protectionist economic controls in Britain. A vigorous campaign led to the repeal in 1846 of the protectionist 'corn laws' which were symbolic of Britain's mercantilist empire. There was no comparable public demand for repeal of the Navigation Act which restricted imports to goods transported on board British ships, and ships registered in the state from whence the goods originated. It was generally recognised that naval defence depended upon a substantial merchant marine. Nevertheless, the reforming spirit of government led to the virtual repeal of the Navigation Act in 1849.

Re-evaluation of naval strategy was stimulated by the collateral damage suffered by both sides in the Anglo-French war as a result of their operations to control trade. Because the strategic value of naval action to control trade depends upon that control being extended over neutral shipping, the power of neutral states to protect their own interests has always been the most important restraint on the abuse of prize law. The cost to Britain of its economic strategy against Napoleon had been a declaration of war by the United States in 1812. Napoleon's 'Continental System' was even more disastrous for the French Empire, as it contributed to the Spanish revolt, and the renewal in 1812 of war with Russia in which the Grand Army was destroyed at Borodino and in the long winter retreat from Moscow. With the return of peace, the arguments resurfaced that the protection the state accorded trade came at an unacceptable cost, economically as well as internationally. US Secretary of State Adams approached the British government in 1823 with a project for a treaty to abolish altogether 'private war' at sea.

The abandonment of protectionist trade policy created a fundamental distinction between the economics of war and of peace. The economic sinews of war are measured less by the absolute wealth of the belligerents than by their economic and production capacity relative to their enemies. In peacetime the wealth of neighbouring nations is an advantage, whereas in wartime even the wealth of neutral nations may pose difficulties. But the dichotomy between the economic strategies for peace and those for war was obscured in mid-nineteenth century Britain by the competitiveness of British industry and trade. The experience of the last war had encouraged a view that enemy traders would always seek to evade state control, so as to be able to get their cargoes to market.

The economist David Ricardo argued that it was unnecessary to protect home production because business interests would always seek to supply a market, even an 'enemy' one in wartime.[1] As war loomed with Russia, voices demanded that trade be permitted to continue without state interference.

The lobby for free trade in wartime on the part of business interests in the only state which had significant naval forces, and which had financed the recent war against Napoleon by trade control, appears to be quixotic. The merchants' demands, however, were a logical consequence of the faith with which *laissez-faire* principles had come to be held. Mercantilist trade war was a system aimed less at injuring the enemy than at maximising national wealth for all purposes, including those of war. If free trade was indeed a significant multiplier of wealth, then to many contemporary minds it appeared that free trade should be regarded as the correct means of paying for war, or at least it should be by states such as Britain which had the commercial and technical resources to play a dominant role in international trade. Free trade in wartime, in that context, was a modification rather than an abandonment of the mercantilist strategy, and it enjoyed the very great attraction as a strategy that it could not provoke conflict with neutral traders.

The relative invulnerability of Russia to British economic pressure encouraged the abandonment of the old trade strategies when war was declared in March 1854. The immediate concern was the threat that Russia would resort to the perfectly legal means of conducting trade war at nominal cost by issuing letters of marque to business interests in neutral countries, authorising their equipment of privateer warships to cruise against British trade. Britain also had to deal with the implications of the alliance with the French, who maintained somewhat different interpretations of international law with respect to maritime prize.

The long-established British doctrine was that enemy-owned cargoes were liable to seizure even if being transported in neutral ships, and that neutral ships were themselves vulnerable to capture if they participated in any trade which would have been closed to them in peacetime by the domestic laws of the enemy state – the 'Rule of 1756'. This was entirely logical, and was essential if naval action in wartime was to deny the enemy the ability to conduct trade. British interpretation of prize law also provided for the release of neutral cargoes taken when an enemy ship was captured. This was less logical as it made it possible

[1]'An Essay on the Influence of a Low Price of Corn on the Profits of Stock, etc'; see William D. Grampp, *The Manchester School of Economics*, Stanford, 1960, p. 23.

for an enemy shipper to earn neutral freights, but it was pragmatic as it reduced conflict with neutrals.

French prize courts, on the other hand, usually asserted the immunity of neutral shipping to arrest even if transporting enemy-owned cargo – the principle that 'Free Ships mean Free Goods'. This policy served the interests of a lesser naval power, and also had the advantage that it reduced conflict with neutral states. The United States favoured the French position, and concluded between 1824 and 1850 a series of treaties with the successor states to the Spanish Empire in South America which recognised the principle. They also recognised the principle favoured by the French that neutral cargoes in enemy ships might be seized.

The opinion of the First Lord in the Earl of Aberdeen's administration, Sir James Graham, was that Britain should not herself issue letters of marque in this war against Russia, and should make it illegal for any Briton to accept a privateer commission from a foreign state [1]. He also suggested that, in order to facilitate co-operation with France, the fleet should be instructed to respect neutral shipping for the duration of the war, provided their cargoes were not contraband intended for the armed forces of the enemy, and that they respect any close blockade imposed on enemy ports. For their part, the French agreed to suspend their practice of condemning neutral-owned goods captured as part of the cargo of enemy merchant shipping. It was also agreed not to employ privateers. This self-denial was conceived of primarily as an inducement to neutrals not to admit Russian privateers into their ports.

Given the decision not to undertake a general sea-denial campaign, the suppression of privateering did not significantly reduce British and French naval power in the Russian war. Its importance lay in the precedent thereby established. In conducting their negotiations, the British and French governments were less interested in the Russian war than they were in the prospect of a future war between themselves. For that reason, the French agreement not to issue letters of marque was made against the objections of the Minister of Marine, Theodore Ducos.[1]

Suppression of privateering was entirely consistent with the belief that war would be won the more quickly if commerce were impeded as little as possible. The long-term implications for Britain of herself adopting the policy of 'free ships mean free goods' were very serious indeed, but the new free trade climate encouraged the risk, and certainly

---

[1]C.I. Hamilton, 'Anglo-French Seapower and the Declaration of Paris', *The International History Review*, vol. IV, No. 1, February 1982, pp. 166–90.

something had to be done to facilitate co-operation with France. Long-term considerations also determined American policy. Secretary of State Marcy would not agree to ban privateers from American ports, and urged that the doctrine of 'free ships *mean* free goods' should be made a permanent doctrine of British prize law. In July the United States concluded a treaty with Russia establishing that principle.[1] During the war, however, no privateers operated out of American ports.

J.L. Ricardo, son of the great economist, was not alone in viewing the blockade of Russia as useless.[2] The Anglo-French blockades did have a fiscal effect on the Russian war economy. Russian exports fell by 80 per cent between 1853 and 1855, to the consternation of British importers of Russian raw materials, and Russian imports fell by 33 per cent. In consequence, Russian customs revenue was injured. However, the failure of the Anglo-French blockade to coerce the tsar's government is consistent with the experience of three centuries. Ricardo *fils* should have been more interested in the success of the Anglo-French strategy in sustaining the cost of their own war effort.

After the conclusion of peace at a congress in Paris in 1856, Tsar Alexander II invited the world powers to conclude an instrument redefining belligerent rights at sea. The Declaration of Paris was the international effort to replace, in part, the case law which had been developed by prize courts over the centuries. It established four principles which in effect made the pragmatic wartime agreement between Britain and France an international norm. Privateering was abolished. The principle that neutral shipping was inviolate was adopted, henceforth 'free ships' would indeed make 'free goods' unless they were carrying contraband of war, or were prevented from entering an enemy port by a formal naval blockade. At the same time, the British principle that neutral cargoes carried by enemy ships should be restored to their neutral owners by prize courts became internationally recognised. The ancient principle that blockades were only legal when enforced by the immediate presence of warships at the approaches to the blockaded harbours was affirmed by states which over the centuries had recognised that naval technology made close blockade a less than effective way of attacking enemy commerce. Lord Palmerston, who had succeeded as prime minister in February 1855, obtained Queen Victoria's approval for the cabinet decision to sign the Declaration. Its critics point out that it was not a treaty, but the government nonetheless felt itself to be committed.

[1] Carlton Savage, *Policy of the United States Toward Maritime Commerce in War*, Washington, 1934, vol. I, p. 68.
[2] 'The War Policy of Commerce', quoted in Francis Piggott, *The Declaration of Paris 1856*, London, 1919, p. 110.

The United States government rejected the invitation to sign the Declaration of Paris because it objected to the ban on the use of privateers to supplement the very limited professional naval forces it controlled. Only if the European states now agreed to Secretary Adams's proposal to extend a complete protection to private property at sea, to the same extent as law protected it ashore, would they accede to the Declaration.

The ban on privateers did not long remain an important constraint on naval strategy. In the years following the signature of the Declaration of Paris, the Imperial Russian navy sought to devise a means not only to dissuade Britain from further interference in Russian foreign policy, but also to prevent a reoccurrence of the close blockade of Russian ports which had marked the last years of the war. In 1860 Tsar Alexander II agreed to Grand Duke Konstantin's plan to construct sail and steam frigates designed for commerce raiding in distant waters. In the event of war between Britain and Russia, the strategic function of the Russian commerce raiders would become that of containing British naval power by obliging the British navy to devote so many ships to trade defence that the resources would not be available for blockade of Russia's widely separated sectors of sea coast. Not only did this strategy work around the ban on privateers, but it was actually made more effective because of it. The role of privateers in trade war had not been limited to predation, as they had also come to play an important part in trade defence under contract to shipping companies, thus relieving regular naval forces for fleet action. Russian naval missions were established in New York and San Francisco, and in 1863, fearing British intervention in support of Russia's Polish citizens, the distant-water squadrons were deployed to those neutral harbours. The deployment also made clear Russia's unequivocal support for the American Union.

The American decision not to sign the Declaration of Paris backfired almost immediately. With the outbreak of civil war, the Confederate states proceeded to demonstrate how the weaker naval power could use privateers against the trade of the stronger. Washington's support of the free-enterprise warriors disappeared immediately, but the efforts of Lord John Russell to obtain Secretary of State William H. Seward's signature to the Declaration of Paris was defeated by the latter's attempt to use adherence as a means of obliging the European states to treat Confederate privateers as pirates.

The Civil War was to be an important theatre for the development of the law of blockade. The Union government, a gamekeeper turned poacher, developed a principle of 'continuous voyage' to stop blockade runners using Bermuda and Nassau as entrepôts. Neutral shipping with clearances for those ports was stopped at sea, and information obtained by the American consuls in Europe was used to identify cargoes ultimately intended for the Confederate states. As recently as the Russian, or Crimean war the American government had objected to the principle of continuous voyage, but President Lincoln ensured that the Supreme Court would not declare the interception of shipping on the high seas a violation of prize law. He delayed hearings on the first prize cases until vacancies occurred on the Supreme Court bench, which he filled with justices on whom he could rely. He even expanded the bench to ten justices in order to strengthen his hand. The bench did not let him down. The British practice was copied of deliberately obscuring the principles upon which the law acted, in order to extend the belligerent claims without openly admitting doing so. Secretary of State Seward added diplomatic procrastination to evasion, especially in order to retain some control over trade into Matamoros in Mexico, which was an easy river connection to Texas.

Only fear of neutral reaction limited the scope of the blockade. Law had some part in defining how the neutrals would react, and power determined which neutrals had to be placated. With the Union fighting a desperate battle for its very existence the peril which had to be avoided above all others was that of driving Britain into the war on the Confederate side. Seward took a very strong line with London and Paris, warning that any recognition of the Confederacy would mean war with the Union. A European war, however, would have been the swansong of the Union. When a Union naval officer boarded the British steamer *Trent* and took prisoner Confederate commissioners bound for London and Paris, the act had to be disavowed. The opportunity was taken to show that the violation was identical to the seizure of British deserters on board US ships during the Napoleonic wars, which had been one of the reasons for the American declaration of war in 1812. Once the Confederacy was defeated, the American government abandoned its restraint. Claims were pressed against the British government for its laxity in permitting Confederates to fit out in British ports warships such as the commerce raider *Alabama*, and London found it expedient to pay a substantial indemnity.

The belligerent control of trade had not been a decisive strategy in the Civil War, for either party, because the blockades were too easily circumvented by blockade runners, by inland transport or by legal subterfuge. Some contemporary accounts attribute the defeat of the Confederacy to the blockade. On the whole this idea can only reflect the enthusiasm of Union naval officers, including the future Admiral Alfred Thayer Mahan, and the reluctance of Confederate military leaders to admit that they had been defeated in the field. There is no doubt that the Civil War caused severe economic dislocation in the Confederacy, and that the high freight rates which could be charged by neutral blockade runners because of the blockade played a part in this ruin. Poor administration, however, and the refusal of the states to pool their resources, probably had more to do with deficiencies in army supply than did the Union blockade. For its part, the commerce raiding by Confederates served to persuade northern commercial interests to reflag their ships in Britain, and led to the boom in shipbuilding and ownership in British North America. But that development did not significantly undermine the Union's capacity to conduct the war.

If anything, the record of the Civil War ought to have served as a caution against high expectations. The attempt made by Confederate committees of public safety to use embargo of the cotton crop as a means of obliging Britain and France to intervene in the war proved singularly unsuccessful. Between 1840 and 1860 the United States had supplied 80 per cent of the raw cotton used in British manufactures. The Confederates were convinced that Britain would be compelled to recognise the Confederacy to prevent revolution in the northern mill towns. This strategy, however, failed. The British business community as a whole was able to make adjustments to cope with the effects of the cotton famine. British labour was less well insulated against the effects of mill closure, but the political effect of the privation was not that for which the Confederacy had hoped. In November 1862, three-quarters of the Lancashire cotton mill hands were out of work, but British working men were developing a degree of political sophistication which was to have important consequences. Sympathies were strongly and vocally hostile to the slave states. Karl Marx brought the fact of this working-class solidarity to the notice of the world, and a *New York Times* editorial led to shiploads of American produce being sent across the Atlantic to the relief of the impoverished mill hands.

But despite the limitations hindsight can see in the utility of the Union blockade and Confederate raiders, the American Civil War was to be a turning point in the history of maritime strategy. The success of Confederate raiders in avoiding battle with superior Union forces, especially the long career of the *Alabama*, impressed naval planners. The need for cruisers for trade defence was underlined. At the same time, a strong impression had been created that a major cause of the defeat of the Confederacy had been the sea denial operations of the Union navy, and specifically the impact on the Confederacy of stoppage of imports. It appeared that the greater sophistication of marketing arrangements which reduced stockpiling and local economic autonomy, and the development of steam-powered navies, had at last made the strangulation of an enemy state technically possible. Despite the fact that the economic strength of the Union had been important it its victory, the interest of naval strategists had decisively shifted away from the proved but outmoded mercantilism of the age of sail.

There was consensus, however, only about the strategic importance of sea control. Concerning the technical requirements of the strategy, and hence which nations profited by the developments, there was less agreement.

When in July 1870 war was declared by Emperor Napoleon III against Prussia, London was advised that the French intended to abide by the provisions of the Declaration of Paris, and extend its protection to Spain and the United States which had not signed it. Prussia announced an intention to raise a volunteer navy, and France objected that this amounted to employing privateers. But in the wake of the US Civil War, London refused to second the French. In 1871 Lord Salisbury described the Declaration of Paris as 'reckless Utopianism,' the result of which was that 'the fleet, valuable as it is for preventing an invasion of these shores, is almost valueless for any other purpose.'[1] In the event, the Prussian scheme never materialised.

The pace of European reassessment of the strategic utility of trade war was set by the *Jeune Ecole*, a group of anti-British officers in the French navy. In the mid-1880s they promoted through publications a belief that Britain's capability to outbuild the French battle fleet was no impediment to France defeating Britain in naval warfare. The new steam-powered torpedo boats could evade the battleships and cruisers and attack the merchant shipping upon which Britain was far more than ever dependent for imports. It was not thought that the enormous British merchant marine could be sunk or captured en masse. In that appreciation the *Jeune Ecole* and the British Admiralty were in agreement. It was the belief of people such as Admiral Aube, however, that dramatic sinkings on the first days of war would force up insurance rates to the point where shipping would be kept in harbour. The result would be food shortages and unemployment, which would reduce the labouring classes to starvation, and to rebellion.

The views of the *Jeune Ecole* were far from universally accepted in France. The British public, however, was impressed by Britain's apparent vulnerability. The French blockade of rice in 1884–85 to bring pressure on the Chinese government was a warning that food supply

---

[1]*Hansard*, 6 March 1871, p. 1364; quoted by Sir Herbert Richmond, *Sea Power in the Modern World*, pp. 63–8.

might be at risk in wartime despite the laws of war. Agitation in parliament led by Sir John Charles Ready Colomb and Admiral Lord Charles Beresford resulted in the formation in 1887 of the Naval Intelligence Division (NID) at the Admiralty. That decision neither allayed the public's fears, nor led to the rapid adoption of measures to defend trade. The naval manoeuvres of 1888 demonstrated how difficult it would be for a British fleet to blockade French commerce raiders into their ports. Admiral Sir George Tryon, in May 1890, pressed the idea of a national war-risk insurance, but the idea was rejected by the government on the grounds that interference in the enterprise of shippers would keep them from finding ways of evading attack. In 1902 a specialist Trade Division was established in the Naval Intelligence Division. The following year an association which numbered amongst its members 40 admirals, 30 peers and 50 Members of Parliament, was formed to press for a Royal Commission on Food Supply in time of War. The Commission once formed, however, did little more than endorse the need for overall naval superiority, although it did decide that it was necessary for the government to indemnify shippers for war losses if they were to be persuaded to risk trading in wartime. It was concerned to make it clear that it was unsound for naval forces to be diverted by enemy attacks on trade from the principal task of fighting the decisive battle for command of the sea. A Treasury Committee was appointed in 1907 with Austen Chamberlain as chairman, but it did not recommend any state intervention in the insurance business. Not until May 1913 did a sub-committee of the Committee of Imperial Defence take up the question again, and not until July 1914 was an arrangement made to provide some governmental reinsurance for mercantile hulls against damage caused by 'the King's enemies'.

At the same time as the defence community was debating the capacity of blockade to defeat an industrial power in a major war, the great powers were actually employing naval control of trade as in instrument for policing their interests when these were threatened by the actions of lesser states. The use of naval blockade to promote limited purposes without resort to war, without abandoning the advantages of a non-belligerent relationship, is known as 'pacific blockade'. The practice was derived from the concept of reprisal, and was most properly directed at such problems as the failure of states to honour international debts. The objective of reprisal is by definition a limited one; one not involving the safety of either party. In the early modern period such reprisal had been carried out by private persons licensed with a letter of marque but, following the signing of the Declaration of Paris banning letters of marque, state navies had come to supply the muscle needed to protect the interests of their nationals. About 20 instances of pacific blockade occurred during the nineteenth century, including the famous Don Pacifico affair in 1850 when the British fleet blockaded Greece to exact reparations for a number of injuries, including that suffered by a British subject at the hands of a Greek mob. What right an act of reprisal, or 'self help', implied for control of the shipping of 'neutral' states was a matter of dispute.

The legal basis of the blockading power's right to expect neutral nations to avoid in any way delaying the submission of the blockaded, even if only by the effect on morale of the passage of its warships through the cordon, lay in the medieval idea of trial by combat. Interference with the combat in any way amounted to violation of the judicial process. Neutral powers did not have a good record in this respect, as the temptation to take advantage of war for their own purposes was great. In the nineteenth century greater recognition was being given to the 'obligations' of neutrals – with the objective primarily of ensuring that their interests would be respected in turn by belligerents.

Despite its name, pacific blockade amounts to the naked use, or abuse, of power. In the context of nineteenth-century international relations, pacific blockade was a relatively successful means of protecting the interests of the great powers. The inchoate rules of pacific blockade minimised the resentment of the developed states which possessed ocean-going merchant marines, and the right of such states to use force to manage relations with less developed states was scarcely questioned. By the beginning of the twentieth century, however, public sentiment began to favour more restraint. Following the Venezuelan crisis at the turn of the twentieth century, which led to the United States government sending a battle fleet into the Caribbean and threatening Canada in order to enforce the 'Monroe Doctrine' of American pre-eminence in the Americas, pacific blockade did not appear to be practicable politics. At the 1907 Hague Conference all the naval powers, with the exception of the United States and Russia, signed a convention proscribing the use of reprisals to exact payment of debts.

In the last decade of the nineteenth century and the first of the twentieth a major effort was made to develop by international convention the restraints upon belligerent rights at sea. Both Britain and the United States were impelled primarily by consideration of the need to ensure the safety and profitability of their shipping as neutral carriers in a world troubled by imperial wars, but both exhibited some inconsistency in their objectives. During the Spanish–American war (1898) the United States had declared a blockade of the north coast of Cuba, but

Washington continued to seek a general ban on 'private war' against merchant shipping. The American delegates to the first Hague conference in May to July 1899, including amongst their number the great apologist of sea power, Admiral Mahan, proposed that 'the private property of all citizens or subjects of the signatory powers, with the exception of contraband of war, shall be exempt from capture or seizure on the high seas.'[1] The British government shunned the temptation during the South African war which broke out later in 1899 to intercept food shipments to the Boers because they had come to see their interest as excluding food from a contraband list. The inconvenience Britain and the United States experienced as neutrals in the Russo–Japanese war in 1904–05 by the Russian government's inclusion of food and fuels on its contraband list produced many complaints by British shipping interests, which could not be satisfied because there was no arbitration agreement in place, and led Secretary of State Hay to circularise a protest amongst European diplomats.[2] When at the end of the war Tsar Nicholas II proposed a second 'Peace' conference at the Hague in 1907 it was accordingly decided to put belligerent rights on the agenda.

Not all Britons were satisfied with Mahan's conviction that a dominant naval power could strangle an enemy by blockading his trade. The lessons he believed had been taught by the Civil War did not altogether convince Britons who knew that there had always been a good chance that suitable ships could run the Union blockade. The experience of the Crimean War had also suggested that the internal communications of Europe had developed to the point where the power of the British navy against trade could have little effect. In 1904 Sir George Sydenham Clarke, secretary of the newly created Committee of Imperial Defence, drafted a paper in which he concluded: 'the sea pressure that can be brought to bear upon a continental enemy appears, therefore, to be far less effective than formerly. If this be admitted the advantage a belligerent state possesses from the right to capture contraband appear[s] illusory.'[3] In 1927 Sir Cecil Hurst, a legal adviser in the Foreign Office, was to write that 'the Russo-Japanese War' had convinced Clarke 'that the power to seize contraband had ceased to be of prime importance to Great Britain.'

---

[1]Carlton Savage, *Policy of the United States Toward Maritime Commerce in War*, Document 152, p. 494.

[2]Carlton Savage, *op. cit.*, p. 106.

[3]A.C. Bell, *A History of the Blockade of Germany and of the Countries associated with her in the Great War: Austria-Hungary, Bulgaria, and Turkey. 1914–1918*, London, 1937, p. 9.

Eyre Crowe, the Senior Clerk of the Foreign Office in 1907, did not share Sydenham Clarke's doubts. He wrote that the publications of Admiral Mahan showed that 'Sea power is more potent than land power . . . No one now disputes it.' The inference Crowe drew, however, was that it was 'but natural that the power of a State supreme at sea should inspire universal jealousy and fear, and be ever exposed to the danger of being overthrown by a general combination of the world.' In consequence, he urged that Britain should be careful to avoid posing any threat to the trade of her neighbours.[1]

The growing prospect of war with Germany did not persuade the British government that it was necessary to reverse the trend towards limitation of belligerent rights. Between 1904 and 1907, the Committee of Imperial Defence and the Naval Intelligence Division reappraised Britain's interests, but concluded that a compromise could be reached between Britain's interests as a neutral, and as a possible belligerent against Germany, if the concept of contraband were eliminated altogether. Germany was not well placed to attack British commerce but had a substantial merchant marine hostage to British attack, the loss of which could be expected to have political effects in Berlin. If contraband control were eliminated as a motive for trade warfare, British shipping would be safe, but Britain would still be able to deny Germany access to military supplies by conducting a close blockade of German ports. The Japanese warned the British government in 1907 that the experience of their late war had shown how difficult it was to enforce a close blockade, but it was not until 1908 that the Admiralty policy of close blockade began to be modified. As late as 1911 Admiral Sir Arthur Wilson, when First Sea Lord, reverted to it.

Prime Minister Asquith's Liberal administration was more interested in removing the causes of conflict than in preserving the legal ambiguities which had been used in the past to support British belligerent rights, but the Foreign Secretary, Sir Edward Grey, feared that it would be impossible to obtain political support for the Hague conventions unless the law of belligerent rights were clarified. Accordingly, the powers were invited to send delegates to a conference on the subject in London in the winter of 1908–09. In the formulation of the Declaration of London, neither the British aim to eliminate contraband as a reason for stopping neutral ships on the high seas, nor the reiterated American suggestion that private property should be considered immune from seizure in war, were satisfied. Later, both countries were to be glad of

[1]G.P. Gooch and H. Temperley (eds), *British Documents on the Origins of the War*, London, 1932, iii, pp. 402–3 and viii, p. 392.

that. Mahan had himself come to oppose according immunity to private shipping because he increasingly saw Britain's capacity to threaten German shipping as the only means available to confront Prussian militarism. He did not trust the British Liberals to sustain the practical means for their own defence and obtained Theodore Roosevelt's permission to publicise his views.

He was right to be concerned. Despite the Japanese warnings about the difficulty of supporting close blockade of enemy ports, the first article of the Declaration of London established that 'A blockade must not extend beyond the ports and coasts belonging to or occupied by the enemy.' The traditional British view that neutral convoys escorted by warships were not exempt from blockade was negotiated away. Inconsistently, on the other hand, article 47 provided that 'Any individual embodied in the armed forces of the enemy who is found on board a neutral merchant vessel, may be made a prisoner of war, even though there be no ground for the capture of the vessel.' Thus was also negotiated away the ground upon which the Union government had been obliged to restore the Confederate officers found on board the *Trent*. Public pressure prevented the British government ratifying the Declaration of London, but the American government did, and its terms were incorporated in the fleet orders distributed by the British Admiralty on the outbreak of the First World War.

Over 20 years later Colonal Maurice Hankey, who was then Secretary of the Committee of Imperial Defence, wrote that 'the Convention for the Establishment of an International Prize Court [drafted at the 2nd Hague Conference] . . . was drawn up at a time when no data existed for examining its effect on our belligerent rights in a war with Germany.'[1] Hankey wrote that the strategic implications for Britain of the emasculation of belligerent rights at sea were never discussed in the Committee of Imperial Defence, to which at the time he was Naval Assistant Secretary. As such, he drew up two long memoranda in which he pointed out that in the technical conditions of contemporary naval warfare Britain could not mount a close blockade of German Baltic ports. 'We can blockade the North Sea ports, but we can do absolutely nothing to prevent the trade of Germany being carried in neutral bottoms to the Baltic ports or through neutral ports in neighbouring countries.' The Royal Navy was not able to impose a close blockade of German ports because the Kiel Canal made it possible for the German fleet to appear in strength in the Baltic or North Sea, while deep draft British dreadnought battleships could not enter the

---

[1]*Belligerent Rights at Sea*, Confidential Print 286 (27). CAB 21/307; CAB 16/79, part 9, p. 290

Baltic through the Belts in the face of mines and submarines. The only way the Royal Navy could influence the course of military affairs on the continent was by exercising belligerent rights over neutral shipping as it approached the North Sea, but the Declaration of London had seriously affected that capability. 'The negotiators of the Declaration of London have made the fatal error of basing their agreement . . . on the experience of a few very recent wars in which the weapon of sea power, as a means of putting pressure on the inferior naval power, had no scope for exertion.' Hankey believed that the British government should not ratify the Declaration of London, or should place virtually all German imports on the contraband list.

Clearly Hankey was heavily influenced by the ideas about maritime strategy generated by the US Civil War, but his assertion that the administration was blinkered by recent experience is open to question. Arguably its perspective was a longer one than was Hankey's focus on the Civil War: its policies were consistent with the experience of the Russian War and the Napoleonic War, not to mention the wars of the previous two centuries, that the strength of maritime power lay in its being a generator of wealth which could support the cost of war. The realities of 1914–15 were apparently to vindicate Hankey because the British commitment of manpower to the army undermined the ability of British industry to grow at the rate needed to meet the requirements of war.

The treaty laws which were developed in the wake of the Declaration of Paris lacked the vitality of even the disputed interpretations of the Course of Admiralty, the precedent law which had guided courts in the previous three centuries, and did little more than undermine respect for a pervasive international law. If indeed naval force put unlimited power into the control of a few favoured states it was improbable, to say the least, that international treaty would be able to preclude its use. The impact of the treaties limiting belligerent rights had less importance then did the enhanced reputation imparted to maritime strategy by the theorists. The provisions of the Declaration of London were to be set aside in stages during the First World War, as rapidly as that could be justified by German violations of the Hague conventions, and the Declaration was itself abrogated in 1916. Following the war, efforts to restrict by treaty the strategic use of naval forces were to become hopelessly entangled by competing national interests, which could only be papered over by limiting the matériel of navies.

The significance of the blockade in the eventual defeat of the Central Powers in the Great War is hard to assess. It is certain, however, that the Entente's blockade was a contributing factor in their eventual victory. The shortage of food contributed to the growth of the civilian peace movement in 1917 and 1918, especially in the Austro-Hungarian empire where it encouraged the food producing areas of Hungary and Croatia to defy central authority. In Germany the socialists found a strong case against the imperial government in their maladministration of the food supply. In April 1917 Emperor Karl appealed to the German government to seek peace at almost any price: 'We are fighting a new enemy, who is more dangerous than the entente: our enemy is international revolution, which is finding a powerful ally in the general famine.'[1] But in retrospect, it can be seen that the blockade was no more than a multiplier of the forces which ultimately brought German surrender. The disillusionment caused by the failure of the German U-boat campaign to starve Britain into submission, and the consequences for Germany of the American entry into the war following the German return to unlimited U-boat operations in 1917, added significantly to the political reaction when the army high command proved unable to bring peace despite its sacrifice of German manhood. Only with victory could the army, the aristocracy and the Prussian monarchy continue to justify their political power. The army, unable to defeat the Entente in the field, found it convenient to blame the blockade for their defeat.

The apparent potential of naval trade control in breaking the impasse on the western front in the First World War, a potential which on reflection was more apparent than real, ensured that during the interwar years the belligerent rights issue was a major point of contention between Britain and the United States. The British believed that at last they had perfected a technique for defeating a continental militarist regime, perhaps bringing an end to the threat of invasion. But the United States viewed the power of the Royal Navy to impose blockade as a mercantilist threat limiting the potential of American commercial growth. For the British, the apparent success of the naval blockade of Germany created the hope that future generations could enjoy security based on naval strength. Britain had always found naval power a weak tool of foreign policy, an army having usually been necessary to translate into international influence the economic power generated by sea control, but in 1918 there was a strong conviction that at last the technique had been perfected by which a great empire could be defeated by naval blockade. The high reputation the war had given, rather unjustifiably, to the power of maritime blockade led to the League of Nations Covenant providing for the use of economic sanctions to express the collective disapproval of the aggressor's actions, and if necessary to oblige the aggressor to desist from its actions. But the

---

[1]Quoted in A.C. Bell, *History of the Blockade of Germany*, p. 694.

the relief of Belgium was the poignant origin of his hatred of blockade as a political instrument, and the continuation of the wartime blockade into 1919 to compel the German government to sign the peace treaty had put an end to his sympathy for Britain. After his election to the presidency, however, he wrote in his memoirs that, 'Believing that elimination of friction with Great Britain must be one of the foundation stones of our foreign policies, I sought ways to end the various gnawing differences between us. The most dangerous of these frictions was of course competitive naval building.'[1]

The dénouement of the belligerent rights dispute with the United States left the legal regime at sea much as it had been prior to the drafting of the Declaration of London, but the realities of the 1930s were very different from the situation 20 years before. The Spanish Civil War and the Sino-Japanese war created problems for the Admiralty, which sought to protect British shipping while undermining as little as possible the ability of Britain herself to employ a distant blockade in future wars. But when the German war was renewed in 1939 the Ministry of Economic Warfare, equipped with a *Handbook* based on the lessons learnt in the Great War, was constrained to limit its efforts out of concern for the sensitivities of the United States and other neutral nations. The American government was not willing to provide passive support for British economic warfare, although it did amend its own neutrality legislation to permit British ships to load munitions in American ports. It imposed restrictions on American ships, and American nationals, to reduce the risk of being drawn into war as it had been in 1917, but it defended the rights of American shipping to conduct its trade unrestricted by the demands of the belligerents. Americans, and American ships, were ordered to stay outside a war-zone which was drawn around most of Europe and included Halifax and ports in Canada east of it. An exception was made of Bergen and the north Norwegian coast, and strong protests were made when British cruisers brought American traders to Bergen into Kirkwall for inspection. In agreement with the Latin American states, Washington declared an American neutrality zone which included southern Nova Scotia. Canadian consent was not considered necessary. Efforts to allow American shipping to be examined in a safe Canadian port were thereby frustrated. The United States Treasury forbade shippers to make agreements with the British government to restrict their cargoes to those covered by a British Navicert. Only when the Japanese attack on Pearl Harbor brought the

[1]H.C. Hoover, *The Memoirs of Herbert Hoover*, 2 vols, New York, 1951–52, vol. 2, p. 342.

United States into the war, under the aegis of a United Nations, called into existence by President Roosevelt and Prime Minister Churchill, could economic blockade be imposed on Germany and Japan without restraint. And only when the United States began to impose embargoes on commodities at source, and to encourage the Latin American states to do so as well, was it possible to attack with any effect the economic base of the German war machine. Until late in 1942, however, the United States government had no agency to provide it with intelligence for economic warfare purposes.

The decision of the United States government, following the defeat of Germany and Japan, to sponsor the formation of the United Nations as a body capable of moving towards world government was to profoundly alter the rule of law at sea. The sanction of the UN Security Council came to be regarded as all the law that was required to guide the strategy of nations fighting in a UN mandated conflict. Because the United States was one of the five permanent members of the Security Council and had a veto over Security Council resolutions, it was certain that the United States would never again need to play the role of champion of neutral rights in the event of 'public' war. Nevertheless, questions of belligerent law at sea continued in the post-war years to be a matter of concern, to a degree because the Cold War between the Soviet Union, the Republic of China and the North Atlantic Treaty Organization powers, led by the United States, greatly limited the occasions on which the United Nations Security Council could take control of international events. Although the Korean War (1950–53) was mandated by the General Assembly of the United Nations, the reality was that naval action had to be circumspect to avoid conflict with the Soviet Union, which was the unofficial sponsor of the North Koreans. In 1962, during a crisis of unparalleled proportions for the world, President Kennedy declared a 'quarantine' of Cuba as a means of persuading the Soviets to withdraw the missiles they were in the process of placing there. One of the honorary editors of *The American Journal of International Law*, Quincy Wright, demolished the special pleading which was used in Washington to justify the quarantine. In particular, he dismissed the claim that it was an instance of pacific blockade. It was applied to the ships of all states and was employed before recourse had been made to all diplomatic means of resolving the conflict. 'The episode,' he concluded, 'has not improved the reputation of the United States as a champion of international law.'[1] Neutrals were not inclined to support

---

[1]Quincy Wright, 'The Cuban Quarantine', *The American Journal of International Law*, 57 (1963), p. 547.

the legality of the quarantine. The Canadian government withheld assent to the blockade but saw that its objective was met by inspecting ships and aircraft in Canadian ports before granting clearances for Cuba. Sweden refused to acknowledge the justice or the fact of blockade, but Poland said it would comply although it could not agree to the quarantine's legality. The British press was especially hostile to Kennedy's action, which stood in such stark contrast to American denunciation of the Anglo-French operation at Suez, and to Kennedy's denunciation of India's takeover of Portuguese Goa. However, Prime Minister Harold Macmillan expressed the predominant view when he told the House of Commons that the American action was 'designed to meet a situation which is without precedent' by means which were 'studiously moderate.'[1] The quarantine was an illegal resort to force, but it was generally recognised to be a soft option compared to the alternatives available to President Kennedy.

In the less threatening circumstances of the Vietnam War (1964–75), the restraints imposed by the Cold War were again observed. When the American government saw the need to stop the flow of military supplies from the Soviet Union into the port of Haiphong in 1972 the United States Air Force bombed the bridges inland from the port, and later the United States Navy mined the approaches to the harbour, but merchant shipping from the Soviet Union was not boarded or searched on the high seas. For its part, the Soviet Navy did not employ naval force against American supply ships.

The Beira patrol, established in 1966 to stop the flow of oil to Southern Rhodesia through the pipeline from the Mozambique port of Beira, is the last instance of maritime blockade for which it is possible to publish official British papers. Because of the ability of the Union of South Africa to supply the necessary oil, this operation was largely symbolic. Its importance to the development of the legal regime at sea lies in the fact that it was authorised by the United Nations Security Council.

* * *

Some notice should be taken of more recent events because they indicate the extent to which the older concepts of belligerent rights have been modified in the new world order. One of the most important is the

---

[1]Carlo Q. Christol and Charles R. Davis, 'Maritime Quarantine: The Naval Interdiction of Offensive Weapons and Associated Materiel to Cuba, 1962', *The American Yearbook of International Law*, 57 (1963), p. 528.

Iran/Iraq war which broke out in 1980, obliging western naval powers to respond to belligerent threats to shipping. Cold War with the Soviet Union was still very much a consideration, and ensured that the Gulf conflict was played out without the effective intervention of the United Nations. In 1984 alone, Iraqi forces carried out 53 attacks on shipping. Iran responded with 18, and intercepted cargo vessels entering the Persian (or Arabian) Gulf to inspect them for contraband bound for Iraq.[1] When in 1990, following the conclusion of the conflict with Iran, the Iraqi government invaded Kuwait to obtain the financial resources it needed to pay for the cost of the war with Iran, the Cold War was over. As a result, the United Nations was able to play a more active role. Its actions serve to indicate how much has changed in the interpretation of belligerent rights, and perhaps just as much, how little has changed.

In response to the Iraqi invasion of Kuwait, the United Nations Security Council passed Resolution 661 (2 August 1990) banning all trade with Iraq and occupied Kuwait, both imports and exports, with the exception of medicines and foods required for humanitarian relief. Resolution 670 extended the controls to the airways, and Resolution 678 made it clear that 'all necessary means' might be employed to enforce the sanctions. These included naval blockade in the Gulf of Acaba and the Persian Gulf.

The proviso in Resolution 661 that food for humanitarian purposes should be permitted to pass through the blockade was made ineffective by the hard policy of coalition states which led to the adoption of Resolution 666 limiting the distribution of food to United Nations approved agencies, which did not in fact have access to Iraq. United States Secretary of State James Baker's statement to the United States Senate, 5 December 1990, that sanctions, to be valuable, would have to 'hurt Iraq so much that Saddam Hussein', the then President of Iraq, 'changes his behaviour and withdraws from Kuwait', indicates that he was formulating his policy in the belief that economic pressure directed indiscriminately at a target state should have the power to coerce hostile governments. The progress of the Kuwait crisis did not substantiate his expectation. Economic pressure did not obviate violent resolution of the crisis, but did contribute very substantially to the horrors of the conflict.

The non-aligned nations did not have the power enjoyed by the United States as a neutral in the world wars, and were not in fact able to

---

[1]General Council of British Shipping, *Guidance Notes for Owners and Masters with vessels in the Arabian Gulf,* 1 October 1985. *The Times,* 6 February 1987, reported that a total of 98 ships were attacked in 1986.

protect the legal right of civilians to food supplies. The ambiguity in which the legal status of food control was left ensured that food supplies to the states bordering Iraq were not rationed, and that Iran, Jordan, Syria and the Lebanon permitted Iraqis to purchase food in their villages and carry it home. After the start of the air battle, however, the road from Jordan was closed, by bombing civilian truckers. In the following years the United Nations attempted to address the needs of the Iraqi population by licensing the sale of Iraqi oil to benefit an escrow account for the purchase of food and medicine. Initially the Iraqi government refused to comply, but at the end of 1996 an oil-for-food programme, authorised by resolution 986, finally commenced after the United Nations and the government of Iraq agreed on the details of implementation. Iraq was initially permitted to sell up to two billion dollars worth of oil in a 180-day period, and the ceiling on oil sales was eased during 1998 and finally lifted in 1999, enabling the programme to move from a focus on food and medicine to repairing essential infrastructure, including the oil industry. The arrangement, however, was far from satisfactory because the government of Iraq was able to manipulate the situation to its advantage, and because much of the money raised through oil sales was used to pay reparations to Kuwait. Following the end of the second Iraq war in 2003 the United Nations Security Council formally ended all economic sanctions on 22 May.

It is doubtful that the sanctions against Iraq satisfied a key proviso in the Aquinian concept of the 'just war', that the means employed can only be considered 'just' if they are capable of obtaining the legitimate objectives of the campaign. Their effect must also be proportional to the ends. The additional protocols to the 1949 Geneva Convention relating to the protection of victims of international armed conflicts should have ensured the security of ordinary Iraqis, but because Iraq is a net importer of food, restrictions on Iraqi exports needed to pay for the food imports could be judged to be a violation of the Convention.

During the debate in the Security Council on 25 August discussing Resolution 665 authorising the use of force against Iraq, Alarçon de Quesada, the ambassador for Cuba, declared that 'no action or decision adopted or to be adopted by this Council can give it the political, legal or moral authority to undertake any kind of action that is in itself inhuman.'[1] Three days later he attempted to persuade his fellow ambassadors that the term 'humanitarian circumstances' should be

---

[1]United Nations, Security Council Verbatim Reports, Provisional, 25 August S/PV 2938 discussion of draft resolution S/21640 (resolution 665).

interpreted not only as applying to a need to avert imminent death, but also 'where withholding food could have long-term effects – on the growth or mental development of children for example.'[1] Mr. Richardson, the British ambassador, objected that 'If the Security Council had intended to exempt foodstuffs systematically, it would not have included the proviso "in humanitarian circumstances"', but on 7 September the chairman of the committee, Marjatta Rasi, wrote to the Secretary-General, Javier Pérez de Cuéllar, that 'All the members of the Committee shared the view that resolution 661 (1990) must be implemented without creating conditions of starvation in Iraq and Kuwait.' However, following the war, a study conducted by the Harvard School of Public Health, using statistics from house-to-house surveys, concluded that infantile mortality rates had more than tripled, to 80 per 1000, as a result of the war and revolt. An estimated 46,900 children under five died in Iraq between January and August 1991, in excess of the peacetime expectation of infantile mortality.[2] The grinding poverty imposed on ordinary Iraqis in the subsequent decade multiplied that figure many times.

In a somewhat analogous case involving the 1992 Security Council ban on arms sales to Bosnia, Justice Lautherpacht, in a summation at the International Court of Justice, posed the possibility that national governments might in some particular circumstances be morally and legally bound to ignore resolutions of the Security Council. The ban on arms sales disabled the Bosnian government from preventing Serbian irregulars effecting 'ethnic cleansing'. Lautherpacht said that the court should not

> overlook the significance of the provision in Article 24(2) of the Charter that, in discharging its duties to maintain international peace and security, the Security Council shall act in accordance with the Purposes and Principles of the United Nations. Amongst the Purposes set out in Article 1(3) of the Charter is that of achieving international co-operation 'in promoting and encouraging respect for human rights and for fundamental freedoms for all without distinction as to race, sex, language or religion'. ... The Security Council resolution can be seen as having in effect called on Members of the United Nations, albeit unknowingly and assuredly unwillingly, to become in some degree supporters of the genocidal

---

[1] United Nations, Provisional Summary Record of the 4th Meeting of the 661 Committee, 28 August 1990. S/AC.25/S2.4

[2] Alberto Archerio et al.,'The Effect of the Gulf War on Infant and Child Mortality in Iraq', *New England Journal of Medicine*, 23 September 1992 (1992; 327:931–6).

activity of the Serbs and in this manner and to that extent to act contrary to a rule of jus cognes.[1]

In the determination of the United States and Britain to enforce the United Nations sanctions against Iraq regardless, there is an echo of Prime Minister Churchill's assertion in 1940 that the only 'agencies which can create famine in any part of Europe now and during the coming winter, will be German exactions or German failure to distribute the supplies which they command.'[2] The justice of the blockade, in both instances, is questionable. In concluding his staff history of the 1914–19 blockade of the Central Powers, Lt Cmdr W.E. Arnold-Forster cautioned against the temptation to use the economic weapon without regard for its consequences for civil society:

> For there is a peculiar danger attaching to the use of this particular weapon, a danger which has not yet been sufficiently realised. It has now been found by experience that blockade is an instrument which can be wielded without any uncomfortable exertion, and can to a large extent be created, by men sitting in offices far from any visible sign of the consequences of its use. Men thus fighting with their pens in London come naturally to thinking that pens are cleaner weapons than bayonets, besides being much more convenient for the amateur. No danger, no mess, merely a Government ukase.
>
> And that is just what makes blockade so dangerous a weapon in bureaucratic hands; it is so infernally convenient.
>
> It would be a good thing if everyone who may have to use this weapon in future, whether at sea or ashore, would devote some serious study to the real nature of its consequences.[3]

It is evident that this caution needs repeated expression.

---

[1]International Court of Justice, 13 September 1993, I.C.J. 325 'Case Concerning Application of the Convention on the Prevention and Punishment of the Crime of Genocide, Bosnia and Herzegovina v. Yugoslavia (Serbia and Montenegro)', p. 440.

[2]*The Food Blockade and the Occupied Territories, Memorandum by the Minister of Economic Warfare*, Hugh Dalton, Secret, W.P. (41) 176, 28 July 1941. CAB 66/17, p. 235.

[3]Lt Cmdr W.E. Arnold-Forster, *The Economic Blockade 1914–1919*, Admiralty Staff History, 1920, ADM 186/603.

PART I

THE RUSSIAN WAR, THE DECLARATION OF PARIS,
THE US CIVIL WAR AND BELLIGERENT RIGHTS IN
THE LATE 19TH CENTURY

INTRODUCTION

The Russian war saw the beginning of great changes in the laws of war at sea. The first document in this chapter, a letter from the First Lord of the Admiralty, Sir James Graham, to the Secretary of State, the Earl of Clarendon, is at once a policy statement and a review of the history of belligerent law at sea [1]. After an exhaustive statement of British traditional claims, Graham recommended the suspension of the right to seize enemy cargoes carried in neutral vessels in order to facilitate co-operation with France, and recommended that letters of marque be outlawed as an encouragement for Russia to do so as well. The implication of this restraint was that the impact of naval action on the trade of Russia was limited, access to the Russian market still being possible through neutral ports. The second document is a notification to the powers of Britain's intent in this respect [2].

The free traders' point of view prevailed to such an extent that no blockade of Russian ports was declared until February 1855, and the priority given to Black Sea operations reduced the capacity of the French and British navies to enforce a blockade in the Baltic. Until the blockade was effective, the only trade restriction imposed was an order in council forbidding the entry of British ships into Russian ports. Britons were permitted nonetheless to conduct trade with Russia via neutral carriers. When a close blockade of Russian ports was declared, preventing access by neutral shipping, Britons were still free to route their commerce through neutral ports. Prussia facilitated the trade by constructing a railway from Danzig. The British government despaired of finding means to close the loopholes, but the free traders insisted in any case that loopholes were necessary so that Russia could continue to supply British industry with raw materials. When in October 1854 consideration was being given to legislation to prohibit Britons continuing to trade with the enemy through neutral middlemen, Viscount Edward Cardwell, President of the Board of Trade in Lord Aberdeen's administration, argued that the consequences would be more injurious to Britain than it would be to Russia [3].

The 'Declaration of Paris,' drawn up by the powers following the peace conference at Paris in 1856 at the suggestion of Tsar Alexander

II, perpetuated the pragmatic wartime agreement between Britain and France. Its terms were bold, and simple: 1. Privateering is and remains abolished; 2. The neutral flag covers enemy's goods, with the exception of contraband of war; 3. Neutral goods, with the exception of contraband of war, are not liable to capture under enemy's flag; 4. Blockades, in order to be binding, must be effective – that is to say, maintained by a force sufficient really to prevent access to the coast of the enemy. At a cabinet meeting in April 1856 to discuss the proposal, both the Secretary of State for Foreign Affairs, the Earl of Clarendon, and the Prime Minister, Lord Palmerston, stated their belief that Britain could never again enforce her traditional maritime claims [4]. The only power to refuse its assent to the Declaration of Paris, which became the first convention controlling the use of armed force, was the United States, which would not agree to abolish privateers unless at the same time it was agreed that all private property should be free from naval control in wartime. As Secretary of State William Marcy explained to the Comte de Sartiges, French ambassador in Washington, on 28 July 1856, the American perspective was that the elimination of privateers would give an advantage to those who supported a navy in peacetime [5].

Accounts of the negotiations ending in the British signature of the Declaration of Paris were drawn up in 1876 and 1893 by Sir Edward Hertslet, the Foreign Office Librarian and Fellow of the Royal Geographical Society who also served as a diplomat [14, 16]. Nevertheless, when in 1918 a war cabinet 'International Law Committee', under the chairmanship of the Right Honourable Viscount Cave, reviewed the events leading to the signature of the Declaration of Paris, it commented on the singular lack of 'information in our national archives as the origin of this Declaration' [33].

There had been considerable criticism of the adoption of the 'free ships make free goods' policy during the war, and the Declaration of Paris was criticised both in parliament and without. The opposition leader, Lord Derby, objected that the elimination of a decisive economic weapon made Britain dependent upon an ally for influence over European affairs. However, in the House of Lords the Foreign Secretary, Lord Clarendon, justified his signing of the convention by claiming that a refusal to do so would have turned every maritime power against Britain: 'and most properly so – because we should have been maintaining a law which was contrary to the public opinion of the world, which was hostile to commerce, and as unfavourable as possible to a mitigation of the evils of war.'[1] British shipping interests complained

---

[1]Quoted in Sir Francis Piggott, *The Declaration of Paris*, p. 126.

that the Declaration gave neutral American shippers a decisive advantage in seeking freights. But when in 1860 the Horsefall Commission of the House of Commons reported on the significance of the Declaration of Paris to the safety of British shipping in wartime, the worst it foresaw was that British shipping would stay in harbour while British trade was carried by neutrals. It recommended that Britain press for a further diminution of belligerent rights in order to protect all private property at sea. John Stuart Mill was one of very few who continued to demand the abrogation of the Declaration of Paris, which he believed had crippled Britain's capacity to be the champion of liberal democracy [16]. It was not until after the American Civil War that opinion in Britain turned strongly against the Declaration of Paris.

The Queen's Regulations and the Admiralty Instructions for the Government of Her Majesty's Naval Service issued in 1862 reflected the provisions of the Declaration of Paris only to the extent that naval officers were instructed to treat as pirates privateersmen who could not produce a valid letter of marque, and to arrest British subjects found on board for trial on a charge of treason [8]. *The Naval Prize Act* of 1864, however, removed any financial inducement to British privateersmen by stipulating in Article 39 that 'Any ship or goods taken as prize by any of the officers and crew of a ship other than a ship of war of her Majesty shall, on condemnation, belong to her Majesty in her office of Admiralty' [9]. At the outbreak of the Franco-Prussian war in 1870 the French government notified the powers of its intention to conform to the principles of the Declaration of Paris, and in 1884 Admiral Corbet declared a formal blockade of the coast of Formosa in terms consistent with the Declaration [12, 15].

There was some feeling in London that Britain should agree to the American proposal to extend a general protection to private property in wartime. The opinion of the Queen's Advocate Sir John Dorney Harding was that the provision of the Declaration of Paris protecting enemy-owned property freighted on neutral carriers had already so degraded the utility of British sea power that there was an argument for extending protection to enemy property even when carried in enemy shipping. If British sea power had been deprived of its effectiveness for offensive economic warfare, it was in the national interest to promote a regime which facilitated Britain's own commerce in wartime. During the Napoleonic War thousands of licences had been issued by the British government facilitating trade with enemy-occupied Europe, and the experience of the Russian war showed that it could be good strategy to permit trade by British merchants with the enemy. It followed that it would be sound policy for Britain to surrender the right to control

enemy-owned shipping, which was a dubious advantage if neutral shipping were free to carry enemy commerce, if in return British commerce
could be for ever made safe from the threat of American privateers. The
opinion of Dr Stephen Lushington, Admiralty Judge, was in agreement
[5].

Harding pointed out that the American proposal implicitly excluded
from the equation any reduction in the right of naval powers to impose
a close and effective blockade of enemy ports. The fact that the rapid
development of inland rail transport systems reduced the utility of
blockades limited to enemy ports had not yet been assimilated by the
defence community. Nevertheless, in 1859 Palmerston expressed strong
disagreement with the American plan to immunise private property at
sea, and the British government's decision was to reject the American
proposal.[1]

The outbreak of the American Civil War had brought the question
of belligerent rights into prominence. Correspondence between Richard Bickerton Pemell Lyons, ambassador at Washington, and Lord
John Russell, the Prime Minister, had to deal with a belated interest
on the part of the Union government in the suppression of privateers,
and the question of blockade running by British merchant ships [6].
The American claim that its blockade of Confederate ports did not
imply a recognition of belligerency and that it should be viewed as a
form of 'Pacific Blockade' was not accepted at the time, and was to
be dealt with exhaustively by Alfred Scrimshire Green, Foreign Office Sub-Librarian, in a paper 'Relative to Certain Statements made
by Mr Sumner in his Speech of the 13th April, 1869, with Regard to
Pacific Blockades' [11]. The seizure of Confederate officers taking
passage to Europe in a British ship, the *Trent*, the fitting out of a
Confederate raider, the *Alabama*, in a British yard and an American
plan to send a cruiser squadron to work in the English Channel, were
all matters requiring adjustment [10]. The Union felt bound to disa-
vow the seizures from the *Trent*, but the Union was more secure by
the time the *Alabama* claims were pressed, and the British government felt obliged to make a major financial settlement [7]. As the
United States was not a signatory of the Declaration of Paris her
claim for compensation from Britain for the depredations made by the
Alabama had little basis in admiralty law, but Canada was a hostage
to American resentment. As always, it was the naval balance of power

---

[1]C.H. Stockton, 'Would Immunity from Capture, During War, of Non-Offending
Private Property Upon the High Seas be in the Interest of Civilization?', *The American
Journal of International Law*, 1 (1907), p. 930.

which lay behind interpretation of law. The concessions made in the Treaty of Washington of 1871 were part of Britain's policy of appeasement of the United States, which was to lead to such important consequences in the wars of the twentieth century. But at the same time, the parallel commitment made by the United States, to prevent a state hostile to Great Britain fitting out or operating warships from American ports, if respected, finally addressed British fears during the Russian war. It was agreed that for the future neutral powers had an obligation to prevent their ports and coasts being used by the naval forces of a belligerent power [13]. In 1871 the United States also concluded a treaty with Italy in which the two countries agreed that their merchant shipping should be immune from capture should war occur between them. And, on the outbreak of the Franco-Prussian war, the French government announced its intention to abide by the terms of the Declaration of Paris [12].

Pacific Blockade, as a middle ground between belligerency and a less invasive form of naval trade control, became a matter of great interest in the later nineteenth century. Green's review of the earlier instances of such action is a useful introduction to the subject [11]. The French announcement of a blockade of rice in 1884–85 to bring pressure on the Chinese government to pay compensation for an 'ambush' of French soldiers in Annam was couched in the terms of Pacific Blockade, but French purposes were in fact political [15]. The Premier, Jules Ferry, admitted in the *Journal Official* (27 November 1884) that 'there are great advantages to following the policy of reprisal without a declaration of war, to waging war as we are now doing without resorting to a prior declaration.'[1] The passivity of the blockade was thrown into doubt when the Port of Kelung was bombarded and captured. Later Foochow was shelled, Chinese ships were sunk, coal mines were seized and rice ships were prevented from carrying their cargoes to northern China. After initial hesitation, Britain decided that French behaviour amounted to war [18]. The Foreign Enlistment Act of 1870, prohibiting any assistance being offered a belligerent at war with a nation at peace with Britain, was enforced, with the result that the French navy was denied the use of Hong Kong harbour. Britain did not declare neutrality, but France, in retaliation for what was taken as British intervention, informed the powers that it claimed the rights of a belligerent. The seizure of coal mines at Kelung was conceived in Paris as a means of enabling the sizeable French fleet in the Pacific to continue its operations.

[1]Quoted in Albert E. Hogan, *Pacific Blockade*, London, 1908, p. 124.

It appears that the blockade of Formosa was not instrumental in the eventual Chinese decision to negotiate, but the rice blockade is credited with having been an effective instrument of coercion. France did not obtain the indemnity demanded, but China signed away sovereignty in Annam and Tonkin.

Hertslet's two memoranda formed part of a general revival of interest in the definition of Belligerent Rights at sea, which was continued in 1894 with another Foreign Office memorandum. The rights of naval powers to exercise constraint over neutral shipping were never entirely certain, even for declared belligerents. In September 1894 the Foreign Office published a confidential *Memorandum on Blockades* in which they reviewed the legal precedents and opinions respecting the rights of nations exercising shipping control without declaring war. The first half was concerned with the 'Right of a Belligerent Power to prevent entrance and exit of Neutral Vessels of War into and from a Blockaded Port.' After reviewing the precedents and the legal authorities, the Foreign Office concluded 'It may be, at all events, taken as established that where one nation is at war with another, or is repressing an insurrection, the blockading Power should be approached for permission to use a blockaded port.' The record, however, was not entirely consistent. The right of diplomatic representatives to a country to communicate with the consular officials in a blockaded port, and to employ a warship for the purpose, was fairly well established. It was also recognised that neutral powers had a valid claim to protect the lives of their citizens caught in war or civil insurrection. 'Her Majesty's Government,' which increasingly identified its interests with those of neutral shippers, concluded that 'any interference with the ships of a third nation may, in their opinion, be properly regarded by that nation as an act of belligerency implying and only to be justified by the existence of a state of war' [17].

The imposition of a 'pacific blockade' on Venezuela in 1902 by Britain, with Germany and Italy, because of the failure of the Venezuelan government to honour its debts, was to be the last of such operations until that term was used in connection with the 1962 Cuban Missile Crisis. It was not a comfortable alliance, because the British government could not agree with the proposal made by Count Metternich, German Ambassador to the Court of St James, to 'sequestre' neutral shipping attempting to enter Venezuelan ports. A precis of the 1894 memorandum was written by persons identified as A.L., W.E.D. and F.H.V., who declared that 'The so-called "pacific blockade" is not really a blockade at all. Blockade is a belligerent right, and unless one is at war with a State one cannot prevent the ships of other States from free communication with the ports of that State' [18]. At the 1907 Hague Conference the western European powers and Japan agreed to the 'Porter Convention' which proscribed the use of reprisals to exact payment of debts. Neither Russia nor the United States, however, signed on.

1.   *Privateers and Letters of Marque*[1]

Sir James Robert Graham, First Lord of the Admiralty, to the Earl of Clarendon, Secretary of State for Foreign Affairs
Confidential

[FO 83/487]   Admiralty
                                                      3 March 1854

My Lord, I have reason to believe that the Emperor of Russia is about to issue letters of marque, authorising the subjects of various States with whose Governments England is at peace, to equip privateers from foreign ports, for the purpose of capturing property belonging to British subjects.

If it be conceded that Russia may pursue this course without infringing the existing law of nations, it is obvious that the only practical result will be, to enrich foreign adventurers in whose welfare she has no interest, at the price of heaping ruin and misery on individuals not necessarily involved in the calamities incidental to the war. Russia, therefore, by this act, will directly augment the horrors or war, and will add to the amount of human suffering, without obtaining a corresponding advantage either to herself or her own subjects; for the naval power of Great Britain is sufficient to prevent any efforts of such privateers from affecting the ultimate event of the war.

The maritime Powers who are still at peace with Russia, are by no means unconcerned in this determination on her part. Even under favourable circumstances, and subject to the strictest regulations, letters of marque are always liable to abuse. The sole object of those who obtain them, is plunder. Effective discipline can rarely be maintained in a privateer's crew; and cruelty towards the enemy, and outrages upon neutrals, too often accompany their success. If adventurers, animated solely by the hope of plunder, are thus allowed to roam distant seas, unchecked by the proximity of a naval force belonging to the Power by whom they are commissioned, it is certain that the commerce of neutral nations cannot long remain exempt from imminent danger.

The *Law of Nations* by which this act of Russia will be justified, has constantly received modifications from the progress of civilization. In modern times its maxims with respect to the mode of conducting war have been more particularly investigated, and, as observed by an eminent writer in the beginning of the present century, 'It is no longer

---

[1]See also C.P. 22 July 1856, 'Papers Relative to International Mediation and Maritime Law, May–June, 1856'. This file contains 116 documents, totalling 88 pages.

thought lawful to annoy an enemy indiscriminately by every means in our power; nor is it enough to justify an act of violence or cruelty, that it has a manifest tendency to weaken or intimidate the nation with which we are at war. We have ceased to poison arms or provisions, to refuse quarter, to massacre women and children, or to sack and burn defenceless towns and villages.' (Jeffery, Edinburgh Review, April 1806.) The questions now arise:

Ought Europe to rest content with what has been done? Shall the nineteenth century, so distinguished by a generous rivalry among nations in commerce, in science, and in arts, pass away without an effort to benefit the human race by a further mitigation of the disasters and cruelties of war? Surely if mankind are forbidden to regard war as an impossible calamity, they are bound to do the utmost in their power to lessen its evils.

Reprisals or Letters of Marque, under which Russia proposes to shelter these privateers, are founded upon a right inherent in every Government to obtain redress for itself, or its subjects, when injured by a foreign State.

History shows that reprisals have undergone several important alterations. In the feudal times reprisals were exercised without any commission from the State. Afterwards in the fifteenth century commissions came to be considered necessary; and Germany, France, and England required all cruizers belonging to their subjects to be furnished with them. Since that time the necessity for letters of marque has become part of the acknowledged law of nations. For though upon the breaking out of a war a subject may, without a commission, attack the public foe, any capture which he makes under these circumstances inures to the benefit of the State to which he belongs, and not to himself, or in the terms of the law of England becomes a 'droit of Admiralty.'

The advance of civilization has also in another particular affected reprisals. They were at first granted to private persons against foreigners with whose States the Government granting them remained still at peace; and sometimes without any previous application for redress to the Government thus wantonly assailed, though this abuse has long been discontinued. The granting of private reprisals, or letters of marque, is characterized by Lord Stowell in his day as 'an exploded practice.'

It has also been found necessary to provide against the abuse of public reprisals or letters of marque by special regulations. The owners of privateers have been compelled to give security for conducting their enterprises according to the laws and usages of war, to regard the rights of neutrals, and to bring in their prizes for adjudication into a port belonging to the State which granted the commission, or into that of an ally. 'These checks (it is well observed by Chancellor Kent in his Commentaries) are essential to the character and safety of maritime nations.'

On the other hand, the right of granting letters of marque has been extended beyond the limits which seem justifiable, when their intent is carefully considered. If the authority of a State to grant them were in itself a sufficient justification, Russia might grant letters of marque to English subjects, and thereby authorize them to capture English property. The enormity of this is apparent. Yet, to prevent such atrocities, England thought it necessary to pass the Act of the 11th and 12th William III, c.7, by which any such acceptance of letters of marque was declared to be piracy; and in April 1790 the United States of America passed an Act of Congress to the same effect.

The case of the subject belonging to a State at peace with both the belligerent powers, and acting against one of them under letters of marque received from the other, seems at first sight to present a less objectionable aspect. This has nevertheless, by 59 George III, c.69, been declared to be a misdemeanour, and the United States, by an Act of Congress of April 20th, 1818, have also forbidden it. France likewise, in her celebrated 'Ordonnance de la Marine' of 1681, declared – 'Détendons à tous nos sujets de prendre commissions d'aucuns Rois, Princes, ou Etats étrangers, pour armer des vaisseaux en guerre et courir la mer sous leur bannière si ce n'est par notre permission, à peine d'être traités comme pirates.'

The alleged intention of Russia involves not only this act, which France, England, and America have all repudiated, but much more; for Russia possesses no ports of her own in the southern seas; and the intended privateers must be manned by the subjects of neutral States, and be equipped in and despatched from ports belonging to States nominally at peace with all the belligerents; and they must either appropriate their prizes without legal condemnation, or carry them into neutral ports, where (whatever may be the practice of particular States), by the Law of Nations, no legal title can be conferred upon the captor. Such a warfare is not to be distinguished from piracy, though, were it to occur, the sole remedy left to Great Britain, under the existing Law of Nations, would be to declare war against every State who thus allowed her neutrality to be abused; inasmuch as the Russian letters of marque would be sufficient to protect the parties acting under them from being treated as pirates, unless there existed some Treaty now in force between their Government and Great Britain by which special provision was made that such hostilities should be considered piratical.

The modifications which the Law of Nations has undergone of late years encourage the hope that other improvements may still be effected.

In furtherance of justice and of morality many States have waived their undoubted right under the Law of Nations, and have consented to deliver up foreign criminals to their own Governments. The Slave Trade, also, which has been pronounced by the highest legal authorities, both in England and America, to be in itself consistent with the Law of Nations, is now branded as piracy.

England has taken a prominent part in effecting both these important changes. The latter, it should be remembered, was carried [that is, agreed to] against the obvious pecuniary interests of many of those States which now call it piracy, and the way to it was opened by the Congress of Vienna in 1815, solemnly announcing that the Slave Trade was 'repugnant to the principles of humanity and universal morality,' and that the 'universal voice of all civilized countries demanded its abolition.'

The using of letters of marque, against a State at peace with the Government whose subjects thus become the aggressors, tends to foster a mercenary, violent, and lawless spirit, uncurbed by any social or moral control, which soon degenerates into that of the pirate. It would seem strange that no general declaration in favour of morality and humanity has as yet been made against this abuse of reprisals. The reason is, that no nation has hitherto practised it on a large scale; and a European peace of nearly forty years has fixed the attention of the maritime Powers on other more pressing subjects. There exists, however, but few maritime nations which have not, at one time or other, recorded a repudiation of acts similar to those which Russia is thus about to sanction.

At the commencement of the seventeenth century the Spanish Courts decided that a privateer, furnished with letters of marque by a belligerent State, if manned with a crew belonging to a neutral country, could not make a legal capture of property belonging to subjects of the State against whom she had been commissioned. (Albericus Gentilis Hisp. Advoc., lib. 1, c.10.) By another decision, the same Court held that a son, born in one of the belligerent States, but whose father afterwards became naturalized in a neutral state, was unable (though acting under letters of marque granted by the country of his nativity), to benefit by a capture made from the enemies of that country. (Albericus Gentilis, *id.*, c.17.) Whether these decisions are, or are not, law at the present time, they serve to mark the opinions of the Spanish Courts upon the point under consideration.

Denmark, as early as the 13th February, 1600, entered into a Treaty with Great Britain to render it penal for the subjects of either State to accept letters of marque from a foreign Power at peace with itself, though at war with the other. The same provision was repeated in the Treaties of the 11th July, 1670, and 11th January, 1814, and again in a Convention of 13th August, 1841. She also, in an early Treaty with Genoa of July 30, 1789, agreed that any of her subjects accepting these letters of marque should be deemed guilty of piracy.

Prussia, by a Treaty with the United States of 10th September, 1785, agreed that her subjects accepting such letters of marque should be treated as pirates, and she renewed this provision in a subsequent Treaty bearing [the] date 11th July, 1799.

Spain, in a Treaty of 27th October, 1795, with the United States, agreed that her subjects acting in this manner should be considered as pirates.

Great Britain, besides the Treaties which have been already noticed, in 1803 made a Treaty with the Republic of the Seven Islands, forbidding her subjects to accept these letters of marque; and in a Treaty with the United States of 19th November, 1794, she declared those of her subjects so acting to be guilty of piracy. The same clause was again inserted in her Treaty with the United States of 31st December, 1806.

To the United States of America must be conceded the honour of having constantly and consistently endeavoured to carry this principle into full effect. Unfettered by considerations which may have hampered European States, American has energetically lent herself to forward the dictates of humanity and of civilization. The numerous Treaties which have already been adverted to abundantly establish this fact to her honour. But if more were needed, on the 8th October, 1782, she made a Treaty with the Low Countries; and on 20th December, 1825, with the Republic of Colombia; and on the 13th June, 1839, with the Republic of the Equator; in all of which she agreed that conduct on the part of her subjects similar to that into which Russia now proposes to inveigle the subjects of certain States in South America, should be treated as piracy.

Russia herself has by no means repudiated the proposed amelioration of the Law of Nations, for by a Treaty of the 1st March, 1801, made with Sweden, she bound herself to allow none of her subjects to act against that State under letters of marque from any other Power.

* * *

These examples may suffice to show that the great Powers of Europe and America have already, on many occasions, acknowledged the principle that friendly Powers may fairly be required to prohibit their subjects, under the penalty of piracy, from assisting to man or equip privateers commissioned against a friendly State. That the acceptance of these Russian letters of marque by their subjects may, if sanctioned, seriously affect neutral States is evident; but it must also be remembered, that the slightest encouragement given to such acts on the part of neutral Governments compromises their neutrality. Accordingly in several of the declarations of neutrality put forward by different States at different periods, they expressly prohibit such conduct on the part of their subjects. This prohibition is inserted in the declaration of neutrality made by the Grand Duke of Tuscany in 1778; and Genoa, in a similar declaration of 1799, and Austria, in another of 1803, inserted it likewise. The same observation applies to the declaration of neutrality made by Denmark on 4th May, 1803.

The present juncture seems to call upon England to adopt a somewhat unusual course. Russia, a great Northern Power, not possessing any ports belonging to herself, or to any ally, situated in the southern seas, engaged in war against this country, is about to commission privateers for the purpose of intercepting our Australian and Indian commerce. To accomplish this object she will be obliged to man these privateers with the subjects of countries at peace with England, and to fit out the ships in neutral ports. If these privateers are unsuccessful and destroyed, Russia is not injured: the cost to her is the paper on which the commissions are written. If they succeed, her subjects reap no benefit: and she leaves these armed vessels, unchecked by the presence of a responsible Russian force, to develop any piratical tendencies they may secretly entertain, and without a Russian port within reach into which even lawful prizes could be carried.

If a distinction is henceforth to be preserved between war and piracy, Great Britain is entitled in this emergency to call upon the other Great Maritime Powers to show that they give no sanction to such an abuse of letters of marque, by making it piracy for their own subjects to accept them.

In this, England must herself lead the way, and, as America has already done, enact that any of her own subjects acting under letters of marque against a foreign Power with whom she is herself at peace shall be guilty of piracy. It is surely not too much to anticipate that the other Powers will respond to this call, and (if Russia should still unhappily persevere in her present intention) that by enforcing these laws they will prevent the success of a piratical design. It is also impossible not to look forward to a future day of peace, in which Russia by her adherence may aid in incorporating this principle in the law of nations, seeing that it is founded in humanity, and is in accordance with the spirit of a more civilized age, which seeks to diminish the cruelties and the evils of war itself.

Vattel long ago declared, that 'it is an infamous proceeding on the part of foreigners to take out commissions from a Prince in order to commit piratical depredations on a nation which is perfectly innocent in respect to them. The thirst of gold is their only inducement; nor can the commission they have received efface the infamy of their conduct, though it screens them from punishment.' *Book III*, c.8, s.138.

The time has arrived when this shelter should no longer be afforded, and in accordance with the unanimous voice of public opinion in every civilized country privateers fitted out and manned in neutral ports should be denounced as pirates, and should be treated by the Law of Nations as the enemies of the human race.

The foregoing considerations naturally suggest a much more extended inquiry; namely, whether it might not be possible altogether to forego the use of privateers. All that has been said of the abuses to which they are liable, and of the strict regulations under which alone they are to be tolerated, seems to point out the advantage, if possible, of putting an end to them altogether. Were civilized nations universally to abandon the system of private warfare, abstain from issuing letters of marque, and limit maritime hostilities to national ships-of-war, many obvious advantages would ensue. The commanders of such vessels, educated in the public service, would be more easily controlled, less liable to be seduced into acts of cruelty and illegal plunder, and many of the frauds resorted to by neutral merchants would cease to be practised.

The right to employ this force is, however, founded upon the primary Law of Nations, and the advantage which it secures to a State by intercepting the enemy's commerce is obvious. In short, as Sir Leoline Jenkyns quaintly expresses it, 'The privateers in our wars are like the mathematici in old Rome, a sort of people that will be always found fault with, but still made use of.' – *Wynne's Life*, vol. ii p. 714.

Whether any nation can dispense with the use of privateers, will, in a great degree, depend upon the extent to which she intends employing the means in her power of annoying the enemy. If she is determined to enforce the extreme of her rights as a belligerent, and capture every portion of the enemy's property which it is possible for her to seize, a greater number of armed vessels will be needed than if she limits herself to the one grand object which is proposed in making war, and repudiates any private gain which her subjects might possibly derive from it.

An attempt on the part of Great Britain to intercept the whole maritime commerce of Russia would be a gigantic undertaking. Our fleet commands the sea; and neutrals would readily offer their vessels and the security of their names, and even be content to risk some loss, for the lucrative employment of being the enemy's carriers. The attempt, under such circumstances, would involve a minute, and therefore vexatious, search of neutral vessels, to an extent which no regular navy could enforce; and would necessarily require, in addition, the employment of a large number of privateers; while the experience of the last war shows that, notwithstanding every precaution, Russian property might still be so concealed as to render the escape of a great portion of it all but certain.

It is wholly impossible to imagine any maritime war during which the enemy's merchantmen shall be permitted unmolested to navigate the sea. It is also vain to hope that the effects of war can ever be wholly confined to the belligerent nations themselves. Even in a war between small States, their immediate neighbours will suffer, more or less; but in hostilities between great nations, and particularly in modern times where the ramifications of commerce are so varied, the whole civilized portion of mankind may possibly be injuriously affected. So long, therefore, as war shall exist, neutrals must be content to suffer some degree of hardship, and to undergo some losses when it occurs.

The point to be considered is how far this inconvenience to neutrals can be mitigated, without infringing upon the necessary rights of either of the belligerent parties. In elucidating this, it may be well briefly to recapitulate certain of the principles upon which Great Britain conducted the last war.

During that great European struggle, England maintained –

1.   That a belligerent State is justified in seizing and appropriating all property belonging to the enemy which she finds afloat.

2.   That a neutral, in time of war, has a right to prosecute with the belligerent powers any traffic which belonged to her in time of peace, but that this right can only be exercised subject to the right of either belligerent to seize the property of the other whenever it is found afloat. – *Per Lord Ellenborough in 'Barker v Blakes,' 9 East, 292.*

3.   That the right to seize enemy's property necessarily includes the right to search vessels sailing under a neutral flag. – *Per Lord Stowell in 'The Maria,' 1 Rob. 360.*

4.   That, if in the prosecution of this legitimate search, British subjects are found on board a neutral ship, they may be required, in the same manner as if they had been met with on shore, to join a British man-of-war; also, that if any irregularity on the part of the neutral be discovered during such search, Great Britain has a right to investigate it.

5.   That the enemy's property found on board a neutral vessel is a lawful prize; but that the vessel, as belonging to a neutral, is entitled to be released, with the freight she would have earned by transporting the goods to their destined port. – *Per Lord Stowell in 'The Twilling Riget,' 5 Rob. 82.*

6.   That the property of a neutral on board an enemy's vessel, is to be restored to the neutral. – *Per Lord Stowell in 'The Fanny,' 1 Dodds, 448.*

7.   That neither belligerent may prosecute hostilities in any territory belonging to a neutral. – *Per Lord Stowell in 'The Twee Gebroeders,' 3 Rob. 163.*

8.   That neutrals have no right to assume in time of war a trade which was not previously open to them in time of peace. – *Per Lord Stowell in 'The Emanuel,' 1 Rob. 298; and in 'The Johanna Sholen,' 6 Rob. 78.*

9.   That neutrals have no right to convey to belligerents contraband articles of war, by means of which one belligerent so assisted may be able to prolong the war against the other. That such contraband articles in all cases involve the loss of freight and expenses to the neutral, and in aggravated cases may work a forfeiture of the ship, and also of the cargo. – *Per Lord Stowell in 'The Mercurius,' 1 Rob. 288; 'The Jonge Tobias,' ib. 329.*

10.   That neutral vessels, if affected with the knowledge of a blockade, are liable to capture for a breach of such blockade, provided that the blockading force is sufficiently large to render approach dangerous. That the breach of blockade by a neutral renders the vessel liable to confiscation, and also the cargo, if it belong to the same owner; and in all cases affects the cargo, if its owner is implicated in the attempt to break the blockade. – *In the High Court of Appeals, 'The Nancy,' 1 Acton, 58; per Lord Stowell in 'The Welvaart van Pillaw,' 2 Rob. 128; and in 'Mercurius,' 1 Rob. 48.*

11.   That no British subject may, directly or indirectly, trade with the enemy, even in a neutral's vessel, without a licence to that effect from his own Government. – *Per Lord Stowell, in 'The Hoop,' 1 Rob. 198; 'Potts v. Bell,' 8 Term Reports, 548.*

12.   That neutrals have no right to convey the enemy's despatches, and that, by doing so, they render both ship and cargo liable to confiscation when belonging to the same owner, and when belonging to different owners they render the ship, or the cargo, or both, liable to confiscation, according as the owner of the one, or of the other, or of both, is implicated. – *Per Lord Stowell, in 'The Atalanta,' 6 Rob. 444, &c.*

13.   That every State engaged in war has a right to employ privateers authorized by regular letters of marque. – *1 Blackstone Comm., 258.*

14. That no prize can be legally condemned in the territory of a neutral by a judge appointed by the Government of the captor. – *Per Lord Stowell in the 'Flad Oyen,' 1 Rob. 135; and with Lord Kenyon's remark in 'Havelock v. Rockwood,' 8 Term Reports, 268.*

These principles, founded as they are upon a sound exposition of the Law of Nations, England cannot relinquish, although other nations have asserted claims at variance with some of them. The first of these is, that a free ship involves free goods; in other words, that enemy's property found on board a neutral ship ought not to be liable to confiscation. This is mainly founded upon the right of the neutral to carry the enemy's property, added to the consideration, that by the capture of that property on board his vessel, the neutral is prevented from performing a contract into which he had a right to enter. It is undeniable that the general usage and practice of maritime States has from the earliest times accorded with the doctrine which Great Britain maintained in the last war; but it is also undeniable that many maritime Powers have, on a variety of occasions, ceded to particular States the rights for which she then contended.

Another maxim has been added to that of 'free ships, free goods,' which is its opposite; viz., 'enemy's ships, enemy's goods.' According to this, the goods of a neutral found on board an enemy's ship, and which he had a perfect right to place there, are, upon the condemnation of that ship, liable to condemnation also. This maxim relies chiefly for its support upon the ground that it affords something like an equivalent to a nation which admits the principle of 'free ships, free goods.'

It is obvious that these two principles are not necessarily connected. A State at war has a perfect right to concede the first in favour of a friendly Power, but can only enforce the second against a friendly Power, after having obtained her consent. We may forego, at any time, a right we possess; but we cannot, except under legitimate circumstances, exercise any right which we never possessed previously. It is doubtful indeed whether the second of these maxims would ever have been advocated, excepting as an inducement to the practice of the first.

The following examples may serve to show to what extent these two maxims have been adopted.

In a Treaty between Edward IV of England and the Duke of Bretagne, dated July 2, 1468, it is stipulated that the property of subjects of either State found on board an enemy's ship should be lawful prize. – *Rym. xi, 622.*

In another Treaty, between Henry VIII and the same Duke of Bretagne, dated July 19, 1486, a similar stipulation is contained. – *Rym. xii, p. 309.*

During the middle ages, the Hanseatic Towns assumed a prominence among the maritime States. Their object was to accumulate wealth as the carriers of other countries. They, therefore, endeavoured to turn to their own advantage the wars arising between powerful and neighbouring States, and they may fairly be considered to have been the first to enunciate as a rule, that free ships make free goods. Whilst they were able to maintain a naval superiority, they endeavoured to enforce this maxim, but it necessarily lost ground as they declined in maritime importance.

By Article 42 of the French Ordonnance of 1543, and by Article 69 of a subsequent Ordonnance of March 1584, goods belonging to a friendly Power, and having enemy's goods on board, are declared lawful prize. This is altered by a subsequent declaration made in 1650, but was re-established by the celebrated Ordonnance of Louis XIV, in 1681 (b.3, tit.9, sec.7), in which neutral goods on board an enemy's ship, and neutral ships carrying enemy's goods, are declared lawful prize.

In the Ordonnance of 1704, France adhered to these provisions, but by the Règlement of 1744, goods belonging to the enemy were alone confiscated, and the neutral vessel was released, together with any portion of the cargo proved to belong to neutrals.

By Article I of the famous Declaration of Neutrality made by the Empress Catherine of Russia, and dated February 28, 1780, the maxim was adopted, that free ships made free goods. To this Declaration, France, Spain, and the United States, acceded as belligerents, and Germany, Portugal, and Naples as neutrals. In 1807 Russia also issued a Declaration in which the principles of the armed neutrality were declared afresh.

On July 8, and November 22, 1796, the Executive Directory of France decreed, that with reference to visit, seizure, and confiscation, neutrals should be treated in the same way as they permitted themselves to be treated by the enemy.

In January 1798 the Council of Five Hundred, upon a message from the Executive Directory and the Council of Ancients, decreed, that the state of a ship, whether neutral or hostile, should depend upon the ownership of its cargo.

A variety of later Treaties have also been concluded between different States, which have sanctioned one or both modifications of the general Law of Nations above-mentioned.

Thus the maxim, 'free ships free goods,' and 'enemy's ships enemy's goods,' is embodied in Articles VIII and XIII of a Treaty dated December 17, 1650, between Philip IV of Spain and the United Provinces.

Similar stipulations are made by Article XXI of a Treaty dated August 6, 1661, between Portugal and the United Provinces.

They occur again in Article XXII of a Treaty between France and the Netherlands, dated August 10, 1678; and again in Article XXVII of a second Treaty, dated September 20, 1697.

They are likewise confirmed by Article III of a Treaty between Russia and Sweden, dated December 4, 1800; by Article III of a second Treaty between Russia and Prussia, dated December 6, 1800; and by Article III of a third Treaty between Russia and Denmark, dated February 20, 1801.

The United States of America, by Articles XI and XII of a Treaty with the States-General of the Low Countries, dated October 8, 1782, made similar stipulations. These were repeated in Articles VII and XVIII of a Treaty, dated April 3, 1783, between the United States and Sweden; and again in Article XII of a Treaty, dated September 10, 1785, between the United States and Prussia. This latter Treaty was, however, modified by Article XIII of a subsequent Treaty, dated July 1, 1799.

The United States also, in Article XII of a Treaty with Spain, dated February 2, 1819, and by Articles XII and XIII of a subsequent Treaty with Spain, dated October 3, 1824, entered into similar stipulations.

The maxim that neutral vessels shall protect hostile goods, coupled with its opposite that hostile vessels shall cause the confiscation of neutral goods, is not wholly unknown in English Treaties. They are both contained in Article XXIII of the Treaty between Cromwell and Portugal dated July 10, 1654. The latter of these provisions occurs by itself in Article XXVI of a Treaty made between Charles II of England and Charles II of Spain, dated May 23, 1667, which was confirmed by Article XV of the Treaty of Peace concluded at Utrecht dated July 2, 1713, and again by a separate Article to a Treaty dated November 9, 1729, and by Article III of a further Treaty dated October 5, 1750. The Treaty of Utrecht was again confirmed by Article II of a Treaty dated February 10, 1763, and by Article II dated September 3, 1783.

Both these principles are to be found in combination in Article X of a Treaty between England and the United Provinces dated February 17, 1674. The same may be said of Articles XVII and XXVI of the Treaty between Great Britain and France dated Utrecht, March 31, 1713, as also of Articles XX and XXXIX of a Treaty between Great Britain and France dated September 26, 1786.

The above numerous Treaties (to which others might be added) demonstrate that; at any rate since the beginning of the sixteenth century, neutral Powers have been constantly endeavouring to obtain a more favourable treatment at the hands of belligerents than the general Law of Nations would allow them to demand. If one of the belligerent Powers may be interested from circumstances in declaring that free ships make free goods, neutrals are more interested in establishing such a rule. Great Britain could never, after having maintained the strict principles of the

Law of Nations which she supported in the former war, allow any neutral to claim such a concession as a right. She may nevertheless voluntarily yield in favour of friendly Powers generally that which she has yielded at different times to friendly States individually.

There are, however, certain considerations which ought to be borne in mind. The less neutrals are incommoded in exercising the right to carry on their accustomed traffic, the more stringently are they bound to preserve an undoubted impartiality. If they are to enjoy the right of trading with the enemy without inquiry as to the ownership of any property on board their vessels, they can claim no dispensation at the hands of a belligerent Power to convey to the enemy the ammunition, stores, or goods, by means of which alone he will be able to prolong the war. Much less can a neutral hope to be allowed to interfere with the direct operations of the war by bearing the enemy's despatches, or breaking an effective blockade to which one of the belligerents has subjected the ports, harbours, or coasts of the other. Any State refusing to observe these restrictions, forfeits her neutrality.

After an anxious consideration of the foregoing observations as applicable to the present position of England, I desire to recommend certain modifications of the existing maritime law for the adoption of Her Majesty's Government with reference to the impending hostilities.

1.   That no letters of marque should be issued during the present war.

2.   That an Act of Parliament be passed by which the crime of equipping, manning, or serving in a privateer, without the licence of Her Majesty, and in order to assist any State not at war with England, shall be declared piracy, and be subjected to the same penalties as may now by law be inflicted upon persons fitting out or serving in vessels designed for carrying on the Slave Trade.

3.   In order to render the situation of friendly States as little disastrous as possible, I further recommend that, during the present war, Great Britain shall concede the principle of 'free ship, free goods;' but I feel no desire to render this concession less beneficial by clogging it with the opposite principle of 'enemy's ship, enemy's goods.'

This latter principle is obviously unjust, and Great Britain ought therefore to forego any advantage arising to herself from its adoption. Neutral property, not contraband or affected with delinquency, would, therefore, be restored as heretofore, wherever the ownership is sufficiently proved.

The difficulties which arose in former times from claiming English seamen found in neutral vessels can hardly arise at the present moment, considering the modified form in which the manning of the navy is now prosecuted. Indeed, the proper remedy for any abuse in this respect, would seem to be stringent instructions to the commanders of cruizers not to search for men, rather than the proposal of any alteration of the existing law.

Neither Great Britain nor any belligerent can concede to a neutral the right of carrying contraband of war, or enemy's despatches, or of committing a breach of blockade with impunity. It is of vital importance for the effective prosecution of any maritime war that these latter principles should be strictly maintained.

To carry these recommendations into effect, I further suggest:

4.   That a declaration be prepared, announcing the intention of Great Britain, during the present war, to exercise the right of search to the extent only of ascertaining the nationality of the vessels searched, and the fact that there are no contraband articles on board; that if in the course of such search enemy's property, not contraband, be found on board a neutral vessel, it shall not be deemed lawful prize; that Great Britain, for the further benefit of friendly Powers, has no desire to obtain from them the corresponding concession that neutral property shall be confiscated when found on board enemy's ships; that for the present Great Britain pledges herself to commission no privateers; that, on the other hand, Great Britain deems it essential to the just exercise of her rights as a belligerent to maintain the law prohibiting neutrals from carrying contraband of war, or the despatches of the enemy, and to permit no infringement of the existing law with regard to blockade as principles which cannot be compromised or waived without a surrender of means necessary to carry on hostilities.

The liberality of a declaration such as that proposed, at the first commencement of the war, ought to produce a favourable impression on our allies and on neutrals; and prove a bond of closer union between England and the maritime Powers both of Europe and America.

We shall enter the contest in close alliance with France, and on friendly terms with the United States, with Prussia, Sweden, and Denmark. If the concession which I advocate be made, that alliance will be strengthened, and those friendly relations will be confirmed.

The fleets of England are now united with those of France in a common cause, and in every sea. History affords no example of such an union; and is this the moment when England can justly insist on the exercise of extreme rights? Is it not rather the occasion when she is bound to forbear from every act and to waive every right by which the harmony existing between the two countries might possibly be disturbed? Prudence and friendship alike dictate the more generous policy. Neutral countries will partake largely of the benefit, whereby the evils of a maritime war will be mitigated; but will not England have her full share of the general good?

She is still the great emporium of the commerce of the world: every expansion of trade stimulates her industry and enlarges her power; every diminution of it, however indirect or remote, is an injury inflicted on her vital interests. But, can we descend from the height of our proud pretensions and forego claims which we have manfully defended against the world in arms? Yet what changes have taken place in the interval! It must be remembered that we have abandoned the system of protective duties; that we are the largest importers of foreign produce; and impressment is all but relinquished; that we have repealed our navigation laws; that we have renounced the monopoly of our Colonial trade; and that we are now about to throw open our coasting trade itself. With changes such as these successfully accomplished, we can well afford to make a timely and a voluntary concession in favour of commerce, to which we owe so much, and in mitigation of the evils of war, which are the scourges of mankind.

We have abolished slavery in the British dominions. We have done more to suppress the Slave Trade than any other nation on the earth. Let us lead the way to extirpate privateering, and to prevent, even during hostilities, the entire suspension of commerce; we then shall have stripped war of a portion of its miseries; we shall have done much in our day and generation to alleviate human suffering and to promote the concord of nations. When will the greatest jurists or the most successful warriors achieve a nobler triumph?

* * *

2.   Draft of Note to be Addressed by British Agents Abroad to Foreign Courts

*Attachment to draft letter from Lord Clarendon to HM Diplomatic
Agents Abroad
Draft*

[FO 83/487]   4 April, 1854

The undersigned, &c, has received orders from his Gov[ernmen]t to make to HE, [His Excellency] &c _____ the following communication.

Her Majesty the Queen of the United Kingdom of Great Britain and Ireland and His Majesty the Emperor of the French being compelled to take up arms for the purpose of repelling the aggression of HM [His

Majesty] the Emperor of Russia upon the Ottoman Empire, and being desirous to lessen as much as possible the disastrous consequences to commerce resulting from a state of warfare, their Majesties have resolved, for the present, not to authorize the issue of Letters of Marque.

In making this resolution known, they think it right to announce at the same time the principles upon which they will be guided, during the course of this war, with regard to the navigation and commerce of neutrals.

Her Majesty the Queen of the United Kingdom of Great Britain and Ireland has accordingly published the accompanying Declaration, which is identical with that published by His Majesty the Emperor of the French.

In thus restricting within the narrowest limits the exercise of their Rights as Belligerents allied Gov[ernment]s confidently trust that the Governments of Countries which may remain neutral during this War will sincerely exert every effort to enforce upon their subjects (the Republics) or citizens the necessity of observing the strictest neutrality.

Her Britannic Majesty's Gov[ernmen]t entertains the confident hope that the Gov[ernmen]t of _____ will receive with satisfaction the announcement of the resolutions thus taken in common by the two allied Gov[ernmen]ts, and that it will, in the spirit of just reciprocity give orders that no Privateer under Russian colours shall be equipped, or victualled, or admitted with its prizes in the Ports of _____; and also that the subjects/citizens of _____ shall vigorously abstain from taking part in armaments of this nature, or in any other measures opposed to the duties of a strict neutrality.
(Signed)

* * *

3. Commercial Policy towards Russia

Remarks by Viscount Edward Cardwell, President of the Board of Trade in Lord Aberdeen's Administration, 1852–1855
Confidential

[PRO 30/29/23/4/181–88]   October 31, 1854

So soon as it was determined, on the part of Great Britain, to waive those doctrines of the last war which aimed at destroying the trade of the enemy with neutrals, it was obvious that we must practically permit the Queen's subjects to trade with the enemy. The consequence of adopting any other course would have been to drive away trade from ourselves to neutrals; in other words, Russia would not have suffered. Her trade would have continued, though diverted into other channels. Our trade would have been destroyed. At the same time a premium upon neutrality would have been created; another result most prejudicial to the allies.

These considerations induced the allied Governments to relax the strictness of the Law of Nations, by Orders in Council, &c.

It is now observed, that British capital is still embarked in trade with Russia, and that the blockade of the Russian ports has driven the trade to the ports of Prussia nearest to Russia. It is therefore proposed to adopt new measures, namely, to prohibit British subjects from trading with Russia, and, by means of a system of certificates of origin, to prohibit the importation of Russian produce, whether through Prussia or through any other channel.

The Orders in Council are framed, as has been said, upon the supposition that the trade of Russia could not be wholly checked; and that it was not expedient to drive away from ourselves, in favour of neutrals, that portion of it which must inevitably continue to exist. Again, when the Russian ports were blockaded, it was known that so much of the Russian trade as could bear the cost of transport, would evade the pressure of the blockade, by passing through the ports of Prussia. Both consequences, therefore, were foreseen, and their actual occurrence only shows that the Orders in Council have answered the intention of their framers, and that the blockade has been effectual.

Have, then, any new considerations arisen, inviting the British Government to adopt new views?

Are we prepared to revert to our ancient doctrines, and, for the purpose of crushing the trade with Russia, to incur the hostility of all neutral Powers, and to sever our maritime policy from that of France?

Are we so dissatisfied with Prussia as a neutral that we are prepared to make her an enemy? Or are we dissatisfied upon the whole with the effect of a blockade which has transferred to the ports of a neutral so much of the enemy's trade as it has not been able to destroy?

I understand that the proposal now under consideration simply is, that we shall prohibit any trade between Russia and ourselves, in the belief that by so doing we shall inflict a greater injury upon Russia than we shall sustain ourselves.

Before this conclusion is adopted, I think the following considerations should be weighed, viz.,

1.   In point of fact, the trade and manufactures of Russia have, by means of the blockade, been seriously injured. It is a mistake to suppose that our measures have failed to inflict commercial pressure upon Russia.

2. The measure now proposed would have little or no effect upon Russia, while it would in no inconsiderable degree injure ourselves. It would also benefit neutrals: and this result, which we deprecate now when the benefit to Prussia is temporary, and obtained at the expense of Russia, would under the new plan be permanent, and would be obtained at our own expense, and not at the expense of our enemy.

1. In illustration of the first point, viz., that Russia is actually suffering a great pressure, I would observe upon –

    a. The annihilation of the Russian merchant navy.

    b. The diminution of the trade and manufactures of Russia.

    c. The diminished price of Russian produce at St. Petersburgh [*sic*], owing to the cost of conveyance through Prussia.

Of these heads, the first needs no illustration; the second is fully set forth in two letters hereto appended: viz., one from the Foreign Office to the Board of Trade, inclosing a despatch from Berlin to the effect that for some months past (*i.e.*, ever since the blockade was established) the transport of raw material was too expensive to be borne, and the manufactories in Russia had been closed; the other letter from the Board of Trade to the Foreign Office, showing the great diminution in the exports and imports of Russia; also the great diminution in the exports and imports of Russia and Prussia together, and the tendency of that diminution to induce a supply to the British market from other parts of the world; in other words, that England is obtaining what she wants, but ceasing to obtain it so much from Russia.[1]

The third head requires some elucidation, and is of great importance. The system of carrying on trade with Russia has been that the English merchant is a year in advance of money to the Russian producer. It consequently follows, that in the first year of hostilities, the contracts being already made, the purchaser must bear the loss occasioned by any unforeseen expenses incurred in bringing the produce from Russia. But so soon as the time for new contracts comes, the English merchant

---

[1]*Imports into this Country, January to September 1853–54.
From Russia and Prussia together.

	Tallow £	Flax £	Hemp. £
1853	288,455	978,447	468,940
1854	113,760	708,443	176,225
Decrease	174,695	270,004	292,715
From other Countries			
1853	249,727	266,937	319,972
1854	334,904	390,170	567,229
Increase	85,117	123,233	247,248

[Notes marked * appear in the original documents.]

will only give such a price as, after allowing for the additional cost of transit, he can pay.

In other words, the pressure will, in the first year, fall upon England, and will in all future years fall principally upon Russia. This is apparent from reflection; but it is illustrated by the following figures, taken from a paper which has been furnished to me by the Governor of the Bank:

		October 1853	1854
		£000	£000
Hemp	St Petersburgh	26½	21½
	London	36	60
Tallow	St Petersburgh	44	29½
	London	58/9	66

These figures show that while the general course of trade in the world has established a great rise both in tallow and in hemp, Russia is so far from participating, that she sells a much smaller quantity at a much lower price. Before I leave this subject I would observe, that the blockade has scarcely been operative at all in the White Sea, and that the apparent pressure upon Russia in another year will be so much greater.

It is then manifest, that already a very serious blow has been inflicted upon the trade of Russia.

2.   Let us inquire what would be the probable effect of attempting to exclude all articles of Russian origin from the English market. First. Is it possible? Did Napoleon succeed in the like attempt? Are not the frontiers of France crowded with smugglers at this time? If it be answered that we have means of exclusion which continental countries have not, I ask in reply, – if that be conceded, would it be wise to establish a stringent law operative in England and inoperative in France? Would it benefit England? Would it be effective against Russia? Would it tend to cement the good understanding between the allies?

But again; let our coast-guard be ever so effective, is not the scheme impracticable? What consular officer can ascertain the origin of tallow? Or even of hemp? The provinces of Prussia, adjacent to Russia, produce both. Who can say from which country a given consignment springs?

Further; suppose it were possible. Is it wise to create a premium on the partial manufacture abroad of those articles which now come here as raw materials? If the fat of a Russian beast may not come to England in its first state of preparation, who can prevent its being boiled up with its Prussian neighbours, and imported as stearine [sic] with a valid certification of origin? Is it desirable to transfer to Prussia either the whole, or any part, of the manufacture of soap, or of candles? Is it for us, who complain of the advantages which Prussia has already derived from the war, thus indefinitely and permanently to increase them?

Once more; suppose all that has above been referred to as impracticable could be effectually accomplished. Why has Russia been, hitherto, the chief producer of hemp and of tallow? Because she produces them best and cheapest. It has been shown that our measures have directly tended to impair her powers of production; and this is a serious injury to her, while we only share it as consumers, *i.e.* as all the world shares it. But upon the new plan we should obviously injure ourselves, while the injury to be inflicted upon Russia is less clear. We recently repealed the restrictions on the import of slave sugar, alleging that it was absurd to maintain here a distinction which was effaced by the operation of the neutral markets. The whole tallow of the world, the whole hemp of the world, would be open to American and German purchasers; that limited part which has hitherto been least desired would alone be available to British purchasers. What a bonus to neutral ports as against London and Liverpool! What an inducement to establish manufactories in neutral countries of all the articles of which Russian produce is the raw material!

Do we not come back to the point from which we started; viz., either we must pursue the trade of the enemy in the hands of the neutral, which we do not propose, or else we must not disturb it in the hands of our own subjects? To do so would simply be to vex ourselves.

I have observed a sort of movement in favour of restriction in quarters where I did not expect it, viz., among those who are engaged in trading in these very commodities. This circumstance naturally led to the inquiry – Are the stocks in the hands of the dealers very large, and is it their object to keep up a monopoly price? From a circular which I have obtained, the London stocks appear:–

	1853	**1854**
	Tons	Tons
Hemp	9,083	15,235
Flax	718	2,198
Tallow	20,160	31,725

Very satisfactory, no doubt, it would be to those in whose favour we suspended the blockade of the White Sea, that so soon as their property is safely in dock the gate should be shut.

Even if the Government see the question in this light, and adhere to their former policy, the effect will to a certain extent have been produced by the mere alarm. I append a letter now lying for answer at the Board of Trade, illustrating this position.

I have seen observations on the state of the Russian exchanges, from which it is inferred that advances continue to be made to Russia; and it is argued that they ought therefore to be stopped in the mode above referred to. My answer is that they will not be stopped, and that if your measures be, which I believe they will not be, efficacious in diverting these advances from their former channels, you will not (for the reasons above given) have injured Russia, but will simply have transferred her trade from yourselves to neutrals. It is possible that in doing so you might affect the appearance of the London exchange, but I doubt even that, since London is now the money market of the world, and its exchanges vibrate with the transactions of trade, even when British capital is not directly engaged in them.

Let us, however, consider this subject of the exchanges. What does a movement of the exchanges indicate? If Russia wants gold, in whatever way she be seeking to obtain it, the exchanges will be affected. If the Emperor were to sell stock in London and order the proceeds to be remitted to St Petersburgh, the exchange would be affected. It cannot be doubted that every effort will be made to obtain gold for Russia. It does not follow from a state of the exchanges indicating a tendency of gold towards Russia, that advances for commercial purposes have occasioned it; not if such a state of the exchanges were due to commercial reasons, would it follow that Russia was deriving a benefit from it. The following state of trade (for example) might not be such as we should be desirous to disturb, and yet its existence would be attended by an exchange favourable to Russia. Suppose the pressure of war in Russia to have diminished the consuming power of her population, and that less sugar and coffee were imported; suppose, therefore (what is, I believe, the case), that capital had been withdrawn from the indirect Russian trade; suppose that (as we have seen) the cotton manufactories were closed in Russia, and that meanwhile hemp (useful for our navy) continued to be exported; and that in other respects what is natural had occurred, viz., that the producers of flax and tallow had continued to export those articles, though at a much reduced profit, *via* Prussia; suppose also that inasmuch as Englishmen are considerable holders of Russian stock, they are receiving their dividends in the shape of consignments of Russian produce: this state of things would be attended with an exchange favourable to Russia, and yet I know not that it would be very desirable for us to disturb it.

But before arguing upon the state of the exchanges, would it not be well to examine the fact? Has the course of exchange any indications tending to excite alarm? In time of peace 38d. is the value of the rouble, at which gold begins to leave St Petersburgh; and 39d. the value at which it begins to leave London. In face of the present difficulties, the exchange may, I am told, be considered inert between 37¼d. and 39¾d. At this time last year the exchange was at 39d., indicating a tendency of gold from London to St Petersburgh. It is now at 36¼d., indicating a tendency of gold from St Petersburgh to London.

It is true that when war first was declared, and the export of bullion prohibited by Russia, the exchange fell to 33½d., from which it has since recovered, though (as we have seen) by no means to the state of equilibrium, still less to the state at which it stood before the war.

It was natural it should recover; for the purchaser who obtained a rouble for 33½d. could make a profit of 10 per cent. by smuggling bullion out of the country.

Still, therefore, the fact remains that the exchanges actually indicate (if they indicate anything) a state of things favourable to England, and adverse to Russia. I am always reluctant to draw rapid conclusions from the state of the exchanges; because so many complicated questions are involved in them. But I see, without surprise, that, in the present instance, they confirm the conclusions which have been above derived from other, and, as I think, less deceiving proofs.[1]

Once more, therefore, I conclude as follows, viz.:

If you operate upon the whole trade of Russia, whether with neutrals or with British subjects – and this is the effect of the blockade – you seriously injure Russia, and you suffer only little yourself; that little being only what all other customers of Russia suffer equally.

If you operate upon your own trade with Russia – and this would be the effect of the proposed regulations – you seriously and permanently injure yourself, while the probability is that you will injure Russia very little, if at all; simply diverting her trade from yourself to neutrals. Indeed, in a political point of view, I doubt whether you do not upon the whole confer a benefit upon Russia, inasmuch as you give to America and other neutrals a positive reason for espousing the side of Russia.

* * *

[1]***Course of Russian Exchanges**

1853			1854			June	25	37
Oct.	2	38¾	Mar.	5	33½	July	9	36¾
	16	39		19	33½		23	37
	30	39½	April	2	34	Aug.	6	37
1854.				16	34¼		20	37¼
Jan.	8	38⅞		30	35	Sept.	3	37½
	22	38	May	14	35½		17	36¾
Feb.	5	37⅛		28	37	Oct.	1	36¼
	19	37¼	June	11	37½			

4.   Cabinet Minutes Respecting the Declaration of Paris of April 1856[1]

The Earl of Clarendon to Viscount Palmerston

[FO 83/487]   Paris
                                                              April 6, 1856

My Dear Palmerston, It is quite clear that we can never again re-establish our ancient doctrine respecting neutrals, and that we must in any future war adhere to the exception to our rule which we admitted at the beginning of the present war, under pain of having all mankind against us. I am, therefore, for making a merit of necessity, and volunteering as a benevolent act of the Congress to proclaim as permanent the principle upon which we have lately acted, adding to it a Resolution against privateering.

The latter will be a good Roland to the Yankees for their Oliver; thinking to do us an ill turn, they sent a Circular to all Maritime Powers asking their assent to the neutral flag covering the goods. Most of these Powers consulted us as to the answer they should give, and we suggested that they should not agree unless the United States at the same time gave up the system of privateers.

Prussia gave that answer, and the President made some impertinent remarks upon it in his Message, so they will be left alone in their system, and have the world against them if the Congress adopts the Resolution. I send you the draft of Resolution, and if you could let me know by the telegraph whether you approve it would be a convenience, although I have told [Napoleon III's Minister, Alexandre] Walewski that it may be two or three days before I can give him a definitive answer.

The Emperor does not like any engagement with respect to mediation before war is declared, but he is willing that some Resolution in favour of the proceeding should be recorded in a Protocol.

Does anything else in the way of declaration of principles by the Congress occur to you?

The signature of peace has put that august Body in high good humour, and I daresay it would agree to anything that could not be called revolutionary.

I need not tell you that the British and Sardinian Plenipotentiaries are the only Liberal members of it.

                                                    Yours sincerely, Clarendon

[1]Published in CP 5104, 18 May 1885, *Cabinet Minutes Respecting the Declaration of Paris of April 1856.*

Minute by Viscount Palmerston

April 7, 1856

Immediate. I should like to have the opinion of the Cabinet on this matter in the course of this day.

I am inclined to agree with Clarendon that the concessions which we have made to neutrals at the beginning of this war can never, or, at least, will never, on any future occasion, be withheld, and that it would be wise in us to take the lead, and to make the proposal which Clarendon suggests.

'P'

The Queen's Approval

April 8, 1856

The Queen approves Lord Palmerston's proposed course.

* * *

5. No. 1 – *Proposal of the United States Government Relative to Maritime Law*[1]

To the Comte de Sartiges, French Ambassador in Washington, from William Learned Marcy, Department of State, Washington

[FO 83/487/968   July 28, 1856

. . . By taking the subject of privateering into consideration, that Congress has gone beyond its professed object, which was, as it declared, to remove the uncertainty on points of maritime law, and thereby prevent 'differences of opinion between neutrals and belligerents, and consequently serious difficulties and even conflicts.' So far as the principle in regard to privateering is concerned, the proceedings of the Congress are in the nature of an act of legislation, and seek to change a well-settled principle of international law.

The interest of commerce is deeply concerned in the establishment of the two principles which the United States had submitted to all maritime Powers; and it is much to be regretted that the Powers repre-

---

[1]CP, United States, International Maritime Law, 1856–57. Foreign Office June 22, 1861. Committee of Imperial Defence, Sub-Committee on Belligerent Rights.

sented in the Congress at Paris, fully approving them, should have endangered their adoption by uniting them to another inadmissible principle, and making the failure of all the necessary consequence of the rejection of any one. To three of the four principles contained in the Declaration there would not probably be a serious objection from any quarter, but to the other vigorous resistance must have been anticipated.

The policy of the law which allows a resort to privateers has been questioned for reasons which do not command the assent of this Government. Without entering into a full discussion on this point, the Undersigned will confront the ordinary and chief objection to that policy, by an authority which will be regarded with profound respect, particularly in France. In a commentary on the French Ordonnance of 1681, Valin says:

'However lawful and time-honoured this mode of warfare may be, it is, nevertheless, disapproved of by some pretended philosophers. According to their notions, such is not the way in which the state and the Sovereign are to be served: whilst the profits which individuals may derive from the pursuit are illicit, or at least disgraceful. But this is the language of bad citizens, who, under the stately mask of a spurious wisdom, and of a crafty, sensitive conscience, seek to mislead the judgment by a concealment of the secret motive which gives birth to their indifference for the welfare and advantage of the State. Such are as worthy of blame as are those entitled to praise who generously expose their property and their lives to the dangers of privateering.' . . .

It is fair to presume that the strong desire to ameliorate the severe usages of war by exempting private property upon the ocean from hostile seizure, to the extent it is usually exempted on land, was the chief inducement which led to 'the declaration' by the Congress at Paris, that 'privateering is and remains abolished.'

The Undersigned is directed by the President to say, that to this principle of exempting private property upon the ocean, as well as upon the land, applied without restriction, he yields a most ready and willing assent. The Undersigned cannot better express the President's views upon the subject than by quoting the language of his annual Message to Congress, of December 4, 1854:

'The proposition to enter into engagements to forego a resort to privateers, in case this country should be forced into a war with a great naval Power, is not entitled to more favourable consideration than would be a proposition to agree not to accept the services of volunteers for operations on land. When the honour or rights of our country require it to assume a hostile attitude, it confidently relies upon the patriotism of its citizens, not ordinarily devoted to the military profession, to augment the army and navy, so as to make them fully adequate to the emergency which calls them into action. The proposal to surrender the right to employ privateers is professedly founded upon the principle that private property of unoffending non-combatants, though enemies, should be exempt from the ravages of war; but the proposed surrender goes but little way in carrying out that principle, which equally requires that such private property should not be seized or molested by national ships-of-war. Should the leading Powers of Europe concur in proposing, as a rule of international law, to exempt private property, upon the ocean, from seizure by public armed cruizers as well as by privateers, the United States will readily meet them upon that broad ground.'

The reasons in favour of the doctrine that private property should be exempt from seizure in the operations of war are considered in this enlightened age so controlling as to have secured its partial adoption by all civilized nations; but it would be difficult to find any substantial reasons for the distinction now recognized in its application to such property on land, and not to that which is found upon the ocean.

If it be the object of the Declaration adopted at Paris to abolish this distinction, and to give the same security from the ravages of war to the property of belligerent subjects on the ocean as is now accorded to such property upon the land, the Congress at Paris has fallen short of the proposed result, by not placing individual effects of belligerents beyond the reach of public armed ships as well as privateers. If such property is to remain exposed to seizure by ships belonging to the navy of the adverse party, it is extremely difficult to perceive why it should not, in like manner, be exposed to seizure by privateers, which are, in fact, but another branch of the public force of the nation commissioning them. ...

The United States consider powerful navies and large standing armies, as permanent establishments, to be detrimental to national prosperity and dangerous to civil liberty. The expense of keeping them up is burdensome to the people; they are, in the opinion of this Government, in some degree a menace to peace among nations. A large force, ever ready to be devoted to the purposes of war, is a temptation to rush into it. The policy of the United States has ever been, and never more than now, adverse to such establishments; and they can never be brought to acquiesce in any change in international law which may render it necessary for them to maintain a powerful navy or large regular army in time of peace. ...

The President, therefore, proposes to add to the first proposition in the Declaration of the Congress at Paris the following words: 'And that the private property of the subjects or citizens of a belligerent on the high seas shall be exempt from seizure by public armed vessels of the other belligerent, except it be contraband.' Thus amended, the Government of the United States will adopt it, together with the other three principles contained in that Declaration.

* * *

No. 5 – Observations of J.D. Harding, the Queen's Advocate, on the Answer of the United States' Government respecting Maritime Law

Doctors' Commons
September 27, 1856

My Lord, I am honoured with your Lordship's commands, signified in Mr Hammond's letter of the 15th September instant, stating that he was directed to transmit to me two despatches from Mr Lumley, Her Majesty's Secretary of Legation at Washington, inclosing a copy of the answer returned by the Government of the United States to the proposal made in regard to maritime law by the Powers represented in the late Conference at Paris, together with despatches which have been received from Her Majesty's Ambassador at Paris upon the same subject; and to request that I would take the inclosed papers into consideration, and furnish your Lordship with any observations I may have to offer thereupon.

In obedience to your Lordship's commands, I have taken this subject into consideration, and have the honour to report –

That I am not aware whether any or what communication was made by the Count de Sartiges to the Government of the United States, when he presented to it the Declaration of Paris.

I propose, however, to address myself, in the first place, to the consideration of that passage of Mr Marcy's answer to the Count de Sartiges in which I understand Mr Marcy to offer to adopt the Declaration of Paris as it stands, with the amendment, 'That the property of the subjects or citizens of a belligerent on the high seas shall be exempted from seizure by public armed vessels of the other belligerent, except it be contraband.' It appears from the context, that Mr Marcy does not mean to propose to extend this exemption to cases of breach of blockade; in that it would seem as if the words, 'or in case of breach of blockade,' should have been added to his (so-called) 'amendment,' in order fully to express its meaning.

It is obvious that the expediency of acceding to Mr Marcy's proposition is a question of Imperial policy of the highest order, for the determination of Her Majesty's Government, and entirely beyond my province. It is, therefore, with great diffidence that I take the liberty of expressing to your Lordship my individual opinion, which is distinctly in favour of accepting the proposal now made by the United States' Government.

When, in March 1854, Her Majesty's Government determined upon making those extensive concessions of belligerent rights in favour of neutrals, and of British subjects trading with the enemy, which were announced in Her Majesty's Declaration of the 28th March, and Order in Council of the 15th April of that year, I immediately formed and stated my opinion, that a general concession of the right of capturing private property on the sea would be more worthy of the character and position of Great Britain, and at all events not more disadvantageous or dangerous to her, than the particular concessions then made. At the same time I expressed my decided dissent from the policy of such concessions to every member of Her Majesty's then Government who did me the honour to converse with me on the subject.

The peculiar opportunities which I afterwards had of observing their practical working and effect during the war (especially from perusing the confidential mercantile and private letters captured on board every prize) only confirmed my opinion; and I accordingly expressed my decided objections to the Declaration of Paris when summoned (with the Attorney-General) to attend a meeting of the Cabinet at which that Declaration (then in draft, and not precisely in its present shape) was the subject of consideration. I still consider that Declaration fraught with future national danger to Great Britain, and as having secured to her no adequate advantages.

I mention these circumstances at the risk of appearing somewhat unnecessarily obstinate or egotistical, simply in order to satisfy your Lordship that my opinions (or perhaps prejudices) on these subjects were and are opposed, in the abstract, to any policy involving succes- sive concessions to belligerent rights. These very extensive concessions, however, having been now finally and irrevocably made, and even trading with the enemy by Her Majesty's subjects having been (for the first time) legalized and encouraged by the Order in Council, April 15, 1854, it is of course necessary to view the United States' proposition in connection with the existing facts, and, as it were, from this new basis; to lay aside those maxims and that system of policy which looked only to the destruction of the enemy's maritime trade in all shapes and at whatsoever cost; which treated neutrals, or subjects who carried on that trade, as enemies in disguise; and which considered that a 'war for arms' was incompatible with a 'peace for commerce;' to take (as a seaman would express it) 'a fresh departure' from the policy of 1854 and 1856; to consider whether, having actually gone thus far, there is any sufficient or unanswerable reason for now refusing to make the proposed concession, viz., that of the right to capture enemies' private property at sea, *when sailing under the enemies' flag*; for it must be borne in mind that enemy's private property, if under a neutral flag is equally secure; and that in the last war Great Britain encouraged her own subjects to trade with the enemy, provided only that they did not, in British ships, actually enter or communicate with the enemy's ports, a privilege of which they amply availed themselves, no less to their own advantage than to that of the enemy.

In the first place, I would venture to submit that this concession would be an immense step in advance, as far as the general interests of humanity and civilization are concerned; it would seriously mitigate one of the harshest features of modern war, and at all events save a number of innocent individuals from the suffering (often amounting to the total ruin of their private fortunes) now unavoidably inflicted by the capture of their private property.

But apart from all such consideration, and considering the proposition from the lower ground (as it were) of national interest and expediency alone, I would observe that the capture of enemy's private property, even if confined to that under the enemy's flag, if carried into effect upon a large scale, is calculated to inflict considerable damage upon the general commerce of the world, in which there is, from the long prevalence of peace and the increased facilities of communication, a rapidly-increasing general sympathy or unity of interest. Great Britain, as the first commercial Power, cannot fail to profit materially (if indirectly) by any general advantage to commerce, and to suffer by any injury to it. Thus (to illustrate my meaning), supposing Great Britain to be neutral in a war between France and the United States, the general interests of British commerce could not fail to be injuriously affected by any very extensive capture of United States' private property by France. In a large proportion of the few captures made during the late war, British capital and British credit were found to be more or less involved.

Assuming that the chief object of the concessions made during the late war was to secure a plentiful supply of important Russian produce, and thus to diminish the pressure caused by the war upon British manufactures, consumption, and commerce, then the proposed concession will be in furtherance of such object.

I need not enlarge upon the obvious application of this principle to two of the staple articles of United States' produce, a regular supply of which is of the utmost importance to Great Britain, viz., cotton and cereals.

On the other hand, if, under the existing system, captures of private property should in future wars not be extensive, then they will, in my opinion, do very little (if anything) towards producing any serious effect whatever upon the enemy. This, I conceive, is the more probable result to be anticipated hereafter; when the enemy merchant can carry on trade with perfect impunity under the neutral flag, he will not be much disposed to run the risk of using his own; and although in the late war only a small proportion of the Russian mercantile marine was captured on the high seas, and although Russian commerce was only partially interrupted by the blockades, yet, by the second year of the war, scarcely a Russian merchant ship was employed. The power of Russia was not, in my opinion, at all seriously affected by the few captures of Russian vessels which were made; and if the proposed concession had been in operation, the general result would not have been different from what it was.

If this should turn out to be the case hereafter in other wars, then the proposed concession may be made without any serious danger to the national interest. It is also to be borne in mind that blockade remains intact, and will in many cases of itself suffice to produce the desired effect.

This concession, however, will, if made, be by no means gratuitous, or without any important equivalent, viz., the irrevocable abandonment of privateering by the United States, a concession of the greatest practical advantage to Great Britain. This country, France, and Russia, having already abandoned privateering, the United States alone amongst great naval Powers retains the use of this somewhat barbarous weapon.

In the event of a war between Great Britain and the United States, either alone or in league with other Powers, the immense advantage to Great Britain, of her commerce being secure from all molestation by privateers, requires no comment. It would go far to render her invulnerable, and one great advantage, which I presume was anticipated as likely to be secured by the Declaration of Paris, will have been realized, which cannot be the case whilst the United States refuses its accession.

Being, however, wholly uninformed as to what are the precise practical advantages which are anticipated as accruing to this country from the Declaration, and being quite ignorant of the principles of policy by which Her Majesty's Government were really actuated in acceding thereto, I feel unable to deal with the subject as its immense importance deserves. Whatever those advantages or those principles of policy may be, I have thus endeavoured (though briefly and imperfectly) to point out what appear to me some reasons why Great Britain should not now refuse to accede to Mr Marcy's proposal, the most prominent of which are:

1.   That the rest of the system and policy of former wars having been abandoned and changed, the capture of private property under the enemy's flag ought, in accordance therewith, to be now abandoned. I cannot (for instance) see the consistency or justice of encouraging British subjects to supply the enemy with goods, and the enemy to carry on his trade under a neutral flag, and at the same time depriving the enemy merchant of those goods (only) which he ships under his own flag. The supposed object of crippling the enemy's resources by every available means being no longer pursued, or only very partially pursued, this particular practice may be safely discontinued. As far as the preventing our own commercial interests from injury by war is the chief or exclusive object of our policy (rather than that of injuring the enemy), this will be best attained by the proposed concession.

2.   That no real national loss will henceforth be incurred by abstaining from capturing private property in enemy's merchant-vessels.

3.   That the general abandonment of privateering, proposed as an equivalent, is a great advantage to the civilized world in general, and of peculiar value to Great Britain, especially in case of war with the United States, and above all in the possible case of a simultaneous war with that Power, France, and Russia combined, in which event France and Russia would (unless privateering be abandoned by the United States) profit by the injury inflicted on British commerce by United States' privateers.

4.   That unless some very stringent necessity exists for continuing the practice of capturing private property, it should (like privateering), in accordance with all abstract and general principles of justice, civilization, and mitigation of the evils of war, regard for the interests of innocent individuals, and progressive amelioration, be discontinued.

. . .

* * *

No. 6 – Opinion of Dr. Lushington

Extract

31 October, 1856

I am perfectly ready to admit that the solution of this question depends upon ascribing their due weight to antagonistic consideration, that on both sides there may be arguments founded in truth. In my judgment, however, the great preponderance is in favour of the acceptance of the proposition, and that opinion is founded upon a firm conviction that the safety, prosperity, and public credit of Great Britain depend on the maintenance and encouragement of her manufactures and trade; that through those means alone can an adequate revenue be raised for the protection of this country in peace and war; that the proposed measure will confirm the stability of those great interests, and consequently tend to their improvement and increase; and that, by the double effect of adding security to our own commerce, and of augmenting that commerce, by the preservation from injury of the commerce of the world. I think that these great and substantial benefits are cheaply bought by the surrender of a right which never can be exercised to its full extent, and the very exercise of which inflicts an injury on ourselves in the proportion that it is destructive to others. . . .

* * *

No. 8 – Heads of Answer to the Proposal of the United States' Government contained in M. Dallas' Note of February 24, 1857

Extract

But the disinclination of the British Government to adopt this proposal, made by the United States' Government, ought not to be a reason why the United States' Government should hesitate as to joining the other Powers in a resolution to abolish privateering; because, independently of the domestic reasons in favour of such a regulation, which reasons apply with as much force to the United States as to any of the nations whose Governments are parties to the Declaration, the abolition of privateering would, to a certain extent, coincide with the views of the Government of the United States, because although it would not exempt private property and private vessels of a belligerent from capture, yet it would, to a certain extent, limit the risk of capture to which they would be exposed, by leaving them only liable to be seized by national ships of war. Her Majesty's Government would much regret if the Government of the United States were to abstain from being parties to a Declaration which lays down principles to all of which that Government entirely assents, merely because other Powers may not be prepared to substitute, for the regulations thus proposed to be established, another and an essentially different principle, bearing upon different interests, and the effects of which it would require much consideration satisfactorily to determine.

* * *

No. 9 – Minute by the Earl of Clarendon

Extract

Acknowledge and recapitulate Mr Dallas' note in which he says that to all of the propositions of the Declaration made by the Plenipotentiaries at Paris the Government of the United States has been for some time, and still is, prepared cordially to accede, excepting only with such an addition to the first as has always seemed to the President indispensable to the attainment of its true and humane purpose, that of diminishing the calamities of war.

With this addition to Article I of the Declaration, viz., that all private property of a belligerent on the high seas shall be exempt from capture by the public armed vessels of the other belligerent, unless it be contraband, the Undersigned regrets to inform Mr Dallas that Her Majesty's Government are not prepared to agree to the Convention which, by Mr Dallas' note, they are invited to conclude. . . .

* * *

6.   Union Blockade of Confederate Ports

Correspondence between Richard Bickerton Pemell Lyons, Ambassador at Washington, and Lord John Russell, Foreign Secretary

Russell to Lyons

[PRO 30/22/96/55]   9 March, 1861

My dear Lord Lyons. I hope you are getting on well with the new President [Abraham Lincoln].

If he blockades the southern ports we shall be in a difficulty – But according to all American doctrine it must be an actual blockade kept up by an effective force.

I do not see how the Southern ports can be declared not to be ports of entry without forcing on the question of recognition. . . .

* * *

Lyons to Russell
Private

[PRO 30/22/35/59–64v]   Washington
                                                      27 April, 1861

My Dear Lord, In common with the most influential of my colleagues I
exhausted every possible means of opposition to the Blockade. The
great North Eastern Cities insisted upon it, not only as a measure of
vengeance, but as one essential to the preservation of their own prosperity. They could hardly be expected to make sacrifices for the contest,
unless they were secured from seeing their Trade diverted to Southern
Ports. . . .

Mr Seward has talked (not to me) of the United States 'being now
willing to adhere to the declaration of the Congress of Paris abolishing
Privateering.' I am always rather afraid of touching upon the principle
laid down in the Declaration. It may perhaps be a good thing to secure
the adherence of the United States to them – though how long after the
present crisis the adherence may be maintained, is, I think, not a little
doubtful. The time at which the offer would be made renders the thing
rather amusing. It would no doubt be very convenient if the navies of
Europe would put down the Privateers, and then leave the whole Navy
of the United States free to blockade the Ports against European merchant vessels. . . .

I have been rather puzzled what to say to the Admiral. Every Consul
and every British subject want to have a Man of War or a Fleet if
possible at his door. I don't see that the Men of War could be of any
practical use, except as places of refuge, in case of a bombardment or
actual fighting in a town. There are naval as well as political objections
to having our Ships here without strong necessity. The temptations to
desert are very strong and very generally yielded to by our Men of Wars
Men in American Ports. With the practice which has grown up here of
putting out lights and removing beacons and buoys, it might be easier
to get a ship into one of these harbours or rivers than to get her out
again. I should like to have ships as near at hand as possible without
being actually in American waters. The case of [that is 'for'] a strong
joint naval demonstration of England and France united [words un-
clear] to any decision they might come to, about Blockades, Privateers
or other matters would be a very different thing. Not that I think even a
joint intervention of this kind of thing [*sic?*] to be desired in itself.

* * *

Russell to Lyons

[PRO 30/22/96/61]   4 May, 1861

I cannot give you any official instructions by this mail – But the Law
Officers are of opinion that we must consider the Civil War in America
as regular war – justum bellum – & apply to it all the rules respecting
blockade, letters of marque &c, which belong to neutrals during a war.

They think moreover it would be very desirable if both parties would
agree to accept the Declaration of Paris regarding the flag covering the
goods & the prohibition of privateers.

You will of course inform our naval officers that they must conform to
the rules respecting Blockade of which they are I believe in possession.

The matter is very serious and very unfortunate.

* * *

Lyons to Russell

[PRO 30/22/96/94–5]   6 May, 1861

Whether we shall think it possible to allow our supplies of cotton to
be materially interfered with by the Blockade, is a question which it is
not for me to prejudge. . . .

[Extract from a letter from a Mr Russell, possibly R. William Russell,
author of *The New Maritime Law: Review of Mr Marcy's Letter to M.
de Sartiges*, to Lord Lyons, New Orleans, 21 May, 1861.] I avail myself
of a few lines by private hand half dazed as I am by long and heated
travel to tell you what I have seen in part at least within the last few
days at [illegible, Prichard?] and Pensacola. The further I travel the
more satisfied I am of the terrible results of the struggle which seems
quite beyond the reach of reason. There is on the part of the South an
enormously exaggerated idea of its own strength and of its 'faut oivre'
for the rest of the world, which nerves its sinus [*sic*], and there is also
the desperation of position which one must feel who sits on a barrel of
powder and who is menaced with a hot poker. They are resolute and
unanimous to a most extraordinary degree – they are stronger than I
expected to find them – but they – I speak of the men – not of the South
as an 'it' – will, I think, discover that they are ill-fitted for a defensive
and protracted contest, more especially will they lose heart, when or if
their sheet-anchor fails them; and England and France permit the blockade for a year or more. Their ideas of political economy are enough to

drive the venerable A. Smith out of his quiet resting place with a fresh edition of the 'Wealth of Nations' in his claw.

* * *

Russell to Lyons

PRO 30/22/96/63   18 May, 1861[1]

[Relating a discussion with US Ambassador Adams] I pointed out that the blockade recently instituted, and the designation applied to the privateers of the southern states, as pirates, might give rise to difficulties. That however the blockade might no doubt be made effective – considering the small number of harbours on the Southern Coast, even though the extent of 3,000 miles of coast was comprehended in the terms of the blockade.

Mr Adams said it was by no means the intention of the US to institute a paper blockade, a measure against wh[ich] they had always protested.

With regard to privateers & piracy I said that general principles might be proclaimed, but that the putting them into execution might be accompanied with that forbearance & humanity wh[ich] might be expected from a nation so cognizant of international relations, & so advanced in civilization as the US.

* * *

Russell to Lyons

PRO 30/22/96/79   6 July, 1861

Mr Adams has not yet made any communication to me – I have suspected all along that P[resident] Lincoln & S[ecretary] Seward wish to keep the power of sending out privateers, in hopes that they may one day be used against British commerce.

As their fears of Southern Privateers have been dispelled by our order that no prizes should be taken into our ports, they will be still more averse to give up privateering – Certain it is that no proposal to adhere to the Declaration of Paris has been made to me, or I believe to [the French Foreign Minister, Edouard] Thouvenel.

* * *

[1]See also f. 71, 25 May; f. 77, 5 July.

Russell to Lyons

[PRO 30/22/96/85]   16 August, 1861

If our ships can go in ballast for cotton to the Southern Ports it will be well. But if this cannot be done by agreement there will be nearly an extent of 3000 miles, creeks & bays out of which small vessels may come & run for Jamaica or the Bahamas, where the Cargoes might be transhipped – But it is not for Downing St. to suggest such plans to Cheapside & Tooley St.

* * *

Russell to Lyons

[PRO 30/22/96/87]   24 August, 1861

I have proposed a declaration to be delivered by me when I sign the Convention concerning the declaration of Paris. But Mr Adams has not yet told me that he would accept this declaration. I do not ask him to agree to it, simply to receive it.

* * *

Lyons to Russell

[PRO 30/22/96/330]   29 November, 1861

The Consuls in the South are crying out for ships again – This is the solution for every difficulty in the Consular mind, as my experience in the Mediterranean taught me long ago – though what the Ships were to do, except fire a salute in honour of the Consul, I could never discover. ... It is quite true that a town may be bombarded some day by the United States Forces, – that British subjects may have their throats cut by the negroes in a servile insurrection, or be tarred and feathered by a vigilance Committee. But we cannot keep a squadron at every point to protect them – and I do not know what points are particularly threatened.

* * *

Lyons to Russell

[PRO 30/22/35/part 1, 371]   27 December, 1861

My Dear Lord, It is of course impossible for me to give an opinion upon the argumentation in Mr Seward's voluminous note. Time barely admits of its being read and copied before the messenger goes. But as the four prisoners are given up, immediately and unconditionally, it is quite clear to my mind that you will not wish me to decide the question of peace or war, without reference to you. A rupture of Diplomatic Relations, not followed by war, would be worse than war itself, for after that, nothing would ever convince the Americans, that there was any limit to our forbearance.

* * *

Palmerston to Russell

[PRO 30/22/106/8]   10 January, 1862

My dear Russell, I see it is said that a fleet of Federal Ships of war are coming to our seas, would it not be well to warn Adams seriously that if his gov.t wish to remain on friendly terms with us their cruizers must not be overhauling our vessels in the Channel or on the high seas, without Rhyme or Reason, & send them to New York for trial. The nation was quick wound up to war Pitch, and though they are satisfied with the settlement they would be irritated beyond measure at any such Proceedings and another Dispute might be brought on.

* * *

Palmerston to Russell

[PRO 30/22/106/9]   10 January, 1862

My Dear Russell, Euc iterum crispinus would it not be well for you to send immediately to Adams, and to tell him explicitly that we cannot permit armed men in the service of a foreign government to land upon British ground, and to request without delay to telegraph to the Captain of this Federal steamer not again to do that which might lead to a collision between his men and the British authorities.

It seems to me also that Adams should be told that no Hostility can be permitted to be committed by the Federal steamer within British waters. That a ship of war of superior force will immediately be ordered to place herself alongside of the Federal steamer to prevent her from starting from British waters till the Endiration [*sic*] of 24 hours after the *Nashville* has sailed and that the Federal steamer will not again be allowed to take on coals or rations of war in a British port. The Admiralty and Customs an[d] Home office should have corresponding instructions.

This Proceeding is too impudent.

* * *

Russell to Lyons

[PRO 30/22/96/112]   11 January, 1862

I congratulate you heartily on the termination of this affair [i.e. the seizure by the Union navy of the *Trent*] – But I do not regret its occurrence – The unanimity shown here – the vigorous despatch of troops and ships – the loyal determination of Canada may save us a contest for a long while to come – & in fact the cost incurred may be true economy.

* * *

Russell to Lyons

[PRO 30/22/96/116]   15 February, 1862

I have just received your letter of the 31st – I hope you may be more comfortable now than you have been. The *Trent* affair was a trial of our patience, & I do not think the same trick is likely to be played again by any ministers of the US.

* * *

Russell to Lyons

[PRO 30/22/96/126]   29 March, 1862

In consequence of the seizure of the *La Brian*? in Mexican waters, we have been obliged to send some ships to protect our vessels & property at Matamoros & its neighbourhood.

I trust, however, neutral ships in neutral waters will be respected in the future.

* * *

Russell to Lyons

[PRO 30/22/96/160]   20 December, 1862

I have signed today our answer to Seward about the *Alabama* – I confess the proceedings of that vessel are enough to rile a more temperate nation & I owe a grudge to the Liverpool people on that account.

* * *

7. *Correspondence Relating to the 'Trent' Affair*[1]

Earl Russell, Prime Minister, to Lord Lyons, Ambassador in Washington

[FO 881/993]   Foreign Office
                                                   30 November, 1861

My Lord, Intelligence of a very grave nature has reached Her Majesty's Government.

This Intelligence was conveyed officially to the knowledge of the Admiralty by Commander Williams, Agent for Mails on board the contract steamer 'Trent.'

It appears from the letter of Commander Williams, dated 'Royal mail contract packet "Trent" at sea, November 9,' that the 'Trent' left Havana on the 7th instant with Her numerous passengers. Commander Williams states that shortly after noon on the 8th a steamer, having the appearance of a man-of-war, but not showing colours, was observed a-head. On nearing her at 1:15 P.M. she fired a round shot from her pivot-gun across the bows of the 'Trent' and showed American colours. While the 'Trent' was approaching her slowly, the American vessel discharged a shell across the bows of the 'Trent,' exploding half a cable's length a-head of her. The 'Trent' then stopped, and an officer, with a large armed guard of Marines, boarded her. The officer demanded a list of the passengers, and compliance with this demand

---

[1]Printed in *The London Gazette*, 14 January 1862.

being refused, the officer said he had orders to arrest Messrs Mason, Slidell, McFarland, and Eustis, and that he had sure information of their being passengers in the 'Trent.' While some parley was going on upon this matter, Mr Slidell stepped forward and told the American officer that the four persons he had named were then standing before him. The Commander of the 'Trent,' and Commander Williams, protested against the act of taking by force out of the 'Trent' these four passengers then under the protection of the British flag. But the 'San Jacinto' was at that time only 200 yards from the 'Trent,' her ship's company at quarters, her ports open and tompions out.

Resistance was therefore out of the question, and the four gentlemen before named were forcibly taken out of the ship.

A further demand was made that the Commander of the 'Trent' should proceed on board the 'San Jacinto,' but he said he would not go unless forcibly compelled likewise, and this demand was not insisted upon.

It thus appears that certain individuals have been forcibly taken from on board a British vessel, the ship of a neutral Power, while such vessel was pursuing a lawful and innocent voyage, an act of violence which was an affront to the British flag and a violation of international law.

Her Majesty's Government, bearing in mind the friendly relations which have long subsisted between Great Britain and the United States, are willing to believe that the United States' naval officer who committed this aggression was not acting in compliance with any authority from his Government, or that if he conceived himself to be so authorized, he greatly misunderstood the instructions which he had received.

For the Government of the United States must be fully aware that the British Government could not allow such an affront to the national honour to pass without full reparation, and Her Majesty's Government are unwilling to believe that it could be the deliberate intention of the Government of the United States unnecessarily to force into discussion between the two Governments a question of so grave a character, and with regard to which the whole British nation would be sure to entertain such unanimity of feeling.

Her Majesty's Government, therefore, trust that when this matter shall have been brought under the consideration of the Government of the United States, that Government will, of its own accord, offer to the British Government such redress as alone would satisfy the British nation, namely, the liberation of the four gentlemen, and their delivery to your Lordship, in order that they may again be placed under British protection, and a suitable apology for the aggression which has been committed.

Should these terms not be offered by Mr Seward, you will propose them to him.

You are at liberty to read this despatch to the Secretary of State, and if he shall desire it, you will give him a copy of it. I am, &c.

* * *

Private Letter from Earl Russell to Lord Lyons

Extract

December 1, 1861

The despatches which were agreed to at the Cabinet yesterday, and which I have signed this morning, impose upon you a disagreeable task. My wish would be that, at your first interview with Mr Seward, you should not take my despatch with you, but should prepare him for it, and ask him to settle with the President and the Cabinet what course they would propose.

The next time you should bring my despatch, and read it to him fully.

If he asks what will be the consequence of his refusing compliance, I think you should say that you wish to leave him and the President quite free to take their own course, and that you desire to abstain from anything like menace.

* * *

Earl Russell to Lord Lyons

Foreign Office
January 11, 1862

My Lord, In my despatch to you of the 30th of November, after informing you of the circumstances which had occurred in relation to the capture of the four persons taken from on board the 'Trent,' I stated to you that it thus appeared that certain individuals had been forcibly taken from on board a British vessel, the ship of a neutral power, while such vessel was pursuing a lawful and innocent voyage, an act of violence which was an affront to the British Flag, and a violation of international law. I concluded by directing you, in case the reparation, which Her Majesty's Government expected to receive, should not be offered by Mr Seward, to propose to that minister to make such redress as alone would satisfy the British nation, namely, first, the liberation of the four gentlemen taken from on board the 'Trent,' and their delivery to your Lordship, in order that they might again be placed under British protection; and, secondly, a suitable apology for the aggression which had been committed.

I received, yesterday, your despatch of the 27th ultimo, inclosing a note to you from Mr Seward, which is in substance the answer to my despatch of the 30th of November.

Proceeding at once to the main points in discussion between us, Her Majesty's Government have carefully examined how far Mr Seward's note, and the conduct it announces, complies substantially with the two proposals I have recited.

With regard to the first, viz.: the liberation of the prisoners with a view to their being again placed under British protection, I find that the note concludes by stating that the prisoners will be cheerfully liberated, and by calling upon your Lordship to indicate a time and place for receiving them.

No condition of any kind is coupled with the liberation of the prisoners.

With regard to the suitable apology which the British Government had a right to expect, I find that the Government of the United States distinctly and unequivocally declares that no directions had been given to Captain Wilkes, or to any other naval officer, to arrest the four persons named, or any of them, on the 'Trent,' or on any other British vessel, or on any other neutral vessel, at the place where it occurred or elsewhere.

I find, further, that the Secretary of State expressly forbears to justify the particular act of which Her Majesty's Government complained. If the United States Government had alleged that although Captain Wilkes had no previous instruction for that purpose, he was right in capturing the persons of the four prisoners, and in removing them from the 'Trent' on board his own vessel, to be afterwards carried into a port of the United States, the Government which had thus sanctioned the proceeding of Captain Wilkes would have become responsible for the original violence and insult of the act. But Mr Seward contents himself with stating that what has happened has been simply an inadvertency, consisting in a departure by a naval officer, free from any wrongful motive, from a rule uncertainly established, and probably by the several parties concerned either imperfectly understood or entirely unknown. The Secretary of State goes on to affirm that for this error the British Government has a right to expect the same reparation which the United States, as an independent State, should expect from Great Britain, or from any other friendly nation in a similar case.

Her Majesty's Government having carefully taken into their consideration the liberation of the prisoners, the delivery of them into your hands, and the explanations to which I have just referred, have arrived at the conclusion that they constitute the reparation which Her Majesty and the British nation had a right to expect.

It gives Her Majesty's Government great satisfaction to be enabled to arrive at a conclusion favourable to the maintenance of the most friendly relations between the two nations. I need not discuss the modifications in my statement of facts which Mr Seward says he has derived from the reports of Officers of his Government.

I cannot conclude, however, without adverting shortly to the discussions which Mr Seward has raised upon points not prominently brought into question in my despatch of the 30th of November. I there objected, on the part of Her Majesty's Government, to that which Captain Wilkes had done. Mr Seward, in his answer, points out what he conceives Captain Wilkes might have done without violating the law of nations.

It is not necessary that I should here discuss in detail the five questions ably argued by the Secretary of State; but it is necessary that I should say that Her Majesty's Government differ from Mr Seward in some of the conclusions at which he has arrived. And it may lead to a better understanding between the two nations on several points of international law which may during the present contest or at some future time be brought into question, that I should state to you, for communication to the Secretary of State, wherein those differences consist; I hope to do so in a few days.

In the meantime it will be desirable that the Commanders of the United States cruizers should be instructed not to repeat acts for which the British Government will have to ask for redress, and which the United States Government cannot undertake to justify.

You will read and give a copy of this despatch to the Secretary of State. I am, &c. . . .

8. *The Queen's Regulations and the Admiralty Instructions for the Government of Her Majesty's Naval Service*

[HMSO]   1862

Chapter XVIII – Prizes and Prisoners

1.

When any Ship or Vessel shall be captured, or detained her Hatches are to be securely fastened and sealed, and her Lading and Furniture, and, in general, everything on board, are to be carefully secured from Embezzlement; and the Officer having charge of such Ship or Vessel shall prevent anything from being taken out of her, until she shall have been tried, and sentence shall have been passed on her, in a Court of Admiralty or Vice-Admiralty.

2.

The Commanding Officer of Her Majesty's Ship shall cause the principal Officers of any Vessel he may detain, and such other persons of the Crew as he shall think fit, to be examined as Witnesses, in the court of Admiralty or Vice-Admiralty, to prove to whom the Vessel and Cargo belong; and He shall send to the said Court all Passports, Custom-House Clearances, Log-Books, and all other Ship's Papers, which shall be found on board, without suffering any of them to be on any pretence secreted or withheld.

3.

The Commanding Officer is to take particular care that all Prisoners of War are treated with humanity; that their personal property is carefully protected; that they have their proper allowance of provisions, viz., two-thirds of all species, except Spirits, Wine, or Beer, of which none shall ever be issued to them; and that every comfort of air and exercise which circumstances admit of, be allowed them; but, to prevent any hostile attempts on their part, they are to be always attentively watched and guarded, especially when many of the Ship's Company may happen to be employed aloft.

4.

If any Ship or Vessel shall be taken acting as a Ship of War or Privateer without having a Commission duly authorizing her to do so, her Crew shall be considered as Pirates, and shall be dealt with accordingly.

5.

If any one of Her Majesty's subjects shall be found serving on board an Enemy's Ship of War or Privateer, he shall be closely confined, until an opportunity shall offer for his being tried as a Traitor. The Commanding Officer shall, by the first opportunity, send an account of him, and of his place of birth, if known, to the Secretary of the Admiralty; and he shall also direct some of the Officers and Men of the Ship to notice very particularly every circumstance of the case, that they may be able to give evidence against such Offender.

* * *

9. An Act for Regulating Naval Prize of War[1]

27 & 28 Victoria, A.D. 1864, Cap. XXV   23 June, 1864

Whereas it is expedient to enact permanently, with amendments, such provisions concerning naval prize, and matters connected therewith, as have heretofore been usually passed at the beginning of a war:

Be it therefore enacted by the Queen's most excellent Majesty, by and with the advice and consent of the lords spiritual and temporal, and commons, in this present Parliament assembled, and by the authority of the same, as follows:

Preliminary

1. This Act may be cited as the Naval Prize Act, 1864.
2. In this Act –
The term 'the lords of Admiralty' means the lord high admiral of the United Kingdom, or the commissioners for executing the office of lord high admiral.
The term 'the High Court of Admiralty' means the High Court of Admiralty of England:
The term 'any of her Majesty's ships of war' includes any of her Majesty's vessels of war, and any hired armed ship or vessel in her Majesty's service:
The term 'officers and crew' includes flag officers, commanders, and other officers, engineers, seamen, marines, soldiers, and others on board any of her Majesty's ships of war:

---

[1]*The Admiralty Statutes, being the Public Statutes Actually in Force Relating to the Admiralty and Her Majesty's Navy, From 5 & 6 Edward VI (A.D. 1552) to 37 & 38 Victoria (A.D. 1874) Inclusive*, Albert Venn Dicey, ed., London: Eyre & Spottiswoode, 1876, pp. 559–71.

The term 'ship' includes vessel and boat, with the tackle, furniture, and apparel of the ship, vessel, or boat:

The term 'ship papers' includes all books, passes, sea briefs, charter parties, bills of lading, cockets, letters, and other documents and writings delivered up or found on board a captured ship:

The term 'goods' includes all such things as are by the course of Admiralty and law of nations the subject of adjudication as prize (other than ships).

I. – PRIZE COURTS

3.   The High Court of Admiralty, and every court of Admiralty or of vice-admiralty, or other court, exercising Admiralty jurisdiction in her Majesty's dominions, for the time being authorized to take cognizance of and judicially proceed in matters of prize, shall be a prize court within the meaning of this Act.

Every such court, other than the High Court of Admiralty, is comprised in the term 'vice-admiralty prize court,' when hereafter used in this Act.

High Court of Admiralty

4.   The High Court of Admiralty shall have jurisdiction throughout her Majesty's dominions as a prize court.

The High Court of Admiralty as a prize court shall have power to enforce any order or decree of a vice-admiralty prize court, and any order or decree of the judicial committee of the privy council in a prize appeal.

Appeal: Judicial Committee

5.   An appeal shall lie to her Majesty in council from any order or decree of a prize court, as of right in case of a final decree, and in other cases with the leave of the court making the order or decree.

Every appeal shall be made in such manner and form and subject to such regulations (including regulations as to fees, costs, charges, and expenses) as may for the time being be directed by Order in Council, and in the absence of any such order, or so far as any such order does not extend then in such manner and form and subject to such regulations as are for the time being prescribed or in force respecting maritime causes of appeal.

6.   The judicial committee of the privy council shall have jurisdiction to hear and report on any such appeal, and may therein exercise all such powers as for the time being appertain to them in respect of appeals from any Court of Admiralty jurisdiction, and all such powers are under this

Act vested in the High Court of Admiralty, and all such powers as were wont to be exercised by the commissioners of appeal in prize causes.

7. All processes and documents required for the purposes of any such appeal shall be transmitted to and shall remain in the custody of the registrar of her Majesty in prize appeals.

8. In every such appeal the usual inhibition shall be extracted from the registry of her Majesty in prize appeals within three months after the date of the order or decree appealed from if the appeal be from the High Court of Admiralty, and within six months after that date if it be from a vice-admiralty prize court.

The judicial committee may, nevertheless, on sufficient cause shown, allow the inhibition to be extracted and the appeal to be prosecuted after the expiration of the respective periods aforesaid.

Vice-Admiralty Prize Courts

9. Every vice-admiralty prize court shall enforce within its jurisdiction all orders and decrees of the judicial committee in prize appeals and of the High Court of Admiralty in prize causes.

10. Her Majesty in council may grant to the judge of any vice-admiralty prize court a salary not exceeding five hundred pounds a year, payable out of money provided by Parliament, subject to such regulations as seem meet.

A judge to whom a salary is so granted shall not be entitled to any further emolument, arising from fees or otherwise, in respect of prize business transacted in his court.

An account of all such fees shall be kept by the registrar of the court, and the amount thereof shall be carried to and form part of the consolidated fund of the United Kingdom.

11. In accordance, as far as circumstances admit, with the principles and regulations laid down in the Superannuation Act, 1859, (1) her Majesty in council may grant to the judge of any vice-admiralty prize court an annual or other allowance, to take effect on the termination of his service, and to be payable out of money provided by Parliament.

12. The registrar of every vice-admiralty prize court shall, on the first day of January and first day of July in every year, make out a return (in such form as the lords of the Admiralty from time to time direct) of all cases adjudged in the court since the last half-yearly return, and shall with all convenient speed send the same to the registrar of the High Court of Admiralty, who shall keep the same in the registry of that court, and who shall, as soon as conveniently may be, send a copy of the returns of each half year to the lords of the Admiralty, who shall lay the same before both Houses of Parliament.

General

13.   The judicial committee of the privy council, with the judge of the High Court of Admiralty, may from time to time frame general orders for regulating (subject to the provisions of this Act) the procedure and practice of prize courts, and the duties and conduct of the officers thereof and of the practitioners therein, and for regulating the fees to be taken by the officers of the courts, and the costs, charges, and expenses to be allowed to the practitioners therein.

Any such general orders shall have full effect, if and when approved by her Majesty in council, but not sooner or otherwise.

Every Order in Council made under this section shall be laid before both Houses of Parliament.

Every such order in council shall be kept exhibited in a conspicuous place in each court to which it relates.

14.   It shall not be lawful for any registrar, marshal, or other officer of any prize court, or for the registrar of her Majesty in prize appeals, directly or indirectly to act or be in any manner concerned as advocate, proctor, solicitor, or agent, or otherwise, in any prize cause or appeal, on pain of dismissal or suspension from office, by order of the court or of the judicial committee (as the case may require).

15.   It shall not be lawful for any proctor or solicitor, or person practising as a proctor or solicitor, being employed by a party in a prize cause or appeal, to be employed or concerned, by himself or his partner, or by any other person, directly or indirectly, by or on behalf of any adverse party in that cause or appeal, on pain of exclusion or suspension from practice in prize matters, by order of the court or of the judicial committee (as the case may require).

II. – PROCEDURE IN PRIZE CAUSES

Proceedings by Captors

16.   Every ship taken as prize, and brought into port within the jurisdiction of a prize court, shall forthwith, and without bulk broken, be delivered up to the marshal of the court.

If there is no such marshal, then the ship shall be in like manner delivered up to the principal officer of customs at the port.

The ship shall remain in the custody of the marshal or of such officer, subject to the orders of the court.

17.   The captors shall, with all practicable speed after the ship is brought into port, bring the ship papers into the registry of the court.

The officer in command, or one of the chief officers of the capturing ship, or some other person who was present at the capture, and saw the ship papers delivered up or found on board, shall make oath that they are brought in as they were taken, without fraud, addition, subduction, or alteration, or else shall account on oath to the satisfaction of the court for the absence or altered condition of the ship papers or any of them.

Where no ship papers are delivered up or found on board the captured ship, the officer in command, or one of the chief officers of the capturing ship, or some other person who was present at the capture, shall make oath to that effect.

18.   As soon as the affidavit as to ship papers is filed, a monition shall issue, returnable within twenty days from the service thereof, citing all persons in general to show cause why the captured ship should not be condemned.

19.   The captors shall, with all practicable speed after the captured ship is brought into port, bring three or four of the principal persons belonging to the captured ship before the judge of the court or some person authorized in this behalf, by whom they shall be examined on oath on the standing interrogatories.

The preparatory examinations on the standing interrogatories shall, if possible, be concluded within five days from the commencement thereof.

20.   After the return of the monition, the court shall, on production of the preparatory examination and ship papers, proceed with all convenient speed either to condemn or to release the captured ship.

21.   Where on production of the preparatory examinations and ship papers, it appears to the court doubtful whether the captured ship is good prize or not, the court may direct further proof to be adduced, either by affidavit or by examination of witnesses, with or without pleadings, or by production of further documents; and on such further proof being adduced the court shall with all convenient speed proceed to adjudication.

22.   The foregoing provisions, as far as they relate to the custody of the ship, and to examination on the standing interrogatories, shall not apply to ships of war taken as prize.

Claim

23.   At any time before final decree made in the cause, any person claiming an interest in the ship may enter in the registry of the court a claim, verified on oath.

Within five days after entering the claim, the claimant shall give security for costs in the sum of sixty pounds; but the court shall have power to enlarge the time for giving security, or to direct security to be given in a larger sum, if the circumstances appear to require it.

Appraisement

24.   The court may, if it thinks fit, at any time direct that the captured ship be appraised.

Every appraisement shall be made by competent persons sworn to make the same according to the best of their skill and knowledge.

Delivery of Bail

25.   After appraisement, the court may, if it thinks fit, direct that the captured ship be delivered up to the claimant, on his giving security to the satisfaction of the court to pay to the captors the appraised value thereof in case of condemnation.

Sale

26.   The court may at any time, if it thinks fit, on account of the condition of the captured ship, or on the application of a claimant, order that the captured ship be appraised as aforesaid (if not already appraised), and be sold.

27.   On or after condemnation the court may, if it thinks fit, order that the ship be appraised as aforesaid (if not already appraised), and be sold.

28.   Every sale shall be made by or under the superintendence of the marshal of the court or of the officer having the custody of the captured ship.

29.   The proceeds of any sale, made either before or after condemnation, and after condemnation the appraised value of the captured ship, in case she has been delivered up to a claimant on bail, shall be paid under an order of the court either into the Bank of England to the credit of her Majesty's paymaster general, or into the hands of an official accountant (belonging to the commissariat or some other department) appointed for this purpose by the commissioners of her Majesty's Treasury or by the lords of the Admiralty, subject in either case to such regulations as may from time to time be made, by order in council, as to the custody and disposal of money so paid.

Small armed Ships

30.   The captors may include in one adjudication any number not exceeding six, of armed ships not exceeding one hundred tons each, taken within three months next before institution of proceedings.

Goods

31.   The foregoing provisions relating to ships shall extend and apply, mutatis mutandis, to goods taken as prize on board ship; and the court may direct such goods to be unladen, inventoried, and warehoused.

Monition to Captors to Proceed

32.   If the captors fail to institute or to prosecute with effect proceedings for adjudication, a monition shall, on the application of a claimant, issue against the captors, returnable within six days from the service thereof, citing them to appear and proceed to adjudication; and on the return thereof the court shall either forthwith proceed to adjudication or direct further proof to be adduced as aforesaid, and then proceed to adjudication.

Claim on Appeal

33.   Where any person, not an original party in the cause, intervenes on appeal, he shall enter a claim, verified on oath, and shall give security for costs.

III. – SPECIAL CASES OF CAPTURE

Land Expeditions

34.   Where, in an expedition of any of her Majesty's naval or naval and military forces against a fortress or possession on land, goods belonging to the state of the enemy or to a public trading company of the enemy exercising powers of government are taken in the fortress or possession, or a ship is taken in waters defended by or belonging to the fortress or possession, a prize court shall have jurisdiction as to the goods or ship so taken, and any goods taken on board the ship, as in case of prize.

Conjunct Capture with Ally

35.   Where any ship or goods is or are taken by any of her Majesty's naval or naval and military forces while acting in conjunction with any forces of any of her Majesty's allies, a prize court shall have jurisdiction as to the same as in case of prize, and shall have power, after condemnation, to apportion the due share of the proceeds to her Majesty's ally, the proportionate amount and the disposition of which share shall be such as may from time to time be agreed between her Majesty and her Majesty's ally.

Joint Capture

36. Before condemnation, a petition on behalf of asserted joint captors shall not (except by special leave of the court) be admitted, unless and until they give security to the satisfaction of the court to contribute to the actual captors a just proportion of any costs, charges, or expenses or damages that may be incurred by or awarded against the actual captors on account of the capture and detention of the prize.

After condemnation, such a petition shall not (except by special leave of the court) be admitted unless and until the asserted joint captors pay to the actual captors a just proportion of the costs, charges, and expenses incurred by the actual captors in the case, and give such security as aforesaid, and show sufficient cause to the court why their petition was not presented before condemnation.

Provided, that nothing in the present section shall extend to the asserted interest of a flag officer claiming to share by virtue of his flag.

Offences against Law Prize

37. A prize court, on proof of any offence against the law of nations, or against this Act, or any Act relating to naval discipline, or against any order in council or royal proclamation, or of any breach of her Majesty's instructions relating to prize, or of any act of disobedience to the orders of the lords of the Admiralty, or to the command of a superior officer, committed by the captors in relation to any ship or goods taken as prize, or in relation to any person on board any such ship, may, on condemnation, reserve the prize to her Majesty's disposal, notwithstanding any grant that may have been made by her Majesty in favour of captors.

Pre-emption

38. Where a ship of a foreign nation passing the seas laden with naval or victualling stores intended to be carried to a port of any enemy of her Majesty is taken and brought into a port of the United Kingdom, and the purchase for the service of her Majesty of the stores on board the ship appears to the lords of the Admiralty expedient without the condemnation thereof in a prize court, in that case the lords of the Admiralty may purchase, on the account or for the service of her Majesty, all or any of the stores on board the ship; and the commissioners of customs may permit the stores purchased to be entered and landed within any port.

Capture by Ship other than a Ship of War

39.   Any ship or goods taken as prize by any of the officers and crew of a ship other than a ship of war of her Majesty shall, on condemnation, belong to her Majesty in her office of Admiralty.

IV. – PRIZE SALVAGE

40.   Where any ship or goods belonging to any of her Majesty's subjects, after being taken as prize by the enemy, is or are retaken from the enemy by any of her Majesty's ships of war, the same shall be restored by decree of a prize court to the owner, on his paying as prize salvage one eighth part of the value of the prize to be decreed and ascertained by the court, or such sum not exceeding one eighth part of the estimated value of the prize as may be agreed on between the owner and the re-captors, and approved by order of the court; Provided that where the recapture is made under circumstance of special difficulty or danger, the prize court may, if it thinks fit, award to the re-captors as prize salvage a larger part than one eighth part, of the value of the prize.

41.   Where a ship belonging to any of her Majesty's subjects, after being taken as prize by the enemy, is retaken from the enemy by any of her Majesty's ships of war, she may, with the consent of the re-captors, prosecute her voyage, and it shall not be necessary for the re-captors to proceed to adjudication till her return to a port of the United Kingdom.

The master or owner, or his agent, may, with the consent of the re-captors, unload and dispose of the goods on board the ship before adjudication.

In case the ship does not, within six months, return to a port of the United Kingdom, the re-captors may nevertheless institute proceedings against the ship or goods in the High Court of Admiralty, and the court may thereupon award prize salvage as aforesaid to the re-captors, and may enforce payment thereof, either by warrant or arrest against the ship or goods, or by monition and attachment against the owner.

V. – PRIZE BOUNTY

42.   If, in relation to any war, her Majesty is pleased to declare, by proclamation or Order in Council, her intention to grant prize bounty to the officers and crews of her ships of war, then such of the officers and crew of any of her Majesty's ships of war as are actually present at the taking or destroying of any armed ship of any of her Majesty's enemies shall be entitled to have distributed among them as prize bounty a sum calculated at the rate of five pounds for each person on board the enemy's ship at the beginning of the engagement.

43.   The number of the persons so on board the enemy's ship shall be proved in a prize court, either by the examinations on oath of the survivors of them, or of any three or more of the survivors, or if there is no survivor by the papers of the enemy's ship, or by the examinations on oath of three or more of the officers and crew of her Majesty's ship, or by such other evidence as may seem to the court sufficient in the circumstances.

The court shall make a decree declaring the title of the officers and crew of her Majesty's ship to the prize bounty, and stating the amount thereof.

The decree shall be subject to appeal as other decrees of the court.

44.   On production of an official copy of the decree the commissioners of her Majesty's Treasury shall, out of money provided by Parliament, pay the amount of prize bounty decreed, in such manner as any Order in Council may from time to time direct.

VI. – MISCELLANEOUS PROVISIONS

Ransom

45.   Her Majesty in council may from time to time, in relation to any war, make such orders as may seem expedient, according to circumstances, for prohibiting or allowing, wholly or in certain cases, or subject to any conditions or regulations or otherwise, as may from time to time seem meet, the ransoming or the entering into any contract or agreement for the ransoming of any ship or goods belonging to any of her Majesty's subjects, and taken as prize by any of her Majesty's enemies.

Any contract or agreement entered into, and any bill, bond, or other security given for ransom of any ship or goods, shall be under the exclusive jurisdiction of the High Court of Admiralty as a prize court (subject to appeal to the judicial committee of the privy council), and if entered into or given in contravention of any such order in council shall be deemed to have been entered into or given for an illegal consideration.

If any person ransoms or enters into any contract or agreement for ransoming any ship or goods, in contravention of any such order in council, he shall for every such offence be liable to be proceeded against in the High Court of Admiralty at the suit of her Majesty in her office of Admiralty, and on conviction to be fined, in the discretion of the court, any sum not exceeding five hundred pounds.

Convoy

46.   If the master or other person having the command of any ship of any of her Majesty's subjects, under the convoy of any of her Majesty's ships of war, wilfully disobeys any lawful signal, instruction, or command of the commander of the convoy, or without leave deserts the convoy, he shall be liable to be proceeded against in the High Court of Admiralty at the suit of her Majesty in her office of Admiralty, and upon conviction to be fined, in the discretion of the court, any sum not exceeding five hundred pounds, and to suffer imprisonment for such time, not exceeding one year, as the court may adjudge.

Customs Duties and Regulations

47.   All ships and goods taken as prize and brought into a port of the United Kingdom shall be liable to and be charged with the same rates and charges and duties of customs as under any Act relating to the customs may be chargeable on other ships and goods of the like description; and

All goods brought in as prize which would on the voluntary importation thereof be liable to forfeiture or subject to any restriction under the laws relating to the customs, shall be deemed to be so liable and subject, unless the commissioners of customs see fit to authorize the sale or delivery thereof for home use or exportation, unconditionally or subject to such conditions and regulations as they may direct.

48.   Where any ship or goods taken as prize is or are brought into a port of the United Kingdom, the master or other person in charge or command of the ship which has been taken or in which the goods are brought shall, on arrival at such port, bring to at the proper place of discharge, and shall, when required by any officer of customs, deliver an account in writing under his hand concerning such ship and goods, giving such particulars relating thereto as may be in his power, and shall truly answer all questions concerning such ship or goods asked by any such officer, and in default shall forfeit a sum not exceeding one hundred pounds, such forfeiture to be enforced as forfeitures for offences against the laws relating to the customs are enforced, and every such ship shall be liable to such searches as other ships are liable to, and the officers of the customs may freely go on board the same, subject, nevertheless to such regulations in respect of ships of war belonging to her Majesty as shall from time to time be issued by the commissioners of her Majesty's Treasury.

49.   Goods taken as prize may be sold either for home consumption or for exportation; and if in the former case the proceeds thereof, after

payment of duties of customs, are insufficient to satisfy the just and reasonable claims thereon, the commissioners of her Majesty's Treasury may remit the whole or such part of the said duties as they see fit.

Perjury

50.   If any person wilfully and corruptly swears, declares, or affirms falsely in any prize cause or appeal, or in any proceeding under this Act, or in respect of any matter required by this Act to be verified on oath, or suborns any other person to do so, he shall be deemed guilty of perjury, or of subornation of perjury (as the case may be), and shall be liable to be punished accordingly.

Limitation of Actions, &c:

51.   Any action or proceeding shall not lie in any part of her Majesty's dominions against any person acting under the authority or in the execution or intended execution or in pursuance of this Act for any alleged irregularity or trespass, or other act or thing done or omitted by him under this Act, unless notice in writing (specifying the cause of the action or proceeding) is given by the intending plaintiff or prosecutor to the intended defendant, one month at least before the commencement of the action or proceeding, nor unless the action or proceeding is commenced within six months next after the act or thing complained of is done or omitted, or, in case of a continuation of damage, within six months next after the doing of such damage has ceased.

In any such action the defendant may plead generally that the act or thing complained of was done or omitted by him when action under the authority or in the execution or intended execution or in pursuance of this Act, and may give all special matter in evidence; and the plaintiff shall not succeed if tender of sufficient amends is made by the defendant before the commencement of the action; and in case no tender has been made, the defendant may, by leave of the court in which the action is brought, at any time pay into court such sum of money as he thinks fit, whereupon such proceeding and order shall be had and made in and by the court as may be had and made on the payment of money into court in an ordinary action; and if the plaintiff does not succeed in the action, the defendant shall receive such full and reasonable indemnity as to all costs, charges, and expenses incurred in and about the action as may be taxed and allowed by the proper officer, subject to review; and though a verdict is given for the plaintiff in the action he shall not have costs against the defendant, unless the judge before whom the trial is had certifies his approval of the action.

Any such action or proceeding against any person in her Majesty's naval services, or in the employment of the lords of the Admiralty, shall not be brought or instituted elsewhere than in the United Kingdom.

Petitions of Right

52.   A petition of right, under the Petitions of Right Act, 1860, may, if the suppliant thinks fit, be intituled in the High Court of Admiralty, in case the subject matter of the petition or any material part thereof arises out of the exercise of any belligerent right on behalf of the crown, or would be cognizable in a prize court within her Majesty's dominions if the same were a matter in dispute between private persons.

Any petition or right under the last-mentioned Act, whether intituled in the High Court of Admiralty or not, may be prosecuted in that court, if the lord chancellor thinks fit so to direct.

The provisions of this Act relative to appeal, and to the framing and approval of general orders for regulating the procedure and practice of the High Court of Admiralty, shall extend to the case of any such petition of right intituled or directed to be prosecuted in that court; and, subject thereto, all the provisions of the Petitions of Right Act, 1860, shall apply, mutatis mutandis, in the case of any such petition of right; and for the purposes of the present section the term 'court' and 'judge' in that Act shall respectively be understood to include and to mean the High Court of Admiralty and the judge thereof, and other terms shall have the respective meanings given to them in that Act.

Orders in Council

53.   Her Majesty in council may from time to time make such Orders in Council as seem meet for the better execution of this Act.

54.   Every Order in Council under this Act shall be published in the London Gazette, and shall be laid before both Houses of Parliament within thirty days after the making thereof, if Parliament is then sitting, and, if not, then within thirty days after the next meeting of Parliament.

Savings

55.   Nothing in this Act shall –

(1)   give to the officers and crew of any of her Majesty's ships or war any right to claim in or to any ship or goods taken as prize or the proceeds thereof, it being the intent of this Act that such officers and crews shall continue to take only such interest (if any) in the proceeds of prizes as may be from time to time granted to them by the crown; or

(2)   affect the operation of any existing treaty or convention with any foreign power; or

(3)   take away or abridge the power of the crown to enter into any treaty or convention with any foreign power containing any stipulation that may seem meet concerning any matter to which this Act relates; or

(4)   take away, abridge, or control, further or otherwise than as expressly provided by this Act, any right, power, or prerogative of her Majesty the Queen in right of her crown, or in right of her office of Admiralty, or any right or power of the lord high admiral of the United Kingdom, or of the commissioners for executing the office of lord high admiral; or

(5)   take away, abridge, or control, further or otherwise than as expressly provided by this Act, the jurisdiction or authority of a prize court to take cognizance of and judicially proceed upon any capture, seizure, prize, or reprisal of any ship or goods, and to hear and determine the same, and, according to the course of Admiralty and the law of nations, to adjudge and condemn any ship or goods, or any other jurisdiction or authority of or exercisable by a prize court.

Commencement

56.   This Act shall commence on the commencement of the Naval Agency and Distribution Act, 1864.

* * *

10.   Short Account of Alabama's Cruise

[ADM 1/8374/103]

Alabama left Liverpool 28th July 1862: on 20th August 1862 she met, off Porto Praya (Azores), her armament and crew, and Semmes assumed command.

The vessel was 900 tons burden, 230 feet long, 15 feet draught, 300 HP, Barkentine [*sic*] rig – Speed under steam 10–11 knots. Armament 6–32 pdrs. on broadside, 1–100 pdr. rifled and 1–8" smooth bore. Complement 244. Cost £50,000.

She commenced depredations off the Azores on the American Whaling Fleet, making her first capture on 4th September.

When the whaling season came to an end in October, *Alabama* proceeded to the Banks of Newfoundland to intercept grain vessels, working gradually South towards the Tropics, reaching Martinique on 18th November, where she was blockaded by the *San Jacinto* which had been ordered to cruise in the West Indies in search of her. She easily escaped during the night of 19th November and joined her collier at the Island of Blanquilla off the Venezuelan Coast, where she coaled and refitted. She then proceeded to the Californian Coast in the hope of picking up a Californian treasure steamer, but in this she was unsuccessful, though she captured several vessels.

A slight machinery defect early in December 1862 compelled Semmes to run in under the North side of Jamaica: on 12th December she made for the Gulf of Mexico, meeting her collier again off the Yucatan Coast. Early in January she made for Galveston to intercept General Banks' expedition. Here she was engaged on 11th January by the USS *Hatteras*, which was sent out from Galveston to investigate; and the *Hatteras* was sunk. Admiral Bell in the *Brooklyn*, with 2 other vessels thereupon chased the *Alabama*, but the latter escaped in the darkness.

Alabama landed her prisoners from the *Hatteras* at Port Royal on 20th January 1863 and sailed again on 28th January. She first cruised in the vicinity, then working her way down to the Brazilian Coast and reaping a rich harvest en route; she coaled at Fernando Noronha, sailing on 22nd April 1863 for a cruise along the Brazilian Coast which again proved most profitable – on 20th June, when in the latitude of Rio, she captured the barque *Conrad* of 350 tons and commissioned her as a cruiser under the name of *Tuscaloosa*.

In connection with this cruise Captain Semmes says – 'If Mr Welles had stationed a heavier and faster ship than the *Alabama* – and he had a number of both heavier and faster ships – at the crossing of the 30th parallel; another at or near the equator, a little to the eastward of Fernando de Noronha, and a third off Bahia, he must have driven me off, or greatly crippled me in my movements. A few more ships in the other chief highways, and his Commerce would have been pretty well protected.' [Admiral Semmes, *Service Afloat*, p. 629.]

In July 1863 the *Alabama* left the East Coast of South America and took the Cape of Good Hope route, capturing vessels as she went and reaching Saldanha Bay on 29th July and Cape Town on 5th August. Several captures were made in these waters and the vessel then passed on into the Indian Ocean and steered for the Straits of Sunda, sighting very little en route and making no prize until close off the Straits, which were reached on 7th November 1863.

The Straits of Sunda being unguarded, the *Alabama* passed through in safety and made several captures in the vicinity, reaching Singapore on 21st December. She left on the 24th, touching at Malacca, and passed out into the Indian Ocean once more. She doubled Ceylon and hauled up the Coast of Malabar, crossed the Arabian Sea and passed down the Straits of Mozambique, reaching her old cruising ground off the Cape on 7th March 1864, again finding the coast clear of Federal cruisers and making many captures.

On 25th March 1864 *Alabama* left the Cape on her return to Europe. The Equator was crossed on 2nd May and Cherbourg was reached on 10th June.

The *Kearsarge* arrived at Cherbourg on 14th June 1864 and the engagement between that vessel and the *Alabama* on 19th June resulted in the sinking of the latter.

Alabama's Cruise

Period: 28th July 1862–19th June 1864.   23 months.
Number of Vessels Destroyed: 69
Total Value: $6,500,000 – approx: £1,300,000.
Sighted by: 3 Federal Cruisers:

1) *San Jacinto* from which she escaped.
2) *Hatteras* which she sank.
3) *Kearsarge*

Remarks on Federal Effort to Capture *Alabama*.

In 1861 the United States Merchant Shipping still occupied second place among the nations. Less than a tenth of this belonged to the Confederates and this rapidly disappeared.

Consequently the Confederates could strike heavy blows against the Federal Commerce without fear of being struck in return.

They therefore took the offensive against Commerce, which they were able to do almost unmolested, the Federals requiring as many vessels as possible to maintain the blockade of Southern Ports.

In consequence of the appearance of the *Alabama* and *Florida*, the Navy Department, in September 1862, despatched a flying squadron to the West Indies and Bahamas under Captain Wilkes, consisting of 2 sloops of war and 5 other vessels. Only the sloops of war were fit to cope with the *Alabama*, but other suitable vessels were despatched later.

Wilkes cruised in the vicinity of the West Indies for 9 months. During 2 months of this time the *Alabama* was in the same waters, while the *Florida*, on leaving Mobile, ran straight into his cruising ground. But the Confederate vessels were never caught by Wilkes. *Florida* was captured later in Bahia Harbour by the *Wachusett* which was at anchor there when *Florida* arrived and anchored: a flagrant violation of the Laws of Neutrality.

Altogether, from first to last, Wilkes had 16 vessels under his orders and accomplished nothing beyond friction with neutrals. [Soley, *The Navy in the Civil War*, Vol. 1, p. 202.]

The fast Federal steamer *Vanderbilt* went in pursuit of the *Alabama*, but, having been delayed by Wilkes, never came up with her though she dogged her to the Cape.

The *Wyoming* was at Batavia when *Alabama* was approaching the Straits of Sunda, but was thrown off the scent and never sighted her.

Ultimately the *Kearsarge* happened to be lying in Flushing when news of *Alabama*'s arrival at Cherbourg reached her. It seems to have been a pure accident. Semmes made no effort to escape in the dark as he had from the *San Jacinto*, but openly challenged *Kearsarge* to action.

Semmes's success was largely due to his careful study of the ocean highways of Commerce: these determined the locality of his successive cruising grounds. He calculated the time required for the news of his presence to reach the United States and before a ship could be sent after him he had moved to a new scene of operations.

Prizes Captured by Confederate Commerce Destroyers[1]

Name of Confederate Vessels	Number of Prizes
Nashville	2
Olustee	6
Alabama	69
Calhoun	3
Florida	37
Tallahassee	29
York	1
Shenandoah	36
Sumter	18
Tacony (tender of *Florida*)	15
Georgia	9
Clarence (tender of *Florida*)	8
Jeff Davis	8
Winslow	5
Chickamauga	4
Retribution	3
Boston	2
Echo	2
Tuscaloosa (tender of *Alabama*)	2
TOTAL	259

* * *

[1]Scharf, *Confederate States Navy*, pp. 814–18.

11.   Memorandum Relative to Certain Statements made by Mr Sumner in his Speech of the 13th April, 1869, with Regard to Pacific Blockades[1]

[FO 881/6378; CP, 6378]   Foreign Office
                                                            May 20, 1869

MR SUMNER, in his speech to the United States' Senate on the subject of the Treaty for the settlement of the 11 *Alabama* and other claims existing between Great Britain and the United States, says, with regard to the British Government having interpreted the Proclamation issued by the United States' Government for the blockade of the ports of the Southern States in the same light as that of a blockade implying belligerent rights, that such assumption was inconsistent with the Proclamation of the President, which, whilst appointing a blockade, was careful to reserve the rights of sovereignty, thus putting foreign Powers on their guard against any premature concession.

Mr Sumner then states what he considers should have been the interpretation of the Proclamation by a friendly Power. In support of these views he proceeds by stating that numerous precedents exist of what the great German authority Heffter calls 'pacific blockade,' or blockade without concession of ocean belligerency, as in the case of France, England, and Russia against Turkey, 1827; France against Mexico, 1837–39; France and Great Britain against the Argentine Republic, 1838–48; Russia against the Circassians, 1831–36, illustrated by the seizure of the *Vixen*, so famous in Diplomatic history (Hautefeuille, *Des Droits et des Devoirs des Neutres*).

Questions like these Mr Sumner states led Heffter to lay down the rule that *blockade* does not necessarily constitute *a state of regular war* (*Droit International*, sections 112–121), as was assumed by the British Proclamation even in the face of the positive words by President Lincoln asserting the national sovereignty and appealing to the 'laws of the United States.'

The existence of such cases, Mr Sumner maintains, was like a notice to the British Government against the concession so rashly made, and an all-sufficient warning which this Power disregarded.

Previously to referring to the cases quoted by Mr Sumner, for the purpose of showing the distinction between each, and their application, if any, to the case of the Confederate States of America, it will be necessary to give a short outline of the events which had occurred

[1]Printed August 1893.

between the two contending parties in America previous to the issue of the Queen's Proclamation of the 13th May, 1861.

The first steps taken by the Confederate States towards obtaining their separation from the United States was at a Convention which met in South Carolina in December 1860, which on the 20th of that month issued an Ordinance proclaiming the repeal of the Union subsisting between that State and the other States of the United States of America.

This Ordinance was issued under the assumption that the right of secession rested upon the doctrine that the Union was a compact between independent States, from which any one of them might withdraw at pleasure in virtue of its sovereignty.

By the end of January 1861 most of the States which subsequently formed the Southern Confederacy had also declared their secession. On the 8th February a Constitution had been voted by the seceding States, and on the 18th of the same month Mr Davis was inaugurated as President of the Southern Confederacy, and by the 21st his Cabinet was completed.

On the completion of the Government of the Confederate States, the Southern Congress proceeded to vote the laws necessary for the organization of the army and navy of the States. On the 6th March the Law for the organization of the army was passed, and on the 16th of the same month a similar Law was passed for the organization of the navy. On the 12th April hostilities commenced by the attack of the Confederates on Fort Sumter. This led to the issue of a Proclamation by President Lincoln, on the 15th April, calling to arms 75,000 men for the coercion of the rebel States. This Proclamation determined the Confederate States to take the most energetic measures for resistance, among which was the issue by President Davis, on the 17th April, of a Proclamation offering *letters of marque* to all persons who might desire by service in private armed vessels to aid the Government.

This proceeding of President Davis was subsequently confirmed by the Confederate Congress passing an Act (on the 6th May) recognizing a state of war with the United States, and authorizing the issue of letters of marque. The consequence of the issue of the Proclamation of President Davis granting letters of marque was the Proclamation by President Lincoln of the blockade of the ports of the Southern Confederacy, dated the 19th April.[1] The preamble of this Proclamation clearly pointed to the probable acts of warfare which would be carried on at sea by the Confederates, as it states: 'And whereas a combination of persons engaged in such insurrection have threatened to grant pretended letters

[1]*Inclosure No. 1, p. 1.

of marque to authorize the bearers thereof to commit assaults on the lives, vessels, and property of good citizens of the country lawfully engaged in commerce on the high seas, and in waters of the United States.'

The blockade was stated to be established 'in pursuance of *the laws of the United States and the law of nations in such case provided.*'

From the foregoing portion of this Memorandum it will be observed that the Confederate States had, previously to the issue of the Proclamation of President Lincoln, established a Government complete in all its departments, which was supported by a population of upwards of 8,000,000.

The Confederate Congress had also made due provision for the establishment of Courts of Justice, and also for the establishment of an army and navy.

All these provisions had been made by the Confederate Congress previous to its adjournment in the month of March. In consequence of the Proclamation issued by President Lincoln, the Southern Congress again met on the 29th April, 1861, for the purpose of making further provisions for the defence of the States.

On the 6th May the Congress passed an Act for 'recognizing the existence of war between the United States and the Confederate States, and concerning letters of marque, prizes, and prize goods.'

The seventh section of the above Act provided that captured vessels should be proceeded against before a competent Tribunal, and provision was made with regard to the Courts which were to have jurisdiction in cases of prizes.

With regard to the army and navy of the Confederate States, Mr Davis declared, on the 29th April, that the former amounted to 34,000 men, but that it was proposed to organize an army of 100,000 men, and that the latter was necessarily restricted by the fact that sufficient time had not elapsed for the purchase or construction of more than a limited number of vessels adapted to the public service. Two vessels had, however, been purchased and manned, the *Sumter* and *McRae*, and were being prepared for sea at New Orleans with all possible dispatch.

It will thus be seen that the Confederate States had already commenced to form the nucleus of a navy, the extent of which, considering the numerous ports which were then in their possession, it was impossible for the British Government to foresee.

It will now be necessary to refer to the proceedings of the American Minister in England. On the 11th May, 1861, Mr Dallas communicated to the British Government the copy of a Circular which he had received from his Government, of which the following is a transcript:

Department of State,
Sir,   *Washington, April 20, 1861*
'As it is not improbable that mercenary or badly enterprising, men, lured by the seductions held out in a recent Proclamation under the pretended authority of the so-called Confederate States of America, may attempt to fit out privateers in the ports of England, for the purpose of aggression on the commerce of the United States, I am directed by the President to instruct you to be vigilant to the extent of your power towards preventing any such unlawful purpose. To this end you will promptly impart to the proper authorities any facts upon the subject which may come to your knowledge. A copy of the President's Proclamation of the 19th instant is herewith inclosed, from which you will perceive that the pains and penalties of piracy will be visited on any person who may molest a vessel of the United States.

I am, &c.
(Signed)   WILLIAM H. SEWARD.'

Three days after the receipt of the above communication, the 13th May, a Proclamation was issued by the Queen declaring a strict neutrality in the contest between the United States of America and certain States styling themselves the Confederate States of America.[1]

Having thus far given an outline of the measures adopted by the Confederate States for their defence, reference is now made to the statements made by Mr Sumner (Pamphlet edition, p. 11) regarding 'pacific blockade' or *blockade without the concession of ocean belligerency.* The precedents which he quotes are:

1.   The case of England, France, and Russia against Turkey, in 1827.
2.   France against Mexico, 1837-39.
3.   France and Great Britain against the Argentine Republic, 1838–48.
4.   Russia against the Circassians, illustrated by the seizure of the *Vixen.*

The authorities on international law quoted by Mr Sumner are Heffter and Hautefeuille.

To show what analogy, if any, exists between these several cases and that of the civil war in America, it will be necessary to give a short outline of each.

1st Case

The insurrection of the Greeks against their Turkish masters commenced in 1821, and very shortly afterwards numerous vessels were

[1]*Inclosure No. 2.

fitted out by the insurgents to make war on Turkish commerce. The result of this naval warfare led to the injury of neutral traders, and particularly of British ships, by the attacks made upon them by the insurgent vessels.

For some time after the commencement of the insurrection the Greeks had no regularly established Government such as was established by the Confederate States of America, the result of which was that many of the insurgent vessels were unprovided with commissions from any legitimate authority.

The British Government, however, maintained a neutral position in the conflict, and recognized the belligerent rights of each of the contending parties.

These belligerent rights were, however, more formally recognized by the issue of a Proclamation on the 30th September, 1825, prohibiting British subjects taking part in the contest between the Ottoman Porte and the Greeks, or between other belligerents.[1] No Proclamation appears to have been issued by the Turkish Government for the blockade of the Greek ports.

In 1827, in consequence of the prolonged struggle between the Greeks and the Turks, and the injury suffered by neutral commerce, Great Britain, France, and Russia resolved to offer their mediation to the Ottoman Porte with a view of effecting a reconciliation between it and the Greeks. If within the space of one month the Ottoman Porte refused the mediation of the three Powers and the armistice which was to follow, it was stipulated in the Treaty between those Powers that they should declare to either of the contending parties which might be disposed to continue hostilities, or to both of them if necessary, that the said High Powers intended to exert all the means which circumstances might suggest to their prudence for the purpose of obtaining the immediate effects of the armistice which they desired, by preventing as far as possible all collision between the contending parties; and, in consequence, immediately after the above-mentioned declaration, the High Powers would jointly exert all their efforts to accomplish the object of such armistice, *without, however, taking any part in the hostilities between the two contending parties*.[2]

Immediately after the signature of the above Article it was stipulated that the High Contracting Powers should transmit to the Admirals commanding their respective squadrons in the Levant conditional instructions in conformity to the arrangements above declared.

---

[1]*In June 1823 a Proclamation had been issued by the British Government declaring its neutrality in the contests which were then being carried on in Europe and America.

[2]*Additional Article to Treaty between Great Britain and France and Russia of the 6th July, 1827. Hertslet's State Papers, vol. xiii, p. 637.

In consequence of the refusal of the Porte to accept the mediation of the three Powers, and its acceptance by the Greeks, instructions to the following effect were sent to the Admirals commanding the squadrons of those Powers in the Mediterranean. They were directed to place their squadrons in such positions as would intercept all ships, whether of war or merchants, having on board troops, arms, ammunition, &c., for the use of the Turkish force employed or intended to be employed against the Greeks either on the continent or in the islands. They were not, however, to use force for such interception unless it should become absolutely necessary by the commanders of those vessels persisting, after having been duly warned to the contrary, to proceed to the place of their destination, but were to take care to abstain, under the then existing circumstances, from giving any interruption to the regular commerce of neutrals with any of the ports of Turkey or of Greece, though occupied by the Turks.

Notwithstanding all the precautions taken by the Admirals to maintain the pacific character of the measures with which they were intrusted, a conflict soon took place, in which the Turkish squadron was destroyed in the Bay of Navarino. The result of the policy of the three Powers towards Turkey is fully explained in a despatch addressed by Lord Aberdeen to Lord Stuart de Rothsay in June 1829. In this despatch his Lordship stated 'that, disclaiming all hostility towards the Sultan, we have, nevertheless, destroyed the fleet of our ally; we have blockaded his ports, we have captured his fortresses, and expelled his garrisons, and we have taken military possession of his provinces, in the occupation of which we still linger. But we have done more: we have placed a portion of the dominion of our ally under the safeguard of our own guarantee, and have made known to him that any hostile attempt against that territory will be considered as a declaration of war against three of the most powerful States of Christendom.'

With regard to blockades, Lord Aberdeen stated

> that Great Britain is the Power which, of all others, gives the greatest facility to the execution of blockades by belligerent States. At all events, His Majesty was the first to recognize the belligerent rights of the Greek insurgents by the acknowledgment of the blockades instituted by their naval forces. The principle which regulates this conduct is simple and obvious. It is conceived that those belligerents who have the power of carrying on a maritime warfare have also the right [to] blockade the ports of their enemies.
>
> The establishment of a blockade being an act of war by a competent authority, we must either respect such blockade or treat as pirates those who attempt to enforce it. In a contest, therefore, in

which we profess to be neutral we respect all blockades, provided only they are established by a competent authority, and a sufficient force is employed to render them effectual.

From the foregoing statement of the proceedings of England and France and Russia in 1827 it would appear that no analogy exists with the circumstances of the civil war in the United States.

The three mediating Powers intervened to stop the conflict then existing between Turkey and her revolted subjects.

In their instructions to their Admirals in the Levant the mediating Powers directed them to prevent the arrival of arms, ammunition, &c., to the Turkish garrisons in the Morea, but they were not to interfere with the commerce of neutrals.

2nd Case

In 1837, in consequence of the complaints of certain French subjects against the Government of Mexico, redress was demanded by the French Government. The Mexican Government having declined to accede to the demands of France, an additional naval force was sent by the latter, under Admiral Baudin, to the coast of Mexico. On the arrival of the French squadron an ultimatum was addressed by the French Minister to the Government of Mexico, which the latter refused to take into consideration until the French naval forces had been withdrawn from the Mexican coasts.

This led to the French Minister, on the 14th April, 1838, demanding his passports and quitting the country, and immediately afterwards the Mexican ports were declared in a state of blockade by the French Admiral.

The blockade of the Mexican ports was declared in April 1838; but with regard to the trade of neutrals, the instructions of the French Government were so conceived as to reconcile the practical exercise of a legitimate right with the respect due to the independence of neutral flags and with the desire of causing the least possible inconvenience to the navigation of neutral vessels.

In the meantime negotiations were being carried on between the two Powers for the peaceful settlement of the questions in dispute, which, however, having failed, in December 1838 war was decreed by the Mexican Congress.

No question of maritime warfare arose out of these hostilities; Mexico, having no fleet, was incapable of carrying on such a warfare, and she abstained from issuing letters of marque, which might have covered the seas with a swarm of privateers bearing her flag. Hostilities between the two nations finally terminated – after the bombardment and capture by the French of the fortress of St. Juan d'Ulloa – through the mediation of Mr Pakenham, the British Minister.

In this case, although actual war was not declared by France, the blockade of the Mexican ports was certainly regarded by the latter as an act of hostility. Mexico was, however, too weak to resist, and she abstained from using the only means of aggressive warfare, viz., the issue of letters of marque.

3rd Case

In 1838, France, in order to enforce certain claims upon the Government of Buenos Ayres, instituted a blockade of the ports of the Argentine Confederation without any formal declaration of war. The proceeding of the French Admiral was, however, considered by the Argentine Government as an act of hostility, but in consequence of its weakness the Republic was unable to resist, and finally conceded the demands of France.

In this case no question of belligerent rights at sea occurred, the Argentine Republic, although protesting against the blockade, having submitted without making use of any belligerent rights.

4th Case

With regard to the case of the *Vixen*, no formal notice of the blockade of the coast of Circassia was issued by the Russian Government; in fact, none did exist.

By the Treaty of Adrianople, Russia obtained from Turkey certain concessions of territory on the coast of Circassia. For the purpose of protecting that coast from the introduction of disease, and also from illicit trade, the Russian Government issued Fiscal Regulations, which confined foreign trade to the ports of Anapa and Redout-Kalé, and declared that all attempts to trade on any other portion of the coast would be considered a violation of the Regulations, and would subject the vessels to the treatment of smugglers. The British vessel *Vixen* attempted to land a cargo at the port of Sourdjouk-Kalé in violation of the above Regulations, which led to her being seized by the Russian authorities and taken to Sevastopol.

After some correspondence with the Russian Government with regard to the seizure of the *Vixen*, the owners were finally informed that, from the explanation which had been received from the Russian Government, His Majesty's Government had come to the conclusion that it would not be justified in demanding from Russia restitution and compensation on account of that vessel.

The reason assigned by the British Government for this decision was that the *Vixen* had entered a Russian port, and attempted to land a cargo, in contravention of a Regulation of the Russian Government which interdicted to foreign ships the entrance of that port where there was no Custom house establishment, while such ships were permitted to trade at the neighbouring port of Anapa.

Under these circumstances, the British Government did not think that there was sufficient ground to question the right of Russia to seize and confiscate the *Vixen* and her cargo.

From the foregoing outline of the cases of 'pacific blockade' quoted by Mr Sumner, it would not appear that they could be applied to the case of the civil war in America.

With regard to the measure adopted by Great Britain, France, and Russia to put a stop to the war between Turkey and the Greek insurgents, it should be observed that no question of the concession of ocean belligerency could have arisen so long as the three Powers maintained the neutral position to which they pretended in their intervention between Turkey and Greece.

No formal blockade was declared by them, but merely a stoppage of vessels conveying munitions of war, &c. The trade of neutrals was respected. Although the Turks considered the proceedings of the three Powers as acts of hostility, still they abstained from declaring war.

In conclusion, it will be interesting to quote the opinion of M.L.B. Hautefeuille on the question of 'pacific blockades,' or 'blocus pacifique':–

'De tout ce qui précéde, je dois conclure que le blocus est un acte de guerre, un mode de la faire, spécialement appliqué à un lieu déterminé; que par conséquent il ne peut exister sans guerre; d'où il suit que l'acte que j'ai appelé *blocus pacifique*, que quelques personnes nomment *blocus simple*, est illégitime, ou plutôt qu'il est un véritable fait de guerre, que les belligérents cherchent à déguiser, dans leur intérêt particulier. Admettre l'existence du blocus pacifique serait à mes yeux une violation de tous les principes de la loi primitive et secondaire, un attentat contre les peuples restés spectateurs, puisque ce serait laisser à la volonté d'une nation le pouvoir de leur imposer des devoirs qui ne peuvent dériver que de la guerre, c'est-à-dire, d'un état de choses déterminé, d'un fait, et non du caprice, de la prépotence d'une nation.

'Les conséquences de l'admission de ce prétendu état mixte entre la paix et la guerre, si elle avait lieu, ne tarderaient pas à se faire sentir; elles seraient de nouveau exploitées contre les peuples commerçants. Ce mode d'action prétendu pacifique doit donc être rejeté.'

With regard to the policy of the British Government in issuing the Proclamation of the 13th May, 1861, the precedents upon which it acted were the civil wars between Spain and her South American Colonies, and the insurrection of the Greeks against the Porte. During those wars the neutrality of Great Britain was frequently proclaimed, and almost from the commencement of the Greek insurrection she had recognized their claim to belligerent rights.

In concluding this Memorandum it will be interesting to refer to the opinion of Mr H. Wheaton, the well-known American author on international law, regarding the position of neutrals during a civil war. A copy of this opinion will be found contained in Inclosure No. _ of this Memorandum.[1]

[Signed] Alfred S. Green [Foreign Office Sub-Librarian]

* * *

12.   Franco-Prussian War

The Marquis de Lavalette to Earl Granville

[FO 188/1778]   London
July 22, 1870

Translation

The undersigned, the French Ambassador in London, has received from his Government an order to address to his Excellency Earl Granville the following communication:

His Majesty the Emperor of the French has felt himself obliged, in order to defend the honour and interests of France, as well as to protect the balance of power in Europe, to declare war against Prussia, and against the Allied States which afford her the co-operation of their arms against us.

His Majesty has given orders that, in the prosecution of this war, the Commanders of his Forces, by land and sea, shall scrupulously observe towards such Powers as shall remain neutral the rules of international law, and shall especially conform to the principle laid down in the Declaration of the Congress of Paris of 16th April, 1856, which are as follows:

1.   Privateering is and remains abolished.

2.   A neutral flag covers enemy's merchandize, with the exception of contraband of war.

[1*]Inclosure No. 3.

3.   Merchandize of neutrals, except contraband of war, sailing under an enemy's flag is not seizable.

4. Blockades, in order to be binding, must be effectual; that is, they must be maintained by a force really sufficient to prevent the enemy from obtaining access to the coast.

Although Spain and the United States did not adhere to the Treaty of 1856, His Majesty's ships will not seize enemy's property sailing on board an American or Spanish vessel, unless such property is contraband of war.

Moreover His Majesty does not intend to vindicate his right of confiscating the property of American or Spanish subjects which may be found on board an enemy's vessel.

The Emperor is confident that, in just reciprocity, Her Majesty's Government will have the goodness to prescribe measures for the exact observance on their part, by the British authorities and subjects, of the duties of strict neutrality during this war.

The Undersigned, &c.   [Signed] LaValette

* * *

13.   Treaty Between Her Majesty and the United States of America

[Harrison and Sons, London]   Signed at Washington, May 8, 1871
                                   (ratified at London June 17, 1871)

Article VI. In deciding the matters submitted to the Arbitrators [i.e. the *Alabama* claims] they shall be governed by the following three rules, which are agreed upon by the High Contracting Parties as rules to be taken as applicable to the case, and by such principles of international law not inconsistent therewith as the Arbitrators shall determine to have been applicable to the case:

Rules: A neutral Government is bound –

First: To use due diligence to prevent the fitting out, arming, or equipping, within its jurisdiction, of any vessel which it has reasonable ground to believe is intended to cruize or to carry on war against a Power with which it is at peace; and also to use like diligence to prevent the departure from its jurisdiction of any vessel intended to cruize or carry on war as above, such vessel having been specially adapted, in whole or in part, within such jurisdiction, to warlike use.

Secondly: Not to permit or suffer either belligerent to make use of its ports or waters as the base of naval operation against the other, or for the purpose of the renewal or augmentation of military supplies or arms, or the recruitment of men.

Thirdly: To exercise due diligence in its own ports and waters, and, as to all persons within its jurisdiction, to prevent any violation of the foregoing obligations and duties.

Her Britannic Majesty has commanded her High Commissioners and Plenipotentiaries to declare that Her Majesty's Government cannot assent to the foregoing rules as a statement of principles of international law which were in force at the time when the claims mentioned in Article 1 arose, but that Her Majesty's Government, in order to evince its desire of strengthening the friendly relations between the two countries and of making satisfactory provision for the future, agrees that, in deciding the questions between the two countries arising out of those claims, the Arbitrators should assume that Her Majesty's Government had undertaken to act upon the principles set forth in these rules.

And the High Contracting Parties agree to observe these rules as between themselves in future, and to bring them to the knowledge of other maritime Powers and to invite them to accede to them.

* * *

14. Memorandum on the Origin of the Declaration of Paris of 1856, respecting Maritime Law

[With reference to Mr O'Clery's Notice of Motion in the House of Commons of 1st June, 1875.]

[Confidential Print 2763, FO 188/2763]   Foreign Office
                                                          February 1876.

No special instructions upon this subject were given to Lord Clarendon as the British Plenipotentiary to the Paris Conference on his proceeding to Paris, as will appear from the following Memorandum, drawn up on the 15th February, 1856, and initialled by his Lordship:

'Foreign Office, February 15, 1856

Her Majesty's confidential servants having had under their consideration a document which had been communicated to Her Majesty's Principal Secretary of State for Foreign Affairs on the 13th of February by the Count de Persigny, French Ambassador at this Court, entitled, 'Indications Générales sur la marche à donner aux différents points de

la négociation,'* came to the conclusion that the observations contained in that document were generally consistent with the views
entertained by Her Majesty's Government on the points to be discussed, and therefore they considered it unnecessary to furnish the Earl
of Clarendon with any special instructions for his guidance, referring
him to the French document as explanatory of the course which they
thought it desirable that he should adopt as far as the circumstances of
the moment might seem to render it advisable for him to do so.

'C.'

[* Pièces Jointes. 1. Mémoire sur l'Organisation des Principautés, 2.
Simple note sur la possibilité de confier à un Prince Italien la
Souveraineté dans les Principautés, 3. Note sur la Servie, 4. Projet de
Traité pour renouveler la Convention des Détroits, 5. Même projet pour
une hypothèse différente, 6. Projet du Traité particulier entre la Porte et
la Russie. Nothing was said about Maritime Law.]

The question of Maritime Law was first mooted by the Count
Walewski at the Conference, at their sitting of the 8th April, 1856
(Protocol No. 22, upon which occasion Lord Clarendon observed that,
like France, England, at the commencement of the war, sought by every
means to mitigate its effects, and that with this view she had renounced,
for the benefit of neutrals, during the struggle which had then come to
an end, principles which, up to that time, she had invariably maintained; and his Lordship added that England was disposed to renounce
them definitively, provided that privateering was equally abolished for
ever; that privateering was nothing else than an organized and legal
piracy; that privateers were one of the greatest scourges of war; and that
our condition of civilization and humanity required that an end should
be put to a system which was no longer suitable to the present day; and
he concluded by saying that, if the whole of the Congress were to adopt
the proposition of Count Walewski, it should be well understood that it
would only be binding in regard to the Powers who might accede to it,
and that it could not be appealed to by Governments who might refuse
their accession. The other Plenipotentiaries having expressed their view
on the subject, Count Walewski expressed a hope that at the next sitting
they would have received from their respective Governments authority
to adhere to an act which, while completing the work of the Congress
of Paris, would effect an improvement worthy of the epoch.

This Protocol was not sent home officially till the 14th April, but the
following entry appears in the Register kept at Paris:
'To Mr Hammond. (Telegram.) April 11. Form of Neutral Declaration
going home.'

But there is no entry in the Register of the Foreign Office of any despatch on the subject having been received.

On the 13th of April the following official despatch was addressed to the Earl of Clarendon:

Foreign Office
April 13, 1856

'My Lord, I have the honour to transmit to your Lordship a copy of the draft of Declaration respecting the maritime and neutral rights which you forwarded to me on the 11th instant, [It will be observed that no official despatch is here alluded to. E.H.] and I have to state to your Lordship that Her Majesty's Government concur in the substance of this proposed Declaration, provided those amendments suggested in the margin be made in it. Her Majesty's Government do not think it advisable to state in the Preamble as strongly as is stated in the proposed draft the assertion that the maintenance of those principles of maritime law, for which in times past Great Britain has invariably contended, must be a permanent cause of disturbance in the relations between neutrals and belligerents, and the word "calamités" seems needlessly strong as applicable to the differences which opposite opinions in regard to these questions have in times past produced. It may, no doubt, be politic for Great Britain to give up for the future doctrines of maritime law which she has in times past contended for and by force of arms maintained; but Her Majesty's Government should not, in doing so, cast any censure upon the former course of the British Government, nor admit that the course which they are prepared to take upon a balance of advantages and disadvantages, is forced upon them by necessity.

Again, it would not be correct to say that a declaration of principles, such as is now proposed, could alter the Law of Nations. That law rests upon foundations wider and deeper than the occasional declarations of a few States, and it could not be altered except by some agreement much more general and much more formal than the proposed declaration; and it would be dangerous for Great Britain to admit that such a Declaration issued by the Representatives of a small number of States could alter the Law of Nations.

An example thus set, and a precedent thus established by the consent and participation of Great Britain, might hereafter, upon other occasions, be used for the purpose of establishing doctrines of international law to which Great Britain might have the strongest objection and repugnance. It is desirable not only that this Declaration should be communicated to other States, but that the States to which it shall be communicated shall be invited to accede to it; and it is highly important to record that the principles thus proclaimed shall not be applicable to the relations of the declaring Powers with States which shall not have acceded to the Declaration.'

The Draft of this despatch and of the following Declaration, with the marginal notes, was in the handwriting of Mr Hammond.

The Project of Declaration ran as follows:

'Les Plénipotentaires qui ont signé le Traité de Paris du 30 Mars, 1856, réunis en Conférence, considérant que le droit maritime en temps de guerre a été pendant longtemps l'objet de contestations regrettables; que l'incertitude sur les droits et les devoirs de neutre ~~est une cause permanente de trouble dans leurs rapports avec les~~ [donne lieu à des discussions entre ceux-ci et les] belligérants et ~~de nature~~ [peut] à amener des difficultés et des conflits; ~~que la nécessité d'une~~ [même qu'il y aurait par conséquent avantage à établir une] doctrine uniforme pour toutes les nations sur un point aussi important ~~est démontrée aussi bien par les suggestions de la raison que par l'histoire des calamités auxquelles l'absence de tout accord a ce aujet a donné lieu dans le passé~~; que par une Déclaration en date du 28 Mars, 1854, leurs Majestés l'Empereur des Français et la Reine du Royaume Uni de la Grande Bretagne et d'Irlande ont émis relativement à la neutralité maritime pour la durée de la guerre qui vient de finir, des principes essentiellement favorables aux intérêts des Etats neutres; que les Plénipotentiaires assemblés dans ce Congrès ne sauraient mieux répondre aux intentions dont leurs Governments sont animés qu'en travaillant à introduire dans ~~le droit public~~ [les rapports internationaux] des maximes dont le monde a pu apprécier les bienfaits dans la dernière guerre.

Les dits Plénipotentiaires sont convenus de se concerter sur les moyens d'atteindre ce but, et sont tombés à cet effet d'accord sur une déclaration solennelle. Dûment autorisés par l'adhésion formelle de leurs Cours aux principes de-dessus énoncés ils déclarent donc, au nom de leurs Governements, qu'en ce qui les concerne ~~ces principes font décormais partie du droit des géns~~ [et entre eux, comme ainsi entre leurs Gouvernements et tout autre Governement qui pourra y adhérer, ces principes seront désormais la règle de conduite dans tous les cas auxquels ces principes seront applicables].

En conséquence ils reconnaissent et proclament:

1. Que la course est, et demeure, abolie.

2. Que le pavillon neutre couvre la marchandise ennemie à l'exception de la contrebande de guerre.

3. Que la marchandise neutre, à l'exception de la contrebande de guerre, n'est pas saisissable sous pavillon ennemi.

4. Que les blocus, pour être obligatoires, doivent être effectifs, c'est-à-dire, maintenus par une force suffisante pour interdire réellemeut l'accès du littoral de l'ennemi.

[This is and always has been acknowledged as international law, and it seems needless to insert it as a new doctrine.]

Les Gouvernements des Plénipotentiaires soussignés s'engagent à porter cette Déclaration à la connaissance des Cours qui n'ont pas été appelées à participer au Congrès de Paris; [et à les inviter à y accéder;] et convaincus que les maximes qu'ils viennent de proclamer ne sauraient être accueillies qu'avec gratitude par toutes les nations, ils nourissent la ferme confiance que leurs efforts pour en généraliser l'adoption seront couronnés d'un plein succès.

[Ils se réservent toutefois de ne pas appliquer les susdits principes à leurs rapport avec des Gouvernements qui n'y auraient pas accédés.]'

At the meeting of the 14th April (Protocol No. 23) the draft of the Declaration was adopted by the Congress, and the question of mediation and other points were also discussed; and on the 18th April Her Majesty's Government 'entirely approved the course taken by Lord Clarendon in regard to the *several points* discussed in the twenty-third Conference.' [Earl of Clarendon, No. 110; April 15.] Before the Declaration was formally signed, Lord Cowley and Lord Clarendon suggested the omission of the 4th Article concerning blockades, but they did not press their objection.

Before closing the Paris Conferences, Count Walewski said it would be necessary to come to an agreement as to whether the Protocols should be made public or not, and he expressed a hope that the original engagement of keeping secret what had passed in the Congress might still be held binding, and that nothing would hereafter be divulged beyond what was contained in the Protocols. To this proposal Lord Clarendon replied that there could be no doubt on the part of Her Majesty's Government as to the publication of the Protocols, which would be laid before Parliament at the same time as the Treaty; and his Lordship added that although, for various reasons, he thought it desirable that the discussions which had taken place in the Congress should not be made known, yet that he could enter into no engagement whatever upon the subject, as Her Majesty's Government were responsible to Parliament, and bound to afford any information that was required and that could be given without injury to public interests.

On the 22nd May, 1856, a debate took place in the House of Lords on the subject of this Declaration, when Lord Clarendon spoke as follows [Hansard, vol. 142, p. 500]:

'Of course I am the last person to complain of the censure being made as general as possible, or that all the Plenipotentiaries are included in a resolution which, I presume, was intended to impute blame to Lord Cowley and myself; but I think that your Lordships will have some difficulty in placing upon record your regret that all the Plenipotentiaries should have renounced a principle to which their Governments objected without the sanction of the Parliament of Great Britain.

In pursuing the course which we have done in Paris, we have adopted precisely the same course which was taken in Vienna, to which the noble Lord (Lord Colchester) referred, when all the Plenipotentiaries agreed to that memorable declaration by which they affirmed that the Slave Trade scourge had too long desolated Africa, degraded Europe, and afflicted humanity; and they agreed among themselves, with the sanction of their Governments, that the most strenuous measures should be taken for its repression. *If we had confined ourselves within the strict limits of our attributions*, we should have lost the opportunity, when the Representatives of the principal Powers of Europe were met together, of discussing *many important subjects*, which, although they did not relate to our quarrel with Russia, it was most desirable should be arranged. If we had acted on that rule, not a word would have been said about Italy, from the discussions on which, I believe, important results will ensue. Not a syllable would have been uttered on the principle of Mediation, and yet I believe that by the discussion of that subject we have opposed a new and not insignificant obstacle to war. But Lord Cowley and myself did not hesitate – *of course with the consent of Her Majesty's Government* – to affix our signatures to a Declaration which changed a policy that we believed it would have been impossible, as well as against the interests of England, to maintain; France renouncing at the same time a principle to which we had always objected, thus placing our maritime law exactly on the same footing, and giving an additional security for the maintenance of our alliance; coupling it, moreover, with that provision with respect to Privateering which will be of the utmost benefit to a commercial nation like England.'

There is nothing further in the archives of this Office which throws any light on the origin of the Declaration of Paris respecting Maritime Law.

[Signed] E[dward] Hertslet [Foreign Office Librarian], June 7, 1875

For Debates on this subject see:

Hansard,	C.	6 May, 1856	Vol. 142	p. 17
	L.	22 May, 1856	142	481
	C.	14 June, 1857	146	1,486

C.	11 March, 1862	165	1,362
C.	16 March, 1862	165	1,599
C.	5 August, 1867	189	876
C.	21 April, 1871	205	1,469
L.	19 June, 1871	207	197
C.	13 April, 1875	223	822
C.	2 July, 1875	225	900

Annex to Protocol No. 23 – Declaration – April 16, 1856

The Plenipotentiaries who signed the Treaty of Paris of the 30th of March, 1856, assembled in Conference, – Considering:

That maritime law, in time of war, has long been the subject of deplorable disputes;

That the uncertainty of the law and of the duties in such a matter, give rise to differences of opinion between neutrals and belligerents which may occasion serious difficulties, and even conflicts.

That it is, consequently, advantageous to establish a uniform doctrine on so important a point;

That the Plenipotentiaries assembled in Congress at Paris cannot better respond to the intentions by which their Governments are animated than by seeking to introduce into international relations fixed principles in this respect;

The above-mentioned Plenipotentiaries being duly authorized, resolved to concert among themselves as to the means of attaining this object; and, having come to an agreement, have adopted the following solemn Declaration:

1. Privateering is, and remains, abolished;

2. The neutral flag covers enemy's goods, with the exception of contraband of war;

3. Neutral goods, with the exception of contraband of war, are not liable to capture under enemy's flag;

4. Blockades, in order to be binding, must be effective; that is to say, maintained by a force sufficient really to prevent access to the coast of the enemy.

The Governments of the undersigned Plenipotentiaries engage to bring the present Declaration to the knowledge of the States which have not taken part in the Congress of Paris, and to invite them to accede to it.

Convinced that the maxims which they now proclaim cannot but be received with gratitude by the whole world, the undersigned Plenipotentiaries doubt not that the efforts of their Governments to obtain the general adoption thereof will be crowned with full success.

The present Declaration is not and shall not be binding except between those Powers who have acceded, or shall accede, to it.

Done at Paris, the 16th of April, 1856.[1]

* * *

15. Notification of the Blockade of the Coast of the Island of Formosa

[FO 97/570]   London Gazette, No. 25407
                                           Friday 24 October 1884

Translation

We, the undersigned, Vice-Admiral Commander-in-Chief of the French Naval Forces in the far East, acting in virtue of the powers which belong to us, declare: that, commencing on the 23rd October, 1994, all the ports and roadsteads of the Island of Formosa included between South Cape or Cape Nan-Sha and the Soo-au Bay, passing west and north (the situation of these points being: the first in 21° 55' north latitude east of Paris) will be maintained in a state of effective blockade by the naval forces placed under our command, and that friendly ships will be allowed a delay of three days to effect their loading and to leave the blockaded places. Any ship attempting to violate the above-mentioned blockade will be proceeded against in conformity with international law and the treaties in force.

On board the French ironclad *Bayard*, October 20, 1884 (signed) Corbet.

* * *

---

[1]See FO 83/487 for the signed instrument.

16. Memorandum on the Declaration of Paris, and the Proposed Exemption of Private Property at Sea from Capture by a Belligerent

Sir Edward Hertslet, Foreign Office Librarian
Confidential

[FO 881/6307, CP 6307]   9 February 1893

The Declaration of Paris of the 16th April, 1856, runs as follows:
1.   Privateering is and remains abolished.
2.   The neutral flag covers enemy's goods, with the exception of contraband of war.
3.   Neutral goods, with the exception of contraband of war, are not liable to capture under enemy's flag.
4.   Blockades, in order to be binding, must be effective, that is to say, maintained by a force sufficient really to prevent access to the coast of the enemy.

The Declaration was signed by the Plenipotentiaries of Great Britain, Austria, France, Prussia, Russia, Sardinia, and Turkey; and it was agreed that other States which had not taken part in the Congress of Paris should be invited to accede to it; and that it was not, and should not be, binding, except between those Powers who had acceded, or should accede, to it.

Forty-two States acceded to it (see 'Map of Europe by Treaty,' vol. ii p. 1284); but the United States and some of the Central and South American States have not done so.

Bolivia has not acceded, but she has concluded a Treaty with the United States, embodying, but enlarging, the principles of some of the points of the Declaration of Paris (though not alluding to that Declaration), but providing for the protection of privateers. [Treaty May 13, 1858, *Articles* IX, XVI to XX, XXV: *State Papers*, vol. xlxviii, p. 759.]

Honduras has not acceded; but she has concluded a Treaty with Italy, in which it is stated that the Declaration of Paris is accepted, without reservation, by the two Parties in their mutual relations; but extended, so as to embrace, among other things, the following understanding between them, that, in the case of war, 'private property of any kind belonging to citizens of one shall be respected by the other, the same as property of neutrals, and that both at sea and on land, on the high seas, as well as the territorial seas, and in any other place whatever, and under whatsoever flag the vessels and the goods are navigating, without any other restrictions than the case of breaking blockade and the case of contraband of war.' [Treaty, December 31, 1868, Articles XII to XVI: *State Papers*, vol. lxi, p. 1049.]

Salvador has not acceded; but she has also concluded a Treaty with Italy, agreeing to be bound by the principles of the Declaration of Paris, although not alluding to that Declaration. [Treaty, October 27, 1860, Article XIX: *State Papers*, vol. lxi, p. 1031.]

Mexico, *Venezuela*, and *Spain* acceded to the second, third, and fourth points, but not to the first point (relating to privateering).

The *United States*, in acknowledging the receipt of the invitation to accede to the Declaration (whilst approving of the second, third, and fourth points), propose to add to Article I the following words: 'and that the private property of the subjects or citizens of a belligerent on the high seas shall be exempted from seizure by public armed vessels of the other belligerent, except it be contraband,' and, a few months later, the American Minister in London renewed the proposal with regard to Article I, and submitted a draft of Convention in which the Article, as amended, would be embodied with the other three Articles; but, before any decision was taken on this proposal, a change took place in the American Government by the election of a new President of the United States, when the American Minister announced that he was directed to suspend negotiations on the subject. [Parliamentary Paper, 'North America No. 3 (1862),' p. 5; See also Parliamentary Paper No. 605.]

A year or two after the Declaration of Paris had been signed, several of the largest and most opulent ship-owners of Lancashire addressed a private and unofficial communication to Lord Palmerston, as head of Her Majesty's Government, entreating his Lordship's earnest attention to the unsatisfactory position in which, it was stated, British shipping was placed by that Declaration, which, they said, it might be presumed would govern the rights of neutrals in the event of an European war. ['Letter from Mr Lindsay to Lord John Russell on Belligerent Rights, with reference to Merchant Shipping, and the Reply thereto.' Laid before the House of Commons, 1860.]

Those gentlemen pointed out, at considerable length, the serious inconvenience and pecuniary loss which resulted from the apprehensions incessantly entertained by their correspondents in different parts of the world, especially in China and India, of any interruption of the peace of Europe. The practical effect of these apprehensions was, they said, that, in the selection of vessels for the transport of produce to European markets, neutral, and especially American, vessels received a great preference, to the serious prejudice of the British ship-owner.

This preference thus given to American vessels arose, it was said, from the fact that, as the American Government had invariably adhered to a policy of non-intervention in European wars, the merchant-ships of the United States, in the event of a rupture between the European Powers, would enjoy pre-eminently the rights and advantages of neutrals. They would, it was urged, absorb almost exclusively the carrying trade of the long voyage, whatever might be the port of destination, and would pass with their cargoes unmolested through the armed cruisers of the European belligerents; it being always presumed that the British and French must inevitably be the parties involved in any hostilities which might supervene.

This was followed by a letter from Mr Lindsay, MP, to Lord J. Russell, dated 14th October, 1859, on Belligerent Rights with reference to Merchant Shipping, which was laid before Parliament, and in which an historical account was given of the views entertained by Napoleon I, and by the United States in 1824 and in 1854–55, on the question of the exemption of private property of an enemy from capture and confiscation in time of war. [Parliamentary Paper, No. 605.]

Mr Lindsay pointed out, among other things, that, in the event of an European war, the trade and shipping of the country would be destroyed by the enormously increased charges of insurance incidental to ships sailing without, or even with, a convoy, if, he said, convoys could be provided consistently with other paramount exigencies of the State, and with the necessity of defending our shores and our Colonies; and he concluded his letter by inquiring whether some steps could not be devised by which Great Britain, without appearing to take the initiative, might succeed in securing the consent of the Governments of the various States of Europe to some compact, by means of a new Declaration of maritime law, proclaimed at a future Congress of the assembled Powers of Europe, whereby, without awakening the envy and jealousy of commercial rivals, or exciting any suspicion of interested motives, the immunity of merchant-ships and their cargoes might be protected from the depredations of both privateers and armed national cruisers.

It was observed that the concurrence of the United States in such an arrangement would be quite unimportant; because, if a general alliance of the great European Powers should establish the authority of a new code of maritime law, in furtherance of the liberal principles already partially approved by the Declaration of Paris, the Americans would thereafter cease to derive undue advantages, as neutrals, from European wars; and the anticipation of hostilities amongst the crowned heads of Europe would no longer prove a source of profitable speculation to their ship-owners.

To this letter from Mr Lindsay, Lord John Russell replied that the observations contained in it would be duly considered by Her Majesty's Government, but that the proposal appeared liable to grave objections.

It was not long before the same question was again raised in another direction.

On the outbreak of the Civil War in North America in 1861, the United States' Minister at Paris proposed to the French Government:

1.   That France should agree to add to the 1st Article of the Declaration of Paris the plan of protecting private property on sea from capture in time of war; and

2.   That privateering being abolished by the adoption of the 1st Article of the Declaration of Paris, amended as proposed, the privateers sent out by the so-styled Southern Confederacy should be considered as pirates. [Parliamentary Papers, 'North America No. 3 (1862)'. For a Memorandum on the question of issuing Letters of Marque and the treatment of Privateers (1815–1874), see Confidential Paper No. 3939.]

On the receipt of these proposals, M. Thouvenel expressed a wish to learn the opinions of Her Majesty's Government regarding them. When he was informed by Lord John Russell that Her Majesty's Government decidedly objected to the first proposition, as it seemed to them that it would reduce the power in time of war of all States having a military as well as a commercial marine, and his Lordship pointed out that, in practice, it would be almost impossible to distinguish between *bona fide* ships carrying merchandize and ships fraudulently fitted out with means of war under the guise of merchant-vessels. [To Mr Grey, 12 June 1861.]

With regard to the second point, it was stated that Her Majesty's Government were not disposed to depart from the neutral character which Her Majesty, as well as the Emperor of the French, had assumed.

M. Thouvenel expressed great satisfaction on finding how completely Lord John Russell's views coincided with his own. [Mr Grey, 14 June 1861.]

Between 1862 and 1885 several debates took place in the House of Commons on the subject of the Declaration of Paris.

For instance, on the 11th March, 1862, Mr Horsfall brought forward a motion that private property of unoffending non-combatants, though enemies, should be exempted from capture; but, after a long debate, the motion was withdrawn. [*Hansard*, vol. clxv, pp. 1362, 1599.]

On the 5th August, 1867, Mr J.S. Mill pronounced the renunciation of a right to seize enemies' goods in neutral vessels to be a 'national blunder,' and said it was not irretrievable; but his motion led to no decision being taken on the subject by Parliament. [*Hansard*, vol. clxxxix, p. 876, cxlii, p. 535, ccvii, p. 203. The late Lord Derby also declared that, in signing the Declaration, England had cut off her right hand, and he called it the 'Capitulation of Paris.']

On the 21st April, 1871, Mr Cavendish Bentinck moved that Clause 1 of the Declaration of Paris, respecting privateering, and Clause 2, which declared that the neutral flag covered enemies' goods, with the exception of contraband of war, should be withdrawn; but his motion led to no result. [*Hansard*, vol. ccv, p. 1469.]

On the 13th April, 1875, Mr Baillie-Cochrane brought forward a motion for the withdrawal by Great Britain from the Declaration of Paris; but, after a debate on the subject, his motion was defeated on a division. [*Hansard*, vol. ccxxiii, p. 822.]

Various other debates in Parliament might be alluded to (see Memorandum 2763).

It has been stated in the House of Lords and Commons, on more than one occasion, as well as elsewhere, that the Declaration of Paris was not in the nature of a Treaty, and that it was not ratified by Her Majesty; but its binding effect between the Signatory and acceding Powers has been admitted in Parliament, as well as in the wars which have taken place since 1856, although it is also admitted that it is not binding upon and between a Government which is a party to it and another Government which is not a party to it; and, although it was not ratified by Her Majesty as an International Treaty, the Queen approved the course which Lord Palmerston proposed to take in the matter, after perusing the Minutes which had been signed by each of the Cabinet Ministers on the subject. [*Hansard*, June 19, 1871, vol. ccvii, p. 197; vol. ccxxx, p. 1462. Italy and Austria, 1866; *State Papers*, vol. lviii, pp. 306, 310; France and Germany, 1870; Berlin Conference, 1878; 'Map of Europe by Treaty,' vol. iv, p. 2751. Law Officers, January 13, 1866: Italy and Argentine Republic. Law Officers, December 3, 1875: Netherlands and Venezuela.]

This is not generally known, and it was not known at this office until April 1876, when Mr Evelyn Ashley handed over to the Foreign Office these Cabinet Minutes, which were found among Lord Palmerston's archives. [Confidential Paper No. 5104.]

With regard to the power of this country to withdraw from the Declaration of Paris, Lord Selborne wrote a Minute, on the 24th April, 1885, in which his Lordship said (speaking of the treatment by the French Government in its war with China, of rice as contraband of war): 'This is a somewhat alarming indication of the way in which the great Continental Powers might be expected to deal with us, if we should be at war. All the concessions made, to the disadvantage of a Maritime Power, by the Treaty of Paris, will be expected to be observed by us; and they will, at the same time, submit, as neutrals, to whatever law of contraband the other belligerent may choose to lay down, as having a tendency to shorten the war by crippling our trade and stopping our supplies of food through neutrals.

'I do not hesitate to say that, if this should happen, we should have to denounce, and shake ourselves free from, the Declaration of Paris; to resume the old rights of taking enemy's goods in neutral bottoms, and of employing privateers against the enemy.' [Law Officers' Reports, 1885, p. 91.]

There is yet one more point which I think should be mentioned, and it is this.

When, in 1884, the Russian Government proposed the assembling of a Conference at Brussels, on the Rules of Military Warfare, Her Majesty's Government consented to send a Delegate to that Conference, and Sir A. Horsford was appointed the British Delegate, whose duty, it was stated, would be 'to guard carefully against the introduction into the discussions of matters relating to *naval* warfare,' and also to abstain from taking part 'in any discussion which might appear to him to bear upon general principles of international law, not already universally recognized and accepted.' [*State Papers*, vol. lxv, pp. 1004, 1023.]

Under these circumstances, I don't think any advantage could be derived by this country in joining a Conference with the object of extending the provisions of the Declaration of Paris, so as to exempt from seizure the private property of subjects and citizens of a belligerent on the high seas.

In my humble opinion, it would be far better that this country should retain a free hand, and not subscribe to any further Regulations which might be prejudicial to its interests in any future wars.

* * *

17.   *Memorandum on Blockades*

Strictly Confidential 6515

[FO 97/570]   Foreign Office
                                                              September 1894

I.   On the Right of a Belligerent Power to prevent entrance and exit of Neutral Vessels of War into and from a Blockaded Port

GENERALLY speaking (although the matter cannot be said to be entirely free from doubt), the better opinion seems to be that a belligerent instituting a '*blockade jure gentium*' has the right, after due notice, to prevent all neutral ships, including ships of war, from entering or leaving a blockaded port when he deems that circumstances require such a course. At the same time, it would be a very unfriendly act to do so with regard to neutral ships of war, unless the circumstances were special and imperative with reference to the conduct of hostile operations.

2.   It is, of course, an essential condition that the vessel visiting the blockaded port shall not communicate news, or commit any act prejudicial to either blockaders or blockaded.

3.   The above general conclusions are founded on the following precedents and opinions, which should be studied for guidance in particular cases, observing, however, the instructions contained in section 4, Chapter X, p. 150, of the Queen's Regulations.

4.   During the course of the civil war in the United States the Law Officers reported several times on subjects involving the point now under consideration.

5.   On the 30th August, 1861, they approved a set of Instructions issued by Admiral Milne, for the guidance of cruisers employed on the coasts of America.[1]

Article 5 of these Instructions ran as follows:

> It will be expedient that you should approach for observation, and, if necessary, communication with the blockading squadrons, within the limits assigned to you; but unless protection to British life should absolutely demand it, you are to avoid entering into any ports in the occupation of Confederate authorities or troops, as the visit of any of Her Majesty's ships might probably be interpreted into a disposition on the part of Her Majesty's Government to give countenance and support to the Secession movement, and consequently any step calculated to convey such an impression is to be avoided.

Sir Alexander Milne was himself of opinion that the blockading Power must, or ought to, have the right to debar all access to, or egress from, the blockaded port, even to a ship of war of a neutral State, and the Admiralty endorsed this view.

The Foreign Office was of opinion that, with a view to British interests, it was not desirable to establish any positive and unconditional right of entering a blockaded port by ships of a neutral Power. The

---

[1]*On the 2nd May, 1861, the United States' Government had informed the Spanish Minister that armed vessels of neutral Powers would have the right to enter and depart from the blockaded ports (Lord Lyons, No. 122, 23 February 1864).

belligerent should be at liberty to object, in certain cases, where the exercise of such a right might be very prejudicial to operations of war.

6.   A question arose, also in 1861, as to the periodical conveyance of Consular correspondence from the Confederate States to Her Majesty's Minister at Washington by means of a British ship of war, when the Queen's Advocate reported that he could not conceive that the United States' Government would object to so reasonable an arrangement; and he added that, should they hesitate to sanction it, it would then be open to Her Majesty's Government, in common with other Powers, to consider the propriety of insisting on the right of communicating with their respective Consuls by means of ships of war, or even of recognizing the Confederate Government as a *de facto* Sovereign Government, and communicating with it, or through it, so as to correspond with all Consulates in its territory, as might be necessary.

7.   In a Report dated the 24th April, 1863, the Law Officers of the Crown, having been consulted on the proposed conveyance to the Southern States in a British ship of war of a person accused of murdering an officer of the Confederate war-vessel *Sumter*, gave it as their opinion that the right of a belligerent to prevent the entrance of neutral vessels of commerce into a blockaded port does not extend to ships of war belonging to a neutral State; that the neutral Government has a right to hold communication with the belligerent whose port is blockaded, and that the reason of the belligerent right of blockade does not apply to a neutral ship of war, which is bound, of course, to carry no merchandize or relief to the blockaded port.

8.   In the following year (1864), however, the Law Officers were asked to take into consideration the decision of the United States' Government no longer to permit Her Majesty's cruisers to communicate with the blockaded ports, and they then made an exhaustive Report dealing with the question of the right of neutral ships of war to communicate with the blockaded port of a belligerent, which, as already stated modified to a certain extent their Report of 1863.

They reported that, although it was not easy to find any positive expression of opinion in the books on international law, or the judgments of International Courts, as to the right of a belligerent to deny all access to neutral ships of war to a blockaded port, they were, after careful consideration, of opinion that this right did, as an abstract proposition of international law, belong to the belligerent who had instituted a blockade. This right seemed to flow from the reason of the thing, and to be supported by usage; from the reason of the thing, because the right of blockade was the right of cutting off, so far as necessary for the objects of the war, all communication whatever with that part of the enemies' dominions, carrying with it, *prima facie*, the right to interdict the access of the neutral foreigner, whether he approached with the authority of the State to which he belonged, or merely as an individual.

With regard to *usage*, they instanced the siege of Acre (1840) and the blockade of the adjoining Syrian coast by the British fleet, when a French ship of war had been prevented from entering, and the French Government recognized the exercise of this right to prevent her doing so. Again, in the case of the French blockade of the Argentine coast, the French Minister for Foreign Affairs issued a manifesto in 1838 to the effect that neutral vessels of war presenting themselves should be requested to depart, and, on their persisting, should be resisted with force, all responsibility for the results resting on the violator of the blockade.

The Law Officers were, therefore, of opinion that, as a general question, the neutral ship of war was under an obligation to respect the belligerent right of blockade, and not to attempt, without permission, to communicate with blockaded places, and to this extent they modified the opinion expressed on the 24th April, 1863.

The Law Officers then turned to the special case of the United States, as apart from the general question, on account of the unprecedented extent of the coast blockaded, and they said that the neutral had an undoubted general right, which the belligerent ought to respect, of communicating with the other belligerent; that no belligerent had ever wholly denied this right, and that there would be just ground of remonstrance if the right of blockade was carried to this extent.

They then quoted Lord Stowell's decision (the *Rolla*, 6 Robinson, 372) that 'a blockade is a uniform universal exclusion of all vessels not privileged by law,' and gave their opinion that a ship of war having the exclusive object of bearing communications from a neutral Government to its Minister resident in the belligerent State ought to be regarded as belonging to this privileged class.

They quoted another case, when England and France were at war in 1811, in which Lord Stowell said: 'This country makes no pretension to any right of interrupting the communication of the American Government with its Minister [in France], and I should be extremely tender of interposing any difficulties in the way of such a correspondence;' and they observed that the neutral State must exercise this right of limited communication so as not to interfere with the general right of the other belligerent, and in whatever way might be opened to it by the blockading Power; but it could not be altogether debarred from its exercise.

9.   In 1865 a blockade was established of the Rivers Parana and Paraguay by Brazil and the Argentine Republic, who were at war with the

Republic of Paraguay, and a question arose in connection with the passage of Her Majesty's ship *Doterel* up those rivers for the purpose of saving the lives of British subjects.

The Queen's Advocate reported on this occasion that the Commander of the *Doterel*, under the peculiar circumstances of the case, was not guilty of a violation of international law; that the right of the neutral subject to protection was as strong as the right of the belligerent to blockade, and the latter right was not infringed by the passage of the *Doterel* for the sole purpose of saving British life; though, as a matter of comity, this should be done, if possible, with the consent of the blockading Power.

This particular case was further complicated by the existence of a Treaty with the Argentine Republic respecting the free navigation of the Paraguay and Parana by the merchant flag in time of war but this point is apart from the present question.

Subsequently another British ship of war ascended the rivers for a similar purpose, having first asked permission of the belligerents (the blockading Powers), which was at once, accorded. This was repeated in 1867.

Similar permission was, however, refused to a French ship of war in September 1866, and she accordingly returned to Buenos Ayres.

In October of the same year the Brazilian Government appear to have yielded, as a matter of grace, to the United States in connection with the passage of Mr Washburn on a mission to Paraguay; while maintaining their right of refusal.

In 1868 an instruction was addressed to Her Majesty's Minister at Buenos Ayres to endeavour to rescue British subjects detained in Paraguay; but not to attempt to send a gun-boat to Asuncion against the wish of the Brazilian Admiral.

The Brazilian Government later on refused to allow the United States' vessel of war *Wasp* to proceed through the blockade to fetch Mr Washburn, the American Minister, from Paraguay; and on this occasion Mr Seward stated to Mr Thornton that he considered that if one country had a Diplomatic Agent accredited to another, the former had a right to communicate with him through such a public highway as the River Paraguay, by means of a ship of war, in spite of a blockade or any other warlike proceedings; but that it would be a matter of comity to consult with the Commanders of the hostile forces as to the time of passing.

The Brazilian Government, on, and apparently under the pressure of, the American Minister at Rio threatening to demand his passports, gave permission to the *Wasp* to proceed.

The French Minister at Buenos Ayres subsequently announced to the Argentine Government his 'intention' of sending a gun-boat to Asuncion, through the blockade, and 'assumed' that no impediments would be placed in her way; and the British Minister addressed a somewhat similar communication to them when sending Mr Gould on a mission to Paraguay. In both cases the necessary orders were given by the Argentine Government, the only reservation being in the event of their desiring to pass at a moment when some important operation was being carried out.

10.   It may be stated, further, with reference to the practice followed by various countries in this phase of the blockade question, that when the Portuguese ports were blockaded in June 1833 by the naval forces of Doña Maria, the 'ships of war of friendly nations, and packets,' were specially exempted in the notification of blockade.

11.   On the Portuguese blockade of the Douro in November 1846, British ships of war were allowed to enter unmolested.

12.   On the Venezuelan blockade of Maracaibo in June 1848, it was stated that 11 vessels of war of friendly and neutral States are permitted to enter, remain at, and leave Maracaibo, the Government being persuaded that they will not in any way render assistance to the conspirators.

13.   The same course was followed on the Venezuelan blockade of the coast of Coro, August 1849.

14.   On the French blockade of the ports of Acapulco and Manzanillas, on the west coast of Mexico, in February 1864, the French Admiral addressed a letter to the Commander of Her Majesty's ship *Devastation*, in which the following passages occurred:

Désireux d'éviter tout malentendu avec les Commandants des navires de guerre d'une Puissance alliée du Gouvernment Française, je vous prie de faire connaitre aux Commandants des bâtiments qu'une nécessité grave appellerait, soit à Acapulco soit à Manzanillas, que tout en conservant en principe le droit que me confirent les lois internationales de défendre l'accès des ports bloqués, j'autoriserai les croisseurs à admettre les bâtiments de guerre de Sa Majesté Britannique dans les ports susmentionnés. Les navire qui se présenterait pour entrer, devrait communiquer préalablement avec le croisseur Français; et dans tous les cas on ne chercherait jamais à entrer de nuit . . .

Dans le cas où je recevrais l'ordre de m'en tenir à l'exécution du droit strict de bloquer d'une manière absolue, je m'empresserai de vous en donner avis;' and

15.   On the blockade of Chile by Spain in 1865, the instructions of the
Spanish Naval Commander (Article 20) ran as follows:
You must not hinder neutral men-of-war from entering the port which
you are blockading.
16.   It remains to examine the views expressed by the principal writers
on international law upon this point:
   Bluntschli writes, as follows:

> Les Etats sont toutefois autorisés à envoyer, s'il y a lieu, des navires
> de guerre pour protéger leurs nationaux, et à réclamer dans ce but le
> passage à travers les eaux bloquées.
> 1.   Cette question a été discutée en 1865, pendant la guerre entre le
> Brésil et Uruguay. Les Puissances qui bloquaient le fleuve de la
> Plata (le Brésil et la République Argentine) avaient au début soulevés
> des difficultés. Mais elles cédèrent plus tard, et l'Uruguay consentit
> de son côté à laisser passer librement un navire Français (neutre)
> envoyé à l'Assomption pour y protéger les Français.

Geffcken, in a note in Heffter's International Law, says:

> Les vaisseaux publics des Etats neutres, parce qu'ils ne font aucun
> commerce contre lequel le blocus est dirigé, ne peuvent jamais être
> capturés, et doivent pouvoir entre et sortir librement pour servir au
> besoin d'intermédiaire entre leur Gouvernment et leur Ambassadeur
> résidant dans le port, et pour protéger leurs nationaux.

Hall says:

> The right possessed by a belligerent of excluding neutral ships of
> war from a blockaded place is usually waived in practice as a matter
> of international courtesy; and for a like reason the Minister of a
> neutral State resident in the country of the blockaded ports is permit-
> ted to dispatch from it a vessel exclusively employed in carrying
> home distressed seamen of his own nation.

Ortolan, referred to by Hall, says:

> En droit, l'accès et la sortie de ce lieu [le lieu bloqué] sont interdits
> aussi bien aux bâtiments de guerre qu'à ceux de commerce. ...
> Néanmoins, la Puissance tenant le blocus affranchit souvent de la
> règle des bâtiments de guerre en raison du caractère dout ils jouissent,
> et cette concession qu'exigent les égards dus aux Gouvernements
> neutres doit ... être faite toutes les fois qu'elle pent se concilier
> avec l'objet de la guerre;

in support of which he cites the action of the United States in 1861, which action, however, afterwards underwent some modification, as has already been shown.[1]

Wheaton and Calvo speak in similar terms, and the latter adds:

Ortolan justifie ainsi cette immunité: 'En fait,' dit-il, 'le but principal d'un blocus étant d'interdire tout commerce par mer avec le lieu bloqué, le moyen d'atteindre ce but reste tout entier si la prohibition d'entrer et de sortir n'est appliquée qu'aux navires marchands.'

In Ferguson's *Manual of International Law*, 1884, it was laid down (vol. ii, p. 486): During the continuance of the state of blockade no vessels are allowed to enter or leave the blockaded place without special licence or consent of the blockading authority. Public vessels or vessels of war of neutral Powers are all equally bound by the same obligation to respect the blockade. When the public vessel of a neutral State is allowed to have communication with a blockaded place, the neutral Commanding Officer is obliged to observe strict neutrality, and to comply with the conditions under which such permission has been granted to cross the lines of the blockading belligerent. The impartiality, which must be the prevailing feature of an effective blockade, prohibits that, except to public vessels, permission to enter the blockaded place be given, otherwise than in extreme cases of positive necessity.

Diplomatic Agents and Consular officers of a neutral State are allowed the amount of communication necessary for the fulfilment of their official duties.

17.   Although, therefore, neither the actual practice of nations nor the opinions of textwriters have been uniform, they both appear, on the whole, to support the proposition that a blockade extends to vessels of war, and is not confined to merchant-vessels.

This has also been the view quite recently expressed by the Law Officers of the Crown, who reported, on the 12th December, 1893, that, in their opinion, vessels of war come within the same rules as vessels of commerce, with this difference, that, as regards the former, they have, by comity or courtesy, been excepted from the strict operation of blockade. The Law Officers saw no reason to doubt that the belligerent right exists to include ships of war, except possibly in the case suggested by Lord Stowell of communication with the Minister of the neutral Power, where no other means of communication exist.

It appeared to them obvious that cases must be frequent where the presence of, and communication from, a ship of war of a neutral, but

[1]*See previous note.

still friendly, Power might have the effect of delaying that submission of the blockaded Power which it was the object of the blockade to accomplish.

18.   It may be, at all events, taken as established that where one nation is at war with another, or is repressing an insurrection, the blockading Power should be approached for permission to use a blockaded port.

* * *

18.   *Discussion with Count Metternich on the Nature and Attributes of Pacific Blockade*[1]

[Notes]
Confidential

[FO 881/7827]   Foreign Office
28 November, 1902

COUNT METTERNICH pointed out that the blockade, which he had previously described as a 'pacific blockade,' should extend to neutral vessels to this extent, that should such vessels attempt to run the blockade they would be turned back or 'sequestrated.' His Excellency pointed out that blockades of this kind had been resorted to by England in 1837 against New Granada; and in 1842–44 against St. Juan and Nicaraguan ports; by England and France in 1845–47 against the Argentine ports; by England in 1882 against Rio; and by France in 1884 against Formosa.

The annexed extract from the Library Memorandum of September 1894 is interesting as bearing on the general signification attached to 'pacific blockades.' The cases cited are then noticed in their order.

On so-called 'Pacific Blockades'

In regard to what are termed pacific blockades, where a State resorts to blockade as a means of coercion while maintaining that a state of war does not exist, Her Majesty's Government do not deny the right of a State to resort to such a measure as a means of coercion while refraining from a declaration of war or other acts of hostility. Great Britain has, in fact, taken part in such blockades. But Her Majesty's Government hold that in such a case the blockading Power has no right to prevent any neutral ship, whether merchant-vessel or ship of war, from using the blockaded port. Any interference with the ships of a third

[1]See original correspondence in FO 97/570 *passim.*

nation may, in their opinion, be properly regarded by that nation as an act of belligerency implying and only to be justified by the existence of a state of war.

Such interference, therefore, in the case of what has been declared to be a pacific blockade, should not be accepted without remonstrance and reference to superior authority for instructions.

The French Government have hitherto held an opposite view, and it must be admitted that there has been some divergence of opinion among writers on international law on the subject. But the weight of authority is in favour of the view taken by Her Majesty's Government, and although the conduct of Great Britain in earlier years, and particularly in the blockade of the River Plate by the British and French forces in 1845, has not been altogether identical with her present attitude, her more recent practice has been in complete accord with it. It may, indeed, be affirmed that since 1850 no Power except France has claimed the right to interfere with neutral vessels in the case of a pacific blockade, and that France now stands practically alone in her contention.

The case of the blockade of New Granada in 1836, was a case of blockade in time of peace. The circumstances which led to the blockade were these:

Mr Russell, the British Pro-Consul at Panama, was imprisoned by the New Granadian authorities. A demand was made for his immediate release, and for other steps to be taken by the New Granadian Government by way of reparation for the insult.

Compliance with these demands having been refused, Commodore Payton, of Her Majesty's ship *Madagascar*, announced his determination to blockade rigorously all the ports of New Granada from Cape Chichibacon to the Rio Dorodos. Two vessels were prevented from entering the port of Carthagena, and two other vessels bound for that port were detained, one a French barque and the other a New Granadian brig.

This had the desired effect: the Pro-Consul was liberated, and the other demands complied with.

In this instance, although the blockade was nominally at least 'pacific,' there was distinct interference with a ship belonging to a third Power. This was, however, at a time when our views on the principles involved were more fluid and elastic than they have since become.

In 1843, several cases of gross denial of justice to British subjects, and of flagrant violation of their rights and property, having occurred in Nicaragua, the Government was, in consequence, given to understand that, if redress were not afforded to the parties, the port of San Juan would be blockaded.

This intimation having been disregarded, the British Admiral accordingly instituted the blockade, which produced the desired result.

In 1844 the British [and] the French Governments joined in an intervention with the Government of Buenos Ayres, in order to induce it to discontinue the blockade of Monte Video, which was so prejudicial to the commerce of the River Plate.

In 1845 a British Minister was sent out to Buenos Ayres; when remonstrances were addressed by him and by the French Minister to the Government, but to no effect.

The Admirals of the combined naval squadrons, in consequence, declared to the Buenos Ayrean Government that an end must be put to the hostilities against Monte Video; and they announced that, if this were not done, they would have recourse to coercive measures; but these intimations were also ineffectual.

They then intimated to the Buenos Ayrean Admiral that the fleet under his command must not depart; but he made the attempt, and was prevented; and the Admirals [of the combined squadron] then took possession of the fleet.

The bombardment and capture of Colonia followed; and Buenos Ayres was placed in a state of blockade.

A joint expedition up the Rivers Uruguay and Parana, which had been closed to commerce, took place soon afterwards, and was attended with success.

The blockade of Buenos Ayres, so far as Great Britain was concerned, ceased in July 1847.

In neither of these cases have I, so far, been able to find evidence of interference with the shipping of third Powers, or to the contrary; but it seems clear from the terms of the notifications of blockade issued in both cases that the operations were in intention, and, in fact, rather in the nature of blockades *jure gentium* than of pacific blockades.

In the case of the Buenos Ayres blockade, indeed, a term of fifteen days was specifically assigned for the departure of *neutral vessels.*

That this was the view taken by Lord Palmerston is evidenced by the language held by him in writing to Lord Normanby, then Ambassador at Paris (as quoted in Lord Dalling's 'Life of Palmerston'):

The real truth is, though we had better keep the fact to ourselves, that the French and English blockade of the Plata has been from first to last illegal. Peel and Aberdeen have always declared that we have not been at war with Rosas; but blockade is a belligerent right, and unless you are at war with a State, you have no right to prevent ships of other States from communicating with the ports of that State; nay, you cannot prevent your own merchant-ships from doing so. *I think it important, therefore, in order to legalize retrospectively the operations of the blockade, to close the matter by a formal Convention of Peace with the two Powers and Rosas.*

Even, however, if it were assumed that these were instances of pacific blockades, and that it could be shown that interference with the vessels of third Powers had taken place, it would scarcely be an argument of much weight, inasmuch as the views of His Majesty's Government have admittedly by degrees undergone a change in this respect, and the decided attitude adopted by Lord Granville towards France in the case of the Formosa blockade in 1884, of which details are given below, is an authoritative record of the principles by which His Majesty's Government have been guided in more modern times, and from which they have not departed in practice.

In fact, as pointed out by Sir E. Hertslet, since 1850 no Power except France has claimed the right to interfere with the vessels of a third Power in the case of a pacific blockade.

I am unable to identify the instance of a British blockade of Rio in 1882, mentioned by Count Metternich, but it seems not improbable that his Excellency refers to the incident mentioned in the annexed extract, which occurred in 1862, but in which the action of His Majesty's Government was in the nature of 'reprisals,' rather than of a 'pacific blockade.'

In 1862 the fact was brought to the notice of the British Government that in the previous year a British barque (the *Prince of Wales*) had been wrecked off the coast of Brazil, and that an outrage had also been committed on some officers of Her Majesty's ship *Forte* by a Brazilian police-guard; the British Government at once demanded from the Brazilian Government compensation for the losses occasioned to the owner of the vessel by the plunder of the wreck and crew. The sum named was at first fixed at £6,525/19/-; but Her Majesty's Government expressed their readiness to allow the actual amount to be fixed by arbitration, provided the Brazilian Government would admit the principle.

The Admiralty were, at the same time, requested to issue instructions to the Admiral at the station to place himself in communication with the British Minister, and to make such arrangements with his ships as should admit of his proceeding, if necessary to have recourse to *reprisals*.

With regard to the wreck of the *Prince of Wales*, the Brazilian Government refused to accede to the principle of responsibility attributed to it, and 'loudly and categorically' protested against it, adding that if they were obliged to yield to force, they would pay, under protest, whatever sum the British Government of the British Minister might choose to demand.

They also refused to give satisfaction for the indignity to which the officers of Her Majesty's ship *Forte* were subjected.

Five merchant-vessels belonging to Brazilians (valued at £12,440) were accordingly forthwith captured and held as prize by Her Majesty's ships of war; but on the Brazilian Government again expressing their readiness to pay under protest, whatever sum the British Government might demand, provided the captured vessels were at once released, and that no further *reprisals* were made; the sum of £3,200 (instead of the £6,525/19/- originally asked for) was then demanded, which was immediately paid.

With reference to the French view of what constitutes 'un blocus pacifique', and to what passed in 1884 with reference to the French blockade of Formosa in that year, the following extracts from Library Memoranda on the subject may be of interest:

What the French Government understand to be a 'pacific blockade' was thus explained in a note from M. Waddington to Lord Granville of the 5th November, 1884.

His Excellency said: 'The fixed resolution of the French Cabinet is to strictly limit the blockade to the arrangements necessary in order to absolutely prevent access to the waters specified in the Notification of the 20th October. It does not intend now, any more than it did before, to claim the right which belongs only to belligerents of searching and capturing foreign ships on the high seas. The action of the French cruisers will be limited to maintaining an effective blockade, and to assuring its being respected either by *driving back* or by *capturing* the ships which may attempt to force the lines.'

This view as to the rights conferred by a pacific blockade was, however, contested by Lord Granville, then Secretary of State for Foreign Affairs, who pronounced it to be opposed to the opinions of the most eminent statesmen and jurists of France, and to the decisions of its Tribunals, and to be in conflict with well-established principles of international law.

Lord Granville on that occasion entered an emphatic protest against the claim of the French Government that their pacific blockade of the coast of Formosa conferred upon them the right to seize and condemn neutral vessels violating the blockade, and intimated that such action, in conjunction with other acts of hostility, would be considered as constituting a state of war.

The question was again raised in connection with the French declaration of a pacific blockade of the coast of Siam in 1893.

On that occasion M. Develle, the French Minister of Foreign Affairs, stated in a note to Her Majesty's Ambassador at Paris that in view of the immediate raising of the blockade the question had no longer any practical interest, yet that such a measure constitutes a method of coercion to which a State has the right to have recourse, without rupture of peace, in order to recall another Power to the observance of its international duties, and he proceeded to cite various instances which, in his opinion, supported that doctrine.

It was not thought desirable to continue a controversy on the point, but the following extracts from the draft of a despatch which was prepared in reply (though, for the reason above stated, it was never actually sent) will show the grounds on which Her Majesty's Government based their contention:

> The views of Her Majesty's Government on this subject were stated in the correspondence which took place between Earl Granville and Mr Waddington in 1884 respecting the French blockade of the Island of Formosa, and they have undergone no modification. Her Majesty's Government do not deny the right of a State to resort to a blockade as a means of coercion while refraining from other hostile measures. This is a measure of reprisal. But they maintain that if the blockading Power claims to interfere with the ships of third nations, the measure may properly be regarded by such third nations as an act of belligerency implying the existence of a state of war.
>
> November 15, 1902   A.L.

Count Metternich's Proposal that the so-called 'Pacific Blockade' of Venezuelan Ports should extend to the Turning Back or Sequestration of Neutral Vessels should they attempt to run the Blockade

I venture to think that it is clear that we should not acquiesce in any such proposal. We have no right, when a state of war does not exist, to interfere in any way with the commerce and shipping of friendly States, and the turning back, to say nothing of the 'sequestration' of the merchant-vessels of nationality other than Venezuelan, British, or German would constitute a very serious interference with such commerce. We could not justify it in any way by appeals to our former conduct on similar occasions, and we have publicly condemned and combated such a practice when it has been attempted by France.

The so-called 'pacific blockade' is not really a blockade at all. Blockade is a belligerent right, and unless one is at war with a State one cannot prevent the ships of other States from free communication with the ports of that State. Pacific blockade is a means of restraint much milder than actual war. The term 'pacific blockade' is inconvenient and misleading, but has now become accepted. The thing itself is not a century old, the first instance of it having taken place in 1827, when the coasts of Greece were blockaded by the English, French, and Russian squadrons while the three Powers still professed to be at peace with Turkey. Since then there have been many instances of like 'pacific blockades,' e.g.:

The Tagus	By France	1831
New Granada	By England	1836
Mexico	By France	1838
La Plata	By France	1838–1840
La Plata	By France and England	1845–1848
Greek ports	By England	1850
Rio Janeiro	By England	1862
Formosa	By France	1884
Greece	By the five Powers	1886

So that, although the measure of constraint known as 'blocus pacifique' had originally no recognized position in the domain of international law, it may now fairly be said to have taken during the last century a recognized place; and it is dealt with on that footing, at greater or less length, in all the principal *modern* textbooks on international law.

In some of the earlier instances of pacific blockade, vessels, both of the State operated against and of the other Powers were 'sequestrated.' But, so far, at any rate as England is concerned, the principle was soon admitted that no State can *in time of peace* endeavour to obtain redress from a second State by means which inflict loss and inconvenience on other countries. And this has been insisted on in public utterances of the clearest kind by (for instance) Lord Palmerston in 1846, and by Lord Granville in 1884. On the latter occasion, Lord Granville, who was then Foreign Minister, said that: 'The contention of the French Government that a pacific blockade confers on the blockading Power the right to capture and condemn the ships of third nations, for a breach of such a blockade, is in conflict with well established principles of international law;' and this pronouncement had, of course, the approval of the then Lord Chancellor Selborne, and of the Attorney and Solicitor-General (Lord James of Hereford and the late Lord Herschell). I do not see how we could now go back on those declarations, even if there were any sufficient object to be gained by so doing. It appears to me, however, that it is materially to our interest, as the nation which possesses by far the largest maritime carrying trade in the world, to maintain the principle enunciated by Lord Granville.

I think that Count Metternich's statements as to the course adopted by England on previous occasions were based on a misapprehension, but this point has been gone into fully in the accompanying Memorandum by Mr Larcom.

M.F. de Martens, the eminent jurist, in a recent work, when dealing with the subject of pacific blockades, has been misled (as pointed out by the late Mr W.R. Hall) by M. Hautefeuille into saying that: 'L'Angleterre ne laisse passer ni les navires de l'Etat bloqué, ni les navires neutres; elle confisque les uns et les autres.'

It is possible that Count Metternich may have been similarly misled. The statement is at any rate clearly inaccurate.

November 18, 1902   W.E.D.

* * *

Assuming that His Majesty's Government should consider that the foregoing Memoranda are conclusive against the adoption in its integrity of Count Metternich's proposal for a so-called 'pacific blockade' of the particular variety which he advocates, the position would then appear to be as follows:

A 'pacific blockade' (so-called) against Venezuelan vessels only would be, *ex concessis*, unavailing.

A 'pacific blockade' involving any interference (as, for example, 'turning back' or 'sequestration') with the vessels of third Powers would be opposed to our declared policy, and, moreover, if employed, would create a precedent, the disadvantage of which to us in the future would altogether outweigh the temporary advantage to us for the moment. We could not, therefore, be parties to any such measure.

On the other hand, His Majesty's Government must be prepared in the last resort to supplement the seizure of the Venezuelan gun-boat or gun-boats by some further measure of coercion of the kind generally known as 'measures of restraint falling short of actual war.'

If no sufficiently effective measure of this description can be found, then nothing will remain but actual war, which state of things would be brought about at once by the establishment of a blockade *jure gentium*, which is the only measure which in strictness can properly be called a blockade. It is, however, desired to avoid any course of proceeding which will inevitably entail or create a recognized state of war.

The only measures which occur to me are (1) the seizure of the Custom-house or Customs-houses, or (2) the seizure of a port or ports in Venezuela – of course, in the latter case, permitting free access to the vessels of third Powers.

There are other measures, such as the seizure and sequestration of those merchant-vessels of the offending State which happen at the time to be in the waters of the offended State, which have been employed on previous occasions, but they do not seem to me to be of much practical utility in a case where the commerce and shipping of Venezuela, or the property, outside of the limits of Venezuela, of Venezuelans are concerned, although they might be of use in the case of a minor State which had a comparatively large mercantile marine.

The various measures mentioned are, no doubt, all of them in essence acts of war; if Venezuela chose so to treat them she would be justified in taking that course.

It is, however, plainly in her interests not to regard them in this light, and they form a convenient *mitior usus* which, while, of course, totally inapplicable in the case of a Great Power which has given serious cause of offence and which will not grant proper redress, is suitable to the case of a recalcitrant petty State in controversy with Great Powers of overwhelming strength, who, while desiring to obtain proper redress, are unwilling to dismember or destroy a puny antagonist.

November 21, 1902   W.E.D.

* * *

On the 21st November the German Ambassador called upon Lord Lansdowne and handed to him a paper, specifically explaining in the following terms the proposals of the German Government for the blockade of Venezuelan ports:

Arrangement between the German and British Commanding Officers with regard to the Blockade of Venezuelan Ports

(Translation)

(A)   Extent of the Blockade

1.   The blockade will apply to the Venezuelan ports of Maracaibo (which will include St. Carlos), Puerto-Cabello, La Guayra, and . . . (any other ports on the east coast of Venezuela).

2.   The ports of Maracaibo (including St. Carlos) and Puerto-Cabello will be blockaded by the German, and those of La Guayra and . . . (any other eastern ports) by the British Naval Commander.

(B)   Enforcement of the Blockade

1.   The blockade will be carried out by the vessels, boats, and other craft sailing under the German or British flag, which are under the orders of the two Naval Commanders.

2.   A decision is reserved with regard to the extent to which maritime traffic shall be further cut off by special military operations against the above-mentioned Venezuelan ports or separate islands.

3.   *The procedure with regard to every merchant-vessel sailing under other than the Venezuelan flag – regardless of nationality or cargo –* will be as follows:

a.   Merchant-vessels, which are found in the immediate neighbour-hood of, or actually in the blockade area, will receive a special notification from one of the blockading ships of war. In such cases an officer will be sent on board, who will enter in the log-book or in the papers of the merchantman the name of the ship of war which makes the notification, a statement of the existence and extent of the blockade, together with the date and place of his visit and his official signature. Simultaneously, ships which are within the blockade area will receive a summons to quit.

After this summons an attempt on the part of the ship to run the blockade renders her liable to confiscation.

b.   A similar summons will be addressed to such ships as – while cruising in a suspicious proximity to the blockade area – appear from their movements to have the intention of running the blockade.

If these ships do not conform to a summons of this nature they may be confiscated, provided that they have crossed the line of blockade.

c.   Ships which run in and break the blockade and reach a block-aded Venezuelan port must expect to be boarded in this case also by the blockading ships of war, and subjected to the Blockade Regula-tions.

d.   The procedure laid down in 3(c) applies also to merchantmen taking in cargo in blockaded Venezuelan ports. The freighting of these merchantmen in blockaded Venezuelan ports will also be pre-vented.

e.   Merchantmen which are within the blockade area expose them-selves to confiscation if they –

– Make an obvious attempt to avoid being searched.

– Forcibly resist being searched.

– Produce false papers or fail to provide themselves with the necessary papers to prove their identity, or destroy, deface, or con-ceal papers.

- Have disregarded a summons conveyed to them to quit the area of blockade.

4.   Merchantmen sailing under the Venezuelan flag shall be taken possession of in all cases in which merchantmen sailing under other flags would be liable to confiscation.

5.   Merchantmen which sail under other than the Venezuelan flag, and which, on being searched, are proved to be in the service of the Venezuelan Government, will be dealt with in a similar manner to ships under the Venezuelan flag.

6.   Confiscated ships will not be released until after the blockade is raised. The care of such ships, their cargo, and crews rests with their owners, who will have no claim of any sort for compensation on the States which take part in the blockade.

7.   A decision is reserved with regard to the further disposal of 'captured' ships.

(C) Exceptions

1.   Ships which are *bona fide* in distress (on account of serious damage, sickness, and so forth) will be permitted, as need shall arise, to enter or leave a Venezuelan port.

2.   The blockade does not affect foreigners, that is to say, persons of other than Venezuelan nationality, who wish to leave the country.

Ships under other than the Venezuelan flag, which have such persons on board, and possess certificates from their Consuls together with papers in proper form, will, after giving previous notice to the blockading ship, be allowed to pass. But such ships may have no cargo on board beyond the baggage of *bona fide* travellers.

3.   The co-operating Powers will insure every consideration, compatible with the exigencies of the blockade, to their own nationals and the subjects of neutral States.

With regard to the French blockade of Formosa in 1884, his Excellency said that the objection of His Majesty's Government that they had themselves protested against the treatment of their merchant-vessels at that time was, in the opinion of the Imperial Government, met by the contention that the British Government in their correspondence with the French Government at the time expressly declared that they regarded that blockade not as a pacific, but as a belligerent blockade, and therefore had no reason then to enter into a discussion as to the real grounds for a pacific blockade. On that occasion the British Government entirely recognized the French measures of blockade after the French Government had explained that they would abstain from searching or capturing British ships on the high seas. But the search or capture on the high seas of neutral vessels would not be required in a blockade of Venezuelan ports as proposed by the German Admiralty.

In a further communication received by Lord Lansdowne on the 23rd November, Count Metternich said that his Government were disposed to have recourse to a belligerent blockade, if absolutely necessary. Such a blockade would, however, imply a state of war which could only be brought about either by hostilities on the part of the Venezuelans or by a formal declaration of war on the part of England and Germany. It seemed, however, doubtful whether the Venezuelans would commence hostilities by opposing the seizure of their war ships, and, on the other hand, his Government could not declare war without the consent of the Federal Council. Valuable time might thereby be lost. In consequence, his Government would prefer to adopt the coercive measures before spoken of: in the first place a pacific blockade, and if that did not seem acceptable to His Majesty's Government, in the second place, the seizure of the Venezuelan Custom-houses.

The facts of the blockade of Formosa were briefly:

On the 3rd October, 1884, a notification of the blockade was issued in the 'Gazette.' In acknowledging a formal communication on the subject made by Mr Waddington, the French Ambassador, Lord Granville used the following language:

I avail myself of this opportunity, M. l'Ambassadeur, to ask your Excellency to be good enough to consider, in communication with your Government, whether it might not be desirable that some understanding should be arrived at between Great Britain and France as regards the exercise of belligerent rights and the obligations of neutrality flowing from the notification of the blockade. The position of affairs up to the present time has been that both France and China have abstained from asserting or exercising those belligerent rights of visit and search over neutral vessels on the high seas which are incident to a state of war.

In these circumstances, Her Majesty's Government have, on their side, abstained from issuing the usual proclamation of neutrality.

They still entertain the hope that some pacific solution may be found of the present difficulty, and they are most reluctant to take any step which could aggravate the situation. But the notification of blockade which has now been issued by France to neutral Powers has created a different situation. It indicates an intention on the part of France of entering upon a new phase of hostilities and of asserting belligerent rights over neutral vessels. If so, it is of the highest importance that British ship-owners and merchants in China should not be left in doubt as to their position and liabilities in regard to their trade with China, which has already suffered severely from the existing state of affairs. On the other hand, it may still be the wish and intention of the French Government to confine the operations of war to particular localities, and while warning off neutral vessels and preventing all access by them to the blockaded ports of Formosa, to refrain altogether from exercising over them the belligerent rights of visit and of capture.

If the French Government should be disposed to limit the exercise of the rights of war over neutral vessels in the manner above indicated, Her Majesty's Government would consider it unnecessary to modify the instructions issued by them for the observance of neutrality during the hostilities, and which are at present confined to the observance of the provisions of the Foreign Enlistment Act.

A note was subsequently received from M. Waddington (5th November, 1884), in which it was stated that, in establishing that blockade, the French Government had no intention of asserting belligerent rights as against neutrals, such as the right of visit and capture on the high seas, but only to effective blockade to be enforced either by driving away or by capturing vessels which should attempt to violate it; and it was added that such blockades might be established without war.

Lord Granville replied on the 11th November:

Your Excellency informs me that in establishing that blockade the Government of the Republic has no intention of asserting belligerent rights as against neutrals such as the right of visit and capture on the high seas, but only to maintain an effective blockade to be enforced either by driving away or by capturing vessels which should attempt it. Your Excellency adds that such blockades may be established without war; that they have been resorted to both by Great Britain and France in similar circumstances, and that their validity was recognized by the Tribunals of both countries.

I regret to have to inform you, M. l'Ambassadeur, that Her Majesty's Government are unable to concur in the views expressed in your Excellency's letter on this subject.

They do not think that it is expedient or necessary to discuss the circumstances and conditions under which what is termed a pacific blockade might be established consistently with the principles of the law of nations. But they cannot admit that the blockade of the ports of Formosa, which has been notified to neutral Powers, can be considered in the light of a pacific blockade. Actual hostilities have already taken place between France and China on a large scale, and of a character which is quite inconsistent with a state of peace.

Moreover, the contention of the French Government that a 'pacific blockade' confers on the blockading Power the right to capture and condemn the ships of third nations for breach of such a blockade is opposed to the opinions of the most eminent statesmen and jurists of France, and to the decisions of its Tribunals, and it is in conflict with well-established principles of international law.

Her Majesty's Government consider that the hostilities which have taken place, followed by a formal notice of blockade, constitute a state of war between France and China, and they are prepared to recognize the blockade of the ports of Formosa as a belligerent blockade, carrying with it the usual belligerent rights as against neutrals.

Nevertheless, for the reasons explained in my note to your Excellency of the 31st ultimo, and considering the present circumstances and the limits imposed by the French Government on their operations in China, Her Majesty's Government will not aggravate the situation by issuing a formal Proclamation of Neutrality, and enforcing all the strict rights of neutrals, so long as the hostilities are confined to particular localities, and both France and China refrain from exercising against neutrals the belligerent right of visit and capture on the high seas.

Her Majesty's Government desire to impress on the French Government in the clearest manner that they cannot admit the right of visit or capture of British ships unless it be founded on the law of nations applicable to a state of war.

In the course of further discussion which ensued Lord Granville, in a note to M. Waddington of the 26th November, said:

Her Majesty's Government cannot admit any such novel doctrine as that British ships are liable to capture for entering certain Treaty ports in China in time of peace. But they maintain that a state of war exists, and therefore they do not deny the right of the French Government to establish an effective blockade of the ports in question according to the laws of war, and to capture neutral vessels attempting to force it. Her Majesty's Government admit that they are bound to recognize the blockade as a belligerent blockade, and to submit to the exercise of either belligerent of the rights of war which the law of nations accords as against neutral vessels. But the French Government, with the view of alleviating the consequences above mentioned as against neutrals, have declared that they do not propose to exercise the right of visit or capture over neutral ships on the high seas, to which they are entitled in order to prevent the carriage of contraband of war to China.

Her Majesty's Government, on the other hand, being reluctant to aggravate the situation, have declared that so long as the hostilities are confined to particular localities, and neutral vessels are not interfered with on the high seas, they will not issue a Proclamation of Neutrality in the usual form and exercise the strict rights of neutrality as regards belligerent vessels in British ports, but will confine themselves to the enforcement of the Foreign Enlistment Act. Such is the precise situation from the point of view of Her Majesty's Government, and it will be understood from what I have stated that the continuance of this state of things depends on the adherence of the French Government and their naval authorities to the declaration above mentioned as to abstention from exercising the right of visit and capture over British vessels on the high seas.

No formal declaration of war was issued either by France or China, but in January 1885 M. Waddington announced that the French Government did not feel themselves any longer in a position to waive the full exercise of the rights accorded to belligerents by international law, and that instructions in that sense were about to be addressed to the French Naval Commanders.

The following Notice was therefore inserted in the 'Gazette' on the 13th February:

It is hereby notified, for public information, that it has been announced to Her Majesty's Government by the Government of the French Republic that it is their intention to exercise, during the continuance of the present hostilities between France and China, the rights of belligerents which are recognized by the law of nations, including the right to search neutral vessels on the high seas for contraband of war.

The views held by Her Majesty's Government in 1884 are set forth at greater length than in the earlier portion of this Memorandum, as the German Ambassador seems to be under some misapprehension on the subject. All the communications made by Lord Granville to M. Waddington support the arguments already used in conversation with Count Metternich, to the effect that His Majesty's Government cannot regard as a so-called 'pacific blockade' any arrangement which interferes with the vessels of third Powers.

November 27, 1902   F.H.V.

PART II

THE HAGUE CONFERENCES
AND THE DECLARATION OF LONDON,
1899–1916

INTRODUCTION

The initial invitation by Tsar Nicholas II to the powers to send delegates to a conference to reform the law and practice of belligerent rights at sea led to their assembly at the Hague in 1899, but the results of the first Hague Conference were limited, being little more than regulation and protection of hospital ships, and the rather vague words of Article 8 of Convention 3 that 'Sailors and soldiers who are taken on board when sick or wounded, to whatever nation they belong, shall be protected and looked after by the captors.' The attempt which was made the following year to clarify British practice in maritime commerce warfare, by a consolidation of the Naval Prize Act, failed to pass in the House of Commons [19]. The 2nd Hague Conference of 1907 reiterated the provisions of the first and tightened them up. Now, by Article 16 of Convention 10, it was agreed that 'After every engagement, the two belligerents, so far as military interests permit, shall take steps to look for the shipwrecked, sick, and wounded, and to protect them, as well as the dead, against pillage and ill treatment.' It was also agreed that belligerents were required to 'see that the burial, whether by land or sea, or cremation of the dead shall be preceded by a careful examination of the corpse.' Marks of identification were to be sent to the authorities of the respective country. The 2nd Hague Conference also placed controls on the conversion of merchant ships to warships to prevent a return to privateer warships, and put in place controls on submarine mines and naval bombardment to protect mercantile traffic and citizens. Convention 11 stipulated that postal communications were not subject to interception and that 'Vessels used exclusively for fishing along the coast or small boats employed in local trade are exempt from capture, as well as their appliances, rigging, tackle, and cargo. They cease to be exempt as soon as they take any part whatever in hostilities. The Contracting Powers agree not to take advantage of the harmless character of the said vessels in order to use them for military purposes while preserving their peaceful appearance.'

More contentious than the other conventions, and of much greater importance to the continued strategic utility of the British navy, was the draft 'Convention concerning the Establishment of an International Prize

Court' which was never ratified. The Admiralty vigorously objected to the idea of naval operations being subject to an international court which would inevitably be dominated by justices from continental states. It was confident of its ability to defend British trade against cruisers and did not want to provide a future enemy with political ammunition which could prevent the effective use of British sea power. For their own reasons, the British public in general allied themselves with the Admiralty. It was impressed by the alarmist views expressed by Admiral Lord Charles Beresford that British trade was defenceless. In 1905 Admiral Mahan himself had retreated a little from the position that only a dominant naval power could effectively execute economic warfare, accepting that *guerre de course* against commerce could form a useful part of an inferior power's strategy by haemorrhaging enemy resources.

By far the most important of the conventions agreed to at the 2nd Hague Conference was Convention 13, 'Concerning the Rights and Duties of Neutral Powers in Naval War.' Its 33 clauses included bans on naval operations within the territorial waters of neutral states, and an obligation on the part of neutrals to ensure that their waters were not so used by belligerents. Article 8 extended to all signatories the agreement made between Britain and the United States when settling the *Alabama* claims that neutrals had obligations to ensure that their ports were not used to support a belligerency, that 'A neutral Government is bound to employ the means at its disposal to prevent the fitting out or arming of any vessel within its jurisdiction' [20].

This has become the bedrock of the law of naval warfare, but it was not framed in terms which could be used by naval officers carrying out trade control activities. The attempt to create an international prize court failed because there was not an agreed basis of law. Accordingly, the Liberal administration of Henry Asquith invited the powers to a conference in London in 1908–09 to develop a code of law which fleshed out the general principles of the Declaration of Paris. When the delegates assembled they addressed the problem by drawing up three lists of commodities which were to be considered as 'absolute contraband,' and could be intercepted by belligerent warships even if being transported in neutral merchant shipping, 'conditional contraband' which could only be intercepted if manifested for the armed forces of the enemy, and 'free' commodities which could never be stopped by a belligerent except as part of an 'effective' blockade of enemy ports. Items of 'conditional contraband' were not to be liable to seizure on the high seas on the basis of intelligence indicating their ultimate destination to the enemy. These principles were embodied in what was known as the Declaration of London, 1909 [21].

The Declaration was thought to serve British defensive interests by eliminating the application of the principle of continuous voyage to 'conditional contraband,' and by including food on the conditional contraband list rather than making it absolute contraband. Most of the primary products Britain imported for industrial purposes were put on the free list. The greater precision imparted to the question of contraband would also benefit British shipping interests when a neutral. The right of belligerent navies to sink neutral prizes was conceded, but it was hedged with enough limitations to render it less of a threat.

The critical view of the Declaration of London held by Colonel Hankey, then in the Naval Intelligence Department, was not shared by his superiors. Rear Admiral Sir Charles Ottley, Secretary of the Committee of Imperial Defence from 1907 to 1912, believed that the danger of confronting neutrals was too great. Hankey's extreme measures appeared to violate not only the spirit of the Declaration of London, but the principles of the Declaration of Paris. Cynically, Ottley argued that, if there were war, once the fleet had succeeded in bringing the German navy to a decisive battle, and won, neutrals could be prevailed upon to accept interference with their trade. Ottley took for granted that events would be decided by a fleet action, after which trade control could be used in the end game [24]. Why the German navy should allow itself to be drawn into a battle it would lose, unless there were some strategic objective such as the defence of trade which forced it to sea, was not explained.

The First Lord, Reginald McKenna, was impressed by Hankey's defence of belligerent rights, but attached more importance to the consideration that the Declaration of London would benefit British interests in a war in which Britain were neutral, and accepted Ottley's cynical argument that it would become a dead letter should Britain be at war and succeed in defeating the enemy battle fleet. Hankey later said that four successive directors of Naval Intelligence recommended that the Declaration be ratified by the government. In a letter to the Prime Minister Ramsay MacDonald, 11 October 1929, Hankey added that Ottley 'and, to the best of my knowledge, every single person who was concerned either in drawing up the Declaration or in trying to put it through Parliament lived to regret that instrument' [61].

Public opinion in Britain reversed its earlier enthusiasm for limitations. 'Resolutions poured in from Chambers of Commerce and other public bodies', recalled Hankey. In January 1908 an 'Imperial Maritime League' had been formed. Its principal concern was a defensive one. In July 1911 it published an open letter to the Prime Minister, signed by 138 admirals, sounding an alarm about the effect of the Declaration on Britain's importation of food. They were concerned that fast merchantmen converted into auxiliary warships on the declaration of war would provide an enemy with resources for trade war on a scale not seen since the abolition of privateers. The failure of the Declaration of London to eliminate this threat was thought virtually to ensure that British merchantmen would be driven from the sea. The inclusion of almost all food, except for nuts and hops, on the 'conditional contra- band' list, liable to seizure if consigned for the armed forces of the state, was seen as a major danger to Britain. The League argued that any enemy cruiser captain would be able to arrest neutral ships carrying food to Britain because the presence in most British ports of defence forces would make it possible to construe the food as destined for the British military. The League also pointed out that, practically speaking, there was little prospect of the enemy being deceived by false manifests to a neutral port, but that it would be easy for a continental enemy such as Germany to receive all she required via the inland transportation systems [25]. In Hankey's opinion the concerns about Britain's food supply were insubstantial, but the threat to Britain's ability to exert influence over European affairs was serious, and this threat was repre- sented to parliament by Arthur Balfour and Andrew Bonar Law. Eventually the House of Lords voted against the bill.

General diplomatic considerations were put forward in the parliamen- tary debates to justify British agreement to the Declaration of London. A Naval Prize Law Committee was struck to apply the principles of the Declaration of London to British municipal law, and when the Naval Prize Bill was introduced in Parliament on 28 June 1911, Thomas McKinnon Wood, then Under-Secretary of State at the Foreign Office, asserted that Britain really could not stand out against world opinion on the matter [22]. He was supported by Sir Edward Grey, who warned critical naval officers that they were forgetting 'what our interference with neutral trade then cost us – world-wide hostility and an extension of the field of war' [46]. Official belief that it was imperative to retain a free hand to suspend the operation of cruiser warfare in order to sustain working relations with neutral shipping states was a prominent consid- eration in discussion of the juridical status of the navies which were being established in Australia and Canada. An Admiralty *Memorandum as to Prizes Captured by Colonial Navies*, drawn up in April 1910 [23], was followed in July by a *Report of Interdepartmental Conference on Status of Dominion Ships of War* to which the dominion governments had sent representatives.[1] The logic seemed clear in London, but was not

[1]See Nicholas Tracy, *The Collective Naval Defence of the Empire, 1900–1940*, NRS, vol. 136, no. 74 and pp. 112–46 *passim*.

acceptable to dominion governments, which were not certain their interests were best served by paying for forces they did not control.

Although the British government did not ratify the Declaration of London, the United States government did, and the Navy Prize Bill and the Declaration of London had profound effects on planning for a war with Germany. In November 1912 the committee which had drafted the Naval Prize Bill was reconstituted to prepare revisions to the existing Prize Court Rules so they could be enacted quickly in an emergency [26]. Despite the parliamentary rejection of the Prize Bill, the Admiralty incorporated the substance of the Declaration of London in its war orders, and printed them in a *Handbook for Boarding Officers and Prize Officers in War Time* [27]. Thus the Declaration of London provided the rules of engagement for trade control on the outbreak of the First World War.

When less than two years later Britain found herself at war, Hankey's fears were to be fulfilled, and Ottley's cynical advice was in fact carried out. On the outbreak of war the British fleet was directed to seize German shipping, and to intercept the supplies upon which the German army depended.[1] It was recognized that the legal definition of blockade could not be stretched to include interception of neutral ships carrying goods on the Free List of the Declaration of London in the waters north of Scotland. Formal blockades in the technically correct usage of the word were eventually declared on the east coast of Africa, in Asia Minor, Greece, Salonica and Tsingtao, but in waters threatened by the German High Seas Fleet British tactics were directed to the exploitation of the long contraband list of the Declaration of London which was now seen to be useful. On 20 August it was proclaimed that 'His Majesty, by and with the advice of the Privy Council, is pleased to order, and it is hereby ordered, that during the present hostilities the Convention known as the Declaration of London shall, subject to the following additions and modifications, be adopted and put in force by His Majesty's Government as if the same had been ratified by His Majesty.'[2] Sir Edward Grey made it clear 'that we have only two objects in our proclamations: to restrict supplies for the German army and to restrict the supply to Germany of materials essential for the making of munitions of war. We intend to attain these objects with the minimum of interference with the United States and other neutral countries.'[3] The additions and modifications referred to in the proclamation

[1]A.C. Bell, *A History of the Blockade of Germany, 1914–18*, London, 1937 (Confidential to 1961), p. 602.
[2]ADM 116/1234. Also ADM 186/603 p. 176.
[3]Bell, *A History of the Blockade of Germany*, p. 45.

were the substitution of a new contraband list, the application of the doctrine of continuous voyage to contraband cargoes, and a provision that prize courts were to condemn ships and cargoes 'on any sufficient evidence'. Commanders-in-Chief were advised that the reason for the change was to make possible the interception of food cargoes [28].

There was no concrete strategic reasoning behind the reversal of policy. It simply reflected the brutalizing impact of war, and the need to impress the French that the British navy was making a contribution to *Entente* defence. Neutral shipping was obliged to submit to search, and contraband manifested to Germany was seized. The extension of the principles of continuous voyage to conditional contraband was protested by the United States government, which declared that the United States would expect its commerce to be protected by the legal regime in force before 1909.[1] But continuous voyage did not become the principal justification for interception of ships, partly because it was learnt that Germany was not controlling food supplies, and partly because of the difficulty of checking neutral consignees. This policy was embodied in an Order-in-Council on 29 October 1914 which also contained a proviso that, if it became apparent that any neutral port had become an entrepôt of conditional contraband destined for the enemy, all ships sailing to it would be seized. This principle, which had no foundation in law, had actually been suggested to London unofficially by Acting United States Secretary of State Robert Lansing. The effect of neutral quiescence to this declaration was that the governing factor in the enforcement of the blockade increasingly became the ability of the belligerents to reach political settlement with the neutrals. Statistical evidence not admissible in a prize court was used to ration imports into neutral countries to ensure that they were not re-exported to the Central Powers.

To these enforcement techniques the British Empire was able to add practical leverage through its control of most of the world's marine bunker wharfs, most of the world's supply of jute sacking and most of the world's cable communications. Neutral shippers who traded with the Central Powers were placed on a 'Black List' and denied the supplies they needed to stay in business.

In the conditions of twentieth-century society, the payment of prize money to naval officers and men engaged in trade control operations

---

[1]Order-in-Council of 20 August 1914, and US Acting Secretary of State Lansing to Ambassador Page, 22 October 1914, in *Supplement to the American Journal of International Law, Diplomatic Correspondence between the United States and Belligerent Governments Relating to Neutral Rights and Commerce* (hereafter cited as *Supplement to AJIL*), vol. 9, p. 7.

while denying it to those in the battle fleets was considered inappropriate, and a Prize Fund was established to divide any prize money
throughout the navy. Prize bounty payed to officers and men who
participated in the capture or sinking of enemy warships, however, was
retained [29].

The only really important neutral state was the United States. All
sections of the American economy were worried about Britain's settlements with European neutrals, which in effect eliminated the difference
between contraband and conditional contraband. The fall in cotton exports was blamed on the British blockade, and the copper mining states
forcefully expressed their grievances. Shippers were exasperated by the
delays which occurred when a ship was detained for inspection. The
Chicago meat packers, who hoped to make vast profits out of using
Copenhagen as a gateway into Germany, were especially irate. The fear
that British objectives were at least partly mercantilist was exacerbated
by British interception of mails and cables, which led American busi-
nessmen to charge that the British censors were deliberately passing on
trade secrets to British firms. However, although the American government sent Britain a strongly worded note, it refused to act in consort with
other neutrals, and belied its strong language with an evident disposition
to give Britain the benefit of the doubt. In January 1915 Secretary of
State William Jennings Bryan advised the Senate Committee on Foreign
Relations that the British practice with respect to continuous voyage was
one which had been enforced by American courts when the United States
was a belligerent. London and Washington reached a 'working arrangement' by which the American government itself tightened up shipping
manifests of American merchant shipping to prevent evasion of the blockade.[1] Strong protest from American shippers at delays caused by British
inspections of neutral ships led the American Consul-General in London,
Mr Skinner, to suggest a system of cargo passports. London welcomed
the suggestion, and in March 1916 the 'navicert' system was established
by which British consuls in neutral ports provided documentation certi-
fying the nature of neutral cargoes. It proved to be a highly effective way
of administering the rationing system.[2]

Eventually the Declaration of London was set aside altogether because in 1916 the Judicial Committee of the House of Lords in the

[1]See Secretary of State Grey to Ambassador Page, 7 January 1915, in *Supplement to
AJIL*, vol. 9, pp. 60–5.

[2]H. Ritchie, *The 'Navicert' System During the World War*, pp. 4–7 and *passim*; H.W.
Carless Davis, *History of the Blockade. Emergency Departments*, London, 1920, pp.
175–98; and Marion C. Siney, *The Allied Blockade of Germany 1914–1916*, Ann Ar-
bour, 1957, pp. 139–42.

Zamora asserted the independence of prize courts from the British government. In its summation it stated:

> The power of an Order-in-Council does not extend to prescribing or altering the law to be administered by the court . . . If the court is to decide, judicially, in accordance with what it conceives to be the law of nations, it cannot, even in doubtful cases, take its direction from the crown, which is party to the proceedings.[1]

By an Order-in-Council of 7 July 1916 the government released itself altogether from the Declaration of London, but this perilous step was not taken until after a 'Legal Assessment' of the advantages and disadvantages to Britain of reverting to traditional Admiralty law, and of the dangers of confronting neutral sensitivities, had been drawn up by Alexander Pearce Higgins, Advisor on International Law, in the Procurator-General's Department [30]. The effect on the conduct of the economic war, however, was marginal because the Foreign Office only rarely sent cargo cases to the prize courts for adjudication. The coercion it relied upon was almost entirely outside the law, which did not sanction arbitrary detentions or the extortion of agreements not to claim damages.

---

[1]A.C. Bell, *A History of the Blockade of Germany, 1914–18*, p. 463.

19. Short History of the Progress of the Naval Prize Bill

NL Branch, M. Brooks

[ADM 116/1236]   15 December 1903

In April 1900 Professor Holland represented to the then First Lord of the Admiralty [William Parker, Earl of Selborne] the desirability of introducing a Bill for regulating Prize of War – the same to be purely a consolidation Bill and its purpose to bring into one Act matter which, under existing legislation, must be gathered from several Acts bearing on Naval Prize of War.

The preparation of such a Bill was entrusted to Professor Holland, and in due course a draft was submitted by him and referred to various legal authorities, and to the Foreign and Colonial Offices.

Several alterations were suggested by the above, the Colonial Office in especial thinking, from recent experience in South Africa, that this would be a good opportunity of extending the provisions concerning preemption of Stores intended for the enemy beyond what was included in existing Acts.

These were, in the main, embodied by Professor Holland in the Bill, but a proposal of the Foreign Office that the Bill itself should be referred to a committee about to consider certain questions of Prize Law was not accepted.

In July the Bill, as revised, was referred to the Attorney General, Solicitor General, Master of the Rolls, and other legal authorities, and also to Foreign and Colonial Offices. Further small additions were made to meet Colonial Office and Foreign Office views; after considerable correspondence the Bill was concurred in by these Departments, and the Parliamentary draughtsman was instructed in February 1901 to place himself in communication with Professor Holland with the view of preparing the Bill for the next Session. Nothing could, however, be done that Session and consideration of the Bill was postponed until October.

In the interim Professor Holland has seen the Lord Chancellor who took exception to many things in the Bill, and in especial to the new matter introduced at the suggestion of the Colonial Office. A great deal of official and private correspondence ensued, and in the end the Bill was considerably altered by Professor Holland in accordance with the Lord Chancellor's instructions. All procedure clauses were cut out of it and embodied by Professor Holland in the 'Rules of Court in Prize Procedure' (which were to be laid in draft as amended on the table of the House when the Bill reached its second reading), and the Bill in its altered shape was eventually agreed to by the Departments concerned and copies of it were distributed to the Cabinet early in 1902.

The Bill, now purely one of consolidation, passed the House of Lords, but was blocked in the Commons and dropped for the time. It is understood that it will be introduced again next Session.

* * *

20. Hague Convention XIII Concerning the Rights and Duties of Neutral Powers in Naval War[1]

[Department of State Publication 8407]   18 October 1907

With a view to harmonizing the divergent views which, in the event of naval war, are still held on the relations between neutral Powers and belligerent Powers, and to anticipating the difficulties to which such divergence of views might give rise;

Seeing that, even if it is not possible at present to concert measures applicable to all circumstances which may in practice occur, it is nevertheless undeniably advantageous to frame, as far as possible, rules of general application to meet the case where war has unfortunately broken out;

Seeing that, in cases not covered by the present Convention, it is expedient to take into consideration the general principles of the law of nations;

Seeing that it is desirable that the Powers should issue detailed enactments to regulate the results of the attitude of neutrality when adopted by them;

Seeing that it is, for neutral Powers, an admitted duty to apply these rules impartially to the several belligerents;

Seeing that, in this category of ideas, these rules should not, in principle, be altered, in the course of the war, by a neutral Power, except in a case where experience has shown the necessity for such change for the protection of the rights of that Power;

Have agreed to observe the following common rules, which cannot however modify provisions laid down in existing general treaties, and have appointed as their Plenipotentiaries, namely:

---

[1]Treaties and Other International Agreements of the United States of America 1776–1949. Compiled under the direction of Charles I. Bevans LL.B., Assistant Legal Adviser, Department of State, Volume 1, Multilateral 1776–1917, Department of State Publication 8407 Washington, DC: Government Printing Office, 1968.

[List of Plenipotentiaries]

Who, after having deposited their full powers, found in good and due form, have agreed upon the following provisions:

Article 1. Belligerents are bound to respect the sovereign rights of neutral Powers and to abstain, in neutral territory or neutral waters, from any act which would, if knowingly permitted by any Power, constitute a violation of neutrality.

Art. 2. Any act of hostility, including capture and the exercise of the right of search, committed by belligerent war-ships in the territorial waters of a neutral Power, constitutes a violation of neutrality and is strictly forbidden.

Art. 3. When a ship has been captured in the territorial waters of a neutral Power, this Power must employ, if the prize is still within its jurisdiction, the means at its disposal to release the prize with its officers and crew, and to intern the prize crew.

If the prize is not in the jurisdiction of the neutral Power, the captor Government, on the demand of that Power, must liberate the prize with its officers and crew.

Art. 4. A prize court cannot be set up by a belligerent on neutral territory or on a vessel in neutral waters.

Art. 5. Belligerents are forbidden to use neutral ports and waters as a base of naval operations against their adversaries, and in particular to erect wireless telegraphy stations or any apparatus for the purpose of communicating with the belligerent forces on land or sea.

Art. 6. The supply, in any manner, directly or indirectly, by a neutral Power to a belligerent Power, of war-ships, ammunition, or war material of any kind whatever, is forbidden.

Art. 7. A neutral Power is not bound to prevent the export or transit, for the use of either belligerent, of arms, ammunition, or, in general, of anything which could be of use to an army or fleet.

Art. 8. A neutral Government is bound to employ the means at its disposal to prevent the fitting out or arming of any vessel within its jurisdiction which it has reason to believe is intended to cruise, or engage in hostile operations, against a Power with which that Government is at peace. It is also bound to display the same vigilance to prevent the departure from its jurisdiction of any vessel intended to cruise, or engage in hostile operations, which had been adapted entirely or partly within the said jurisdiction for use in war.

Art. 9. A neutral Power must apply impartially to the two belligerents the conditions, restrictions, or prohibitions made by it in regard to the admission into its ports, roadsteads, or territorial waters, of belligerent war-ships or of their prizes.

Nevertheless, a neutral Power may forbid a belligerent vessel which has failed to conform to the orders and regulations made by it, or which has violated neutrality, to enter its ports or roadsteads.

Art. 10. The neutrality of a Power is not affected by the mere passage through its territorial waters of war-ships or prizes belonging to belligerents.

Art. 11. A neutral Power may allow belligerent war-ships to employ its licensed pilots.

Art. 12. In the absence of special provisions to the contrary in the legislation of a neutral Power, belligerent war-ships are not permitted to remain in the ports, roadsteads, or territorial waters of the said Power for more than twenty-four hours, except in the cases covered by the present Convention.

Art. 13. If a Power which has been informed of the outbreak of hostilities learns that a belligerent war-ship is in one of its ports or roadsteads, or in its territorial waters, it must notify the said ship to depart within twenty-four hours or within the time prescribed by local regulations.

Art. 14. A belligerent war-ship may not prolong its stay in a neutral port beyond the permissible time except on account of damage or stress of weather. It must depart as soon as the cause of the delay is at an end.

The regulations as to the question of the length of time which these vessels may remain in neutral ports, roadsteads, or waters do not apply to war-ships devoted exclusively to religious, scientific, or philanthropic purposes.

Art. 15. In the absence of special provisions to the contrary in the legislation of a neutral Power, the maximum number of war-ships belonging to a belligerent which may be in one of the ports or roadsteads of that Power simultaneously shall be three.

Art. 16. When war-ships belonging to both belligerents are present simultaneously in a neutral port or roadstead, a period of not less than twenty-four hours must elapse between the departure of the ship belonging to one belligerent and the departure of the ship belonging to the other.

The order of departure is determined by the order of arrival, unless the ship which arrived first is so circumstanced that an extension of its stay is permissible.

A belligerent war-ship may not leave a neutral port or roadstead until twenty-four hours after the departure of a merchant ship flying the flag of its adversary.

Art. 17. In neutral ports and roadsteads belligerent war-ships may only carry out such repairs as are absolutely necessary to render them seaworthy, and may not add in any manner whatsoever to their fighting force. The local authorities of the neutral Power shall decide what repairs are necessary, and these must be carried out with the least possible delay.

Art. 18. Belligerent war-ships may not make use of neutral ports, roadsteads, or territorial waters for replenishing or increasing their supplies of war material or their armament, or for completing their crews.

Art. 19. Belligerent war-ships may only revictual in neutral ports or roadsteads to bring up their supplies to the peace standard.

Similarly these vessels may only ship sufficient fuel to enable them to reach the nearest port in their own country. They may, on the other hand, fill up their bunkers built to carry fuel, when in neutral countries which have adopted this method of determining the amount of fuel to be supplied.

If, in accordance with the law of the neutral Power, the ships are not supplied with coal within twenty-four hours of their arrival, the permissible duration of their stay is extended by twenty-four hours.

Art. 20. Belligerent war-ships which have shipped fuel in a port belonging to a neutral Power may not within the succeeding three months replenish their supply in a port of the same Power.

Art. 21. A prize may only be brought into a neutral port on account of unseaworthiness, stress of weather, or want of fuel or provisions.

It must leave as soon as the circumstances which justified its entry are at an end. If it does not, the neutral Power must order it to leave at once; should it fail to obey, the neutral Power must employ the means at its disposal to release it with its officers and crew and to intern the prize crew.

Art. 22. A neutral Power must, similarly, release a prize brought into one of its ports under circumstances other than those referred to in Article 21.

Art. 23. A neutral Power may allow prizes to enter its ports and roadsteads, whether under convoy or not, when they are brought there to be sequestrated pending the decision of a Prize Court. It may have the prize taken to another of its ports.

If the prize is convoyed by a war-ship, the prize crew may go on board the convoying ship.

If the prize is not under convoy, the prize crew are left at liberty.

Art. 24. If, notwithstanding the notification of the neutral Power, a belligerent ship of war does not leave a port where it is not entitled to remain, the neutral Power is entitled to take such measures as it considers necessary to render the ship incapable of taking the sea during the war, and the commanding officer of the ship must facilitate the execution of such measures.

When a belligerent ship is detained by a neutral Power, the officers and crew are likewise detained.

The officers and crew thus detained may be left in the ship or kept either on another vessel or on land, and may be subjected to the measures of restriction which it may appear necessary to impose upon them. A sufficient number of men for looking after the vessel must, however, be always left on board.

The officers may be left at liberty on giving their word not to quit the neutral territory without permission.

Art. 25. A neutral Power is bound to exercise such surveillance as the means at its disposal allow to prevent any violation of the provisions of the above Articles occurring in its ports or roadsteads or in its waters.

Art. 26. The exercise by a neutral Power of the rights laid down in the present Convention can under no circumstances be considered as an unfriendly act by one or other belligerent who has accepted the articles relating thereto.

Art. 27. The Contracting Powers shall communicate to each other in due course all laws, proclamations, and other enactments regulating in their respective countries the status of belligerent war-ships in their ports and waters, by means of a communication addressed to the Government of the Netherlands, and forwarded immediately by that Government to the other Contracting Powers.

Art. 28. The provisions of the present Convention do not apply except between Contracting Powers, and then only if all the belligerents are parties to the Convention.

Art. 29. The present Convention shall be ratified as soon as possible. The ratifications shall be deposited at The Hague.

The first deposit of ratifications shall be recorded in a procès-verbal signed by the representatives of the Powers which take part therein and by the Netherlands Minister for Foreign Affairs.

The subsequent deposits of ratifications shall be made by means of a written notification addressed to the Netherlands Government and accompanied by the instrument of ratification.

A duly certified copy of the procès-verbal relative to the first deposit of ratifications, of the ratifications mentioned in the preceding paragraph, as well as of the instruments of ratification, shall be at once sent by the Netherlands Government, through the diplomatic channel, to the Powers invited to the Second Peace Conference, as well as to the other Powers which have adhered to the Convention. In the cases contemplated in the preceding paragraph, the said Government shall inform them at the same time of the date on which it received the notification.

Art. 30. Non-Signatory Powers may adhere to the present Convention. The Power which desires to adhere notifies in writing its intention to the Netherlands Government, forwarding to it the act of adhesion, which shall be deposited in the archives of the said Government.

That Government shall at once transmit to all the other Powers a duly certified copy of the notification as well as of the act of adhesion, mentioning the date on which it received the notification.

Art. 31. The present Convention shall come into force in the case of the Powers which were a party to the first deposit of the ratifications, sixty days after the date of the procès-verbal of that deposit, and, in the case of the Powers who ratify subsequently or who adhere, sixty days after the notification of their ratification or of their decision has been received by the Netherlands Government.

Art. 32. In the event of one of the Contracting Powers wishing to denounce the present Convention, the denunciation shall be notified in writing to the Netherlands Government, who shall at once communicate a duly certified copy of the notification to all the other Powers, informing them of the date on which it was received.

The denunciation shall only have effect in regard to the notifying Power, and one year after the notification has been made to the Netherlands Government.

Art. 33. A register kept by the Netherlands Ministry for Foreign Affairs shall give the date of the deposit of ratifications made by Article 29, paragraphs 3 and 4, as well as the date on which the notifications of adhesion (Article 30, paragraph 2) or of denunciation (Article 32, paragraph 1) have been received.

Each Contracting Power is entitled to have access to this register and to be supplied with duly certified extracts.

In faith whereof the Plenipotentiaries have appended their signatures to the present Convention.

Done at The Hague, 18 October 1907, in a single copy, which shall remain deposited in the archives of the Netherlands Government, and duly certified copies of which shall be sent, through the diplomatic channel, to the Powers which have been invited to the Second Peace Conference.

* * *

21. *Declaration of London Concerning the Laws of Naval War*[1]

[208 Consolidated Treaty Series, 338 (1909)]   26 February 1909

[List of Contracting Parties]

Having regard to the terms in which the British Government invited various Powers to meet in conference in order to arrive at an agreement as to what are the generally recognized rules of international law within the meaning of Article 7 of the Convention of 18 October 1907, relative to the establishment of an International Prize Court;

Recognizing all the advantages which an agreement as to the said rules would, in the unfortunate event of a naval war, present, both as regards peaceful commerce, and as regards the belligerents and their diplomatic relations with neutral Governments;

Having regard to the divergence often found in the methods by which it is sought to apply in practice the general principles of international law;

Animated by the desire to ensure henceforward a greater measure of uniformity in this respect; Hoping that a work so important to the common welfare will meet with general approval;

Have appointed as their Plenipotentiaries, that is to say: [Here follow the names of Plenipotentiaries] Who, after having communicated their full powers, found to be in good and due form, have agreed to make the present Declaration:

PRELIMINARY PROVISION

The Signatory Powers are agreed that the rules contained in the following Chapters correspond in substance with the generally recognized principles of international law.

CHAPTER I   BLOCKADE IN TIME OF WAR

Article 1. A blockade must not extend beyond the ports and coasts belonging to or occupied by the enemy.

Art. 2. In accordance with the Declaration of Paris of 1856, a blockade, in order to be binding, must be effective – that is to say, it must be maintained by a force sufficient really to prevent access to the enemy coastline.

Art. 3. The question whether a blockade is effective is a question of fact.

[1]Henry Dunant Institute for Humanitarian Dialogue.

Art. 4. A blockade is not regarded as raised if the blockading force is temporarily withdrawn on account of stress of weather.

Art. 5. A blockade must be applied impartially to the ships of all nations.

Art. 6. The commander of a blockading force may give permission to a warship to enter, and subsequently to leave, a blockaded port.

Art. 7. In circumstances of distress, acknowledged by an officer of the blockading force, a neutral vessel may enter a place under blockade and subsequently leave it, provided that she has neither discharged nor shipped any cargo there.

Art. 8. A blockade, in order to be binding, must be declared in accordance with Article 9, and notified in accordance with Articles 11 and 16.

Art. 9. A declaration of blockade is made either by the blockading Power or by the naval authorities acting in its name.

It specifies –

(1)   The date when the blockade begins;

(2)   the geographical limits of the coastline under blockade;

(3)   the period within which neutral vessels may come out.

Art. 10. If the operations of the blockading Power, or of the naval authorities acting in its name, do not tally with the particulars, which, in accordance with Article 9(1) and (2), must be inserted in the declaration of blockade, the declaration is void, and a new declaration is necessary in order to make the blockade operative.

Art. 11. A declaration of blockade is notified

(1)   To neutral Powers, by the blockading Power, by means of a communication addressed to the Governments direct, or to their representatives accredited to it;

(2)   To the local authorities, by the officer commanding the blockading force. The local authorities will, in turn, inform the foreign consular officers at the port or on the coastline under blockade as soon as possible.

Art. 12. The rules as to declaration and notification of blockade apply to cases where the limits of a blockade are extended, or where a blockade is re-established after having been raised.

Art. 13. The voluntary raising of a blockade, as also any restriction in the limits of a blockade, must be notified in the manner prescribed by Article 11.

Art. 14. The liability of a neutral vessel to capture for breach of blockade is contingent on her knowledge, actual or presumptive, of the blockade.

Art. 15. Failing proof to the contrary, knowledge of the blockade is presumed if the vessel left a neutral port subsequently to the notification of the blockade to the Power to which such port belongs, provided that such notification was made in sufficient time.

Art. 16. If a vessel approaching a blockaded port has no knowledge, actual or presumptive, of the blockade, the notification must be made to the vessel itself by an officer of one of the ships of the blockading force. This notification should be entered in the vessel's logbook, and must state the day and hour, and the geographical position of the vessel at the time. If through the negligence of the officer commanding the blockading force no declaration of blockade has been notified to the local authorities, or, if in the declaration, as notified, no period has been mentioned within which neutral vessels may come out, a neutral vessel coming out of the blockaded port must be allowed to pass free.

Art. 17. Neutral vessels may not be captured for breach of blockade except within the area of operations of the warships detailed to render the blockade effective.

Art. 18. The blockading forces must not bar access to neutral ports or coasts.

Art. 19. Whatever may be the ulterior destination of a vessel or of her cargo, she cannot be captured for breach of blockade, if, at the moment, she is on her way to a non-blockaded port.

Art. 20. A vessel which has broken blockade outwards, or which has attempted to break blockade inwards, is liable to capture so long as she is pursued by a ship of the blockading force. If the pursuit is abandoned, or if the blockade is raised, her capture can no longer be effected.

Art. 21. A vessel found guilty of breach of blockade is liable to condemnation. The cargo is also condemned, unless it is proved that at the time of the shipment of the goods the shipper neither knew nor could have known of the intention to break the blockade.

CHAPTER II   CONTRABAND OF WAR

Art. 22. The following articles may, without notice*,[1] be treated as contraband of war, under the name of absolute contraband:

(1)   Arms of all kinds, including arms for sporting purposes, and their distinctive component parts.

(2)   Projectiles, charges, and cartridges of all kinds, and their distinctive component parts.

(3)   Powder and explosives specially prepared for use in war.

---

[1]*In view of the difficulty of finding an exact equivalent in English for the expression 'de plein droit', it has been decided to translate it by the words 'without notice', which represent the meaning attached to it by the draftsman as appears from the General Report see p. 44.

(4)   Gun-mountings, limber boxes, limbers, military waggons, field forges, and their distinctive component parts.

(5)   Clothing and equipment of a distinctively military character.

(6)   All kinds of harness of a distinctively military character.

(7)   Saddle, draught, and pack animals suitable for use in war.

(8)   Articles of camp equipment, and their distinctive component parts.

(9)   Armour plates.

(10)   Warships, including boats, and their distinctive component parts of such a nature that they can only be used on a vessel of war.

(11)   Implements and apparatus designed exclusively for the manufacture of munitions of war, for the manufacture or repair of arms, or war material for use on land or sea.

Art. 23. Articles exclusively used for war may be added to the list of absolute contraband by a declaration, which must be notified.

Such notification must be addressed to the Governments of other Powers, or to their representatives accredited to the Power making the declaration. A notification made after the outbreak of hostilities is addressed only to neutral Powers.

Art. 24. The following articles, susceptible of use in war as well as for purposes of peace, may, without notice,[1] be treated as contraband of war, under the name of conditional contraband:

(1)   Foodstuffs.

(2)   Forage and grain, suitable for feeding animals.

(3)   Clothing, fabrics for clothing, and boots and shoes, suitable for use in war.

(4)   Gold and silver in coin or bullion; paper money.

(5)   Vehicles of all kinds available for use in war, and their component parts.

(6)   Vessels, craft, and boats of all kinds; floating docks, parts of docks and their component parts.

(7)   Railway material, both fixed and rolling-stock, and material for telegraphs, wireless telegraphs, and telephones.

(8)   Balloons and flying machines and their distinctive component parts, together with accessories and articles recognizable as intended for use in connection with balloons and flying machines.

(9)   Fuel; lubricants.

(10)   Powder and explosives not specially prepared for use in war.

(11)   Barbed wire and implements for fixing and cutting the same.

[1]*See note relative to Article 22.

   (12)   Horseshoes and shoeing materials.

   (13)   Harness and saddlery.

   (14)   Field glasses, telescopes, chronometers, and all kinds of nautical instruments.

Art. 25. Articles susceptive of use in war as well as for purposes of peace, other than those enumerated in Articles 22 and 24, may be added to the list of conditional contraband by a declaration, which must be notified in the manner provided for in the second paragraph of Article 23.

Art. 26. If a Power waives, so far as it is concerned, the right to treat as contraband of war an article comprised in any of the classes enumerated in Articles 22 and 24, such intention shall be announced by a declaration, which must be notified in the manner provided for in the second paragraph of Article 23.

Art. 27. Articles which are not susceptible of use in war may not be declared contraband of war.

Art. 28. The following may not be declared contraband of war:

   (1)   Raw cotton, wool, silk, jute, flax, hemp, and other raw materials of the textile industries, and yarns of the same.

   (2)   Oil seeds and nuts; copra.

   (3)   Rubber, resins, gums, and lacs; hops.

   (4)   Raw hides and horns, bones, and ivory.

   (5)   Natural and artificial manures, including nitrates and phosphates for agricultural purposes.

   (6)   Metallic ores.

   (7)   Earths, clays, lime, chalk, stone, including marble, bricks, slates, and tiles.

   (8)   Chinaware and glass.

   (9)   Paper and paper-making materials.

   (10)   Soap, paint and colours, including articles exclusively used in their manufacture, and varnish.

   (11)   Bleaching powder, soda ash, caustic soda, salt cake, ammonia, sulphate of ammonia, and sulphate of copper.

   (12)   Agricultural, mining, textile, and printing machinery.

   (13)   Precious and semi-precious stones, pearls, mother-of-pearl, and coral.

   (14)   Clocks and watches, other than chronometers.

   (15)   Fashion and fancy goods.

   (16)   Feathers of all kinds, hairs, and bristles.

   (17)   Articles of household furniture and decoration; office furniture and requisites.

Art. 29. Likewise the following may not be treated as contraband of war:

(1)   Articles serving exclusively to aid the sick and wounded. They can, however, in case of urgent military necessity and subject to the payment of compensation, be requisitioned, if their destination is that specified in Article 30.

(2)   Articles intended for the use of the vessel in which they are found, as well as those intended for the use of her crew and passengers during the voyage.

Art. 30. Absolute contraband is liable to capture if it is shown to be destined to territory belonging to or occupied by the enemy, or to the armed forces of the enemy. It is immaterial whether the carriage of the goods is direct or entails transhipment or a subsequent transport by land.

Art. 31. Proof of the destination specified in Article 30 is complete in the following cases:

(1)   When the goods are documented for discharge in an enemy port, or for delivery to the armed forces of the enemy.

(2)   When the vessel is to call at enemy ports only, or when she is to touch at an enemy port or meet the armed forces of the enemy before reaching the neutral port for which the goods in question are documented.

Art. 32. Where a vessel is carrying absolute contraband, her papers are conclusive proof as to the voyage on which she is engaged, unless she is found clearly out of the course indicated by her papers, and unable to give adequate reasons to justify such deviation.

Art. 33. Conditional contraband is liable to capture if it is shown to be destined for the use of the armed forces or of a government department of the enemy State, unless in this latter case the circumstances show that the goods cannot in fact be used for the purposes of the war in progress. This latter exception does not apply to a consignment coming under Article 24 (4).

Art. 34. The destination referred to in Article 33 is presumed to exist if the goods are consigned to enemy authorities, or to a contractor established in the enemy country who, as a matter of common knowledge, supplies articles of this kind to the enemy. A similar presumption arises if the goods are consigned to a fortified place belonging to the enemy, or other place serving as a base for the armed forces of the enemy. No such presumption, however, arises in the case of a merchant vessel bound for one of these places if it is sought to prove that she herself is contraband.

In cases where the above presumptions do not arise, the destination is presumed to be innocent.

The presumptions set up by this Article may be rebutted.

Art. 35. Conditional contraband is not liable to capture, except when found on board a vessel bound for territory belonging to or occupied by the enemy, or for the armed forces of the enemy, and when it is not to be discharged in an intervening neutral port.

The ship's papers are conclusive proof both as to the voyage on which the vessel is engaged and as to the port of discharge of the goods, unless she is found clearly out of the course indicated by her papers, and unable to give adequate reasons to justify such deviation.

Art. 36. Notwithstanding the provisions of Article 35, conditional contraband, if shown to have the destination referred to in Article 33, is liable to capture in cases where the enemy country has no seaboard.

Art. 37. A vessel carrying goods liable to capture as absolute or conditional contraband may be captured on the high seas or in the territorial waters of the belligerents throughout the whole of her voyage, even if she is to touch at a port of call before reaching the hostile destination.

Art. 38. A vessel may not be captured on the ground that she has carried contraband on a previous occasion if such carriage is in point of fact at an end.

Art. 39. Contraband goods are liable to condemnation.

Art. 40. A vessel carrying contraband may be condemned if the contraband, reckoned either by value, weight, volume, or freight, forms more than half the cargo.

Art. 41. If a vessel carrying contraband is released, she may be condemned to pay the costs and expenses incurred by the captor in respect of the proceedings in the national prize court and the custody of the ship and cargo during the proceedings.

Art. 42. Goods which belong to the owner of the contraband and are on board the same vessel are liable to condemnation.

Art. 43. If a vessel is encountered at sea while unaware of the outbreak of hostilities or of the declaration of contraband which applies to her cargo, the contraband cannot be condemned except on payment of compensation; the vessel herself and the remainder of the cargo are not liable to condemnation or to the costs and expenses referred to in Article 41. The same rule applies if the master, after becoming aware of the outbreak of hostilities, or of the declaration of contraband, has had no opportunity of discharging the contraband.

A vessel is deemed to be aware of the existence of a state of war, or of a declaration of contraband, if she left a neutral port subsequently to the notification to the Power to which such port belongs of the outbreak of hostilities or of the declaration of contraband respectively, provided that such notification was made in sufficient time. A vessel is also deemed to be aware of the existence of a state of war if she left an enemy port after the outbreak of hostilities.

Art. 44. A vessel which has been stopped on the ground that she is carrying contraband, and which is not liable to condemnation on account of the proportion of contraband on board, may, when the circumstances permit, be allowed to continue her voyage if the master is willing to hand over the contraband to the belligerent warship. The delivery of the contraband must be entered by the captor on the log-book of the vessel stopped, and the master must give the captor duly certified copies of all relevant papers.

The captor is at liberty to destroy the contraband that has been handed over to him under these conditions.

CHAPTER III   UNNEUTRAL SERVICE

Art. 45. A neutral vessel will be condemned and will, in a general way, receive the same treatment as a neutral vessel liable to condemnation for carriage of contraband:

(1)   If she is on a voyage especially undertaken with a view to the transport of individual passengers who are embodied in the armed forces of the enemy, or with a view to the transmission of intelligence in the interest of the enemy.

(2)   If, to the knowledge of either the owner, the charterer, or the master, she is transporting a military detachment of the enemy, or one or more persons who, in the course of the voyage, directly assist the operations of the enemy.

In the cases specified under the above heads, goods belonging to the owner of the vessel are likewise liable to condemnation.

The provisions of the present Article do not apply if the vessel is encountered at sea while unaware of the outbreak of hostilities, or if the master, after becoming aware of the outbreak of hostilities, has had no opportunity of disembarking the passengers. The vessel is deemed to be aware of the existence of a state of war if she left an enemy port subsequently to the outbreak of hostilities, or a neutral port subsequently to the notification of the outbreak of hostilities to the Power to which such port belongs, provided that such notification was made in sufficient time.

Art. 46. A neutral vessel will be condemned and, in a general way, receive the same treatment as would be applicable to her if she were an enemy merchant vessel:

(1)   if she takes a direct part in the hostilities;

(2)   if she is under the orders or control of an agent placed on board by the enemy Government;

(3) if she is in the exclusive employment of the enemy Government;

(4) if she is exclusively engaged at the time either in the transport of enemy troops or in the transmission of intelligence in the interest of the enemy.

In the cases covered by the present Article, goods belonging to the owner of the vessel are likewise liable to condemnation.

Art. 47. Any individual embodied in the armed forces of the enemy who is found on board a neutral merchant vessel, may be made a prisoner of war, even though there be no ground for the capture of the vessel

CHAPTER IV   DESTRUCTION OF NEUTRAL PRIZES

Art. 48. A neutral vessel which has been captured may not be destroyed by the captor; she must be taken into such port as is proper for the determination there of all questions concerning the validity of the capture.

Art. 49. As an exception, a neutral vessel which has been captured by a belligerent warship, and which would be liable to condemnation, may be destroyed if the observance of Article 48 would involve danger to the safety of the warship or to the success of the operations in which she is engaged at the time.

Art. 50. Before the vessel is destroyed all persons on board must be placed in safety, and all the ship's papers and other documents which the parties interested consider relevant for the purpose of deciding on the validity of the capture must be taken on board the warship.

Art. 51. A captor who has destroyed a neutral vessel must, prior to any decision respecting the validity of the prize, establish that he only acted in the face of an exceptional necessity of the nature contemplated in Article 49. If he fails to do this, he must compensate the parties interested and no examination shall be made of the question whether the capture was valid or not.

Art. 52. If the capture of a neutral vessel is subsequently held to be invalid, though the act of destruction has been held to have been justifiable, the captor must pay compensation to the parties interested, in place of the restitution to which they would have been entitled.

Art. 53. If neutral goods not liable to condemnation have been destroyed with the vessel, the owner of such goods is entitled to compensation.

Art. 54. The captor has the right to demand the handing over, or to proceed himself to the destruction of, any goods liable to condemnation found on board a vessel not herself liable to condemnation, provided that the circumstances are such as would, under Article 49, justify the destruction of a vessel herself liable to condemnation. The captor must enter the goods surrendered or destroyed in the logbook of the vessel stopped, and must obtain duly certified copies of all relevant papers. When the goods have been handed over or destroyed, and the formalities duly carried out, the master must be allowed to continue his voyage.

The provisions of Articles 51 and 52 respecting the obligations of a captor who has destroyed a neutral vessel are applicable.

CHAPTER V   TRANSFER TO A NEUTRAL FLAG

Art. 55. The transfer of an enemy vessel to a neutral flag, effected before the outbreak of hostilities, is valid, unless it is proved that such transfer was made in order to evade the consequences to which an enemy vessel, as such, is exposed. There is, however, a presumption, if the bill of sale is not on board a vessel which has lost her belligerent nationality less than sixty days before the outbreak of hostilities, that the transfer is void. This presumption may be rebutted.

Where the transfer was effected more than thirty days before the outbreak of hostilities, there is an absolute presumption that it is valid if it is unconditional, complete, and in conformity with the laws of the countries concerned, and if its effect is such that neither the control of, nor the profits arising from the employment of the vessel remain in the same hands as before the transfer. If, however, the vessel lost her belligerent nationality less than sixty days before the outbreak of hostilities and if the bill of sale is not on board, the capture of the vessel gives no right to damages.

Art. 56. The transfer of an enemy vessel to a neutral flag, effected after the outbreak of hostilities, is void unless it is proved that such transfer was not made in order to evade the consequences to which an enemy vessel, as such, is exposed.

There, however, is an absolute presumption that a transfer is void –

(1)   If the transfer has been made during a voyage or in a blockaded port.

(2)   If a right to repurchase or recover the vessel is reserved to the vendor.

(3)   If the requirements of the municipal law governing the right to fly the flag under which the vessel is sailing, have not been fulfilled.

CHAPTER VI   ENEMY CHARACTER

Art. 57. Subject to the provisions respecting transfer to another flag, the neutral or enemy character of a vessel is determined by the flag which she is entitled to fly.

The case where a neutral vessel is engaged in a trade which is closed in time of peace, remains outside the scope of, and is in no wise affected by, this rule.

Art. 58. The neutral or enemy character of goods found on board an enemy vessel is determined by the neutral or enemy character of the owner.

Art. 59. In the absence of proof of the neutral character of goods found on board an enemy vessel, they are presumed to be enemy goods.

Art. 60. Enemy goods on board an enemy vessel retain their enemy character until they reach their destination, notwithstanding any transfer effected after the outbreak of hostilities while the goods are being forwarded. If, however, prior to the capture, a former neutral owner exercises, on the bankruptcy of an existing enemy owner, a recognized legal right to recover the goods, they regain their neutral character.

CHAPTER VII   CONVOY

Art. 61. Neutral vessels under national convoy are exempt from search. The commander of a convoy gives, in writing, at the request of the commander of a belligerent warship, all information as to the character of the vessels and their cargoes, which could be obtained by search.

Art. 62. If the commander of the belligerent warship has reason to suspect that the confidence of the commander of the convoy has been abused, he communicates his suspicions to him. In such a case it is for the commander of the convoy alone to investigate the matter. He must record the result of such investigation in a report, of which a copy is handed to the officer of the warship. If, in the opinion of the commander of the convoy, the facts shown in the report justify the capture of one or more vessels, the protection of the convoy must be withdrawn from such vessels.

CHAPTER VIII   RESISTANCE TO SEARCH

Art. 63. Forcible resistance to the legitimate exercise of the right of stoppage, search, and capture, involves in all cases the condemnation of the vessel. The cargo is liable to the same treatment as the cargo of an enemy vessel. Goods belonging to the master or owner of the vessel are treated as enemy goods.

CHAPTER IX   COMPENSATION

Art. 64. If the capture of a vessel or of goods is not upheld by the prize court, or if the prize is released without any judgement being given, the parties interested have the right to compensation, unless there were good reasons for capturing the vessel or goods.

FINAL PROVISIONS

Art. 65. The provisions of the present Declaration must be treated as a whole, and cannot be separated.

Art. 66. The Signatory Powers undertake to insure the mutual observance of the rules contained in the present Declaration in any war in which all the belligerents are parties thereto. They will therefore issue the necessary instructions to their authorities and to their armed forces, and will take such measures as may be required in order to insure that it will be applied by their courts, and more particularly by their prize courts.

Art. 67. The present Declaration shall be ratified as soon as possible.

The ratifications shall be deposited in London. The first deposit of ratifications shall be recorded in a Protocol signed by the representatives of the Powers taking part therein, and by His Britannic Majesty's Principal Secretary of State for Foreign Affairs. The subsequent deposits of ratifications shall be made by means of a written notification addressed to the British Government, and accompanied by the instrument of ratification.

A duly certified copy of the Protocol relating to the first deposit of ratifications and of the notifications mentioned in the preceding paragraph as well as of the instruments of ratification which accompany them, shall be immediately sent by the British Government, through the diplomatic channel, to the Signatory Powers. The said Government shall, in the cases contemplated in the preceding paragraph, inform them at the same time of the date on which it received the notification.

Art. 68. The present Declaration shall take effect, in the case of the Powers which were parties to the first deposit of ratifications, sixty days after the date of the Protocol recording such deposit, and, in the case of the Powers which shall ratify subsequently, sixty days after the notification of their ratification shall have been received by the British Government.

Art. 69. In the event of one of the Signatory Powers wishing to denounce the present Declaration, such denunciation can only be made to take effect at the end of a period of twelve years, beginning sixty days after the first deposit of ratifications, and, after that time, at the end of successive periods of six years, of which the first will begin at the end of the period of twelve years. Such denunciation must be notified in writing, at least one year in advance, to the British Government, which shall inform all the other Powers.

It will only operate in respect of the denouncing Power.

Art. 70. The Powers represented at the London Naval Conference attach particular importance to the general recognition of the rules which they have adopted, and therefore express the hope that the Powers which were not represented there will accede to the present Declaration. They request the British Government to invite them to do so.

A Power which desires to accede shall notify its intention in writing to the British Government, and transmit simultaneously the act of accession, which will be deposited in the archives of the said Government. The said Government shall forthwith transmit to all the other Powers a duly certified copy of the notification, together with the act of accession, and communicate the date on which such notification was received. The accession takes effect sixty days after such date.

In respect of all matters concerning this Declaration, Acceding Powers shall be on the same footing as the Signatory Powers.

Art. 71. The present Declaration, which bears the date of 26 February 1909, may be signed in London up till 30 June 1909, by the Plenipotentiaries of the Powers represented at the Naval Conference.

In faith whereof the Plenipotentiaries have signed the present Declaration, and have thereto affixed their seals.

Done at London, the twenty-sixth day of February, one thousand nine hundred and nine, in a single original, which shall remain deposited in the archives of the British Government, and of which duly certified copies shall be sent through the diplomatic channel to the Powers represented at the Naval Conference.

[Here follow signatures]

* * *

22. Naval Prize Law Committee, Interim Report

[ADM 116/1231A]   21 December 1909

Sir, In pursuance of your instructions, we have commenced the consideration of the legislation and of the alterations in the Prize Court Rules, which will be rendered necessary by the Convention for the establishment of an International Prize Court at The Hague and by the Declaration of London.

2.   Copies of a Bill have been laid before us which, we are informed, was prepared some years ago to consolidate and amend the enactments relating to naval prize of war. We think that it is desirable that the legislation required in connection with the International Prize Court should form part of a general revision of the existing Statutes concerning Prize Courts, and for this purpose we have been placed in communication with the Parliamentary Counsel in order that a fresh

draft may be prepared of the Naval Prize Bill. This Interim Report is presented on certain points as to which we think further instructions should be given to us, before the final text of a Bill on the above lines is prepared.

3.   We assume it to be intended that the legislation should be enacted by the Imperial Parliament alone, and that it should operate throughout the British Empire, including the self-governing dominions. At present, jurisdiction in matters of prize is conferred upon Courts of Justice in the Colonies by virtue of Imperial legislation, and therefore it would appear natural that any alteration or extension of that jurisdiction should be effected by an Imperial Act. It is a question, however, on which His Majesty's Government may think it expedient to communicate with the self-governing Dominions without delay.

4.   At present, outside the United Kingdom, prize jurisdiction is exercisable by Courts possessing Admiralty jurisdiction under 'The Colonial Courts of Admiralty Act, 1890.' That Act abolished the Vice-Admiralty Courts, except in New South Wales, Victoria, St. Helena, and British Honduras, in which Colonies the coming into operation of the Act was, and is still, delayed. In view of the importance of simplifying as far as possible the machinery of the Prize Courts, we think it very desirable that these Vice-Admiralty Courts should be abolished, and we should be glad to receive instructions as to whether there is any objection to this being done.

5.   Article 6 of the Convention for the establishment of the International Prize Court prevents there being more than one appeal to a National Court in a prize proceeding where the International Court has jurisdiction in accordance with Article 3 of the Convention. By virtue of section 5 of 'The Colonial Courts of Admiralty Act, 1890,' there can be an intermediate local appeal between the Prize Court of First Instance, and the ultimate appeal to His Majesty in Council. We are strongly of opinion that there should be one Supreme National Prize Court, to which alone all appeals should lie, and that the jurisdiction of the Judicial Committee of the Privy Council for this purpose should be maintained. This will necessitate the elimination of any local appeal. We observe that the draft of the Naval Prize Bill prepared in 1906 contained a provision to this effect, and, unless instructed to the contrary, we shall proceed on these lines.

6.   The introduction of a system under which an appeal will lie from His Majesty in Council to the International Court at The Hague renders it, in our opinion, desirable that, so far as concerns jurisdiction in Prize cases, the constitution of the Judicial Committee of the Privy Council should be altered.

The judgments of the Privy Council are recommendations to His Majesty, and the decisions, when approved, become the decisions of His Majesty, and are embodied in an Order of His Majesty in Council. We think it would be derogatory to the Crown that an appeal should lie from decisions which in form are the decisions of the Sovereign, or that orders should be made upon His Majesty by a foreign Court for the transmission of papers or for the payment of compensation.

We therefore think it is desirable that in all matters relating to prize the Judicial Committee of the Privy Council should be constituted as a Court, and we recommend that when exercising these functions it should be termed the Supreme Prize Court.

7. Article 64 of the Declaration of London, and Article 8 of the Prize Court Convention, render it certain that from time to time orders for the payment of compensation (or, as it is termed under the English practice, 'costs and damages') to the owners of captured ships or goods will be made by a Prize Court. The phraseology of the existing rules draws a distinction between the captors and the Crown, but the practice which these rules embody dates, to a large extent, from Napoleonic times, and will, in our opinion, require far-reaching revision.

8. In the days when privateering was one of the usual modes of conducting naval warfare, a very real distinction existed between the liability of the captors to pay damages, and the liability of the Crown. Since 1856 this distinction has no longer existed, and all captures will (with possible rare exceptions, in the case of unauthorised captures by non-commissioned ships) in future be effected by naval officers acting under the authority of the Sovereign. We are informed that, even before the Declaration of Paris, it was the custom of the Crown to assume liability for damages ordered to be paid in the case of captures effected by naval officers, despite the fact that it was also the custom of the Crown to make a grant which deprived it of all interest in ships or goods condemned as prize.

9. In view of the right conferred upon the International Prize Court to assess the compensation which it may find to be due in respect of invalid captures, and of the obligation upon His Majesty's Government to carry out the orders of that Court, we feel some doubt whether it will not be necessary for the Crown to accept the responsibility of the captors in all cases, except in the case of unauthorised captures. Even if such responsibility were accepted, it would not prevent, as between the Crown and the actual captors, disciplinary powers being exercised against naval officers who went beyond their instructions.

10. We feel that this question requires careful consideration by His Majesty's Government. Matters must clearly be taken into account

which do not fall within the scope of those committed to our consideration, and upon which we do not therefore feel it open to us to make suggestions.

11.   Another circumstance, which may require to be borne in mind in connection with this question, is the possible creation of Colonial navies, as this may affect the question as to which Government is to bear the ultimate responsibility for the acts of the officers of such squadrons.

12.   If responsibility for the acts of captors were accepted in all cases, we do not think it would be necessary that any machinery should be inserted in the Act for enforcing the rights of claimants, under the orders of the Court, by Petition of Right or otherwise. Payment would follow as a matter of course, upon the making of an order by the Court for the payment of compensation.

13.   The preparation of a Bill and of a revised set of Prize Rules is at present being taken in hand, but we should be glad, before submitting our final report, with the final text of the Bill and of the Rules, to receive further instructions on the proposals contained in this report.

14.   We understand that the Law Officers of the Crown are considering whether the Declaration of London effects an alteration of the law without further statutory sanction, and the draft Bill may require reconsideration after their opinion is obtained.

Gorell, H. Bertram Cox, A.H.
Dennis, W. Graham Greene, C.J.B.
Hurst, Charles Neish, E.S. Roscoe
   Edward Lt. Gibbon, *Secretary*

* * *

23.   *Memorandum as to Prizes Captured by Colonial Navies*

[ADM 116/1231A]   April 1910

The Conference dealing with Colonial Navies has not yet arrived at any definite recommendation as to the position of these Navies in time of war, but it may be assumed that in time of war they will be placed by the Colonial Government under the control of the British Admiral and will in fact form an integral part of the British Fleet, subject to the Naval Discipline Act and the Admiralty Instructions. In the alternative it is intended that they should cease to be British ships of war and should have no belligerent rights as such. It is suggested in the Colonial Office letter of February 14th that the Colonial Governments might be asked in certain cases to assume responsibility for compensation payable in respect of invalid seizures made by ships of the Colonial Navy. The following objections seem to occur with regard to this proposal:

1)   It is necessarily limited to cases where the ships either transgress the standing instructions, or where the capture is found invalid by the Hague tribunal. The former question would give rise to very difficult disputes which it might be very undesirable to raise. Further, it would be impossible to make the Colonial Government liable in a case where His Majesty's Government thinks it desirable to assume the liability to compensation and to pay it at once without the judgment of a Court, as was done in the Boer War, and as might be done in many cases where there was clearly an unjustifiable seizure. This compensation would probably be paid at the earliest possible moment in order to maintain friendly relations with neutrals. The suggestion that it is fair that the Colonies should bear these expenses is a good deal weakened if the ships are to be placed under Admiralty control.

2)   The liability to compensation would necessarily involve the right of the Colonial Government to dispose of the value of prizes taken. This seems to raise two serious difficulties – (a) His Majesty's Government must have an absolutely unfettered right of releasing prizes at any stage of the proceedings, whether or not the capture appears to be unjustifiable. To exercise this right to the detriment of the Colonial Government might be a source of continual friction. (b) Any such arrangement with a Colonial Government necessarily involves placing it in the power of the Colonial Government to regulate the distribution of proceeds of prize among the officers and men of their ships. It is not at all certain that the present system of dividing the whole of the proceeds of prize among officers and men will be maintained in the future: at all events, His Majesty's Government must be absolutely free to alter it if they think fit, and it would also be very undesirable that the officers and men in the Colonial ships of war should be in any different position in respect of profiting from prizes from the officers and men of other ships of the Navy.

3)   Generally speaking the discussions which have taken place at the meetings of the Colonial Navies Conference point to the conclusion that the fewer subjects of discussion and possible friction that exist between the Home Government and the Governments of the Dominions the better, and on that ground it may be desirable not to raise any question as to prizes at all, but to assume that as the Colonial ships will be brought into the Royal Navy for all purposes in case of war they will be subject to the same regulations as other ships of the Navy, and that proceeds of prize, or the prize bounty or whatever else is divisible, will be divisible among

them in exactly the same way as it is among other officers and men of the Navy and, subject to that, the benefit of the prize will go to the Imperial Government or as it directs, the Imperial Government taking all the liability in cases of invalid captures. Having regard to the importance of keeping the whole region of prize procedure and jurisdiction as an Imperial concern it is suggested that this may be the wiser course to pursue. It is even possible that the decision of the Colonial Prize Courts might be influenced by the fact that the Colonial Exchequer might be benefited by condemnations. If in time of war the question was raised by the Colonial Governments the matter might then be considered and some financial adjustment might possibly be made, but it is suggested that for the present it is advisable to leave it alone.

* * *

24.   Papers on the Ratification of the Declaration of London[1]

Sir Charles Ottley to Mr McKenna

[ADM 116/1236]   17 February 1911

Dear Mr McKenna, The attached rather voluminous paper consists of two parts – the first being an extremely interesting investigation conducted by Captain Hankey upon an aspect of the Declaration of London which has been brought into prominence during our recent enquiries here; and the second being some remarks of my own on Captain Hankey's suggestions. You will notice that, valuable as those suggestions are, they are in my opinion impracticable in the form which he presents them. But, on the other hand, (as I have endeavoured to show) the objects which he seeks to attain can be achieved by a less violent and drastic up-rooting of existing international conventions with equal efficacy and at a [crossed out] less risk of involving this country in hostilities with powerful neutrals.

The subject however is of such importance that I venture to send the two papers (Captain Hankey's suggestions and my own remarks thereon) for your confidential use, in case you, or any of the naval members of the Board, or the DNI may think the matter needs more minute and official investigation.

---

[1]Captain (later Colonel) Hankey's paper has not been copied because Sir Charles Ottley provides a précis, and Hankey himself reviews the argument in later papers written at a time when he had more influence on affairs.

With may apologies for troubling you with so lengthy a document, Believe me, Yours very sincerely, C.L. Ottley

Remarks by Sir Charles Ottley on Captain Hankey's paper (attached herewith)
Secret

The question raised by Captain Hankey is interesting.

Investigations conducted by the Defence Committee, subsequent to the London Conference, showed that one of the most effectual means by which this country could strike at Germany in an Anglo-German War would be by putting economic pressure upon the masses of the German people through the seizure of German oversea supplies.

In view of British naval preponderance, and of the highly disadvantageous geographical situation of her enemy, there seems fair ground for the prediction that, in all probability, very shortly after the outbreak of war the German mercantile flag will be driven from the seas.

As soon as that condition has been established, Germany will have to rely thenceforward and until the war comes to an end, upon neutral vessels for her oversea supplies of commodities of all sorts.

The problem with which we shall then be confronted will be, how far it is possible to strangle Germany's *neutral* sources of oversea supply.

There are but two ways by which such neutral supplies can be interfered with, viz:

1. By blockading the German Coast,
2. By so wide an extension of the definition of absolute contraband as to bring within that definition all commodities essentially necessary to feed the complex industrial system of the German Empire and to sustain her rather dense industrial population. If we are prepared to thus stretch the doctrine of contraband, every neutral ship consigned to a German port will be liable to seizure by our cruisers whenever met with.

The Admiralty have recently informed the Defence Committee that in a war with Germany it would be impracticable for a British fleet to operate in the Baltic. In other words, whereas economic pressure could be very effectually brought to bear on the North Sea Coasts of Germany through the agency of a blockade, a blockade of the Baltic seaports of Germany is out of the question. Goods entering the Baltic in German bottoms would of course be liable to capture, but goods consigned to German Baltic ports in neutral bottoms could not be seized unless they were of a contraband nature. Moreover, however effective our blockade of the mouth of the Elbe, goods in neutral bottoms could still find their way to Hamburg, via the Kiel Canal, so long as we were unable to also blockade the port of Kiel.

This being the situation laid down by the Admiralty, Captain Hankey urges that there still remains another means by which, without blockading the Baltic ports of Germany, neutral vessels could be effectually denied access to those ports.

The means he suggests we might employ would be by a wholesale proclamation placing all the staple commodities and raw materials usually imported by Germany under a common definition of *absolute* contraband, and by insisting that such commodities and raw materials were liable to seizure in neutral ships under the doctrine of continuous voyage, even if consigned to neutral ports in the Baltic.

Such is Captain Hankey's remedy for the difficulty with which we shall undeniably be confronted owing to our inability to blockade the German Baltic seaports.

As a first step towards carrying out this drastic policy, he recommends the rejection of the Declaration of London, since that Declaration places many important raw materials and commodities on the 'free list' (so that they can never be captured in neutral bottoms) and consigns nine-tenths of all remaining commodities to the list of conditional contraband, only liable to capture in neutral ships if destined for the use of the *armed forces of the enemy*. This is of course the existing British Doctrine, but is now for the first time placed in an International Code of Maritime Law.

The attitude which Captain Hankey suggests that Great Britain might take up towards neutrals in some future Anglo-German War would be very similar to that which she adopted towards neutrals during the Napoleonic epoch and which in the sequel involved us in the American War of 1812.

Captain Hankey fully recognises this. He admits that such an attitude on our part could *not* be announced on the outbreak of war without the gravest risk of bringing the entire neutral world into belligerency against us. Powerful neutrals might with justice urge that our action in putting practically every kind of merchandise into the category of absolute contraband was tantamount not merely to a rejection of the Declaration of London, but to a destruction of the whole edifice of international maritime law built up since the days of the Armed Neutrality and consecrated by the Declaration of Paris in 1856.

For, if *all* commodities destined for the enemy are liable to seizure in neutral ships, the article of the Declaration of Paris which stipulates, 'that the Neutral Flag covers the goods except *contraband* of war', becomes a dead letter; and all the neutral immunities for which civilised nations have struggled during the last century would be brought into question once more. Captain Hankey is not unaware of this objection but – he urges – if we simply hold back these extreme Contraband Proclamations for a few weeks while the command of the sea is in dispute, not much loss will accrue to our warlike operations. And, sooner or later he submits – we may confidently count on establishing complete mastery over the German Fleet in the North Sea.

He looks forward to some latter-day Trafalgar or Western Battle of the Sea of Japan which shall bring out before the eyes of all Europe the incontestable superiority of the British Fleet over that of Germany. And, once that condition is established Great Britain will be in a position of such maritime preponderance and secure triumph that she will be able to afford to run the risk of neutral indignation, and will be prepared to issue her tremendous Contraband Proclamations in defiance of the whole neutral world.

In transmitting this interesting suggestion for consideration, I am bound to add that, in my opinion Captain Hankey has not sufficiently weighed the political and international difficulties which stand in the way.

The relegation of peaceful commodities notoriously intended for the use of the civil population, to the category of absolute contraband, not only violates the Declaration of Paris, but runs counter to the policy to which we have ourselves consistently adhered for the last hundred years, and it is I fear quite hopeless to imagine that any British Government could be induced to contemplate a reversal of that policy.

We have, as neutrals, too often and too recently appealed to the idea of the inviolability of the neutral flag as a fundamental principle of international law, when our own shipping has been unjustifiably interfered with by a belligerent, to render it possible for us to make so sudden and violent a volte-face as Captain Hankey's suggestion implies.

But – and this is indeed the essence of the question – if we assume that, after winning a victory a[t] sea so final and crushing in its effects as to not merely bring our enemy to his knees, but to overawe an entire world of powerful neutrals and terrorize them so completely that they would be ready to acquiesce in the tremendous Contraband Decrees to which Captain Hankey suggests we might resort then, surely, it is clear that the mere fact, that, under very [?] conditions in peace time perhaps three or four years before[,] Great Britain had become a party to the Declaration of London, would not suffice to stir neutral powers to the pitch of taking up arms in support of their rights.

To declare all commodities without distinction to be contraband of war is a violation, not of the Declaration of London so much as of the

Declaration of Paris; the mere fact that we had not signed the former Declaration would be no palliative of our action in tearing up the latter. Captain Hankey's proposed Contraband Decrees unquestionably violate the whole principle of the Declaration of Paris. By that Declaration we are already practically, if not juridically bound. Surely a British Government, face to face with some tremendous crisis in a naval war on the grand scale – if they felt themselves so strong vis-à-vis the neutral world that they would be prepared to tear up the Declaration of Paris – would not boggle over the additional stigma implied in a technical violation of the Declaration of London, which latter is of course merely a corollary to the Declaration of Paris.

In view of these considerations I am inclined to think that motives of prudence and national self-interest indicate the following policy as that which we ought now to adopt, rather than the more violent measures suggested by Captain Hankey.

There appears no reason to reject the Declaration of London in order to obtain the liberty of action which Captain Hankey desires, for – as will be shown – that liberty of action can be equally obtained without any repudiation of the benefits derivable from the Declaration.

On the contrary in the event of an Anglo-German War we ought in *our own interests* loyally and consistently to abide by the terms of the Declaration of Paris and London so long as the issue of the naval operations hung in the balance. Under those two instruments we should be able to capture all the enemy's merchant ships, to blockade his coasts and to seize all contraband going to his ports. If the rigours of our grip on neutral commerce due to the vigorous exercise of our rights of blockade and capture brought about disputes with powerful neutrals, the existence of the International Prize Court would constitute a safeguard against a dangerous explosion of public opinion in the neutral countries. It cannot be too plainly pointed out that until fortune had [sic] declared unmistakably in our favour at sea, it would be sheer madness to risk the hostility of powerful neutrals by wholesale violations of the neutral flag, such as would be implied in Captain Hankey's Extreme Contraband proposals. Those proposals quite transcend in rigour the British Orders-in-Council issued in the Napoleonic Wars, and whereas the Orders-in-Council were admittedly a reply to Napoleon's more outrageous Berlin and Milan Decrees, it does not appear that we should have any such excuse for the action proposed in the circumstances contemplated by Captain Hankey.

But, when once our command of the sea had been effectively established, it would be for the consideration of the Board of Admiralty if they felt themselves strong enough at sea, and if – on a careful assessment of all the considerations of the moment – they considered it to the public interest to do so – to move His Majesty's Government to make an appeal in the following sense to the Neutral Maritime Powers –

A British proclamation might be issued pointing out that the British Government had hitherto throughout the war in progress loyally and consistently adhered to the stipulations of the Declarations of London and Paris. The success of the British arms at sea had been so far effective that the enemy's fleets had been destroyed or driven into port and his mercantile flag had disappeared from the seas. A position had therefore been reached when no further means were at His Majesty's Government's disposal to put further pressure upon the enemy unless it were by seizing all commodities of every kind in neutral ships destined for the German ports. The proclamation might go on to declare that, since it was plainly in the interests not merely of the two belligerents but of civilisation at large that the war should be brought to a close as soon as possible, they had now reluctantly come to the conclusion that it had become incumbent upon them to abrogate for the time being the Articles of the Declaration of Paris and London dealing with Contraband and Continuous Voyage. It would be for the consideration of the British Government of the day to add the further announcement of their wish to mitigate the rigours of this policy towards neutral shipping, by the payment of compensation for all cargoes of a non-contraband character destined for the enemy ports. But, (whether with or without this mitigation of the severity of our attack upon the neutrals), from the date of that Proclamation and until the close of the war no neutral vessels would be permitted to carry commodities of any kind to any German destination, either directly, or for transhipment after discharge at any neighbouring neutral port.

It seems that action of this kind would be open to us at any time whether we had signed the Declaration of London or not. As regards this proposal to pay compensation for non-contraband neutral cargoes, although not essential, such a measure would I believe be politic and would rob the neutrals of a very large part of their grounds for complaint. Of course the compensation would presumably be re-imbursed to the British Exchequer if a war indemnity could be exacted in the terms of peace.

* * *

25.   The Navy's Warning Against the Declaration of London

[ADM 116/1236]   2 Westminster Palace Gardens,
                                                            London, S.W.
                                                            3 July 1911

THE IMPERIAL MARITIME LEAGUE
*Founded to Secure the Maintenance of British Sea-Power, 27 January
1908*

The following is the text of a letter now signed by *one hundred and
thirty-eight Admirals*, whose names are appended. This letter, with the
names of the signatories, has been forwarded by the Imperial Maritime
League to the Prime Minister and to the Secretary of state for Foreign
Affairs, and to every Member of both Houses of Parliament, and has
been published in the press.
To the Right Honourable
    The Prime Minister,
        10, Downing Street, S.W.   29th May, 1911

THE DECLARATION OF LONDON

Sir,
    We, the Undersigned, venture to appeal with the utmost respect to
His Majesty's Government to consider the reasons stated in this letter
which render it, in our opinion, urgently necessary, for the preservation
of the food of this people during war, that the Declaration of London
should be repudiated.
    These reasons are:

1.   That by far the larger proportion of the food consumed by the
population of the United Kingdom is derived from over-sea sources
and that any serious interruption of its safe transit on the high seas is
likely, if not certain, *to create at once famine prices in this country,*
owing to the rise in rates, freightage, and insurance, which would be
the inevitable and immediate sequel. In this connection we would
recall the fact that, in the Memorandum recently published by the
Secretary of State for War, the present First Sea Lord gave public
warning of the gravest character that the danger of such interruption
exists.
2.   That, as shown by the current number of the Navy List, the total
number of cruisers belonging to the Royal Navy, capable of acting as
commerce protectors, which are stationed for the defence of the trade

routes in all the non-European waters of the world is but 27 (against the far larger number similarly stationed a hundred years ago). Of these 27, three are at the Cape, five in the East Indies, six in Chinese waters, nine in the South Pacific for the defence of vessels leaving or approaching ports in the many thousand miles of coast line of Australia and New Zealand, three (attached to the Fourth Cruiser Squadron) in North American waters and the West Indies, and one, with a roving commission, cruises off the West Coast of South Africa and the East Coast of South America.

3.   That, in view of the immense areas of ocean which this disposition leaves *practically devoid of any naval protection*, it is clear that any sudden and unexpected outbreak of hostilities would find the greater part of our sea-borne trade defenceless against any attacking force existing in its neighbourhood.

4.   That the presence of such attacking force, in the unhappy event of a war with a great maritime Power, appears now to be assured by the Convention signed on behalf of England in November, 1909, which leaves it open to any foreign power to convert its merchantmen into men-of-war (whenever it chooses to begin hostilities) without previous notification of the vessels to be so employed.

5.   That this state of affairs manifestly renders it impossible to continue to rely on the British Mercantile Marine as the means of maintaining that uninterrupted supply of foodstuffs during war which is essential if famine prices are not to prevail in these islands.

6.   That therefore *our dependence on the neutral Flag is immeasurably increased*, the importance of leaving food free to reach our ports in the ships of friendly countries having now become matter of paramount national necessity.

7.   That this freedom of food is *in substance and effect entirely destroyed by Article 34 of the Declaration of London*, which makes all foodstuffs conditional contraband (with the two exceptions of nuts and hops), and imposes liability to capture on neutral vessels carrying food to any port of the United Kingdom serving as a base for armed forces.

8.   That since all such ports are in railway communication with armed forces, and most of them may actually have, during war, armed forces of some kind stationed for their protection, it follows that all our ports will become construable as serving as bases for those armed forces, and therefore that all neutral ships carrying food, or any other conditional contraband to them, will become capturable.

9.   That this construction will absolutely certainly be placed upon Article 34, since the effective agent who will have to decide the point

will be the hostile captain of a hostile cruiser or converted merchant-man.

10.   That this officer will have the strongest motive to make the seizure, and no motive at all in any other direction, since the easiest road to victory over this country is by inflicting starvation upon its people.

11.   That the fact that the owners of the captured neutral ships and cargoes may have right of appeal to an International Court on the Continent, and may possibly be awarded compensation at a later date by that Court, will afford no consolation at all to the famished population of Britain.

12.   That the argument is vain which has been used in defence or palliation of this Article 34, namely, the argument that neutral vessels carrying conditional contraband for our service may acquire immunity from capture during their long passage over the high seas by means of bogus consignments to neutral continental ports, and that, when they have thus reached the area of British naval protection in the narrow seas, they may then be convoyed from those neutral continental ports to our own shores.

13.   That this argument is futile in the case of an attack on Britain by Germany, because it assumes the acquiescence of the greatest military power in the world in a transparent evasion of the terms of the Agreement which that Power (in common with this country and with the other parties to the Declaration of London) will have signed, and in an international deception calculated to prevent its victory in the war in which it is engaged.

14.   That there is nothing in the modern history of Germany to justify any expectation of such acquiescence, but on the contrary much to suggest the probability of its refusal.

15.   That the habitual flow of trade is well known, and that diversion of that habitual flow, such as would be occasioned by the consignment of great quantities of foodstuffs, or other conditional contraband, intended for consumption here, to ports in such countries as France, Belgium, Holland, or Denmark, would be immediately noted and its real object perceived.

16.   That in these circumstances, Germany would naturally instruct at once all vessels acting as her cruisers in any part of the world to seize all neutral merchantmen carrying cargoes of such suspicious destination.

17.   That she would also most certainly employ her immense military power by way of threat and pressure to deter the neutral countries named from thus frustrating the success of her plan of campaign.

18.   That for all these reasons, no reliance whatever can be placed upon this suggested method of escaping the inevitable effects of Article 34 of the Declaration of London, if that Declaration be ratified.

19.   That the list of articles immune from capture which is comprised in Article 28 does not include any foodstuffs except the two already mentioned, namely, nuts and hops, which are insufficient in themselves for the nutriment of our people, and that, therefore, the free list does not affect the one supreme vital point of our food supply during war.

20.   That the argument that the immediate avenues of approach to our shores cannot be blockaded is wholly inapplicable to this point, on which the life of our population will depend in war, because what we have to fear is the inevitable effect on prices here of interference with shipping on the high seas.

21.   That, if the Declaration be ratified, nothing short of the purchase by the Home Government of all food in the country and its subsequent sale at fixed rates could palliate that effect, and even this measure could not prevent immense suffering if the war continued, since the food supply in the United Kingdom is at all times very limited.

22.   That Article 35 differentiates between Island States such as Britain, Australia, and New Zealand, and continental States, such as Germany, to the extreme disadvantage of the former, and the extreme advantage of the latter. It imposes, as already shown, liability to capture, on food and other conditional contraband on its way to Island ports, but gives immunity from such capture to like cargoes on their way to a belligerent via any neutral Continental ports. Under this article, foodstuffs and many other goods of the highest utility, consigned to the naval and military authorities of a Continental enemy of this country's, could pass without arrest through a British Fleet.

23.   That these various disadvantages which we should incur as Belligerents enormously outweigh any possible advantage which can be alleged as likely to accrue to us as neutrals.

24.   That such alleged advantage is certainly to a large extent illusory, since under Article 49 we agree in advance (if the Declaration be ratified) to the sinking of any neutral British merchantmen (held by the cruisers arresting them to be liable to capture) whenever the cruiser captain chooses to affirm that to send them into port would involve danger to the success of his operations.

25.   That since under modern conditions, vessels of war do not habitually carry more than the number of men required to work and to fight the ship, and since to part with a prize crew would always cripple efficiency and therefore involve peril to the success of subsequent

operations, this article practically authorises the destruction of neutral merchantmen at the discretion of their captors.

We are, Sir,
Your obedient servants, signed: [signatures not copied]

* * *

26. *Naval Prize Court Procedure*

Proposed new reference to Naval Prize Law Committee as reconstituted

[ADM 116/1231A]   27 November 1912

MISSION AND MINUTES

The failure to pass the Naval Prize Law Bill renders it necessary to consider the action to be taken to effect the revision of the procedure in the Prize Courts, which was included in the Bill. The legal advisers of the Public Departments concerned are agreed that a revision is necessary and this can only be carried out by rescinding certain parts of the existing Prize Act, a short bill being passed for this purpose. Lord Gorell was Chairman of the Committee which drafted the Naval Prize Bill and he was also engaged in the drafting of the revised rules of Court, but his state of health renders it out of the question that he should be called upon to undertake any work at present and he is going to spend the next six months abroad. In the circumstances the Treasury Solicitor has consulted Mr B.C. Aspinall, KC, who has previous knowledge of this matter, and he is willing gratuitously to act as Chairman of the Committee for the purpose indicated. It is proposed, therefore, that the Committee be reconstituted, with Mr Aspinall as Chairman in place of Lord Gorell, with an instruction to prepare a new set of rules of Court together with a short Bill which might be passed in an emergency, or when possible. Sir E. Grey concurs in such a Bill being prepared and proceeded with.

It is proposed at the same time to send an official letter of thanks to Lord Gorell for his services as Chairman of the former Committee expressing regret at his illness.

Admiralty Permanent Secretary [Signature indecipherable]

* * *

27. Handbook for Boarding Officers and Prize Officers in War Time[1]

[ADM 186/11]

I. POWERS OF OFFICER IN COMMAND OF HM SHIPS

In time of war the Officer in Command of any of HM Ships of War (including any vessel, boat, &c., for the time being in the service of His Majesty) may cause any private vessel – except vessels in neutral territorial waters and neutral merchant vessels under convoy of a warship of their own nationality – to be *visited* and, if necessary, *searched* with a view to ascertaining whether she is liable to *detention*. (See Section II.)

Should circumstances not admit of every vessel sighted being visited, the OC will, in the absence of more definite instructions, cause those vessels to be visited which he suspects of coming within the category of Section II.

Movements of suspicious vessels will, as far as possible, be communicated by the Admiralty to H.M. Ships concerned in Home Waters, and by Intelligence Centres to H.M. Ships concerned on Foreign Stations. (*See* N.I.D. 940 of September 1913, 'Intelligence arrangements at Ports abroad.')

Every care is to be taken not to subject the commerce of Great Britain or her allies, or of neutral States, to vexatious interference.

The steps necessary for detaining vessels in British, Indian, or Colonial *ports* will, as a general rule, be taken by the Customs or other local port authorities, the intervention of naval or military force being only necessary in the event of force being required to ensure compliance with the directions of the local authorities.

II. VESSELS LIABLE TO DETENTION*

* As the information in this section is summarised, the O.C. should consult the Naval Prize Manual for further details before approving the detention of a vessel. [8, 9]

The following vessels are liable to detention, subject to the explanations and exceptions here given. (For exceptions see Section III.)

---

[1]*Note by editor.* – References in the margin (placed in square brackets [ ] in this transcript) are to Articles in the Naval Prize Manual, 1914, and the following abbreviations in the text appear throughout the book: OC means any officer who, for the time being, is in command of any of HM ships; NPM means Naval Prize Manual (1914 edition).

1)   *Any enemy vessel* irrespective of destination or cargo. [12-18]

Under this heading would come, in addition to vessels flying the enemy flag, enemy vessels that have been transferred to another flag for the specific purpose of escaping the risk of capture as an enemy vessel (see Section V); a vessel sailing under the pass of an enemy State (except British or allied vessels granted passes under the 'Days of Grace' Convention, see p. 65, NPM); and vessels acting as specified in clause 4 (d) to (g) below.

Enemy vessels encountered at sea, before they are aware of the outbreak of war, should be detained.

2)   *Any British vessel or vessel of an ally trading with or acting in the service of the enemy without a licence.* [19-25]

'Trading' includes any intercourse with the enemy not necessitated by stress of weather or other like cause.

'Acting in the service of the enemy' includes carrying enemy despatches (not carried as postal correspondence) or persons in the naval or military service of the enemy.

3)   *Any neutral vessel which is*: [6-30];

   1)   *herself contraband*, [43-45]

   i.e., if she can be shown to be destined for the use of the enemy's army, navy, or Government departments, but not otherwise. *or*

   2)   *carrying contraband.* (See Section VI.) [31-42]

Contraband only includes articles having belligerent destination and purpose.

As a guide, the list included in the 'Declaration of London (1909)' is given in Section VI, but definite lists will be issued on the outbreak of war, *or*

   3)   *Rendering un-neutral service* [43–46]

   i.e., if she is on a voyage specially undertaken with a view to the transport of individual passengers who are embodied in the armed forces of the enemy, or with a view to the transmission of intelligence in the interests of the enemy;

   or if, to the knowledge of either the owner, the charterer, or the master, she is transporting a military detachment of the enemy, or one or more persons who in the course of the voyage directly assist the operations of the enemy;

   or if she is acting in any of the ways specified in clause 4 (d) to (g) of this section.

   If a neutral vessel is carrying 'enemy despatches' (that is to say, official communications between officers and officials in the service of the enemy not carried as postal correspondence), they must be handed over to the Visiting Officer, and the vessel may then be allowed to proceed. If the master refuses to hand them over, the vessel should be detained. [23, 46] *or*

4)   *engaged in breach of blockade* (See Section VII)

A vessel must not be detained for breach of blockade –

1)   except within the area of operations of the blockading force; but she is liable to capture so long as she is pursued by any ship of the blockading force, and

2)   unless she can be presumed to have known of the existence of the blockade. This must be ascertained by enquiry on board.

4)   *Any vessel, irrespective of nationality, destination, or cargo, which* [9, 33, 44]:

1)   *forcibly resists visit or search, or*

2)   *sails under enemy convoy, or*

3)   *produces false or no ship's papers, or if papers are in any way deficient or irregular.*

If papers produced are inconsistent with each other or with statements of the master, the ship should be detained. NID 883 of February 1912 gives specimen papers carried by vessels of the principal nations. (See also Section XXVI.) *or*

4)   *takes a direct part in hostilities, or*

5)   *is under the orders or control of an agent appointed by the enemy Government, or*

6)   *is in the exclusive employment of the enemy Government, or*

7)   *is exclusively engaged at the time either in the transport of enemy troops or in the transmission of intelligence in the interest of the enemy.*

III.   VESSELS EXEMPT FROM DETENTION

The following vessels are in general exempt from detention provided they have taken no part whatever in hostilities [10]:

(They can at any time be visited and, *if desirable, searched,* to ensure that they are entitled to exemption. *Public* enemy ships cannot be searched.)

a.   *Ships protected by a British licence*

For one form of licence, see Form No. 15, Appendix. To claim exemption, a ship must strictly conform to the terms of licence.

b.   *Hospital ships*

A belligerent may restrict the movements of such ships and in other ways exercise control over them. For international convention dealing with hospital ships, sick bays, and the sick and wounded, see p. 66, NPM.

c. *Enemy vessels*:

1. *if temporarily protected as mail packets under certain Postal Conventions.*

(For conventions at present in force, see p. 106, NPM), *or*

2. *if exclusively employed in coast fisheries or petty local trade, or*

3. *while exclusively engaged on religious, scientific, or philanthropic missions, or as cartel ships (i.e., engaged in the exchange of prisoners, &c.)*

A cartel ship is more fully defined on p. 4, NPM.

IV. POSTAL CORRESPONDENCE EXEMPT FROM SEARCH AND DETENTION

The postal correspondence found on board any vessel must not be searched, and, if the vessel is detained, the mail bags, &c., must be forwarded to their destination with the least possible delay.

This exemption does not extend to parcels sent by post, nor does it apply in the case of postal correspondence addressed to or emanating from a blockaded port, found in a vessel detained for breach of blockade.

A vessel carrying mails is not on that account exempt from search or detention, but she should only be searched when there are strong grounds for suspecting that she is liable to detention [11].

V. ENEMY VESSELS TRANSFERRED TO ANOTHER FLAG

If, on boarding a British, allied, or neutral vessel, it appears from her papers or other circumstances that she was shortly before, or has been at any time since, the outbreak of war an enemy vessel, there would be ground for suspecting that the transfer had been made for the specific purpose of escaping risk of capture as an enemy vessel, and if such suspicion can be confirmed, as indicated below, the vessel should be detained. (See Section II, 1) [16–18]:

Interrogate Master and any other person and examine ship's papers, particularly certificate of registry (as every vessel sold from one country to another must fly the flag of the country from which bought until she has received a new certificate of registry) and bill of sale for date and particulars of transfer, &c. Observe the general appearance of the vessel, and the names and notices (if any) placed about in the ship.

If it appears that the transfer has been made –

i.   during the voyage or in a blockaded port; or

ii.   without the proper fulfilment of the requirements of the laws of the countries concerned (see ID 669, 'Nationalisation of Merchant Vessels'); or

iii. after, or within 60 days before, the outbreak of hostilities and the bill of sale is not on board;

the vessel should be detained.

In all other cases the Visiting Officer should generally satisfy himself –

i.   that the alleged transfer and new control over the vessel is genuine and irrevocable; and

ii.   that possession has been taken by the new owner or his agent; and

iii. that the vessel is not under enemy control, and that the master is not in the service of the enemy.

If there is reasonable ground for suspecting that any of these conditions are not fulfilled, the vessel should be detained, unless the transfer took place more than 30 days before the outbreak of hostilities, in which case she should only be detained if it is clearly shown that at least one of these conditions is not fulfilled.

VI.   CONTRABAND

1.   The term 'Contraband of War' only includes articles having belligerent destination and purpose. Such articles are classed under two heads – absolute contraband and conditional contraband – the former consisting of goods that are primarily and ordinarily for warlike purposes, the latter useful indifferently for warlike and peaceful purposes.

     The term 'contraband' is applied to neutral property on board ship on the high seas or in the territorial waters of either belligerent which (1) is by nature capable of being used to assist in, and (2) is on its way to assist in, the naval or military operations of the enemy [31].

2.   *Absolute contraband* is liable to capture when destined to territory belonging to or occupied by the enemy, or to the fleets or armies of the enemy. It consists of the following articles, with such additions or alterations as may be notified by the Admiralty:

     1.   Arms of all kinds, including arms for sporting purposes, and their distinctive component parts.

     2.   Projectiles, charges, and cartridges of all kinds, and their distinctive component parts.

3. Powder and explosives specially prepared for use in war.
4. Gun-mountings, limber boxes, limbers, military waggons, field forges, and their distinctive component parts.
5. Clothing and equipment of a distinctively military character.
6. All kinds of harness of a distinctively military character.
7. Saddle, draught, and pack animals suitable for use in war.
8. Articles of camp equipment, and their distinctive component parts.
9. Armour plates.
10. Warships, including boats, and their distinctive component parts of such a nature that they can only be used on a vessel of war.
11. Implements and apparatus designed exclusively for the manufacture of munitions of war, for the manufacture or repair of arms, or war material for use on land or sea.

A vessel carrying absolute contraband is not exempt from detention merely because her own destination is neutral, and she should be detained –

i. when such goods are documented for delivery to an enemy destination*; or
ii. when the vessel is to call at enemy ports only, or when she is to touch at an enemy destination* before reaching a neutral port for which such goods are documented; or
iii. if it appears (from information gathered on board, &c) that such goods, although documented for discharge in a neutral port, are in fact intended for an enemy destination*; or
iv. if the circumstances under which the goods are carried give reasonable ground for suspecting enemy destination*.

*'Enemy destination' here means enemy territory or the fleets or armies of the enemy [31–34].

3. *Conditional contraband* is only liable to capture when shown to be destined for the use of the fleets or armies of the enemy or of a Government department of the enemy State. It consists of the following articles, with such additions or alterations as may be notified by the Admiralty:

1. Foodstuffs.
2. Forage and grain, suitable for feeding animals.
3. Clothing, fabrics for clothing, and boots and shoes, suitable for use in war.
4. Gold and silver in coin or bullion; paper money.
5. Vehicles of all kinds available for use in war, and their component parts.

6. Vessels, craft and boats of all kinds; floating docks, parts of docks, and their component parts.

7. Railway material, both fixed and rolling stock, and materials for telegraphs, wireless telegraphs, and telephones.

8. Balloons and flying machines, and their distinctive component parts, together with accessories and articles recognisable as intended for use in connection with balloons and flying machines.

9. Fuel; lubricants.

10. Powder and explosives not specially prepared for use in war.

11. Barbed wire and implements for fixing and cutting the same.

12. Horseshoes and shoeing materials.

13. Harness and saddlery.

14. Field glasses, telescopes, chronometers, and all kinds of nautical instruments [31(b), 36–41].

A vessel carrying conditional contraband should be detained, provided she intends herself to call at an enemy destination, if – [39]

i. such goods are consigned to authorities or agents of the enemy State; or to a fortified place belonging to or occupied by the enemy or serving as a base for her fleets or armies; or

ii. it appears (from information gathered on board, &c.) that such goods are in fact intended for, or if the circumstances under which such goods are being carried give reasonable ground for suspecting that they are intended for, the enemy's fleets, armies, or Government departments.

4. *Goods not to be treated as contraband.* – The following are not to be treated as contraband:

a. Articles serving exclusively to aid the sick and wounded.

b. Articles intended for the use of the vessel in which they are found, or intended for the use of her crew or passengers during the voyage.

c. The following articles:

1. Raw cotton, wool, silk, jute, flax, hemp, and other raw materials of the textile industries, and yarns of the same.

2. Oil, seeds, and nuts; copra.

3. Rubber, resins, gums, and lacs; hops.

4. Raw hides and horns, bones, and ivory.

5. Natural and artificial manures, including nitrates and phosphates for agricultural purposes.

6. Metallic ores.
7. Earths, clays, lime, chalk, stone, including marble, bricks, slates, and tiles.
8. Chinaware and glass.
9. Paper and paper-making materials.
10. Soap, paint, and colours, including articles exclusively used in their manufacture, and varnish.
11. Bleaching powder, soda ash, caustic soda, salt cake, ammonia, sulphate of ammonia, and sulphate of copper.
12. Agricultural, mining, textile, and printing machinery.
13. Precious and semi-precious stones, pearls, mother-of-pearl, and coral.
14. Clocks and watches, other than chronometers.
15. Fashion and fancy goods.
16. Feathers of all kinds, hairs, and bristles.
17. Articles of household furniture and decoration; office furniture and requisites.

d. Articles which are not susceptible of use in war.

VII.   BLOCKADE

1. Blockade consists in the prevention by a belligerent of access to, or egress from, territory of, or in occupation of, his enemy.

It may be instituted to prevent ingress only ('blockade inwards') or egress only ('blockade outwards'), though it is generally instituted to prevent both ingress and egress.

It must be maintained by a force sufficient to create evident danger to vessels attempting to obtain access to the blockaded coast-line.

It must not extent to neutral territory.

The Government or Officer in Command of a blockading force having duly notified a blockade, it rests with Commanding Officers to detain every vessel, irrespective of nationality, *knowingly* engaged in breach of such blockade. (*See* notes to clause 3, d, of Section II.)

Permission may, however, be given to neutral warships to enter or leave a blockaded port.

Any neutral vessel compelled to seek shelter by stress of weather or other circumstances of distress may be allowed by an officer of the blockading force, on proof of such distress, access to a blockaded port provided she does not discharge or take on board cargo whilst within the blockaded area. An officer is to board such a vessel and enter in her log a memorandum of his visit and of the circumstances necessitating her entry into the blockaded area; also a notice that cargo must not be shipped or discharged, and that it will be checked on her departure from the blockaded area, for which purpose steps must be taken to obtain a reliable list of her present cargo.

A vessel is presumed to know of the existence of a blockade that has been duly notified to the authorities of the blockaded area and to neutral Governments –

i.   if she is coming out from the blockaded area; or
ii. if, when she left her last port, the existence of the blockade could have been known there.

2.   The procedure on sighting and boarding vessels is laid down in Sections IX, X, XI.

In the case of suspected breach of blockade, it is first necessary for the Visiting Officer to ascertain by enquiry and by examination of the ship's papers whether the vessel has knowledge of the blockade.

If such knowledge can be presumed, then the vessel should be detained if – without proper authority or reason –

a.   she attempts to approach or leave a blockaded area; or
b.   her position gives grounds for suspecting that she intends to enter the blockaded area by evading the blockading squadron; or
c.   she discharges cargo into lighters, &c, to be conveyed by them to the blockaded area; or
d.   whilst lying outside the line of blockade, she takes cargo on board from lighters, &c., which have been sent out from within.

Examine certificate of registry for nationality, also manifest, and charter party (if any), and bills of lading, to see whether they contain any reference to the blockade.

If necessary, examine also chart, engine-room registers, and wireless and signal logs (if any), and ascertain last port of call and date (*see* notes to clause 1); and, if still uncertain, it is possible a newspaper or some document might be found on board that contains reference to the blockade.

Examine the official and deck log-books to ascertain if there is any warning of the blockade (clause 3).

3.   a.   If the vessel is to be detained, then the OC and the Visiting Officer should proceed as in Sections XIV and XVI.

b.   If the vessel is not to be detained because there is no evidence that she intends knowingly to break blockade, or because the Master is acting in consequence of erroneous information as to the blockade previously given him on the same voyage by a British or allied officer, the Visiting Officer will enter in her official log-book a

Warning of Blockade

This vessel has to-day been visited by me, and the master has been warned that the coast of *_____ is under blockade, and that he must not proceed thither.

Date and time _____
Place or lat. and long. _____
(Signature and rank) _____
of H.M.S. '_____'

*Here insert full extent of blockade. Great care should be exercised that the correct limits of the blockade are invariably entered in the notices made on ship's papers, as any irregularity in this respect will invalidate any seizure.

c.   If the vessel is to be allowed to enter or leave the blockaded area under the terms of the Proclamation of Blockade, the Visiting Officer will enter in her official log-book an

Authorisation to Pass

This vessel has this day been visited by me and has been authorised to enter (or leave) the blockaded area, being considered by me not to be liable to detention for the following reason _____

Date and time _____
Place or lat. and long. _____
(Signature and rank) _____
of H.M.S. '_____'   [47–70]

VIII.   CONVOY

Neutral merchant vessels under convoy of a warship of *their own* nationality are exempt from visit and search; but a neutral warship cannot claim exemption for vessels of a nation other than her own [71–74].

All vessels under enemy convoy are liable to detention [9].

On meeting a neutral convoy, an officer is to board the neutral warship and request information as to the destination and cargo of each of the vessels under convoy. The Officer in Command of the convoy is bound to furnish this information.

If the Visiting Officer suspects that some of the vessels under convoy are liable to detention, he should give reasons, and ask the Convoying Officer to cause an examination to be made, and request a written statement of the result of the examination, which must be forwarded to the Senior Officer, and a copy sent to the Admiralty.

If the Convoying Officer admits that any of the vessels under convoy are liable to detention and withdraws his protection from them, such vessels should be detained; but, in the event of any difference of opinion between the Visiting Officer and the Convoying Officer, the decision of the latter must be accepted, and the incident reported (if urgent, by telegraph) to both the Admiralty and Senior Officer.

If a neutral merchant vessel of a nationality other than that of the convoying warship is amongst the convoy, she should be visited.

IX. PROCEDURE ON SIGHTING AND CHASING SUSPICIOUS VESSELS

1. The OC should require the vessel to bring to and to hoist her colours, and at the same time he should chase her. Should the vessel not bring to at once, the warship should fire in succession two blank charges, and then, if necessary, a shot across her bows, but before firing the British ensign and pendant must be flying. At night the OC must use his discretion as to stopping and boarding vessels.

   If the vessel still neglects to bring to coercion may be used.

   A warship may chase, but must not fire under false colours. A capture may not be effected in neutral territorial waters.

   The name of the vessel should, if possible, be ascertained, so that her description can be looked up in 'Lloyd's Register' before boarding. The confidential book 'Foreign Mercantile Marine' also contains information on this point. A vessel must bear her name visibly, so that it can be identified from a distance.

   If on boarding it is found that the vessel has been sailing under false colours, or has signalled a wrong name, she cannot for that reason alone be detained, but there would be grounds for regarding her with suspicion [81–90, 182–186].

2. An officer is to be directed to observe and note in writing:

   a. *When a vessel is first sighted.*
   Time and where she was first sighted; her bearing and distance from his ship; and her course.

Whether any other British or allied ship of war was in sight, and, if so, her bearing and distance from his ship and course; and whether she was chasing the suspected vessel.

b.   *During pursuit.*

Whether any alteration took place in course of vessel chased.

Whether any other British or allied ship of war came in sight, and, if so, time and her bearing, distance, and course; and whether she joined in the pursuit, and, if so, to what extent.

c.   *At the capture.*

Time and where vessel was overtaken.

Whether any other British or allied ship of war was in sight, and, if so, her bearing, distance, and course.

If another British or allied ship of war is the actual captor, what was the bearing and distance of his own ship from the chase and the course his ship was steering.

This information is partly required in case any claims of joint capture arise. (See Proclamation as to Prize Money in Quarterly Navy List which, *inter alia*, says: 'Ships or vessels being in sight of a prize, as also of the captor, under circumstances to cause intimidation to the prize and encouragement to the captor, shall be alone entitled to share as joint captors.' [82]

3.   Two officers should be warned to get ready to board the vessel.

If the vessel appears to be a foreigner, one of the officers should, if possible, be an interpreter of the required language.

They should be each supplied with a copy of this Handbook, and take a notebook and pencil.

The boat's crew should, if necessary, be supplemented, in case it is required to search the vessel. (See Section XIII.)

The OC will decide whether to arm the boat or crew.

Before boarding, the two officers should make themselves acquainted, from the book of reference 'Merchant Ship's Papers (NID 883),' with the form of certificate of registry issued by the country whose colours the vessel is flying.

X.   BOARDING THE VESSEL

When the vessel has been brought to, the Officer in Command should, weather permitting, send a boat (flying the white ensign) to her with two officers in uniform (hereinafter called the 'Visiting Officer' and the 'Witnessing Officer').

In the first instance these two officers should alone board the vessel.

If impracticable to lower a boat or board the vessel, the Officer in Command will decide whether to stand by her or allow her to proceed.

He will under no circumstances order the vessel to send any persons or papers to the war ship.

Care must be exercised that no avoidable delay or deviation from her course is caused to the vessel, and the visiting officers should be warned to show all possible consideration to those on board.

If, upon boarding, the Visiting Officer is at once satisfied that the vessel is not liable to detention, he should immediately quit her and report accordingly to the OC, who may then allow the vessel to proceed.

Whilst the vessel is being boarded and during the whole time that the Visiting Officer is on board, the warship will stand by her, and the OC will order a constant look out to be kept from his ship on the vessel [86–90].

XI.   DUTIES OF THE VISITING OFFICER

1.   As the object of visiting a vessel is to ascertain whether she is liable to detention for any of the reasons set forth in Section II, the duties of the Visiting Officer comprise: Examination of ship's papers and interrogation of the Master; and – if considered necessary for the elucidation of doubtful points or suspicious circumstances – interrogation of *any* other person on board, and inspection of the vessel, cargo, crew, and passengers.

If at any time during his visit or search, the Visiting Officer considers the vessel is exempt from detention, he should at once quit her and report accordingly to his Commanding Officer, so that the vessel may be allowed to proceed without delay.

It will be seen from Section II that, subject to the few exceptions in Section III, the following vessels can be detained:

i.   Any enemy vessel.
ii.   A British or allied vessel, engaged in unlicensed trade or inter-course with enemy.

.... (continued)

* * *

28. Wartime Adjustments to the Laws of Contraband Control

Admiralty to All Commanders-in-Chief
Confidential

[ADM 116/1234]   August 1914

[Draft Memorandum 15498]

With reference to the accompanying copy of an Admiralty telegram No. — of the 19th instant, the effect of which is to maintain the doctrine of continuous voyage for conditional contraband, I am commanded by My Lords Commissioners of the Admiralty to acquaint you that the object of His Majesty's Government in issuing this instruction is to enable foodstuffs to be intercepted which are consigned to places in Germany through neutral ports as there is reason to believe that the German Government have taken over the control of all foodstuffs in the country.

All foodstuffs, therefore, consigned as above may be captured on the presumption that they are destined for the use of the armed forces or of a Government Department of the enemy State.

The conditions prevailing at Rotterdam necessitate a different rule for vessels on their way for that port. Destination to Germany may be presumed in the case of all foodstuffs consigned to Rotterdam unless they are covered by a guarantee from the Dutch Government that neither they nor their equivalent will be exported from the Country. Where no such guarantee is found on board the vessel should be detained and the circumstances reported without delay.

In the case of goods other than foodstuffs consigned to Germany, and in the case of any goods, including foodstuffs, consigned to an enemy country other than Germany, neutral vessels are not to be detained on the ground of carriage of, nor cargo seized as, conditional contraband unless there is evidence, actual or presumptive, of destination in accordance with Article 39 of the Naval Prize Manual.

I am at the same time to enclose a copy of an Order of His Majesty in Council dated the 20th instant, the provisions of which are to be applied to and read as part of the Naval Prize Manual, and all officers are to be guided thereby accordingly.

The effect of the Order-in-Council upon the provisions of the Manual is as follows:

a)   The list of contraband contained in the Proclamation of August 4th, 1914, should be substituted for the lists contained in Article 31 of the Manual.

b)   The following should be substituted for Article 39 (a) of the Manual 'if such goods are consigned to authorities of the enemy state or to or for a merchant or other person under the control of the authorities of the enemy state'.

c)   Articles 37, 38, the first two lines of Article 39 down to the words 'are fulfilled,' and Article 40 of the Manual should be regarded as cancelled.

The effect of this last paragraph (c) is that the doctrine of continuous voyage will apply to conditional contraband as well as to absolute contraband.

* * *

29.   Naval Prize

[ADM 116/1234]   3 December 1914

At a meeting of the Finance Committee (assisted by the Fourth Sea Lord, Admiral Sir Edmond Slade, and Mr Evans, head of NL Branch) on 1st December, the question of the constitution of a Naval Prize Fund and of the distribution of the Fund was considered, the Committee having before them Memoranda prepared by Sir E. Slade and Mr Evans. After discussion it was agreed that the following recommendations should be placed before the Board in connection with the proposed establishment of a Prize Fund in consequence of the Order in Council of 26th August, 1914, cancelling the provisions of the Royal Proclamation of 17th September, 1900, with regard to the distribution of the net proceeds of Naval Prizes:

I – Establishment of a Naval Prize Fund

1.   There shall be one general Naval Prize Fund, into which shall be paid the net proceeds of the sale of all ships and cargoes condemned by any Prize Court in the United Kingdom, the Dominions, Colonies, or Indian Empire as the result of action taken by his Majesty's ships and armed forces, together with any freight earned by prizes before they are sold.

2.   The distribution of the Fund shall be made on the same basis for all the naval forces of the Crown.

3.   Although each individual prize will be dealt with separately by the Prize Court and a separate account will be kept for each, as in former wars, the net proceeds of each, after all claims are satisfied, shall be paid into the Prize Fund.

4.   The Prize Fund will bear the cost and damages awarded for ships and cargoes where the captors of ships taken as prize have been unable to make good their case.

It will not bear any costs and damages awarded in respect of ships and cargoes sent into the Prize Court by direct order of the Crown and not condemned.

5.   The Prize Fund will not be concerned with either the value of ships detained under the terms of The Hague Conventions or the cost and expenses thereof.

6.   The costs and expenses arising out of cases where ships have been brought in and subsequently released, but were not the subject of prize proceedings, will be paid by the Crown and not by the Fund.

7.   The charitable funds of Greenwich Hospital shall receive any benefits from unclaimed or forfeited prize money, &c., as has been customary heretofore.

8.   The Prize Fund thus composed shall, except for the payment of costs and damages under Clause 4, be inviolable, that is to say, that any money taken out of it prior to the final distribution or allocation is to be repayable into the Fund with interest.

9.   The prizes not captured by His Majesty's naval forces, and the ships detained under The Hague Convention rules will not come within the purview of the Naval Prize Fund, and accordingly must be dealt with in a separate account, any necessary funds required being provided by the Exchequer. The administration of the business connected with these latter ships requires to be defined and placed on a proper footing.

II – Distribution of Prize Fund

10.   Prize gratuities should be payable to all officers and men borne on ships' books in any sea-going fleet, squadron, or flotilla, including air craft engaged in flights or taking part in warlike operations, also the staff of War Signal stations.

11.   This description will cover all those who may be regarded as having any claim for the full gratuity. The unit of the full gratuity should be not less than £1. The scale which is proposed later on would admit of a grant of £5 to every A.B. and 1st Class Stoker, the other ranks and ratings sharing in due proportion.

12.   The description will include all the crews of the mine sweepers and armed patrols, and others performing risky service, but it will exclude many who are performing distinctly good work of an arduous and exacting nature, but without the same degree of risk, such as that in Auxiliaries which are not commissioned, colliers, hospital ship carriers, &c., and Coast Guard Stations.

13.   In order to provide a reward for the efforts of the men employed in non-commissioned vessels, the Coast Guard, the staff of the home depôts and other naval establishments on shore and in harbour (including the Transport Staff abroad and air stations), there should be a smaller gratuity – say, half that mentioned in paragraph 11 above.

14.   This would be conferred on deserving classes of men who might have preferred taking the more risky service, but have been compelled to remain on shore and do their duty to the State in less prominent, but none the less necessary, positions. The description suggested will cover most cases of the kind under consideration, but it is possible that when the matter comes to be more fully investigated there may be found to be other deserving cases which are not provided for. In no case should any officer or man receive both gratuities.

15.   A change from the old distribution is required in the case of Flag Officers, Commanding Officers, and Executive Officers in big ships. Under the old rules, the Flag Officer, or Flag Officers, have received one-thirtieth of the total, and of the remainder one-tenth has been appropriated to the Captain and Commander, the residue being divided into shares for the reward of the ship's company.

16.   With one general Prize Fund, it is better to assign a definite number of shares out of the whole to these Officers, as the award of a percentage of the total is impracticable. A scale has been devised with a maximum of 500 shares for the Commander-in-Chief, the amount allotted to the Field-Marshal Commander-in-Chief in the South African War. The army scale has not been followed with close adherence to relative rank, but consideration has been given to the responsibility attached to the services performed by the various classes of Officers. For instance, having regard to the position occupied by Captains, Commanders, and Lieutenants, during a naval engagement, and the heavier risks they are likely to incur than do non-executive Officers of the same relative rank, it is fair that the award should be somewhat larger.

17.   Apart from this, the principal new feature in the scale is the subdivision of the old 9th Class into two, in order to recognise the difference in fighting value of A.B.'s and Stokers (1st Class) from Ordinary Seamen and Stokers (2nd Class). It has, therefore, been proposed to assign five shares to the former and three shares to the latter class.

18.   Besides Appendices (A), (B), and (C) giving the old scale, the South African War Army Scale, and the proposed new scale of distribution, a statement has been prepared of the total cost of paying the proposed full gratuity to the total number of ranks and ratings borne on the 1st April, 1914, and a statement showing the amount payable to

certain typical ships. An estimate of the total cost can only be considered as an approximation, because the total number of men in the Service is now vastly larger than on the 1st April, but, on the other hand, all will not be entitled to the full gratuity if the foregoing proposals are adopted.

19. Under the Naval Agency and Distribution Act it is provided that a percentage of £2/10s on the net amount distributable shall be paid to the ship's agents as his sole and full remuneration. As the ship's agent does not, in the circumstances which now obtain, perform any work in connection with the condemnation of prize, no payment to him is justifiable, and action should be taken accordingly. Legal opinion as to the interpretation to be placed on the wording of the Act is undecided, and if the agents press their claim legislation may be necessary.

Appendix (A)

Present Scale for all Ranks other than Flag Officers
or Commanding Officers, &c.

	Shares
1st Class, *i.e.*, ranking with Captain	45
2nd Class, *i.e.*, ranking with Commander	40
3rd Class, *i.e.*, ranking with Lieutenant over eight years (now Lieutenant-Commander)	35
4th Class, *i.e.*, ranking with Lieutenant	30
5th Class, *i.e.*, ranking with Warrant Officer	20
6th Class, *i.e.*, ranking with Chief Petty Officers, Midshipmen, &c.	12
7th Class, *i.e.*, ranking with Petty Officer	10
8th Class, *i.e.*, ranking with Leading Rate	7
9th Class, *i.e.*, ranking with A.B., Stoker, &c.	4
10th Class, *i.e.*, ranking with Kroomen and Supernumeraries	2
11th Class, *i.e.*, ranking with Boys	1

Appendix (B)

Army Gratuities for South African War	Shares
Field-Marshal	500
General	400
Lieutenant-General	152
Major-General	76
Brigadier-General	57
Staff Officer paid at rate VI or X, Article 115, Pay Warrant; Colonel, R.A.M.C.; Departmental Colonel; Ordnance Officer 1st Class	40

Colonel (except as above defined); Lieutenant-Colonel –
Regimental or Departmental; Staff Officer paid at rate XI,
Article 115, Pay Warrant; Ordnance Officer, 2nd Class   32
Major-Regimental or Departmental; Staff Officer paid at rate
XVI or XLII, Article 115, Pay Warrant; Ordnance Officer,
3rd Class   16
Captain – Regimental or Departmental; Staff Officer paid at rate
XIV, Article 115, Pay Warrant; Ordinance Officer 4th Class 12
Lieutenant   7.5
Second-Lieutenant   6
Warrant Officers   4
Non-commissioned officers and men according to the
classification of Article 144, Pay Warrant – Class I   3
 Class II   2.5
 Class III   2
 Class IV   1.5
 Class V   1

Appendix (C)

Proposed Scale	*Shares*
Admiral, Commander-in-Chief of Home Fleets	500
Admiral, Commanding squadron or fleet	300
Vice-Admiral Commanding	200
Vice-Admiral not in independent command	175
Rear-Admiral Commanding	150
Rear-Admiral not in independent command, and Commodores, 1st Class	90
Commodore, 2nd Class	85
Commanding Officer, if a Captain	80
Captain, not in command, and officers of corresponding rank	40
Commander, if in command or under a Captain	40
Officers of relative rank of Commander	30
Lieutenant-Commander, if in command, and First Lieutenant when serving as Executive Officer in ships commanded by Captains	30
Lieutenant-Commander, and officers of relative rank	25
Lieutenant in command	25
Lieutenants and officers of corresponding rank	20
Mates, Sub-Lieutenants, Chief Warrant Officers, and Warrant Officers in command (including Skippers in command)	15
Warrant Officers	12
Chief Petty Officers	10

Petty Officers	8
Leading rates	6
A.B.'s and Stokers, 1st Class	5
Ordinary Seamen and Stokers, 2nd Class	3
Supernumeraries, including Canteen Attendants	2
Boys	1

NAVAL PRIZE BOUNTY

Prize bounty is payable to the extent of £5 for each person on board the enemy's ship sunk or captured, and distributed among the officers and crew of the ships engaged in the action. The scale recommended for the prize money should also be adopted for prize bounty, which is payable in addition to the shares received from the general Prize Fund.

Under the Navy Prize Act of 1864, to bring the prize bounty system into operation an Order-in-Council or Proclamation declaring the King's intention to grant prize bounty to the officers and crews of His Majesty's ships of war in relation to this present war is required. A memorial to council making such declaration and adopting the system of distribution above recommended should be prepared at once for approval. Orders could then be issued to the fleet in order that the case for the grant of prize bounty in respect of any ships present at the action may be brought before the Prize Court under section 43 of the Act.

The rules for dealing with claims for prize bounty are given in Order 33 of the Prize Court Rules. Apparently, agency might still survive in the case of prize bounty in order that each claimant ship may present its case. The Order is as follows:

'In claims for prize bounty the procedure shall be as follows:

(1)   Where the ship is brought in for adjudication, the application for a decree under 'The Naval Prize Act, 1864', section 43, shall be made in Court at the hearing of the principal cause, or as soon thereafter as possible.

(2)   Where the ship has been destroyed, or, having been taken, has not been brought in for adjudication, the application for a decree as aforesaid shall be made by motion in Court.

(3)   Not less than four clear days before such application, notice thereof shall be served upon the proper officer of the Crown.

(4)   The witnesses in support of the application shall be examined before the Judge in court, or their evidence may be taken by affidavit.

(5)   If the Judge makes a decree in favour of the application, and there are no parties other than the original applicants claiming to

share in the bounty, the Judge may, upon the hearing of the application, or at a later date, if he shall see fit, make a decree declaring the title of the applicants to the prize bounty, and stating the amount thereof. If there are other persons claiming to share in the bounty, the Judge may make a decree that bounty is due, stating the amount thereof, but reserving the question to whom the said bounty is due. Forms of decree will be found in Appendix (A), No. 53 (XXV) to (XXVIII).

(6) All claims to share as joint captors in prize bounty shall be, as far as possible, subject to the same procedure and rules, and be heard and determined in the same manner as hereinbefore provided in the case of claims to share as joint captors in prizes.

* * *

30.   The Repeal of the Declaration of London Order in Council[1]

Legal Assessment by Alexander Pearce Higgins, Advisor on International Law

[ADM 116/1234]   Procurator-General's Department
                                                         8 March 1916

In the event of the repeal of the Declaration of London Order in Council and the restoration of the rules of English Prize Law being decided on it will be necessary to ascertain what are the gains and losses to Great Britain as a belligerent Power. It is proposed in the following to take each of the Chapters of the Declaration of London and examine them with this object.[2]

1.   BLOCKADE

As regards the formalities attendant on the Declaration of a blockade English Prize Law recognises a *de facto* blockade without any special notification or declaration as is required by Article 9. The knowledge of the existence of a blockade on the part of a neutral is a question of fact but if the blockade has been diplomatically notified to the Government of the State to which the vessel belongs and sufficient time

---

[1]See also: E.J.W.S., 'The Modifications of the Declaration of London – Present Position', 20 April 1916, ADM 116/1234.

[2]*Cases are not referred to as a rule, for fuller discussion see Mr Bentwich's Note on 'Anglo-American practice'.

has elapsed for communication to the subjects of their State, knowledge is presumed.

While it is doubtful whether there is a binding custom as to giving time to neutrals to leave a blockaded port, except those in ballast or with cargo loaded before the institution of blockade, modern practice has been in favour of specifying such days of grace, and the provisions of Article 9 might with advantage be observed.

As to presumption of knowledge of the existence of blockade the English rules are more rigorous than those contained in Articles 14–16. *Area of Capture.* The English rule is more favourable to the belligerent than the Declaration of London. Sailing with intent to break blockade inwards renders a vessel *in delicto* until the intention is abandoned. Similarly the English rule as to liability to capture for breach of blockade outwards is more favourable to the belligerent than the Declaration of London; a vessel is liable to capture until the conclusion of her return voyage.

As regards *the application of the doctrine of continuous voyage* to blockade, the repeal of Article 19 leaves the British Court free to follow or extend the American practice if it so thinks fit.

Liability of Cargo. The English rule is more severe than that of Article 21, as the owners of the cargo are concluded by the illegal act of the master, though it may have been done without their privity and contrary to their wishes (*Panaghia Rhomba*, 2 E.P.C. at p. 641).

2. CONTRABAND

The lists of contraband articles, absolute and conditional, as well as the 'free list' have already been repealed and the Order in Council continues in force the existing contraband lists.

The repeal of Article 23 which appears to narrow absolute contraband down to Articles '*exclusively* used for War' enables a full return to be made to the older practice of making goods absolute contraband which are in their nature peculiarly serviceable for war, e.g. – materials for making munitions of war. The doctrine of *Continuous voyage* in the Declaration of London is only applicable to absolute, and not to conditional contraband except where the State for which it is destined has no seaboard. The President has already held that the doctrine is applicable to conditional contraband by the Law of Nations, the doctrine will therefore come into full vigour on the repeal of the Declaration of London. The presumptions of hostile destination set forth in the Declaration of London have been increased by those of the Order in Council of the 29th October and it is proposed to repeat and extend all in the Order in Council now under consideration. The former presumptions are rebuttable and the President has held in the *Kim* that they are not violations of any rules of International Law.[1]

The repeal of Article 38 which declares that a vessel may not be captured on the ground that she has carried contraband on a previous occasion if such carriage is in fact ended brings again into operation the English and American rule that if a vessel has carried contraband with false papers on her outward voyage she can be condemned if taken on her return voyage.

The liability of the ship to condemnation if the contraband carried forms more than half the cargo (Article 40) is different from the English rule which will be restored by the repeal of this Article. In English Prize Law the penalty on the ship for carriage of contraband was (a) loss of freight, (b) confiscation, if owner of the ship was owner of the contraband, or of his share if part owner, (c) confiscation, if contraband goods are carried with false papers, (d) confiscation, where contraband is carried in contravention of a treaty.

The repeal of Article 43 which relates to capture of contraband on a vessel whose master was ignorant of the existence of war or of the fact that the articles seized were contraband raises the question of restoring the practice of pre-emption (see Naval Prize Act 1864, section 37 *Holland's Manual of Naval Prize Law* p. 24).

Article 44 introduced a mitigation of the old rule as to taking a ship in for Prize Court proceedings where she carried contraband by allowing the captor to remove the noxious articles. It is contrary to the old practice; Article 81 of *Holland's Manual of Naval Prize Law* expressly forbids commanders to remove contraband goods and allow vessels to proceed. . . . Under existing circumstances it is doubtful if Article 44 has been of much practical value, but instructions to Commanders might still be given in this sense and their execution could be defended on the ground of convenience to the neutral in avoidance of the delay of taking into port.

3. UNNEUTRAL SERVICE

The repeal of these articles will enable the court to treat a vessel guilty of unneutral service as an enemy vessel in cases where under Article 45 she would be condemned as a neutral. The English rule was more severe and more flexible than the provisions of articles 45 and 46.

---

[1]This refers to the court ruling on the legality of the capture of the *Kim*.

4. *DESTRUCTION OF NEUTRAL PRIZES*

Repeal of Chapter IV restores the old rule that destruction of a neutral prize is justifiable only by the gravest importance of such an act to the public service and only on condition of making full compensation. The English rule is more favourable to neutrals.

5. *TRANSFER TO A NEUTRAL FLAG*

The Declaration of London as regards transfers from an enemy to a neutral flag *after* the outbreak of war is more severe against neutrals than the English Prize Law. The French rule accords with the Declaration of London.

6. *ENEMY CHARACTER*

Article 57 on the conclusive character of the flag has already been repealed. The repeal of Article 60 which allows a former neutral owner of goods on an enemy vessel to exercise a right of stoppage *in transit* on the bankruptcy of the enemy consignee will restore the English rule which does not qualify the general rule that enemy goods retain their enemy character till they reach their destination.

7. *CONVOY*

The Declaration of London (Articles 61 and 62) recognizes that neutral vessels convoyed under warships of their own state are exempt from search. The English practice was the reverse.

8. *RESISTANCE TO SEARCH*

The English rule is more severe than that of Article 63 which renders the cargo on a vessel which has forcibly resisted search liable to be treated as the cargo on an enemy vessel, *i.e.* – raises a presumption against it. The English rule condemns the whole cargo.

9. *COMPENSATION*

The rule of the Declaration of London is little different from the English Law, though in its wording more favourable to the neutral as the English rule provides for costs and damages where there was no reasonable grounds for the capture, whereas the Declaration of London awards them 'unless there were good reasons' for the capture.

SUMMARY

It appears from the foregoing that Great Britain as a belligerent *gains* by the repeal of the Declaration of London.

(1)   *Blockade* – Area of capture, and possibility of application of continuous voyage – greater flexibility as to declaration of blockade, severer penalties as to cargo.

(2)   *Contraband* – Fuller powers as to issue of lists of absolute contraband, power to condemn on return voyage a vessel carrying contraband with false papers.

(3)   *Unneutral Service* – Wider powers as to appreciation of unneutral service and severer penalties for it.

(4)   *Enemy Character* – Restoration of power to go behind flag.

(5)   *Convoy* – Power to search convoyed ships (possibly of little value).

(6)   *Resistance* – Severer penalties.

The *losses* to Great Britain as a belligerent appear to be:

(a)   *Contraband* – No power to condemn ship where contraband cargo exceeds half; no special presumptions throwing burden of proof on claimants.

(b)   *Transfer of Flag* after outbreak of war – gives the Transferee right of proving his *bona fides*.

(c)   *Destruction of neutral prizes*. The English rule is more favourable to neutrals.

   [Signed] A. Pearce Higgins

Lord Robert Cecil's Reasons for Rescinding Order-in-Council

[ADM 116/1234]   26 March 1916.

(a)   The effect of a code such as the Declaration of London is to limit the exercise of belligerent power, as apart from the application of the provisions themselves a presumption arises that what is not specifically mentioned is not recognised by International Law.

(b)   The formal adoption of the Declaration, even though to a modified extent, will fetter us in any negotiations which we may have to enter upon at the end of the war in regard to belligerent and neutral rights on the seas.

(c)   The result of following the procedure of adopting and then amending the Declaration of London by Orders-in-Council is irritating to Neutrals who look upon it as a grievance that after formally adopting the provisions of the Declaration we proceed to revise them whenever it appears to be to our interests to do so.

(d)   Since the decision of the Judicial Committee of the Privy Council in the 'Zamora' case, the Orders-in-Council cease to have any independent authority in the Prize Courts and are only valid when in conformity with the principles of previous decisions of British Prize Courts; consequently an Order-in-Council cannot enlarge our powers under International Law as defined in the Prize Courts, while in certain cases it may restrict them.

* * *

PART III

WARTIME LESSONS AND
ANGLO-AMERICAN DISCORD, 1918–1930

INTRODUCTION

The years between 1918 and 1930 constitute the third chapter of this volume because of the ongoing and heated discussion during that period with the United States about the legitimacy of naval belligerent action to control neutral trade, a discussion made all the more acerbic because the experience of the Great War appeared to show that naval trade control was a strategy of such power that it could bring a great continental empire to defeat. Britain had no intention of giving up the proven means of national survival, but the United States was concerned that it was also a means of threatening her own economic potential. President Woodrow Wilson's plan to create a League of Nations did not fully address the problem because it was unproved, and because in the end the United States did not join it. Nor did the 1928 Kellogg–Briand pact outlawing aggressive war fundamentally change the situation, although it did complicate it.

The American declaration of war in April 1917 had made possible the near perfection of the blockade, despite the insistence of the American government that they were co-belligerents rather than allies and that they could not go against their own declared principles of free trade. The American navy did not participate in the work of interception and inspection of shipping, but there was no need for it to do so and the American government used its control over commodities produced in the United States to coerce the neutral European states into making formal agreements not to re-export to the Central Powers. Eventually American practice was brought into line with that of the *Entente*. The American government brought in and censored mail, instituted bunker control to oblige neutral shipping to sail on routes useful to the war effort of the 'Associated' powers, and even went so far as to use embargo of food supplies and other commodities to coerce neutral states into employing their merchant shipping within the danger zone. The final treaty imposed by the coercive efforts of the United States and her associates was concluded with Sweden, 29 May 1918.

Colonel Hankey was the great apologist of sea power during this period. In 1908 he had been appointed Assistant Secretary to the Committee of Imperial Defence, and he was to continue from 1912 to 1938 as its Secretary. In 1916 he had been appointed to the War Cabinet, and between 1917 and 1918 to the Imperial War Cabinet. From 1919 to 1938 he was also Cabinet Secretary, and between 1923 and 1938 he was Clerk of the Privy Council. In 1939 he was made Minister without Portfolio, in 1941 Chancellor of the Duchy of Lancaster and in 1941 to 1942, Paymaster General. He was a man of immense influence, and energy, which he repeatedly deployed to defend the widest possible interpretation of belligerent rights at sea.

The opening paper in this series was not, in fact, drawn up until 1927, when Colonel Hankey prepared for the Committee of Imperial Defence Sub-Committee on Belligerent Rights an account of the discussions in 1918 between the Allied and Associated Powers. They met to consider an armistice with Germany based on Wilson's 'Fourteen Points', number two of which was 'Absolute freedom of navigation upon the seas, outside territorial waters, alike in peace and in war, except as the seas may be closed in whole or in part by international action for the enforcement of international covenants' [31]. At that date, neither Prime Minister Lloyd George, nor President Clemenceau of France, would agree to make 'The Freedom of the Seas' the basis of negotiations, and defied a threat on the part of Wilson's advisor, Colonel House, to make a separate peace. Lloyd George said that 'he could not accept this clause under any conditions. If this clause had been in operation at the present time, we should have lost the power of imposing a blockade.' When agreement on the terms of the Armistice was reached on 5 November, the Americans had temporarily submitted. The German government was advised that the Allied Governments 'reserve to themselves complete freedom on this subject [that is the Freedom of the Seas] when they enter the Peace Conference.'[1] The draft of a December 1918 report to the Imperial War Cabinet, which was entitled 'Freedom of the Seas', was taken by Sir Cecil Hurst to the Paris Peace Conference. But when President Wilson did not press there the matter it was thought better to avoid any formal international review of belligerent rights [33].

The effects of the allied naval action against trade had been most severe during the winter of 1918–19 after the internment of the German fleet. The second paper in the series is an Admiralty memorandum pointing out that the situation gave Britain, as the dominant naval power in the Baltic, the capability of effecting long-term commercial gains in the north of Europe [32]. Although the idea was dismissed, the

---

[1]Quoted in H.W.V. Temperley, *A History of the Peace Conference of Paris*, London, 1920, I, p. 133.

fact that it was even discussed gives some colour to American concerns about the long-term mercantilist implications of post-war British naval power.

Hankey was almost certainly the author of the report on 'The Freedom of the Seas,' and he was definitely the author of a 1927 'Memorandum by Sir M. Hankey on Blockade and the Laws of War,' in both of which he exhaustively examined the early discussions of the Declaration of London and the actual conduct of the Great War at sea [33], [46]. These papers are central to understanding British policy on belligerent rights at sea during the inter-war period. His attitudes are also reflected in a paper written in 1928 by Sir Arthur Steel-Maitland, Minister of Labour in Stanley Baldwin's second administration [50].

In his 1918 memorandum, which was an important statement of the strategic role of naval forces, Hankey wrote:

> If it is true that the object of maritime war is to exert pressure on the enemy, the corollary follows that the destruction of the enemy's naval forces is merely a means to an end, and that the real and final aim of naval strategy is one or both of the following objects: –
>
> (a)   Prevention of enemy trade.
>
> (b)   The support of direct military attack in the form of invasion across the sea, and the maintenance of the requisite oversea communications . . .
>
> The pressure arising from the grip of sea-power is, in fact, the antecedent cause of most naval operations; and if it is not applied in one form or another, naval war ceases to have any real meaning [33].

In 1915, before the American entry into the war, President Wilson had proposed that Britain should exempt food ships from the effects of the blockade, and in return Germany should abandon submarine attacks on merchant shipping. The idea was communicated by 'Colonel' Edward Mandell House, Wilson's emissary, who visited London and Berlin. Both sides rejected the deal, in London first by the Liberal Cabinet, and then later by the Coalition cabinet. According to an account Hankey prepared in October 1929, 'It was never claimed that the Central Powers would be brought to terms by starvation alone, but it was held that in combination with military success it might become a decisive factor' [61, 62].

Far from curtailing the naval action against German supplies, British thinking was moving in the opposite direction. In April 1918 the Admiralty had recommended the abrogation of the Declaration of Paris, and the possibility of doing so formed part of Hankey's 1918 'The Freedom of the Seas' memorandum [33]. The International Law Committee under the Chairmanship of Lord Cave, which reported to the Attorney-General in December 1918, backed the idea of abrogation. There was some idea that abrogation could be justified on the grounds that blockade was to become a primary tool of the League of Nations, and ought therefore to be unlimited by any agreement dating from the era of *realpolitik*. Sir Cecil Hurst took a draft memorandum to that effect with him to the peace conference but returned without using it when it appeared that the Americans were not going to press the issue of Freedom of the Seas [66]. However, there was no provision in the Declaration for unilateral denunciation, and it was felt that even Britain's allies would not approve.

The Admiralty Staff History published in 1920, *The Economic Blockade 1914–1919*, written by Lt Cmdr W.E. Arnold-Forster, did not depart from Hankey's opinion that the blockade of the Central Powers had been decisive in their defeat. Here it has only been possible to reproduce its concluding section on 'the future'. The author warned against any attempt at predicting the conditions in which a future blockade would be conducted, or at attempting to define them by treaty: 'it seems hopeless to attempt to frame a complete fixed code of rules like the Declaration of London. The history of that unhappy document is indeed the best proof of this truth.' The somewhat tentative conclusion was that the creation of the League of Nations permitted the perfection of blockade strategy because it reduced the difficulty of dealing with neutral states [34].

The next in the series of papers on 'lessons learnt' dates from 1923 when the Standing Sub-Committee on the Co-ordination of Departmental Action on the Outbreak of War, which had been formed by the Committee of Imperial Defence on 11 February 1920, completed a *Summary of Recommendations; Trading, Blockade and Enemy Shipping* [35]. The nature of the discussion about methods which was to continue well into the years of peace is illustrated by two private letters, beginning with one in May 1926 from Cecil E. Farrer, Senior Intelligence Officer, Department of Overseas Trade, to Cmdr Claude Preston Hermon-Hodge, RN, Assistant Secretary, Committee of Imperial Defence [38]. Economic warfare is highly dependent on the smooth interaction of civil and military departments of government, and the structures developed during the war, although effective, were liable to interdepartmental power struggles. Farrer iterates the seemingly obvious fact that 'the blockade depends ultimately upon the navy,' but continues, asserting that it 'is equally obvious that the Foreign Office must be the department in control of the policy of blockade.' A year later Sir Charles Hipwood, Mercantile Marine Department, Board of

Trade, sent Commander Hermon-Hodge a copy of a 15 June 1927 paper to the Imperial Defence College on *Shipping Control in Time of War* in which he noted the need for continual development of plans for the conduct of economic warfare [41]. He noted, for instance, that the most powerful lever employed during the Great War to oblige neutral shippers to carry cargoes for British customers had been the ability of Britain because of its near monopoly on coal bunker stations to deny coal to them should they refuse to cooperate. But this lever was losing its value as ships were increasingly employing oil for bunker. He also pointed out the importance of keeping abreast of the marine insurance industry as that alone had made it possible for Norwegian shippers to continue in British trades.

President Wilson's interest in the 'Freedom of the Seas' had been muted because he had come to the conviction that future peace could only be ensured by the formation of a League of Nations to moderate the Westphalian system of national sovereignty. The development of a system of collective defence would eliminate the old concept of neutrality. Robert Cecil, Under-Secretary of State for Foreign Affairs in 1916–18 and Minister of Blockade from July 1918, was a leading British advocate of a League. Lloyd George's views were more cautious. His position was, or at least he said it was, that he wanted 'to see the League of Nations thoroughly established and proved before any discussion took place' about belligerent rights [31]. The recommendation of the Committee of Imperial Defence was

> that it would be inverting the proper order of procedure, if any agreements were made tending to limit British naval rights, before the League [of Nations], not only is an accomplished fact, but has proved that it is capable of fulfilling all the high ideals which its supporters expect to see accomplished by its establishment [33].

But the decision of the United States Senate not to authorise signature of the League Covenant complicated the situation immeasurably. In a minute drawn up by Alex Hunt, PAS Admiralty Secretarial Branch, in September 1924, attention was called to the fact 'that although the aggressor is deemed to have committed an act of war the opinion of committees who considered this subject in 1921 was that a state of war was not created and that the members of the League were not embarking necessarily on war.' If no state of war was deemed to exist, could members of the League enjoy the rights of belligerency? But even if they were entitled by law to exercise belligerent rights, could they in fact do so over the objection of a neutral as powerful as the United States. Captain Dudley Pound, the Director of Plans, minuted that:

'The Admiralty has always maintained that *economic* blockade as referred to in Article 16 does not involve Naval operations as such operations cannot be embarked on without going to War with the Aggressor nation' [37].

The Admiralty was even alarmed by the trend of discussion at the League of Nations in 1924 suggesting that the navy would be called upon to maintain the sea communications of victims of international aggression. Even that defensive action, which entailed the risk of attack without warning, had very serious implications. The risk was one which would necessitate the navy taking pre-emptive action against the forces of the aggressor state. Such acts of war would have to be planned for, and provided with legal justification, but inevitably would also create political and international difficulties. The idea that sanctions would amount to 'pacific blockade' did not eliminate the difficulty of dealing with the United States. It had to be remembered that the position adopted by the British government in the French intervention in Formosa, and in the Venezuelan crisis of 1902, was that belligerent rights could only be exercised by a declared belligerent. In 1927 there was discussion in London about the effectiveness of pacific blockade as a means of influencing the Nationalist government of south China, but it was recognised that control of external trade with China would probably have only a marginal effect on a country capable of self-sufficiency [40].

The Washington Conference concentrated on naval arms limitation because it could not address the issue of belligerent rights with any prospect of success, but agreement was reached to address British, and American, concern about the threat of submarines to trade. A subsidiary treaty 'Relating to the Use of Submarines and Noxious Gases in Warfare,' 6 February 1922, embodied the principle that submariners are bound by the provisions of the Hague conventions on 'visit and search' that provided for the safety of merchant mariners. But the convention did not address the question of what was a merchant ship, or what actions on the part of a merchant ship might void its protected status; it was to prove an inadequate defence. A Committee on Limitation of Armament formed by the Washington powers attempted to regulate the use of aircraft for trade warfare, but could not find a satisfactory formulation [36].

The provision that failure to comply with the requirements of the Hague Convention rendered naval commanders liable to conviction as pirates was implemented by British municipal legislation in the Treaties of Washington Act 1922, but not by similar acts in any other country, and in September 1926 Paymaster Captain Manisty wrote a minute to the C-in-C Portsmouth urging reconsideration. He argued that, as the act was in advance of international practice, it placed British naval officers at a disadvantage. No action was taken, however, as Alex Hunt held the danger to British officers to be insignificant [39]. In August 1927 Manisty, who had recently been lecturing on international law at the RN Staff College, Greenwich, returned to the charge with a letter to Victor Weekes, Secretary to the First Sea Lord, urging the need to address the question of the legal liabilities of naval officers enforcing any sort of trade control [43].

As a consequence of the failure of the 1927 Geneva naval disarmament conference, the United States Senate turned to consideration of a cruiser building programme, during which a strong opinion developed in favour of the adoption of a resolution asking the President to summon an international conference for the purpose of a 'restatement and codification of the rules of law governing the conduct of belligerents and neutrals in war at sea'. The Naval Construction Bill was amended to the effect: 'First, that Congress favours a Treaty or Treaties with all principal maritime nations regulating the conduct of belligerents and neutrals in war at sea, including the inviolability of private property thereon. Second, that such Treaties be negotiated, if practically possible, prior to the meeting of the Conference on Limitation of Armaments in 1931' [60].

Austen Chamberlain, Foreign Secretary in Stanley Baldwin's second ministry, was impressed. In October 1927 he drew up a paper for Cabinet in which he stated his conclusion that the failure of the Three-Power Naval Conference at Geneva had been occasioned by the fundamental disagreement between Britain and the United States about belligerent rights at sea. 'It cannot be denied,' he wrote, 'that the present difference on this subject between the United States and ourselves is the only matter which makes war between our two nations conceivable. But I go further; I believe that General Preston Brown [US Army] does not exaggerate when he says that any attempt by us to enforce our rights in a future war where the United States were neutral, as we enforced them in the late war, would make war between us "probable".' Chamberlain was fully aware of the difficulties which would be involved in any attempt to reach a general agreement with the United States on the matter of belligerent rights, but he argued that it was essential to make the attempt [44].

It was in response to Austen Chamberlain's paper that in November 1927 Colonel Hankey, who strongly opposed reopening the subject in discussions with the United States, drafted his second major review of the history of Britain's exercise of belligerent rights during the century.[1] This in turn produced a response by Sir Cecil Hurst. He did not dispute the importance of the blockade in defeating Germany. However, he pointed out that the tolerance of British action, both by neutral nations and by Britain's own prize courts, was consequential upon Germany's violations of the laws of war, which justified British reprisal. Hurst asked whether it was meaningful for Britain to assert traditional belligerent rights now that the United States was in a position to outbuild the British fleet. And he asked whether, if Britain's naval position was weakening, in future it might not be in Britain's interest that belligerent rights should be curtailed. He also believed that the eventual growth of the League of Nations would significantly affect the implications of neutrality. But although he differed from Hankey in his intellectual apparatus, he was no less convinced that it would be best to avoid any immediate discussion with the United States which would tie British hands in the future [46].

The advice of the British Ambassador in Washington, Sir Esme Howard, was that common ground could 'never be accomplished by a regular staged conference, on account of the public excitement that would be certainly created by the press in both countries.' He recommended 'quiet conversations, about which the press should be kept in ignorance until an agreement is in sight.' An article in the 21 November 1927 edition of the *New York World* which he paraphrased ended with the line: 'If one nation were clearly right and the other nation clearly wrong the solution would be much easier to find.'[2] In May 1928 Howard warned that the 'intransigent enemies of the League' in the United States were campaigning against the Senate's ratification of the Kellogg Pact precisely because it was 'nothing but a back door entrance into the League for the United States' [54]. In the long term the Locarno and Kellogg–Briand treaties were significant in transforming the legal belligerent rights at sea regime, Hankey acknowledged, but in more immediate terms their significance was not so clear [56].

As part of the examination of the belligerent's rights issue, in 1927 Sir Robert Leslie Craigie, the head of the American department in the Foreign Office, had written a commentary on Hankey's and Hurst's papers in which he pointed out that the Admiralty had compared British and American naval practice with respect to interception of trade, and found relatively little difference, and he argued that the American hostility to British attitudes to belligerent rights was changing as their own

---

[1]Hankey's correspondence with Chamberlain and others is reviewed in Stephen Roskill, *Hankey, Man of Secrets*, London: Collins, 1972, Vol. II, p. 451 *et. seq.*
[2]CAB 16/79, Sir E. Howard to Sir Austen Chamberlain, 2 December 1927.

naval power grew [46], [60]. His reading of the Admiralty's assessment, however, had been somewhat selective, its conclusion not being so sanguine [49]. Far from the two navies feeling an underlying commonality of purpose, the First Sea Lord, Admiral Sir Charles Madden, had placed in the Sub-Committee's files a 'Note' in which he characterised the American concept of 'Freedom of the Seas' as 'freedom to prolong the war and amass wealth at the expense of the belligerents, who, when exhausted by war, may be at the mercy of the Power which has been allowed this freedom.'[1]

On 5 December 1927 Baldwin had formed a Sub-Committee of the Committee of Imperial Defence, under the chairmanship of Lord Salisbury, to consider the problem of belligerent rights [59]. A few days later, apparently as a result of Hankey's representation to Baron Stamfordham, the king's Private Secretary, King George V spoke to Austen Chamberlain about the importance of great caution on making commitments about belligerent rights. On Chamberlain's advice, Baldwin instructed Hankey to forward to Admiral Sir Herbert Richmond all the papers relating to the subject [60]. Richmond was commandant of the Imperial Defence College, and Hankey wrote to Madden that he was 'a very old friend of mine (we were shipmates in 1898 and have been pals ever since) and he is as sound as a bell on the question' [48]. Presumably Hankey had engineered this reference to Richmond.

The urgency of the cabinet's problem with respect to belligerent rights was increased when on 21 February 1928 United States Senator Borah, Chairman of the Senate Committee on Foreign Relations, submitted a resolution 'That there should be a restatement and recodification of the rules of law governing the conduct of belligerents and neutrals in war at sea' prior to the meeting of the Conference on the Limitation of Armaments in 1931.[2] In March 1928, in advance of the expiration of the Root-Bryce General Arbitration Treaty between Britain and the United States of 1908, a draft of a new treaty was received from Washington for British consideration.[3] The Americans wanted to reserve from the arbitration treaty their special interests in the Americas. They also insisted that the US Senate would have to approve resort to

[1]CAB 16/79 ff. 203–204. Note by First Sea Lord, B.R. 16, 1 February 1928, CID Sub-Committee on Belligerent Rights.
[2]CAB 16/79 f. 221, enclosure in *Note by the Secretary of State for Foreign Affairs*, CID Sub-Committee on Belligerent Rights, March 1928.
[3]CAB 16/79 ff. 258–61, *Revised Draft Arbitration Agreement between the United States and Great Britain submitted to His Majesty's Government by Mr. Kellogg in March, 1928*, CID, Sub-Committee on Belligerent Rights.

arbitration in every individual instance. But their draft deleted the old reservation of 'vital interests', and this was taken primarily to refer to disputes arising out of the exercise of belligerent rights. The dilemma for Stanley Baldwin's cabinet was very great. Refusal to accept the American draft was felt to ensure that the Americans would call a conference on belligerent rights, in which British interests would be overwhelmed by the alliance of American opinion with those of continental military powers that had everything to gain by emasculating the Royal Navy. The American draft did exclude from arbitration British action taken in compliance with resolutions of the League of Nations, and this might have been thought to have shown the way forward, but Britain was not ready to put its security entirely into the hands of the League. Had the United States been a member, the view from London might have been different. Safety could not be found in refusal to participate, because over time arbitration courts settling disputes between other countries in other wars would inevitably bring changes to international law – changes which were not likely to be in Britain's interest.

In February 1928 Sir Arthur Steel-Maitland submitted the Foreign Office memorandum in which he noted that 'the only force which was effective in imposing any limit on belligerent rights at sea was that exercised by neutrals.' His recommendation was that Britain only seek a more defined law of belligerent rights if British needs were 'swinging towards freedom of the seas' [50]. This attitude was consistent with the advice being received from Sir Esme Howard, ambassador in Washington [51]. However, the paper submitted in May 1928 by Maurice Gwyer, the Procurator-General, on the 'Havana' treaty concluded by the United States on 'Maritime Neutrality' suggested that the United States was not diametrically opposed to British ideas about belligerent rights [53].

Richmond submitted two reports, in March and April 1928. In the latter he made the obvious point, which Hankey had earlier made, that the free exercise of belligerent rights was the only way in which Britain had been able to use her naval power in support of allies, to increase the financial resources of the alliance and diminish those of the enemy. Any significant constraint on the rights of belligerents to control maritime trade would oblige Britain to build up her army to a size where it could fight on the continent in support of her allies, 'or, as some will have it, to fight by destroying the towns, with their historic buildings and treasures of irreplaceable value, and killing the citizens of both sexes and all ages' [52].

It appeared to Sir Esme Howard that American politics were being propelled less by a concern for neutral rights than by the demand of the

'Big Navy' lobby for a 'Navy Second to None'. He believed that the lobby was only able to mobilise public support for a large cruiser building programme by appealing to anti-British sentiment. The lack of any show of interest in the British press for the American cruiser programme appeared to lie behind a sudden revulsion amongst the American electorate for the costs involved. He reported on 29 February 1928 that the House of Representatives Naval Construction Bill provided for building no more than five light cruisers and one small aircraft carrier. The programme had been expected to be 25 cruisers and five carriers [51]. When the House passed the Naval Construction Bill up to the Senate in May, a slightly amended version of Senator Borah's resolution was tacked to it.[1] [58]. On 17 October 1928, the Cabinet referred to the Sub-Committee on Belligerent Rights the question of the renewal of the Arbitration Treaty with the United States.

Herbert Hoover's election in 1928 added further urgency to the need to come to terms on belligerent rights, and the Senate's resolutions made it unavoidable that the question of belligerent rights had to be addressed if naval competition were to be controlled. But an immediate crisis was deflected by instructing Sir Esme Howard to communicate confidentially to Hoover the British concern about a conference being called prior to an opportunity being made to discuss the matter fully and confidentially with the United States government[2] [59, 60].

London was alive to the need to keep the Dominions on side.[3] The security of a thalassic empire depended absolutely on the effectiveness of imperial naval forces, but at the same time Canada's security depended absolutely on the health of Anglo-American relations. In November 1927 Herbert B. Taylor, at the Naval Intelligence Division, Department of National Defence, Ottawa, Canada, advised Admiral Sir Barry Domvile, Director of Naval Intelligence, that the perspective from Ottawa was not encouraging. American attitudes to the exercise of belligerent rights by Britain were so negative that, if the empire and the United States did not reach an agreement protecting both their interests, it would be necessary in the event of the empire becoming engaged in a major war for Canada to adopt a neutral stance. Any other course of action would mean that all her resources and more would be required to defend her frontier to the south [45]. In January 1929, on the other hand, Sir Harry Batterbee, the Dominion's Secretary, sent a note to Hankey passing on the opinion of a

[1]CAB 16/79 f. 243v., Howard to Chamberlain, 4 May 1928, 12:37 p.m.
[2]CAB 16/79 ff. 245–6, Howard to Chamberlain, 25 April 1928.
[3]See CAB 16/79 f. 291, *Despatch*, Leo S. Amery to Dominion governments, 15 March 1928.

Canadian journalist that the way to address American concern was to point out that if the regime now wanted by the United States had been in force in 1914, and the United States had then had a 'navy second to none', Britain would have been unable to prevent German militarism dominating the world [57, 59].

The Sub-Committee on Belligerent Rights tabled its 'First Report' on the Arbitration Treaties to the Committee of Imperial Defence in February 1929, and its 'Second', on Belligerent Rights, in March [59, 60]. Considerable attention was paid to the distinction which had come, *de facto* if not yet *de jure*, into existence between 'public' and 'private' wars as a result of the Covenant of the League of Nations and the Locarno and the Kellogg–Briand pacts. This distinction was as much operational as it was legal, because economic warfare was only a practicable strategy against an enemy at once surrounded by hostile states, and under intense military pressure. These circumstances were only likely to recur in wars of collective defence as authorised by the League of Nations. Hankey had addressed the subject in a memorandum of 31 December 1928, but his conclusion was that the distinction would not be practicable. He believed the American public would view it only as an excuse for perpetuation of the powers Britain had asserted in the Great War, and feared that the League's capacity to protect British interests was inadequately tested [56]. The Sub-Committee apparently accepted his argument. But, although it did not think there was much potential in the idea, the Sub-Committee recognised its bargaining value, as discouraging the American public's interest in calling a conference on belligerent rights. It preferred the hope that discussions in private between the British and American governments would make it possible to develop an effective *modus vivendi*. The First Sea Lord, Admiral Sir Charles Madden, was part of a minority who objected to any concession to American interests. His view, that 'No code can really be produced which can foresee the contingencies of war twenty, thirty or fifty years hence,' was spelled out in an appendix to the first report [60].

It was not in fact to be the Baldwin cabinet which in the end had to meet the challenge from the United States, for the Conservative party was defeated in the general election of 30 May 1929. Ramsay MacDonald formed his second Labour administration on 5 June, and on 28 September he set off for a visit to Ottawa and Washington. Hoover did not pursue the matter of a codification of belligerent rights, but he pressed the case for their modification to the extent that 'food ships should be declared free from interference during times of war and thus remove starvation of women and children from the weapons of warfare.'[1] At Hoover's summer 'camp' on the Rapidan River it was agreed that a conference should be held in London in 1930 at which no naval officers should be present. The delegations should be made up of political leaders who could be trusted to prevent technical arguments obstructing an accord. The main subject was to be cruiser strengths.

Hankey sent a 'heads up' to MacDonald in October 1929 which was very nearly a threat, couched in kindly words, that 'Whenever the subject [of belligerent rights] has been opened its tendency has been to create either dissension in the Cabinet, or in Government Departments, or in Parliament, or public outcry, or international ill-will, and sometimes several of these evils at once' [61]. In Parliament MacDonald felt obliged to reassure Lloyd George that he had made no concessions to Hoover on belligerent rights. He warned the President that 'our people have a deep sentimental regard for their historical position on the sea and ... the simple fact of a re-examination is apt to unsettle and stampede them.'[2] Hankey exceeded norms of behaviour for a civil servant when he threatened to resign if any concession were made on belligerent rights, or if any further, and in his view futile, appeasement was attempted of the United States.

In a CID memorandum of December 1929 Hankey rehearsed the arguments against treating food ships like hospital ships. Some of the material in this memorandum was a recital of his earlier observations, but the tone was tailored to address Ramsay MacDonald's peculiar sensitivities. He began with the important point that Britain had undertaken under the Covenant of the League of Nations to sever all trade, financial transactions and personal contacts with an offending state. Along with the other members of the League, Britain had undertaken to intercept all communication between the nationals of the Covenant-breaking state and of any other state, whether a member of the League or not. 'President Hoover's proposal, then, has to be considered primarily in the light of our commitments under Article 16 of the Covenant of the League.' To Hoover's assertion that the exemption of food ships from the effects of war would weigh the balances on the side of peace, Hankey objected that fear of starvation was one of the greatest deterrents to adventurism, and in the particular circumstances of the time, diminution of the international influence of the two great naval powers, Britain and the United States, would diminish their capacity to work for peace. To Hoover's argument that starvation was a weapon which most

---

[1]Herbert C. Hoover, *The Memoirs of Herbert Hoover*, New York, 1951–52, Vol. II, p. 342.

[2]S.W. Roskill, *Hankey, Man of Secrets*, vol II, p. 48.

hurt the weak, the women and children, Hankey replied that in modern war all civilians are part of the great organisation of the state, and that women's enfranchisement meant that they were just as responsible for the outbreak of war as were their men. Hoover's argument that neutral food exporters were hurt by wartime trade control was no more substantial, as the disruption of food production in belligerent states due to the diversion of labour to the army ensured that there would always be a wartime market for food. Hoover's plan would only serve the war profiteers who sought to use their neutrality to exploit people's misery [62].

Britain was, of course, the nation most vulnerable to the effects of naval action against food supplies, but the experience of the Great War showed that the security of food supplies had to be ensured by something more substantial than treaties. 'If this proposal were adopted, there is a real danger that we should enter into a fool's paradise, in which we should be trusting our very existence to a "scrap of paper" instead of making proper provision for the defence of our vital interests.' But even if a treaty protecting food shipments were respected, it would be useless unless Britain were able to export manufactures to pay for the import of food, or import the raw material for manufacture.

The practical problems associated with Hoover's scheme had to be taken seriously: how were food ships to be identified without their being searched at sea, how were they to be spared air attack once they had reached harbour, how could Britain afford to send her own food ships back across the Atlantic in ballast, or permit an enemy to send theirs across laded with exports? And were armies to be able to block food shipments through their lines, while naval powers were prevented from using their own best strategy? Hoover's proposal lacked even the inducements of Wilson's 1915 proposal, for there was nothing offered in compensation for Britain's concession to American demands. Hankey dismissed, from experience, any thought that a generous act on Britain's part would produce any improvement in the attitude of the United States towards the British Empire.

The threatened invitation to a conference on belligerent rights never materialised. The American government had begun to move towards the idea of denying violators of the Kellogg–Briand Pact access to American manufactured arms. On 16 January 1929 congressman Korell introduced a resolution entitling the President to declare a signatory of the pact in violation, and interdict.[1] But, while a redefinition of bellig-

---

[1]CAB 16/79 ff. 420–24, Sir Esme Howard to Sir Austen Chamberlain, 25 January, 1929, CID, Sub-Committee on Belligerent Rights.

erent rights was avoided, it was only at the price of a further naval arms limitation treaty. At the conference in London in 1930 British and American political leadership agreed to reduce the British plan to maintain a fleet of 70 light cruisers. The backroom dealing between British and American leaders was seen as a major insult to the Japanese, and contributed to the deterioration of conditions in the Far East. And this was to put belligerent rights back into the spotlight.

Included in the Treaty of London of 22 April 1930 was a reassertion of the rules of submarine warfare. The arms limitation clauses of the Treaty of London were only to last until 31 December 1936. In consequence, the Rules of Submarine Warfare were renewed on 6 November 1936 by a procès-verbal signed over the following two years by all the naval powers, and still in force.[1]

---

[1]Canada, Directorate of Law Training, Department of National Defence, *Collection of Documents on the Law of Armed Conflict*, 1999 edition, p. 57.

31. *Armistice Discussions, 1918*

Committee of Imperial Defence Sub-Committee on Belligerent Rights
Secret – B.R. 2

[CAB 16/79]   2 Whitehall Gardens, S.W.1
                                               December 9, 1927

With the authority of the Chairman I circulate herewith, for the information of the committee, extracts from the discussions in Paris during the Armistice negotiations, October–November 1918, on the subject of Freedom of the Seas.

(Signed) M.P.A. Hankey,

Extract from Notes of a Conversation in Mr Pichon's Room at the Quai d'Orsay, Paris, on Tuesday, October 29, 1918, at 3 p.m. – (I.C. 83)
Present:

France:

M. Clemenceau, President of the Council and Minister of War.
M. Pichon, Minister for Foreign Affairs.
M. Berthelot.

Great Britain:

The Right Honourable D. Lloyd George, MP, Prime Minister.
The Right Honourable A.J. Balfour, OM, MP, Secretary of State for Foreign Affairs.
Lieutenant-Colonel Sir M.P.A. Hankey, KCB, Secretary, War Cabinet.

Italy:

Baron Sonnino, Secretary for Foreign Affairs.
Count Aldrovandi, Chef du Cabinet.

America:

Colonel E.M. House.
Mr. A.H. Frazier, First Secretary, USA Embassy, Paris.
Mr. Gordon Auchincloss.

Lieutenant P. Mantoux, *Interpreter.*

FREEDOM OF THE SEAS

M. PICHON then read the second of the fourteen points:

(II) Absolute freedom of navigation upon the seas, outside territorial waters, alike in peace and in war, except as the seas may be closed in whole or in part by international action for the enforcement of international covenants.

Mr LLOYD GEORGE said that he could not accept this clause under any conditions. If this clause had been in operation at the present time, we should have lost the power of imposing a blockade. Germany had broken down almost as much from the effects of the blockade as from that of the military operations. She was short of copper, rubber, tungsten, wool, cotton, leather, and many other materials. This was a cause of very great popular discontent in Germany, and the same was even more true of Austria. The suggestion was to hand this power over entirely to the League of Nations. If Great Britain was fighting for life, no League of Nations could prevent her from applying a blockade. When Holland had been pouring foodstuffs into Germany, and Scandinavia had been doing the same, we had been obliged to put a stop to it. So far as Clause II was concerned, therefore, he would like to see the League of Nations thoroughly established and proved before any discussion took place. Even after the establishment of the League of Nations he would only be prepared to begin discussing it. He was not prepared to discuss this question with Germany, or to give Germany this great advantage. If a League of Nations had been formed and was thoroughly established, then Great Britain might discuss the question, but after the Fleets of Great Britain, France, Italy, America and Japan had exercised this great weapon with so much success, to hand it over as one of the conditions of peace to a League of Nations was to deprive ourselves of a most powerful weapon. . . .

COLONEL HOUSE said that the discussions were leading to this, that all the negotiations up to this point with Germany and Austria would have to be cleaned off the slate. The President would have no alternative but to tell the enemy that his conditions were not accepted by his Allies. The question would then arise whether America would not have to take up these questions direct with Germany and Austria.

M. CLEMENCEAU asked if Colonel House meant to imply that there would be a separate peace between the United States of America and the enemy.

COLONEL HOUSE said it might lead to this. It would depend upon whether America could or could not agree to the conditions put up by France, Great Britain and Italy.

Mr LLOYD GEORGE said that, so far as he was concerned, it was impossible for the British Government to agree. If the United States of America was to make a separate peace, we should deeply regret it, but, nevertheless, should be prepared to go on fighting. (M. CLEMENCEAU here interjected: 'Yes.') We could not give up the one power which had enabled the American troops to be brought to Europe. This was a thing we were prepared to fight through and could not give up. Great Britain was not really a military nation. Its main defence was its Fleet. To give up the right of using its Fleet was a thing which no one in England would consent to. Moreover, our sea-power had never been exercised harshly. He thought there was no serious complaint to be made by neutrals against the British, French, or Italian Fleets, or the American Fleet, which was now engaged in close concert with them. . . .

That was the end of the matter so far as the Armistice discussions were concerned, and the subject never arose during the Peace Conference. It will be noted that Colonel House's attitude was at one time rather menacing, and that he even hinted that the United States of America might make a separate peace. President Wilson's telegrams, however, quoted in the above Minutes, do not indicate that he was as keen on this matter as Colonel House, which we suspected at the time, and which is borne out by the President's omission to raise the question at the Peace Conference.

* * *

32. *Memorandum on Blockade*

to be considered on the 26th November, 1918

[ADM 116/3619]

The entry of the British fleet into the Baltic has raised a new question in regard to the Blockade.

It is now possible, for the first time, to prevent traffic to and from Germany across the Baltic and this fact, coupled with the provision in the Armistice that the blockade is to continue, has already had the effect of preventing Swedish and Norwegian ships sailing for Germany owing to fear of capture. German fishing vessels have also withdrawn from trade and the position of all German ships which have hitherto traded in the Baltic is affected.

The problem as affecting neutral ships has been considered by the Allied Blockade Committee in London who decided that the trade of such ships to and from Germany should be rendered subject to the concurrence of the Inter-Allied Trade Committees in Copenhagen, Stockholm and Christiania.

The position of German ships is being considered by the Admiralty.

But a wider question arises in regard to outward cargoes from Germany, and in particular those consisting of manufactured articles.

It has been suggested that the control of the Baltic should be used to prevent exports from Germany and to secure allied predominance in

Scandinavian markets. It is argued that, even if exports from Germany cannot altogether be prevented owing to the necessity of allowing her to pay for such imports as are considered necessary, German exports should at all events be confined to raw materials (e.g. coal) and that manufactured goods should be absolutely excluded. Even as regards raw materials it is pointed out that Germany has complained to the Allies of the serious internal situation created by shortage of rolling stock and that the Allies should either compel her to use her rolling stock for purposes of internal relief or point out that her complaint is unfounded as she continues to carry coal etc. to Baltic ports for export.

On the other hand it has been argued that the blockade has now attained its object and that it would be impolitic to introduce a new form of pressure at the present juncture; also that blockade pressure cannot fitly be employed for trade purposes.

The Allied Blockade Committee who discussed this question on November 19th were unable to reach a decision and felt that the policy to be adopted during the armistice in regard to German exports was too wide a matter for them to decide.

It is suggested that exports from Sweden in Swedish ships should be permitted as heretofore and that safe conducts should be granted by the Inter-Allied Trade Committee accordingly.

As regards exports from Germany it is suggested that licences by the Inter-Allied Trade Committee should be made necessary and that licenses should be granted without reference to London for raw materials except gold and that Sweden should be informed that we do not desire to withhold any manufactures of which she is in need and licences will be granted for such manufactures after reference to London, each case of necessity being judged on his merits.

* * *

33.   The Freedom of the Seas

[CAB 21/307; CAB 16/79, Part 11/181–8]   Imperial War Cabinet
21st December 1918

Contents

I DEFINITIONS

1. Freedom of the Seas. The term 'freedom of the seas' is used in various senses, but it may be said generally to mean complete freedom of passage to neutral trade in time of war. As its extreme advocates also demand the immunity of all enemy private property at sea it involves in its widest sense freedom of passage to all belligerent trade.

2. The Term 'Private Property.' The word 'private' is used here in a misleading sense which is well refuted by Captain Mahan in 'The War of 1812.' He says: 'Property belonging to private individuals but embarked in the process of transportation and exchange, which we call commerce, is like money in circulation. It is the life-blood of national prosperity on which war depends, and as such is national in its employment and only in ownership private. To stop such circulation is to sap national prosperity, and to sap prosperity on which war depends for its energy is a measure as truly military as is the killing of the men whose arms maintain war in the field.'

3. Freedom of the Seas in Peace. The question of the freedom of the seas in peace arises in those cases in which coasting trade ('cabotage') is closed to foreign shipping, a generally recognised right enforced by nearly all countries except Great Britain. This is in practice, if not in law, an abridgment of complete freedom of the seas outside territorial waters, since coasting trade is held to include trade between any ports in the same territory, as, for instance, between Petrograd and Vladivostock, or between New York and San Francisco. The USA go so far as to extend the term 'coasting trade' to include the whole of their trade with their colonial dependencies, including the Philippine Islands. Freedom of the seas in peace would appear to mean the universal adoption of Great Britain's policy.

4. The Demand for Freedom of the Seas. By the declaration of war both belligerents cut themselves off from some of their usual sources of supply. At the same time they require increased supplies of various kinds for the support of their armies and peoples. Consequently the belligerent who is debarred by his weakness at sea from sharing the products of oversea neutrals, and the neutral trader in contraband whose share in the large profits of maritime trade during war would be greatly increased by free competition between the belligerents, combine in a constant struggle to escape from the pressure of sea power and to diminish the exercise of belligerent rights at sea.

The main support, however, of the demand for 'freedom of the seas' is the belief that it will lead to a reduction in naval armaments and the removal of a dangerous source of friction between belligerents and neutrals. This idea is based on a misunderstanding of the nature and meaning of maritime war.

II THE NATURE OF MARITIME WAR

5. Object of Modern War. Nothing can be clearer than the fact that modern war resolves itself into an attempt to throttle the national life. Waged by the whole power of a nation, its ultimate object is to bring pressure on the mass of the enemy's people, distressing them by every possible means, so as to compel the enemy's government to submit to terms.

6. Comparison of Invasion and Maritime War. Of all forms of pressure, invasion is the most effectual and most complete, for it strangles the life of a nation at its source; and as a nation's armies generally stand between it and invasion, their defeat is the final object of military strategy. In naval warfare, the strategical object cannot be reached so directly, for the enemy fleet may refuse action indefinitely; and even if it is eventually brought to battle and defeated, victory on the sea can exercise no influence on a war except by permitting the execution of measures which bring direct pressure to bear on the enemy's population.

7. Object of Maritime War. If it is true that the object of maritime war is to exert pressure on the enemy, the corollary follows that the destruction of the enemy's naval forces is merely a means to an end, and that the real and final aim of naval strategy is one or both of the following objects: –

(a) Prevention of enemy trade.

(b) The support of direct military attack in the form of invasion across the sea, and the maintenance of the requisite oversea communications.

8. Control of Communications. Though the first of these aims may be partly achieved by economic measures, yet such measures must rest ultimately on naval force. In each of the above cases, therefore, the real question at issue is the control of communications; and it is the function of the fighting ships to obtain that control by destroying or masking their opponent's naval forces, with the definite object of securing the uninterrupted passage of one's own trade and transports and denying such passage to the enemy.

9.   Maritime war is sometimes incorrectly visualised as a series of detached and isolated contests between the opposing fleets or vessels, but viewed in their right perspective, naval battles are merely the culminating points of a series of operations for the prevention of traffic and, in some cases, the passage of transports. The pressure arising from the grip of sea-power is, in fact, the antecedent cause of most naval operations; and if it is not applied in one form or another, naval war ceases to have any real meaning.

10.   Futility of Naval Warfare without Commerce Attack.   It is clear from the foregoing that the abolition of the capture of sea-borne trade would limit naval war to coastal bombardments, the transport of troops, and resistance to these forms of attack. One or both of the belligerents, however, may be practically invulnerable to coastal bombardments (for example: Germany in the late war), or may not have an army capable of exercising any serious military pressure (for example: the British in the early stages of the war), or their geographical situation may render the oversea transport of troops unnecessary. In both of these cases, the abolition of commerce prevention would be tantamount to the abolition of naval war. At the outset of the present war the prevention of German trade was the only means by which pressure could be applied to Germany; and until Britain raised a large army it was her primary means of offence.

11.   Efficacy of Conventions doubtful.   Any agreement therefore to abolish restrictions on belligerent trade must not only react unfairly on the nations that trust to naval rather than military power for exercising pressure on their enemies, but it must infallibly break down under the strain of a great war. Can it be imagined, for example, that a strong naval power engaged in a life-and-death struggle is going to abstain from using its Navy against maritime trade if the ability of its opponent to carry on the war depends on the continuance of oversea supplies? Under such circumstances, conventions forbidding attack or sea-borne trade are bound to be repudiated.

12.   Distinction between Legislation for the Prevention and for the Conduct of War.   So long as there is war there must be interference with trade. If Universal security from attack can be ensured by some international agreement it is worth striving for, but until it is achieved, proposals for the freedom of trade merely constitute an attempt to abolish one of the principal methods or functions of naval war without abolishing war itself. If, on the other hand, a 'League of Nations' is evolved, its authority must depend upon ability to coerce a recalcitrant nation; and this will necessarily include the right to cut off supplies by sea. *In any case, a careful distinction should be drawn* *between legislation for the prevention of war and legislation for the conduct of war.*

III THE RIGHT TO PREVENT BELLIGERENT TRADE IN NEUTRAL SHIPS AND THROUGH NEUTRAL PORTS

13. Replacement of Belligerent by Neutral Shipping. Having considered the great part which the restriction of enemy maritime commerce plays in the conduct of a war, we can proceed to examine the more particular case of belligerent trade in neutral ships. The only result of granting freedom of passage to neutral vessels and leaving belligerent merchant vessels liable to capture would be the replacement of belligerent by neutral shipping, without affecting the nature or bulk of any enemy's maritime commerce. The commerce would still go on under a neutral flag, except in the case of the belligerent mercantile marine being too large for neutral shipping to replace in its entirety. The following table illustrates this point:

Foreign Shipping Employed by Britain, USA, and Germany

Nationality of Carrier	Percentage of Foreign Trade Carried		
	British*	U.S.A.[†]	German[‡]
British	56.4	51.9	25.3
U.S.A.	–	13.8	–
German	11	12	48.4
Norwegian	7.1	7.5[§]	5.2
Swedish	4.2	[§]	6.5
Danish	3.8	1.3	8
Dutch	3.9	2.8	2.5
French	2.8	2.7	0.7
Spanish	2.2	1	0.46
Other Nationalities	8.6	7	2.9

* Annual Statement of Navigation and Shipping, 1913
[†] Statistical Abstract of the United States, 1914
[‡] Statistisches Jahrbuch für das Deutsche Reich, 1911
[§] Norwegian and Swedish classified together as 7.5%

14. Previous to 1914, Great Britain as a neutral could have kept the essential maritime trade of the smaller maritime Powers going, very much to the disadvantage of their opponents.

Similarly, before the war, about 25 per cent. of German foreign trade was carried in neutral ships; and German trade statistics show that this proportion was capable of carrying Germany's oversea food supplies and a very large proportion of the raw material required for military purposes, provided all non-essential trade was excluded. If this neutral shipping had been allowed free passage, Germany would have experienced very little difficulty in the supply and revictualment of her people and armies. Entire freedom of passage to neutral ships would therefore have had a very great influence on the outcome of the war.

15.   Besides the normal allocation of neutral shipping, additional neutral tonnage as well as new construction would tend to gravitate into the service of belligerents. Immunity of neutral shipping would therefore have the same effect as the abolition of commerce attack. Besides handicapping one belligerent more than another and causing intense friction with neutrals, a limitation of this sort must inevitably break down when vital issues are at stake. In land warfare, an analogy could be found if two equally matched armies refrained from attacking each other's commercial and military communications so long as they were maintained by neutral labour, vehicles, and railways.

16.   **Transfer of Belligerent Trade to Neutral Ports.**   Now, just as a belligerent may attempt to outflank an opponent's sea power by the use of neutral ships, she may endeavour to carry on her oversea trade circuitously through neutral ports. Before the war, over 20 per cent. of Germany's total sea-borne trade passed up the Rhine through the neutral port of Rotterdam. In 1910, 6 million tons of iron ore out of a total 9.8 millions, and 52 per cent. of her grain imports entered by this channel.[1] Similarly, as the Allies were unable to extend their control to the Baltic, Swedish and Danish ports became available to Germany as entrepôts for her trade. *In fact, if it had not been for the enforcement of the doctrine of 'Continuous Voyage,' and other measures, Germany would have been able to get all her essential supplies through neutral ports, thus completely outflanking the Allies' naval power. It therefore appears that any attempt to limit the enforcement of blockade and capture of contraband to ships proceeding direct to belligerent ports must not only give an advantage to a favourably-situated belligerent, but would render the old-established right of blockade and seizure of contraband absolutely worthless and would nullify naval war.*

If it is in the power of a belligerent to prevent it, he cannot be expected to allow a neutral to perform for the enemy a service which the enemy has been rendered impotent to perform for himself. The doctrine of continuous voyage and adjudication according to final destination is therefore an essential corollary of the doctrines of contraband and blockade.

---

[1]*These figures are deduced from the Jahresbericht für die Rheinschiffahrt, 1916. [Notes marked * appear in the original documents.]

17. These conditions are not peculiar to Europe; for if the USA were fighting Mexico and the immunity of neutral ships trading through neutral ports were established, Great Britain would be entitled to supply Mexico with all the munitions and material of war required through the neutral ports of Guatemala.

18. Summary of Principles Deduced. *The foregoing examination may be summarised by saying that the restriction of an enemy's maritime commerce is the most vital operation in maritime war; that the continuance of belligerent trade in neutral ships or through neutral ports may completely outflank naval power; and that, therefore, rules designed to protect a neutral assisting a belligerent by these means must inevitably break down when vital issues are at stake and the opposing navy is in a position to dispute them.*

19. Relation of these Principles to the Future. If the influence of commerce restrictions on maritime war has been correctly interpreted, this country cannot bind itself to any limitation of belligerent rights, and in the event of a League of Nations materialising, the necessity for any such limitation will be less apparent than ever, since the League itself will require the power to exercise the rights of maritime war. Sea power will still have to be exercised by individual States if such a League is not prepared to or is unable to act. This conclusion, however, does not prevent an examination of the lessons of the war in order to devise measures for the elimination of unnecessary friction between belligerents and neutrals.

IV ATTEMPTS TO LIMIT BELLIGERENT RIGHTS

20. Declaration of Paris. Previous to the Declaration of Paris in 1856, this country claimed and exercised the full belligerent right of stopping all trade with an enemy, no matter under what flag it sailed. By that Declaration we practically limited interference with neutral ships to contraband and blockade, but the absence of any exact definition of contraband and the different views of blockade taken by the various Powers left the question in a vague and undecided state.

21. Declaration of London. As a result of difficulties with Russia on questions of contraband in the Russo-Japanese War, the institution of an International Prize Court was proposed at the second Hague Peace Conference. In order to arrive at some agreement as to the rules which should guide it, a conference was assembled at London in 1908. It resulted in the Declaration of London of 1909, which was an attempt to codify the customs of maritime war so far as neutrals were concerned. By introducing a definite list of contraband articles under the headings 'absolute' and 'conditional' and a free list that could not be declared contraband, and by renouncing the doctrine of continuous voyage in the case of conditional contraband and blockade, it greatly limited the application of the principles of contraband and blockade previously in force.

22.   The Declarations of Paris and London may therefore be correctly viewed as a step towards 'Freedom of the Seas'; and as this country put in force the provisions of the Declaration of London, with certain modifications, on the outbreak of war, an examination of the practical working of the Declaration under the stress of war should facilitate a judgment on the larger issue, and will also indicate the extent to which the applications of the principles of contraband and blockade have been modified by modern conditions.

23.   Failure of Codified System in the Present War.   The Appendix shows in tabular form the gradual development of the blockade of Germany. Numerous Orders-in-Council[1] followed one another closely; and these, combined with the initial attempts to reconcile the actual requirements of war with the Declaration of London, as adopted by the Orders-in-Council with certain modifications, were responsible for confusion and uncertainty in the minds of neutral merchants as to what they could or could not do. As stated by Sir Edward Grey[2] in his instructions to the Delegates at the London Conference: 'What the commerce of the world desires above all is certainty'; and it was just this lack of certainty which was partly responsible for friction with neutrals.

24.   Probable Failure in Future Wars.   A similar uncertainty will always arise if a country clings to a codified system which it has to abandon in time of war. Weapons develop so rapidly, and different wars vary so greatly, *that the efficacy of international law can only be preserved by holding fast to a few elementary principles whilst retaining elasticity in their actual application.* The attempt to embody the rules of maritime war in a rigid code definitely failed in this war. If in 1909, we were willing to renounce rights which, independently of Germany's illegal submarine warfare, were essential to the exercise of British sea power six years later, there is no guarantee that another code of rules may not mean the abandonment of some other doctrine essential to our future salvation. Such mistakes are inevitable once legislation departs from the broad principles governing the doctrines of contraband, blockade, &c., and binds itself rigidly to the terms of a convention.

---

[1]*The fact that these orders were not necessarily binding on the Prize Courts added to the uncertainty of the situation. (*Vide* 'Kim' and 'Zamora' in Lloyd's Reports of Prize Cases.)

[2]*Correspondence and documents respecting the International Naval Conference held in London, 1909, Cd. 4554, p. 23.

25. Danger of the Code System. Although, before the war, this country recognised the absolute necessity of maintaining intact the weapon of blockade,[1] she was ready to renounce the application of 'Continuous Voyage' to blockade, on the grounds[2] that it had not been previously applied by British Prize Courts, thus illustrating the danger of 'the code and agreement system' as opposed to the application of general principles. If it be admitted – and it was admitted – that a belligerent has the right to enforce a blockade, it was entirely illogical to abandon a principle which safeguards a blockade from indirect infringement.

26. Proposed Return to Broad Principles. It is considered that the only satisfactory solution is a return to the old method, which consisted in claiming certain specific rights – namely, search, seizure for adjudication, blockade, &c. – leaving the Prize Court to base its judgment on general principles modified by the circumstances of the particular case. This system is recommended as being more adaptable to varying conditions and more likely to elicit an intelligible and consistent policy. It presumably would have been followed in 1914 if the Declarations of Paris, London, and The Hague had been non-existent.

27. Lord Stowell expressed the same idea when he said in the 'Atalanta' (6 C. Rob. 440, 1 E.P.C. 607): – 'All law is resolvable into general principles. The cases which may arise under new combinations of circumstances, leading to an extended application of principles, ancient and recognised by just corollaries, may be infinite; but so long as the continuity of the original and established principles is preserved pure and unbroken, the practice is not now nor is it justly chargeable with being an innovation on the ancient law, when, in fact, the Court does nothing more than apply old principles to new circumstances.'[3]

28. *It is considered, therefore, that Great Britain should refuse to bind herself to any hard-and-fast code governing the conduct of naval war, but should withdraw from the Declaration of Paris, denounce The Hague Conventions,[4] and declare her intention of being guided in the future by certain recognised principles and rights, the interpretation of which must be left to the judgment of the Prize Courts.*

---

[1]*Correspondence and documents respecting the International Naval Conference held in London, 1909. Cd. 4554, p. 25.

[2]*Ibid. p. 27. The reason why Britain had not previously applied this doctrine was because geographical conditions had not required it. This illustrates the danger of being guided only by precedent.

[3]*Memorandum for HM Procurator-General on Contraband Trade and Continuous Voyage by Dr A. Pearce Higgins.

[4]*According to the terms of the Hague Conventions they may be denounced by any of the contracting parties, subject to one year's notice.

V   BELLIGERENT RIGHTS AND THEIR PRACTICAL APPLICATION

29.   It is considered that any exposition of our claims should confine itself to general principles covering only the salient points, and should avoid anything in the shape of an elaborate code. The actual draft would, of course, require to be drawn up by competent counsel in close consultation with the Admiralty, but the following outline is suggested as embodying the main points:

30.   Great Britain claims the following to be the fundamental rights of a belligerent:

(1)   A Belligerent has the right to bring every possible pressure to bear on an enemy, consistent with due regard for innocent inter-neutral trade and in accordance with those dictates of humanity which modern opinion regards as imperative.

(2)   A belligerent has the right to prevent oversea supplies reaching the enemy, which may assist him in the prosecution of the war, and to attack his credit and resources by the restriction of his exports.

(To permit the execution of this right in the case of goods of enemy origin carried in neutral ships it will be necessary to abrogate Article 2 of the Declaration of Paris.)

(3)   The Government of a neutral state must refrain from assisting belligerents or shielding them from the pressure of their enemy's hostility, but it is not incumbent on such Government to prevent its subjects from trading in contraband. The responsibility rests with the belligerents concerned.

31.   Great Britain claims that these rights should be enforced in accordance with the following general methods and principles:

(a)   Safety of Neutrals and Non-combatants.   They must be exercised in such a manner, and only in such a manner, as to secure the safety of the lives of neutrals and non-combatants and the property of neutrals, subject in the case of property to interim seizure for adjudication before a proper court.

Corollary to (a).   A submarine can only become a legitimate weapon against commerce provided that it places in safety all persons and relevant papers before destroying a prize, nor can ships' boats be considered a place of safety.

(b)   Visit and Search.   The right[1] of visit and search is an essential preliminary in order to ascertain the true nature of the vessel and cargo.

[1] "The right to visit neutral ships is a necessary presupposition of the right to capture enemy merchantmen as well as of the right to prevent neutral ships from breaking a blockade, carrying contraband, and rendering unneutral service.'

When sea conditions render such visit or search impracticable, a vessel may be conducted into harbour for the purpose.

Corollary to (b).   The promulgation of a notice that all shipping in a given area (barred zone) will be subject to attack *without individual preliminary warning* is illegal.

(c)   Removal of Enemy Subjects and Suspicious Persons.   Enemy subjects capable of bearing arms, suspected of espionage or other belligerent service, may be arrested on the high seas. Neutral subjects may be similarly dealt with for espionage or when acting as enemy agents, but information of any such action must be conveyed as soon as possible to their Minister and they must be brought to trial before a competent court. Enemy mails and correspondence are also liable to seizure in a neutral ship.

(d)   Contraband.   Any articles may be declared contraband which assist or support the enemy directly or indirectly in the prosecution of the war.

Corollary to (d).   Not only does the nature of modern war prevent any clear distinction between absolute and conditional contraband, but the attempt to differentiate between the two introduces an endless source of friction between belligerents and neutral traders. Belligerents must publish their lists of contraband as soon after the commencement of hostilities as possible. Any list of contraband articles issued in peace time must be recognised as provisional, for its extent must depend partly on the nature and scope of the war.

(e)   Blockade.   The restriction on enemy commerce may be further enforced by a blockade, *i.e.*, an absolute restriction of all maritime trade with the whole or any portion of his coast, duly promulgated to neutrals. A blockade must be initiated as a distinct operation of war, and it must be maintained by a sufficient force.

(f)   Ultimate Destination.   The capture of goods of other than enemy origin whether by right of blockade or contraband is governed by the ultimate destination of the goods concerned or of goods which they replace, as accepted in what is known as the doctrine of continuous voyage.

Corollary to (f).   The difficulty of producing definite evidence as to the ultimate enemy destination of goods consigned to neutrals has been a serious cause of friction in the present war; but if belligerent maritime

'But whereas belligerents have not, in addition to the right of capture, a *right* to stop and visit enemy merchantmen, it is nevertheless their *duty*, before they apply force for the purpose of capturing them, to call upon these ships to stop.'

(The Position of Enemy Merchantmen in Naval War, Professor L.F.L. Oppenheim, Zeitsschrift fur Volkerrect, Vol. VIII, pp. 154–69.)

rights are to be preserved, means must be found to check imports in excess of a neutral's domestic requirements. New conditions arising from increased facilities of transport must be met by new methods, such as those built up during the present war (*vide* Appendix for description of blockade), and maritime powers should organise, in peace time, systems of control which would eliminate, as far as possible, the element of doubt and suspicion and would facilitate the passage of *bonâ fide* inter-neutral trade.

Governments should view favourably any efforts on the part of their merchants to safeguard and accelerate *bona fide* neutral trade; while remaining neutral, they should not hinder in any way, but rather encourage, the organisation of guilds to inspect, load, and guarantee such goods as may be intended for use and consumption only in their own country.

Governments should also undertake, and specially provide for, the compilation and publication of trade statistics by which the domestic requirements of neutrals can be measured and supplied by rationing. Intelligence is at the basis of accelerated passage of neutral goods and statistics are an essential part of the machinery of acceleration.

APPENDIX: DEVELOPMENT OF THE BLOCKADE

Note. – This appendix is included in order to enforce the lesson that instead of binding itself to any hard and fast code of international maritime law, this country should prepare in peace time different methods of blockade, suitable to the conditions of different wars, in conformity with the general principles laid down under the heading, 'Belligerent Rights and their Practical Application.'

The mere fact of promulgating a clear and logical policy to neutrals will do much to remove friction and distrust.

First Stage: Up to 20th August 1914

British vessels on the way to the North Sea or Baltic were warned not to continue their voyages, and to seek safety in a British port. This warning was reinforced by the refusal of Government insurance.

In the case of neutral vessels, goods shipped before the war broke out could not be seized as contraband, but we were able to use the right of pre-emption to take over a large amount of perishable goods which would otherwise have reached the enemy.

Enemy shipping came to a standstill. A large proportion was captured by the Allies or was laid up in neutral ports.

Second Stage: 20th August to November 1914

On 20th August an Order in Council put into force most of the rules contained in the Declaration of London, with the important exception that the doctrine of continuous voyage was made applicable to conditional as well as to absolute contraband. In view of the fact that practically all German trade had been diverted through neutral channels, it would have been impossible under the Declaration of London to have seized anything but absolute contraband.

The contraband lists were extended by successive proclamations, iron ore, copper, and rubber being declared conditional contraband on September 21st.

On 29th October, a further Order in Council was issued directing the seizure of goods consigned to a neutral port 'to order' or to a consignee in enemy territory. This unfortunately rendered it impossible to interfere with conditional contraband consigned to a named consignee: its effect therefore was to weaken the blockade. Further, instructions were issued on November 3rd that no foodstuffs consigned to a neutral port 'to order' were for the time being to be detained, with the result that all foodstuffs were free to pass through.

From this time onward, until the Order in Council of March 11th, 1915, no consignments of conditional contraband, except a few special items, were placed in prize.

These measures were at first executed largely by the traditional method of naval search; that is to say, the decision to send a vessel in for adjudication by the Prize Court generally rested with the Commanding Officer of the boarding vessel, guided by the instructions in the Naval Prize Manual.

Neutral shippers took steps to defeat this method of search by consigning goods to an apparently neutral destination, so that there was nothing to indicate that the destination of the articles mentioned in the manifest was other than the neutral country for which the ship was bound. There was no alternative under the old methods but to send in all such cargoes for adjudication, a measure which caused grave inconveniences to legitimate neutral trade and supply.

The methods which were gradually developed may be described as methods of guarantee, methods of evidence *re* particular cargoes, and finally methods of rationing by statistics.

The first step was to obtain guarantees in the case of each cargo from the neutral government concerned that the goods would not be re-exported. To do this it was necessary to wire the contents of the manifest to the Admiralty, thus transferring the decision as to whether a ship

should be released to the State. By November 1914, when this procedure became the regular practice, a radical change had therefore taken
place in the functions of the fleet, since the responsibility for seizing
ships and cargoes had been transferred from officers at sea to committees sitting in London. An additional reason for this procedure was the
difficulty and danger involved in the most superficial search of a modern ship at sea, subject to attack by submarines.

This was a departure from the traditional customs of maritime war,
but it was thoroughly justified by the new conditions, and made for the
convenience both of the belligerent and of the legitimate neutral trader.

Third Stage: November 1914 to 11th March 1915

The examination system developed rapidly. It was soon found that,
except in the case of Norway, the guarantees given by neutral governments in Europe against re-export were worthless, either from weakness
or complicity. Our blockade, instead of being directed simply to prevent the passage of contraband from overseas, had to be used with the
wider object of backing up our diplomatic pressure on the Scandinavian
neutrals.

In such cases as came before them, the Prize Court had little difficulty in brushing aside the pretences of neutral destination based on the
literal reading of the Declaration of London, and showing that the
goods were in fact destined for the German Government. In other
words, modern developments transformed the doctrine of Continuous
Voyage into a doctrine of Ultimate Destination.

On the naval side regular examination stations had been developed in
the Downs, at Falmouth, Kirkwall, Gibraltar, and Port Said, at which
all shipping was forced to call. In the case of the Downs, this call was
enforced by making use of the presence of British and German mine-
fields in the Narrow Seas. Elsewhere the work was performed by Cruiser
Squadrons. On November 4th an agreement was made with the United
Steamship Company of Denmark, in return for facilities for rapid handling, that their ships would voluntarily call for examination. This was
the first of many similar agreements with shipping lines, merchants,
and associations, in which we granted increased facilities for rapid
handling to traffic which was submitted to our supervision.

On 12th December the Netherlands Oversea Trust [NOT] was formed
to take charge of all contraband entering Holland, all contraband not
consigned to the Trust or the Dutch Government itself being liable to
seizure. Though hampered at first by lack of supervising staff, the
Netherlands Oversea Trust may be said to have reconciled the rights of
belligerents and neutrals with a considerable degree of success. Had all

the neutrals been able or willing to follow the example of Holland, the problem of the blockade would have been greatly simplified.

On the 13th November, as a result of all copper shipments being held up at Gibraltar, Italy decreed that goods arriving at an Italian port consigned 'to order' or to a destination in Italy were not to be re-exported. This order enabled Allied sea power to control the imports to Switzerland at Gibraltar and at sea.

Although the three Scandinavian countries had given guarantees not to re-export various kinds of contraband, their prohibition lists were not identical, and by the liberal granting of exemptions for export to one another, a brisk trade in contraband was still kept up. Norway appears to have meant well by us, but Denmark through weakness, and Sweden through a preference for Germany, made a satisfactory arrangement impossible. More pressure had therefore to be applied to them. In the case of Denmark this led to the conclusion of a series of private agreements with manufacturers.

No attempts had yet been made by us to control the export from European neutral countries adjacent to Germany of their own products, in regard to which the direct use of sea-power was inapplicable.

News was received early in November 1914 of the sinking by the enemy of two cargoes of grain intended for the civil population of Dublin. Under the Order in Council of October 29th, 1914, we had practically lost the power of stopping foodstuffs and other conditional contraband. The arrival at the end of January 1915 of the SS 'Wilhelmina' with a cargo of foodstuffs for the civil population of Hamburg drew attention to the impossibility of distinguishing, under the conditions of modern war, between the food supplies of the civil and of the military population.

Just before the arrival of the ship in British waters news was received of an announcement by the German Government (afterwards withdrawn) that all stocks of corn and flour in Germany would be seized by the German Government on February 1st. The cargo was placed in prize and the shippers compensated. On February 1st Germany announced the commencement of the submarine blockade as a retaliation against the closing of the North Sea by this country. The British Government thereupon made a statement, in announcing the seizure of the cargo of the 'Wilhelmina,' that the apparent intention of the German Government to sink merchant ships by submarine without bringing them into port or providing for the safety of their crews had made it necessary to consider retaliatory measures. On March 11th the Retaliatory Order was announced.

Fourth Stage: 11th March 1915 to 1st February 1917

Under the Declaration of London, the technicalities involved in declaring a blockade had rendered it impossible of application under the existing circumstances. As the best means of avoiding this tangle, the Order in Council of 11th March 1915 set up a system tantamount to a blockade, which enabled us to seize all goods of German origin, and to exert more pressure on neutrals such as Sweden and Denmark, who were acting as bases of supply to the enemy, by seizing *all* German imports instead of contraband only.

This necessitated a greater degree of control being executed by the British Government, and an organisation was developed to deal with it, including the War Trade Intelligence Department.

The illegality of the methods pursued by German submarines rendered it less invidious for us to adopt these necessary measures, which might otherwise have been more bitterly contested.

In the summer of 1915 we extended our supervision of neutral shipping by the municipal act of refusing facilities for bunker coal to ships which did not accept our arrangements. By October 1915 this system was in full operation.

Our next step was the development of agreements with neutral merchants or associations of merchants, both as regards re-export and export of their own produce. Our power to have these agreements carried out depended mainly on our maritime rights, but to a greater extent on the control of our own exports, principally coal. We also used the power to *purchase* goods.

In the case of Holland, the arrangement with the NOT was extended, and from 20th July 1915 they took charge of all overseas trade. Agreements in regard to the export of agricultural produce, fish, and glycerine followed. In the case of Denmark, an agreement was signed on 19th November 1915 with the Merchants' Guild of Copenhagen and the Chamber of Manufacturers. Other agreements followed, including some with the Danish Government and the Governments of Iceland and Greenland.

In the case of Sweden negotiations with the Government broke down in October 1915, and we were forced to rely entirely on the use of our maritime rights. The situation was complicated by the question of transit to Russia.

In the case of Norway a large number of agreements were signed with the various Trades Associations and Shipping Lines, and an understanding was come to with the Government Food Commission.

In the case of Switzerland an organisation similar to the NOT, the SSS (Société de Surveillance Suisse), was formed on 17th November

1915, but constant pressure was necessary to prevent leakage through the German-speaking cantons.

In the case of USA a series of agreements were made with trades associations to prevent the re-export of products of the British Empire to suspicious destinations, and agreements were made with the Meat Packers and other trades as regards export to Scandinavia. On 13th April 1916 a system of Letters of Assurance was instituted to minimise the delays of approved cargoes.

In addition to these agreements we were able to exercise a great degree of control over trade throughout the world by means of jute, its products being used to pack or cover the majority of goods for transport.

This stage involved little change in our means of executing our maritime rights, except in so far as the conclusion of agreements enabled us to exercise them more effectively with regard to our object and with less inconvenience to neutrals. It may be observed that it was necessarily to our own advantage to facilitate all trade which was not to the advantage of Germany.

We began to enforce rationing in certain commodities in March 1915, and the system was gradually extended and confirmed by means of agreements.

The final step was to institute a system of rationing imports by agreements with the importing countries. In view of the extreme difficulty of ascertaining the destination of any particular cargo, it was fairer to the neutrals and more satisfactory to us to allow a definite quantity to enter. This was, in fact, the logical consequence of our previous measures.

The rationing agreement with the NOT came into force on 5th November, 1915, that with the Danish Associations on 29th February, 1916, that with the Norwegian Food Commission on 7th April, 1916. Sweden refused to furnish statistics, but the system was applied to her, and was in general operation by the end of 1916.

Our blockade could now be described as effective up to the limit of the pressure which it had been held desirable to put upon the neutrals.

It should be noted that our agreements were working moderately well whenever we were able to make them directly with individuals or associations, as in Norway. A large organisation, such as the NOT, necessarily suffered from leakage, while no Government agreement was satisfactory.

Under the Order in Council of 7th July 1916 we abrogated the Declaration of London and resumed our traditional maritime rights. This did not affect what we were doing, but is important as a matter of principle.

Fifth Stage: 1st February 1917 to 29th August 1917

The declaration of the Unrestricted Submarine Campaign did not affect the principles of our blockade, but led to important modification in practice. The ports of examination had to be transferred outside the war zone, namely, to Halifax, Kingstown, Jamaica, Sierra Leone, and elsewhere. The development of the convoy system somewhat facilitated our control of neutral shipping. The shortage of shipping, however, hampered us in carrying out our agreements and supplying Scandinavia with coal. A series of measures became necessary to prevent neutrals (with the exception of Norway) from laying up their shipping.

Dutch shipping in Allied waters was seized by right of augury in March 1917. In June a shipping agreement was concluded with Denmark, in November with Norway, whose shipping had, however, been to a great extent at our disposal previous to the agreement. Under these arrangements we undertook to supply coal in return for the use of shipping. In May, after several months' pressure had been applied, Sweden released British shipping from the Baltic through the Kogrund Channel.

Final Stage: 29th August 1917 to the end

The United States of America entered the war on 6th April 1917. On 29th August 1917 the US War Trade Board prohibited the export of all goods except under license. This action cut off practically all imports to Scandinavia at the fountain head, and the use of naval force to exercise our maritime rights became largely superfluous. The Tenth Cruiser Squadron was finally withdrawn on 30th January 1918. The USA action, which, it should be noted, was purely municipal in appearance, forced Holland and Denmark to consume all, or practically all, their own home products, and led to a series of agreements with Norway (30th April 1918), Sweden (29th May 1918), and Denmark (18th September 1918), under which they handed over a proportion of shipping for our use, and limited their exports to Germany to a definite schedule, in return for rations.

The treatment meted out to neutrals by the US War Trade Board, though carried out by municipal acts not involving the use of force, was actually more severe than that applied by means of our maritime rights.

Imports to Germany were now reduced to the lowest limits possible.[1]

* * *

[1]Graphic display of 'Development of the Blockade' not copied.

Committee of Imperial Defence
Sub-Committee on Belligerent Rights: Report of Lord Cave's
Committee of December, 1918

Note by the Secretary, Committee of Imperial Defence

[CAB 21/307; CAB 16/79, part 7/231]   2, Whitehall Gardens, S.W.1
January 18, 1928

A report, dated the 18th December, 1918, to the Attorney-General by a Committee known as the International Law Committee, of which Lord Cave was Chairman, has recently been brought to my notice and is circulated herewith for the information of the Sub-Committee. This report covers a good deal of the ground under consideration by the present Sub-Committee. Its origin appears to be as follows:

2.   The establishment of the International Law Committee was suggested by Sir John Macdonell, who, in August, 1917, wrote to Lord Robert Cecil pointing out that it would be useful to the Government if a careful examination were made of the Hague Conventions, the Declaration of London and the decisions of the Prize Courts, in order to ascertain the chief changes in the rules of international law which the experience of the European War had shown to be desirable. It was at first decided to put off consideration of these questions until after the end of the War; but Lord Robert Cecil considered it advisable to get on with the Inquiry, and the Committee was appointed. Its terms of reference were:

> To consider what additions and amendments would be desirable, in the interests of Great Britain, to the established rules of international law on the subject of the conduct of hostilities, whether those rules rest on treaty or custom.

Although a formidable list of questions for discussion was drawn up, the Committee really dealt with only two matters – the Declaration of Paris of 1856 and the Freedom of the Seas.

3.   It will be seen that the Committee included, among others, Lord Cave, Sir Thomas Inskip, the late Sir Eyre Crowe, Sir Cecil Hurst, Sir John Mellor, Mr Pearce Higgins and the late Sir Erle Richards.

4.   It is perhaps worth mentioning that in November, 1918, the Imperial War Cabinet, while considering the second of President Wilson's Fourteen Points, namely, 'Freedom of the Seas,' decided, *inter alia*, to invite the Law Officers of the Crown to prepare a Memorandum dealing with the historical and legal side of the question. This conclusion

was transmitted by the Secretary to the Attorney-General, but the Office files contain no reply to his letter. The Report circulated herewith, however, which is addressed to the Attorney-General, deals with the very questions on which the Imperial War Cabinet requested information. Whether it was intended as the Law Officers' reply to the Imperial War Cabinet is not known, since, shortly after the signature of the Report (the 18th December, 1918), the Imperial War Cabinet came to an end and the question of Freedom of the Seas receded in urgency. For, on the 30th December, 1918, Mr Lloyd George informed the Imperial War Cabinet that, as regards Freedom of the Seas, President Wilson, who was then in London, was very vague and did not oppose his suggestion that the matter should be left for further consideration after the League of Nations had been established and proved its capacity in actual working (*Imperial War Cabinet*, 47 (1)). At a meeting on the following day Mr. Lloyd George stated that –

> As regards the freedom of the seas, his (President Wilson's) views did not really seem now to clash with the view we had put to M. Clemenceau, namely, that our Navy must be able to do in a future war what it had done in the present one.

(signed) M.P.A. Hankey

* * *

The Freedom of the Seas[1]

Enclosure
Memorandum by the International Law Committee*

18 December 1918

*The Committee is constituted as follows:

Right Hon Viscount Cave, *Chairman*

Rear-Admiral G.P.W. Hope, CB	Admiralty
Rear-Admiral Sir Reginald Hall, KCMG, CB	Admiralty
T.W.H. Inskip, Esq. KC	Admiralty
Brigadier-General G.K. Cockerill, CB	War Office
Sir Eyre Crowe, KCB, KCMG	Foreign Office

[1]Part II, *The Argument in Support of the Recommendations*; and Appendix, *Extracts from an Inter-Departmental Committee report of the 21st March, 1907, on the Right of Capture of Private Property at Sea*, not reproduced.

C.J.B. Hurst, Esq., CB, KC   Foreign Office
Sir J.P. Mellor, KCB, Procurator-General
A. Pearce Higgins, Esq., CBE, LL.D.   Procurator-Gen Dept
Colonel E.H. Davidson, MC   Air Ministry
C.R. Brigstocke, Esq.   Air Ministry
Sir John Macdonell, KCB, LL.D.
Sir H. Erle Richards, KCSI, KC
W.A. Steward, Esq., *Secretary*
R.F. Roxburgh, Esq., *Assistant Secretary*

* * *

16. Article 2 of the Declaration of Paris. The concession made by Great Britain by article 2 of the Declaration of Paris, 1856, providing that 'the neutral flag covers enemy goods ('la marchandise'), with the exception of contraband of war' is an example of the ill-considered adoption of a principle of the 'freedom of the seas' type.

There is singularly little information in our national archives as to the origin of this Declaration. The draft was sent from Paris to London by Lord Clarendon with a private covering letter to Lord Palmerston, and is preserved in the Foreign Office, together with the minutes of all the members of the Cabinet, and the Queen's acceptance on Lord Palmerston's recommendation. It is clear from the minutes and the covering letter, that the principal argument in favour of acceptance was the conviction that Great Britain, after agreeing to the temporary arrangement with France in 1854, would be unable to re-assert her old practice against neutrals. The Declaration was sprung upon the public, and was accepted in spite of some opposition.

Great Britain in this way abandoned her traditional practice – an abandonment which has embarrassed the navy in the prosecution of the present war, and, but for the illegal conduct of Germany, which enabled His Majesty's Government to justify its action as reprisals, would have made the Order in Council of the 11th March, 1915, difficult, and that of the 16th February, 1917, impossible to justify.

17. Its Abrogation is desirable. The abrogation of this article was discussed at length by us on the 11th October last, and we were of opinion that the paramount interest was the interest of this country as a belligerent, rather than as a neutral, and that, from the point of view of the conduct of war, the opinion of the Admiralty, expressed decidedly in favour of withdrawal from the Declaration of Paris in their letter to the Foreign Office of the 30th April, 1918, should prevail. We, therefore, passed the following resolution:

The Committee are of the opinion that, in view of the experience of the present war, it is desirable that the Declaration of Paris should, if possible, be abrogated, and they recommend that the Foreign Office should be requested to consider what steps should be taken for this purpose.

* * *

6. GENERAL CONCLUSIONS

24. Arguments against Restrictions and Compromises. The Committee feel that there are fundamental arguments against making any binding undertakings for the conduct of future naval wars which may shortly be summed up as follows:

(1.) During the present war Conventions regulating belligerent rights have broken down No success has attended the well-meant efforts hitherto made to formulate conventional stipulations regulating the exercise of belligerent rights.

This may be attributed partly to the failure of States, in making Agreements in anticipation of war, rightly to appreciate the conditions and circumstances under which war may be carried on; and partly to the fact that, as the experience of the present war has shown, International Agreements become incapable of execution in the face of entirely novel conditions.

(a.) The Declaration of Paris and other International Agreements. For example, the doctrine of the Article of the Declaration of Paris accepting the rule 'free ships, free goods,' has broken down in practice [see above paragraph 16]; numerous rules of the Regulations attached to the Hague Convention on the laws and customs of land warfare have been found to be impracticable. The meaning of the terms of the XIth Hague Convention (1907) on enemy ships at the outbreak of war has been found difficult of appreciation, and the Prize Courts of this country have so far refrained from adjudicating upon them in view of their ambiguity, and the possibility of compromising a settlement of the difficulties relating to such vessels; there are marked lacunae in the Hague Convention relating to hospital ships; the Convention relating to bombardment of coast towns in naval warfare has been violated by the enemy; and in the XIth Hague Convention relating to certain restrictions on the exercise of the right of capture in naval warfare a most striking instance is to be found.

(b.) The XIth Hague Convention. This Convention was drawn with the approval of the British naval authorities, whose opinion at the time was that it would inflict no injury upon British belligerent rights; but, speaking broadly, there is no single provision in it which His Majesty's Government have not found to be unworkable, and which they have not been compelled to ignore. Postal correspondence has been seized, and over a million packages are at this moment in this country, because it was found that the Germans were making use of the immunity given by this Convention to cloak their contraband trade, and as a means of disseminating propaganda in neutral States, and seditious literature in British possessions. Fishing boats have been captured, and destroyed, or strictly controlled, both by the Germans and by ourselves. The crews of merchant ships have not been released but detained as prisoners of war.

(c.)   The Declaration of London.   Another noteworthy illustration is provided by a study of the views put forward by His Majesty's Government, on the recommendation of the Admiralty, at the Naval Conference of London. It was then believed that the whole subject of Contraband would be of secondary importance, as compared with Blockade, and that, if the British views in regard to Blockade were adopted, the power of the Navy would be secured. In fact, however, Contraband has been found to be of vital importance; and if the abandonment of the doctrine of 'Continuous Voyage' in relation to Conditional Contraband, which was embodied in the Declaration of London, had received legal sanction, its observance would have completely paralysed the operations of the Fleet. On the other hand, a blockade of Germany, under the conditions provided by the Declaration of London, was found to be impracticable.

Probably the best and most striking comment on this point is to be found in the joint memorandum issued by the British and French Governments* respecting the withdrawal of the Declaration of London Orders in Council. After stating that the Allied Governments, at the beginning of the war, decided to adopt the provisions of the Declaration of London, as appearing to present in its main lines a statement of the rights and duties of belligerents, based on the experience of previous naval wars, the memorandum says:

> As the present struggle developed, acquiring a range and character beyond all previous conceptions, it became clear that the attempt made at London in time of peace to determine not only the principles of law, but even the forms under which they were to be applied had not produced a wholly satisfactory result. ... The rules laid down in the Declaration of London could not stand the strain imposed by the test of rapidly changing conditions and tendencies

which could not have been foreseen. The Allied Governments were forced to recognize the situation thus created, and to adapt the rules of the Declaration from time to time to meet these changing conditions. These successive modifications may perhaps have exposed the purpose of the Allies to misconstruction; they have therefore come to the conclusion that they must confine themselves simply to applying the historic and admitted rules of the Law of Nations.

*Appended to the note addressed by His Majesty's Government to neutral representatives in London on the 7th July, 1916 (*Parliamentary Papers, 'Miscellaneous, No. 22 (1916)'*).

All these attempts at codification or amendment of the laws of warfare, especially of naval warfare, having been put to the test of war, have been found wanting; and, had we been engaged with an enemy whose conduct was honourable, and who, by observing these Conventions, had given us no ground for receding from them without discredit, the power of the British Navy would have been seriously curtailed.

(2.)   **The strong view expressed by the Admiralty.**   In the course of their deliberations upon article 2 of the Declaration of Paris [Above paragraph 17], the Committee had before them a letter from the Secretary to the Admiralty [.............], dated the 30th April, 1918, which contains the following observations:

In their Lordships' opinion, it cannot be questioned that all conventions and declarations which place limitations on the exercise of sea power are to the disadvantage of the country which has the strongest naval force, and therefore, so long as we maintain our superiority on the seas, the provisions of the Declaration of Paris are necessarily to our disadvantage when we are at war. Modern developments of naval warfare have, indeed, produced new conditions, in which the restrictions directly and indirectly resulting from the Declaration are an incalculable hindrance to a proper naval policy.

In their Lordships' views, our aim should be to rid ourselves of all that has been shown by the experience of this war to be detrimental to the exercise of our full sea power, rather than to attempt to fetter, by rules of international law, the sea power of the future, the conditions of which with the progress of science, no man living can foresee.

The Committee attach great importance to the very strong opposition which the Admiralty make in this letter to any proposal to limit, or define, by international agreements, belligerent rights in naval warfare. Their opinion is based, both on the practical experience derived from the present war, and also upon the supreme importance to Great Britain, as an Island and an Empire whose only means of intercommunication is the sea, that the fleet, which is the Empire's safeguard, should not be hampered, or its power limited, by agreements which, as experience has shown, can never fully take into account all the possible circumstances and conditions of a future war.

(3.)   The Navy and popular Opinion.   There is also the question whether popular opinion, both in Great Britain and in the whole of the Empire, would not be against the abandonment of any rights which Great Britain may claim as a belligerent. This Committee prefer on this point to repeat the finding of the Inter-Departmental Committee of 1907:

> We feel that we should be guilty of presumption if we offered advice upon such a question. The subject is, however, one of great importance; involving as it does traditional national sentiment in regard to the Navy and the services to be expected from it in case of war.

(4.)   The Danger of Conventions without a Sanction, and the unjustified expectations hitherto raised at Conferences are now becoming everywhere understood.   We have so far approached the question chiefly from the standpoint of Great Britain; but this is not the point of view from which other States can be expected to approach it, and nations who have benefited in the past by the use of British sea-power sometimes have short memories.

Nevertheless the atmosphere which surrounded the Hague and London Conferences has been dispelled by the course of the war. The feeling that Conventions without a sanction are worse than useless is not confined to any one country or party. Their dangerous effect, in inducing a false feeling of security, has been revealed, and the admirable sentiments expressed by delegates, and embodied in speeches and preambles, have unfortunately proved to be only a method of concealing the real intentions of States.

This has been strikingly illustrated by the action of Germany, whose Delegate at the Second Hague Conference loudly proclaimed that the officers of the German Navy would always fulfil, in the strictest fashion, the duties which emanate from the unwritten law of humanity and civilisation. At the same time Baron Marschall laid his finger on a really weak spot in all international conventions designed to regulate the conduct of maritime war when he stated that they should only contain clauses the execution of which is possible from a military point of view, even in exceptional circumstances. Otherwise the respect for law would be lessened, and its authority undermined.*

Parliamentary Papers, 'Miscellaneous No. 4 (1900)', p. 55: Protocols of the Hague Conference, 1907, i, pp. 280, 281. A. Pearce Higgins, *The Hague Peace Conferences,* p. 342.

(5.)   Restrictions on Naval Power should not precede the establishment of a League of Nations.   We have considered the 'freedom of the seas' in relations to the proposed establishment of a League of Nations. As to this aspect of the case, we feel that it would be inverting the proper order of procedure, if any agreements were made tending to limit British naval rights, before the League, not only is an accomplished fact, but has proved that it is capable of fulfilling all the high ideals which its supporters expect to see accomplished by its establishment.

We feel that this is a very powerful argument in favour of obtaining a delay in discussion the questions connoted by the phrase: the 'freedom of the seas.' Should the League obtain the success which is hoped and expected from it, the whole international situation will assume a new phase, and the whole question will then need to be re-examined.

In our opinion the first essential is to assure the founding and successful working of the League of Nations, before any attempt is made to interfere with existing belligerent rights in naval warfare.

If the League is successful, it will diminish the chances of war, and ultimately abolish war itself. Disarmament will naturally follow the growth of international confidence, and the increased stability of the international régime, and, ultimately, the laws of naval warfare will thus automatically vanish. If war is carried on by, or with the authority of, the League, all the means of bringing pressure on its adversary will be at its disposal. But until this result is assured, it appears to be premature to discuss the means which a naval belligerent may employ, for the purpose of bringing about the overthrow of his enemy.

(6.)   Great Britain's Record in the Past.   The Committee feel that great importance attaches to the use which Great Britain has made of her maritime rights in the past. The record shows that seapower in her hands has been used in the defence of liberty, and, as in the present war, for the freedom of the world. They desire to draw attention to the following extract from a speech made by the present Prime Minister [Lloyd George] at the Mansion House on the 21st July, 1911:

I believe it is essential in the highest interests not merely of this country, but of the world, that Great Britain should at all hazards maintain her place and her prestige amongst the Great Powers of the World. Her potent influence has been many a time in the past and may yet be in the future invaluable to the cause of human liberty. It has more than once in the past redeemed continental nations, who are apt sometimes to forget that service, from overwhelming disaster and even from national extinction.

This influence has once again been asserted; and, by means of the British fleet and the British mercantile marine, France, Belgium, and other continental nations have been enabled to be rescued from overwhelming disaster – some of them from national extinction. British sea-power made possible the entry of the United States into the war by the side of the *Entente* Allies; and British transports, protected by ships of the Royal Navy, brought to Europe the greater part of the American troops, with singularly slight loss of life.

The overthrow of Napoleon was similarly brought about by the power of the British navy. Admiral Mahan says:

I should say that foremost amongst the cause of Napoleon's fall was the fact that to the products of France, so wealthy in her fields, vineyards, and manufactures, circulation was denied by the fleets of Great Britain. The cessation of maritime transportation deranged the entire financial system of France largely dependent on foreign custom.*

Some Neglected Aspects of the War, Chapter vii.

In the same way, it was, in the long run, due to the superiority of the Federal fleet, that American unity was preserved, and slavery abolished on the North American Continent in 1865.

25.   These arguments point to the desirability of carefully revising existing Conventions and avoiding further codification.   In view of these considerations, the Committee are of opinion that the existing Conventions dealing with naval warfare all need careful re-examination in the light of the experiences of the present war. These Conventions cover but a small part of the field of naval warfare, and in so far as this field is untouched by Conventions, we think that any attempt at codification of the rules and principles applicable should be avoided.

26.   The 'Freedom of the Seas' and the United States of America. The question of the 'freedom of the seas' is one of the fourteen points forming the basis of the proposals of peace with Germany enunciated by President Wilson, and although His Majesty's Government have made reservations upon it, doubtless the United states Delegates will wish to raise a discussion on it.

It does not appear that the United States Government is stopped by its conduct during the present war from doing so, as, since they became a belligerent, although they have materially assisted the enforcement of the Allied blockade policy, they have done this by means of municipal action in regard to restricting exports; their naval forces have not taken part in the patrol, and, as far as is known, they have not made any seizures of neutral or enemy ships, and have had no case in their Prize Courts.

27.   Pending the establishment and effective working of a League of Nations, British Naval Power should not be diminished by further legal restrictions.   The 'Freedom of the Seas' is a wholly misleading phrase, and we think that we have shown that, as used by revolutionary France, by Napoleon, or, in recent times, by German writers and statesmen, it has always been a direct attack on British maritime rights.

What meaning is to be attached to it, when used by President Wilson in his second 'Point,' we do not know. Should it mean no more than a desire for certain alleviations in the methods in which belligerent rights have been exercised by Great Britain during the course of the present war, we append [See Part II] a statement, by no means exhaustive, of the most important questions on which belligerent and neutral rights have been in conflict, and a summary of the measures which have been taken by the Allies to intercept all enemy commerce while causing the minimum of interference to *bona fide* neutral trade. These measures seem suitable for adaption in the future.

But if the phrase is used in the old French or modern German sense, as indicating an attack upon the maritime rights of a sea Power, we can only observe that, in our opinion, it should be strenuously resisted, and that, until a League of Nations is established, and has proved itself capable of fulfilling the rôle which it is hoped it may play in bringing about a complete change in the international system, British naval power, and the corresponding maritime rights, should not be diminished, or the power of the British fleet to protect the freedom of the world weakened. Until that condition of affairs has been reached, we think that discussion of the questions relating to maritime belligerent rights should, if possible, be postponed.

C.

* * *

34. The Economic Blockade 1914–1919

Admiralty Staff History by Lt Cmdr W.E. Arnold-Forster

[ADM 186/603] 1920[11]

INTRODUCTION The writer of this history, Lieutenant-Commander W.E. Arnold-Forster, RNVR – was appointed to the Trade Division of the Admiralty in the early months of the war, and was charged with the duty of making a comprehensive study of the subject of the Blockade in its various phases. He served at different times on the Contraband Committee, Licensing Committee, Black List Committee, and in the Restriction of Enemy Supplies Department, &c.; also on the Blockade and Raw Materials Sections of the Supreme Economic Council in Paris in 1919. . . .

p. 161 *Part III – THE FUTURE*

Chapter XXXI
PRINCIPLES OF A FUTURE BLOCKADE

It is, of course, extremely difficult to draw any conclusions from the history of the past blockade which will stand even a remote chance of proving applicable to a future blockade. It seems safe to assume that if a blockade does occur again it will be of a very different character to the last one; naval and aerial weapons and means of transport will have developed, the grouping of the powers will have changed, and if the League of Nations has become truly effective, blockade by separate nations will presumably be replaced in most cases by some form of co-operative international boycott.

Before attempting to draw any conclusions as to the nature and methods of a future boycott by the League of Nations or of a blockade by separate states, it may be worth setting down a few broad principles deduced from the past blockade which seem likely to prove applicable in any future case.

1. *The Impossibility of Detailed Codification of Rules of Blockade.* The first conclusion which may safely be drawn from the history of this blockade is that it would be worse than useless to try to define in advance with any great precision the rules upon which a future block-

---

[11]*Circulated to the Cabinet prior to the inception of the Sub-Committee on Belligerent Rights, and re-circulated to its Members by its Secretary, C.P. Hermon-Hodge, 19 January 1928.

ade may have to be conducted. Some broad, generally accepted, understanding as to maritime law will of course be needed; but it seems
hopeless to attempt to frame a complete fixed code of rules like the
Declaration of London. The history of that unhappy document is indeed the best proof of this truth; for even in the interval between the
signature of the Declaration in 1909 and the outbreak of war in 1914,
naval opinion as to the feasibility of a close blockade of the type
contemplated in the Declaration of London appears to have undergone
a fundamental change.

The weapons of naval warfare will not cease to develop, and the
relations of the nations one to another will not cease to change. If we
bind ourselves to the observance of some narrowly defined code incapable of a corresponding development, then we may find ourselves
again embarrassed, as we were embarrassed in this war, by a set of
obsolete rules based on principles which have become fallacious. Only
the most elastic and broadly defined code will stand a chance of surviv-
ing the test of another maritime war.

2. *The Fallacy of Dividing the Instrument of Blockade.* A second
conclusion, which it seems safe to draw, is that the arbitrary distinctions which theorists used to make between private property and state
property, and between civil and military supplies, are wholly inapplicable to the conditions of war between highly organised modern states. A
shipment of copper or of lard imported in the name of a private German
firm during the war served precisely the same function in the economy
of the state as an import in the name of the German War Ministry; and
the maintenance of the civil population at home was just as much the
concern of the German Government as that of the army in the field.

It is useless to try by means of a code of rules to cut the weapon of
blockade in half; if this weapon is retained by the nations, we shall
have to recognise, as the Covenant of the League of Nations does in
fact recognise, that it may have to be used for no less a purpose than the
prevention of the whole of the enemy's commercial life. This, and
nothing less than this, was the objective of the blockade which we
ourselves developed during the war; and it is precisely this sort of
blockade which is contemplated in the Covenant of the League.

Article XVI of the Covenant provides that, if a member of the League
resorts to war in disregard of its Covenants, the other members 'undertake immediately to subject it to the severance of all trade or financial
relations, the prohibition of all intercourse between their nationals and
the nationals of the covenant-breaking state, and the prevention of all
financial commercial or personal intercourse between the nationals of

the covenant-breaking state and the nationals of any other state, whether a member of the League or not.'

There are no reservations here, no distinctions between contraband and non-contraband, or between civil and military needs; such a 'blockade' or boycott aims at nothing less than the destruction of the enemy's commerce.

Thus with its first gesture the League has swept away all that tangle of restrictions based on fallacious theory which had been allowed to hamper the use of the blockade instrument for its full and proper purpose.

3. *The Fallacy of the 'Effective Blockade.'* Thirdly, we may conclude that it is necessary to abandon the old theory that blockade is *only* permissible when it amounts to the close and 'effective' investment of the enemy's coasts. The kind of blockade which used technically to be described as 'effective,' namely, the prevention of all passage of ships to or from the enemy's coasts, has proved impossible to maintain in face of the submarine and the mine; the blockading Power's reply to these weapons has been, and seems certain to be again, the long-distance blockade.* Although we never made an 'effective' blockade of Germany in the technical sense, our blockade was of course effective enough in the non-technical sense; and although a number of neutral states lay within the ring of our long-distance blockade, we did on the whole find means of avoiding undue injury to those neutral's interests.

It is, of course, not intended to suggest that an 'effective' close blockade will never be possible and should never be declared. It did, in fact, prove possible to make and to declare such a blockade during this war in several areas, such as the Red Sea, in which the submarine and the mine did not constitute a serious menace. But the point is that we ought not to let ourselves be tied down by a definition of the legality of blockade which would exclude the long-distance blockade.

*The point is of some importance, for there is some reason to suppose that in certain eventualities the United States might still seek to maintain the attitude that the long-distance blockade is illegal. They have never recognised as legal the form of blockade which we found it necessary to develop during the war, although they eventually co-operated in maintaining it; and though their position would be somewhat illogical, they may not impossibly try to re-establish the old rules of 'effective' blockade.

Chapter XXXII
A FUTURE BLOCKADE BY THE LEAGUE OF NATIONS

Whether the magnificent experiment of the League of Nations will prove successful or not remains at present uncertain. At the time of writing, some of the greatest Powers of the world are still outside the League, notably the United States, Germany, and Russia, as well as Austria and Hungary. It appears very unlikely, however, that the whole structure of the League, to the support of which our own country, like so many other states, is deeply pledged, will be suffered to crumble into ruin: we may assume that the League will in one form or another remain as a permanent institution. The creation of the League has profoundly changed the prospects of blockade in the future. The weapon which the members of the League have definitely bound themselves to employ in certain contingencies is the weapon of economic and financial war; if this economic war by the League does ever take place it will be fundamentally different from the blockade which we have lately seen, for the conflict between the interests of neutrals and belligerents, which constituted the fundamental problem of that blockade, will have been to a great extent, though probably not wholly, swept away. So far as the League extends, there will be either no belligerency, or else, in effect, no neutrality.

Cases in which League of Nations Blockade is contemplated. Let us examine first what are the circumstances in which an economic war by the League of Nations is contemplated in the Covenant of the League as it now stands.

Article XVI of the Treaty embodying the Covenant runs as follows:
Observance of Covenants
16.   Should any Member of the League resort to war in disregard of its covenants under Article XII, XIII, or XV, it shall, *ipso facto,* be deemed to have committed an act of war against all other Members of the League, which hereby undertake immediately to subject it to the severance of all trade or financial relations, the prohibition of all intercourse between their nationals and the nationals of the covenant-breaking State, and the prevention of all financial, commercial, or personal intercourse between the nationals of the covenant-breaking Member of the League and the nationals of any other State, whether a Member of the League or not.

It shall be the duty of the Council in such case to recommend to the several Governments concerned what effective military or naval force the Members of the League shall severally contribute to the armed forces to be used to protect the covenants of the League.

The Members of the League agree, further, that they will mutually support one another in the financial and economic measures which are taken under this article, in order to minimise the loss and inconvenience resulting from the above measures, and that they will mutually support one another in resisting any special measures aimed at one of their number by the covenant-breaking Members of the League, and that they will take the necessary steps to afford passage through their territory to the forces of any of the Members of the League which are co-operating to protect the covenants of the League.

Any Member of the League which has violated any covenant of the League may be declared to be no longer a Member of the League by a vote of the Council, concurred in by the Representatives of all the other Members of the League represented thereon.

The following are 'the Covenants under Article XII, XIII or XV' which are referred to in the foregoing passage:

Any Member of the League which has violated any covenant of the League may be declared to be no longer a Member of the League by a vote of the Council, concurred in by the Representatives of all the other Members of the League represented thereon.

Arbitration

12. The Members of the League agree that if there should arise between them any dispute likely to lead to a rupture, they will submit the matter either to arbitration or to enquiry by the Council, and they agree in no case to resort to war until three months after the award by the arbitrators or the report by the Council.

In any case under this Article, the award of the arbitrators shall be made within a reasonable time, and the report of the Council shall be made within six months after the submission of the dispute.

Dispute

13. The Members of the League agree that whenever any dispute shall arise between them which they recognise to be suitable for submission to arbitration and which cannot be satisfactorily settled by diplomacy, they will submit the whole subject matter to arbitration.

Disputes as to the interpretation of a treaty, as to any question of international law, as to the existence of any fact which, if established, would constitute a breach of any international obligation or as to the extent and nature of a reparation to be made for any such breach, are declared to be among those which are generally suitable for submission to arbitration.

For the consideration of any such dispute the court of Arbitration to which the case is referred shall be the Court agreed on by the parties to the dispute, or stipulated in any convention existing between them.

The Members of the League agree that they will carry out in full good faith any award that may be rendered, and that they will not resort to war against a Member of the League which complies therewith. In the event of any failure to carry out such an award, the Council shall propose what steps should be taken to give effect thereto.

* * *

Mediation of Council
15. If there should arise between Members of the League any dispute likely to lead to a rupture, which is not submitted to arbitration as above, the Members of the League agree that they will submit the matter to the Council. Any party to the dispute may effect such submission by giving notice of the existence of the dispute to the Secretary-General, who will make all necessary arrangements for a full investigation and consideration thereof.

For this purpose the parties to the dispute will submit to the Secretary-General, as promptly as possible, statements of their case with all the relevant facts and papers, and the Council may forthwith direct the publication thereof.

The Council shall endeavour to effect a settlement of the dispute, and if such efforts are successful, a statement shall be made public giving such facts and explanations regarding the dispute and the terms of settlement thereof as the Council may deem appropriate.

If the dispute is not thus settled, the Council, either unanimously or by a majority vote, shall make and publish a report containing a statement of the facts of the dispute, and the recommendations which are considered just and proper in regard thereto.

Any Member of the League represented on the Council may make public a statement of the facts of the dispute and of its conclusions regarding the same.

If a report by the Council is unanimously agreed to by the Members thereof other than the Representatives of one or more of the parties to the dispute, the Members of the League agree that they will not go to war with any party to the dispute which complies with the recommendations of the report.

If the Council fails to reach a report which is unanimously agreed to by the Members thereof, other than the Representatives of one or more of the parties to the dispute, the Members of the League reserve to themselves the right to take such action as they shall consider necessary for the maintenance of right and justice.

If the dispute between the parties is claimed by one of them, and is found by the Council, to arise out of a matter which by international law is solely within the domestic jurisdiction of that party, the Council shall so report, and shall make no recommendation as to its settlement.

The Council may in any case under this Article refer the dispute to the Assembly. The dispute shall be so referred at the request of either party to the dispute, provided that such request be made within 14 days after the submission of the dispute to the Council.

In any case referred to the Assembly, all the provisions of this Article and of Article XII, relating to the action and powers of the Council, shall apply to the action and powers of the Assembly, provided that a report made by the Assembly, if concurred in by the Representatives of those Members of the League represented on the Council and of a majority of the other Members of the League, exclusive in each case of the Representatives of the parties to the dispute, shall have the same power as a report by the Council concurred in by all the Members thereof other than the Representatives of one or more of the parties to the dispute.

Economic War by the League against a Member of the League.   It is clear that these clauses do not expressly contemplate the use of the economic weapon by the League against one of its members *unless that member should 'resort to war in disregard of its Covenants'* under certain specified articles. There is no express provision for the use of the economic weapon against a member which merely defies the general verdict of the League.

(It should be noted, however, that 'any war or threat of war, whether immediately affecting any of the Members of the League or not' has been declared by Article XI of the Covenant to be 'a matter of concern to the whole League, and the League shall take any action that may be deemed wise and effectual to safeguard the peace of nations.' Moreover, Article XIII provides that when a dispute has been submitted to arbitration and there has been failure to carry out the award, the Council of the League 'shall propose what steps should be taken to give effect thereto.' We may take it, therefore, that even in cases in which a member of the League did not actually 'resort to war in disregard of its Covenants' but defied the League's verdict, the League would have to consider the desirability of employing economic pressure. But the prospects of that pressure being actually employed by the League in such a case appear somewhat remote, since the decision of the Council on such a matter *must be unanimous* (except for the parties interested); if, as seems not unlikely, that unanimity is not secured, then the parties to the dispute are fully entitled under the Covenant to go to war; the League could take not objection.)

Economic War by the League against Non-Member of the League.   Besides these provisions as to economic war by the League against an offending member, the Covenant provides for the use of the League's economic weapon in certain contingencies against a state which is not a member. Article XVII lays down that in the event of a dispute between a member and a non-member, the non-member 'shall be invited to accept the obligations of membership in the League for the purposes of such dispute, upon such conditions as the Council (of the League) may deem just'; if the non-member refuses to accept these obligations and resorts to war against the member 'the provisions of Article XVI shall be applicable as against the State taking such action.' The economic weapon of the League would, in fact, be employed in such a case, even though the offending state were outside the League altogether.

It should be noted also that the Covenant does provide (in Article XVI) for the use of the economic weapon by the League in order to prevent intercourse between an offending member and the states which are not members. Thus, if the Argentine were to remain outside the League and the League were to be blockading, say, Jugo-Slavia, the members of the League would be called upon to prevent Argentine trade with Jugo-Slavia.

These, then, are the conditions under which the Covenant contemplates the use of the League's economic weapon against members and against non-members of the League.

Strength of League's Economic Weapon.   It is important that the enormous strength of the weapon which the League already possesses should be fully realised. Some have expressed the view that the League will have no powerful weapon unless it directly controls a great international naval and military force. It is, of course, true that some naval co-operation will almost certainly be necessary if the League's economic weapon is to be made wholly and immediately effective; but even without naval assistance at all the League will be able, if unanimous, to exercise a tremendous pressure on a recalcitrant state. Even in the late war, when the work of the naval patrols was of course the essential foundation of the blockade, the effectiveness of the whole instrument was due in far larger measure than is generally known to the use of weapons which were quite independent of naval operations; in a future blockade by the League, when an even larger alliance will be co-operating against the enemy, the power of these purely economic weapons will be enormously increased, and the blockade will be proportionately less dependent upon naval action.

The power of the League's economic weapon will of course depend very largely upon whether the Great Powers which now lie outside it have by that time become members of the League or are co-operating with it. Yet even without the co-operation of these great states, the League blockade will be from the beginning a much more complete and irresistible instrument of pressure than was our blockade of Germany in its early days. Instead of dealing with an enemy partly surrounded by neutral states the League may reasonably hope to have to deal with an enemy surrounded by loyal members of the League. Instead of having at every turn to attempt solutions of the sometimes insoluble problem of reconciling neutral and belligerent rights all over the world, the League will begin its blockade under conditions in which this problem has already been resolved to a great extent, if not entirely. Instead of waiting for eight months before deciding to stop the enemy's exports and many of his principal imports, the League will begin with the stoppage of all imports and exports whatever. Instead of waiting for sixteen months before stopping the enemy's mails, the League will from the start cut off all enemy communications which come within its reach. The refusal of facilities for finance and for insurance, instead of being confined at first to London and Paris, will apply from the outset to most if not all of the financial centres of the world.

The power of the League's economic weapon will indeed be so great that no single Power (with the possible exception of Russia) could hope to withstand it for long. A power such as Italy would be deprived of the necessaries of life in a few weeks or months; the mere stoppage of coal supplies would paralyse those of her factories which are not dependent on electrical power. Above all, the financing of her trade would immediately become impossible.

As for our own islands it is needless to point out that no amount of naval power would suffice to maintain our vital supplies or our overseas commerce, if the nations of the world simply refuse to deal with us. Even if we were able to maintain all the supplies which we derive from the various parts of the British Empire we should still be dependent upon American food, Spanish ore, and other foreign imports; and in any case our commercial position which depends upon export trade and on communications, would be at the mercy of the League, if the League were hostile to us.

Some Weaknesses of the League's Economic Weapon.   Such is the strength of the economic weapon which the League already possesses. It is evident, on the other hand that, there are also certain elements of weakness against which the league will have to guard.

The first and most obvious weakness lies in the fact that some of the greatest trading states, notably the United States, Germany, and Russia, are at present outside the League. The completeness of the League's economic weapon will of course depend largely upon whether these powers become members or are willing to co-operate in a particular blockade. It is reasonable to hope, though it is by no means safe to assume, that in course of time these states will come in: if they were to remain outside, the problems of the blockade by the League would tend to approximate towards those of the late blockade of the Central Powers. If there is one conclusion which may safely be drawn up from the past blockade it is that the effective blockade of a continental state is absolutely impossible unless a large measure of international co-operation can be secured. We should never have been able to make this weapon a decisive factor in the war against Germany unless we had had the co-operation of Germany's greatest neighbours, France and Russia. This difficulty in the way of making the blockade effective without international co-operation was largely due in the late war to the development of modern methods of transport; it appears certain that the future developments of applied science will accentuate this tendency. For example, unless all the world's great states are co-operating in the blockade, the development of wireless communications and of aerial and submarine postal services will complicate the problem of censorship, and may render the task of preventing all communications with the enemy insuperably difficult. In the same way, unless a large measure of co-operation is secured, the further development of transport by electricity or oil or other sources of power may be expected to reduce the value to the League of that control of coal (and oil) which proved so powerful a factor in the late war.

A second danger lies in the possibility that a block might be formed against the League so powerful and so self-supporting that it would be able to withstand, for a long time at any rate, the pressure of the League's economic weapon if unsupported by naval and military action. Even Russia alone would probably be impossible to coerce within a short period; and the same would apply with much greater force in the case of an alliance between Germany and Russia or between Germany, Russia, and Japan.

There remains a third danger against which it will be difficult to guard. The essence of the covenant is that a period of delay shall take place after the outbreak of the dispute and before the outbreak of war. It seems certain that a state which became involved in a dispute and which might presently have to face the blockade of the League would take good care to lay in an ample stock of the principal commodities during the period of delay. It is difficult to see what measure the League could take to prevent such a weakening of the power of its economic weapon unless, as seems rather improbable, it could secure the co-operation of all its members in rationing supplies to the disputants, whilst at the same time preserving sufficiently friendly relations with the states thus forcibly rationed.

This is a question which may be expected to become prominent in future discussions as to the employment of blockade by the League.

Machinery of the League for Economic War.   It will, of course, be necessary for the League to create some machinery for the proper use of its economic weapon. The terms of the covenant clearly indicate the intention that each Power shall be free to determine the precise nature of the blockade measures which it will take in order to give effect to Article XVI; but it is certain that some preparation beforehand and a close co-operation of the blockade measures of the co-operating powers will be essential if the League's economic weapon is to be properly used.

The machinery of the League for this purpose has not yet been created; but it seems fairly safe to assume that it will comprise, firstly, a standing blockade committee for the study in time of peace of questions relating to the economic war; and, secondly, a temporary blockade council which will be assembled on the outbreak of a League war and whose function will be to co-ordinate the blockade measures of the co-operating countries.

Standing Blockade Committee of the League.   The Standing Blockade Committee of the League (whatever the name that may be chosen for it) will presumably be an international body. It will have to consider the measures which ought to be taken in concert by the members of the League in the event of an economic war; it will be particularly concerned in the study of the vital trades and trade routes of each country, and of the control of finance and of communications.

Blockade Council of the League.   The Blockade Council of the League (to give it a name) will also be an international body and will presumably consist of the Blockade Ministers of the co-operating Powers, or their deputies. It will, in fact, be analogous to the Superior Blockade Council which sat in Paris in 1919.

Measures of Economic War by the League. Let us now consider what steps the League is likely to have to take in the event of an economic war becoming necessary. A dispute has, perhaps, arisen between two members, one of which has broken its undertaking to submit its dispute to arbitration or to inquiry by the Council of the League; or else, after having submitted the dispute to arbitration, it has refused to wait for the appointed three months after the award before having resort to war.

(It may be observed here that this provision for delay, which is of course the most valuable feature of the covenant, is likely, in very many cases, to prevent the outbreak of war altogether by giving time for the public opinion of the world to mobilise and to arrive at a settlement of the dispute by reason rather than by force.)

The offending country, having resorted to war in disregard of its covenants, would be 'deemed to have committed an act of war against all other members of the League.' The state of war would therefore already exist when the economic pressure has to be applied. But the Powers which are thus brought into a state of war are not *obliged* to employ more than the economic weapon; the employment of naval and military forces is a matter for the Council of the League to *recommend* to the several Governments.

Prohibition of Trade with the Enemy. We will deal first with the economic weapons which the members of the League would have to use in order to fulfil their pledges under Article XVI.

The first step would be for the members to prohibit their nationals from having any intercourse whatever with the nationals of the enemy state.

If the League includes all the great trading states, and if all its members are loyal and unanimous, this simple prohibition should be enough to paralyse the whole of the enemy's foreign trade and cut off all his imported supplies. After the first few weeks there would then be no more trouble about the interception of shipments from League countries to the enemy; such shipments would simply cease to be made.

But the position is not likely to be so simple as this. The mere prohibition of trade with the enemy by all the members of the League would be an immensely powerful weapon; but it would almost certainly need some reinforcement.

Finance, Insurance, Communications, Black List. The prohibition would, of course apply to the whole field of financial relations, and to insurance business and to communications. The financial weapon might often be sufficient of itself for the coercion of the offending state: its use will presumably be one of the most important and the most technical of the problems to be studied by the Standing Blockade Committee of the League. The interception of mails and cables will also require study and seems likely to present considerable difficulties, if some neutral states remain, and if (as is certain to be the case) communication by wireless and by aeroplane and submarine becomes much commoner and easier than at present. If censorship is necessary it will be difficult to ensure uniformity of treatment in a number of different centres.

If some countries should still be neutral, it might be necessary for the League to discriminate against enemy nationals or firms of close enemy association in those countries by means of a League Black List.

Prohibitions of Export.   The simple prohibition of trade with the enemy would presumably have to be reinforced by some other civilian measures. One such measure would be the prohibition of exports to certain destinations except under licence.

Some prohibitions might be required in order to conserve supplies or to control the allocation of articles specially needed by members of the League; but we need not deal here with these defensive measures.

Other prohibitions would be necessary if there were any neutral states which might export to the enemy. It may be noted in this connection that mere geographical propinquity is likely to be of much less importance in this respect than in the past: in a future blockade of Germany, for example, it would be necessary in view of submarine developments to keep a watch upon the imports of quite distant countries (such as Morocco or Iceland) which have a comparatively unguarded coast.

Apart from this, it would probably be necessary to exercise a further control over exports to weak though friendly states adjacent to the enemy country. It would often be desirable to prevent the accumulation of excessive stocks in such states, especially if they happened to be for any reason in a weak position in relation to their neighbour, or had a frontier convenient for smuggling traffic or were of doubtful loyalty to the League. This would apply with special force in respect of those articles of high military value which are comparatively easy to smuggle, such as rubber, tungsten, and nickel.

Another case for control of exports might arise if a friendly state should lie within the danger zone of the enemy's operations, so that shipments to a friendly port would be liable to capture by the enemy. Shipments would presumably have to be sent forward under some sort of convoy to a country so situated, for it would obviously be the duty of the League to co-operate in maintaining the supplies and the commerce of that country at a normal level if possible. In many cases it might be sufficient for this purpose if the Customs were merely to take steps to ensure that ships bound for that country would only proceed under convoy; but it is not difficult to imagine circumstances of this kind which would make it necessary to impose some prohibitions of export as a measure of friendly co-operation rather than as a restriction.

Chapter XXXIII
A FUTURE BLOCKADE BY SEPARATE STATES

As has been seen in the last chapter, the Covenant of the League of Nations, as at present constituted, greatly reduces, but by no means rules out, the possibility that this country may again have to employ the weapon of blockade acting not as a member of the League but as a separate state. It is obviously necessary to consider the prospects of such a blockade, in which we should not have the support of the League of Nations,

The following attempt to forecast the methods which may prove applicable to a future blockade has been based upon two assumptions. Firstly, it is assumed that, for a long time to come at any rate, the transport of bulky commodities, such as cereals, fodder, and fertilisers, will continue to be made by sea and land, not by air; and that, therefore, blockade is likely to continue to be a potentially effective weapon of offence in appropriate cases. Secondly, it has been assumed that any future blockade in which the League of Nations does not participate is likely to present the problems of a long-distance blockade; even if such developments as the submarine and the mine do not render the close blockade of the enemy's coast impracticable – as they will surely do in the majority of cases – it will still be necessary to control imports into any neutral countries that may be adjacent to the enemy. For the theory of the close blockade has been exploded not only by such developments as the mine but also by the development of modern transport.

I. Methods of Control

(A) Naval Control. It would of course be quite useless to attempt here to forecast the amount of naval force which might be required for purposes of blockade in so hypothetical a case. All that can well be said is that, in proportion as this country finds itself more isolated in its blockade measures, the larger its naval force is likely to have to be; if we could secure the co-operation of other powerful states, as in the late war or as in the event of a blockade by the League of Nations, then we should be able to reduce the amount of naval force required, especially in the later stages of the war. It will be remembered that in the late war

we were able, after the co-operation of the United States and our Allies had been secured, to withdraw the Tenth Cruiser Squadron from its station on the Northern Patrol; and it is perhaps not yet sufficiently realised to how surprisingly great an extent we found ourselves able in the later stages of the war to rely for 'blockade' action upon weapons other than that of naval force.

(B) Export Prohibitions from Great Britain and the British Empire. The export trade of Great Britain and of the British Empire forms so large a proportion of the world's commerce that its control must obviously be one of the most powerful weapons of a blockade. It has been seen in previous chapters how the importance of this control was very imperfectly realised, or at any rate imperfectly secured, during the early part of the war, with the deplorable result that the German army was at one time being supplied with cocoa of British origin, and that the enemy's principal supplies of commodities such as tin and linseed oil were being derived from this country. It seems very desirable that, among the plans which may be worked out on paper for the enforcement of a future blockade or boycott, special attention should be given to the preparation of schemes for the prompt control of exports of vital commodities in accordance as far as possible with the requirements of each hypothetical case.* Such a scheme would have to be prepared in co-operation with the Board of Trade, and it would of course be advisable to consult the Colonial Office as to the adoption of corresponding measures by the British Dominions and Colonies.†

*It may be noted here that it is of great importance that all British exports which are likely to be of high importance in a blockade should be separately recorded by HM Customs; for unless this is done there is no means of keeping abnormal exports under statistical observation. No British export during the war deserved a more careful scrutiny than that of nickel, yet it is the singular fact that the Board of Trade have no record of the amounts exported up to the time when the War Trade Statistical Department began its work. The Customs schedule included nickel under the heading of ferro-alloys, and so the metal is impossible to identify in the export returns of the Board of Trade, even though its export was specifically prohibited by the Board of Trade on the very first day of the war.

†A complete set of the lists of prohibited exports, which were issued by the Board of Trade from time to time during the war, is filed at the Admiralty, for use in this connection.

(C) Export Prohibitions in other Countries. In the early chapters of this book attention was drawn to some of the weaknesses inherent in a system of blockade which relied too much upon prohibitions of export by neutral countries: if we failed to prevent the neutral countries contiguous to Germany from becoming flooded with perishable imported goods which they could not consume themselves, then we could not always safely rely upon prohibitions of re-export from those countries. Moreover, if we succeeded in inducing one of the neutral states in question to prohibit the export of a commodity to the enemy, we were liable to find that prohibition to be ineffectual until a similar measure had been adopted by the other neutral countries as well.

This amounts to saying that such a system of prohibitions of export cannot be relied upon as the principal method of enforcing a long-distance blockade. It is, of course, a most valuable adjunct to such a blockade, but the blockading power must retain the means and the right of stopping all goods destined for its enemy, and must be prepared to shoulder the whole of the responsibility for doing so.

(D) Agreements and Guarantees against Re-export. It would certainly be necessary in a future blockade to resort again to the system of guarantees against re-export. Presumably, too, it would be necessary again to create a series of agreements with importing associations and individual consumers so that the guarantees might be more readily collected and enforced. In any blockade involving neutral as well as belligerent states it is likely that private or semi-private associations in the neutral countries might find it easier to come to an arrangement with the blockading power than their respective Governments; for the Governments might be too much concerned with the maintenance of their neutrality to risk giving offence to the blockaded power by entering into such arrangements. It is most important however that, if private organisations, such as the Netherlands Overseas Trust, are formed, they should have at least the recognition and the assurance of support of their Government; otherwise they will be likely to find themselves, like the Netherlands Overseas Trust, in danger of being thrown over by the Government as soon as pressure from the blockaded power becomes inconvenient.

(E) Letters of Assurance. The system of letters of assurance has proved itself so valuable a means of reconciling neutral and belligerent interests, and is capable of so wide an application, that it seems safe to prophesy that efforts would have to be made to revive it in the event of a future blockade of the type we are considering. The working of the 'navicert' system of advance bookings, which is outlined in Chapter

XXVI, deserves careful study, for this proved to be one of the most successful innovations in the whole course of the blockade.

There is one point which may be worth special attention in this connection. The practical result of the system of letters of assurance was to eliminate the use of the Prize Court almost completely and to render it unnecessary, except in a trifling proportion of cases, even to detain consignments under the terms of the Order of March 11th, 1915. It has been questioned whether this system could still be made to function if we retained only the right of *detaining* suspect consignments, and did away altogether with the right of *confiscating* them. The system did in fact come into existence not so much by reason of the fear of shippers or importers that their consignments would be condemned as Prize, but by reason of the fear of shipowners that their vessels would be delayed, and the desire of traders to eliminate uncertainty as to whether their neutral trade would be interrupted or not.

If the risk of detention would in fact suffice to induce shippers to submit their booking in advance to the blockading power, and if the rationing principle could be effectively applied, then the blockader could perhaps afford to make a concession to the neutrals by abandoning the right of confiscation altogether. Looked at from a detached standpoint, the practice of confiscating neutral property destined for an enemy, or obtained from an enemy, appears a somewhat barbaric survival; and a blockading power might find it advantageous for political reasons to agree to the waiving of this practice, and of the Prize Fund, *if* the alternative of detention could be relied on to secure an adequate result. But there can, of course, be no doubt that if the condemnation of contraband were abolished, neutral traders would be much less shy of trading, or trying to trade, with a blockaded state; and it seems likely that the stimulus thus given to trading with the enemy would outweigh any political advantage which the blockader might derive from making the concession to neutrals.

Opinions will differ as to how far mere detention would be likely to suffice for the purposes of a blockading power; but, in any case, the principle is one which cannot in future be ignored by the international jurist. It was this principle which the Allies chose to adopt as the basis of their policy of reprisals in March, 1915; and the possibility of its effective application has undoubtedly been greatly increased by the development of the systems of rationing and of advance bookings. From an international point of view the reciprocal abandonment of the right of confiscation might have much to recommend it; and in considering such a change from the purely national standpoint it would be necessary of course to consider the prospective interests of Great Britain, not only as a possible belligerent and a blockading power, but also as a neutral and as a blockaded power.

(F) Bunker Control. It will have been seen from the chapter on bunker control that the power which we found ourselves able to exercise by means of the control of fuel was far greater than had been generally anticipated. Some such control could probably be employed in a future blockade; but the whole situation may of course be changed by some cause impossible to foresee, such as the development of new means of locomotion. In the same way the power which the control of coal would give us in dealing with countries dependent on British coal for their industrial life will probably be reduced or destroyed by the development of new sources of power.

(G) Censorship. It is unnecessary to add here to what has been said in the pages on censorship, except to note that any legal limitations which would interfere with the exercise of a control of an enemy's communications at least as strict as that which we developed during the war ought if possible to be avoided. The object of the blockade will presumably be nothing less than the prevention of the enemy's commerce, and communications are an indispensable part of that commerce.

(H) Finance. The value of British financial control over the enemy's means of purchasing and shipping commodities has already been emphasised. Some study of the possible future use of the financial weapon will be an important part of the preparations to meet the contingency of a future blockade; it is needless to add that no part of the task will be of a more technical and difficult character.

(I) Insurance. The importance of insurance control as a means of paralysing the movement of recalcitrant ships and preventing the shipment of undesirable commodities has been indicated in Chapter XXIX. Whether the conditions which made the effective use of this weapon possible in the late blockade will recur in another case is of course impossible to predict; much depends upon whether British insurance business retains its present predominant position.

The control of information communicated in insurance correspondence, especially as regards the movement of shipping and the real destination of consignments, is a subject which deserves exhaustive study, for the international character of re-insurance business makes it exceptionally difficult to prevent the leakage of information of vital importance. It has been seen in the late war how the re-insurance bordereaux of a neutral insurance agency may be of immense value to a belligerent in identifying consignments of enemy destination, and may, in certain circumstances, assist a belligerent in tracing the movement of shipping. The methods of control of insurance correspondence, and, if possible, the nationality and record of foreign insurance companies, should, therefore, receive some study in time of peace.

II.   *Methods of Discrimination*

We have now dealt in summary with the principal methods of controlling the movement of goods towards an enemy country through a future long-distance blockade. The methods of distinguishing between such goods when destined for the enemy and when destined for genuine neutral consumption, remain to be considered.

(J)   Rationing.   It has been emphasised throughout this book that the basis of the whole of the recent blockade was the system of rationing. If there is one prophecy which may safely be made as to a future blockade of similar character, it is that the statistics of trades vital to the enemy will again afford the best guide in doing injury to the enemy, and that the statistics of the normal requirements of neutrals will furnish the only satisfactory means of avoiding injury to the neutrals.

The statistics of the world's vital trades will therefore be the basis of any future offensive operation of blockade. It will not be enough merely to collect the import and export returns of the various countries; it will be necessary for those engaged in this study to follow at the same time the inter-relations of the different commodities one to another, and to keep in touch with the scientific developments which will continually be altering the relative importance of these commodities. During the past blockade, the lack of a scientific adviser to the blockade was felt on many occasions. It seems possible that those who are charged with the task of studying the requirements of the world's vital trades will do well to keep in touch with some body (such as the Department of Industrial and Scientific Research) which could advise as to the changing importance of each commodity.

The rationing in itself is not very difficult to apply, provided that the difficulty of distribution can be got over by arranging for the consignment of the whole of the appointed quota of each commodity to a distributing agency in the country in question. It seems likely that even one of the great Powers, if it remained neutral in a further blockade, could be restricted to fixed rations of the principal commodities without incurring its hostility, provided that the negotiations were carefully handled, and that a distributing agency could be formed.

It has been seen in the chapter on rationing, that there is one fundamental difficulty which attaches to the application of the rationing principle by any means other than the system of letters of assurance. The Prize Court is not able at present, and presumably will not be able in future, to regard statistical evidence as being of itself sufficient to justify the condemnation or detention of specific consignments. The difficulty is one which can be got over by means of the system of letters of assurance, and by means of rationing agreements with importers, and (in some cases) with exporters.

There is, however, one further difficulty, which will always embarrass a blockading power, if it is necessary to employ the rationing system in its fullest development. The treatment of 'produits similaires' is a subject which is likely to occupy the attention of jurists whenever the problem of a long-distance blockade has to be considered. It is comparatively easy to defend the stoppage of imports of margarine material into Sweden, or of feed-stuffs into Denmark, if it can be shown that a normal and sufficient quantity of these articles has already reached Sweden and Denmark. But it is by no means easy to defend in the Prize Court the stoppage of these commodities if it can only be shown that Sweden has a surplus of butter which she is exporting to the enemy, and that Denmark will use some of the fodder for the fattening of cattle and the increasing of dairy produce which she is exporting to the enemy: such a stoppage may seem easy enough to justify from the point of view of common sense, but it will not pass the test of international law. It appears, therefore, that the extension of the rationing principle to cover products similar to those which are being exported to the enemy is likely to meet with much opposition in a future blockade, and could probably only be made effective in a case in which the blockading power occupied an overwhelmingly strong position.

(K) Evidence against particular Shipments.   In a future blockade the rationing system, no matter how perfectly worked out, would presumably have to be supplemented by a system of collection of evidence with regard to specific shipments. The supply of such evidence will be of special importance during the first few months, for it is the weakness of the rationing system that it cannot become effective in a moment but is dependent upon the collection of statistics over a considerable period.

The nature of the organisation created for the purpose of supplying information against particular shipments during the last blockade has been indicated in a previous chapter. An attempt was there made to indicate some of the defects which had to be overcome and the remarkable efficiency of the organisation which was gradually evolved. This may serve to suggest the lines on which the embryo of such an organisation for use in a future blockade might be formed in time of peace.

It is essential that the nucleus of this organisation should be prepared in advance. The mass of material to be dealt with will be enormous, and if the machinery for dealing with it has to be improvised after the outbreak of war, it is perfectly certain that much of the information which might otherwise be made available for stopping shipments intended for the enemy will remain lost in the files, and will only be identified long afterwards, when it has ceased to be of practical value. The experience of the recent blockade furnishes the most painful evidence of this truth; to look back now at any of the early series of German telegrams which have since been arranged is to feel once more deeply depressed at the magnitude of the opportunities missed, and at the injury done to the blockade owing to the lack of proper organisation for the use of the evidence available.

(L) Black Lists. It would obviously be desirable, in the event of a future blockade of the type of the last one, that the Admiralty (or some other Department which may be concerned with the preparatory study of blockade) should have knowledge from the beginning not only as to which trades are vital to the enemy, but also which trades the enemy is likely to depend upon, and which are of enemy character or association. It cannot be expected that a watch will be kept upon the commercial ramifications of all important foreign enterprises; but it would be very desirable that the Admiralty should have available for future use, in case of need, some sort of record of the principal industrial concerns of foreign powers outside their own territory. The sort of material accumulated during the war in the Index of the War Trade Intelligence Department, in that Department's printed volumes, and in the Cable Censor's Handbook, and Black List Committee Minutes, will very soon be quite out of date; but it may serve for a few years at any rate as a starting point for further studies of some foreign trade connections.

One further point may be noted in this connection. During the past blockade it was found that this country was unfortunately so dependent upon the services of certain firms (notably W.H. Muller & Co.) which were more or less closely associated with enemy interests that it was impossible to treat those firms with the severity which the case required. It may be found possible in the course of the Admiralty's work during peace time to make special study of the potentially dangerous connections of foreign firms, especially shipping firms, upon which this country may be specially dependent.

(M) Enemy Imports from within the Blockade. That part of a future blockade which is concerned with the restriction of an enemy's supplies from neighbouring neutral countries is even more difficult to

foresee than the part which concerns the stoppage of supplies from overseas.

The method of buying up the output of the neutral countries in question is obviously applicable only in exceptional cases; for the blockaded power will generally be prepared to pay a higher price than its opponent, and the cost of purchase to the blockading power will therefore tend to become more and more unremunerative. As was seen in the chapter on the restriction of the enemy's supplies, there may be some instances in which the commodity is so important, or the supply so limited, that purchase may be desirable as an exceptional expedient; but it is generally better to avoid so direct a conflict with the laws of supply and demand, and to make use of some other form of bargaining in addition to or instead of purchase.

The minutes of the Restriction of Enemy Supplies Committee in 1914–15 and the history of the Restriction of Enemy Supplies Department in 1916–18 afford plenty of material for the study of such problems. The vast purchases of Norwegian fish, Swedish iron ore, and Argentine grain, and the schemes by which Dutch and Danish and Danish, Icelandic, and Norwegian produce was prevented from reaching the enemy, illustrate the variety of the expedients employed. But no generalisations can safely be drawn from these past experiences: future cases will have to be dealt with on their merits.

Besides the method of purchase there is of course the method of bargaining and of agreement. The Dutch, Danish, Icelandic and Norwegian agreements show how the control of British exports was employed as a lever in obtaining favourable terms. From the point of view of a country specially anxious to maintain its neutrality the Danish policy which aimed at maintaining the pre-war proportion of exports to the two parties in the struggle had much to recommend it. The policy of neutrals in a future blockade of the same type would very likely approximate to this Danish compromise.

But in truth such speculations as to the treatment of neutral states which might lie within the ring of a future long-distance blockade can hardly be of any substantial value; the hypothetical case is too vague to be examined.

British Dependence on Foreign Supplies. There is, however, one closely related subject which might well be studied in peace time, namely, the dependence of this country upon certain vital supplies from foreign sources.

The recent blockade has furnished many proofs of the damaging effect to the blockading power of being absolutely dependent on certain sources of foreign supply. The statement is indeed a truism; but the blockade has illustrated it in unexpected ways. Thus, in our negotiations with Sweden as to the blockade we were always at a disadvantage owing to the fact that, throughout the war, we were dependent on supplies of Swedish iron ore, steel, and ball-bearings. Our policy with regard to Denmark was crippled early in the war by our dependence on Danish dairy products; and the measures which we should have liked to take in dealing with Holland were for a long time impracticable owing to our unfortunate dependence on Dutch margarine and on oil from the Dutch Indies.

It is obvious that this country could never hope to become 'self-supporting,' and even the idea of a 'self-supporting' British Empire, independent of American cotton, Spanish ore and foreign grain, appears to be fundamentally unsound. But it is clear too that the military departments cannot afford to ignore the problems created by our dependence on foreign supplies, and that in certain cases, where our military efficiency is conditional upon our continuing to obtain some key article from a foreign firm, every effort should be made to stimulate the production of that article at home. Our dependence during this war upon a neutral firm, such as the Svenska Kullager Fabrik for ball bearings, or Messrs. Jurgens and Van den Bergh for margarine, was a perpetual complication in our foreign policy and a source of injury to our blockade.

Necessity for a Ministry of Blockade.   In conclusion a word may be said as to the organisation required in the event of another great blockade by this country. It is safe to predict that, if it should ever be necessary for the State again to co-ordinate all its resources for such a purpose, another Ministry of Blockade would have to be formed, and that that Ministry would have to be in the very closest connection with the Foreign Office.

For although blockade is a weapon made up of many parts it can only be used effectively if used as a single weapon directed by a single policy. Every step in a blockade means interference with the trade of a foreign state and so affects our foreign relations; it is the Department of Foreign Affairs, not the Board of Trade or even the Admiralty, which must be the most closely associated with the Minister of Blockade.

* * *

Other Forms of Economic Pressure.   We have not dealt in summary with the possible future of a blockade of the type of the one recorded in this book; that is to say, a blockade directed by governments and involving the problem of reconciling neutral and belligerent rights. We have also considered the possible future of the weapon of boycott or blockade as it might be applied by the governments of the League of Nations, when the conflict between neutrals and belligerents would arise only in a moderated form or not at all.

These are the forms of open economic warfare which principally concern the Admiralty as an instrument of the State; but there are of course many other kinds of economic pressure by governments, such as the manipulation of tariffs, the withholding of shipping facilities, and other varieties of more or less veiled economic war in which the Admiralty will be deeply interested.

No attempt will be made to deal here with this far-reaching and vitally important subject of economic 'war' waged by (or with the connivance of) governments in time of 'peace.' But before ending this book it is necessary to allude to the possible developments in the future of another kind of blockade or boycott, the boycott imposed not by governments but by the private organisations of capital or labour. The League of Nations will perhaps succeed in retaining the weapon of national boycott in the hands of the governments of its component states. Yet it must not be ignored that capitalist organisations which control the supply of essential commodities may easily exploit their monopoly by boycotting a particular country; the League of Nations will have to be constantly on guard against such violations of its cardinal principle of the 'open door.'

Moreover, it is not only the forces of capital which may be expected to employ national boycott as a weapon; that weapon is already being used by the organised forces of labour. For the war has vividly demonstrated the possibilities of a co-operative boycott; and now the growth of organisation is beginning to give to the national and international labour movements new power to impose certain boycotts if they so choose. Already there are many evidences of this new tendency, such as the recent boycott by international labour organisations of a reactionary government in Hungary, and the incidents in regard to the shipment of munitions to Poland and to Ireland. The only means of checking this anarchic tendency towards the assumption of the functions of government by any one section of the community appears to lie in making the government more truly representative of the national will, especially in the field of foreign affairs, and in strengthening the League of Nations, and for this reason there are many who hold that it would be desirable to institute a Foreign Affairs Committee of the House of Commons, and to make the constitution of the League of Nations more democratic. Be this as it may, there can be no doubt that as matters stand there is a real, and perhaps not very remote possibility that the weapon of national boycott may in certain circumstances be taken out of the hands of the national governments and even of the League of Nations, and that organised international labour may co-operate across the frontiers in applying or withholding pressure at its own discretion.

In short, whilst the international state boycott and blockade may be expected to supersede the national state blockade in almost every case, both of these forms of pressure might, in certain circumstances, be replaced by the national or international political strike.

CONCLUSION

This book will presumably come into the hands of those concerned, not only with the history of the weapon of blockade in this war, but also with the problems of its possible use in future. The task of these readers is a professional one and will have to be studied professionally; in this blockade we were fighting for our lives against the enemy's attempt to starve us, and there was only one way, the coldly professional way, in which we could regard the process of starving him.

Yet it is permissible for one moment, at the end of this professional book, to refer to the other more human side of the matter, to the consequences of the blockade as well as to its methods. For there is a peculiar danger attaching to the use of this particular weapon, a danger which has not yet been sufficiently realised. It has now been found by experience that blockade is an instrument which can be wielded without any uncomfortable exertion, and can to a large extent be created, by men sitting in offices far from any visible sign of the consequences of its use. Men thus fighting with their pens in London come naturally to thinking that pens are cleaner weapons than bayonets, besides being much more convenient for the amateur. No danger, no mess, merely a Government ukase.

And that is just what makes blockade so dangerous a weapon in bureaucratic hands; it is so infernally convenient.

It would be a good thing if everyone who may have to use this weapon in future, whether at sea or ashore, would devote some serious study to the real nature of its consequences.

There is plenty of material at hand for such a study; Europe is full of it. As General Smuts has said, 'It is the most awful spectacle in history, and no man with any heart or regard for human destiny can contemplate it without the deepest emotion.'

This is not a mere rhetorical phrase, it is the truth; and everyone who touches the weapon of blockade should try to realise it. For if suffering were a communicable experience, another such blockade would be impossible.

* * *

35.   Summary of Recommendations: Trading, Blockade and Enemy Shipping

Committee of Imperial Defence, Standing Sub-Committee on the Co-ordination of Departmental Action on the Outbreak of War Secret 428-B

[CAB 15/21]   30 May 1923

55.   (a)   The existing system as regards the custody and sale of Prize Court goods should be enforced in any future war, and provision should be made for special assistance to be given to Collectors of Customs at certain ports on the outbreak of war. (Paragraph 23 and Appendix V.)

(b)   Full powers to prohibit all trading with the enemy should be taken at the outbreak of war, but they should be administered so as to meet the particular circumstances, and the changing conditions, of that war. (Paragraph 27.)

(c)   The Parliamentary Counsel should settle the Draft Proclamation forbidding trading with the enemy, and the Draft Bill to give statutory effect to any trading with the enemy Proclamations which are annexed. The Draft Proclamation and Bill should then be approved provisionally for use in any war of any magnitude. When war is imminent, the duty of putting forward the Draft Proclamation Bill would rest on the Board of Trade. (Paragraph 30 and Appendix VI.)

(d)   The Draft Customs War Powers Bill should be settled by Parliamentary Counsel, and provisionally approved for use in an emergency. The duty of taking the necessary steps to bring the Bill forward being placed on the Commissioners of Customs and Excise. (Paragraph 30 and Appendix VII.)

(e)   The Board of Trade and Board of Customs and Excise should formulate proposals as to the bodies to be charged with the duty of granting Export and Import Licenses and place them before the Advisory Committee. (Paragraph 31.)

(f)   The Draft Bill to restrict the transfer of British ships should be settled by Parliamentary Counsel and approved for use in case of war. (Paragraph 32 and Appendix IX.)

(g)   The Draft Instructions to Consular Officers as to certificate of origin should be considered and settled by the Advisory Committee. (Paragraph 33 and Appendix IX.)

(h)   Care should be taken to balance the advantages against the disadvantages before any machinery for interfering with finance is put in motion. (Paragraph 38.)

(i)   The Board of Trade should be responsible for arranging for a liaison between the Government and the insurance market on the lines of the Insurance Intelligence Department which was established in the late war. (Paragraph 38.)

(j)   The Board of Trade, which contains within itself the nucleus from which a Ministry of Shipping will develop when required, should be responsible that the requisite powers for controlling the movement and trading of British ships are obtained. (Paragraph 39.)

(k)   In all future war plans particular regard should be paid to the commercial side of such wars, and the question of chartering neutral ships should not be overlooked. (Paragraphs 40 and 46.)

(l)   On the outbreak of war a Bunker Committee should be established. (Paragraph 41.)

(m)   The Colonial Office and the India Office should either be represented on, or in the closest possible touch with, any Committees dealing with economic pressure. (Paragraph 45.)

(n)   The effect of the war itself on our supplies and the extent to which our economic pressure on a hypothetical enemy may be weakened by our need of essential commodities are most important parts of the commercial side of any future war of any magnitude. These questions should always be included in the list of subjects to be studied in connection with any future hypothetical war. (Paragraph 47.)

(o)   An Advisory Committee should be appointed to co-ordinate all war trade work. (Paragraph 48.)

(p)   War trade organisation should allow necessary weight to be given to political and diplomatic considerations. (Paragraph 49.)

(q)   In the initial stages of the war use should be made of the peace time Advisory Committee, with the addition of a strong Chairman, who might or might not be of Ministerial rank. (Paragraph 50.)

(r)   Further consideration to be given to questions affecting aliens in articles 29–32 of the instructions to collectors and officers of Customs and Excise – Appendix XI. (Paragraph 52.)

(s)   A small Committee should be appointed *ad hoc* to consider the question of the British Empire, when a neutral, cutting off the supply of essential commodities to belligerents in those cases when such action may be advisable. (Paragraph 53.)

* * *

36.   Revision of the Laws of War

Note by the Secretary, Committee of Imperial Defence, Colonel Sir
Maurice Hankey
Secret No. I.L./J/3.

[ADM 116/3619]   7 February 1924

Contents: Part I   Previous History
              Part II Questions for Decision

Part I   PREVIOUS HISTORY

At the Washington Conference, 1921, the representatives of the United States of America, the British Empire, France, Italy and Japan on the Committee on Limitation of Armament agreed that a Commission composed of not more than two members representing each of the above-mentioned Powers should be constituted to consider the following questions:

a.   Do existing rules of International Law adequately cover new methods of attack or defence resulting from the introduction or development (since the Hague Convention of 1907) of new agencies of warfare?

b.   If not so, what changes in the existing rules ought to be adopted in consequence thereof as a part of the law of nations?

The following Resolution was also passed by the Committee on the Limitation of Armament:

'That it is not the intention of the Powers agreeing to the appointment of a Committee to consider and report upon the rules of International Law respecting new agencies of warfare that the Commission shall review or report upon the rules or declarations relating to submarines or to the use of noxious gases and chemicals already adopted by the Powers in this Conference.'

These Resolutions were adopted by the Conference on the Limitation of Armament at their 6th Plenary Session on 4th February, 1922.
2.   The question was considered by the Committee of Imperial De-

fence at the 156th Meeting, held on 14th March, 1922, when it was agreed:

a. That the Foreign Office should be asked to appoint a diplomat of adequate rank and a jurist as British Delegates to the Commission.

b. That a Sub-Committee of the Committee of Imperial Defence should be appointed, composed of the two Delegates appointed by the Foreign Office, together with two representatives each of the Foreign Office, the Admiralty, the War Office and Air Ministry to study the question.

3. In accordance with the foregoing Conclusions the Foreign Office nominated the Right Hon. Sir Rennell Rodd and Sir Cecil Hurst as the Delegates of the British Empire to the Commission to consider the revision of the Laws of War; and a Sub-Committee of the Committee of Imperial Defence was appointed under the Chairmanship of Sir Rennell Rodd to study the question.

4. This Sub-Committee examined the whole question exhaustively, and in August, 1922, presented its Report for consideration by the Committee of Imperial Defence, (CID Paper No. 359-B)

The laws of naval warfare, land warfare and aerial warfare were dealt with in separate sections of the Report, and where it was considered that aerial warfare impinged upon operations by land or by sea, recommendations were made with a view to bringing the rules of naval, land and air warfare as far as practicable into harmony.

A draft Code of Laws of Aerial Warfare was also included in the Report.

5. The Report of the Sub-Committee was considered by the Committee of Imperial Defence at the 165th Meeting, held on 30th November, 1922, and the Committee recommended: 'That the discussions of the International Commission to revise the Laws of War should be confined to aviation and wireless telegraphy.'

Certain minor amendments were made in the draft Code of Laws, and Article 8 which dealt with the Right of Visit and Search of Merchant Ships at Sea by Aircraft, was referred for further consideration by the Naval Staff.

With the above-mentioned exceptions the Report was approved by the Committee, and was adopted for the guidance of the British Delegation.

6. The Inaugural Meeting of the International Commission was held at the Hague on the 11th December, 1922. The American Delegation, as representing the State which convened the Commission, insisted on

using their own draft Code of Laws of Aerial Warfare as a basis of discussion. The draft Code in the possession of the British Delegation (CID Paper 379-B), amended in respect of Article 3 in accordance with CID Paper 392-B) was also submitted, and in the discussion of the various Articles adopted by the Commission the provisions contained in each of these drafts were taken into consideration, as well as amendments and proposals submitted by other Delegations.

7.   The International Commission completed its labours on 17th February, 1923, and in due course issued a Report which, together with a covering letter from the Foreign Office, a despatch from Sir Rennell Rodd and a Memorandum prepared by the Foreign Office explaining the action of the Delegates with regard to certain outstanding questions, is reproduced in CID Paper No. 418-B.

This Report is now for consideration by the Committee of Imperial Defence.

Part II   QUESTIONS FOR DECISION

... VISIT AND SEARCH OF MERCHANT SHIPPING BY AIRCRAFT, Chapter VII

15.   The Commission were unable to arrive at agreement with regard to the question of the use of aircraft for the exercise of the belligerent right of visit and search of merchant vessels.

The course of the discussion on this subject is given in Chapter VII (Pages 31 to 34) of the Report (CID Paper 418-B), the concluding paragraph relating to the subject reading as follows:

'Although all the Delegations concurred in the expression of a desire to adopt such rules as would assure the observance of the dictates of humanity as regards the protection of the lives of neutrals and non-combatants, the Commission, by reason of a divergence of views as to the method by which this result would best be attained, was unable to agree upon an Article dealing with the exercise of belligerent rights by aircraft against merchant vessels. The Code of rules proposed by the Commission therefore leaves the matter open for future regulation.'

The question is also dealt with at some length in the Foreign Office Memorandum on pages 47 to 49 of CID 418-B.

16.   Considerable difficulty had been experienced by the Government in arriving at a decision with regard to the instructions to be issued to the British Delegation on this subject. The advice given to the Commit-

tee of Imperial Defence by the Sub-Committee which first considered the question, was that the use of aircraft for the visit and search, attack, seizure, destruction or forcible control of merchant vessels and generally for any operations against merchant vessels should be prohibited.

The Committee, however, adopted the opposite view and recommended that the Article in question should read as follows:

'The use of aircraft against merchant vessels must be regulated by the following provisions, which, being in conformity with the rules adopted by civilized nations for the protection of the lives of neutrals and non-combatants at sea in time of war, are to be deemed an established part of International law:

A merchant vessel must be ordered to submit to visit and search to determine its character before it can be seized.

A merchant vessel must not be attacked unless it refuses to submit to visit and search after warning or to proceed as directed after seizure.

A merchant vessel must not be destroyed unless the crew and passengers have been first placed in safety.

Belligerent aircraft are not under any circumstances exempt from the universal rules above stated; and if an aircraft cannot capture a merchant vessel in conformity with these rules, existing law of nations require it to desist from attack and seizure and to permit merchant vessels to proceed unmolested.

Provided, however, that this prohibition does not preclude belligerent military aircraft from replying to an attack first made by a merchant vessel, nor from bombarding enemy shipping in a dock or harbour.'

The above Article is an application to aircraft of the clauses dealing with submarines with regard to the rules of seizure and search as laid down in the Washington Convention.

17.   Subsequently, after the actual departure of the British Delegation to the Hague, the Admiralty wished to re-open the question, and expressed the view that the use of aircraft for the visit and search, attack, seizure, destruction or forcible control of merchant vessels at sea should be prohibited; thus reverting to the original proposal of the Sub-Committee of the Committee of Imperial Defence contained in (CID Paper No. 359-B).

The question was discussed by Lord Salisbury, Chairman of the Committee of Imperial Defence, with Mr Bonar Law, the Prime Minister, and the latter decided that the Conclusion arrived at by the Committee of Imperial Defence at the 167th Meeting should be adhered to and that

Article 8 of the British Draft Code of Laws of Aerial Warfare should remain in the form quoted in paragraph 16 above.

The Foreign Office were informed of this decision and requested to inform the British Delegates at the Hague accordingly (CID Paper 397-B).

18. The Air Ministry in their paper CID 426-B call attention to the fact that it will be necessary, in view of the failure of the Commission to agree to any rules upon the subject, to consider, in conjunction with the Admiralty, what instructions should be given to air force commanders in regard to operations against sea-borne commerce.

It is understood also that the Admiralty attach the greatest importance to the settlement of the question.

It is for consideration, therefore, first what action (if any) the Committee of Imperial Defence should recommend be taken by His Majesty's Government to reach agreement on the subject with other Powers, and second what should be the basis of the instructions to be issued by the Admiralty or Air Ministry to Air Force Commanders in time of war.

FOREIGN OFFICE LETTER OF 5th APRIL, 1923

19. Two further points on which it is necessary for the Committee of Imperial Defence to make recommendations are raised in the Foreign Office letter of 5th April, 1923, (Page 1 of CID Paper 418-B).

APPROVAL OF ACTION TAKEN BY SIR R. RODD AND SIR C. HURST AND EXPRESSION OF THANKS

20. The first of these is with regard to the proposal contained in paragraph 2 of the above-mentioned letter that His Majesty's Government be moved to approve the action taken by Sir Rennell Rodd and Sir Cecil Hurst in the important question of visit and search of merchant vessels by aircraft; and in the general conduct of the negotiations, and to state that an expression of thanks of His Majesty's Government should be conveyed to them.

The Committee of Imperial Defence might recommend that effect should be given to the above proposal made by the Foreign Office.

PUBLICATION OF THE GENERAL REPORT

21. The second is with regard to the suggestion contained in paragraph 3 of the Foreign Office letter that should it be considered desirable for the General Report of the Commission on the Laws of War to be laid before Parliament the Report should be published as an enclosure to the despatch dated 19th February, 1923, (Appendix A pages 2 & 3 of

CID Paper 418-B), which was specially written by Sir Rennell Rodd with this object.

The Air Ministry have, however, made some comments on this proposal (vide CID Paper 426-B, paragraph 7).

* * *

37. Naval Enforcement of Article 16 of the League Covenant

Admiralty Minute Sheet

[ADM 1/8671/215]   7 September 1924

As regards present Article 16 of the Covenant the Admiralty views have been that the economic boycott does not involve Naval Operations (See Papers M.11038/23 and letters enclosed therein).

2.   The new suggestion in telegram of the 15th September from Geneva is not that Naval Forces shall carry out Military measures against the State which is declared the aggressor, but that the safety of the sea communications of the threatened State shall be ensured, i.e. presumably that a Naval Force shall be employed in the protection of the sea communications of the threatened State. The emphasis is now being transferred from Naval Activities against a State (the aggressor) to Naval activities for the protection of a State (i.e. the attacked); also instead of the Council merely recommending what Naval Forces the members of the League shall contribute to the Armed forces to be used to protect the Covenants of the League, there is intended to be a definite undertaking both individual and collective to supply a force to ensure the sea communications.

3.   Will Director of Plans please consider the position of such a protecting force and remark generally? Prima facie it is not clear whether such a protective Naval Force would be expected to prevent intercourse between the Nationals of the aggressor and the Nationals of any other State or not. Unless such activities are definitely ruled out we should have troubles with the USA, etc.

4.   In connection with this question it has to be remembered that although the aggressor is deemed to have committed an act of war the opinion of committees who considered this subject in 1921 was that a state of war was not created and that the members of the League were not embarking necessarily on war.

5.   The bearing of the Straits Convention on this subject relative to the sea communications of Straits bordering on the Black Sea will have to

borne in mind as the number of warships passing through in peace is limited.

6.   From consideration of other nations, e.g. Poland, China (vis-a-vis Japan) etc. the proposal would appear to render the protecting ships fairly vulnerable or alternately ineffective.

[signed] Alex Hunt

Concur with PA.S.(S)

It is proposed therefore to inform Foreign Office in the following sense:

'By the new interpretation of Article 16 the part that the British Fleet may be required to take is open to the gravest objections.'

Under Article 16 the economic measures that can be applied are far reaching and can be put into effect by Domestic action without incurring responsibility and risks of Naval operations on the high seas. The Admiralty has always maintained that *economic* blockade as referred to in Article 16 does not involve Naval operations as such operations cannot be embarked on without going to War with the Aggressor nation.

In 1921 an attempt was made to include in the Covenant a clause which read as follows:

'Where the Covenant-breaking state has a seaboard it will be necessary to institute an effective blockade thereof and the Council will forthwith consider which member of the League can most conveniently be asked to discharge this duty.'

When this proposal came to the notice of the Admiralty Their Lordships immediately declared their strong dissent from the proposed clause. The reasons that prompted Their Lordships to enter a strong protest against the proposal of 1921 apply with added force to the new proposal which renders the British Fleet liable to be called upon to ensure the Sea communications of the attacked or threatened state.

To ensure the sea communications of a threatened state entails the use of a Naval Force for the purpose of preventing the aggressor state from interfering with the sea borne commerce of her opponent under whatever flag it may be carried.

To be effective this force must operate within reach of the Naval forces of the aggressor state and will be open to attack by the Naval forces of the Aggressor state at any moment.

My Lords cannot protest too strongly against the British Fleet being placed in such a dangerous position.

My Lords are aware that in the opinion of the Committee who considered this subject in 1921 the Members of the League, would not, in operating against an aggressor nation be necessarily embarking on War and the same claim might be made when operating in Defence of a threatened state. As was stated by My Lords at the time of the Corfu incident it is not possible without running the gravest risks to conduct operations on the high seas which may at any moment result in an attack on our ships without warning until a state of war is known to exist.

As an example (amongst many) of the demands involved in the proposed new clause to the Covenant Their Lordships would invite attention to the case in which for instance China and Japan were in disagreement and Japan were to be declared the Aggressor. In these circumstances the sea communication of China would have to be safe-guarded against interference by Japan. This would necessitate the presence of Naval forces in the Sea of Japan and in active control of the Straits [of] Tsushima. These forces would be liable to interference in the execution of the function allocated to them by the League from the whole Fleet of Japan, and they would therefore require to be in suffi-cient force to withstand attack from the Japanese Fleet at the latter's selected moment.

In the case of both nations being declared the aggressor the situation becomes still more impossible.

Finally, Their Lordships would point out that, apart from all other objections the adoption of a one power standard of strength for the British Navy is entirely inconsistent with the assumption of such great responsibilities by the proposed new clause in the Covenant, which in their opinion would involve the gravest risks to the fleet on which the safety of the Empire depends.

[signed] Dudley Pound, D[irector] of P[lans] 9/24

* * *

Extract from 'The Times'

Geneva
September 16 1924

The news of the offer of the British Navy for the Service of the League of Nations is causing keen discussion here. League enthusiasts are jubilant and exclaim that at last Great Britain has realized her obligations under Article 16 of the Covenant. The extreme enthusiast is a difficult person to argue with, for the moment any objection is raised to the proposal he jumps to the conclusion that one is 'out to smash the League.'

The objections to placing the Navy at the unreserved discretion of the League are, of course, numerous and obvious, and its best friends, even at Geneva, realize that these objections must be met. The first and foremost is the position in which Great Britain would find herself in regard to the United States. The United States, not being in the League, would in no case find itself bound by the orders or recommendations of the League, and if the country outlawed by the League were one with which American citizens habitually traded the British Navy would at once find itself involved in every sort of vexatious complication.

Then there is the further difficulty of the Dominions to which inquiries were despatched on Sunday night, but which it is obviously difficult to consult adequately on the matter.

The negotiations here since the Third Committee broke ...

Extract from 'The Times'

Geneva
September 15 1924

I understand that in the negotiations now taking place in the sub-committees of the Third (Disarmament) Committee of the League of Nations it is contemplated that the British Fleet shall be placed entirely at the disposal of the League as prescribed by Article 16 of the Covenant. This can, of course, only happen after a case of 'aggression' has been declared by the Council against an offending State; and the list of disputes which can be brought before the League at all is being carefully considered by the First Committee (Legal and Constitutional).

Some days may elapse before either Committee has finished its work. But the probability is that when the proposed protocol is finally ready for presentation to the assembly it will be found – unless modifications are made between now and then – that the British Fleet, in case of aggression, is to be put unreservedly at the service of the League. This, it is claimed, is simply a recognition of the obligations which this country long since incurred under Articles 10 and 16 of the Pact. I understand, however, that this protocol will contain a clause that it shall not be binding upon any country, even if adhered to at Geneva, until it has been ratified by the Parliament of that country.

It is a singular fact that the remarkable departure from traditional British policy involved in Lord Parmoor's proposal should not have been made publicly in a Committee meeting, but should have fallen from his lips incidentally in a semi-official conversation. It has received, as it were, official endorsement by implication from Sir Cecil

Hurst's speech in the First Committee, in which he spoke of the possible complications for a maritime nation carrying out penal economic measures at the behest of the League. I understand that no reservations are now contemplated as to the nature of the sanctions.

There is a rumour in Geneva to-night that Mr MacDonald and M. Herriot are to return here during the first week of October.

* * *

Telegram – No Distribution

Decode. His Majesty's Consul (Geneva). 20th September 1924.
O.   1.00 p.m. 20th September 1924.
R.   2:30 p.m. 20th September 1924.

Following for Admiralty from A. Smith.
Newspaper reports based on misunderstandings when Lord Parmoor interviewed press representatives. Details of all proceedings in committees together with texts etc., are in the hands of Foreign Office. I have not been consulted or expressed any opinion.

* * *

38. The Execution and Management of Economic War

Cecil E. Farrer, Senior Intelligence Officer, Department of Overseas Trade, to Cmdr Claude Preston Hermon-Hodge, RN Assistant Secretary, Committee of Imperial Defence

[CAB 21/319]   20 May 1926

Secret and Confidential
Dear Hermon-Hodge, I enclose herewith a copy of the memorandum which I have submitted to Hipwood through Crowe.

In this private letter, I would like to take at random various points of a nature which renders them unsuitable for incorporation in an official document and you will no doubt regard this letter as a purely personal communication.

Memorandum. Paragraph 2 Section a.   You may wonder why it is necessary to mention such an obvious fact, that the blockade depends ultimately upon the navy. The answer is, that in the early stages of the war there was a great deal of unnecessary friction caused by a feeling in the Navy that the 'mandarins' at Whitehall were stultifying their work and, in some of the Departments, that the Navy were trying to interfere in matters of foreign affairs. Again, as the machine improved in efficiency, I do not think that it was always realised what a difficult and trying time the members of the 10th Cruiser Squadron had and how our organisation relied as a last resort on their bravery and endurance. I earnestly hope that this will never happen again but obviously if it is realised and admitted from the outset that without the Navy we would be powerless, a much better spirit of co-operation may be expected to ensue.

Memorandum. Paragraph 3.   It is equally obvious that the Foreign Office must be the department in control of the policy of blockade. This again needs stating with reasons because since the termination of hostilities, there seems to have been a certain tendency on the part of other departments [the Board of Trade] to endeavour to get hold of a certain amount of patronage, in fact, a kind of 'option' on any new blockade ministry. I hope that my reasons are obviously convincing because I am quite sure that whether or not they are accepted in the long run, the logic of facts will confirm the object of my thesis.

Memorandum. Paragraph 3 (a).   There is a real reason against having a secretary to the Contraband Committee. He could not be a man of such weight as to rival the official forces of the Foreign Office as a department and he might be rather badly shot at by departments who disagreed with decisions of the Committee. Therefore, I think it is very desirable that the Contraband Committee should have on paper no other secretary than its own department, which in turn is a branch of the Foreign Office. A committee who are sitting daily to 7:30 or so has no time to deal with correspondence, which had better be left to the departmental machine. There seems to be no reason why the Board of Trade should be represented on the Contraband Committee, and, indeed, their representative on it in the late war himself told me that he thought his function was a useless one. Trade and blockade are absolutely opposed.

Memorandum. Paragraph 3 (d). Intelligence Department.   The staffing of the Intelligence Department in its more confidential aspects is a matter which will need very careful consideration. I have said that I think the Department of Overseas Trade can provide a considerable proportion of the staff and would be the right department to draw upon for that purpose but I am not myself familiar with the relations existing between MI5.C. and the Special branch of Scotland Yard. It seems highly desirable that they should each have a 'finger in the pie' in order to avoid any sort of competition and even our more anonymous friends, of whom I spoke to you, ought also to consider the best means of liaison very carefully. I think that I could give them a notion of the kind of information which would be wanted and they might then consider what plans to draw up to obtain it in case of need. Some of the best information which I got through them in the late war took just nine months to obtain after being asked for.

Memorandum. Paragraph 3 (e). Lord Emmett's memoranda in your possession and, indeed, his conversations with myself on many occasions, have made it plain that he did not quite like the attitude of the Foreign Office on certain blockade questions but I have always felt that that was due to the fact that he did not really understand the impossibility of splitting up rations so as to give a fair share to the British Empire on the one hand and to foreign countries on the other. The reason for this is not obvious; but it is that the Contraband Committee cannot start detaining cargoes until the total rations from all sources is exceeded. Therefore, if neutral countries choose to order more than their normal imports from foreign sources, there is no means of preventing them from doing so in International law, provided that their total imports do not exceed their legitimate requirements. That is one reason why it seems desirable that the Contraband Committee and Department and the Licensing Department should both be placed in a subordinate position to the Central Blockade Department from the very beginning. They will both take their orders from one chief and he will 'knock their heads together' if there is any nonsense.

Memorandum. Paragraph 5. I am personally of [the] opinion that the success of the late blockade organisation in its later stages was due to the fact that each department by then had a very clear and definite idea of what its job was and that this came about through their chiefs having access to the winning personality of Lord Robert Cecil and his own clearness of mind. It seems to me that we ought to hope for 'thrusters' as heads of these departments and if that is so they are much better controlled on really important matters by the Minister of Blockade himself than by a Permanent Secretary, who is probably an elderly man steeped in the routine of a peace-time department. I know this is arguable but I give it as my opinion for what it is worth. Besides, the head of such a department as the Restriction and Purchase Department must almost inevitably be a business man. Towards the end of the late war, for example, it was Sir William Mitchell Thomson, and frankly, I cannot see him taking orders from most of the permanent officials at present in His Majesty's Service, yet he was extraordinarily efficient and it is difficult to think of a better choice.

Memorandum. Paragraph 5. It may seem unnecessary to insinuate that reports of the Intelligence and Statistical Departments would be shelved unless the heads of those departments had direct access to the Minister but I can assure you that I have myself worked in departments where this has been done, not in the Blockade Department, though even in the latter there have been times when pressure has been brought by interested sections to prevent certain facts being brought to light.

I have said nothing about blockade outwards, i.e. an enemy's exports; – that is a separate matter more closely connected with 'trade war.'

With apologies for so long a letter, . . .

* * *

39. *Amendment of the Naval Prize Manual*

Paymaster Captain H.S. Manisty, Superintendent, Secretaries' Course,
to Commander-in-Chief, HM Ships & Vessels, Portsmouth
Confidential

[ADM 1/8700/132, No. 067] 27 September 1926

1. With reference to the following extract from Addendum No. 1 to O.U.5316 – Naval Prize Manual: RULES FOR GUIDANCE OF OFFICERS COMMANDING SUBMARINES WHEN OPERATING AGAINST TRADE.

a. The Washington Treaty regarding the use of Submarines and Noxious Gases in War (see Appendix VIII, pages 114 and 115) becomes effective only after ratification by all the Powers concerned in the Treaty. Such ratification has not, as yet, taken place.

b. Pending notification to the Fleet of general ratification, Submarines have the same rights and obligations in regard to the action they take, vis-à-vis merchant ships, as have other ships of war.

c. Attention is drawn to Article 118, page 27.

I beg to submit the following remarks for consideration.

2. It is understood that France is the only one of the five powers which signed the second Washington Treaty of February 1922 which has not ratified it. From publications and information accessible to the ordinary individual there does not appear to be any probability of France ratifying in the near future if ever; and also there is no information that any non-signatory power has accepted the invitation contained in Articles II and IV of the treaty to adhere to its provisions regarding submarines.

3. As far as is known no country except Great Britain has taken legislative measures to create the necessary municipal law to enforce

the restrictions placed on the use of submarines (and the penalty incurred by their abuse) as set forth in the second Washington treaty. Such action was taken by Great Britain in the Treaties of Washington Act 1922, Section 4 of which reads as follows:

> Any person in the service of any power who violates any of the rules contained in Article 1 set forth in the Second Schedule to this act whether or not such person is under a governmental superior, shall be deemed to have violated the laws of war, and shall be liable to trial and punishment as if for an act of piracy, and if found within His Majesty's Dominions may be brought to trial before any civil or military tribunal who would have had jurisdiction to deal with the case if the act had been an act of piracy.

The second schedule is a reprint of Articles I and III of the Second Washington Treaty.

The Act came into force on 15 October 1925 by Order in Council of 11 October 1925.

4.   The present position therefore appears to be:

a.   The second Washington Treaty is not binding on any of the Signatory powers.

b.   If, however, any person, e.g. a British Naval Officer, violates the rules of warfare against commerce as set forth in the treaty, he is liable to be tried and punished for piracy if found within the United Kingdom or any British possession other than India and the self-governing Dominions not having, so far as available information goes, taken any legislative measures.

5.   There are, however, other points which seem to affect the matter and which place British submarine officers in an invidious position:

a.   Great Britain has by her municipal law extended the crime of piracy to any person in the service of any power who violates certain rules of warfare set forth in a treaty which is not binding on any power. In the event of war, therefore, in which Great Britain is a belligerent, an Officer Commanding a British submarine would become a pirate by the law of his country if he sank an enemy merchant ship without visit *and* search or without placing the crew in safety, whether or not such action was carried out in compliance with the orders of superior authority. No such stigma would attach to an officer commanding an enemy submarine if he committed a similar act, but if he were later taken prisoner and brought to the United Kingdom he could be tried in Great Britain as a pirate. It is, however, improbable that this would be done as it would lead to retaliatory measures against British prisoners. The more rigorous imprisonment imposed at one time on German submarine officers taken as prisoners during the late war had to be abandoned for this reason.

b.   Under International Law, pirates, irrespective of nationality, can be tried and punished by the Courts of any country. One of the objects of the Washington Treaty would appear to have been to treat as a 'universal pirate' any person who violates rules of warfare set forth therein, and that any such violations should be treated as world wide piracy is recognised by Great Britain in Section 4 of the Treaties of Washington Act 1922. To apply this to an extreme example – the CO of an enemy submarine could, in the event of war, engage in unrestricted submarine warfare against commerce without the risk of being treated as a pirate by any nation other than Great Britain, while the CO of a British submarine, who on his own initiative or under orders, successfully attacked an enemy convoy carrying contraband of vital importance for the prosecution of the war would not only be liable to be tried in Great Britain for piracy, but if his submarine visited the port of a neutral (a Central or South American Republic for instance) the Government of that country could arrest and try the officers and crew as pirates; and in view of her municipal law Great Britain would, logically, have no cause of complaint, and could be faced with the answer that such an act was acknowledged as world wide piracy by her own laws. A convoy protected by armed ships is possibly not a good example, as theoretically the presence of the latter can be argued to constitute resistance to visit and search. The elements set forth above could, however, be applied to other cases, if a neutral state wished to be unpleasant and considered that submarines should not be employed as 'commerce destroyers' (Article 4 of the Treaty) notwithstanding that they might be in a position to conform to the accepted rules of warfare on commerce. The meaning of 'commerce destroyers' is not clear and is capable of being interpreted that submarines cannot be used against commerce under any circumstances, e.g. ordinary visit and search, detention, capture, blockade, minelaying (a merchant ship – enemy or neutral – might explode a mine laid off a base of the enemy's fleet) etc.

6.   That action by some States as outlined above is not beyond the bounds of possibility appears to be shown by the recent action of Turkey in the case of Lieutenant Demons the first officer of the French steamer *Lotus* which sank by collision the Turkish steamer *Bozhurt* on the high seas at the beginning of August 1926 and was tried and committed for manslaughter in the Courts at Constantinople, there having been loss of life from the *Bozhurt*.

7.   I submit that the repeal of Section 4 of the Treaties of Washington Act is a matter for consideration. British Naval Officers are less likely

than those of any other nation to depart from the customary rules of naval warfare and laws of humanity, and it appears undesirable to afford any pretext for a neutral (possibly a not over-scrupulous one) desirous of adopting a tone of high morality as against Great Britain in international affairs, or to curry favour with our enemy, to stigmatise and treat our officers as pirates. There may not be the slightest possibility of this country being engaged in a Naval war in the near future, but the repeal of the section, if left to the outbreak of war or after, might be liable to lead to misunderstandings amongst neutrals of this country's intentions as to the method of conducting war on the enemy's trade. At the present time, from our past Naval history, there can be no suspicion that British Naval Officers would be likely to depart from the ordinary rule of visit and search and placing the crew of a ship in safety before destruction.

Minute by Alex Hunt

[M.02398/26]   11 10 1926

I have on several occasions thought about this question and it has always seemed to be expedient to leave the Treaties of Washington Act, 1922, as it stands, especially as disarmament conferences might reconsider very soon the question of submarine activities.

The enclosed letter is not quite as clear as it might be. Thus, in paragraph 5 (a) reference is made to certain rules of warfare set forth in a Treaty which is not binding on any power. Whilst this is strictly correct, it fails to bring out the fact that these rules of warfare really are the rules adopted by civilised nations, (i.e. that they are the customary law of nations). Though the Treaty in which these rules are set forth is itself not binding, the rules as set forth are a very summarised statement of the rules that are in force, and certainly they correspond to our rules, and I agree with the views in the last paragraph that 'at the present time, from our past naval history, there can be no suspicion that British Naval Officers would be likely to depart from [these] rules'. As regards the idea stated in paragraph 5 that the Government of a neutral could arrest and try certain British Officers and crew as pirates, this overlooks the fact that (1) in this aspect the conditions existing at present are not different from those that would have existed if the Treaty had been ratified; (2) that unless the legislation of the neutral had provided by Statute for trying such officers and crew as pirates the courts would in all proability not take action, as courts do not try a person for a crime which is not a crime under the nation's Statutes. If the courts did deal with such a case Great Britain would have cause to complain. Great Britain, similarly, by her municipal laws has made slavery piracy, but until other nations have adopted the same attitude and either by international agreement or by their statutes have declared it to be piracy, the courts of these other nations do not treat slave trading as piracy or try British slave traders as pirates. Admittedly, it is wrong that the municipal law should be in advance of international obligations. The last clause of paragraph 5, in so far as it refers to commerce destroyers, and article 4 of the Washington Treaty is misleading. Article 4 does not come into this question at all. Article 3 (i.e. the piracy clause) only refers to a violation of the rules in Article 1. Paragraph 6 of the letter does not seem to strengthen the matter; it merely indicates that local Turkish law was adopted by the courts at Constantinople. I doubt if foreigners could treat the British Officers in the contingency contemplated as pirates unless they are pirates according to the law of nations. (When in 1858, before the abolition of slavery in America, British men-of-war molested American vessels suspected of carrying slaves, the United States rightly complained.) As the piracy sanction for the violation of the laws of war has not been internationally recognised, I feel that the matter would not be justiciable in the courts of any country except possibly Great Britain, where we have provided for the matter by our own municipal law. The risk, such as it is, that British officers would be tried in this country can be taken with equanimity for some time yet: the Statute is a threat to our enemies that might be useful.

The subject can be watched. At the time the Treaties of Washington Act was being prepared it was, for Parliamentary reasons, thought desirable to incorporate in the Bill all parts of the two Treaties signed at Washington which required to be implemented by municipal statute. A copy of the Bill which later became the Treaties of Washington Act, 1922, is attached. It would be difficult to get amended legislation through Parliament.

* * *

40. Possibilities of Exerting Economic Pressure on the Nationalist Government of South China

Committee of Imperial Defence Advisory Committee on Trading and Blockade in Time of War

[CAB 21/299]   February 1927

11 c. *Pacific Blockade*   There would be no difficulty in dealing with the ships of Powers participating in the blockade. Further, a case could be made out for stopping Chinese ships, because it would be difficult for the Chinese Government to make an effective protest against steps taken to prevent violation by the Cantonese authorities of treaties to which China is a party. China might, of course, appeal to the League of Nations, and though such an appeal might not be well-founded it ought not lightly to be provoked. The real difficulty would arise, however, if an attempt were made to interfere with the trade of States not partici- pating in the blockade, such as Russia or the United States. . . .

34 *General Remarks on the effect of Economic Pressure against South China*   In the circumstances, we are considering, viz., a state of war, a blockade of South China could probably be made effective so far as the sea is concerned. The opinion of the Chinese experts is that even such an effective external blockade would produce very little influence on the Cantonese, and that they could quite well get on without any for- eign trade, as indeed they did during the 18th Century.

* * *

41. Shipping Control in Time of War

Sir Charles Hipwood, Mercantile Marine Department, Board of Trade, to Commander Hermon-Hodge, forwarding a copy of Hipwood's 15 June paper to the Imperial Defence College

[CAB 21/299]   17 June 1927

p 11.   During the last war our control of bunker coal was a most potent lever for persuading the neutrals to follow the right road. During the next war it will not be nearly so effective, as oil is displacing coal, and we have not yet succeeded in getting oil from coal on a paying basis. Insurance, that is, War Insurance, was also a very influential consideration with neutrals in the war. At one point in the war the Norwegians all but stopped running owing to the breakdown of their War Insurance Scheme, which was a million pounds to the bad. We kept them running by taking over their scheme, in effect, and paying their debt. We took the risk for the remainder of the war on the condition that we settled the rates, and we were able to keep the boats running and made a profit. We must be prepared in any future war of any magnitude to provide insurance for friendly neutrals, but we must not expect more from this measure than it will yield. London is the main insurance market, but not the only insurance market of the world, and neutrals can go elsewhere.

* * *

p. 17.   Each industry knows where it gets its raw material and what processes it goes through from start to finish, and there are trade associations and organisations of various kinds in which all this knowledge is centralized. In these associations there are a certain number of leading men, and it is the business of the Government, if it has to take over the work of controlling supplies and the transport of supplies, to keep in touch with these men. . . .

* * *

p. 21.   A great deal can be done beforehand. (a) We can study the commercial side of possible wars, and this study is essential if we are to have an intelligent blockade policy or an intelligent supply policy. We must know what are the important supplies which we can cut off from the enemy and what are the important supplies which are closed to us or which he can close or hamper. (b) Secondly, we must have a suitable official machine, which can be developed rapidly in case of war into a Ministry of Shipping and a Ministry of Supply. The nucleus of a Ministry of Shipping is in the Board of Trade, and it could be expanded very rapidly if occasion arose. If war came soon, we should probably use very much the same kind of machine that we had in the last war as it worked well, but there should be definite schemes on paper for a Ministry of Shipping and a Ministry of Supply and they should be overhauled from time to time to see that they are up to date. (c) Thirdly, we must learn all we can of the mechanism of the transport and main supply trades, and keep in touch with the men in those trades who count most. This sounds a tall order, but it is part of the regular business of my Department as regards shipping, and a great deal has been done in the same direction as regards the important supply trades.

* * *

42. Enforcement of Article 16

Minute by Alex Hunt, Principal Assistant Secretary, Admiralty Secretary's Department

[ADM 1/15037] 11 June 1927

1. This Legal Report tends in the direction I rather anticipated. A new International Law rather different from the Traditional International Law is being introduced very largely based on Article 16 of the Covenant.

2. I think the Admiralty should continue to maintain that the economic sanctions have nothing to do with blockade, that the measures contemplated in Article 16, paragraph 1, are measures taken within the jurisdiction of an individual State.

3. As the Legal Sub. Committee of the CID [Committee of Imperial Defence] said, 'when a future war is waged with the support of the League every other member of the League will be bound to exclude enemy exports from its territory, but the first paragraph in Article 16 appears to contemplate measures taken within the jurisdiction of individual States without necessarily being accompanied by a Declaration of War.' 'It would not appear to touch belligerent Naval measures on the High Seas.' Of course the importance to Great Britain of this Legal Report in emphasizing the compulsory obligation to break off financial and commercial relations on the one hand and the obligation to submit to such interruption at the hands of the other members to the full extent contemplated by the Article cannot be exaggerated from the point of view of the Board of Trade and the Treasury as this country depends on Trade and on the delicate mechanism of London as the financial centre of the world.

4. It would be tragic if paragraph 1 was literally acted upon and this country had to take similar steps to those taken during the war in preventing financial facilities, cutting off trade relations etc.

5. As regards however the special point of a pacific blockade I suggest that the Admiralty should adopt the view that paragraph 1 of Article 16 relates to action that is taken within the jurisdiction of a State and there is no justification for the view that there is any obliga-

tion to apply a pacific blockade, i.e. that the Admiralty should resist a pacific blockade being included as one of the *normal* measures to be taken in the event of action (prior to war being declared) under Article 16. The Memorandum in Annex 2 on pacific blockades is really not unfair, although it has a bias in favour of pacific blockades, whereas personally I have a bias against them, though reserving as a matter for consideration whether on the merits of an actual case a pacific blockade might not be on occasion put into force by this country. The question of such a blockade has come up recently in connection with action in China and the disadvantages regarding third parties are familiar within the Admiralty. I see the Memorandum brings out what I stated regarding the pacific blockade in China that the U.S.A. had never declared a pacific blockade and I do not think that the US Executive could declare a blockade without the consent of Congress.

6. I believe the point has never been gone into in law, but I am not quite certain as to whether a British ship owner could not bring a case against the Government, if a pacific blockade was declared, for demurrage, and I am slightly doubtful as to what the attitude would be of the Dominions if a vessel registered in the Dominions was held up by a ship of the Royal Navy during a pacific blockade with which the Dominions (being members of the League) were not in sympathy. As a first action the Admiralty might ask the Foreign Office for their views on this report and might suggest an Interdepartmental Conference should be held at which the Board of Trade, Treasury, Admiralty and Foreign Office might be represented.

[Number 7 not used.]

8. The report seems most vulnerable as regards Page 3(b) dealing with the position as regards members of the League themselves, seeing that it is left to each State to decide whether a casus foederis has really arisen; yet it really was an implied condition in Article 16 that all other Powers would take similar and simultaneous action. Of course Article 16 is far too rigid in its absolute obligation to cut off economic relations, and several Powers have felt the need of toning down this compulsory obligation, but Great Britain is the most affected, and it is a moot point whether we ought to have signed the Covenant as regards Article 16 seeing that the U.S.A. stood outside the League.

9. As she and other Powers stand outside there is a gap in the effectiveness of the economic boycott under paragraph 1. There will thus be a tendency for it to be stated that the economic boycott must be supplemented by the pacific blockade, i.e. to bring in the Navy to help the Board of Trade and Post Office and Treasury and yet the gap in the effectiveness will remain as long as third parties' interests must be

consulted and Great Britain will be put to a great economic and financial loss to carry out measures, the efficacy of which will be blunted by the activities of the United States, Russia, and other Nationals.

10.   Another point to be remembered is that the sanctions referred to in this Report which deal with the case of a Nation which has resorted to war contrary to the Provisions of Articles 12, 13 or 15 may be used, if present Geneva tendencies mature, to prevent war under Article 11 of the Covenant.

* * *

Admiralty Secretary to the Under-Secretary of State, Foreign Office

[H.2221/27]   10 August 1927

Sir, I am commanded by My Lords Commissioners of the Admiralty to acquaint you that they have had under their consideration the report C.241.1927.V., forwarded in your letter W.5126/61/98 of 8th June, 1927, on the legal position arising from the enforcement in time of peace of the measures of economic pressure indicated in Article 16 of the Covenant of the League of Nations, particularly by a maritime blockade.

2.   When the Covenant of the League of Nations was originally drafted, it was apparently contemplated that the measures of economic pressure under Article 16 of the Covenant should be limited to measures taken within the jurisdiction of the individual states.

3.   The fact, however, that the United States did not adhere to the League of Nations, threatened to make such provision valueless, since the USA and the other non-adhering nations could as a rule supply all the needs of the offending Power.

4.   For this reason Article 16 of the Covenant has been interpreted as also implying a pacific blockade to be enforced by the members of the League.

5.   In the Report under consideration the facts of such a policy under International Law are examined. The authors of the Memorandum conclude that non-adhering States may be led to acquiesce by sympathy with the motives of the League, taken in conjunction with the fact that a formal declaration of war would enable the members of the League to apply the recognised blockade rights of belligerents.

6.   My Lords think it desirable that HM Government should make it clear that they cannot recognise pacific blockade as one of the normal measures to be taken in the event of action under Article 16. The

burden of any such action would certainly fall upon this country as well as the consequences in the form of disputes and claims for damage from non-adhering states.

7. It is suggested that questions connected with League Document C.241 should in the first instance be discussed by an interdepartmental conference at which the Treasury, Foreign Office, Admiralty and Board of Trade should be represented.

8. Copies . . .

* * *

43. *International Law as Affecting Naval Warfare*

Paymaster Captain Manisty, Port Accountant Officer, Portsmouth, to Secretary to First Sea Lord

[ADM 116/3619]   13th August, 1927

My dear Weekes, With reference to my interview yesterday, I enclose a copy of the Treaties of Washington Act, 1922, which is a British *municipal* Act. You will see by Section 4 that a Naval Officer is placed in some peril of being tried 'before the military authorities of any Power within the jurisdiction of which he may be found', if he violates (or, I suppose, if he is *accused* of violating) 'any of the rules contained in Article I of the Second Schedule'; you will also see that these rules are 'universal rules' and apply to all ships of war including submarines.

Admiralty papers M.02398/26 will show the reply sent to Portsmouth when this point was raised.

I drew up the enclosed paper on 12th March 1927, but as far as I know it has not been used officially, and I did not know to whom it could be addressed with advantage.

Since then, owing to the absence of Professor Pearce Higgins temporarily in the USA, I was asked to lecture in his place to the War Course and Staff Course at Greenwich, six lectures to each, and this matter, among others, was discussed with the two Courses, and I gathered that the Officers felt that the Act placed them in a very invidious position. The USA Naval Officer, from an article in one of their Magazines, is fully alive to this danger and is therefore glad that France did not ratify the Treaty, and as far as [the] USA or any other country is concerned the Treaty has no force. It is difficult to understand why our country alone has enforced the Treaty by municipal legislation.

The question arose also on the point whether a warship may attack merchant ships, either neutral or belligerent, when in a convoy under the escort of an enemy warship without giving such ship warning; if the Act is taken literally 'a merchant vessel must not be attacked unless it refuse[s] to submit to visit and search after warning, or to proceed as directed after seizure'. Rear-Admiral Pound, ACNS, saw me in connection with this, and afterwards, in response to his request, I drew up an agenda of points which I consider to be of vital importance in the conduct of Naval Operations, but on which there is uncertainty of guidance from any Admiralty instructions.

Among them is the point mentioned by you yesterday, that of diverting a merchant ship into port for search instead of searching her at sea, called 'detention' in the Prize Manual, 1923. How does the Act affect this? Supposing a USA liner with a cargo of millionaires, USA being a neutral, is ordered by a belligerent Destroyer off the Philippines to proceed into Hong Kong for search and refuses to do so, her destination being ostensibly Honolulu, what is the Commanding Officer of the Destroyer to do?

I think that Admiral Pound is considering the question of the appointment of a Committee to look into the points in the agenda.

Another important point is the status in war of state-owned merchant ships, e.g. the USA Shipping line. Are they immune from visit and search, or if not immune from visit are they immune from search once it is established by visit that they are state-owned.

Of course, these problems must also be considered, though perhaps not so important, from the point of view of our being a neutral. Would the British community acquiesce in British liners passing through the Mediterranean, during a war between two Mediterranean Powers, being diverted to a belligerent port for search merely because they could not be searched at sea.

Could you see Admiral Pound and ascertain the present position before I attempt to draw up anything for the First Sea Lord. In my view the present position of the Admiralty instructions, including the Prize Manual, as a guide to Naval Officers afloat is most unsatisfactory, and though this view is also held by many Naval Officers to whom I have lectured, or with whom I have discussed the matter, you will see by some of the correspondence in 'M' Branch that my view is not the official Admiralty view.

I suggest you should also see the DTSD [Director of Training and Staff Duties] as regards the instruction in International Law at the War Course and Staff Course at Greenwich. While acting as 'locum tenems' for Professor Pearce Higgins as lecturer to the two courses this year I took a different line to him, and though, of course, he is a world-wide authority on the general subject of International Law, I think that of necessity he must be academic.

The War has taught Naval Officers that International Law in its effect on Sea Power is anything but academic, and post-war developments at Versailles, Lausanne, Washington, Geneva, and the Hague have taught the same lesson. Those of us who had to give advice on the Bridge of a Ship, or at the Admiralty, which affect *immediate* action, cannot forget this, and it forces us to take the subject seriously. Actual knowledge of the sea and ships, fighting or trading, and of foreign countries, distances, weather conditions, etc. make it much easier for Naval Officers to visualise the future than for those who remain on shore and in England. But here again my view may not be the Admiralty view.

Before I do draw up anything on paper for the First Sea Lord, would you kindly explain my position.

All International Lawyers are self-constituted, mainly by writing books – of which there is no limit especially by USA writers; as regards Prize matters the best authorities are the Prize Court Judges, Lord Stowell and his contemporaries and his successors, practical, and not academic, lawyers.

But under modern conditions, particularly in a future war, say, in the Pacific, the leisurely process of taking ships into ports of the belligerent, and then trying them in a prize Court, will, I think, form but a small part in the methods of economic pressure which a belligerent will have to exercise. Wireless telegraphy and the speed of warships and the assistance of aircraft, will make recapture more feasible, and the sinking of captured ships therefore more necessary. The distinction between warships (including 'Q' ships), offensively and defensively armed merchant ships, fleet auxiliaries, government-owned ships, transports, oil-tankers, etc. (and even hospital ships) tended, as regards their status, to diminish in the last war, and judging by the disarmament discussions at Geneva may be even more difficult in the next, just as the distinction between the fighting forces and the civil population tends to disappear.

Prize Law and the Prize Court may, therefore, take a small share in the next war, and, in a short war in any case, most of the Prize Court work is Post Mortem or Post Pacem.

As you yourself know I was 'self-constituted' as an International Law lecturer at the Secretaries' Course; as Superintendent I was responsible for seeing the Class was instructed in International Law, and as I was not allowed enough funds to obtain the services of Professor Pearce Higgins, and there seemed to be no one else available I had to take it on myself, and did it for over three years. It meant, of course, much more than merely lecturing; there were discussions, individual precis and personal correction thereof for each member of the Course, and examinations at the end of the Course. With Students, many of whom had definite War experience of points under discussion, I could not help acquiring a good deal of knowledge; I also joined certain International Law Societies so as to keep in touch with the academic side; and also kept in touch, as far as possible, with Admiralty developments.

This work was undertaken by my successor, Paymaster Captain Measham, who again has succeeded me as Deputy Judge Advocate of the Fleet [DJAF], and who in that capacity has been asked to lecture in International Law to the Staff Course at Greenwich.

The instruction in International Law at the Secretaries' Course will now be given by the new Superintendent, Paymaster Commander Bennett, who was for two years my Assistant at that Course. Both these Officers have had very considerable experience as Secretaries to Flag Officers in peace and war.

All Paymaster Lieutenants are required to pass an examination in International Law before promotion to the rank of Paymaster Lieutenant Commander, this examination being arranged by the DJAF and Supt. of Secretaries' Course in conjunction.

There is, thus, a definite 'school' of instruction and thought in the Accountant Branch, on International Law, under the guidance of Senior Officers of that Branch. It is hoped that this will produce competent advisers to Flag Officers on this subject.

I feel, however, that the time has come when there should be more liaison between the Admiralty, Greenwich and the 'school' and more guidance from Admiralty.

* * *

44. Belligerent Rights at Sea and the Relations Between the United States and Great Britain[1]

Austen Chamberlain's Conclusions
SECRET

[CAB 21/307/157–66; Confidential Paper 258(27)]　　October 26 1927[2]

As one result of the failure of the Three-Power Naval Conference, I was led to consider what was the real ground for the apparently unreasonable attitude of the United States towards the British proposals for limitation of armaments. This consideration quickly brought me to the conclusion that the difference between us centred in the use which we make of our naval forces to enforce our view of the rights of a belligerent at sea. This at once raised the question whether it was desirable, and, if desirable, possible, to attempt to reach an agreement with the United States upon the disputed points of international law. On my return home I found that the same problem had been raised independently alike in private letters from the Ambassador at Washington and within the Foreign Office itself.

Sir Esme Howard had set out his views in two private and confidential letters to Sir William Tyrrell, which I print for the information of the Cabinet (Appendix I).

I set out my own line of thought in the memorandum which is printed as Appendix II, and in Appendix III will be found a memorandum by Mr Craigie which gives a much more detailed examination of the points of difference between ourselves and the Americans, and the possibility of reconciling them.

I know the immense difficulties which surround this question, and I realise that there must be a most careful examination of all that is involved before any such negotiations could be undertaken, but I hold strongly that the examination ought to be made and that the new factors introduced by the rise of United States naval and financial power and by the cost and extent of modern warfare must be taken into account. It cannot be denied that the present difference on this subject between the United States and ourselves is the only matter which makes war be-

---

[1]*Circulated to the Cabinet prior to the inception of the Sub-Committee on Belligerent Rights, and re-circulated to its members by its Secretary, C.P. Hermon-Hodge, 19 January 1928.

[2]Esme Howard's letters of 15 and 22 September 1927 and Appendix III, 'Memorandum respecting the Possibilities of an Anglo-American Agreement regulating the Exercise by either Power of its Belligerent Right to Intercept Private Property at Sea', not reproduced here.

tween our two nations conceivable. But I go further; I believe that General Preston Brown does not exaggerate when he says that any attempt by us to enforce our rights in a future war where the United States were neutral, as we enforced them in the late war, would make war between us 'probable'. The world position has been altered to our disadvantage and what was possible in the past may have become impossible for the future. I would, therefore, urge that the question should be referred for consideration by a special Committee of the Cabinet or the CID. I am advised that, if it should appear that there is any possibility of entering upon pourparlers or negotiations with the United States, the sooner we can take action the better would be our chances of success.

A.C. [Austen Chamberlain]

* * *

Colonel R. Pope-Hennessy, Military Attaché, to Esme Howard in letter from Esme Howard to . . . Tyrrell, 22 September 1927

Manchester, Mass.
September 20 1927

H.E.,

I submit the following memorandum of a conversation with General Preston Brown on the outcome of the Geneva Conference:

1. By invitation of Major-General Preston Brown, commanding 1st Corps Area (Boston), I visited him at Fort Ethan Allen from the 24th to 26th August in order to inspect the troops training at that post.

2. General Preston Brown is an experienced and educated soldier. He has read and thought a great deal about war, and has not allowed his mind to lie fallow since he left the University of Yale to enter the American Army some thirty-three years ago. In the late war he saw something of the British army in France, and has retained happy recollections of his contact with it. He gives me the impression of being a Southern gentleman, very friendly to England, and with genuine appreciation of what the British Empire stands for. He has been most courteous to my predecessor and to me; my relations with him are cordial and almost intimate, as we find that we have many interests in common.

3. On the evening of the 25th August, when I was sitting alone with him in his room at Fort Ethan Allen discussing some questions of the late war in which we were both interested, I guided the conversation to

the subject of the Geneva Conference to find out how an American soldier of his type had reacted to the breakdown of the conference. What he said amounts to this:

4.   The conference failed because neither side would tell the truth; you (British) want numerous cruisers not only to protect your trade routes – which is obvious – but [also] in order to apply in war your historic weapon of blockade. Small cruisers can do that. We (Americans) want a smaller number of big cruisers to ensure that your blockade does not interfere with our commerce as a neutral. The 10,000-ton cruisers are necessary to us to break your blockade. This country is never again going to put up with what it had to put with in 1914–15 from both sides. It was the mercy of God and the co-operation of Walter Page and Grey that kept America from coming in on the wrong side last time. Next time He may not be so kind, and Page and Grey aren't there. You have no idea how remote we were from the war. In 1914 I was in the Philippines, and in 1915 in Texas, and all we know of the war there was that British cruisers were stopping American trade and German submarines were sinking our people. If the Germans had not made that mistake we would have come in on the wrong side.

5.   General Preston Brown made it clear to me that, in his opinion, war between Great Britain and the United States was 'unthinkable' only as a result of disagreement between those two Powers alone; as an issue arising out of a state of war between Great Britain and a third party, he considered it 'probable', unless Great Britain modifies her practice of blockade so as to conform with the wishes of the United States.

6.   To my remark that, if that was the case, it would be a pity to wait until national passions were at white heat before trying to come to an understanding on the question of blockade, he replied that the blockade question could not be taken up between the two countries too soon 'before the anti-British hot-air campaign gets going'. He added: 'We know all about blockade in this country. I remember the South after the Civil War. It is a thing we ought to be able to agree about, as we too may not always be neutrals and may want to use the weapon ourselves as we have in the past.'

7.   I would like to emphasize the fact that throughout this conversation General Preston Brown spoke about Great Britain and British policy in a most friendly, and indeed sympathetic, way. The impression he left on me was that of a friend anxious to open my eyes to the danger of living in a fool's paradise by assuming that war between our two countries is 'unthinkable', when, as a matter of fact, in the eventuality which he

indicated, it is 'probable', unless steps are taken now to clear up the question of blockade.

* * *

Appendix II
Memorandum by the Secretary of State

October 16, 1927

Sir W. Tyrrell,

I am much interested by Sir Esme's letters of the 15th and 20th September.

As you know from our first conversation on my return, my mind had been occupied by the same problem and had reached very similar conclusions. I had, indeed, already spoken to the Prime Minister about it at our meeting at Talloirs, and he recurred to it on my return home in consequence of a conversation which he had had with Mr Vansittart.

It may be useful that I should summarise my own line of thought. It was as follows:

(i.)   The United States entered the recent conference with a plan of naval limitation rather hastily put together, proceeding from no principle (unless 'parity' be dignified with that name), and based on no clear strategic view of America's policy or need.

(ii.)   Only late in the discussions did they become aware of their real case, viz., that whilst 'parity', when interpreted to mean equality of numbers or tonnage, might be necessary to satisfy national pride, but had no basis in strategic necessity, our small cruisers were the instruments of our blockade policy and not, as we claimed, a purely defensive force. It would seem to me that our representatives were so preoccupied about our food supplies that they had really failed to take the offensive tasks of the small cruisers into consideration at all.

(iii.)   Blockade is, therefore, at the root of our difference with the United States over naval limitation, and is the one question which might lead to war between us. Unless they are belligerents, the United States will never again submit to such a blockade as we enforced in the Great War.

(iv.)   After every considerable war, military and naval authorities are prone to think in terms of that war – till another has been fought, teaching new lessons. Now it is extremely unlikely that, if and when we are again engaged in a serious war, the conditions governing the application of blockade will be at all comparable to those of the last great struggle, in which all the great land frontiers of our enemies were closed to trade. The present tendency is to exaggerate the potency of the blockade weapon, even when the attitude of the United States is left out of account.

(v.)   But it cannot be thus excluded from consideration, for

(a.)   The United States have the means and the will to create a navy equal to our own. Their one existing difficulty is men. If there is no agreement between us, they will in time get the men by developing, at no matter what cost, their mercantile marine. We shall, therefore, stimulate a double rivalry – naval and mercantile.

(b.)   If we are engaged in a life and death struggle such as the last, it would be suicidal to add the United States to our enemies. Whatever we contend are our rights, we cannot, in fact, afford to exercise them if it involves war with the United States when the United States possesses a navy equal in combative force to our own, and we are at war with a first-class Power.

(c.)   But it is not even necessary for the United States to declare war to bring us to destruction. They have only to refuse us supplies and credits in order to deal us a fatal blow.

(vi.)   Not all these arguments apply with equal force to minor conflicts, but the blockade weapon is itself of less consequence to us in such lesser wars and we can in such cases more readily abandon our extreme claims.

(vii.)   Whilst hitherto we, whether as neutrals or belligerents, have consistently supported the highest doctrine of belligerent rights, the attitude of the United States has been inconstant. They have put those rights high when they were belligerents; they have sought to minimise them when they were neutrals. But now that they have with us the equal-largest navy of the world and like us a very small army; now that with the growth of their international interests they are less certain of being always neutrals, their interests approach our own and this approach should render agreement between us more easy. Our great weapon is their great weapon. They must ask themselves the same question as we have put to ourselves and answered: Sea-power being our great strength and decisive weapon, shall we bear with the sacrifices which its assertion by others entails when we are neutrals, *i.e.*, the majority of cases, in order to keep it effective for the rare occasions upon which it is our only means of salvation, or shall we take the risk of not being able to use it when its use is vital sooner than suffer the inconvenience of its use by others in circumstances in which that use may cause us some loss and annoyance, but can do us not vital injury!

Differing here from Sir Esme, I should say that the higher the United States will put belligerent rights, the better for us, but their doctrines must be the same in peace and in war.

I am strongly in favour of an endeavour to reach agreement with them and that as early as possible. The first step is to get our own ideas clear in the Foreign Office; next to approach the Cabinet and/or the Committee of Imperial Defence. Only then can we open discussions with the United States of American in whatever manner may seem best.

It will be seen that

1st. I reject the first of the alternatives stated by Sir Esme in his letter of the 15th, *i.e.*, to pursue a blockade policy regardless of the United States of America.

2nd. That I approve his second, *i.e.*, to endeavour to come to an agreement with them.

3rd. I would reserve consideration of the suggestion for an international conference until we see the result of our pourparlers with the United States. Incidentally is not Sir Esme making a rather bold assumption when he speaks in this connection of 'the rules of International Law as established before 1914 . . . '? Was there in fact any general agreement as to these rules? Perhaps he is thinking only of the measures of agreement then reached between the United States and ourselves. This in any case would be the starting-point for any reconsideration of our position.

Sir Esme should be supplied with a copy of Mr Malkin's valuable article on the Declaration of Paris.

(Initialled) A.C. [Austen Chamberlain]

* * *

45. *A Canadian Perspective*

Herbert B. Taylor to Admiral Domvile, Director of Naval Intelligence
Secret

[ADM 116/3619]   Naval Intelligence Division,
                        Department of National Defence, Ottawa, Canada
                                                 8 November 1927

Dear Admiral Domvile, . . .

(2)   My second reason in writing to you is in connection with a memorandum enclosed under cover of the Director of Naval Intelligence,

Ottawa's secret letter S.No. 110/27 of the 3rd November 1927, addressed to the Director of Naval Intelligence, Admiralty. This relates to the freedom of the seas versus blockade controversy. A good deal of thought has been given to the question recently by the Department of National Defence of Canada. While our sympathies are entirely with Great Britain in this respect, one is, comparatively speaking, close to the United States of America here in Ottawa and one sees their point of view to a certain extent. After this matter had been under consideration here for some time, I was sent down to Washington to ascertain the ideas on this subject at the British Embassy, and I found these synchronise very close with our own. Briefly, these may be summarised as follows:

(a)   The responsible administrators of the United States of America do not mean to allow belligerents to interfere with their neutral trade in any future war. This (apart from the purely Big Navy party) is the real reason why the Americans want a big navy and why they will not agree with any limitation in the eight-inch gun cruiser which is intended to protect their trade against our six-inch gun cruisers or armed merchantmen.

(b)   Unless through diplomatic channels we come to some arrangement suitable to both sides, and one which the Americans are willing to observe (very difficult), we feel in Canada that the United States of America will throw in her weight on the side of our enemies. It appears to us that they hold the balance of power, as we do not see how, in addition to other enemies, we could take on a country with unlimited resources and which has, on paper, a navy equal to our own.

(c)   Realizing that the United States of America would probably be an enemy of Great Britain if she insists on her blockade policy, I do not see how responsible Ministers in Canada can, in the future, recommend that Canada should join in a war with the remainder of the British Empire. If they decide to do so, I cannot see how they could spare troops for any oversea military expedition. It seems more natural that Great Britain would have to send them here. I believe that the majority of people in Canada are extremely loyal to the British Crown and but for the menace of the United States declaring war, I have no doubt, when the time comes, they would act in the future as they have always done in the past.

(3)   In the last war we objected to the United States trading with Germany, no matter how the goods went. In the Civil War, the North objected to us trading with the South. If the United States goes to war with Mexico, they would certainly object to us trading with the latter

country. It appears to me, our demands are so similar, under different conditions, that we should be able to reach some agreement.

(4) True, we in Great Britain starve if we do not get our food, but equally, from my short acquaintance with the United States of America, I shudder to think what would happen to them if the clockwork machinery went wrong and they could not carry out their normal trade.

(5) In 1809 President Jefferson of the United States of America put an embargo on trade going to Great Britain. Their trade dropped to about one-fifth of its normal value with the result that they had very grave internal difficulties. I think these would be very much worse to-day than they were then.

* * *

46. Belligerent Rights at Sea

Memorandum by Austen Chamberlain
Confidential Print 286 (27)

[CAB 21/317; CAB 16/79, part 9/290]   14 November 1927

While C.P. 258 was being printed for circulation, I mentioned to Sir M[aurice] Hankey that I was proposing to bring this subject before the Cabinet. He was good enough to supply me within a few days with a memorandum embodying his strongly-held view that we should enter into no new engagement restrictive of our liberty.

I believe the Cabinet will be glad to have his opinion as well as the observations made upon it and on the whole subject by Sir Cecil Hurst, who is also opposed to negotiation. I therefore circulate them with my own paper.

On one thing we are all agreed – that the question is of immense importance, and that the answer, whether negative or affirmative, is fraught with grave possibilities. I have formed no definite conclusion. I ask the Cabinet for no decision until the question has been thoroughly examined by the most competent committee that we can choose; but I cannot take the responsibility which would be mine if, because I am not prepared at present to give a definite answer to the question which I have raised, I refrained from calling the attention of the Cabinet to it and by my inaction, in fact, decided it in the negative. A.C.

Memorandum by Sir M[aurice] Hankey on Blockade and the Laws of
War[1]
Confidential Print 258 (27)

2, Whitehall Gardens, S.W.1
October 31, 1927

For several decades before the outbreak of the Great War, a period during which there was no unlimited war and, indeed, no great war in which sea power was a paramount consideration, there grew up a tendency to assume that war was a matter solely for fighting men and that the civil population ought to be exempted from its hardships. Professor Oppenheim, in his Treatise on International Law (First Edition, Part II, Chapter II, Section 178) shows how, after the Declaration of Paris, 1856, the Continental Powers and the United States of America worked for the abolition of the right of capture of property at sea. 'It cannot be denied,' he continues, 'that, as the matter stands, it was the opposition of Great Britain which has prevented the abolition of the rule that private enemy vessels and goods may be captured.' By the beginning of the present century there were many people of liberal and pacific tendencies even in this country who, in the absence of any modern experience to bring home the importance of economic pressure to this country as a weapon of offence, inclined towards some alleviation of the old rigours of naval warfare.

2.   The exercise in the Russo-Japanese War by both countries of what they conceived to be their belligerent rights in the search, capture and sinking of neutral vessels, and the protests made by the business community, tended to rivet attention on the neutral aspects of the question, with the result that international law took a definite turn in the direction of limiting the freedom of belligerents. The situation, so far as this country was concerned, is explained in the following extract from a speech by Earl Beauchamp in the House of Lords on the 12th December, 1911:

> During the Russo-Japanese War the Foreign Office was inundated with a number of complaints from British traders and British merchants, who complained of various acts which were done in the course of the war, but, still more, they complained of the want of certainty with regard to the state of the law. . . . There was very little that the Foreign Office could do. There was no arbitration possible;

[1]Appendix, 'Blockade: Extracts from the Writings of German Leaders Bearing on its Results', not reproduced here.

and if the belligerents in that case or in any other case refuse arbitration, there is very little that any Foreign Office can do in such circumstances. . . . That was the position to which the present Secretary of State succeeded when he came into office, and he came to the conclusion that it was eminently desirable that, if possible, some means should be devised by which the decision of a belligerent's Court should be subject to an appeal in cases relating to neutrals; and when the Second Peace Conference at The Hague took place, the British delegates, and also the delegates from other nations, went there with instructions to see if something could be done in the matter.[1]

3.   The Second Peace Conference (1907) drew up a draft 'Convention concerning the Establishment of an International Prize Court,' which was signed by the representatives of all the Great Powers except Russian and many of the smaller Powers. Eleven States did not sign the Convention.

4.   The International Prize Court, however, had no agreed code of law to administer, and, before the Convention could be ratified and the Court set up, it was felt to be necessary to compile such a code. The British Government, accordingly, summoned a Conference on the subject, which drew up the famous Declaration of London, 1909.

5.   In 1907, when the Second Peace Conference met, we were in a transition state in regard to our preparations for war. Prior to the *entente* with France, our thoughts had been directed across the Channel. And although by 1907 much had been done in the direction of adjusting the distribution of the Fleet and coast defences to the new situation, no comprehensive study had yet been made of the questions of blockade and economic pressure in a war with Germany. The Convention for the Establishment of an International Prize Court, therefore, was drawn up at a time when no data existed for examining its effect on our belligerent rights in a war with Germany.

6.   In the course of an enquiry (conducted by Mr Asquith's Chairmanship) in 1908–09 by the Committee of Imperial Defence into the Military Needs of the Empire as affected by the Continent of Europe, the Admiralty submitted a powerful Memorandum as to the possibilities of economic pressure on Germany, which made a strong impression on the Committee, with the result that a series of enquiries was undertaken by the Committee into some of the means by which such pressure could be exercised.

[1]*Parliamentary Debates, Lords*, 1911, Vol. X.

7. In these circumstance, it is somewhat surprising that the Declaration of London was never at any stage referred for examination by the Committee of Imperial Defence. Perhaps it was thought that the inclusion in the British Delegation of Sir Charles Ottley, the Secretary of the Committee, and of Admiral Slade, the Director of Naval Intelligence, was a sufficient safeguard. However this may be, the Declaration never was referred to the Committee of Imperial Defence. But, when it was published, the present Secretary of the Committee of Imperial Defence (at the time the Naval Assistant Secretary) wrote two long Memoranda pointing out the adverse effect which the Declaration would have on our power to put pressure on an enemy, as revealed by the detailed enquiries of the Committee of Imperial Defence. They are too long to give in full, but the following extract from one of them sums up on one of the most formidable heads of the indictment:

The fact is that, if the Declaration of London is ratified, we shall, in the event of even a successful war with Germany, be in a most humiliating position. We can blockade the North Sea ports, but we can do absolutely nothing to prevent the trade of Germany being carried in neutral bottoms to the Baltic ports or through neutral ports in neighbouring countries. While we are carefully watching the mouth of the Elbe the trade of Hamburg will continue in neutral ships, which will pass through the Belt and the Kiel Canal, the only additional cost being the enhanced freight due to the withdrawal of its German flag, and the slightly lengthened voyage round the Skaw. The first of these causes of additional cost will be reduced as time goes on and more neutral vessels are attracted, and, no doubt, by the *bona fide* purchase by neutrals (possibly with capital supplied from Germany) of German merchant ships, which will take the place of the neutral vessels in their ordinary routes.

These questions were insufficiently studied before the Declaration of London was entered into. There is no instance to be found in modern history of a war in which commerce has played a vitally important part, owing to the fact that recent wars have not been fought between nations susceptible – as are Great Britain and Germany – to attack through their commerce, and there are no data on which to calculate what means it will be necessary to adopt in such a war. The difficulties of blockade, due to modern inventions, suggest that even greater latitude may be necessary in the future than in the past. The negotiators of the Declaration of London have made the fatal error of basing their agreement not on the experience of past wars (for in the Napoleonic wars and all previous wars, when commerce was an important consideration, the greatest latitude was claimed and exercised) and *not* on a scientific appreciation of possible future wars, but have rested themselves on the experience of a few very recent wars in which the weapon of sea power, as a means of putting pressure on the inferior naval power, had no scope for exertion.

Yet, in a Continental war, Great Britain has no other weapon of bringing an enemy to terms except that of her sea power. The position is still that described by Mahan in his *Influence of Sea Power upon the French Revolution and Empire* (Vol. II, p. 284):

The battle between the sea and the land was to be fought out on commerce. England had no army wherewith to meet Napoleon; Napoleon had no navy to cope with that of his enemy. As in the case of an impregnable fortress, the only alternative for either of these contestants was to reduce the other by starvation.

On these grounds alone there would appear to be the strongest possible case for a rejection of the Declaration of London. The objections to this instrument, however, do not end here. Sir Charles Ottley, who did not agree with these criticisms, nevertheless forwarded them to several people in authority. They fell on deaf ears. The writer was advised verbally by a very high officer in the Admiralty, who had read his Paper, to drop the matter, as no instrument of this kind could possibly survive the test of war – a remark which, though prophetic, was not a good ground for allowing the Convention to pass.

8.   If the criticism of the Declaration of London in inside circles was numerically feeble, it was far otherwise outside. The publication of the Declaration was followed by a storm of public criticism and adverse propaganda promoted by Mr. Thomas Gibson Bowles. One hundred and twenty retired Admirals signed a protest. Resolutions poured in from Chambers of Commerce and other public bodies. The Conservative party, then in opposition, took the course – very unusual in matters of this kind – of opposing ratification until after an examination by a Commission of experts. So great was the interest, that in a crowded Parliamentary Session no less than three days were given up to a Debate in which the leaders on both sides took part. As a result the Naval Prize Bill, which was intended to put the Declaration into effect so far as this country was concerned, was rejected by the House of Lords, and the Declaration of London, in consequence, had not been ratified when war broke out.

9.   The public criticism of the Declaration of London, as revealed by a study of the Parliamentary Debates, did not, for the most part, touch its main defects. Instead of attacking the limitation it imposed on our own

power to put pressure on an enemy, most of the critics directed their denunciations against the effect it would exercise on our own supplies in time of war, or on our position as a neutral, and on a number of alleged technical defects in the instrument. These criticisms were easily met. Whether this misdirection of criticism was due to lack of knowledge and insight of the conditions of modern war, or to a natural restraint in tackling such a delicate subject as the full implications of sea power, it is impossible to say. There were, however, two exceptions to the general rule. Mr. Balfour and Mr. Bonar Law both dwelt briefly on the real ground for criticism:

> *Mr Balfour*: Take first the argument about imported food supplies to a Continental country. There are great Continental countries which habitually import such corn as they require through neutral ports. They cannot be touched under this Declaration. You may say that, after all, they import a small fraction of their supplies, and that that fraction will be very well supplied from friendly neighbours on the Continent, and that the matter is of legal but not of practical importance. The whole trend of modern industry is to make the Western European nations more and more manufacturing countries, and therefore to make those zones in which the population is increasing more and more dependent upon overseas supplies. It is perfectly true that corn can come in, whatever you do, through these ports to Continental nations. Will any human being deny that to give them absolute security under this treaty, to make it impossible for them to have any moments of anxiety, to make it unnecessary to raise either the insurance or the freights of the neutral bottoms carrying these supplies, is to give them an advantage absolutely and formally denied to us by the same instrument?
>
> (*Parliamentary Debates, Commons*, 1911, Vol. XXVII, Cols. 846 and 847.)

Mr Bonar Law touched the spot even more closely:

> *Mr Bonar Law*:   Every article written on this subject by sailors has declared that the blockade in modern times is not of the value which it used to be, and that owing to the danger of submarines you cannot have a close blockade, *while by this very Declaration it is impossible for us to have a widely extended blockade, because it is not allowed to cover neutral coasts.*
>
> (*Parliamentary Debates, Commons*, 1911, Vol. XXVII, Col. 914.)

10.   Some of the reasons used by the defenders of the Declaration of London are very pertinent to the present day controversy. We are told

to-day, for example, that the United States of America will never again stand our interference with their trade as neutrals with an enemy, or at any rate with another neutral State. In private the same argument was used by the supporters of the Declaration of London in the controversies of 1910–11. In public these arguments were also used, though in a slightly veiled form, as shown by the following extracts from the Parliamentary Debates.

In introducing the Naval Prize Bill on the 28th June, 1911, Mr McKinnon Wood said:

Their ideal [namely, that of naval officers] is that we should be free to act as we did a century ago in the French war. They forget what our interference with neutral trade then cost us – world-wide hostility and an extension of the field of war. Even then we could not maintain the licence we assumed. They do not recognise how impossible it would be to assume that licence now, with the general development of naval power and the vast extension of sea-borne commerce.

Later in the Debate, Sir Edward (now Lord) Grey spoke as follows:

I see two intelligent grounds of opposition to the Declaration of London which I must discuss. One is, as Mr Gibson Bowles has said, 'We have no rules, we impose them; we make our own rules.' The time is gone for that. If you press that you are doing something which you will not be able to carry out. *You will be increasing the risk, by failing to get an international agreement, of interference with belligerents.* . . . I have never contended, and I have carefully abstained from contending, that the Declaration of London or the International Prize Court Convention would enable us to reduce naval expenditure; but I do say if you defeat an international agreement of this kind which other nations are anxious to have, because you wish to keep your hands free and impose your own rules on the world – if you will have no agreement with them unless you get your own way in everything because you will make no concessions – you will be increasing the tendency, not of one or two Powers, but of several Powers to enlarge their naval expenditure, *and you will be adding to the risk that you will be interfered with in time of war by neutral Powers.*

11.   Another argument which was used in private by the supporters of the Declaration of London was that the adaptation of the principle of blockade to modern conditions (which the writer of these notes had advocated) was really impracticable, that, so long as countries like

Belgium, Holland and Denmark remained neutral, there were no means by which the passage of supplies to and from Germany could be stopped, even if there were no Declaration of London. By the time the Committee of Imperial Defence got on to this aspect of the question the Government of the day was already deeply committed to the Declaration, and the subject was never examined on any other hypothesis. In fact, Lord Desart, who had led the British Delegation at the London Conference, was the Chairman of the Sub-Committee of the Committee of Imperial Defence on Trading with the Enemy, and several of the other delegates were members. This is certainly one reason why the implications of a blockade under modern conditions were not examined in greater detail before the War. We had put 'the cart before the horse,' and had committed ourselves to the rules without studying their application, and when the study of war with Germany was made it had to be based on the new rules, notwithstanding that they were found on a conception of naval warfare which was already obsolescent and becoming more obsolete every day.

The War

12.   The experience of actual war bore out in one respect the forecast of the high officer of the Admiralty, to which allusion has been made earlier in these notes; that is to say, the Declaration of London proved incompatible with the full exercise of sea power under modern conditions. But it was not jettisoned at once, and for nearly two years exercised a baneful influence on our policy. Here was a great code of International Law drawn up at an International Conference held in London under the auspices of the very Government which was conducting the war. How could it be thrown overboard at the first actual test? How could it fail to exercise the greatest moral influence on our relations with neutrals? Moreover, it was the only code in existence on which we and the French had ever reached agreement, and our Naval Prize Manual had been revised in accordance with its provisions. To revise the Prize Manual and to come to terms with the French would have required much time. Consequently, though still unratified, the Declaration was tacitly adopted at the outset of the War as the basis of our action, and the contraband lists issued at the outset of the War were in accordance with its provisions.

13.   Very soon, however, the Declaration began to crumble. Experience almost at once revealed its shortcomings, and public opinion would not stand this cramping of our belligerent rights. The action of the enemy, first in the indiscriminate laying of mine-fields, and later on in the adoption of the submarine campaign, provided the necessary

excuse. In spite of the efforts of the enemy to force us to a return to the Declaration of London (described by Admiral von Tirpitz as the 'Alpha and Omega' of the German Foreign Office), in spite of the many protests of neutrals, and more especially of the United states of America, the measures of economic pressure were gradually tightened up until, after the lapse of two years or more, the full rigour of blockade adapted to conditions of modern warfare foreseen as necessary by some of the critics (including Mr. Bonar Law and the present writer) were applied.

14.   Modifications in the Declaration of London were introduced as early as the 20th August, 1914:

> In the course of a few weeks it became evident that the right to capture conditional contraband on vessels was derisory so long as supplies were permitted to flow into Germany without interruption, through neutral countries. Accordingly, an Order in Council was issued on the 20th August in which the position arrived at by consultation between the Allied Governments was defined. The position was, in effect, an acceptance of the provisions contained in the Declaration of London, with the very important modification that conditional Contraband having an ultimate enemy destination would be liable to capture to whatever port the vessel was bound and at whatever port the cargo was to be discharged, whether in belligerent or neutral territory.
>
> (*The Official History of Sea-borne Trade. Fayle. Chapter IV.*)

On the 29th October two more Proclamations modifying the Declaration of London were promulgated. The first transferred to the list of contraband a number of articles which had been on the free list in the Declaration of London, including a number of metals required for the manufacture of war material, motor vehicles of all kinds, rubber, and mineral oils other than lubricants. The contraband list in the Declaration of London had corresponded closely with the lists of the 16th and 17th centuries. That it should have included in the free list articles such as the above is a glaring example of how completely the requirements of munitions manufacture and transport in modern war had been overlooked.

The second Proclamation of the 29th October, 1914, related chiefly to the treatment of conditional contraband and the circumstances in which enemy destination could be assumed. It modified articles 33, 35 and 38 of the Declaration of London. Another Order in Council of the 20th October, 1915, abrogated article 57 of the Declaration providing that the neutral or enemy character of a ship should be determined by the flag she was entitled to fly. An Order of the 30th March, 1916,

made further provision for stiffening up the procedure as regards contraband, whether absolute or conditional, and *inter alia*, included
provisions directly contrary to article 19 of the Declaration:

By this time (July 1916) the Allied Governments had come to the
conclusion that the application to warfare, under modern conditions, of
the rules laid down in the Declaration of London could no longer be
upheld. . . .

> So numerous and so far-reaching were the modifications now in
> force that little was left of the original rules, and for the purpose of
> avoiding friction and misconstruction it appeared better to lay the
> Declaration on one side and rely only on the application of princi-
> ples underlying the historic and admitted rules of International Law.
> (*Official History of Sea-borne Trade. Fayle. Vol. II Chapter 20.*)

15.   The final disappearance of the Declaration of London was effected by an Order in Council dated the 7th July, 1916. But the
Declaration of London was by no means the only great international
instrument affecting naval warfare to be overthrown by war experience.
The greater part of the Declaration of Paris, 1856 (drawn up, like the
Declaration of London, after a war – the Crimean War – in which
economic pressure played only a minor part), was very early sub-
merged by the experience of actual warfare, and those who before the
War had advocated its repudiation were justified. Similarly, the provisions of The Hague Convention forbidding the capture of enemy mail
bags on the high seas had been circumvented by the subterfuge of first
bringing into port the ships carrying them! It is no exaggeration to say
that every International Law which was not to the mutual benefit of
both belligerents was overridden, notwithstanding the protests of the
injured party – and so it always has been, and always will be, once
unlimited warfare holds sway!

16.   The extraordinary difficulties which our diplomacy encountered,
and the dangers we ran of interference by neutrals, especially by the
United States of America, must not be underrated. Those difficulties
were enormously increased, and in all probability the War was lengthened, by the haphazard way in which before the War we had entered
into engagements without proper examination or the exercise of sufficient forethought and imagination. Nevertheless, by the skill of our
diplomacy and the blunders of our enemy, these difficulties were sur-
mounted. The United States had the power, if they had desired to
exercise it, by escorting their merchant ships, to frustrate and paralyse
our blockade. We could not have afforded to interfere with her convoys.
She did not resort to this expedient, as the defenders of the Declaration

of London had insisted she might do. She might have entered the War against us. She actually joined in on our side. The difficulties of adapting blockade to modern conditions so as to put the maximum economic pressure on the Central Powers did not prove insuperable, as the supporters of the Declaration of London had insisted they would.

17.   In the long run the blockade proved to be one of the most essential means for supplementing the action of the military forces in bringing the War to an end. It was the home front in Germany which broke first. Anyone who doubts the efficacy of economic pressure is referred to the extracts in the Appendix from the accounts of the War by the leading enemy figures therein.

Observations

18.   The chapter of history summarised above deserves to be carefully studied in connection with any fresh proposal to reopen the question of belligerent rights at sea.

In the years before the War we entered on a slippery slope. The protests against the action of the belligerents during the Russo-Japanese War (which some people at the time regarded with misgiving) led to the International Prize Court Convention; the Convention to the Declaration of London; the Declaration to the verge of disaster. On the edge of the abyss we were saved from the final catastrophe of ratification by the instinct of the British people in regard to naval matters and the wisdom of the Conservative party and of the House of Lords.

The arguments used to support the Declaration of London were precisely the same as those used to-day. It was said that neutrals, and above all the United States of America, would never stand the full exercise of belligerent rights. The answer given at the time by the present Secretary to the Committee of Imperial Defence was as follows:

It is extraordinary how much neutrals will endure, and instances could be multiplied to show how the Powers have allowed even their legitimate interests to be trampled on rather than go to war.

We overlooked that, if our general cause was just, neutrals would stand a great deal. We overlooked our own prestige and tradition, to which Admiral von Tirpitz ascribes the fact that we were not interfered with more than we were by neutrals. We overlooked that we might find in the action of our enemies the excuse for our own methods. When war came, America could at any moment have compelled us to give up the exercise of belligerent rights by escorting her vessels through a neutral zone, or even more easily by putting an embargo on the export of war material. The fact that she did not do so under the greatest provocation shows how false the argument was.

Another argument was that, owing to modern developments of communication and international trade, we could not, in future wars, bring full economic pressure to bear on an enemy. We were never allowed to test that out, because by the time the Committee of Imperial Defence was studying the question of putting economic pressure on Germany the Government was deeply committed to the Declaration of London. The experience of the War shows how false the argument was. Meanwhile our preparations for war were being based on false premises. The Declaration of London was their foundation, and the Declaration was based on assumptions as to naval warfare which were obsolescent at the time of the London Conference and completely obsolete when the War broke out.

When the War came we discovered at once how great a handicap the Declaration of London was. Although unratified, the Government were deeply committed to it, and it was not easy to shelve. Its retention naturally became, to use von Tirpitz's phrase, 'the Alpha and Omega of the (German) Foreign Office,' and their diplomacy with neutrals was directed to securing its retention. We were fortunately able gradually to get rid of the Declaration on the plea of retaliation to the enemy's breaches of the laws of war. In spite of the fact that we had not ratified the Declaration, every German writer accuses us of bad faith in advocating it before the War and throwing it over after. They have the justification that we took the first step in the competition by our Proclamation of the 20th August, 1914. But it took us nearly two years finally to rid ourselves of the Declaration of London and to bring the full pressure of sea-power to bear. It could hardly be contested that we should have been in a stronger position if we had never taken the first step on the slippery slope to which allusion has already been made and had insisted that our action in a future war was too difficult for us or for anybody else to foresee and that we must have our hands free.

The War showed how enormous was the importance of sea power and the full exercise of belligerent rights. They were one of the decisive factors of the War, as all the writings of our late enemy testify. It is sometimes said, as, indeed, it was said before the War, that there is no prospect of these circumstances ever arising again. French opinion, at any rate, seems to hold the contrary. They believe in Germany's war of revenge. The Locarno policy may avert this, but does not the ultimate sanction of the Locarno policy, in the event of a German aggression, visualise a reproduction, so far as the position of Germany is concerned, of the war situation? Great Britain, France, Belgium, Italy, with possibly Poland and Czechoslovakia, hemming Germany in! If we deplete our armoury by weakening the factor of economic pressure, do we not at once deprive the sanction of part of its value? These eventualities, it is true, may never arise, or they may be postponed for an interval comparable to that which elapsed between the Napoleonic Wars and the Great War. This, it is submitted, is no argument for hampering the exercise of sea power. The Declaration of Paris, 1856, which collapsed with the Declaration of London, was no less baneful because of its antiquity. Wars in which sea power is a decisive factor are few and far between, but when they come the nation's existence may be at stake. For this very reason, because we cannot see what changes the future will bring, the longest views and the utmost caution are necessary.

In conclusion, it may be useful to quote what Lord Grey, after discussing the Declaration of London, says:

> One lesson from the experience of the War is that we should not bind ourselves to observe any rules of war, unless those who sign them with us undertake to uphold them by force if need be against an enemy who breaks them.
>
> (*Twenty-five Years, Vol. II Chapter XXII, p. 102.*)

II.   Memorandum by Sir C[ecil] Hurst on Sir Maurice Hankey's Paper on 'Blockade and the Laws of War'

Foreign Office
November 10, 1927

The thesis maintained by Sir Maurice Hankey in his paper is that no agreement should be negotiated with the United States on the subject of belligerent rights at sea, because an agreement would hamper this country in applying economic pressure against the enemy, and if the struggle in which Great Britain was engaged was one of vital importance to her, it would be essential to apply such pressure.

2.   It is no doubt true that throughout the greater part of the XIXth century a belief was widely spread among the public at large that war was a struggle between the contending armed forces and not between the nations concerned. Consequently, there was a movement in favour of excluding so far as possible civilian non-combatants from the effects of the war. The idea dates back to the time of Rousseau. There is, I

think, no chance of any similar delusion prevailing in the future. At present all modern States are disposed – some even outwardly – to organise themselves for defence upon the basis that the whole nation is to share in the burden. This point is one which is not without importance, as it affects the vulnerability of this country in time of war owing to the extent to which Great Britain depends upon imported seaborne foodstuffs.

3. Sir Maurice Hankey traces the history of the Declaration of London in a way which suggests that the movement in favour of the Declaration emanated from those who thought principally of the protection of Great Britain's neutral trade when other States were engaged in war, and, secondarily, of protecting Great Britain's seaborne commerce, particularly her imports, from the ravages of her enemy when she herself was engaged in war. This is not correct.

4. The movement which culminated in the Declaration of London originated with the first Secretary of the Imperial Defence Committee (Sir George Sydenham Clarke, now Lord Sydenham). The experiences of the South African War, and perhaps the early experiences of the Russo-Japanese War, had convinced him that the power to seize contraband had ceased to be of prime importance to Great Britain and that the risk of antagonising neutrals by belligerent seizures effected by British naval forces, coupled with the power which it gave to an enemy to interfere with the commerce of this country in time of war, and also with the injury done to the commerce of this country when a neutral by seizures by foreign belligerents, outweighed the advantages which the right to seize contraband and thereby impose economic pressure upon the enemy conferred upon this country in time of war. In a CID paper, Secret 41-B, of December 1904, reprinted with additions in April 1906, there is a memorandum by the then Secretary of the Defence Committee on the question of 'The value to Great Britain as a belligerent of the right of search and capture of neutral vessels', in which he examines the problem at length and, after a reasoned argument of six pages of print, arrives at the conclusion in paragraph 40 that an international arrangement under which neutral bottoms covered contraband would be to our advantage. There is in the same paper an Admiralty letter, dated the 10th June, 1905, expressing doubt upon the problem, and indicating that they were not yet convinced. The value of this letter is that it shows that the proposal raised by the Secretary of the Defence Committee must at least have been considered by the Admiralty.

5. The policy then indicated must have been accepted by His Majesty's Government. It was examined at length by an interdepartmental committee appointed for the purpose of framing the instructions to the

British delegates to the Second Peace Conference at The Hague in 1907, and the recommendations of that body were in favour of international agreement for the purpose of allowing a neutral's trade to be subject to no other restraint than the exercise of the right of visit and of effective blockade (see Report, dated the 21st March, 1907, of the 'Interdepartmental committee appointed to consider the subjects which may arise for discussion at the Second Peace Conference', p. 2, paragraph 8 (b)). The members of this committee included Sir Charles Ottley, who was at the time Director of Naval Intelligence at the Admiralty. It was in pursuance of the policy originated in the Defence committee paper referred to above and renewed in the report of the interdepartmental committee of 1907 that the British delegates were sent to The Hague in 1907 to propose the total abolition of the right to seize contraband of war, leaving sea power to be exercised solely by means of blockade in the old-fashioned sense of the term, *i.e.*, the blockade of an enemy coast-line. Great Britain being thus committed to the principle of restricting the exercise of sea power in time of war was naturally also in favour of curbing the pretensions of belligerent prize courts by the creation of an international prize court, which should be entitled to review the decisions of national prize courts and award compensation to those whose rights had been ignored by such national prize courts. It was for the purpose of providing this international prize court with a code of rules which it was to apply that the Naval Conference was summoned to meet in London in 1908–9 and framed the Declaration of London. Primarily, it is no doubt true that the Declaration of London was intended only as a code to be applied by the international prize court, but the whole situation was controlled by the belief that Great Britain stood to gain by the total abolition, or, if that were impossible, the restriction, of the right to seize contraband of war.

6.   The policy pursued in 1907 may have been right or may have been wrong. The events of the war of 1914–18 certainly suggest that the policy was wrong; but the circumstances of the war of 1914–18 were very peculiar in that at the time when the application of economic pressure to the enemy was at its highest every Power of any importance was a belligerent. From the moment that the United States came in, there was no neutral State of sufficient weight to oppose the Allied operations at sea or to oppose the Allied measures for the purpose of securing control of enemy imports intended to reach the enemy country through neutral territory. No man, before the war, could have foreseen the situation as it emerged during the war, and it would be a bold man who would prophesy that similar circumstances will arise in any future war.

7. Sir Maurice Hankey's paper seems to me to underestimate one difficulty with which British naval operations against neutral commerce must always contend in time of war, that is, that the legality of the operations will always be controlled by the prize courts, and that any action which the prize courts are pleased to determine to be inconsistent with international law will be invalidated and the Government, in the form of the captors, will be ordered to pay costs and damages. One has only to remember a case like the *Zamora* in 1916 (where the Privy Council held to be invalid a measure which His Majesty's Government had taken for the purpose of requisitioning neutral property and thereby increasing the economic pressure on the enemy) to see that such restrictions as the naval authorities suffered from during the late war were not all due to international engagements, whether ratified or unratified, by which His Majesty's Government had bound themselves in time of peace. People are apt to forget to-day the extent to which all through the late war the enemy played into our hands by the successive blunders which he committed at sea, thereby enabling His Majesty's Government to introduce all manner of novel measures under the guise of retaliation which no British prize court would have tolerated if the enemy had not made these mistakes. It is true that in time the United States came in on the Allied side, but there, again, we have to thank our enemy for the blunders which brought in the United States against them. British measures at sea for the purpose of harrying American commerce were certainly not the element which made the United States join in the struggle against Germany.

8. I do not for a moment contest the view that it was by means of the Blockade that the war was won, but Sir Maurice Hankey's paper does not seem to me to state fully the case *against* the proposal to sound the United States as to the possibility of an agreement on the subject of belligerent rights at sea. The arguments which he marshals against the Declaration of London are not in my opinion the points of primary importance at the present stage, and the case against attempting to negotiate an arrangement with the United States as proposed in the Craigie memorandum should rest, I think, on other grounds.

9. For one Power to exercise effective economic pressure upon its opponent by means of sea power two conditions must be fulfilled: (a) the Power exercising the pressure must have the superiority at sea, and (b) the measures which it takes must be measures which are within the admitted principles of international law, or such as for exceptional reasons the prize court will uphold. These two conditions do not operate on a footing of equality: the first is the more essential. Unless the Power which is anxious to effect economic pressure on the enemy has

the superiority at sea, it is the enemy which will exert the economic pressure and not the first Power. If Great Britain were engaged in a naval war with a Power which was superior at sea, it is Great Britain which, by reason of her vulnerability on account of her necessary importations of foodstuffs, would feel most economic pressure which sea power can effect, and the more that the whole nation participates in the struggle and not merely the armed forces, the more precarious becomes the position of foodstuffs which theoretically are intended only for the civilian non-combatant population. Furthermore, without that superiority at sea, the neutrals would not tolerate the interference with their commerce which the exercise of sea power entails.

10.   The proposed agreement with the United States would only affect the second of the conditions postulated above. It is useless to make such an agreement unless it is certain that Great Britain will in the future maintain that superiority at sea which she has exercised in the past. Without that superiority sea power can and will be exercised to Great Britain's economic disadvantage.

11.   To what extent does superiority at sea depend on the mere multiplication of ships? I suppose it must now be admitted that, if the United States chose to do so, they could outstrip Great Britain in any shipbuilding race in which they chose to engage. Does the problem of manning the ships built, and does the problem of sailing and fighting the ships when built and manned, so weigh down the scales against the United States and in favour of Great Britain that Great Britain could afford to ignore numerical superiority on the part of the United States and feel that she could maintain her superiority at sea despite American preponderance of ships and guns? These are questions which no layman can answer, but they seem to be to be questions upon which His Majesty's Government must be clear in their own minds before any decision is given on the question of whether an agreement as to belligerent rights at sea would be to our advantage.

12.   If the question indicated in paragraph 11 is answered in the affirmative, there must be taken into consideration another question. The type of agreement contemplated in the Craigie memorandum is based wholly on the experience of the past, that is to say, it is proposed to come to an agreement as to the extent to which the belligerent practices of the late war are to be acknowledged to be in accordance with the accepted principles of international law. The problem of past wars in connection with economic pressure at sea was in reality that of the rights of neutrals. To what extent will neutrality prevail in future wars in the way that it has done in the past? To what extent will nations be entitled to appeal to the rights of neutrals? As a contrivance for the

maintenance of peace the League of Nations is an attempt to organise
general concerted action against a State which goes to war in breach of
its undertakings. If the League were universal, there would be no neutrals.
That was the hope of its founders, and the intention with which article
16 of the Covenant was drafted. The greater the extent to which the
League becomes general, the greater the number of States which will
have debarred themselves and their nationals from any attempt to trade
with the State against which the concerted action is being taken.

13.   The League has not become universal because the United States
has not, and so far as one can see at present, is not likely to, become a
Member, but from the point of view of naval warfare the United States
is the only State now standing outside of the League which is of real
importance. Spain and Brazil are likely to come back in time; Turkey,
Russia and Mexico are not of first-class importance so far as concerns
seaborne commerce. The problem comes back, as before, to that of the
United States. At present the League is only seven years old; on the
whole it is tending to become stronger rather than weaker, and there is
no reason for assuming that within the Membership of the League the
covenants of the League will not be enforced. Assume a war, therefore,
in which there is an enemy State against which Great Britain, in col-
laboration with the rest of the League, is endeavouring to exercise
economic pressure, and the United States is standing out and maintaining all the rights of a neutral Power. What is the position?

14.   Every State except (a) the one against which concerted action is
being taken, and (b) the United States, will be co-operating to sever all
trade and financial relations between the Covenant-breaking State and
the outside world. Consequently, it will be bound to prevent the use of
its territory for transit purposes for foreign trade with the Covenant-
breaking State. No doubt can arise as to the right of a State to control
the use of its territory for this purpose. There can be no doubt as to the
right in international law of a State to control exports from its own
territory, and to impose such conditions as it may choose upon exports
from its own territory. There can equally be no doubt as to the right of a
State to control imports into and transit through its own territory, and to
impose such conditions upon import and transit as it chooses. The only
neutral American trade, therefore, with the Covenant-breaking State
which, if stopped or controlled by Great Britain, can give rise to dispute
is American seaborne trade transported directly to or from the enemy
ports.

15.   The extensions of belligerent practice which Great Britain was
forced to introduce during the late war, and as to the legality of which
disputes arose, were wholly concerned with neutral trade on its way to

or from the enemy territory *via* the territory of other neutral States. If one can assume that the League will gradually become stronger and that its Members will fulfil the obligations of the Covenant and stop all transit trade with the enemy across their territory, the difficulty which arose during the late war will not arise in the next war in the same form, if it arises at all, as it arose in the war of 1914–18. The right of a belligerent to control neutral trade on its way to or from the enemy country when in the course of direct transportation to or from enemy ports, is a matter upon which the rules of international law are sufficiently well settled, and are adequate. It is a branch of the law in which it is unlikely that our own prize courts would tolerate unreasonable innovations. It therefore follows that if we can count on the development of the power of the League in the interval before the next Armageddon is likely to break out, this proposed agreement with the United States will be unnecessary. The existing rules of international law give us all we want.

16.   If the proposed agreement with the United States is unnecessary, it is obvious that it is undesirable to try and negotiate it, because the attempt to negotiate it would inevitable involve great risk. The effect on the mind of the American people would probably be to make them think that Great Britain was ready to negotiate because she was afraid of the United States and felt that she could not compete. The Big Navy party in America would exploit the situation accordingly. If the attempt to negotiate an agreement failed, the situation would be worse than before.

17.   To my mind, therefore, the situation comes to this:

(1.)   Firstly, leaving out of account the anticipated strengthening of the League, an agreement with the United States is undesirable at the present time, because (a) if we maintain our naval superiority as against the United States in the future, an agreement would tie our hands and prevent the exercise of economic pressure by the use of sea power, *i.e.*, Sir Maurice Hankey's thesis would hold good; (b) if we cannot maintain our naval superiority as against the United States, an agreement of the type proposed would prevent the influence of Great Britain being used to swing the belligerent practice in the direction of what the United States have hitherto meant by the phrase 'the freedom of the seas.' If we lost our superiority at sea, it would be to our advantage to safeguard our own imports by curtailing belligerent rights as much as possible.

(2.)   Secondly, if the League of Nations develops in strength, as one may at present anticipate that it will do, the problem arising from British action under article 16 of the Covenant for the purpose of severing intercourse between the outside world and the Covenant-breaking State, reduces itself to interference with American sea-borne commerce in the course of direct transportation to or from the enemy State. As regards the rights of a belligerent to interfere with this form of neutral sea-borne commerce, the rules of international law are adequate and well established and require no agreement to supplement them.

18.   I leave out of account one possible eventuality, namely, that the League will continue to grow in strength, and that in the next war it is Great Britain which will be the Covenant-breaking State with the whole world arrayed against her. In such a war Great Britain would never carry the Dominions with her, and it is an eventuality which need not be considered.

C.J.B. Hurst

Some Observations by Sir Robert Leslie Craigie, head of the American Department in the Foreign Office, on Sir C. Hurst's Memorandum of November 10 (C.P. 286 (27)) on the suggestion for an Agreement with the United States in regard to the exercise of Belligerent Rights at Sea
(Circulated by Direction of the Secretary of State for Foreign Affairs.)

[SECRET C.P. 287 (27)]   Foreign Office
                                                                                        16 November 1927

Leaving on one side the more purely legal aspects of the case, there are in this memorandum certain points of a political or semi-political character with which, I think, it is difficult for this Department fully to agree. After discussing the matter with Mr Vansittart, I venture to put forward the following considerations, which might perhaps be discussed verbally with Sir Cecil Hurst:

1.   Sir Cecil Hurst's memorandum is in the main based on the assumption that, in order to secure an agreement with the United States on this subject, we must necessarily be called upon to abandon some important right which we have hitherto exercised. Sir Maurice Hankey also looks upon the conclusion of such an agreement as merely a repetition of the errors committed in signing the Declaration of London. But can either assumption be taken for granted at this time?

Taking the Declaration of London first, it is only necessary to mention that one of the most powerful criticisms directed against the Declaration by opponents in this country was that it abandoned the application to conditional contraband of the doctrine of continuous voyage. This abandonment was, however, at the time more distasteful to the United States Government than to His Majesty's Government, and I see no reason to think that the United States views on this point have changed. This and other criticised points in the Declaration represented concessions to the 'continental' Powers – departures from our hitherto accepted doctrine which need not, and indeed should not, be repeated in any Anglo-American Convention.

In my memorandum of the 17th October (Appendix III in C.P. 258/27) I endeavoured to show that, on the basis of our experience during the war, it would be wrong to assume that no agreement with the United States was possible unless it departed from the principles of law which have hitherto been observed by either country when a belligerent and which have received the sanction of the British and American Prize Courts. Since then an examination of the United States Naval Prize Code of 1900 (as modified in 1903) has reinforced the above conclusion. Only in the matter of the immunity of convoys from search and immunity of coast fishing vessels from capture does there appear to be any fundamental divergence in so far as the rules of contraband blockade and the capture of enemy vessels are concerned. Writing in the *Times* of the 10th April, 1901, Professor Holland, referring to the Naval War Code, stated that 'on most debatable points the rules are in accordance with the views of this country.' This naval code was, on the eve of the London Naval Conference of 1908–09, submitted to His Majesty's Government by the United States Government as representing their view on these questions at that time. In communicating this document, the State Department quoted a passage from the instructions sent to the United States delegate at the second Peace Conference, from which I extract the following:

> The Order putting this code into force was revoked by the Navy Department in 1904, not because of any change of views as to the rules which it contained, but because many of those rules, being imposed upon the forces of the United States by the Order, would have put our naval forces at a disadvantage as against the forces of other Powers, upon whom the rules were not binding.

The State Department's note to our Embassy added that the attitude of the United States had not changed since the second Hague Peace Conference and that the relevant portions of the above instructions [including the code] were as applicable to the London Naval Conference as they were to the Hague Conference. There is nothing to show that the United States Government have since gone back on the views expressed in 1908. Indeed, their relative naval strength having enormously increased since that date, it is reasonable to suppose that the old American thesis of 'freedom of the seas' is also sinking into the background; an America drawing rapidly up to an equality of naval strength with this country is on the whole unlikely in the future to show much enthusiasm for securing the immunity from capture of private enemy ships. If this proves to be the case, I cannot see what important belligerent right we are likely to be asked by the Americans to abandon.

As stated in the earlier memorandum, the principal difficulties to be anticipated relate to the diversion of ships to a home port for visit and search, the substitution of a 'long-distance' blockade for the earlier type of close blockade and the censorship of mails, as exercised during the war. These are all extensions of our earlier practice necessitated by the changing conditions under which both modern trade and modern warfare are carried on. If we play our cards carefully, we may well succeed in bringing the United States along with us as a partner in a logical adaptation to present-day necessities of old-fashioned rules no longer capable of giving full effect to the principles on which they were based. But such a result would only be possible at a time when both countries are at peace; not when we are already engaged in a life and death struggle.

2. The example of a full League war quoted by Sir Cecil Hurst in paragraphs 14 and 15 of his memorandum is certainly one in which an agreement with the United States would prove less useful than in the case of other types of war. Even in this case, however, it is difficult to agree that such an understanding would be entirely useless from a political point of view. United States dislike of the League and all its works is a factor with which we – who will have to apply the naval pressure in a League war – must count.

But can we afford to neglect the possibility of our being engaged in a war in which the League takes no part?

Under the Covenant as it stands there are several possible ways in which a war could be waged without the League States taking an active part. Thus Article 15 of the Covenant, dealing with disputes between members of the League contains the following paragraphs:

> If the Council fails to reach a report which is unanimously agreed to by the members thereof, other than the Representatives of one or more of the parties to the dispute, the Members of the League reserve to themselves the right to take such action as they shall consider necessary for the maintenance of right and justice.
>
> If the dispute between the parties is claimed by one of them, and is found by the Council, to arise out of a matter which by interna-

tional law is solely within the domestic jurisdiction of that party, the Council shall so report, and shall make no recommendation as to its settlement.

Again, Article 17, dealing with disputes between a member of the League and a State which is not a member of the League, contains the following paragraph:

If both parties to the dispute when so invited refuse to accept the obligations of membership in the League for the purposes of such dispute, the Council may take such measures and make such recommendations as will prevent hostilities and will result in the settlement of the dispute.

In none of the cases mentioned in the above paragraph does Article 16 (which imposes what for want of a better term one may call a 'League War') come automatically into operation, and it seems more than probable that in such cases the war may be confined to the parties immediately interested in the dispute. Apart from the above it seems necessary to reckon with the possibly remote contingency that, when League opinion in regard to any particular dispute is fairly evenly divided, the machinery for League intervention may break down at an early stage, thus paralysing any corporal action by the League of Nations.

Types of war other than that cited by Sir C. Hurst seem therefore to merit consideration before we can conclude that an Anglo-American agreement is unnecessary.

3.   In paragraph 16 of his memorandum Sir C. Hurst states:

The effect on the mind of the American people would probably be to make them think that Great Britain was ready to negotiate because she was afraid of the United States and felt that she could not compete. The big navy party in America would exploit the situation accordingly.

I do not believe that this would be the predominating effect on the mind of the American people, but, even if it were, this circumstance would hardly assist the big navy party in America as suggested. The success of that party's propaganda depends not on a realisation that Great Britain may be afraid of the United States, but on the opposite consideration, namely, that the United States have something to fear from the British navy. There is ample evidence to show that it is precisely this danger of a dispute with the British Empire in regard to the treatment of private property at sea which is being used by the big navy party to exert pressure on the Administration and Congress to increase the United States navy to 'parity' of strength with the British navy.

4.   At the end of paragraph 16 Sir C. Hurst states: 'If the attempt to negotiate an agreement failed, the situation would be worse than before.' This, of course, is true of almost any attempt to negotiate an agreement on any controversial subject, but the danger might be reduced to a minimum if the cautious method of approach which has been proposed were to be adopted and no formal British proposals were to be put forward until we were certain that the United States Government were ready to talk – and to talk reasonably.

5.   Paragraph 17 (1) (b) of the memorandum states:

> If we cannot maintain our naval superiority as against the United States, an agreement of the type proposed would prevent the influence of Great Britain being used to swing the belligerent practice in the direction of what the United States have hitherto meant by the phrase 'the freedom of the seas.'

With the conditions in which naval warfare and commercial enterprise are conducted constantly shifting, it would be reasonable to suggest to the United States Government that any agreement come to should be subject to denunciation or revision every five years. If at the present moment the Committee of Imperial Defence should recommend that our claims in the matter of contraband and blockade should be put at the maximum, it seems unlikely that before the expiration of five years the position could have so changed as to necessitate His Majesty's Government urging a revision of the rules of war in the direction of 'the freedom of the seas.' In other words, if the experts are content now with the rules and practices which emerged from the Great War, it seems hardly likely that they would have completely reversed themselves by the year 1932 or thereabouts.

The above points are submitted with all due deference in case they may be considered worthy of further consideration or discussion.

R.L. CRAIGIE

* * *

47. Sir Arthur Stamfordham, Private Secretary to King George V, to Lieutenant-Colonel Sir Maurice Hankey

SECRET

[CAB 21/310]   Buckingham Palace
                                                17 December, 1927

My Dear Hankey, The result of our recent conversation is: that the King spoke as strongly as you could have wished to A.C. [Austen Chamberlain] on Thursday last, but of course without reference to you, and elicited that at all events nothing would be done in a hurry. His Majesty will talk to you after the Council on Tuesday.

Meanwhile, although probably you know all about it, I send two extracts from Henry Wilson's Diary. If I were Prime Minister I should be inclined to have no more discussions and merely tell America that she may do what she likes and we also will go our own way. I see they have announced a comprehensive 5 years' programme, but it may be partly bounce.

* * *

48. Sir Maurice Hankey to Admiral of the Fleet, Sir Charles Madden, First Sea Lord

PERSONAL

[CAB 21/310. Original in ADM 116/3619]   22 December 1927

Dear C[hief of]. N[aval]. S[taff]Many thanks for your personal letter of to-day's date. I have not been able to establish definitely whether the articles in question were produced under official inspiration or not. I have however now established on absolutely reliable information, that the press section of the Department in question is now exercising great discretion in this matter. They have been bombarded by the press on the subject, and have contented themselves with talking vaguely about the Declaration of Paris and the Declaration of London, which can do no harm.

It will interest you to know that this morning I received an instruction from the Prime Minister, at the suggestion of the Secretary of State for Foreign Affairs, to send copies of all the papers on the belligerent rights question personally to Admiral Richmond at the Imperial Defence College. Richmond is a very old friend of mine (we were ship-mates in 1898 and have been pals ever since) and he is as sound as a bell on the question.

* * *

49. Belligerent Rights at Sea – American and British Practices Compared[1]

Committee of Imperial Defence Sub-Committee on Belligerent Rights [Memorandum]

[CAB 21/317; CAB 16/79, part 141;192–9]   Admiralty, S.W.1
                                                      14 January 1928

5.   We claim the following belligerent rights, by the use of which the great war was won:

	United States Views
(a.) *The right of visit and search*	Agree.
(b.) *The right of detention: i.e.,* if for any sufficient reason it is not practicable to visit or to conduct a satisfactory search, vessels may be detained and sent into port in order that further investigation may be made. It is contemplated that vessels would only be deflected to convenient ports.	Disagree.
(c.) *The right of seizure in prize.*	Agree.
(d.) The right to blockade, with the object of striking at the enemy's commerce and weakening his resources; the blockading ships may be at some distance from the blockaded port or coast.	Agree, but this subject requires further consideration as given in Appendix I.
(e.) The right to prevent a neutral from carrying to an enemy articles calculated to aid him in the conduct of war, *i.e., Law of Contraband.*	Agree. But the United States would probably wish the lists of contraband to be

---

[1]Forwarded under cover of a note by the First Lord of the Admiralty, W.C. Bridgeman, 17 January 1928.

The contraband list may vary with the particular war and be flexible.	strictly limited.
(f.) The right to prevent unneutral service.	Agree.
(g.) The application of the doctrine of 'continuous voyage' or 'transportation' both to (i)contraband and (ii) blockade.	Agree as to (g) (i), not as to (g) (ii).
(h.) *The right to rely on other evidence than is available in the ship's papers, by interrogatories of the personnel, and actual search on the spot of the ship*	Disagree.
(i.) The right to examine ships under convoy of neutral warships.	Now disagree.
(j.) The right to censor mails in merchant ships and to seize seditious literature.	Disagree generally. Have probably not considered seditious literature.
(k.) The right to arm defensively British merchant ships.	Agree generally.
(l.) The right to retaliate against a belligerent who breaks international law, treaty obligations or the customary usages of naval warfare.	Disagree, in all probability, on principle in large sense in which Great Britain has applied Retaliation.

The Declaration of Paris and The Hague Conventions to which we are a party will bind us when belligerent, if the other belligerents are also parties. The Declaration of London will, of course, not be binding. Customary usages in naval warfare, *e.g.*, the securing of the safety of the lives of neutrals and non-combatants, will be observed. . . .

* * *

11.   The Dominions are vitally interested in everything that affects the British Navy and anything that limits its effectiveness. Their position is as stated by Sir Littleton Groom (Australia) at the British Empire Delegation Meeting at Geneva in September 1924, when he said, 'It was impossible for the British Government to make any decision concerning the fleet without involving the whole Empire.' Great Britain, moreover, cannot make an agreement with any Power affecting belligerent rights from which the Dominions could stand out, for it is

unthinkable that one part of the Empire should carry out warfare according to one set of rules and another part according to a different set of rules. The Empire as a whole must apply British Prize Law. The New Zealand Division of the Royal Navy will automatically operate with the Royal Navy in the event of war, and it is to be anticipated that Australia will place all or some of her ships at the disposal of the Admiralty in war.

The interest of the Dominions in belligerent rights at sea was shown at the Imperial Conference in 1911, when the Commonwealth of Australia tabled a resolution which stated that 'It is regretted that the Dominions were not consulted prior to the acceptance by the British Delegation of the terms of the Declaration of London.' The absolute need of consulting the Dominions has been strengthened by the Resolutions of the Imperial Conference of 1923 regarding the procedure to be observed in the negotiation, signature and ratification of International agreements and in their defence resolutions, reaffirmed in 1926, which laid down, as a guiding principle, the desirability of the maintenance of a minimum standing of naval strength, namely, equality with the naval strength of any foreign Power.

Since a possibility exists that there may be a divergence of opinion between the Dominions on the advantages or disadvantages of coming to some agreement with the USA, which might involve a limitation of the belligerent rights of the Royal Navy, the idea of an agreement needs, if only for this reason, the most careful consideration, as it would be a misfortune to occasion a cleavage of opinion between the various parts of the British Empire.

12.   The Admiralty do not believe that there is at present any likelihood of the American Government and Senate agreeing to detention, rationing, seizure and censorship of mails, retaliation, or that any agreement would be possible about contraband or blockade, or the use of evidence not found on board the intercepted ship. The Admiralty believe that the USA Government and Senate (if approached) will press the 'Neutral' view and that there is no firm basis for an agreement. Discussions will mean that we get on to a slippery slope and that to secure American concurrence in one right we have to sacrifice something considerable. The possibilities of agreement are hypothetical in the extreme and the dangers of starting negotiations considerable; they are a leap in the dark; an unsatisfactory result is the probable outcome. . . .

* * *

APPENDIX I, BLOCKADE

1. Several formal blockades were declared during the Great War in various parts of the world, e.g., East Coast of Africa, Asia Minor, Greece, Salonika and Tsingtao, and it is impossible to give up the formal type of blockade as understood at the time of the Declaration of Paris and as applied by the USA in the Civil War.

2. The view of Great Britain and, it is understood, of the USA in the past has been that the area of operations of the blockading forces does not need to be limited to the close neighbourhood of the blockaded port or coast, and that the true criterion of the legality of a blockade is not the place where the blockading ships are situated, but the capability of the forces wherever stationed to maintain the blockade. Even in Nelson's time his blockade of Toulon when he stationed his ships 100 miles off the port was recognised as valid. Distances such as 100 miles and 800 miles were suggested in conversations at the Hague Conference in 1907, and in connection with the Declaration of London the United States representatives suggested 1,000 miles as the maximum. *Prima facie*, there is thus a considerable measure of agreement between the USA and this country that a long distance blockade may be carried out, and during the war the United States Secretary of State, on the 30th March, 1915, stated that 'the Government of the United States might be ready to admit that the old form of close blockade with its cordon of ships in the immediate offing of the blockading ports is no longer practicable' (copy of telegram attached as Annex 1). It will be seen, in so far as this telegram is of value, that America would allow the blockading squadrons to be practically placed at any distance, but the squadron would let through all outward traffic from a neutral country and all inward traffic to a neutral, except contraband; the blockading squadron would apparently have full rights against vessels going direct to and from the enemy blockaded coast and have only the right of interception of contraband in the case of vessels going to neutral contiguous territory. This proposition does not allow the idea of 'continuous voyage' or 'transportation' in connection with long distance blockade; the United States of America also probably intended, and, in the opinion of the Admiralty, would now demand, that visit and search should be carried out on the spot in the case of vessels going to neutral contiguous territory.

3. In the opinion of the Admiralty, both the doctrines of 'continuous voyage' (vessel) and of 'continuous transportation' (goods on board) should be applied to blockade in cases where it has been considered essential to adopt a long distance blockade, where the blockading ships lie across the lines of approach to neutral as well as enemy territory. The

British Courts in Lord Stowell's time held that 'continuous sea voyage' but not 'continuous transportation' (including both land and sea) to – or from – a port under blockade would be the ground of condemnation and confiscation. If a long distance blockade was formally declared in the future it is presumably a matter of some doubt whether the Prize Courts would now accept either the doctrine of 'continuous sea voyage' or 'continuous transportation.' It is anticipated that they would probably adopt the doctrine of 'continuous voyage' and possibly the doctrine of 'continuous transportation.' In this connection there are portions in the judgment of Sir Samuel Evans in the case of 'The Leonora' which are attached in Annex 2 for convenience of reference. It seems wrong to make the character of the voyage rather than the destination of the goods the test. Whilst this blockade might be conducted by ships mainly operating at a distance, it may be, in fact, anticipated that belligerents may employ a number of submarines near the blockaded coast to add to the effectiveness of the blockade by turning back vessels that have passed the outlying ships. Such a blockade does not deny access to neutral ports, except in so far as the goods are for the purposes of the enemy.

5.[*sic*] A blockade is very necessary to prevent the enemy sending exports from the country and thus increasing the enemy's financial resources. It cuts off all commerce, whereas, under the Law of Contraband, no outward commerce in neutral ships can be intercepted.

6. As regards the USA, it is felt that either the Executive or the Senate (or both) would resolutely oppose the doctrine of 'continuous voyage' or 'transportation' in reference to Blockade. American protests during the war are considered to represent American views rather than one or two of their Prize Court decisions during the Civil War. It is also gravely doubted whether, if now approached, the USA authorities would not endeavour to restrict the distance at which blockading ships may be stationed.

7. As regards Article 16 of the Covenant and the application of the words therein – 'Prevention of all financial, commercial or personal intercourse between the nationals and the Covenant-breaking State and the nationals of any other State, whether a Member of the League or not' – the view of the Admiralty has been stated in Admiralty letter M. 02587 of the 24th September, 1927 (Annex 3). This coincides with the view of the Legal Sub-Committee, namely, that the first paragraph of Article 16 appears to contemplate measures taken within the jurisdiction of individual States. If the policy contained in the above-quoted Admiralty letter is carried out, there should be less occasion for possible friction with the USA.

* * *

Annex 3 – Copy of a Letter from the Admiralty to the Foreign Office
(CONFIDENTIAL AND IMMEDIATE)

[M.02587]   September 24, 1927

6.   In connection with the question of blockades [and Britain's obligations under the Covenant of the League of Nations], I am to invite
attention to the USA attitude regarding blockade questions (see, for
example, Sir Esme Howard's despatches numbered 1512 of the 3rd
August, 1927, and 1549 of the 12th August, 1927). It is quite important
that there should be no commitment to carry out a blockade, in order
that the issues commonly known in U.S.A. as the 'freedom of the seas,'
should not be unnecessarily raised with that country, and any tendencies at Geneva to regard a maritime blockade, whether pacific or
otherwise, as one of the measures to be taken under Article 16 or
Article 11 of the Covenant should be resisted. In particular, as regards
paragraph 1 of Article 16, it should be maintained that the measures of
economic pressure indicated therein do not include any naval measures
at sea, whether of the nature of a pacific blockade or otherwise. This
view can well be supported by the contention that the aim of the
Covenant is not to involve countries in war, and this country, if it
carried out a pacific blockade, would be involved in disputes possibly
in war, with USA and nations not adhering to the Covenant. The probability of trouble with America is too real to be risked.

My Lords request that the British Representatives at Geneva be
informed of these views, and that the present opportunity at Geneva be
taken for stating definitely the above understandings as to the existing
situation under the Covenant, at the same time resisting M. Paul
Boncour's suggested resolution and any formula to imply any military
obligation. There is every reason to think that these views are in accordance with the views of the Dominions and of various members of
the League.

(Signed) Charles Walker

* * *

50.   Belligerent Rights at Sea

Memorandum by Sir A. Steel-Maitland circulated to the Sub-Committee on Belligerent Rights by direction of the Secretary of State for Foreign Affairs, Committee of Imperial Defence

[CAB 16/79, part 19/362–5]   24 February 1928

1.   No consideration of the subject of belligerent rights at sea can be adequate unless it takes as its starting point the lessons of the recent war. Some of these have been discussed in the three memoranda which were circulated to the Cabinet recently. But no analysis is complete without an appreciation of the extent to which international law or the rules of war at sea have stood the test of actual hostilities on a great scale.

2.   One clear conclusion follows inevitably from a consideration of the facts of the late war. The observance by a belligerent of any restraint or limitation on practices which he thinks may prove to his advantage depends on force and force alone. In the last war, each belligerent was driven step by step by the pressure of circumstances, and was prepared to evade, on one pretext or another, any of the recognised or asserted rules of war at sea. It is true that there was no uniform and agreed code. A conflict of doctrine existed on some important points. On others there was much vagueness and lack of precision. Evasion was thus made easier. The truth of the main conclusion remains unaffected, however, that in a life and death struggle the only limitation to the practices adopted depended on the force or the apprehension of the force which might support the limitation.

3.   It is also evident that in the last war the only force which was effective in imposing any limit on belligerent rights at sea was that exercised by neutrals. And this will be true in the future. Neutrals may be composed of the body of individuals that constitute the League of Nations (other than the 'aggressor' or 'aggressors' if they are members of the League). In such circumstances, if the members of the League act up to their obligations, their influence will, in all probability, be overwhelming. The problem of practical importance, however, is that of a non-League war, *i.e.*, one in which the League does not declare one party to be the aggressor, or in which possibly it has itself ceased to function.

4.   The natural tendency of neutrals is to assert the 'freedom of the seas.' Protests of this nature were made by Great Britain during the Russo-Japanese war. Under what circumstances then can neutrals be

compelled to tolerate interference with their trade, and if they cannot be compelled, what influences, if any, will affect them? The first and foremost consideration is the reluctance of a neutral country to run the risk of being brought into a war in which she is likely to suffer, as contrasted with the enjoyment of a trade which is very profitable even if it be liable to interruption. This reluctance depends on the power of the neutral and also on her geographical position. It was possible for Portugal to go to war with Germany; it was impossible for Denmark. On the other hand, the power of the United States made her attitude vital. In the end, the predominance of sympathy in the United States of America with Great Britain and France won the day, but only after years of critical relations. During those years, the whole course of the war might have been changed vitally to our detriment at any moment by a decision on the part of the United States of America to enforce the rights which she claimed as a neutral by convoying her commerce with the Central Powers.

* * *

13. CONCLUSIONS

a.   A decision upon the desirability of wide or restricted belligerent rights depends on the best forecast that can be made of the conditions under which another 'non-League' war would be fought as regards blockade of an enemy and interception of our own supplies.

b.   The balance of probability is in favour of our adopting a policy of 'swinging towards freedom of the seas.'

c.   If so, it is desirable to make an early attempt at an agreement on these lines with the United States.

d.   Such an agreement should also aim at and perhaps also be made conditional on an international convention to abolish submarine and aircraft warfare on commercial vessels, and to restrict the construction of submarines.

e.   It will be open to consider whether preparatory conversations should be held on the subject of a new cruiser conference.

* * *

51.   *Sir Esme Howard to Sir Austen Chamberlain*

[CAB 16/79, part 23, no. 480/321–2]   29 February 1928
                                                                  (Received 12 March)

Sir,   I have the honour to refer to my telegram No. 77 of to-day's date, stating that the Naval Committee of the House of Representatives yesterday reported out the Bill for Naval Construction. This measure, as now advocated by the committee, provides for the construction of fifteen cruisers and one aircraft carrier before the 1st July, 1931, at an estimated cost, distributed over three years, of 274 million dollars. Thus the original proposal backed by the Navy Department, amounting to twenty-five cruisers and five airplane carriers at a cost of 740 million dollars, spread over five years, has been reduced as regards cruisers more, perhaps, in appearance than in actual fact, but, nevertheless, greatly reduced as far as airplane carriers are concerned. The total result is, of course, to produce a reduction of expenditure which will allay the alarm of the taxpayers. . . .

11.   The lack of any excitement in Great Britain over the original naval programme has undoubtedly immensely upset the Big Navyites, who had counted on British criticism to stir up the flagging interest of the Middle West into supporting the Bill. It would have probably made all the difference if they could have said that the British were trying to prevent the United States citizen from having the navy he was entitled to. . . .

* * *

52. Blockade – Memorandum by Vice-Admiral Sir Herbert Richmond, Commandant, Imperial Defence College[1]

Committee of Imperial Defence, Sub-Committee on Belligerent Rights Circulated to the Sub-Committee by direction of the First Sea Lord

SECRET, B.R. 30,   April 1928
[CAB 16/79/235–6; CAB 21/320]

It is being suggested we should severely limit or give up our old rights of preventing trade between neutrals and the enemy. What this amounts to, in practice, is that we are to restrict our means of bringing pressure upon an enemy to the action of land forces or of air forces. As a member of a coalition of nations, we are to be debarred from exercising upon the enemy that pressure which results from stopping his oversea commerce. The possession of sea power under these conditions is, therefore, strai[gh]tly restricted to enabling our army, or the armies of our allies, to cross the sea, and to prevent the enemy's armies from doing so. We, therefore, in a future great war, must be prepared to become a military power, to raise large armies and to fight on land, or, as some will have it, to fight by destroying the towns, with their historic buildings and treasures of irreplaceable value, and killing the citizens of both sexes and all ages. While this is in progress, the enemy is to be allowed the free use of the sea to refresh and maintain his national life. His industries are to continue to receive those raw materials they need, and he is free to export their products; and by thus keeping his commerce alive, he is to be enabled to maintain the financial means of continuing the war, and to avert those social upheavals which result – as they did in Russia and Germany, and came near to doing in Italy – in a crumbling of the powers of resistance.

Whether at the present day any importance is attached to the weight which this country carries in the councils of the world I do not know. But it is quite obvious that, as Sir Julian Corbett remarked in 1917, 'since the influence of Naval power in the world is measured by the extent to which it can exercise command of the sea, every restriction in this direction tends to diminish the influence of the Naval Powers. And as it diminished the influence of Naval Powers, so it gives fresh relative strength to the Military Powers.'

[1]A letter from Hankey to Chief of Naval Staff, 5.5.28, asks in Richmond's absence for permission to circulate his 'second' paper to the Belligerent Rights Committee, ADM 116/3619. Richmond's 'First' paper, dated 13 March 1928, is located at PRO CAB 16/ 79, ff. 217–19.

The most important wars are those in which some great principle is at stake – such as freedom from the domination of some power or principle of Government – and these have always been fought between great coalitions of Powers.

In all of these, the weapon which this country has primarily furnished to the common cause has been her Sea Power. The value of that power lay in the fact that it could not only maintain the financial strength of the coalition, but could weaken both the financial power and the resistance of the enemy. Under the proposal to rescind the right of capture, we are to look upon war purely as a struggle between armies. We shall still be under the necessity of providing a navy stronger than our enemies, since without it we cannot defend ourselves against invasion, whether or no our trade was secured by international agreement. But, in addition, we must also provide a great army; and that army cannot move to aid our Allies without definite superiority at sea. If, therefore, we are to give assistance and support to a great cause, we must become at once both a naval and a military power. . . .

* * *

53.   The Havana Convention

Note by Maurice Gwyer, Procurator-General[1]

[CAB 16/793/244; Secret, B.R. 33]   Storey's Gate, S.W.1
                                                            May 1, 1928

1.   This Convention is described as a 'Convention on Maritime Neutrality,' and accordingly emphasizes the rights and duties of neutrals rather than the rights of belligerents. It is divided into four sections: Section I deals with the Freedom of Commerce in Time of War; Section II with Duties and Rights of Belligerents; Section III with Rights and Duties of Neutrals; and Section IV with the Fulfilment and Observance of the Laws on Neutrality. Section II, however, is more concerned with the restrictions which are to be imposed upon belligerents in their relations with neutrals than with any positive rights which may be asserted against the latter.

2.   An examination of the terms of the Convention does not disclose any change in the attitude of the United States with regard to maritime

---

[1]Committee of Imperial Defence Sub-Committee on Belligerent Rights. Circulated in accordance with B.R. 3rd Minutes, Conclusion (b).

warfare or the rights which belligerents are or may be entitled to assert. The Articles of the Convention itself, as printed in Paper No. B.R. 27, are frequently ill-drawn and clumsily expressed, and have the appearance of being translated from some other language (it is stated to have been drawn up in Spanish, English, French and Portuguese); but its meaning is reasonably clear.

3. Article 1 lays down that warships of belligerents have the right 'to detain and visit on the high seas, or in territorial waters that are not neutral, any merchant vessel for the purpose of ascertaining its character and nationality, and whether it carries cargo prohibited by international law, or has committed any violation of the blockade.' The word 'detain' in this Article appears to mean no more than 'stop' or 'cause to stop,' and not to refer in any way to the right of 'detention' in the sense in which that word is used in the Admiralty memorandum (Paper No. B.R. 14). That this is so is shown by the sentence which follows: 'If the merchant vessel does not heed the hint to stop, the warship may pursue it and detain it by force.' It would also be reasonable to expect the phrase to be 'visit and detain' instead of 'detain and visit' if anything more than the right to stop a merchant vessel for the purpose of visit and search were intended. The 'right of stoppage, search and capture' in Article 63 of the Declaration of London is, in the French version, 'droit d'arrêt et de saisie' and 'detain' is no doubt a translation of the French phrase. There is nothing, therefore, in Article 1 of the Convention which indicates any change in the United States attitude, unless, indeed it is to be inferred from the absence of an express prohibition of the right of a belligerent to take a vessel into port for the purpose of examination.

4. It will be observed that the right of blockade and the right to seize contraband (which is presumably what is meant by 'cargo prohibited by international law') are recognised by Article 1, but there is nothing in the Convention which defines or restricts either right. It may be assumed, therefore, that the intention is that these two matters should continue to be regulated by the existing rules of international law, whatever they may be.

5. Article 2 provides that 'The detention of a vessel, as well as its crew, due to a violation of neutrality shall be made in the manner which best suits the State effecting the same, and at the expense of the offending vessel. Said State, save in the case of a serious fault on its part, is not responsible for damages suffered by the vessel.' It is not clear whether this Article is intended to relate to unneutral service by neutrals, or to the commission in neutral waters by belligerents of acts of war. Possibly it is intended to include both, in which case it is to be pre-

sumed that the 'detention' referred to means either detention with a
view to bringing the offending neutral vessel before a Prize Court for
condemnation on the ground of unneutral service, or the detention of a
belligerent vessel by a neutral State in a port belonging to the latter in
accordance with the provisions contained in Section II of the Convention, which imposes conditions upon the right of belligerents to enter
neutral ports in time of war. It appears more likely, however, that the
Article is intended to deal with the cases of merchant vessels which
make an improper use of neutral ports as a base of supplies for warships of a belligerent, as the vessels of the Kosmos Line did of Chilean
ports during the war. In any event, the Article seems out of place in
Section I and belongs more appropriately to Section II.

6.   There is no Article in the Convention which deals either expressly
or by implication with the question of continuous voyage, evidence in
Prize Courts, convoy, mails or the right of retaliation. With regard to
armed merchant ships, Article 12 provides that: 'As regards the stay,
supplying and provisioning of belligerent ships in the ports of jurisdic-
tional waters of neutral, the provisions relative to warships shall be
applied equally to [among others] armed merchant ships'; but the United
States have signed the Convention with an express reservation on this
point. Presumably, therefore, they are not prepared to admit that defensively armed merchant ships are in any different position from merchant
ships not so armed.

7.   The rest of the Convention defines the rights and duties of neutral
States in time of war at some length, but it does not appear to go
beyond the generally recognised rules of international law, except perhaps in Article 27, which imposes an obligation on a belligerent to
indemnify for any damage caused by a violation of the provisions of
the Convention. Several of the Articles are no more than a restatement
of provisions in The Hague Convention XIII of 1907.

8.   If the comment may be allowed, the Convention is a singularly
barren production, and its framers appear to have been careful to avoid
all reference to any controversial subjects. It is, however, satisfactory
that it does not seek to embody in terms any of the views of the United
States upon those topics which were a matter of dispute between the
United States and this country during the war, and it may or may not be
legitimate to draw the inference that those topics are intended to be left
open for further discussion. It is certainly remarkable that in a Convention of this kind to which the United States is a party not the slightest
attempt should have been made to lay down any rule with regard to
visit and search, blockade, or the doctrine of continuous voyage; and if
the omission to deal with these subjects is not to be regarded as having

any significance, it can only be assumed that the Convention (if it is permissible so to describe a Convention signed by twenty-one sovereign States) is little more than a piece of window-dressing.

* * *

54. Sir Esme Howard to Sir Austen Chamberlain

[CAB 16/79, part 35, no. 1042/425]   17 May 1928
(Received 30 May)

Sir,   With reference to previous correspondence on the subject of the proposed treaty to outlaw war, I think it well to inform you that more than one writer in the press of this country has recently insisted on the value of such an instrument to Great Britain because it would disarm the United States as against a British blockade of an aggressor nation on behalf of the League of Nations. So far this point has generally been made by persons who are both ardently in favour of the treaty and convinced advocates of the League. There is, however, clearly an element of considerable danger in the airing of such arguments. The intransigent enemies of the League may be relied on to make use of them to prove that the treaty is nothing but a back door entrance into the League for the United States, and to attempt in this way to defeat the treaty in the Senate. There are already signs of the adoption of such an attitude. Ready allies are likely to be found by the opponents of the League among the big navyites, and the patriots who see in all persons or societies, who merely wish to further efforts to promote peace, 'pacifists', in the sense of the word as used during the war. It is interesting to notice the surprising number of patriots of this sort that seems to be springing up in Washington. To us they appear curiously old-fashioned; and their sentiments, and the manner of their expression, an echo of voices from the dim distance of the years before the war. I believe the club-chairs occupied by their prototypes in Great Britain have for some time been emptying, and that they are not being retenanted.

* * *

55. *Renewal of Arbitration Treaties*

Memorandum by Sir Cecil Hurst, and Minute by Lord Cushendun,
Chancellor of the Duchy of Lancaster
CONFIDENTIAL, C.P. 303 (28)

[CAB 16/79/435–7]   Foreign Office
                                                           October 5, 1928

In view of the approaching expiration of our arbitration treaties with
several Foreign States, I circulate to the Cabinet the subjoined memorandum, prepared at my request by the Legal Adviser to the Foreign Office.

If the proposals contained in paragraph 6 of Sir Cecil Hurst's memorandum are approved by my colleagues, I propose to initiate negotiations
with all the States whose arbitration treaties are expiring, and also with
Germany, with whom we have no treaty in existence. The renewal of
the treaty with the United States will require separate consideration.
Cushendun.

* * *

6. I am disposed to think that the conclusion of the Kellogg Pact
renouncing resort to war as an instrument of national policy offers an
opportunity of overcoming the difficulty about disputes rising out of
belligerent action at sea in another way, and the result of some unofficial
enquiries and conversations which, at the request of Lord Cushendun, I
held while at Geneva with my French and German colleagues, leads me
to think that a solution of this problem on the lines indicated below
would not be unacceptable to the French and German Governments.
Politically it is advantageous for His Majesty's Government to treat the
Kellogg Pact as opening a new chapter in international relations. If the
Pact is treated as a reality, His Majesty's Government will be entitled to
assume that this country will not become involved in war in future,
except in self-defence or in co-operation with the League of Nations in
pursuance of our obligations under the Covenant or under the treaties of
Locarno. His Majesty's Government are, therefore, justified in maintaining exceptional matters, to be dealt with as political disputes rather than
as disputes which are purely justiciable and susceptible of decision by
the application of a rule of law. I would therefore propose that the basis
on which our arbitration treaties should be concluded would be that of
providing that all justiciable disputes should be referred to the Permanent
Court of International Justice at The Hague, and that all other disputes

should be referred to conciliation commissions, with a further provision that if the parties are not prepared to accept the recommendations of the conciliation commission, the dispute should be submitted to the Council of the League. It will also be necessary to add a further exception as regards disputes arising in respect of countries in which Great Britain has special interests, by reason of the necessity of maintaining the safety of her inter-Imperial communications.

* * *

56. 'Public' and 'Private' Wars

Memorandum by Sir Maurice Hankey, Secretary, Committee of Imperial Defence

[CAB 16/79, part 57/515–20]   2 Whitehall Gardens, S.W.1
December 31, 1928, published January 1929

I have been asked to write a commentary on the proposal discussed and tentatively approved at the last meeting of the Sub-Committee for dividing wars into 'public' and 'private' wars, and approaching any conversations on the question of belligerent rights from this point of view.

The Circumstances in which the Proposal has been made
2.   The proposal must, of course, be considered in the light of the Sub-Committee's conclusion as a whole, and of the position reached in the present Inquiry. The Sub-Committee has decided in effect that it is in our interest to maintain belligerent rights as high as possible, and that the question should be discussed on this basis; that at any international Conference, in order to reach agreement, we should almost certainly have to make some concessions which would make a gap in the full exercise of belligerent rights, and that in consequence a Conference may become inevitable. The likelihood of this is accentuated by the Borah Resolution, now awaiting consideration by the American Senate, in favour of the summoning by the United States Government of a Conference for 'a restatement and recodification of the rules of law governing the conduct of belligerents and neutrals in war at sea,'[1] to be

---

[1]*The preamble to the Borah Resolution refers specifically to the Declaration of London and the Second Hague Conference. This opens a much wider range of subjects than Belligerent Rights as discussed by the Sub-Committee.

brought about, 'if practically possible, prior to the meeting of the Conference on the Limitation of Armaments in 1931.' It is true that the Borah Resolution has been before the Senate for ten months and its consideration has again and again been postponed, but His Majesty's Ambassador in Washington has several times advised that it will be passed, and that, if it is passed, the Administration will probably act upon it, but most likely not before the new President has assumed office. The Sub-Committee are understood to hold the opinion that an invitation to a Conference could not be refused,[1] and that, if a Conference becomes inevitable, it should, if possible, be preceded by conversations, with a view to an alignment of the views of the United States of America and ourselves.

3. Uncertainty regarding the American attitude towards the question of Belligerent Rights has throughout been one of the main difficulties which confront the Sub-Committee. There is a good deal of evidence to show that their position does not differ widely from our own, but it is rather vague and uncertain. In the Great War the United States co-operated to the full in the general policy of putting economic pressure on the enemy. 'It took Great Britain three years to reach a point where it was prepared to violate all the laws of blockade,' said Mr Polk to Mr Balfour. 'You will find it will only take us two months to become as great criminals as you are.'[2] They co-operated also, indirectly, by laying a minefield across the North Sea as an anti-submarine measure, but with the additional effect of restricting the movements of shipping approaching enemy ports, and so assisting the blockade. They also sent a Battle Squadron to join the Grand Fleet, on which our Cruiser Squadrons depended for support. But they took no action which weakens their previous attitude towards the more controversial aspects of the question of maritime belligerent rights. The American Naval Prize Manual, though differing on some important technical points from our own, is based on fairly high belligerent rights. The Havana Convention on Maritime Neutrality, 1928, though a flaccid document evading the real difficulties, is based on the exercise of maritime rights by a belligerent. There is also a good deal of evidence that thinking people in the United States are beginning to see that to a great Naval Power, such as they have now become, high belligerent rights are an advantage, though it has to be remembered that there has always been a school of thought

[1]I should prefer to keep an open mind on this point until we know more about the American attitude. It might be necessary to discuss the matter at an Imperial Conference before accepting an invitation, particularly if the differences between the two nations on questions of principle prove greater than we now contemplate. – M.P.A.H.
[2]'Life and Letters of Walter H. Page,' vol. II, p. 265.

in favour of the views of which Admiral Mahan was so powerful an exponent.

4.   Against this evidence is the 'traditional view' of the United States in favour of 'freedom of the seas' as pressed by Colonel House during the War and included in President Wilson's Fourteen Points, though accepted by the Allies only with a reservation as to its meaning. That this view is still widely held is shown by Sir Esme Howard's statement to the Sub-Committee on the 27th July in regard to the Borah Resolution, to the effect that 'there was no doubt that the Senate had the United States Press at the back of their minds when they decided on their policy, and there was no doubt that the sympathies of the Press were entirely on the side of neutral rights against Belligerent Rights' (Minutes of 4th Meeting).

5.   All the evidence that the Sub-Committee has been able to collect seems to indicate that the Administration, up to last summer at any rate, had thought very little about the matter, had not made up its mind, and did not particularly desire a Conference. Mr. Hoover, it is understood, is more likely to stand for high belligerent rights than low, and Sir Esme Howard reports that Mr. Garfield, a friend of Mr. Hoover, indicated in private conversation that no great divergence was likely to be found between the two countries.

6.   In view of the above, the Sub-Committee have decided to prepare for the possibility of conversations. A technical Conference has been asked to consider what concessions on maritime belligerent rights as hitherto exercised by this country could be made, and the proposal, which forms the subject of this Memorandum, has been adopted tentatively.

Origin of the Proposal

7.   The present proposal undoubtedly has its origin in the uncertainty just referred to regarding the American attitude. It was felt by many people that to enter a Conference or even on conversations on the purely technical issues of belligerent rights at sea without any political background might only have the result of intensifying antagonism and mutual suspicion. To quote Mr Philip Kerr, who is one of the parents of the present proposal:

   I don't believe that you can solve the question [i.e., of Anglo-American relations] by having a new Conference about belligerent and neutral rights. In fact, such a conference will only repeat in an intensified form the exacerbation of feeling which has already been caused by the discussion about cruisers.

8.   The proposal, however, is perhaps not so new as some of us have thought. President Wilson seems to have had in mind something of the kind at the time of the Paris Peace Conference. In a footnote to a passage in 'The Intimate Papers of Colonel House,' Volume IV, discussing the reasons why the President never raised the question of Freedom of the seas at the Peace Conference, occurs the following:

> Wilson explained his policy on the ground that there would be no more wars except those conducted by the League against an 'outlaw' State, and therefore, no neutrals. Hence the problem of the interference with neutral trade would not arise.

The failure of the United States to ratify the Covenant no doubt caused the idea to drop out of sight.

9.   A year ago, however, I myself thought of something similar to the present proposal. Mr Philip Kerr, who had just returned from a long tour in America on behalf of the Rhodes Trust, and who makes a special study of Anglo-American relations, came to see me about this time and had, I found, evolved the same idea. I spoke of the matter to some of the parties concerned in the Foreign Office and elsewhere, but not much interest was awakened and the idea was allowed to drop. Recently Sir Ronald Lindsay formulated it in greater detail in a private conversation with Lord Salisbury and myself, and that is the origin of the present proposal. That very morning I had received a letter from Mr Philip Kerr (an extract from which is appended to this Memorandum), developing his idea in more detail.

The Proposal in Detail

10.   The present proposal is founded on the idea that the Kellogg Pact opens a new era in international relations. Throughout the ages the folly of war and the advantages of peace have been admitted. Thucydides, writing of events in BC 424, says, 'That war is an evil is a proposition so familiar to everyone that it would be tedious to develop it,' and then speaks of 'the universal consent that peace is the first of blessings.' Universal peace was all but achieved during nearly 200 years by the Roman Empire at the beginning of the Christian era; it was aimed at in the best days of the Holy Roman Empire; and it was the ideal that brought the Holy Alliance into existence. But the Kellogg Pact carries these age-long aspirations further, for, with almost negligible exceptions, the nations of the world have agreed to outlaw war and to renounce it as an instrument of policy. In parenthesis it may be admissible to express private doubts as to whether nations may not, nevertheless, find themselves at war, each in the honest belief (so complicated are the

events which almost invariably precede hostilities)[1] that it has not broken the Pact. One may also prefer to have more confidence (even though not complete confidence) in the efficacy of the League of Nations, with its personal contacts and elaborate machinery of delay, and conciliation, than in the Kellogg Pact as preventive of war. However this may be, it is justifiable, for purposes of international discussion, to assume that the nations who signed the Kellogg Pact mean what they say, and that the Pact will be observed. If so, the only wars that can break out are wars of defence against a nation that has broken the Kellogg Pact and become an outlaw state. War against such a State, which has broken faith with the whole world, so the argument runs, would be a 'public' war, fought in the interest of the good faith of the world. It is unthinkable that the nations of the world (even thought they do not feel called to take part in the war) should succour an outlaw State. If they happened to be members of the League of Nations they would be bound, under Article 16, to suspend relations with a declared aggressor. If they are not members of the League the least they can do is to allow the fullest exercise of belligerent rights at sea in order to end the war as soon as possible. Such, in general terms, would appear to be the argument on which the proposal is based that breaches of the Kellogg Pact should be described as 'public' wars and that belligerent rights should be exercised in full against the recalcitrant State.

11.   Other wars, which for some reason or another may break out, are to be termed 'private' wars. In regard to these, if Mr Philip Kerr had his way, we should propose the abandonment of the exercise of maritime belligerent rights, a view which is shown later to be unsound. The Sub-Committee, while not going so far as this, think that we ought to be willing to make concessions.

12.   A third class of hostilities has been proposed under the title of 'Police Measures' to cover the case of the American operations in Nicaragua, or our own measures in Arabia, Aden Protectorate, China, the Sudan, or, possibly, Egypt. It should be noted that in the course of the Persian Gulf Inquiry the point has come out that our main security for the good behaviour of Ibn Saud is his complete dependence on imported foodstuffs. Presumably, a pacific blockade, such as was exercised against Greece during the War, would fall within the definition of 'police measures.'

---

[1]*For example: to protect their compatriots in Afghanistan, Russia might enter into the country, remaining there permanently. Circumstances might arise which made it very difficult for us, as an essential measure of self-defence, to avoid an invitation from Afghanistan to help in driving them out. Both sides would claim it as a war of defence.

Lord Balfour's View of the Principle

13. At this point the Sub-Committee may like to know the views of an absent colleague on the principle of the proposal. In reply to a communication as to the latest developments of the present Inquiry, Lord Balfour, on the 22nd December, writes a letter (from which he has given me permission to quote) as follows:

> I wish we could have a moratorium in respect of certain international questions. Discussions on them only lead to bad blood and a false perspective of international relations. A passion for defining is not the mark of a really acute mind; though acute minds, no doubt, are under the sad necessity of often having to deal with definitions.
>
> By the way, has it ever occurred to you that an over-zeal for the intellectual exercises may, in certain cases and in certain controversies, be cooled by laying down the principle that if we are determined to improve the definitions of international law there is one phrase with which we ought to begin, namely the Monroe Doctrine? Have our American friends ever agreed among themselves as to what they mean by it; or as to how the International court of Justice would be likely to interpret it? I personally am in favour of the Monroe Doctrine and am in favour of leaving it alone. But if the world is going to insist upon an agreed system of international jurisprudence, the Monroe Doctrine is the subject with which they should begin. The next one would be the distinction between measures of international police and measures of international war.

Balfour adds the following postscript in his own handwriting:

> I shall like to see the classification of wars into 'public' wars and 'private' wars worked out – it is perfectly sound in theory.

The Practical Application of the Plan

14. Sound though the plan may be in theory, it is with its practical application that the Sub-Committee is now concerned, and it is to this aspect that attention must now be directed. Perhaps the best plan will be to try and imagine a conversation between a British and an American representative in which the former tries to steer the discussion of belligerent rights into the plane of 'public' and 'private' wars. ...

* * *

26. What a pity it would be to raise a controversy which might so easily be used by mischief-makers and even by the most patriotic

elements in the populations of the two countries to make trouble, especially upon a question like maritime belligerent rights, which may never arise, and can only arise in an acute form in some remote war of a probably distant future! But if this problem must be discussed, and if differences must arise, let it be in the spirit of Mr Kellogg's pronouncement, and with a full public realisation of its remoteness and insignificance in comparison to the absence of disagreement between the two countries on any live issue.

27.   The Prime Minister some little time ago pointed out, in a public speech, as one of the difficulties in Anglo-American relations, the inevitable lack of personal contact between its statesmen. If by some means such personal contact could be achieved, and a discussion could take place over the whole field of Anglo-American relations, so as to precede or accompany technical conversations on maritime belligerent rights, and some publicity could be given to the results, it might be possible to emphasize how secondary in importance are the differences in comparison to the vast field of sympathy and understanding that exists between the two nations.

* * *

57.   Sir Harry Batterbee, Secretary of State for the Dominions, to Lt Col Maurice Hankey

PRIVATE

[CAB 21/310]   28 January 1929

My Dear Hankey, The other day I asked a prominent Canadian journalist how he would deal with the question of Anglo-American relations if he were the Secretary of State for Foreign Affairs. His reply was somewhat surprising. 'I should tell them,' he said 'that the reason why we were hesitating and deliberating so carefully is because, if the state of affairs which the United States wish to bring about, viz. the establishment of the principle of the freedom of the seas, backed up by a powerful American Navy, had existed fifteen years ago, we should not have been able to have prevented Germany from drawing the supplies which she required, Germany would have won the War and military imperialism would have been triumphant to-day. It is because of the line which you took fifteen years ago that it is impossible for us to accept the solution you offer to-day. We are arguing, not for ourselves, but for humanity and for you. If the Americans retort that the situation is altered by the Kellogg Pact, the answer is that you cannot rely on nations to keep their word, and it was simply because Germany did not keep her word that Great Britain declared war on her.'

I confess I was at first very surprised at this answer, but he persisted that smooth words were of no use with the Americans, and that a declaration of the above kind, something that would stir the conscience of the United States, was the only possible way of arriving at a lasting settlement. The United States would be terribly excited for six months, but in the end the conscience of the United States would rally to our side.

I send you this for what it is worth. There may conceivably be something in the idea that the line we should take is that we cannot accept the solution the United States now offer, because in the past such a solution would have spelled disaster to the world.

You will, of course, regard this as very private as it would not be fair to quote what was said at a private lunch.

* * *

58. Sir Esme Howard (Washington), to the Secretary of State for Foreign Affairs

[Telegram]

[CAB 16/79/367–9]   received 11:45 a.m. January 26th, 1929

My telegram No. 59.

Senator Borah opened resumed debate on cruiser bill in Senate yesterday by offering following amendment:

> First that the Congress favours a restatement and recodification of rules of law governing conduct of belligerents and neutrals in war at sea; second that such restatement and codification should be brought about if practically possible prior to meeting of the conference on limitation of armaments in 1932.

United States were on verge of naval race with Great Britain; both nations were building with the other country in view, whatever governments might say. Situation was similar to Anglo-German situation from 1905 to 1914. Senator quoted from Commander Kenworthy's 'Peace or War' and referred to statements in United States to prove existence of war-mindedness in both countries and this fear of war between them. He ascribed it to present conditions with reference to maritime law.

Was neutral commerce in war time to rely for protection on law or only on navies? He wishes to try protection of law, and to seek agreement on this law in spirit of friendliness and not antagonism. He would at once vote for present bill if time limit clause were eliminated. This would give time for further negotiations during next year or two for limitation of armaments and for attempt at regulation of maritime law, and United States taxpayer might be saved cost of building unnecessary cruisers. He would proceed in negotiations with such clarity and certainty of purpose that if they failed, failure would and could be regarded as final and therefore a challenge to United States to build. United States would know where their duty lay, construction could and should then proceed and there would be need for many more than fifteen cruisers for United States would inevitably and undoubtedly build navy superior to Great Britain. Washington conference had failed to deal with the one question viz. neutral rights, about which people had been thinking and organising ever since. This unsolved question had been real cause of failure at Geneva. He was not of those who fear aggressive attacks by Great Britain on US or vice versa, but was thinking of wars, e.g. between Great Britain and other countries. Without solution number of ships necessary was unlimited. Only satisfactory definition of freedom of the seas was right of neutrals to carry commerce in war as freely as in peace except when carrying actual munitions of war or seeking to break blockade which however must be of kind sufficient to prevent actual passage of ships. Enlargement of the contraband list by a belligerent was obnoxious to idea of freedom of the seas, but it had been done in Great War. United States had done so and would always do so again as long as freedom of seas question remained unsolved. Great Britain contested for right to interfere at will with neutral trade in war. This might be justified in past but it could not stand now against cause of peace. Borah then quoted Lord Wester Wemyss's speech of November 10th 1927, to show British attitude now. According to this speech they wished command of seas not only to defeat enemy but to force neutral nations to join with them to bring enemy's defeat about. But command of seas was obsolescent if not obsolete term. United States would not let their commerce be subject to other Power's whim. Great Britain might soon be able to see that theory of command of seas could work as much to her disadvantage as that of others; full neutral rights might be as essential to her safety as command of seas. There was tremendous sentiment in England in favour of freedom of seas, but he did not know whether British Government shared it. The only way to avoid tremendous armaments was to settle question of freedom of seas and use of navy in relation thereto. Senator Hale accepted Borah's amendment but advocated building cruisers now as best means of persuading Great Britain to agree to recodification of maritime law. Senators Bruce and Metcalf took same line. Borah said construction should be delayed till it was clear no agreement could be reached. During debate Senator Watson accused Great Britain, of violating spirit of Washington treaty by building more cruisers. Senator Robinson refuted this.

* * *

59. The Renewal of Arbitration Treaties. First Report

Committee of Imperial Defence Sub-Committee on Belligerent Rights
SECRET, 943-B

[CAB 16/79]   February 1929

INTRODUCTORY

1.   This Interim Report does not deal specifically with our main refer-ence on the question of Belligerent Rights at Sea, but only with a cognate subject which was referred to us by the Cabinet at its meeting on the 17th October, 1928 (Cabinet 47 (28), Conclusion 5), namely, the question of the renewal of our Arbitration Treaties which have expired or are about to expire.

2.   The Root-Bryce General Arbitration Treaty of 1908 expired on the 4th June, 1928, and in March 1928 the draft of a new Treaty was received from Washington for the consideration of the British Govern-ment. While the draft was under consideration by the Cabinet, the Kellogg Pact for the Renunciation of War was proposed. As it cut across the question of the renewal of the Root–Bryce Treaty further examination of the latter was postponed for a while.

3.   Meanwhile, the Arbitration Treaty with France expired on the 14th October, though steps have been taken to renew it indefinitely until such time as a new Treaty is negotiated. The Arbitration Treaties with Italy and Spain will expire this month, and we have at present no Arbitration Treaty with Germany.

4.   So far as we ourselves are concerned, we should feel no difficulty in renewing these Treaties approximately in their original form. The present difficulty arises owing to the desire of other parties to the Treaties to exclude from the new version the existing reservation of questions involving the 'vital interests, the independence, or the hon-our' of the contracting parties. The draft Treaty forwarded by Mr Kellogg

in March 1928 excludes certain other matters from the scope of the Treaty, such as those within the domestic jurisdiction of either of the high contracting parties, those involving the interests of third parties, the Monroe doctrine, and our commitments under the Covenant of the League of nations, but does not exclude matters of 'vital interest.' The similar exception of 'vital interests' has been dropped from the Franco-American Treaty, and from Treaties concluded between the United States and Albania, Austria, Czecho-Slovakia, Denmark, Finland, Germany, Italy and Poland, and is likely to be excluded from a number of treaties with other States which are now in course of negotiation. The Foreign Office have also received a private intimation that the French Government would be disappointed if His Majesty's Government asked for a renewal of the Arbitration Treaty on the old terms, and we are satisfied that the United States of America would refuse to renew the Root-Bryce Treaty on those terms.

5.   It is clear, therefore, that, whether wisely or unwisely, whether as a temporary phase or as a definite stage in the advance of arbitration, the opinion of the world, under American inspiration, has set against the reservation of 'vital interests.' For the British Government, therefore, to refuse to enter on new Arbitration Treaties unless 'vital interests' were reserved would be a very serious matter. In view of the attitude of the United States of America, it would, in the opinion of the Foreign Office, amount to a refusal to negotiate any arbitration Treaty with America. Both at home and abroad, it would be represented as a reactionary step running counter to the current of a great world movement. Before taking such a step we felt bound to examine every alternative course, in order to discover which will produce the best results and involve the least risk. In this respect we have received valuable assistance from the Governments of the Dominions.

6.   Before setting forth the various courses open to us, it will be convenient to consider what our own 'vital interests' are. In Sir Cecil Hurst's memorandum, which was referred to us by the Cabinet (Paper No. B.R.40), they are described as the maintenance of our belligerent rights at sea, which it has always been considered unsafe to submit to an international tribunal, and our 'special interests' in certain countries, due to the necessity of maintaining the safety of our imperial communications. This definition may (or may not) be correct to-day. It is, however, impossible to foresee where 'vital interests' may arise in the future. In the days of sailing-ships, who could have foreseen the vital importance of coal and then oil. Even ten or twelve years ago who could have foreseen the importance of the countries of the Middle East to our imperial air communications? Who, to-day, would venture to forecast

what 'vital interests' may arise out of developments in such directions, for example, as aviation, wireless telegraphy, Antarctic discovery, or some new source of power? We return to this aspect of the question in examining the detailed proposals submitted to us.

* * *

13.   One proposal, which was submitted by the First Lord of the Admiralty and supported by the high authority of Lord Balfour (who, unfortunately, was prevented by indisposition from taking any active share in this part of our enquiry), was that the Kellogg Pact (assuming that it will be ratified) renders unnecessary the renewal of the Root–Bryce Arbitration Treaty. In support of this thesis it is pointed out that the Kellogg Pact rules out war and provides for the settlement of conflicts by pacific means; that ample pacific means are available, whether for conciliation or arbitration, in the Bryan Treaty and The Hague Courts; that the elastic plan of leaving to the occasion the precise machinery to be adopted is the better one; that the attempt to bring these disputes beforehand within hard and fast provisions of legal procedure is a mistake; and, above all, that by avoiding renewal all these delicate matters of 'belligerent rights' and 'special interests' to which we have alluded would be avoided.
14.   Attractive as this proposal is at first sight, we do not feel able to recommend it for adoption. . . .

* * *

31.   The Arbitration Treaty which the majority of the Committee are prepared to recommend for the approval of the Committee of Imperial Defence and the Cabinet does not exclude Belligerent Rights from amongst the subjects to which, in the last resort, arbitration could be claimed by either party. A substantial minority of the Committee, however, do not accept this solution and make an alternative proposal that the Treaty should be signed subject only to a formal intimation that Belligerent Rights are reserved from arbitration until agreement has been reached as to what those rights are. The First Sea Lord, speaking on behalf of the Naval Staff, demurs to the submission of belligerent rights to compulsory arbitration under any condition. His reasons are stated in full in Appendix II. Sir Maurice Hankey asks that his agreement with Sir Charles Madden may be recorded.
32.   Before setting forth the alternative theses in detail it is necessary to state that on certain fundamental questions of principle the

two sections of the Committee are agreed. All are agreed in regretting that we cannot renew the Arbitration Treaty in the old form, excluding vital interests. With the exception of Lord Cushendun, who is in favour of wide concessions by this Country on Belligerent Rights, all are agreed that it is important to maintain these in the highest form that is possible – a matter that will be dealt with in detail in our main Report. The difference then arises not on the principle of maintaining Belligerent Rights high, but on the best method of achieving that end. Those who support the method of concluding an Arbitration Treaty applicable to Belligerent Rights do so with reluctance and only to avoid what they regard as greater risks. Those who oppose this do so because they consider that the risks of injuring our belligerent rights in the long run are greater than those involved in the alternative course that they propose. At best it is a choice of evils that the Committee of Imperial Defence and the Cabinet have to make. We proceed to state in detail the different views which have been laid before us.

Proposals of the Majority

33.   The majority of the Sub-Committee includes the Chairman (Lord Salisbury), the Secretary of State for Foreign Affairs, the Lord Chancellor, the President of the Board of Trade and the Chancellor of the Duchy of Lancaster, who though differing widely from his colleagues as to the desirable standard of belligerent rights supports the majority on this question. The arguments which have convinced the majority are as follows.

34.   In the first place they are satisfied that if Belligerent Rights are withdrawn from arbitration an International Conference will be called together by the United States on the subject of these rights, the invitation to which we must surely accept, and that there will inevitably be a demand from nearly all the Powers participating in the Conference that these rights should be placed at a lower level than we could to-day obtain from a Court of Arbitration, and that American public opinion will support this demand; and for this reason, that public opinion is looking towards Freedom of the Seas, whilst the finding of a Court could not be at a lower level than is prescribed by the American Naval Instructions, and would probably be upon an even higher standard. As will be observed from the Report we are about to submit on the general question of Belligerent Rights, the Committee have carefully examined these Instructions with the result that they turn out to differ less from our own than we have had reason to expect. We have therefore not so much to fear from arbitration upon the uncertain law as it stands as

from being faced with the amended law which American public opin-ion would demand at the Conference.

35.   We could, of course, resist the demand, but, if we were to take such a course whilst at the same time leaving the United States no ultimate appeal upon any belligerent rights issue except to force, we should not be supported by our own people.

36.   It is no doubt true that we might, after signing an arbitration Treaty not excluding belligerent rights from arbitration, still be invited to a Conference on the subject of these rights, and certainly in that event, as in the former case, we could not afford to reject the invitation. But in this case we need only accept on the understanding that the subject-matter should be limited to the codifying or bringing into har-mony existing practice, and we could refuse to attend any Conference which had as its object an alteration or amendment of the law. For having shown ourselves so amenable as to allow Belligerent Rights to be arbitrable, we could confidently anticipate support from public opin-ion, at any rate in England, in refusing to attend a Conference which had as its object amendment outside the practice not only of England but of America herself. In other words, if belligerent rights are not to be controlled by arbitration, the case for their careful scrutiny and amend-ment upon the plea of placing them upon an equitable basis is immensely strengthened. If, on the other hand, arbitration is admitted, all that can be required is that the law and practice should be made clear as they stand, and we have a strong case to refuse to move from that position. In fact, our situation would be so strong that not only could we resist anything below the level of the American Instructions, but even in the solution at the Conference of the ambiguous points that lie between ourselves and the United States we ought to do very well. In the interests, indeed, of high belligerent rights, it may not unreasonably be contended that the only way to secure them in these negotiations and conferences is to avoid coalescing all neutral Powers against us by refusing to allow issues, which are so clearly justiciable as Belligerent Rights, to be subject to some form of arbitration.

37.   It must not be forgotten that Prize Courts, in deciding a question of Belligerent Rights, purport to be administering International law. To refuse to allow questions depending entirely upon International Law to be settled by impartial decision will be represented as equivalent to an announcement to the world that we do not intend to be bound by International Law, but only by the standard of our own necessities. This has often been alleged against us in the past, to give substance to the charge by a refusal of arbitration will go very far to provide the incen-tive needed to make the citizens of the United States resolve to do their

utmost to prevent us from ever again exercising the rights we claim. The truth must be faced that we shall be less able in the future than we were in the late war to enforce Belligerent Rights against United States commerce beyond the limits permitted by the United States. If an Arbitration Treaty exists we can at least rely on the exercise of those rights which are recognised by their own Prize Court decisions and Naval Instructions: if there is no Arbitration Treaty, the United States may dispute even this measure of liberty for our Navy, and might conceivably even claim for their commerce that freedom of the seas which a large section of their public opinion already demand. In the absence of an Arbitration Treaty, we should have no redress against such a claim. In this view, the existence of an Arbitration Treaty, including Belligerent Rights, is a protection to rights which we have no other means of enforcing against the will of the United States.

38.   But beyond these points broadly the majority are convinced that, if Belligerent Rights are excluded, the Arbitration Treaty will not be accepted by the American Government at all and with the Treaty, the whole structure of a new departure in cordial relations with that country in the near future would fall to the ground. On the other hand the signature of the Treaty would produce great advantages not only in the sphere of general policy, but even in respect of Belligerent Rights themselves. As regards general policy the conclusion of the Treaty would tend to ease the situation in the cruiser controversy by removing the argument, which has been used with so much effect during the debates in Congress, that a great American Navy is required in order to prevent Great Britain, when engaged in war, from interfering with neutral trade. The existence of the Treaty would clearly cut away this contention. The Secretary of State for Foreign Affairs indeed believed that this would so far improve the situation that the President might even refrain altogether from summoning a Conference notwithstanding the general attitude of the Senate. However, that may be, even if a Conference were summoned, we would repeat what has already been indicated in paragraph 36, namely, that we should be in a strong position to insist that the subject-matter should be limited to codification and that even that codification should fairly take account of the British side of the case.

39.   There is this further point. If we were engaged in war and there were to be an outcry against our exercise of Belligerent Rights, an American Government, being anxious not to break with us, would be in a better position to stand up to popular pressure in favour of drastic action if it could remind the public that arbitration lay behind its diplomatic endeavour. There would be no risk of precipitate executive action.

Indeed, far from this, there can be nothing remotely resembling precipitation in the operation of the American Arbitration Treaty. First diplomacy must be tried. After its failure the nature of the dispute may be such that resort can be had to the Bryan Conciliation Commission, which is allowed a year for its efforts. Then the 'agreement' as to what is to be arbitrated has to be settled between the two Governments and approved by the Senate, and, if the Committee's proposals are adopted, by the Parliaments of all parts of the Empire concerned. Then only is it referred to arbitration whether by the Permanent Court of Arbitration established at the Hague or some other competent tribunal, and, when that point has been reached, there is no reason why the result should be adverse to our claim.

40.   At this point it must be said that, whatever the Cabinet decide upon the question which has divided the Committee, we cannot escape having regard to the Court of International Arbitration. If we are parties to an arbitration there is always a British Judge upon the tribunal, and his influence, indeed his mere presence, is no inconsiderable guarantee of an equitable decision. But it should be remembered that if we are not parties, even if we have no arbitration treaty at all and are not technically amenable to the decisions of the Court, these decisions cannot fail to weigh with us. The point of view of the world opinion which would accept them and the attitude of neutrals generally must react upon any inclination of ours to exercise Belligerent Rights in defiance of those decisions even though we may not have recognised their validity.

41.   Finally, the amendment to which we have referred, under which the last word as to the reference of a particular issue to arbitration would lie with the Parliaments of Great Britain or her Dominions, as the case may be, is of the essence of the proposed Treaty which the majority submit to the Committee of Imperial Defence and the Cabinet. If it were true that, once the Arbitration Treaty is signed without the exclusion of Belligerent Rights, every issue in respect of those rights, whatever the circumstances of it, however vital it may be, however great our want of confidence in the tribunal that will adjudicate, must upon the demand of the American Government be compulsorily referred to arbitration, the Cabinet might well shrink from such a conclusion. But in these democratic days such an abdication cannot be defended. The American Government do not attempt to defend it. We have only to follow their example, and if the circumstances are strong enough and the issue important enough we may, under the shield of this amendment, confidently rely upon our Parliaments to protect us.

Proposals of the Minority

42.   The minority of the Committee is composed of the First Lord of the Admiralty, the Secretary of State for Dominion Affairs and the Secretary of State for India. They, too, are in favour of omitting from the Arbitration Treaty itself any qualification which, overtly or covertly, would exclude belligerent rights from its purview. But they would accompany the Treaty by a separate reservation declaring that we cannot regard the Treaty as applying to cases arising out of the exercise of belligerent rights at sea pending agreement as to what those rights are, but intimating our readiness to enter upon the discussion of this whole question at an early date. Lord Balfour, who, to the great regret of all his colleagues, has, for reasons of health, as already mentioned, not been able to take any active part in the discussions on arbitration, has also expressed doubts in regard to the proposals of the majority. After perusing the Minutes of the Meeting at which the majority scheme was discussed, Lord Balfour expressed views which have been summarised by Sir Harry Batterbee, of the Dominions Office, in the following terms:

> Although he had always been opposed to a conference if it could be avoided, it might be preferable to obtain a definite codification of belligerent rights at a conference, provided that it did not fall appreciably below the United States Naval Instructions of 1917, rather than to rely upon arbitration. If arbitration were accepted, it might result in our losing the rights we needed by the reference of disputes to The Hague in wars in which we took no part. He fully realised the extreme difficulty of the situation, but he hoped that before any decision were reached to allow belligerent rights to go to arbitration, every other avenue would be very fully explored.

43.   The views of Mr Bridgeman, Mr Amery and Lord Peel are based on similar doubts. They believe that to include Belligerent Rights among the questions liable to compulsory arbitration is the beginning of concessions which will afterwards make it difficult for any Government to stand firm. In time these rights will be whittled away, not only in arbitrations to which we are a party, but in arbitrations arising out of wars in which we are not engaged, the decisions of which will become established precedents. The Permanent Court of International Justice, the Court that would normally be appealed to by all Powers other than the United States of America, consists of Judges elected from Spain, Italy, Brazil, Cuba, Great Britain, Switzerland, Holland, United States of America, Denmark, Japan, France. What prospect is there, the mi-

nority of the Committee ask, that a Court so constituted would endorse
a high level of maritime rights? As Mr Malkin wrote in 1924:

> It is very difficult for a Court composed of international lawyers,
> when dealing with cases of this nature, to realise that what they have
> got to do is not to apply the rules which they will find in text-books,
> based as they are entirely on the experience of the past, but to
> endeavour to discover what should be regarded as the applicable
> rules of international law in the circumstances of the present. If, for
> instance, a really serious attempt had been made to test before an
> arbitral tribunal the validity of the decisions of the American Prize
> Courts in the Civil War in relation to contraband and blockade, I
> think there can be little doubt that these decisions would at that time
> have been condemned; but even before the last war there was almost
> general agreement that the development of the old rules embodied in
> those decisions was sound.

44.   The Minority hold that to entrust the future employment of Belligerent Rights to the decisions of some such tribunal as that described
above would be to run too great a risk. They point out that any nation,
however small, will be able to bring us to arbitration. The American
Arbitration Treaty will not stand alone. It will provide a model which
will have to be followed in similar Treaties with other countries. There
is no doubt that the existence of Compulsory Arbitration Treaties with
Holland and Denmark, for example, would have proved an immeasur-
able handicap during the War to the exercise of Belligerent Rights,
which, though contrary to precedent, were justified by the circumstances of the situation. The decisions of arbitrations under the new
Treaties will handicap us in future wars, since they will be binding for
all time and in all wars.

45.   If the Minority feel the gravest anxiety in regard to the risks
involved in the Majority proposals, they are profoundly sceptical as to
the realisation of the advantages claimed for them. They do not believe
that the great sacrifice we are making in submitting Belligerent Rights
to arbitration is going to produce any permanent difference to our
relations with the United States of America. Since the war the British
Empire has made considerable concessions to American opinion – the
abolition of the Anglo-Japanese Alliance, the funding and regular service of the debt, the extension of the operations of liquor prohibition
vessels beyond the three-mile limit. During the same period France has
adopted a very different attitude. She has always held firmly to her
principles on matters of national defence in refusing to discuss land
armaments at Washington, in declining to agree to the abolition of

submarines, or to ratify the Washington Convention applying to submarines the rules for the capture of merchant ships at sea. In addition, she has not yet funded her debt. Yet, which nation is the more suspect, which the more respected, in America? Which is the more frequent object of attack in Congress? There is no ground, in the opinion of the Minority, to believe that one more great concession is going to change American opinion or to lead to any permanent reduction in the American naval programme.

46.   The Minority do not take the view that the Americans will refrain from summoning a Conference on the subject of Belligerent Rights because we agree to include that subject within the scope of the Arbitration Treaty. The Americans will be just as aware as we are ourselves that the concession is made to *force majeure*, and it will not render them less anxious to compel further concessions. Moreover, the fact that we have accepted arbitration will make them the more anxious to clear up the whole question of what is to be the law and practice of the future. For similar reasons the Minority scout the idea that we shall in fact be able to limit the discussions to a so-called 'codification.' There is so much uncertainty that, at the best, there is bound to be a certain amount of rewriting. Much as the Minority, like the Majority, regret a Conference, they believe it is necessary to face the fact that we are very likely to receive an invitation, and that we cannot refuse it. Their plan, therefore, is frankly based on a recognition of the fact that a Conference is unavoidable. If the Conference results in a code of international law acceptable both to the Americans and ourselves, then they would consent to the inclusion of Maritime Belligerent Rights within the scope of the Arbitration Treaty. If the results of the Conference are not acceptable to us, or are rejected by the American Senate, then we remain free. They do not see that the Americans have any reasonable ground for objecting to our desire to have the inclusion of belligerent rights postponed for a year or two until this question is cleared up. By offering to conclude an 'all-in' Arbitration Treaty, subject to the amendments proposed in this Report and subject to this one temporary exception, we shall have put ourselves right with our own public opinion. The delay will also give us time for a proper consultation with our Dominions and India, which, in any event, we ought to have before we enter a Conference on Belligerent Rights.

47.   It is also contended, on behalf of the Minority, that their method of procedure would retain for us a larger measure of initiative in dealing with the whole question. The reservation accompanying the Treaty of Arbitration would afford some opportunity for a dignified and reasoned statement of the case for our historic policy. If the Senate refused

to accept the Treaty because of the temporary reservation, the onus of having caused a breakdown would clearly rest with them. The declaration of a willingness to enter a conference, which would necessarily have to accompany the reservation, would enable us both to declare that we could only do so after we had discussed the matter among ourselves at the next Imperial Conference, and to intimate that we regarded it as a Conference for the purpose of codifying and clearing up and not of modifying or revolutionising the existing maritime law.

48.   The Minority attach importance to the delay, which their proposals involve, in reaching a final decision from another point of view. They believe that the last few months of a Government's term of office is an extraordinarily bad time for announcing a great concession to a foreign State. The acute differences between members of the Committee are bound to be reflected outside, and at the present time they will be discussed in an atmosphere that is wholly unfavourable to the formation of a steady and balanced public opinion.

Statement of the Issue

49.   In conclusion, the alternative proposals between which the Committee of Imperial Defence and the Cabinet are asked to decide may be summed up as follows:

Alternative 'A'. The proposal of the majority of the Sub-Committee (Lord Salisbury, Sir Austen Chamberlain, Lord Hailsham, Sir Philip Cunliffe-Lister and Lord Cushendun) that the American draft, as amended in the form given below, should be accepted, and that Maritime Belligerent Rights should not be excluded from the Arbitration Treaty.

Alternative 'B'. The proposal of the minority of the Sub-Committee (Mr. Bridgeman, Mr. Amery, Lord Peel, who based themselves on a point of view similar to Lord Balfour's) that the American draft, as amended below, should be accepted, but subject to an intimation that Maritime Belligerent Rights must be reserved from its operation until such time as agreement has been reached as to what those rights are.

APPENDIX NO. 2

*Remarks by Admiral Sir Charles Madden, the First Sea Lord, on the
Proposal to allow Belligerent Rights to go to Arbitration if
International Maritime Law becomes Codified*

Admiralty, S.W.1
February 9, 1929

The Minority Report in paragraph 46 contains suggestions of a willingness to arbitrate on Belligerent Rights if an International Maritime
Conference produces a code of law.

I strongly recommend that such ideas be deleted.

2.   No code can really be produced which can foresee the contingencies of war twenty, thirty or fifty years hence.

The Declaration of London in 1909 and the war in 1914 made
manifest the impossibility of such foresight even for so short a period
as five years ahead. Had our Belligerent Rights been admitted as subject to arbitration in 1909 following on the Declaration of London, we
should have been taken to arbitration by neutrals in 1914, and been
deprived of our principal weapons for exercising economic pressure,
thereby materially prolonging the war.

3.   A code of law lays down technical legal rules to give effect to the
principles, which are the essence of these rights. Just as development in
municipal law must come with time, so also must this be so with other
law. Unfortunately, development of belligerent rights only materialises
with war, when it is too late to revise rules for the guidance of arbitrators, who must presumably, therefore, abide by what is then probably
obsolete, and insufficient to safeguard the vital principles at stake, and
any modern applications of these principles.

4.   If we must attend a Conference to discuss with many other Powers
codification of maritime rights, is it not better to go there unfettered by
the knowledge that the compromise arrived at, which is the most that
can be expected, will perhaps subsequently be the subject of arbitration? If this is not so, will not contentious details be fought out to the
detriment of good relations?

5.   Further, if the principle that belligerent rights can be arbitrated on
is conceded by the great maritime Powers, may not pressure be brought
to eliminate belligerent rights from reservation under the optional clause
of the Statute of the Permanent Court?

6.   I view with the gravest misgivings from the point of view of the
Naval Officer the idea of arbitration, particularly as I feel convinced
that a body constituted like the Permanent Court of International Jus-

tice would give an adverse decision on the following issues that arose in the Great War, and may be important in another war –

Retaliation.

Continuous voyage in relation to conditional contraband.

Diversion.

Inclusion of many articles in the list of absolute contraband.

Examination of mails.

Convoy.

Mining.

Angary.

7.   Such decision may be given by such a body largely constituted of biassed neutrals in the early stages of a long war, and even pending the arbitral decision, the Court or the Neutral will ask us to stop the practice complained of, and the Navy will almost certainly be instructed accordingly.

8.   As I see it, our sea power will be stultified.

The Freedom of the Seas
NOTE BY THE SECRETARY OF STATE FOR DOMINION AFFAIRS

Committee of Imperial Defence,
Sub-Committee on Belligerent Rights
9 February 1929

I notice that Sir Esme Howard in his letter of January 25th, circulated to the Sub-Committee, is afraid that the 'freedom of the seas' as a slogan might easily cause 'as much furore' in the United States as the once famous '55°50' or fight.' Sir Esme does not add that if we had been impressed by that furore then and accepted the American slogan we should have sacrificed all of the prairie region of Canada and of British Columbia that was worth having. By sticking to 49°50', and not being bluffed, we made it possible for the Canadian Dominion to come into being with incalculable consequences on the whole development of the British Empire since. As for the Americans they soon forgot all about '55°50' or fight' and, possibly, may forget all about the 'freedom of the seas' before very long if we, while maintaining a conciliatory attitude, refuse firmly to abandon our vital interests.
(Initialled) L.S.A. [Leo Amery]

* * *

60.   *Maritime Belligerent Rights. Second Report*

Committee of Imperial Defence – Sub-Committee on Belligerent Rights
SECRET 944-B

[CAB 16/79]   6 March 1929

Composition and Terms of Reference

The Prime Minister desires that a Sub-Committee of the Committee of Imperial Defence, composed as follows:[1]

(*Chairman*)

The Most Hon the Marquess of Salisbury, KG, GCVO CB,	Lord Privy Seal
The Right Hon Sir Austen Chamberlain, KG, MP,	Secretary of State for Foreign Affairs,
The Right Hon the Earl of Balfour, KG, OM,	Lord President of the Council,
Right Hon W.C. Bridgeman, MP,	First Lord of the Admiralty,
Right Hon Sir Philip Cunliffe-Lister, KBE, MC, MP,	President of the Board of Trade,
Right Hon Viscount Peel, GBE,	First Commissioner of Works,[2]
Right Hon Lord Cushendun,	Chancellor of the Duchy of Lancaster,
The Right Hon Sir Douglas Hogg, KC, MP,	Attorney-General,[3]

with the following expert assessors[4]

Admiral of the Fleet, Sir Charles Madden, Bart, GCB, GCVO, KCMG,	First Sea Lord and Chief of Naval Staff,
Sir Cecil Hurst, GCMG, KCB, KC,	Legal Adviser, Foreign Office,

---

[1]*The Right Honourable L.S. Amery, MP, Secretary of State for Dominion Affairs and the Colonies, was added to the membership of the Sub-Committee on October 17, 1928 (Cabinet 47 (28), Conclusion 5).

[2]*Now Secretary of State for India.

[3]*Now the Right Hon Lord Hailsham, Lord Chancellor.

[4]*Sir William Tyrrell, GCMG, KCB, KCVO, Permanent Under-Secretary of State for Foreign Affairs, was added to the Expert Assessors on January 19, 1928, on the authority of the Prime Minister, and was succeeded on July 26, 1928, by the Right Hon Sir Ronald Lindsay, GCMG, CB, CVO, who had taken his place as Permanent Under-Secretary of State for Foreign Affairs.

Lieutenant-Colonel Sir Maurice P.A.   Secretary, Committee of
  Hankey, GCB,   Imperial Defence,
Commander the Hon C.P. Hermon-   (*Secretary*),[1]
  Hodge, DSC, RN.

should meet to consider the question of Belligerent Rights at sea, as
raised in Cabinet Papers C.P. 258 (27), C.P. 286 (27), and C.P. 287 (27).

December 5, 1927

REPORT

Part I – Introductory

The Sub-Committee was appointed by the Prime Minister on the 5th
December, 1927, with the composition shown on the previous page, to
consider the question of belligerent rights at sea as raised in Cabinet
Papers C.P. 258 (27), C.P. 286 (27) and C.P. 287 (27).
2.   On the 17th October, 1928, the Cabinet referred to the Sub-Committee, in addition, the question of the renewal of our Arbitration Treaties
which have expired or are about to expire. This aspect of the question
has already been dealt with in a separate Report (Paper C.P. 40 (29)).
[The origin of the inquiry is stated to have been Chamberlain's paper of
26 October 1927 quoted above, [1927–10], C.P. 258 (27).]

* * *

Procedure

6.   The subject of our investigation is one of great magnitude. Nearly
every aspect is controversial. Many volumes have been devoted to neutral
and belligerent rights and freedom of the seas, and the standard works on
naval history and international law contain many references to the subject. Space prohibits us from dealing with the earlier history of the
question, a summary of which is to be found in vol. XXIII of the Peace
Handbooks prepared under the auspices of the Foreign Office for use at
the Peace Conference, under the title 'Freedom of the Seas.' Nevertheless, we have collected much additional documentary evidence. The
Secretary to the Committee of Imperial Defence has furnished material
from the archives in his custody, including particulars of the breakdown
during the War of a number of international agreements previously concluded; an account of the incident at the Armistice discussions when the
Allies, on the initiative of Mr Lloyd George, reserved the second of

---

[1]*Succeeded on March 1, 1928 by Commander L.E.H. Maund, RN.

President Wilson's Fourteen Points relating to Freedom of the Seas, notwithstanding Colonel House's threat that America would withdraw from the War; papers prepared for the Imperial War Cabinet before the Peace Conference by the Admiralty and by a Legal Committee under the Chairmanship of the late Lord Cave; a recent Report by the Legal Sub-Committee of the Advisory Committee on Trade and Blockade on our blockade practice during the War; as well as comments on other papers presented to the Sub-Committee. The Admiralty have formulated in detail their present claims in regard to the exercise of belligerent rights, and have expressed their views as to the effect of any abatement of these claims to meet American views, as well as on other aspects of our Inquiry. The Foreign Office have kept us constantly informed of all developments of this question in the United States of America. In addition to a number of despatches from Sir Esme Howard in regard to American opinion, we had the advantage of the Ambassador's presence at one meeting. We also received a written report, as well as verbal commentary thereon, from Mr Craigie, the head of the American Department in the Foreign Office, on his return from a visit to the United States of America. The Foreign Office reports include full particulars of a Convention of Maritime Neutrality drawn up at the Pan-American Conference in Havana in February 1928. In addition to memoranda by the Chairman and several members of the Committee, we have received memoranda from outside, from the Minister of Labour and the Parliamentary Under-Secretary for Foreign Affairs. At the suggestion of the Secretary of State for Foreign Affairs, the whole of our proceedings were sent to Admiral Sir Herbert Richmond, until recently the Commandant of the Imperial Defence College, who has contributed valuable memoranda on Blockade. In addition, a Legal Technical Sub-Committee has compiled a most important Report on the technical aspects of our terms of reference, to which we frequently refer in this Report.

7. The results of our deliberations on these matters will now be summarised.

Part II – GENERAL POLICY

High or Low Belligerent Rights?

8. The first matter to which we directed attention, and one to which we more than once returned, is the fundamental question of principle as to whether it is in the interest of the Empire to maintain belligerent rights high, as in the past, or to recede from our previous attitude.

9. Historically, as the Cabinet and Committee of Imperial Defence are aware, the argument is in favour of high belligerent rights. In the

greatest wars of our history the exercise of these rights has often proved
a decisive factor:

> 'For two hundred years,' wrote Admiral Mahan, 'England has been
> the great commercial nation of the world. More than any other her
> wealth has been entrusted to the sea in war as in peace; yet, of all
> nations, she has ever been most reluctant to concede the immunities
> of commerce and the rights of neutrals. Regarded not as a matter of
> right, but of policy, history has justified the refusal; and if she
> maintain her Navy in full strength, the future will doubtless repeat
> the lesson of the past.' ('The Influence of Sea Power upon History.')

Although some concessions were made, by international agreement, to
the position of neutrals between 1815 and 1914, these failed to stand
the test of unlimited war, and, before the end of 1916, partly owing to
their vagueness and partly in retaliation for breaches of the laws of war
by the enemy, they had disappeared. In spite of immense pressure from
neutrals, and more especially during the first part of the War from the
United States of America, who were in the last resort in a position to
enforce their claims owing to the dependence of the Allies upon them
for supplies, the Allies, nevertheless, were able to increase their economic pressure every year of the War until, and this time with the
co-operation given by the United States from April 1917 onwards, the
economic weapon again became once more one of the decisive factors
in victory.

10. It has been suggested, however, that times have changed. An
essential factor in maintaining high belligerent rights is sea supremacy.
That, it is said, we no longer possess, since we have accepted equality
with the United States of America; and, indeed, not only so, but owing
to the vast increase of population and wealth in the United States it is
going to be more and more difficult to maintain even equality in sea-
power. Moreover, America is now conscious of her power, and there is
a strong public movement, against allowing her trade to be interfered
with by a belligerent. This is, in fact, one of the main arguments by
which public opinion in America is being induced to support the movement for the expansion of the Fleet. In these circumstances it is suggested
that for us to insist on our right to interfere with neutral trade is simply
to stimulate American naval competition. The question is put, 'Would it
not be better to bow to the inevitable and make all the concessions that
may be asked of us?' By doing so, it is pointed out, we may hope to
remove the argument in favour of naval expansion, which makes the
strongest appeal to moderate opinion in the United States, and so free
ourselves from the risk of a competition in armaments with a country

richer than ourselves. This aspect is strengthened by the speeches made in the recent debates in the Senate at Washington. In support of this view it has also been urged that the circumstance of the late war are never likely to recur, that it is impossible to imagine circumstances in which it would be worth while to adopt a policy of economic pressure against an enemy, and that in any event it would be ineffective.

11.   These arguments in favour of concessions are carried still further by a reference to our dependence on oversea trade even for the prime necessities of existence. It is recalled that during the War our trade suffered severely from the depredations of surface raiders and submarines, and that at one time the position became one of extreme peril. In these circumstances it has been urged that this danger can best be removed by entrusting our security primarily to international law, and that our best course is to work for Conventions based on lower belligerent rights. This, it is contended, would have the further advantage of liberating our trade from the restrictions to which it is liable from belligerent action in wars in which we ourselves are a neutral.

12.   Finally, much has been made, particularly in public discussions, of the alleged cruelty of economic pressure, and some stress has been laid on the iniquity of interfering with neutral trade. Attention has been drawn to the strength of public opinion on this subject in the United States, whose views may be shared in some quarters in the Dominions and have a considerable echo in this country.

13.   To each of these arguments in favour of a policy described as 'swinging towards Freedom of the Seas,' an answer has been given, and, in addition, counter-arguments have been brought forward in favour of the maintenance of high belligerent rights, which the Sub-Committee (with the exception of Lord Cushendun) consider conclusive.

14.   Taking first the reply to the arguments summarised in paragraph 10, it is not disputed that the United States now share with us the supremacy of the seas, nor that they would have the power in a future war to interfere with the exercise of belligerent rights. The supporters of high belligerent rights point out, however, that this is no new factor. Long before the War we knew that neutrals, and particularly the United States, had the power to make the exercise of belligerent rights very difficult, if not impossible. This was in effect the argument used by Lord Clarendon as long ago as 1856 in order to justify acceptance of the Declaration of Paris. It was also an argument used in defence of the Declaration of London. During the War America had the power to interfere with the so-called blockade. She possessed the third fleet in the world, and, as already mentioned, complete control of supplies on

which the Allies depended. She could, if she had so desired, have refused to sell to the Allies that indispensable war material of to-day – oil – without which warships, submarines, armies, tanks and aircraft cannot move. She could have refused transportation through her ports of Canadian grain, or to sell her own grain. She could have refused to furnish munitions or machinery for their manufacture. She could, in fact, have returned to Jefferson's Non-Intercourse Policy, which, though indecisive at the time, would to-day produce results far greater than they could at the beginning of the last century. There is also ample evidence that she was fully conscious of her power, and that there was a strong movement in favour of exercising it. Nevertheless, for one reason or another – predominance of sympathy with the cause of the Allies, irritation at the enemy's breaches of the laws of war, internal prosperity due to supplying the Allies, the political influence of interested traders, and so forth – she lacked the will to exert pressure actively. Why then, it is asked, should we assume that in a future and probably distant war every circumstance is going to be against us? Why should we trust to arguments which were used before the War and were disproved by the experience of the War? Why should we base ourselves on the assumption that in a future war, however odious and provocative may be the aggression of an enemy, we shall never have America as an ally, or as a sympathiser, or even in a state of reluctance to become embroiled in a distant conflict? Wars in which high belligerent rights are a decisive factor are few and far between. The next occasion in which they may be required is almost certainly remote; its conditions are impossible to forecast; and it would be folly by international agreement to preclude ourselves from using what has often proved our principal means of putting pressure on an enemy. Of course the arguments must not be pressed too far. The Secretary of State for Foreign Affairs points out that it cannot be inferred because she had the power and did not use it in 1914–17, that, therefore, she will not use it in a future struggle. Throughout the early years of the Great War the situation was always delicate and often critical. In the last resort we were saved not so much by the large concessions which we made as by the greater irritation caused by German outrages. It would be unsafe to base our policy on the assumption that the conduct of our enemies will always be more offensive to neutrals than our own, and that diplomacy will always be able to judge the exact extent to which we can avoid an open breach.

15.   The contention that, by advocating low belligerent rights, or Freedom of the Seas, we should permanently remove the basis of the American 'Big Navy' movement, is also contested. American naval

competition will not be prevented by paper concessions in the negotiations. . . .

* * *

22.   As regards the trend of public opinion in the United States, in certain quarters in the Dominions and to some extent in this country, it is thought by some that if the other side were put properly even the United States of America would see how much they have to lose from the surrender of belligerent rights. The Secretary of State for Foreign Affairs does not reject this possibility, though he is advised by the Foreign Office that they do not believe this to be the case in the present state of American opinion or without long and careful preparation. The more one studies the conduct of nations the more does it become clear that their attitude towards the question of immunity of commerce is determined purely by their own situation and conditions, by the advantages they derive from immunity. National advantage, not a philosophic attitude towards war or humanity, was ever the spring of the policy of nations. As neutrals we see them advocate immunity to its utmost lengths. As belligerents, allied to strong Naval Powers, they advocate the strongest measures of coercion. America, as a neutral, disputed the legality of black-lists. When she became a belligerent her black-list was far more comprehensive than that of any of her European allies. It is possible that if the United States could be got to study some of the problems which may confront them in the future, they would discover their own need for the retention of belligerent rights, and this, perhaps, is the reason for the lukewarmness of the 'Big Navy' Party on this particular proposal, of which we have some evidence.

* * *

Part III – The Attitude of the United States Towards Belligerent Rights in Comparison with Our Own

The American Attitude

29.   Before setting forth our recommendations as to how belligerent rights can best be maintained at a high level, it is necessary to examine the American attitude towards this question. As a result of our efforts in this direction, we have come to the conclusion that, although the Big Navy Party, and some thinkers outside it, are probably beginning to realise that the interests of the United States in future are likely to be best served by high belligerent rights, the trend of United

States opinion, both in Congress and in the country, is in the opposite direction. . . .

* * *

31.   'Public' and 'Private' Wars – In the course of the public discussions in magazines and the Press that have taken place recently on both sides of the Atlantic, a new theory has been evolved regarding the effect on the nature of war of the Pact for the Renunciation of War [the Kellogg Pact]. While we do not hope that this theory will provide a solution of the belligerent rights difficulty, we feel that, in view of all that has been said upon the subject, we ought in this Report to take note of the difference between 'public' and 'private' wars. The proposal is based on the suggestion that the Kellogg Pact has changed the whole situation in regard to war, and has opened a new era in international relations. The nations of the world, with the exception of the Argentine and Brazil, have pledged themselves to renounce war as an instrument of national policy. The only wars, then, in which it is said that the signatories of the Pact can become engaged are wars of defence against nations that have violated their engagements. War against such a State, which has broken faith with the whole world, so the argument runs, would be a 'public' war, fought in the interest of the good faith of the whole world. It is unthinkable that the nations of the world (even though they do not feel obliged to take part in the war) should succour an outlaw State. If they happen to be members of the League of Nations they would be bound, under Article XVI, to suspend relations with a declared aggressor. If they are not members of the League, the least they could do would be to allow the fullest exercise of maritime belligerent rights in order to end the war as soon as possible. Other wars, which may for some reason or another break out in spite of the existence of international machinery to prevent them, are, under this proposal, to be deemed 'private' wars. The more extreme advocates of the theory suggest that maritime belligerent rights should be abandoned for such wars, and a more moderate proposal is that they should be reduced to a lower level.

32.   If the United States of America had become a member of the League of Nations there might be something to be said for the theory that all wars would be 'public' wars. From Colonel House's Memoirs it appears that President Wilson at the Peace Conference had something of the kind in mind:

'Wilson explained his policy' (i.e., of not pressing Freedom of the Seas at the Peace Conference) 'on the ground that there would be no more wars except those conducted by the League against an 'outlaw' State, and therefore no neutrals. Hence the problem of the interference with neutral trade would not arise.' (The Intimate Papers of Colonel House, Vol. IV, p. 432.)

The abstention, however, of the United States from the League invalidates the whole plan so far as they are concerned. . . .

* * *

35.   In addition to 'public' and 'private' wars, a third category of belligerency has been proposed, under the heading 'Police measures,' to include minor operations, such as the recent employment of American Marines in Nicaragua, the use of international forces in China, our own operations in the Aden territory, and so forth. In these cases narrow limitations of belligerent rights might well seem to the Americans to be as much out of place as it does to ourselves, and here again in considering these cases an educative effect may be hoped for as to the importance of our view of belligerent rights. In the next section of this Report we examine the British and American attitude towards some of the technical aspects of the application of belligerent rights at sea.

British and American Views Regarding the Application of Maritime Belligerent Rights

36.   For a detailed comparison of British and American views regarding the application of maritime belligerent rights we are indebted to a Technical Sub-Committee under the Chairmanship of Sir Maurice Gwyer, His Majesty's Procurator-General and Treasury Solicitor. The subject was further explored by a Technical Committee under the Chairmanship of Sir Cecil Hurst, the Legal Adviser to the Foreign Office, whose task was to re-examine, for possible use in discreet conversations with the United States officials, the ground covered in the Report just referred to and other papers, in order to see whether it was not possible to arrive at a policy in connection with belligerent rights which would safeguard the essentials of the Admiralty, and at the same time afford some reasonable prospect of an agreement with the United States. Both these Reports are attached hereto (Appendices I and II).[1]

37.   In pursuing their investigations the Hurst Sub-Committee used as a basis of their work the Declaration of London of 1909, which, though never ratified by this country, is an important landmark in the history of

[1]These reports have not been reproduced in this volume.

maritime law. They have done so because Senator Borah's Resolution in regard to belligerent rights, which at the time the Report was prepared had remained on the table of the Senate for ten months, had taken the Declaration as a point of departure, and because Sir Esme Howard had intimated in a private letter that this was the Senator's intention. For the purposes of their Report the Sub-Committee, for reasons stated therein, limited their enquiry to the questions which might arise if Great Britain found herself at war with another State in circumstances which entail no breach of the Covenant on either side and therefore entitle other States members of the League to claim to adopt an attitude of neutrality. They accordingly take as a hypothetical case for the purposes of their enquiry a war between Great Britain alone and some other powerful European State alone, there being no allies on either side, a war in which the extent to which belligerent rights could be exercised by Great Britain would be very different from that to which she exercised them in the late war. On these assumptions the Sub-Committee have considered each of the matters dealt with in the Declaration of London in the light of the United States Naval Instructions of 1917 and of a Memorandum submitted by the United States Government to the London Conference of 1908–9 as embodying its views on the correct rules of international law relating to the various matters to be discussed at the Conference.

'8.   The United States Naval Instructions of 1917,' the Technical Sub-Committee's Report explains, 'are in this connection of particular importance. These instructions comprise rules covering practically all the matters dealt with in this Report. In the extent to which they recognise the right of the naval forces to exercise belligerent rights, they show an appreciable advance upon the standpoint adopted by the United States Government in the diplomatic notes exchanged during the war, and on many points they formulate rules on which it would be possible for the British Navy to act effectively in time of war. They thus provide a useful guide as to the view which the United States Government may be expected to maintain in any conference. Even if they were withdrawn by the United States Government, they would remain on record as the instructions which were in force for ten years during and after the war. No Government could maintain that the instructions it had issued to its own fleet and maintained in force for so long a time as ten years were contrary to international law.'

38.   Great as is the importance of these considerations in arriving at an agreement with the United States Government, it is necessary to bear in

mind that, at an International Conference, other Powers would have to be considered, and that there is a greater difference of view between continental nations and ourselves than between ourselves and the United States on this subject.

39. *Visit, Search and Detention* (paragraphs 16 to 18 of the Technical Sub-Committee's Report). – The Technical Sub-Committee draw attention to a difference between British and American practice on this matter. Before 1914 there was no established practice of diverting neutral vessels from their course and holding them in part pending a decision. During the Great War, however, owing to the impossibility of making a thorough examination of a ship's cargo in the open sea, where even boarding was often impossible or dangerous owing to the presence of submarines, this practice was adopted by the principal belligerents on both sides. The United States, when neutral, denied the validity of this extension. Their Naval Instructions of 1917 provided that the boarding officer shall first examine the ship's papers. If they furnish conclusive evidence of the innocent character of the vessel, cargo and voyage, the vessel shall be released; if they furnish probable cause for capture, she shall be seized and sent in for adjudication:

> If the papers do not furnish conclusive evidence of the innocent character of the vessel, the cargo, and voyage, or probable cause for capture, the boarding officer shall continue the examination by questioning the personnel or by searching the vessel or by examining her cargo. If such further examination furnishes satisfactory evidence of innocency, the vessel shall be released. Otherwise she shall be seized and sent in for adjudication.

The difference, then, between the two practices is this: that the British divert into port any neutral vessel which cannot establish its innocency, as, for example, by some form of navicert, whereas the American regulations provide, in the first place, for some kind of actual examination at sea, though, if the ship cannot then establish innocency, it is seized and taken into port. In the second place, under the American rule the ship is sent in for Prize Court Adjudication, whereas under the British practice the decision as to Prize Court Proceedings is not taken until after the examination in harbour.

40. The objection to the American rule is twofold. The Admiralty have a practical objection that it is impossible to examine a ship at sea with sufficient thoroughness to establish innocence or guilt, and that to attempt this in waters frequented by enemy submarines is dangerous. The second objection is the weight of responsibility which the adoption of this rule would impose upon the boarding officer. Every ship de-

tained would have to be sent in for adjudication by the Prize Court, and since, if the Prize Court held that she was sent in without sufficient justification, a claim for heavy damages might follow, the boarding officer would always have before him the fear that his action might not receive the support of his Government. On the other hand, it is material to note that under American rule the vessel has always to prove her innocency, and unless the examination furnishes this evidence she is just as surely sent into port as under the British rule.

41.   We agree generally with the conclusions of the Technical Sub-Committee on this subject, particularly in regard to the importance of not excluding the use of extraneous evidence in effecting a capture; that the difference between the two Governments is not so much one of principle as in the application of a principle; that some form of navicert system is of importance in this matter and should be explored in any informal conversations between the two Governments; and that the difference between the British and American practice is mainly represented by the increased risk of claims for damages by neutral shipowners if the Prize Court should hold that their ships had been improperly detained and sent in for adjudication.

42.   *Blockade* (paragraphs 19 to 23 of the Sub-Committee's Report). – We concur with the views of the Sub-Committee on this subject, and we note that the rules for blockade, as laid down in the United States Naval Instructions, are more satisfactory than those laid down in the Declaration of London. [The Technical Sub-Committee noted that wartime condemnation of conditional contraband was not challenged by the Americans – who did not differ in principle to British practice.]

43.   We think it right, however, to draw the attention of the Committee of Imperial Defence and the Cabinet to the fact that these rules would not enable us to carry out all the measures of economic pressure adopted during the Great War, many of which were imposed in retaliation for the enemy's illegal actions, and we are satisfied that it would be impossible to obtain the assent of an International Conference to the embodiment of these retaliatory measures as a legitimate extension of the right of blockade. One of the criticisms of the Declaration of London was that it weakened the effects of seapower by its failure to provide for the adaptation of the blockade rules to the conditions of modern naval warfare, and the same criticism might be directed against a Convention based on the Sub-Committee's proposals. In a future war many of the more drastic measures of 1914–18 could only be taken in retaliation for contravention of the laws of war by an enemy – a matter to which we return later.

44.   *Contraband* (paragraphs 24 to 28 of the Sub-Committee's Report). – We concur generally in the Report on the subject of contraband,

and we take particular note that 'it would be possible for His Majesty's Government to achieve all that is necessary at the outset of a war on the bases of the existing American classifications.' Nevertheless, we feel some doubts whether the United States Government would contemplate adhering to their own list. They might find this particularly difficult in the event of an International Conference on belligerent rights, especially if it were held in Washington. There is no doubt the nations that are consistently neutral, such as Holland, Denmark, and the smaller continental Powers and probably the South American Republics, would wish to restrict the lists of contraband, an attitude which it would not be easy for the Americans to resist. During the debate on the Cruiser Bill Senator Borah is reported to have said: 'The enlargement of the contraband list by a belligerent was obnoxious to the idea of freedom of the seas, but it had been done in the Great War'; but he proceeded to add: 'The United States had done so and would always do so again as long as the freedom of the seas question remained unsolved.' In view of the difficulty of blockade under modern conditions, except in wars with very weak States, the contraband list becomes a matter of great importance. The list in the Declaration of London was based on the 17th Century list and was completely out of date. The vast extension of engines and materials of war in modern times necessitates a reasonably extensive list if it is to be of any value whatsoever. It is very desirable that we should obtain a list not lower than that provided for in the American Instructions.

45. *Unneutral Service. Destruction of Neutral Prizes* (paragraphs 29 to 31 of the Sub-Committee's Report). – We have no observations to make on the remarks of the Sub-Committee on these questions. Agreement would appear to be not impossible.

46. *Transfer of Flag. Enemy Character Defined* (paragraphs 34 to 37 of the Sub-Committee's Report). – We agree generally with the recommendations of the Technical Sub-Committee in regard to transfer of an enemy vessel to a neutral flag, whether effected before or after the outbreak of hostilities.

In regard to the question of enemy character, it is laid down in the Declaration of London that, subject to the provisions respecting transfer to another flag, the neutral or enemy character of a vessel is determined by the flag which she is entitled to fly. Great Britain did not observe any such rule in its entirety in the late War, and reverted to the old English rule that the enemy flag is conclusive against the vessel, but the neutral flag is not conclusive against the captor. The Americans in their Instructions have adopted the rule of the Declaration of London, and a divergence with the United States over this question is not impossible. The difficulty is stated by the Technical Sub-Committee in the following terms:

> The practical importance of this question is whether it would enable any appreciable number of vessels to escape capture by the British naval forces where, without there having been any change of flag during the war, the vessels belong to subsidiary companies organised in neutral States by a corporation or individual in the enemy State.

In order to assist us in determining whether this question was one on which it was vital for His Majesty's Government to insist on the maintenance of the rule followed during the War, we obtained a Joint Report from the Admiralty and Board of Trade. They are unable to say to what extent maritime countries at the present time run ships under the flag of another State in which they have subsidiary trading or shipping companies, but they report that there is an increasing tendency in this direction. They consider that the Covenant of the League of Nations and the Kellogg Pact have increased the delay likely to occur between the first indications of trouble and the outbreak of hostilities, and that such increased delay makes the likelihood of a change of flag greater, and that it would not always be possible to deal with such changes under Article 55 of the Declaration of London if it were in force. For these reasons they think that the rule should be that the character of the vessel[1] should depend upon the character of the controlling interest, as in the case of cargoes. They cannot tell us how much we should lose without this rule, because we have no real idea how much belonging to one country is invested in ships of another. They believe, however, that the rule is likely to be more important in the future than at present or in the past, and that, although there may not be a great amount of money on the whole invested in non-national ships, nevertheless, we should abide by the principle, though it is possibly not a vital one in any discussions. Sir Charles Madden and Sir Charles Hipwood sum up by stating that in any discussion we should use this question of enemy character as a bargaining factor. We accept these views.

47. *Evidence and Procedure in the Prize Courts (Admissibility of Extraneous Evidence)* (paragraphs 38 to 44 and paragraph 57 of the Sub-Committee's Report). – We concur in the Report of the Sub-Committee on this subject, and we draw special attention to the following paragraphs referring to the admissibility of extraneous evidence:

---

[1]*I.e.*, a vessel entitled to fly the neutral flag.

'43. This question of the admissibility of extraneous evidence is one of the few points upon which Great Britain cannot give way, and if no basis of accord can be found with the United States, the question must be considered whether it is essential that the point should be covered in any agreement which is come to on the subject of belligerent rights, either in the form of a preliminary agreement with the United States or in a convention emerging from a conference. There seems a fair chance that if the British prize rules provided for the admissibility of extraneous evidence, and the right to use such evidence were disputed by a neutral Power and submitted as the result to international arbitration, His Majesty's Government would succeed in demonstrating that, under modern conditions, the refusal to admit extraneous evidence in determining the validity of the seizure was tantamount to denying the belligerent right of capture. The evidence establishing the destination would never, under modern conditions, accompany the ship or cargo. On the other hand, it is impossible to say that an international tribunal, whose bias might be in favour of the neutral claimants, would not decide that modern conditions did not justify any enlargement of the old belligerent right of capture, and that the rules, as laid down in Napoleonic times, admitted capture only where proof of destination accompanied the shipment.

44. In view of the above, we recommend that this is a point which must be discussed with the United States Government, and every effort made to secure their acceptance of the view of the admissibility of extraneous evidence. If the effort fails, His Majesty's Government must then re-examine the situation and consider whether it is safe to allow an agreement to be concluded without mention of the question.'

We incline to the view that the Americans would find it difficult to exclude extraneous evidence, even under their own Instructions, and we think that a naval officer requiring proof of innocence could hardly be prevented from using extraneous evidence. [Extraneous evidence included statistical evidence of changes to neutral traffic patterns.]

48. *Convoy* (paragraphs 45 to 50 of the Sub-Committee's Report). – The Technical Sub-Committee draw attention to the difficulties in regard to the right of convoy. The principle that neutral vessels under convoy of vessels of war are exempt from search was temporarily admitted by Great Britain in the unratified Declaration of London and by the United States Naval Instructions of 1917, subject to the safeguards provided by the Declaration of London; that is to say, the

Commander of the neutral convoy is bound to give the Commander of a belligerent warship all particulars as to the character of the vessels and cargoes which could be obtained by search; if the belligerent suspects that the confidence of the Commander of the convoy has been abused, he communicates his suspicions, and it is then for the Commander of the convoy, and for him alone, to investigate the matter, though he is bound to communicate a copy of his report to the Captain of the belligerent warship, and, if guilt is proved, to withdraw the protection of the convoy.

49.   In the light of our experience in the Great War this procedure is open to strong objections. With the right to convoy, the neutral Governments would be besieged by exporters wishing to take part in a lucrative business, and the neutral Government would be likely to accept the assurance of the exporters regarding the honesty of the consignees rather than the evidence of one of the belligerents. There are many dodges by which the exporters might get goods through to the enemy country which it would be difficult for their Governments to discover. Evidence against the goods carried would be very difficult to obtain prior to their arrival at their destination. During the late War we often had the barest suspicions about a cargo, and it was not until the Prize Court proceedings had developed that we were able to prove, by means of the evidence which had by then been collected after seizure, or which became available in the course of the proceedings themselves, that the goods were destined for the enemy State. Another objection is that neutrals might not accept our list of contraband and their convoys might cover goods which we had declared to be contraband.

50.   We feel that to trust to the responsibility of the Commander of the neutral warship would be most uncertain. It is true that in fact we could not stop a convoy escorted by an American warship except at the risk of going to war. Nevertheless the actual admission of the right of a neutral warship to escort a convoy would be very formidable. It would be tantamount to an invitation to all neutral States to break the blockade. To give a free hand to every State of whatever size or respectability to escort convoys would involve such overwhelming possible consequences that we hesitate to believe that American negotiators would face it. We doubt, therefore, whether the American rule would survive discussion.

51.   *Examination of Mails* (paragraphs 52 to 55 of the Sub-Committee's Report). – We concur with the general conclusions of the Sub-Committee on this question. The examination of mails, within such limits as are possible, is essential to Great Britain, because it is through such an examination that the evidence for Prize Courts is obtained, but we accept the opinion of the Sub-Committee that the

point is not one on which it should be impossible to come to agreement with the United States.

52.   *Retaliation* (paragraph 56 of the Sub-Committee's Report). – In discussing blockade (paragraphs 42 and 43) we have already drawn attention to the importance of the right of retaliation. Without it we cannot exploit the advantages of sea-power to the full against an enemy which, as in the late War, has violated the laws of war and placed us at a disadvantage. The Technical Sub-Committee point out that the only means by which this can be accomplished is to introduce a provision which will render the agreement inapplicable in case the rules of war are not observed by the other side.

53.   *Armed Merchantmen.* – We understand that no substantial difference exists between the Americans and ourselves on this question.

Remarks

54.   On the whole, the result of the above comparison indicates that the difference between the point of view of the Americans and ourselves on the questions dealt with in the Declaration of London, though not unimportant, may be less than we had anticipated at the outset of our Inquiry: It must be remembered, however, that this comparison is based on the assumption that the United States Government will adopt the same general standpoint as they have done in the past. If they should adopt the so-called Freedom of the Seas, or some low basis of belligerent rights (the possibility of which has already been discussed in paragraph 29) there would be no basis of agreement. In that event, however, the Americans must repudiate their Naval Instructions of 1917, following on the whole of their previous practice as belligerents. They would, we presume, seek to justify this by pointing out that these Instructions were drawn up at the time of their entry into the War; that the nations associated with them had already irretrievably compromised the situation by their blockade measures, and that they themselves had really no alternative but to co-operate – a course to which they were reconciled by the fact that they had only entered the War owing to the flagrant breaches by the enemy of the laws of war; that now the matter had to be considered not in an atmosphere of retaliation but of justice. Their case would certainly not appear to be a strong one, but the possibility of its being advanced is by no means out of the question.

55.   Apart from the considerations discussed above, there are, as the Technical Sub-Committee state, a certain number of matters affecting the relations between belligerents and neutrals which lie outside the Declaration of London. From our point of view, the narrower the scope of any conference or conversations the better will our interest be served,

and therefore there is no reason why our representatives should take the initiative in bringing up these subjects for discussion. Nevertheless, it is by no means unlikely that the Americans themselves, or, at a Conference, other Powers, might raise some of them, and our representatives ought to be aware of the views of His Majesty's Government with regard to each of them. Among them we may mention the right of visit, search and detention by submarines and aircraft; visit, search and detention of Government-owned vessels; submarine mines; belligerent warships in neutral ports; *matériel* and personnel of a belligerent State salvaged or rescued at sea; conversion of merchant ships on the high seas or in neutral ports; the rule of the War of 1756; limits of the right and angary; radio-telegraphy; war zones; test of enemy character of goods. We have not yet investigated in detail any of these matters, nor does the above list purport to be exhaustive. If desired, we are prepared to examine them and to deal with them in a third Report so that the Cabinet may have before them all aspects of the question. Our attention has also been drawn to such matters as the rationing of neutral nations, the navicert system and bunker control, as being liable to cause difficulties with neutrals in time of war; but since, in our view, these questions do not fall within the domain of international law, it would be impossible for any Conference to deal with them which had for its object the revision, or even the codification, of international law. Nor have we attempted to deal with matters which exclusively affect the relations of belligerents *inter se*, since these appear to be outside the scope of our terms of reference. We refer, for example, to such topics as days of grace, sinking of enemy merchant ships, and the use of neutral flags by belligerent warships and merchant ships.

56.   Finally, when we consider the possibilities of agreement, we cannot exclude from view a subject that has only lately been raised, but which appears in the Senate's resolution quoted below in paragraph 58, namely *the immunity from capture of private property at sea.* We cannot overload this long Report with a full dissertation on this question. The proposal was made at The Hague Conference of 1907, but although it obtained a majority of votes, it was not adopted. The fallacies underlying this proposal were exposed at the time by the late Admiral Mahan and Sir Julian Corbett in articles that have since been reproduced in the former's volume on 'Some Neglected Aspects of War.'

Part IV – Conclusions and Recommendations

57.   Having dealt in Part II with the larger question of policy and in Part III with the attitude of the United States, in comparison with our own, towards Belligerent Rights both as regards the principles and their

application, we are now in a position to summarise our conclusions and recommendations on the question of what should be our attitude towards an International Conference or conversations or negotiations with the United States Government.

58.   Throughout our inquiry we have had to consider whether a Conference would be to our advantage or not. As time went on, the probability that the Americans would take the initiative in summoning a Conference increased. During the discussions in the American Senate on the Cruiser programme, as Sir Esme Howard had warned us was likely to be the case, a strong opinion was developing in favour of the adoption of a resolution asking the President of the United States of America to summon an International Conference for the purpose of a 'restatement and codification of the rules of law governing the conduct of belligerents and neutral in war at sea.' At the last moment, however, the Senate changed its plans and the resolution was converted into an amendment to the Naval Construction Bill and assumed the following form:

> First, that Congress favours a Treaty or Treaties with all principal maritime nations regulating the conduct of belligerents and neutrals in war at sea, including the inviolability of private property thereon. Second, that such Treaties be negotiated, if practically possible, prior to the meeting of the Conference on Limitation of Armaments in 1931.

This amendment, which was proposed by Senator Reed of Missouri, was passed with the Bill that has now become law. The amendment, however, merely expresses the view of Congress that Treaties on this subject should be negotiated, 'if practically possible,' and is not mandatory upon the President, who remains free to act upon this advice or not, as he thinks fit.

59.   The principal argument in favour of a Conference on this subject is that if a settlement could be arranged, not only should we dispose of a difficulty that is claimed to be at the root of both the Cruiser problem and the Arbitration Treaty (which, apart from belligerent rights, are the only serious outstanding points between the United States of America and ourselves), but we should also secure ourselves against the risk of interference in a future war. To obtain this latter result it has been urged that it would be worth while for us to make considerable concessions. Suppose, for example, that we could secure by agreement 75 per cent. of the belligerent rights we exercised in the Great War, it would be well worth while to abandon 25 per cent. of our claims. The alternative of going without a settlement and leaving the problem to be settled when

the emergency arose might be to place ourselves in the dilemma of having to abandon the whole or risk bringing the United States of America into the war against us.

60. We found, however, that strong reasons could be urged against a Conference. The late Lord Cave's Committee, which considered the whole question very carefully just after the War, reached a definite conclusion that the discussion of questions relating to maritime belligerent rights should, if possible, be postponed, and that was the trend of opinion at the Imperial War Cabinet between the armistice and the Peace Conference. At the present time the reasons against a Conference may be summarised as follows:

(1) The laws of war as they exist at present are only in a small measure the result of definite international treaties. The great body of international law in this sphere is merely the expression of the fact that certain principles, and in a less degree particular applications of them, have in course of time come to be generally accepted. To reduce to the rigidity of a detailed code this necessarily elastic and developing system is to court certain failure. It is as impossible to-day to foresee the conditions and developments of the future as it would have been at the close of the Napoleonic wars to forecast the weapons, methods and conditions of the Great War. A code made in such ignorance of the conditions in which it will be invoked is certain to be inapplicable and to become a dead letter.

(2) It is in the interest of the Empire that belligerent rights should be kept as high as possible.

(3) The present trend of opinion in the United States is favourable to drastic limitation of the rights of a belligerent to intercept private property at sea, and in such a conference this tendency would be irresistibly strengthened by the support of the Scandinavian and other Powers, including, perhaps, Italy. In these conditions and in the present circumstances it is very doubtful whether the United States would take their own naval instructions as a basis for codification.

(4) No agreement for codification could in any case be reached without concessions being made by both sides from extremes of high and low belligerent rights, and a compromise of this kind, even if reached by the two Governments, is likely to be repudiated either by Congress or Parliament or both.

(5) There is a serious risk that any agreement reached with the United States in the present state of public opinion in that country would have the effect of curtailing the field of action open to mem-

bers of the League under Article 16, or Great Britain under the Locarno Treaty and other Treaty obligations.

(6)   There is at present a movement in the United States towards a recognition of the corporate responsibility of nations for the imposition of sanctions against a violation of the Kellogg Pact; an international agreement on maritime law, by crystallising the old conception of belligerency or neutrality, would have the effect of arresting the growth of this new conception of corporate national responsibility not only in the United States itself, but throughout the world.

61.   The proposal set forth in the Resolution passed in the United States Senate (paragraph 58) for separate Treaties with the principal maritime nations appears to us to offer no advantages, since it could not achieve codification, while it would be open to all the objections of disagreement.

62.   At the moment when our first Report on Arbitration Treaties was being compiled, information was received from Sir Esme Howard to the effect that Mr Hoover, the President-Elect, had intimated to Senator Borah (Chairman of the Senate Committee on Foreign Relations) that he intended to take up the question of codifying maritime law at an early date and that he was personally anxious to get a settlement. After consulting the sub-Committee, Sir Austen Chamberlain replied by instructing Sir Esme Howard to communicate confidentially to Mr Hoover, either directly or through the State Department, the reasons for which His Majesty's Government deprecated the issue of invitations to a Conference at an early date, and, above all, without their having been given an opportunity of discussing the matter fully and confidentially with the United States Government before a decision is taken.

63.   Having thus taken steps to deter the United States Government from undue precipitation, we had to consider, in the light of the recent Senate Resolution and the present agitation in the United States, the question how can a Conference be avoided?

64.   In the first instance, by explaining to Mr Hoover the serious risks of disagreement and by pointing out that at any such conference the question of the distinction between public and private wars is bound to come up and with it a perfectly logical demand that the United States should at least remain passive in face of a rigorous application of economic sanctions against an acknowledged violator of the Kellogg Pact. The following point could, indeed, be put to the United States Government with some force:

What is presumably suggested by those who favour a conference is the formulation of a code of general application governing belligerent and neutral rights at sea; in other words, a code which is to be applicable in all future wars. This has been the object of all past attempts to codify this branch of international law, and it is necessarily based on the theory, which will be found in all the text books, that whatever the rights and wrongs of the war and the merits and demerits of the belligerents, the rights of belligerents and neutrals are unaffected thereby. This is, in fact, the 19th century doctrine of neutrality, and it is really based on the view which has prevailed until recently that any State is entitled to go to war in support of its national policy if it thinks fit to do so. But how can the nation which has produced the Kellogg Pact contend that this is the state of affairs to-day? The object of the Kellogg Pact is to abolish the legitimacy of war as an instrument of national policy, and to ensure that, if war occurs at all, the country which goes to war in support of its national policy will be universally regarded as having done something which is wrong and as having violated a solemn international obligation. Is it, therefore, conceivable that the United States should seriously propose that, in the event of war breaking out in consequence of a violation by one Power of the Kellogg Pact, that Power should be entitled to exercise the rights of belligerents, and that States which may desire to trade with it should be entitled to claim the rights which were conceded to neutrals, under the old state of affairs? But if a code of general application is adopted this is exactly what would happen, and such a state of affairs is surely more likely to lead to trouble between the 'innocent party' to the war and neutrals than anything else.

These are possibilities and considerations which Mr Hoover's Administration will be unable to brush aside or ignore.

65.   Nevertheless, the Foreign Office believe that something more will be necessary to avoid the summoning of a Conference. It is their considered opinion that, apart from representations in the above sense, the only means by which we can hope to avoid a conference in present circumstances are (1) the early conclusion of an arbitration treaty containing no reservations in regard to belligerent rights (as recommended by the majority in our first Report dealing with the draft Arbitration Treaty with the United States); and (2) the early conclusion of an Anglo-American agreement, or, if that be impossible, a *modus vivendi* with regard to the limitation of naval armament.

The Admiralty, however, hold that the conclusion of an Arbitration Treaty as in (1) would endanger in war and, perhaps in the long run, destroy our belligerent rights, being convinced that a body constituted like the Permanent Court of International Justice – which, moreover, in war, would contain many biassed neutrals – would give an adverse decision on rights exercised by the Allies in the Great War and essential in a future important war.

We forbear to discuss this question, which has already been fully dealt with in our first Report on the renewal of Arbitration Treaties, and on which we have been unable to reach agreement.

66.   Assuming, however, that for one reason or another the summoning of an International Conference on this subject or the negotiation of separate treaties in accordance with the Senate's resolution quoted in paragraph 58, which might have substantially the same effect, should prove to be inevitable, what will be the best procedure?

67.   Firstly, an endeavour should be made to enter into private and confidential discussions with the United States Government in the hope of persuading them to conclude a separate treaty in the first instance with this country on the basis of their existing naval instructions.

68.   Should this prove impossible, an attempt should be made to secure the limitation of the Conference to the five Great Naval Powers for the reason that in a conference composed in this manner we should hope to gain a certain amount of support to our policy of high belligerent rights, and at any rate the number of Powers arrayed against us would be smaller than at a Conference at which the lesser States were also represented.

In any event, an endeavour should be made to enter into private and confidential conversations with the United States Government, in the hope of harmonising beforehand, as far as possible, the views of the two Governments. In any case also, it should be made quite clear to the United States Government that this country will refuse to enter upon any negotiations or conferences having for their object a revision as opposed to a recodification of maritime law. By 'codification' is meant the codification of the alleged existing rules of maritime law and the bringing of the recognised principles of international law, as shown in the customary law, up to date and into harmony, so that the ideas emerging from the principles may be formulated in articles which have some relation to modern conditions and modern war practices.

Beyond this point it is difficult to define in advance what will be the best procedure, since this must necessarily depend on the course of subsequent events and, in particular, on the attitude assumed by the United States Government.

69.   But whether it is ultimately found possible to avoid a Conference or not, it is essential that on a matter of such importance as belligerent rights we should reach complete agreement with the Dominions as to

the policy to be pursued, either by means of correspondence or by discussion at an Imperial Conference. For reasons which we indicate in paragraph 23 above, we do not anticipate that there will be any insuperable difficulty in bringing into complete agreement, which is essential, the views of the various parts of the Empire on this issue. . . .

* * *

61. Maurice Hankey, Secretary to the Cabinet and the Committee of Imperial Defence, to Ramsay Macdonald

SECRET

[CAB 21/352/212–23]   11 October 1929

Dear Prime Minister,

You will have received a Private and Personal telegram from me about the Belligerent Rights question, and as we shall no doubt be much concerned in this matter in the not distant future I should like to expand it a little in a letter which you can read on your way home before you are once more immersed in the overwhelming cares of State.

I have a little reproached myself for not speaking to you on this subject before you left. It is true that at the beginning of your conversations with General Dawes I did send to you at Lossiemouth the CID Committee's Reports and warned you that it was a most prickly subject. The telegrams exchanged towards the end of June with Howard seem to make it clear beyond doubt that this question would not be raised in the present series of conversations. One of the first questions I enquired about on returning from the Hague was as to whether it was likely to come up, and I was told there was nothing new on the subject. I was therefore reluctant, when you were so tremendously busy and I was seeing you so little, to drag in what appeared a problem of the past, and conceivably of the future, but not of the present. However, I did coach Tom Jones a little about it, and gave him the two Reports of the CID Committee to take with him. Everyone here felt the greatest sympathy with you in having these difficult questions thrust upon you unexpectedly and certainly without sufficient warning. From this end it really looked like sharp practice on Hoover's part.

I said in my telegram that in my 21 years at the Committee of Imperial Defence I have found this to be the most controversial question of all. Perhaps I may expand this a little.

I got into close grips with the subject in 1909, quite soon after I joined. My beloved Chief, Sir Charles Ottley, had been at the Second Hague Conference and was one of the negotiators of the Declaration of London. He, and, to the best of my knowledge, every single person who was concerned either in drawing up the Declaration or in trying to put it through Parliament lived to regret that instrument. On this question alone I always differed strongly from Ottley, as I knew the Declaration must break down in time of war. I still have the very prophetic Memoranda I wrote. Ottley, though he disagreed with them, nevertheless sent them to the Admiralty. I was myself told by the heads of the Admiralty that they agreed with every word I wrote, but it really did not matter much, because if war ever came the thing would break down. Their prophecy, like my own, turned out to be correct, but to my mind it was a horribly cynical thing to enter into a solemn international engagement knowing that it could not stand the only test for which it was devised – that of war. This is the touchstone by which all such Agreements must be judged. They must be practicable under war conditions, when intense national feeling is aroused. Although, owing to the Lords' rejection, the Declaration was never ratified, it committed us morally and embarrassed us greatly in the early part of the war.

My next contact with the question was in 1915, when House put forward a proposal very similar to Hoover's, but more advantageous to us than the latter. House wanted to get an arrangement whereby the Germans should give up using submarines against merchant ships if we would give up the *food* blockade. The complete story, which I pieced together a couple of years ago from all the different sources, is rather entertaining, but too long to repeat here. It is sufficient to say that the Cabinet rejected the proposal in February, 1915; that House nevertheless continued to press it; that Grey, in spite of the Cabinet's decision and without again consulting the Cabinet, continued to encourage House and even allowed him to make the suggestion, through Ambassador Gerard, that the Germans should themselves propose it; that House carried out an intensive propaganda in this country in favour of it, but that the Germans themselves turned it down. After the Coalition Cabinet was formed in May, 1915, Grey's eyes went, and he had to go away for a month. Crewe, who was acting for him, put up to the Cabinet in June practically the same proposal, except that in return for our giving up the food blockade he suggested Germany should be asked to give up mine-laying in the open sea, poison gas, and one or two other things. The arguments for it were almost exactly the arguments that I imagine are used by Hoover today. Many of them are dealt with in the CID Committee's Report, but by no means all. I have not time or space to repeat them here, but I shall be making a big summary of the whole thing before your return. So far as the War was concerned, however, the following argument, in one of the Memoranda circulated to the Cabinet, was, I think, decisive:

> Whether the starvation of Germany is a practicable policy or not, the curtailment of her food supplies must be a cause of weakness and, above all, of anxiety, to the Central Powers. It is therefore an essential element in our system of blockade. The object of our blockade is psychological as well as material. It aims at inflicting on the enemy the maximum of inconvenience, dislocation of trade and finance, waste of effort, depression and despair. The process may be slow, but its effects are cumulative and certain. When the psychological moment of military success arrives and the enemy population is no longer sustained by victory and hope, the blockade may well prove the decisive factor. To withdraw foodstuffs from the scope of the blockade would be to blunt the edge of this important weapon.

The latter forecast of how the blockade would work proved absolutely correct. In Germany today the explanation of their downfall is, 'We were never beaten, but we had not enough to eat.' The German books show that it was not the army that was beaten, nor man-power that was lacking, but [that] the home front was broken by the blockade, and the men who had been combed out from the factories would fight no more. Some time ago I compiled extracts from some of the German books to prove this, but I have since accumulated much additional evidence on the subject.

The question came up again in the Armistice discussion, when there was a terrible scene between House and Lloyd George, which is described, but not done justice to, in House's book. What House did not know was that Lloyd George had sent Eric Geddes to Washington and just before the meeting he had received a telegram showing that the President [Woodrow Wilson] did not really know what he meant by 'Freedom of the Seas' and was not very keen about it. Consequently Lloyd George was in a position to 'call House's bluff', and he and Clemenceau reduced House to pulp, as I well remember. Wilson, on coming to Europe, agreed, as Geddes had hinted he would, not to take the question up at the Peace Conference, and Lloyd George always refused to have the question brought up internationally (e.g., at the Washington Conference, where Balfour avoided it most adroitly) because as he knew it to be so bitterly controversial.

Towards the end of 1927, however, as the result of correspondence between Howard and Tyrrell (in which, needless to say, House's intervention is once more apparent) the subject was forced up again, (un-necessarily, as I thought, if the question had been properly handled in America) and there was a prolonged Inquiry which resulted in the two Reports you have seen. At the outset of the Inquiry opinion was by no means unanimous and there was a good deal of rather bitter dissension but eventually whole-hearted agreement was reached, with one absten-tion. One saw, however, once more, what one had seen in all these controversies – what bitter feelings this subject arouses.

Please note that since 1915 House is to be found in the background every time the question is raised, and nearly always with this food proposal thrust forward. It is an obsession with him. I have been specu-lating whether he is in some way behind Hoover's proposal. There is no such clever propagandist as House.

I have had every detail documented of all these affairs and could substantiate the statements I have made in regard to every one of them with a wealth of detail.

I also dared to say in my telegram to you that in my opinion the inclusion of Hoover's announcement would greatly weaken the na-tional front by which you are supported on the Disarmament question. Here I speak from absolute knowledge. The attitude of the Unionists is revealed in the CID Report which it was my duty to pass on to you. A year ago Lloyd George consulted me about a book he was talking of writing on Episodes of the War, and among others he mentioned this question of Freedom of the Seas, which at that time was being dis-cussed in the Press. He spoke in no unmeasured terms as to his conviction that his attitude at the Armistice Conference and in keeping this subject off the Agenda of the Peace Conference had been dead right, that the situation had not really changed today, as some claimed, and that it was a vital matter on national grounds.

If a controversy arose, it would not be short or sudden, but probably rather slow in developing. There would be a much better-instructed criticism than that levelled against the Declaration of London, which was singularly feeble to those who knew the truth. There are numbers of people about with a vast war experience of this question, not only Naval Officers, but Judges and lawyers who were concerned in Prize Court cases, business men, Professors, and others, who volunteered for service in such institutions as the War Trade Intelligence Department, and Trade Licences Department, the Blockade Department, and so forth. There are people who would at once start to organise all this instructed opinion against concessions. It is interesting to know that Thomas Gibson Bowles' son has written a book on the subject, but far abler people than he would take the lead.

I think, then, that I was not exaggerating in what I said in the telegram. I confess that I dread nothing so much as the public reopening of this question *if* it means concessions on our part; and, especially after the revelation of Hoover's foolish plan, I doubt if we can reach agreement without considerable concessions. I do not see how, in a bitter controversy, we could expect to escape from home truths and even cruel things being said about the Americans, and I cannot conceive that Anglo-American relations could benefit from such a controversy. People here would point to the breakdown within six months of the outbreak of war of all the Conventions of The Hague, the Declaration of Paris and London, etc., with regard to Belligerent Rights. They would say that in war the new arrangement must break down, that public opinion would never allow us to maintain it, and so forth. That would be repeated in America. Mr Britton has already said this in order to cast doubt on our *bona fides*. Of course if we can reach agreement *without* serious concession it would be all right, but either a failure to agree or big concessions on our part would be disastrous.

I have given you this hasty sketch in order to show how very troublesome the question has been to your predecessors. Whenever the subject has been opened its tendency has been to create either dissension in the Cabinet, or in Government Departments, or in Parliament, or public outcry, or international ill-will, and sometimes several of these evils at once.

Some people have been wondering whether, if we can get the Naval Agreement through all its phases – the Five-Power Conference, the Geneva Disarmament Conference – it would not be possible to avoid tackling this question, with all its dangerous possibilities of embitterment of relations. Blockade, in its grand lines, is only required in unlimited wars, such as the Napoleonic Wars and the Great War. From 1815 to 1914 it never became a decisive factor except in the American Civil War. Whatever happens, it is unlikely to be required again for a long time to come. So much is being done to banish wars, and especially these great wars, that it seems rather absurd to worry ourselves with so remote a problem. The trouble is that you simply cannot discuss it without thinking out every detail of a war, and I cannot believe that this intensive study of war – particularly if it gets into the phase of public controversy – can conceivably contribute to that mind towards peace which I understand to be the basis of your policy. No-one of importance has ever taken this line publicly here, though I have seen it mentioned in American publications. I believe that there is an immense opportunity to put the case on those lines in both countries, but time will be required for it to sink home.

I end by wishing you a very pleasant voyage. You have had a wonderful success.

Yours very sincerely, M.P.A. Hankey.

* * *

62.   The Food Factor in Blockade[1]

Memorandum by the Secretary to the Committee of Imperial Defence. Committee of Imperial Defence Sub-Committee on Belligerent Rights at Sea

[CAB 21/328]

2 Whitehall Gardens, S.W.1
23 December 1929

INTRODUCTORY

In the course of his Armistice Day address, President Hoover repeated in public the aspiration he had already expressed in his private conversations with the Prime Minister, that food ships should be declared free from any interference in time of war. His proposal is that all vessels laden solely with food supplies should be on the same footing as hospital ships, thus removing the starvation of women and children from the weapons of war and reducing the necessity of naval arms for the protection of avenues of food supplies.

2.   The President's proposal is, of course, intimately bound up with the general question of maritime belligerent rights, which was the subject of a Report by a Sub-Committee of the Committee of Imperial Defence (C.I.D. Paper No. 944-B) to the late Government, and which has been circulated to the present Cabinet. Since then, however, the Government have taken a long step towards the formulation of a policy in regard to Belligerent Rights by the issue of the White Paper on the subject of the Optional Clause (Cmd. 3452/1929). In that document His Majesty's Government in the United Kingdom have made clear that their policy is based on a determination to fulfil their obligations under the Covenant of the League of Nations and the Kellogg Pact. The former includes, in Article 16, an obligation to subject any Member of the League which resorts to war in disregard of its Covenants under Articles 12, 13 or 15 to the severance of all trade or financial relations,

---

[1]Following this report Hankey wrote to Henderson at the FO, 21 October 1930, and was answered 28 Oct. These are important letters relative to the question of a conference with the US on belligerent rights.

the prohibition of all intercourse between their nationals and the nationals of the Covenant-breaking State, and the prevention of all financial, commercial or personal intercourse between the nationals of the Covenant-breaking State and of any other State, whether a member of the League or not.

3. President Hoover's proposal, then, has to be considered primarily in the light of our commitments under Article 16 of the Covenant of the League. It becomes a League question rather than a purely British question, and the issue can be presented in the following form: 'Would the pressure exercisable by the League of Nations be seriously impaired or not by the adoption of Mr Hoover's suggestion?'

PART I – COLONEL HOUSE'S PROPOSAL IN 1915

4.[1] The proposal is no new one. It closely resembles suggestions put forward by Colonel House in 1915, which were rejected twice by the British Cabinet and once by the German Government. In February 1915 President Wilson, following hints from Ambassador Bernstorff, made a proposal to the British Government that if the British food blockade could be raised the German submarine campaign would be abandoned. Colonel House, who arrived in England about this time, supported the proposal actively. Sir Edward Grey gave him personal encouragement, but made clear that the proposal was not acceptable to public opinion in England. On the 15th March, according to Colonel House's Memoirs, the Cabinet refused the proposal, and there is evidence to support this, although in those days Cabinet decisions were not recorded.

5.[2] In spite of the Cabinet's adverse decision, Colonel House did not abandon his project, and embarked on an intensive campaign of propaganda on this subject, both in this country (where it fell very flat) and in Germany. In May 1915, when the submarine situation was more serious, he again discussed the matter with the Foreign Secretary. Notwithstanding the Cabinet's rejection of the proposal two months before, Sir Edward Grey again gave House's proposal a sympathetic reception, and actually allowed him to telegraph on his own responsibility to Mr Gerard, in Berlin, asking the Ambassador if he could not induce the German Government to propose that, if England would permit foodstuffs in the future to go to neutral ports without question, Germany should discontinue her submarine warfare on merchant ships and also the use of poisonous gases. The German Government, however, refused to make the proposal.

---

[1]*This paragraph is based primarily on Colonel House's Memoirs.
[2]*This paragraph is based primarily on Colonel House's Memoirs.

The Liberal Government at this time was in process of dissolution, and Sir Edward Grey made it clear that he could not commit the Cabinet. It is practically certain that he did not consult the Admiralty or the Prime Minister (Mr Asquith), who were always opposed to concessions on this point.

6.   In May 1915 the first Coalition Cabinet was formed, and Colonel House, believing the atmosphere unfavourable for pushing his favourite theory, sailed on the 5th June for the United States. Sir Edward Grey had to take a long rest, and Lord Crewe acted for him at the Foreign Office. The diplomatic difficulties resulting from our blockade policy, however, were increasing, and during June Lord Crewe circulated to the Cabinet a Memorandum prepared in the Foreign Office containing a proposal somewhat similar to Colonel Houses's, namely, that we should cease to prohibit the import of food-stuffs to Germany through neutral ports, and fall back, so far as food-stuffs were concerned, on the ordinary rules for conditional contraband, in return for abandonment by Germany of the submarine campaign against merchant ships, of the use of poison gas, of the poisoning of water supplies, the spreading of disease by scientific means, and the abolition of minelaying. This proposal was rejected by the first Coalition Cabinet, just as Colonel House's proposal had been by their predecessors in March.

7.   From Memoranda in the archives of the Committee of Imperial Defence, the reasons which influenced the two successive Cabinets may be summarised as follows: There were two methods in operation for winning the War, namely, military pressure and economic pressure. Germany possessed the advantage as regards military pressure, as she had long been preparing for war. The Allies had the advantage as regards economic pressure because they exercised command of the sea. Germany had won many victories on land, and had only sustained one serious reverse – the Marne. She showed no sign of military weakness, but, from an economic point of view, she was already in difficulties. The Central Powers had already been driven to the rationing of food. In these circumstances the Allies could not afford to weaken the only obvious advantage they possessed. The War had already become a struggle not merely between armies, but between nations. It was the enemy's boast that he had mobilised his nation on a scale unprecedented in the history of war. The men of military age were being absorbed into the fighting line, and the remainder of the population, female as well as male, were being organised with the object of maintaining his armies at the utmost possible efficiency. To relax the blockade in respect of food would have increased the store of food from which the enemy nation, both military and civil, was fed, and would also have

enabled the enemy to divert to the army considerable resources that were devoted to agriculture. It was never claimed that the Central Powers would be brought to terms by starvation alone, but it was held that in combination with military success it might become a decisive factor. The situation is explained in a nutshell in the following extract from a Memorandum on Lord Crewe's proposal which was submitted to Mr Asquith and communicated by him to the Cabinet:

> 'In short, it is only by the cumulative effect of every means of pressure at our disposal that we can hope for success, and in view of the moderate degree of success which has attended our military pressure, we cannot afford to forgo any of these means. It is not only that we deprive ourselves of the particular means, but we diminish the effect of all the others.'

The following passage from a second Memorandum submitted to the Prime Minister about the same period shows how the blockade policy was expected to work out:

> 'Whether the starvation of Germany is a practicable policy or not, the curtailment of her food supplies must be a cause of weakness and, above all, of anxiety, to the Central Powers. It is therefore an essential element in our system of blockade. The object of our blockade is psychological as well as material. It aims at inflicting on the enemy the maximum of inconvenience, dislocation of trade and finance, waste of effort, depression and despair. The process may be slow, but its effects are cumulative and certain. *When the psychological moment of military success arrives and the enemy population is no longer sustained by victory and hope, the blockade may well prove the decisive factor.*[1] To withdraw food-stuffs from the scope of the blockade would be to blunt the edge of this important weapon.'

8.   The truth of latter forecast was completely borne out by the results of the War. In Germany to-day a common explanation of their downfall is: 'We were never beaten, but we had not enough to eat.[2] This is an exaggeration. Their armies *were* beaten, though not routed, in the field, and when this occurred (as forecast in the extract quoted above) the full

---

[1]*The italics are not in the original.

[2]*'The *Entente* has defeated us by means of the British ships of the line, which made the starvation blockade possible and whose prestige yoked to England's chariot all the peoples of the world. The economic war had become the main fight, while the military front, in spite of the tremendous forces which were necessarily employed in the defensive fighting, was now the secondary theatre.' (*Admiral von Tirpitz's Memoirs*, Chapter 18.)

effect of the blockade was realised and the home front broke. There was still available considerable man-power, but the men combed out from the factories, &c., could no longer be relied on to fight. And many of those who returned to the front from leave, with first-hand knowledge of what their families were suffering, even though they had hitherto been fighting well, could not stand up against the combined effect of adversity in the field, short rations, and knowledge of the hardships that their families were enduring. There is abundant evidence in the German writers that the fighting power of the soldiers was affected by shortage of food.[1] And so the German resistance came to an end far sooner than the military necessities of the case compelled.

9.   Apart from the effects of food shortage on the will to win of the German nation and on the fighting power of the troops, the strategy of the Central Powers in 1918 was affected profoundly by the food situation. For example, writing of Autumn 1917, Ludendorff says:

> 'Only by offensive action in this war which had been forced upon us, and by expanding to the East and West, had we been able to exist; we should certainly have lost had we remained within our own frontiers.' (*Ludendorff, 'My War Memories, 1914–1918,'* p. 517.)

Later on the shortage of food compelled the Germans to penetrate further and further into Russia, and, for the collection of food, considerable forces had to [be] kept there, which otherwise would have been available to reinforce the final throw, which as it was, so nearly succeeded in March 1918.[2] In the final stage of the war, as can be seen from General Ludendorff's and Prince Max's accounts, the decision whether to accept President Wilson's terms or to fight on turned mainly on the fact that 26 German Divisions were locked up in Russia for economic reasons. In short, the food blockade acted like a very formidable diversion to keep large forces away from the decisive theatre at the decisive moments of the war. In addition, the constant withdrawal of supplies from Bulgaria to Austria and Germany was one of the causes of Bulgaria's disaffection; and the more closely the German accounts of the last phase of the war [are read?], the more important does the Bulgarian collapse appear. If in 1915 the food blockade had been withdrawn, the contest could undoubtedly have been prolonged, and no one can tell when the War would have come to an end or what

[1]*Extracts from the German accounts to support this statement have been compiled and are available, if desired.

[2]*Ludendorff, 'My War Memories,' Chapter headed 'The Offensive in the West, 1918.' Also Minutes of German War Cabinet published in Prince Max of Baden's Memoirs, Vol. II.

the result would have been; for, apart from the immediate effect of the blockade, if Germany had desisted from the submarine campaign it is probable that America would never have come into the War.

10.   To sum up, the food element in the blockade, which President Wilson and Colonel House wanted us to surrender in 1915, became in the last year of the war one of the decisive factors, first in averting defeat in March, and afterwards in bringing the war to an end in November 1918. Without the food blockade we should perhaps have lost the war; but even if we had not lost it, the war would certainly have been prolonged. With this recent experience in the greatest crisis of our national history, confirming the experience of earlier wars, it seems incredible that anyone could be so lacking in foresight as to contemplate blunting the edge of the blockade weapon.

PART II – THE HOOVER PROPOSAL AS APPLIED TO FUTURE WARS

11.   The arguments which convinced the Cabinet in 1915 are equally applicable to the future. There are, of course, some wars, for example, those waged against nations that are normally self-supporting, or which depend for their supplies upon a food-exporting neighbouring country, where the food factor may be quite unimportant in a blockade. From 1815 to 1914 food was not an essential factor in any of the wars of this country. But even in such cases events may alter the situation. Who could have foreseen, for example, that during the Great War, France, normally a self-supporting country in the matter of food, would become dependent on the good offices of the United Kingdom, which normally imports most of its food? Who could have foreseen that Russia, formerly an exporter of huge food supplies, would, as in recent years, frequently come into the market for imports of food-stuffs? It is, however, mainly in great unlimited wars, such as the Napoleonic wars, the Great War, and the war of the future, in which the League is confronted with a group of aggressor States, that blockade in general, and the food factor in particular, may become decisive.

12.   We will now examine in detail some of the claims made by President Hoover in support of his proposal, and the arguments he employs to substantiate it.

Will the Hoover Proposal Prevent War?

13.   The President claims that his proposal 'would act as a preventive as well as a limitation of war.' This claim is believed to be devoid of any foundation. In principle it is open to argument whether attempts to humanise war ever do anything at all to prevent war. To make the

attempt now, when the world is trying to abolish war and to represent it as a disreputable proceeding, is like drawing up a code for duelling when you are trying to abolish it. But apart from the question of principle there are special reasons why this particular proposal tends to increase rather than to lessen the prospects of war. Fear of economic pressure, and especially of a food shortage, is one of the strongest deterrents to war. That is why economic pressure was included in Article 16 of the Covenant as one of the principal sanctions at the disposal of the League. By removing this tremendous deterrent; by promising to a violator of the Kellogg Pact and the Covenant of the League that at least he shall not suffer the rigours of food shortage, we make war more and not less probable.

14.   In addition, by blunting the edge of the weapon of blockade we reduce the importance of sea-power without any corresponding reduction in land-power. In other words, the influence (so far as influence depends in the last resort on exercise of force) of great sea Powers like the United States of America and ourselves, which happen to be the Powers with the strongest will to peace, is reduced in comparison with the great land Powers. This is a point to which we return later, in paragraph 31.

The 'Cruelty' Argument

15.   The effectiveness of the food blockade, however, will probably not be seriously questioned, nor its influence as a deterrent to war. President Hoover's case rests rather on the assumption that it is too effective, or, as he puts it, too cruel. The exemption of women and children from starvation in war must at first sight appeal to every humane mind. But when the matter is probed deeper this first impression weakens, and finally disappears, for the proposal can be shown to increase instead of decreasing the cruelty, even to women and children, by prolonging a general suffering in which food shortage is only one of the items.

16.   It has already been shown that in the Great War the food shortage was one of the decisive factors in shortening the period of hostilities. Let us think for a moment of what the civil populations of the belligerent countries were suffering. Vast tracts of territory were devoted to the operations of the contending armies. In these areas every town, village and house was blasted; all vegetation destroyed; industry brought to an end; the very shape of the land altered beyond recognition. For miles behind the lines cities, towns, and villages were exposed to long-range bombardment. And miles beyond the fighting zones, great capitals like London and Paris were the object of frequent aerial bombardments.

Every advance or retreat involved an extension of the devastated areas. To many, however, the loss of property, the discomforts, privations and even the dangers of the war were a small matter compared with the haunting and unrelieved dread for the fate of husbands, parents, children and relations at the front. That is the worst cruelty. To prolong that is incomparably more cruel than to exercise economic pressure on a nation. and anything that increases the general store of food of a nation which otherwise would be suffering from a shortage must end to prolong the war.

17.   Apart from this the force of the 'cruelty' argument is weakened when the conditions under which modern warfare is declared and maintained are considered. For in 1929, even more than in 1915, war, in principle, has become a matter between nationals rather than between armed forces. The old autocracies have passed away and war can only be waged by the will of a democracy, in which, in most countries, women have their full share of responsibility. Moreover, war is now everywhere organised on a national basis. It is no longer a contest of armed forces. America set the pace by creating a gigantic organization for the mobilisation of all the resources of the nation in time of war. France followed with an elaborate law designed for the same purpose. Other nations are following suit. Even we, in a less blatant manner, have had to make our preparations. When the Powers are preparing to mobilise every man and woman and to organize every resource the 'cruelty' argument is somewhat unconvincing.

The Historical Argument

18.   President Hoover, in his Armistice Day message, speaks of the dependence of nations upon imported food as a modern development resulting from 'the rapid growth of industrial civilisation during the past century.' The cutting off of such supplies is referred to as a feature of wars 'of recent years.' Nothing could be further from the truth. It has been the case from remote antiquity. Athens, for example, at the zenith of its power, depended upon overseas supplies, and the collapse of Athenian power in BC 405 was brought about almost entirely be a food blockade. Lysander, the Spartan at the head of the hostile coalition, first defeated the Greek fleet in the Dardanelles, which gave him control of the food supplies of Athens from the Black Sea, and shortly after invested Athens and blockaded the Pyraeus with a fleet based on the island [of] Aegina. After a disastrous famine, Athens had to capitulate, the terms including the surrender of the fleet, the destruction of the Long Walls which had rendered safe the communications between the Capital and its ports, and the abandonment of all overseas Possessions.

Similarly, Imperial Rome was dependent upon imported food. The principal granary was Egypt, and under a dispensation made by the Emperor Augustus this country was maintained under the personal supervision of the Emperor, 'as he apprehended that Italy might be distressed with famine by any who seized that province, the key to the Empire by sea and land, and defensible by a small garrison of men against large armies.'[1] The following extract from a letter from the Emperor Tiberius to the Senate illustrates the point:

> It is wonderful that nobody lays before the Senate that Italy stands in need of foreign supplies; that the lives of the Roman people are daily exposed to the mercy of uncertain seas and tempests; were it not for our supplies from the provinces – supplies by which the masters and their slaves and their estates are maintained – will our groves, forsooth, and villas maintain us? This duty, Conscript Fathers, devolves upon the Prince; and if it were neglected the utter ruin of the State would follow.[2]

When Vespasian in Palestine decided to wrest the Imperial power from Vitellius, his first step was to stop the Egyptian and African supplies. By the time Vitellius fell, Rome's food-stocks were reduced to 10 days' supply.[3] In fact, all through history food has been one of the decisive factors in the policy of nations.[4] It may be possible to eliminate war; at any rate, it must be tried; but once war has broken out it is impossible to eliminate the food factor, since it is one of the decisive elements in war.

The Alleged Injury to Exporting States

19.   President Hoover's apprehension that the economic stability of States which produce surplus food are adversely affected by a blockade is, it is believed, devoid of foundation. The truth is that in a great war like the last all the belligerents, even those that are normally self-supporting, require food imports, as vast resources of men and material required have to be diverted to sustain the war, and national industry, including agriculture, languishes. As already mentioned, France, though self-supporting in normal times, became dependent during the war upon imported food, and the provision and transportation of foodstuffs for all our European allies (except Europe) [sic] became a very serious preoccupation for the British Government. Judging by the experience

---

[1]*Tacitus, 'The Annals', Book II, paragraph 59.
[2]*Ibid, Book III, paragraph 54.
[3]*Tacitus, 'History,' Book III, paragraph 48, and Book IV, paragraph 53.
[4]*Venice, 'Knights of Malta,' Holland, &c.

of the Great War, the producing countries would always find ample markets for their supplies in spite of a blockade. The real difficulty in disposing of foodstuffs arose in very distant countries, like Australia and New Zealand, and was due not to the blockade at all but to the shortage of shipping resulting from the submarine campaign and to the demands on tonnage of the Allied navies and armies, as well as of the Allied nations for wheat, coal, raw material and war supplies. In the autumn of 1917, notwithstanding the shutting off by the blockade of markets in enemy countries, there was a world shortage of foodstuffs, and it was difficult to supply the full requirements even of the Allied countries over the next twelve months. Mr. Hoover's proposal, if it had been in operation, would merely have raised prices all round. Apart from the enemy countries (who, as already shown, might then have won the war), the only beneficiaries would have been the war profiteers, who, in any event, have everything to gain from this plan.

The Argument in Regard to British Supplies

20.   The claim for the freeing of food from interference in war will no doubt be supported to-day, as in the past, by the argument that we, as the Power most dependent upon imports for the essentials of existence, have the most to gain by securing our own food supply and so removing a source of real anxiety. That argument has, of course, been used from time immemorial in support of similar concessions. To quote Mahan:

> For 200 years England has been the great commercial nation of the world. More than any other, her wealth has been entrusted to the sea in war as in peace; yet, of all nations, she has ever been most reluctant to concede the immunities of commerce and the rights of neutrals. Regarded not as a matter of right but of policy, history has justified the refusal, and if she maintained her Navy in full strength, the future will doubtless repeat the lesson of the past.

The argument has always been used to support every concession in the direction of Freedom of the Seas, such as the Immunity of Private Property at Sea, the Declaration of London, Colonel House's proposals of 1915, &c. Its fallacy has been ruthlessly exposed by Admiral Mahan and Sir Julian Corbett.

21.   No one, however, would contest the truth of President Hoover's suggestion that the need for protecting foodstuffs is one (though only one) of the most compelling reasons for naval armaments. But the substitute he suggests, namely, an international agreement, unsupported by any kind of guarantee or sanction, was shown by the experience of

the Great War to be absolutely worthless. At the outbreak of war there were in existence no less than eight international Conventions bearing on sea warfare, seven of which had been drawn up within the preceding decade. All of them were broken – most of them within a few months of the outbreak of war.[1] Not a single one of the neutral Powers, including America, which had signed and ratified them, and whose moral force was supposed to be behind them, moved a step in their defence unless their own interests were assailed. With that recent experience behind us, it seems incredible that anyone could contemplate entrusting the security of the Empire in its most dangerous point to an international agreement instead of to our own forces. If this proposal were adopted, there is a real danger that we should enter into a fool's paradise, in which we should be trusting our very existence to a 'scrap of paper' instead of making proper provision for the defence of our vital interests.

22.   But even supposing the passage of food supplies was guaranteed, how far would this avail? Our people depend for their livelihood on two things besides food supply – raw materials for manufactures, and exports wherewith to pay for our food and raw materials. Food would not be very comforting if we were deprived of all the raw materials required to sustain the war and to maintain our industries which furnish the exports to pay for our food. The truth is that sea-power is a necessity to us. It is insufficient to obtain protection for food alone – even if it were a real protection, which international law never will be. While doing all we can to avoid war we must be in a position, if war comes, to protect our maritime communications and the whole of the traffic along them, whether military or civilian. This problem, of course, presents difficulties of its own, but in the past we have never failed to surmount them, and there is no reason to suppose we shall fail in the future. Food ships do not form a very large proportion of our total shipping (certainly nothing like the 25 per cent. mentioned by President Hoover), and, as the remainder of our shipping would still be liable to attack, we should not realise any disarmament out of this plan, except by an incredible lack of foresight.

PART III – PRACTICABILITY

23.   The President's suggestion is that all vessels laden solely with food supplies should be protected in the same manner as hospital ships are now protected. Even hospital ships, however, were not immune

[1]*Full particulars have been compiled and can be circulated in a separate paper, if desired.

from attack in the War. Several times they were fired at with torpedoes, and three British hospital ships were hit. In some cases, at any rate, the ships were fired at deliberately because the enemy believed the hospital ships were breaking neutrality.

24.   President Hoover supports his plan by reference to the success of the Belgian Relief Scheme during the War. This scheme, however, was to the advantage of both sides. The Germans were relieved thereby of the necessity to provide from their scanty resources for the Belgian population, and the Allies ensured the fidelity of the Belgian Government and army, which otherwise might have been tempted to succumb. Moreover, the distribution of the Belgian supplies was under the immediate supervision of a neutral whom everyone trusted – Mr Hoover himself. The present proposal is accompanied by no corresponding guarantee. It is a proposal to increase the total stock of food in a belligerent country, on which both the fighting forces and the civilian population depend. And here it may be remarked that the army will always get the lion's share.

25.   In another instance that occurred during the War a plan resembling Mr Hoover's was less successful than the Belgian Relief Scheme. In April, 1917, arrangements were made whereby the German Government promised a safe passage to certain neutral wheat ships leaving United Kingdom ports for Sweden on or shortly after the 1st May. These ships were painted in red and white vertical stripes and were to follow pre-determined courses. On the 25th May, 1917, the Admiral Commanding Orkneys and Shetlands reported that the '*Vesterland Sverige*,' painted with red and white vertical stripes and its name painted on the hull, was torpedoed and sunk while in convoy with seven other ships. He continued as follows:

> I would remark that out of eight neutral ships which were painted with red and white stripes and reported to Admiralty in accordance with message 2030 of the 29th April, six have now sailed from examination ports; two of these have been sunk and one damaged by torpedo, the remaining three left Lerwick with escort forces and arrived safely.

Thus three out of six ships that sailed were attacked by the Germans. These instances well illustrate the precariousness of such arrangements in time of war.

26.   If the President's proposal were carried out on a large scale it seems certain that the right of visit and search would have to be exercised. Otherwise the special mark for food ships (even if covered by a 'navicert' from a neutral Government) would be abused and contraband

would be carried in vessels masquerading as food ships. *Consequently, the proposal would not even have the effect of eliminating the old diplomatic difficulties which have arisen in the main from the exercise of the right of visit, search and detention.*

27.   So far as British imports of foodstuffs are concerned the proposal is believed to be impracticable from another point of view. It is distinctly stated in the President's armistice day address that the immunity refers to ships 'laden solely with food supplies.' It is understood, however, that a large proportion of our foodstuffs are carried, not in food ships, but in 'parcels' on board liners. This applies to practically all imports of meat and refrigerated produce, and to a large proportion of grain imports and minor foodstuffs.[1] The question of the return voyage of the food ships also raises points of great difficulty. If they are to return empty the cost of the food would be raised considerably and a most wasteful employment of tonnage would be involved. In the later war, when the issue turned largely on the provision of sufficient tonnage (for example, in 1918 to bring over the American troops), such waste of tonnage could not have been afforded. We should have been compelled to bring our foodstuffs in ships which could be employed more economically and the Hoover proposal would have been valueless to us. On the other hand, if the food ships were allowed to take return cargoes, the effects of a blockade or of economic pressure would be largely frustrated. These are points on which it is hoped that the advice of the Board of Trade will be sought.

Impracticability Illustrated by Test Cases

28.   We now come to the other side of the question of practicability, namely, the interruption of the enemy's communications. Would such an indiscriminate exemption of foodstuffs be watertight? It can be tested by the following hypothetical cases:

Case I.   An enemy army has effected a landing in British territory, (e.g. Hong Kong or Singapore), but has failed to achieve a decisive result before the arrival, some time later, of the British fleet, which is blockading this strongly-defended landing base. The British garrison, outnumbered, is hard put to it to hold the position and military reinforcements are still far distant. The enemy, though numerically superior to the British garrison, is short of food, and is living from day to day on what is brought through the British blockade by food ships covered by the Hoover Convention. Is it conceivable, in such

---

[1]*See a most interesting article in the 'Nation' of November 23, 1929, by Mr C. Ernest Fayle the author of the 'Official History of Seaborne Trade.'

circumstances, that the Convention could be allowed to stand for a moment? Everyone knows that it would at once be torn to shreds! The gap would be closed, and the enemy would be compelled to surrender by food shortage. The same principle applies to an invasion of the Mother Country. It is interesting to recall that one of the points on which Lord Roberts' case regarding the danger of invasion broke down most seriously in the Inquiry of 1907–8 was that the enemy, though he might slip through our fleet and effect a disembarkation, would inevitably be cut off from his supplies. But under the Hoover proposal he would (in theory) be free from embarrassment so far as food supplies were concerned.

The Americans might be faced with an identical problem if a Japanese expedition were landed in the Philippines before the main American fleet could arrive.

Case II.   America is attacking an enemy port, as she attacked Santiago de Cuba in 1897. Her army has surrounded the port on the land side and cut it off from supplies, but can make no impression on the powerful defences. The port is blockaded by sea. Is it conceivable, when their husbands and sons were dying in thousands in the trenches or from disease, that American citizens would stand for the indefinite prolongation of the siege by permitting food ships to enter the port? Could we and the French have allowed food ships to pass into Sebastopol in the Crimean War, or into the Dardanelles in 1915? Could Japan have allowed food ships to enter Port Arthur during the siege? We all know that in none of these cases would a wartime public opinion have stood it.

In connection with this case it is pertinent to ask whether a port which is normally supplied from markets in the interior is to be allowed to bring supplies through the enemy's lines. If not, why not? On what logical basis is it to be permitted to cut the food communications by sea but not by land?

Case III.   War with a country like Italy or Greece, or even with Arabia, the country of Ibn Saud, which is dependent on imported foodstuffs. The alternatives are a costly war, heavy land fighting, severe loss of life, on the one hand, or a short blockade (such as was applied by the Allies during the War when King Constantine was troublesome), on the other. But the Hoover proposal would make the latter course illegal.

Case IV.   Is a repetition of the circumstances of the Great War. An immensely powerful and ambitious military State like Germany, surrounded by enemies on most of her land frontiers, and without command of the sea. Secure to her food supply and she can devote her whole forces to the conquest of her enemies' territory, without anxiety in regard to her most vulnerable point. She has now but little to fear from sea-power. Her greatest deterrent from making war is removed. That would be the effect of the Hoover proposal.

29.   The above cases have been devised as a progressive illustration. In cases I and II the effects of exempting food from blockade are shown to be palpably ridiculous, because one side is asked to surrender an overwhelming advantage without getting anything in return, since, in any event, possessing command of the sea, he could satisfy his own needs. The same principle applies in only a slightly different degree in cases III and IV.

PART IV – GENERAL OBSERVATIONS

30.   We come now to certain observations and criticisms of a more general character, which do not fall within any of the headings under which the proposal has hitherto been discussed.

The Proposal Enures to the Benefit of the Land Powers

31.   It has already been pointed out in paragraph 14 that, by blunting the edge of the blockade weapon, the proposal weakens the Sea Powers, which happen to be the more pacifically minded nations of the world, without imposing any corresponding diminution of power on the Land Powers. This point requires elaborating.

32.   First, there arises the difficulty that a ship is liable to attack when in harbour just as much as on the high seas. For example, a food ship has passed up the Channel and arrived in the port of London. Is she to be immune from air attack? In that event, how are the aircraft, attacking probably by night, to distinguish food ships from other ships? Again, is a food ship to be exempt from attack in territorial waters? If not, the enemy will merely await her chance to deal with her as she crosses the three-mile limit. One result of the adoption of the Hoover proposal would be a great increase in the use of the submarine mine, which does not discriminate between different kinds of ships – as Hospital Ships found to their cost during the War. The mine barrage, laid mainly by the Americans across the North Sea, could not respect either a hospital ship or a food ship.

33.   One would wish to know, also whether food is to be allowed to pass freely on land also. If Germany is at war with Czecho-Slovakia, is she to allow food-stuffs to pass freely across a no-man's-land which separates the armies? Is a city which is besieged by land, as Paris was besieged in the war of 1870, to be supplied across no-man's-land? Presumably not. Neither, then, would it be allowed in the case of the

land side of a besieged seaport. In other words, a country could obtain all the results of a blockade by occupying an enemy's ports with military forces or by cutting the land communications of those ports, and refusing to allow food landed at a port to reach its destination. Again the advantage is to be with the Land Powers.

34. The whole tendency of the Hoover proposal, then, is to weaken sea-power without any corresponding diminution in land or air power. At sea, where Great Britain is strong, the food ship is to be immune. In harbour the same ship is liable to bombardment from the air or to capture and confiscation by a land army. The sea communications to a port are to be free for the passage of food; but the land communications (whether by rail, road, canal or river), by which the food cargo is to be passed on to its ultimate destination, are to be liable to interruption by land or by air. It is therefore an unfair arrangement, which weights the scales in wartime in favour of the Land Powers and against the Sea Powers.

The Proposal could not Stand the Test of War

35. The fundamental causes of the failure in the Great War of the Declaration of Paris and the Declaration of London are admirably summed up in the following passage from the Labour Party's pamphlet on Freedom of the Seas:

> By the time the Great War came, the assumptions on which the framers of the Declaration of Paris had based their compromises had really become obsolete. The framers had assumed, with Rousseau, that war is 'not a relation between man and man, but a relation between State and State'; so that the individual would be only indirectly affected. They had assumed, with Grotius, that commodities could be so divided in war time as to leave private property and civil supplies untouched, while State property and miliary supplies were stopped; so that the belligerents' weapon of commerce-prevention would be conveniently cut in half.

36. To adopt President Hoover's proposal would be to fall into an equally serious error. As the breakdown of the pre-war agreements proves, it is useless to adopt in time of peace provisions that cannot stand the test of war. Most of those agreements and codes were entered into after a century of freedom from unlimited war. In drawing them up, the atmosphere of war was ignored. To-day we are in danger of repeating the same errors. We are rightly anxious to forget the War. But if we are to try and regulate these war questions without it making the same mistakes as our predecessors, it is essential that

we should reconstruct in our minds the atmosphere of war and the national psychology that is inevitably and invariably induced by it. Everyone who had responsibility for the control of our war effort knows well that during an unlimited war, when the existence of the nation is at stake, public opinion would not stand a measure which allowed ships crammed with food to sail through our lines to an enemy port when the people realised that this meant prolonging a war. If British soldiers were again dying in tens of thousands in France or Flanders, the British fathers and mothers would refuse to permit the resources of the enemy to be increased and the war prolonged by allowing the free passage of food ships up the Channel and through our Fleets. Means would be found to evade, or excuse to denounce, the paper Treaty. It would be a gross deception, and an insult to international law, to enter into an agreement for time of war which we know cannot stand the test of war.

The Proposal Offers no Compensation for the Sacrifice of Belligerent Rights

37.   One curious feature of the Hoover proposal is that we are apparently to receive nothing in return for the sacrifice of our historic attitude towards blockade, for the blunting of the one immediately ready offensive weapon that we possess. Under the proposals of 1915 we were to get in return the abandonment of the submarine campaign against merchant ships, desistence from the use of poison gas (in which the enemy then had the advantage), cessation of mine-laying, &c. On the present occasion there is no corresponding inducement. The proposal is not even linked up with the abolition of submarines. No guarantee or sanction is offered. We are to make this sacrifice as a mere makeweight in negotiations for a Naval Treaty, which is already supposed to rest on a basis of mutual sacrifice and advantage, as defined by the term 'parity,' in order to satisfy or disarm the criticism of a group of Senators who are intensely hostile either to the Treaty or to the President, or both.

Limited Effect of Concessions to American Opinion

38.   It is pertinent to ask whether the Senators are likely to be satisfied even with this concession. Is it not more likely that, when the day comes, they will say (what is true) that, under the stress of war, Great Britain will find means to evade it? This has already been said in the American newspapers and journals. For example, on the 27th January (1929), Congressman Britten declared that a sea-law agreement would be 'another gesture towards peace which will be ignored and broken by

powerful belligerents in war time . . .'[1] It will no doubt be said in the public controversies here, as it was said (prophetically, as it turned out) in the controversy over the Declaration of London. After the experience of the War it might prove a decisive factor against the Treaty instead of a solvent.

39.   If the temporary effects of a great concession are uncertain, can anyone say that the permanent effects are likely to be great? Recent years have seen one concession after another to what was supposed to be American opinion – the sacrifice of the Anglo-Japanese Alliance, against the desire of almost all members of the Imperial Conference, 1921; the Articles of Agreement with the Irish Free State (concluded on different grounds, but which, it was said, would make a permanent improvement in our relations with America); the Debt Settlement; the Liquor Traffic Agreement. The writer has heard responsible Americans of the highest position say beforehand of some of these concessions that they would remove the main cause of friction and suspicion. Yet in no case was any lasting effect produced, and by the time the present Government came into office, in spite of all these concessions, it was generally agreed that Anglo-American relations were in a deplorable state. France, who had flouted Washington by refusing discussion of land defence, by rejecting the abolition of submarines, and by refusing to ratify some of the Washington Treaties, and who for years refused to ratify a Debt Agreement, was apparently no more unpopular than we were. In a matter of this kind history is certain to repeat itself. We might, by the food concession, possibly, but by no means surely, do something to help President Hoover's tactical position in the Senate, but it is submitted that we should derive no permanent advantage in any way commensurate with the humiliation of the surrender, the loss of prestige and potential strength, and with the strain on our good faith if once again we found ourselves under the overwhelming compulsion of war necessity to act contrary to our agreement.

PART V – SUMMARY

40.   The objections to the proposal may be summed up as follows:

(1.)   A similar proposal, but in a more attractive form, offering considerable advantages, was twice rejected during the War. If it had not been rejected we should probably not have won the War. In any

---

[1]*Article in the 'News Bulletin' of the Foreign Policy Association of New York of February 1, 1929.

event, it must have been prolonged, and the loss of life and universal distress would have been correspondingly increased.

(2.)   The reasons for which it was rejected are applicable to future wars of a similar character. The sanctions of the Covenant would be seriously impaired by the adoption of the proposal.

(3.)   By prolonging wars, and the universal suffering and distress engendered thereby, the proposal would involve greater cruelty than that which it sets out to remove. In any event, the 'cruelty' argument is unconvincing under modern conditions, when the whole nation is organised in support of the fighting forces. To quote the Labour Party Pamphlet on the Freedom of the Seas:

'In February 1915 the Foreign Office declared (*with perfect justice*)[1] that "the reason for drawing a distinction between foodstuffs intended for the civil population and those for the armed forces or enemy Government disappears when the distinction between the civil population and the armed forces itself disappears". . . .'

As Ludendorff wrote: 'In this war it was impossible to distinguish where the sphere of the army and navy began and that of the people ended.'

This is even more true of future wars, which are everywhere being prepared for by a national organization.

(4.)   Blockade in general, and food blockade in particular, are the greatest deterrent to war and are recognised as such by the adoption of economic pressure as a sanction in the Covenant of the League of Nations. To remove or weaken the greatest deterrent is not to make war less probable. To tell a potential enemy that in all circumstances you will feed him, is not to reduce the risk of an aggression.

(5.)   In view of the complete breakdown during the war of the various treaties drawn up before the war to govern the rules of war, we could not entrust the security of our food supplies to a new treaty. In any event we should require protection for our trade other than food, which is the life-blood of the nation and would remain unprotected under this proposal. There is no real disarmament to be obtained from the proposal, but only a fictitious sense of security which in time would tend towards neglect to provide the proper defensive means.

(6.)   The proposal is open to many criticisms from the point of view of practicability, and is believed to be unworkable (see Part IV). In some cases, such as those given in paragraph 28, it is palpably absurd and could never stand the test of war. It would not even

---

[1]*The italics are not in the original.

get rid of the necessity for visit, search and detention, which have always been the main cause of international difficulties.

(7.)   Unless accompanied by corresponding provisions in the case of land and air warfare of so sweeping a nature that no military Power could concede them, the proposal would weaken the Sea Powers without any corresponding diminution in the strength of the Land Powers. In their influence on the maintenance of peace, which in the last resort rests upon potential force, the Sea Powers (which, as it happens, are the more pacific) would have their strength diminished as compared with the Land Powers.

(8.)   No comparable *quid pro quo* is offered in return for what the world would regard as a humiliating surrender of our strength.

(9.)   It is by no means certain that by this sacrifice we should even secure the passage through the Senate of the Naval Treaty. The argument already used in America, that when the day came we should, judged by the precedent of the Great War, find means to evade our obligations, would be the more deadly because it is true. But once we have made this offer, even if it is not ratified, we shall have sacrificed the principle.

(10.)   To enter into a treaty which we know from experience less than fifteen years old we should have to evade in certain kinds of wars, if it could be managed by hook or by crook, would be an unthinkable act of hypocrisy and bad faith.

* * *

PART IV

THE USE OF BELLIGERENT RIGHTS, 1937–1970

INTRODUCTION

Despite the concern felt in the 1920s that the Royal Navy might be called on to exercise belligerent rights on behalf of the League of Nations, during the period between the two world wars it was only as a neutral that the British government was obliged to take practical measures with respect to belligerent rights, to deal with the needs of British shipping during the Spanish Civil War and the Sino-Japanese war. The near simultaneous calls for naval action to deal with Italian aggression in Ethiopia, the civil war in Spain and the intervention there of Italy and Germany, and the Japanese war in China, placed an impossible burden on the Royal Navy. League of Nations sanctions against Italy could have been a much more effective instrument of collective action had naval force been employed, and the Mediterranean fleet was deployed to Alexandria, but following the election of the Nazi Party in Germany in 1933 there was little appetite for alienating Mussolini. There was also concern that the United States would challenge a naval blockade. The humiliated British Mediterranean Fleet was on its way home from Alexandria when developments in the Spanish Civil War led to British nationals, and British shipping, coming into danger. Both the Republican government of Spain and the Nationalist mutineers led by General Franco attempted to use naval forces to deny to the other side access to foreign sources of supply.

This chapter opens with the minutes of a Cabinet meeting called in April 1937 to discuss the problem of the activity of the navy of the Spanish Nationalist Mutineers. The question of escorting food ships into Bilbao was especially provocative given British resistance to President Hoover's efforts to obtain immunity for food ships in wartime. There was a general recognition that 'where a port or district was beleaguered by land and effectively blockaded by sea, action to enforce the admission of British food ships might well be interpreted in some quarters as tantamount to intervention.' It was agreed that the Secretary of State for Foreign Affairs should advise General Franco's insurgent government in writing that 'We cannot recognise or concede belligerent rights and we cannot tolerate any interference with British shipping at sea. We are, however, advising our shipping that, in view of the conditions at present prevailing in the neighbourhood of Bilbao, they should not go into that area so long as these conditions continue' [63]. The attempt to evade the issue, however, proved inadequate. Public opinion in Britain forced the government's hand. The bombing of Guernica led to a further reversal of government policy, and orders to the navy to escort refugee ships leaving Basque towns.

Despite the outcome of the Ethiopian crisis, the First Lord of the Admiralty, Sir Samuel Hoare, continued to set a high priority on detaching Italy from Germany, and persisted in this policy even when it became evident that Mussolini was employing Italian forces to support General Franco. So long as the Spanish Republican government possessed naval dominance the Admiralty preferred to deny Spain belligerent rights on the high seas, but when the Nationalists acquired significant naval assets of their own the Admiralty recommended to the cabinet that both sides be accorded the status of belligerents. This recommendation was not implemented, but in an attempt to make a policy of non-intervention compatible with a denial of belligerent rights British shipping was forbidden by act of parliament from carrying contraband to either side of the civil war. The denial of belligerent rights on the high seas to the combatants in a civil war was without precedent, and led to clandestine acts of naval force by and on behalf of the mutineers [65].

The Japanese war against China had added to Britain's problems as a neutral shipping state, and as a naval power. The Board of Trade was informed that the Admiralty wanted to establish a navicert system which would satisfy Japanese contraband control without necessitating boarding and searching British ships, but that there was concern this would severely injure relations with China. The shipping industry was being sounded on whether they could establish a Navicert system on a commercial basis without official sponsoring, but it was doubtful whether that would satisfy the Japanese. On 26 August the Japanese government informed the British government that it intended to blockade the Chinese coast, but that it would respect the immunity of neutral flag shipping. Neutral ships would only be inspected to ensure that they were entitled to the flags they were flying, and if a British warship were present to guarantee the nationality of the ship, that right would be waived [64].

These events proved to be the prologue to the outbreak of the Second World War. Economic intelligence had been secretly collected during the 1920s and 1930s. In 1929 a Ministry of Blockade had been reestablished at the Foreign Office, and in 1931 an Industrial Intelligence Centre had been established under the direction of Major Desmond

Morton, which became the Intelligence Division of the Ministry of Economic Warfare when it was officially established on 3 September 1939.[1] A *Handbook of Economic Warfare*, prepared by the Advisory Committee on Trade Questions in Time of War, had been printed the previous July [67]. It amounts to a definitive statement of the methods of economic warfare, especially with respect to the methods of enforcement practicable within the political, legal and geographical limitations of the British Commonwealth, based on the experience of nearly a century since the Declaration of Paris in 1856. The Intelligence Division was subdivided into a Blockade Branch responsible for the minutiae of contraband control and an Enemy Branch which was tasked with appraising the expected performance of the German economy.[2] Concern about the American attitude to restraints on trade, however, and also the feeling that coercion of small neutral states was inappropriate in a war which was being fought to defend the freedoms of small states, led to the measures of trade control Britain ordered against Germany on the outbreak of war in 1939 being restricted to contraband control as it had been in 1914. Despite the detailed description of the system published only that summer in the *Handbook of Economic Warfare*, no attempt was made to recreate the apparatus for rationing the imports of neutral states bordering Germany, nor was pre-emptive purchasing of war supplies pursued.

Prize courts functioned in virtually the same manner as they had in the First World War, but the destructive nature of the conflict meant that relatively few cases were brought before them. The precedents established in the First War were in general applicable to the Second. The reprisal orders of the First War having lapsed, the Declaration of Paris was recognised as protecting enemy goods in neutral ships [66]. The distinction between contraband and conditional contraband was recognised as part of the course of Admiralty, but the Declaration of London was not recognized following its denunciation in 1916. In this new war, however, for the first time in British naval history, the *The King's Regulations and Admiralty Instructions For the Government of His Majesty's Naval Service* (Clause No. 894) made it clear that 'The officers and crews of His Majesty's ships have no right or claim to the proceeds of Prize of War, except as may from time to time be granted by the Crown' [74].

[1]Minister of Economic Warfare Order, 1939 (SR & O 1939, No. 1188) under the Ministers of the Crown (Emergency Appointments) Act 1939 (2 & 3 George VI, Chap. 77). The ministry was dissolved 28 May 1945.
[2]F.T. Hinsley, *British Intelligence in the Second World War*, 3 vols, Cambridge, 1979, vol. 1, pp. 223–48.

In January 1940, as a necessary concession to Anglo-American relations, Winston Churchill was constrained to order the Admiralty to stop
bringing in American ships. The less powerful neutrals could complain
with good reason that Britain showed special deference to American
might. Lord Halifax, the Foreign Minister, also insisted that the Board
of Trade should not pass on to British businesses information obtained
from censorship or from intelligence which would threaten American
trade interests. He was, however, ready to facilitate British trade taking
the place of German exports. Immediate strategic considerations had to
outweigh long-term economic ones, and it was to be the Americans
who profited from the war [68, 69, 71]. When in April 1940 the American government banned sailings to Bergen, the problem of American
exports to Germany receded, but the Italian entry into the war made
contraband control in the Mediterranean impossible, and led to the
focus of economic warfare being placed on long-range contraband
control. The *First Monthly Report submitted by the Minister of Economic Warfare Covering the Period 10th June–10th July 1940* noted
that the invasion of the Netherlands and Belgium had brought their
empires to co-operate with the British Empire embargo of strategic
commodities at source, but also that the fall of France ended the co-
operation from the French Empire [70, 71]. These catastrophic events,
on the other hand, reduced American resistance to the British naval
control of trade, and brought the American government to consent to
compulsory navicerting of cargoes, and the establishment of bunker
control.

The spectre of starvation in occupied Europe was a concern to the
Secretary of State for Foreign Affairs, Anthony Eden, primarily because of the effect it might have on relations with the United States,
and the effect it could have on the morale of allied merchant seamen
whose families were in occupied countries [72]. However, Hugh Dalton,
the Minister of Economic Warfare, was confident that there would be
no starvation, 'nor even acute shortage, unless the Germans fail to
distribute the supplies fairly.' 'The food blockade,' he reminded the
Cabinet, 'is an essential weapon of economic warfare. If we let in food,
we make possible the transfer of German man power from food production to the production of munitions or service in the armed forces;
also we ease the strain on the enemy's transport system' [73].

The German attack on Russia, the Japanese attack on Pearl Harbor
and the American entry into the Second World War did what the formation of the League of Nations had failed to achieve, and virtually put an
end to the nineteenth-century concept of neutrality. With it went the
only force which was capable of imposing restraint on belligerent

action at sea. On receipt of word of the Japanese attack on Pearl Harbor, Admiral Stark, US Chief of Naval Operations, signalled 'Execute Unrestricted Air and Submarine Warfare against Japan.'[1] Japanese militarist barbarism, and no doubt racism, eradicated any sense of a humanitarian morality behind international law. American resort to unrestricted war on trade freed the British from their restraint in the European theatre. Whole areas of ocean were declared to be 'dangerous to shipping,' within some of which enemy vessels were liable to be sunk on sight. This departure from international law was justified as reprisal for German excesses.[2] Following the war, however, when German leaders were brought to justice at Nuremberg, it was found expedient not to charge Admirals Raeder and Dönitz with violation of the 1937 Protocol on Submarine Warfare. As Admiral von Lanz wrote in an appeal directed to Admirals Cunningham, Nimitz and Lemonnier, condemnation on that charge would have implicated the allied commanders. A conviction would 'be of such a nature as greatly to impair the honour and the reputation of the Naval Commands of all nations who participated in this war, and influence the future development of Naval warfare principles in a decisive manner' [76].

When the Economic Warfare Division (EWD) of the Admiralty Trade Division was wound down in 1945, it was considered essential that a staff monograph of the Contraband Control Service should be drafted so as to record 'Lessons Learnt'. It was also agreed by the Director of Trade Division, Peter Skelton, that the two most senior members of the EWD Registry staff should be absorbed into the Trade Division staff so as to retain a living memory of the service.[3] Two years later, with the Cold War a grim reality, the Trade Division again looked at the question of Contraband Control [75]. The experience of the last war suggested that there was no need to plan for the scale of operations envisaged in the 1930s, especially as it was expected that only rubber, tin and uranium would be useful targets for control. It was also anticipated that those commodities would have been stockpiled by an enemy. On the other hand, with the formation of the United Nations the potential for blockade strategy appeared to be strengthened by the prospect that there would be no neutrals in a

[1]W.T. Mallison, Naval War College International Law Studies 1966, *Studies in the Law of Naval Warfare: Submarines in General and Limited Wars*, Washington, 1968, pp. 87–91.

[2]See William O. Miller, 'Belligerency and Limited War', United States Naval War College International Law Studies, vol. 62, *The Use of Force, Human Rights and General International Legal Issues*, [Richard B. Lillich and John Norton Moore, eds], Newport, 1980, p. 164.

[3]ADM 1/17741, 4 and 8 August 1945.

future European war. It was even suggested by the Director of the Trade Division, Captain Robert Jocelyn Oliver Otway-Ruthven, that the Ministry of Defence should make a ruling to that effect. But the Director of Plans, Captain Thomas Leslie Bratt, could not agree with the supposition, believing it possible 'that some countries in Europe would remain neutral even in a major war.'

In April 1950 a draft memorandum was prepared at the Foreign Office on the dependence of Great Britain upon American munitions during the war [79]. The drift of the paper suggests that there were those who were optimistic that in different conditions Britain might be able to return to a more independent foreign policy, but the 1956 Suez crisis was to make it absolutely clear that Britain was no longer able to mount military operations without at least the tacit agreement of the United States. There were few conflicts in which the United States did not adopt the stance of a protagonist.

In the late 1940s the major concern for the British government was the freedom of British maritime commerce in wars and 'police actions' conducted by other countries, beginning with the French use of naval forces to control shipping during the Algerian civil war. The Chinese civil war forced the Admiralty to adopt measures to protect British trade, while being careful not to undermine the rights of belligerents to control trade. In June 1949 the C-in-C Far East Station circulated a general message advising HM ships that the British Government did not recognise the 'Nationalist' blockade of Communist controlled ports, and setting out the rules of engagement, which were limited to self-defence and defence of British merchantmen actually under attack [76]. By September consideration was being given to escorting British merchant shipping into Shanghai, to prevent the breakdown of civil government and to help British business in the city. It was recognised that the Americans might not be happy with a development which could only help the Communist insurgents, but it was also hoped that accommodating the Communist masters of Shanghai might be useful, at least in so far is they might release HMS *Amethyst*, which had been shelled by the Communists in the Yangtse in April 1949. Her crew later fought their way out to sea [77, 78].

The additional protocols to the Geneva Convention signed on 12 August 1949, relating to the protection of victims of international armed conflicts, finally fulfilled President Wilson's and President Hoover's objective of establishing formal legal impediments to the use of starvation of populations as a means of war. Protocol I Article 54 established that

1. Starvation of civilians as a method of warfare is prohibited.

2. It is prohibited to attack, destroy, remove or render useless objects indispensable to the survival of the civilian population, such as food-stuffs, agricultural areas for the production of food-stuffs, crops, livestock, drinking water installations and supplies and irrigation works, for the specific purpose of denying them for their sustenance value to the civilian population or to the adverse Party, whatever the motive, whether in order to starve out civilians, to cause them to move away, or for any other motive.

3. The prohibitions in paragraph 2 shall not apply to such of the objects covered by it as are used by an adverse Party:

(a) as sustenance solely for the members of its armed forces; or

(b) if not as sustenance, then in direct support of military action, provided, however, that in no event shall actions against these objects be taken which may be expected to leave the civilian population with such inadequate food or water as to cause its starvation or force its movement.

4. These objects shall not be made the object of reprisals.

Article 14 of Protocol II extended protection to the victims of non-international armed conflicts. However, the brutalising effect of war tended to reduce the efficacy of the provisions.

The outbreak of war in Korea in 1950 involved Britain in naval control of trade operations, as part of the United Nations Emergency Force led by the United States. This was not, however, to become an unlimited exercise of belligerent rights because of the realities of the Cold War. The Korean war was a United Nations operation only because the Soviet Union had withdrawn from its seat in the Security Council. With the Soviet Union actively, but covertly, supporting Communist North Korea, belligerent rights had to be exercised with a degree of discretion not unlike that imposed on belligerents in conflicts prior to the creation of the United Nations.

United Nations forces mounted a coastal blockade of both North Korean coasts, that on the east being the first blockade operation mounted under US Navy command since the Civil War. By June 1951 the British commander on the West Coast regarded the blockade as all but complete [80]. There was no general economic campaign mounted on the high seas. The focus of United Nations action was upon battlefield logistics, but the only limitations placed on the blockade were geographical. Because of North Korea's long border with China, and because of the economic support provided by the Soviet Union and China, the naval blockade could be of strategic value only to the extent it obliged the North Korean government to devote more inland transport to military and civilian food supplies. Its only utility was as a multiplier of the simultaneous efforts which were made with aircraft and gunfire to isolate the Korean battlefield.

The quasi-belligerent operations undertaken by the powers during the Cold War rarely involved any interference with maritime commerce. The history of conflict over belligerent rights made it too likely serious escalation would follow on stopping, let alone torpedoing, Soviet or American shipping. Citing grounds of 'Defence and International Sensitivity' historians are still blocked from an Admiralty file on 'Naval blockade and maritime countermeasures against USSR 1959–1961'.[1] The principal exception to this rule of restraint was the 'Quarantine' imposed on Cuba in October 1962 as a technique for persuading the Soviet government to remove intermediate range ballistic missiles which it was in the process of installing, purportedly to prevent the United States attempting another invasion of Cuba. The reaction of Sir Harold Macmillan's administration was highly supportive, but he warned President John F. Kennedy that the technique left Chairman Krushchev with dangerous options: 'his obvious method would be to escort his ships and force you into the position of attacking them. This fire-first dilemma has always worried us and we have always hoped to impale the Russians on this move. We doubt you have thought of this but I would be glad to know how you feel it can be handled.' Kennedy, in his reply, admitted that he knew 'of no sure escape from the problem of the first shot' [81, 82, 83].

Cuban civilian imports were not blocked, but insurance for voyages to Cuba became hard to get, and the United States government ordered that no ship which continued in the Cuba trade would be chartered to carry United States government funded exports. Some attempt was made to persuade the British government to discourage British flag-ships from participating in Cuban trade, but this was resisted [84, 85]. In February 1963 Edward Heath, answering a question in the House of Commons, said 'We have made clear throughout that Her Majesty's Government do not approve of any restriction on freedom of navigation in times of peace' [86]. The Americans expressed particular concern about shipments of Leyland buses being exported from Britain with a British Credit Guarantee.[2] Three years later the Royal Navy was ordered to blockade the port of Beira in Mozambique, but this was not a

[1]ADM 205/221.
[2]See CAB 21/558, Jeremy Thomas, Foreign Office, to W.I. McIndoe, Cabinet Office, 11 October 1963.

national initiative, having been authorised by the United Nations Security Council as part of sanctions intended to put an end to the unilateral declaration of independence by the government of Southern Rhodesia [87, 88].

Although the Beira patrol cannot be said to have had much impact on the Rhodesian economy, because it was bypassed by oil shipments from South Africa, operations in support of economic sanctions are now considered a major role for naval forces with international reach. Those conducted against Iraq following the 1990 invasion of Kuwait and continuing until the 2003 Anglo-American invasion of Iraq may well become a pattern for the future. But restrictions on scholarly access to papers relating to the subject preclude their inclusion in this volume.

63. The Spanish Crisis

CABINET MEETING

[CAB 23/88/64–79]   11 April 1937

The President of the Board of Trade [Viscount Walter Runciman] said that we had no legal right to compel British ships to avoid certain ports. The owners of British ships already in Spanish waters or proceeding thereto had already incurred a liability in respect of the cargo, as it was unusual for the charter party to contain a diversion clause. Consequently, the shipowners could not take their cargo to another port without incurring liabilities. He would expect that British shipowners were likely to protest that they had every expectation of Naval protection. At the same time, the President said that up to the present time those owners with whom he had been able to communicate had adopted the advice of the Board of Trade though they would expect not to be bullied out of their traffic by General Franco.

The Lord Chancellor [Lord Sankey] pointed out that ships were bound to go only as near to a port as they could safely get. It was pointed out, however, that this was generally assumed to apply to physical conditions.

The First Lord of the Admiralty [Sir Bolton Eyres-Monsell] suggested that the question of diversion of ships and compensation therefore was a secondary issue. If the suggestion of the Secretary of State for Foreign Affairs was accepted, questions of compensation or otherwise might have to be considered later. For example, it might be possible to include a sentence in the Order-in-Council adding to the list of goods that British ships were not to carry to Spain a new category, namely food stuffs, but applying only to the particular port of Bilbao. On the main issue, we had tried to hold to the position that we should protect British shipping on the high seas but not in territorial waters. Now, however, General Franco had challenged it. Information of that challenge had not been available to the Cabinet Committee at the meeting on the 7th April. The more the matter was considered, the more difficult did the attempt to hold to the original position appear. The Chief of the Naval Staff [Admiral Sir Ernle Chatfield] urged strong objections against the policy of protecting our shipping up to the edge of Spanish territorial waters and then allowing ships to enter them and be captured within sight of their escorts. That would be bad for the prestige of the Navy. In view of General Franco's challenge, therefore, it was difficult to continue the differentiation between the high seas and territorial waters. Owing to General Franco's challenge, diversion of ships from Bilbao gave an impression of giving way, but the alternative of using the Navy to force an entry into Bilbao would raise grave issues. The establishment at Bilbao of an effective blockade by General Franco's forces created a new situation, since this was the first occasion in the war when there had been an effective blockade of a port by sea and land. Off Bilbao, the insurgents now had one new battleship armed with 12-inch guns, a modern cruiser, a light cruiser and a destroyer as well as armed trawlers. In view of General Franco's threat, he and the Chief of the Naval Staff had decided that it would be advisable that the British Navy in that region should be [there in] overwhelming strength. First, HMS *Shropshire*, an 8-inch cruiser and now HMS *Hood* were being sent there. He assured the Cabinet that there was no doubt that we should possess overwhelming strength so that whatever decision the Cabinet might reach, it would be based on strength and not on weakness. The British ships en voyage to Bilbao were mostly of small tonnage and one or two had been transferred recently from foreign flags. One of the ships was reported by the General Staff to be carrying munitions clandestinely. Some Scandinavian Governments already wished to place their ships bound for Spain under armed protection. If we were to start giving protection, we should get many such requests. A serious point which ought to be considered by the Cabinet was, he said, the effect of any decision on non-intervention policy. Admittedly, the International non-intervention policy applied only to munitions of war. But if we were to interfere at a beleaguered port, it would be interpreted as taking sides and this might provoke Germany and Italy to break away from non-intervention. He himself had no desire that General Franco – or the other side – should win, but he did not want to appear as a protagonist against General Franco, if only for the reason that the insurgents held the part of Spain in which this country was more especially interested. He believed that General Franco was anxious to avoid antagonising us. This view was borne out by the apology offered at Palma for the bombing of a British destroyer. Even in the present case, there was evidence that General Franco wished to avoid a clash and here he referred to the telegram, referred to above, announcing a communication from the Spanish to the British Naval authorities. He urged, therefore, that in order to keep non-intervention alive, it was important to avoid an incident. Our aim should be to play for time, to see whether General Franco found it possible to maintain the blockade effectively and, within the next few days to avoid any action that could be interpreted as intervention by forcing our food ships into Bilbao. He contemplated that in the event of a corresponding situation arising at some port where the positions of contending parties were reversed, our policy should be the same. Our object always being to avoid an incident that would break up the policy of non-intervention.

The Chancellor of the Exchequer [Neville Chamberlain] reminded the Cabinet that there were two cases to consider:

(i)   that of particular ships now in their way to Bilbao;

(ii)   the general policy as to ships not yet on their way.

Some of the proposals before the Cabinet dealt with the first case and some with the second. The latter was the more important, and if that could be decided the first case could be settled on the same lines.

The Secretary of State for Foreign Affairs [Sir John Simon] said that at the moment he was aiming at a day to day arrangement. He was disturbed at the fact reported in the telegram from the Senior Naval Officer that the Spanish Naval authorities classed Santander with Bilbao as regards the entry of British ships in ballast, as it seemed to point to a doubt whether General Franco would allow British food ships to proceed to Santander. If General Franco would accept this then he would advise all British ships bound for Bilbao to go to Santander.

The Minister for Co-ordination of Defence [Sir Thomas Inskip] doubted whether General Franco would allow Santander as a substitute for Bilbao.

The Secretary of State for Foreign Affairs pointed out that General Franco was not in a position to make the blockade effective at Santander.

The Lord Privy Seal asked whether it would not be possible whenever a blockade was effective as at Bilbao to recognise belligerent rights locally in respect of that blockade. That would clear up the difficulty as to international law. He agreed that it was illogical in present circumstances to try and maintain the distinction between the protection of ships in territorial and non-territorial waters: that was why he suggested the principle of a local grant of belligerent rights.

The Chancellor of the Exchequer pointed out that an agreement might be reached with General Franco without granting belligerent rights.

The Minister for Co-ordination of Defence suggested as a possible course to tell General Franco that we did not recognise his blockade as legal, but that we proposed to inform British shipping that a *de facto* blockade existed. There had been a precedent for this action in the case of a Chilean revolution in about 1860–70.

The Secretary of State for Foreign Affairs read a communication he had received as to the attitude of French Government, which was to the effect that in principle the blockade was inadmissible: that in practice they would protect their shipping on the high seas, but that this was more doubtful as regards territorial waters. Generally speaking, they would follow British practice.

The First Lord of the Admiralty said that the French attitude was not important as no French ships were proceeding to the North Spanish ports.

The Home Secretary [Sir John Gilmour] suggested that a basis might be found for an arrangement with General Franco, under which we should undertake that if General Franco would admit our ships in ballast to Bilbao and Santander we should agree that where a *de facto* blockade had been established we would advise our nationals not to send their ships. We should do this, however, without recognising belligerent rights.

The President of the Board of Trade said that out of six British ships at St. Jean de Luz and Bayonne four were not in ballast and could not go to Bilbao under any such arrangement. One contained food and the last was suspected of containing munitions of war, which might be taken to some British port for examination. Probably there were three more ships in voyage to the Spanish coast.

The Minister for Co-ordination of Defence urged the importance of keeping Bilbao open for obtaining iron ore, which was much needed in this country.

In the course of the discussion most of the proposals for dealing with this question were found open to objections from one point of view or another.

The Naval objection to continuing at a blockaded port the policy of protecting British shipping outside, but not inside, territorial waters, met with much sympathy. It was suggested, however, that this created a new situation which virtually compelled us to protect British ships both on the high seas and in territorial waters, or in neither.

The possible course of compelling the insurgent forces to admit British food ships met with little or no support, though it was pointed out that General Franco was unlikely to jeopardize his ships by resistance to a well-supported demand. The probable consequences on the international policy of non-intervention, however, were generally conceded to rule out this course. The contention was felt to be valid that, in cases where a port or district was beleaguered by land and effectively blockaded by sea, action to enforce the admission of British food ships might well be interpreted in some quarters as tantamount to intervention.

One suggestion was that British merchant ships might be warned against proceeding to Bilbao owing to the dangers from submarine mines and air bombing, against which no protection could be offered by the Navy. From a Parliamentary point of view this course offered attractions, because it would avoid any apparent yielding to General Franco's demands. Against this, however, two objections were urged: either British ships in ballast would be deterred, even though permitted, from going to Bilbao for mineral ore, or, alternatively, their owners might decide to run the risk and it might be shown in practice that the warning had been totally unfounded. It was thought better that the warning, if it were issued, should be based more broadly on the general conditions existing at Bilbao today. Such a warning was compared to a storm warning: a battle was going on at Bilbao and it was obviously dangerous to enter a battle area, which might even extend beyond the three-mile limit. A warning on these grounds could be accompanied by a statement that, so far as our information went, Santander was not yet a battle area.

In connection with the proposal to advise British shipping to proceed to Santander instead of Bilbao, the First Lord of the Admiralty informed his colleagues that a telegram had been received indicating that mines were being laid at various places along the Spanish coast, including probably Santander.

While the use of Santander was favoured, it was recognised that, before a final decision could be taken, further technical information would be required which the Foreign Office and Admiralty were asked to obtain. It was felt that anything in the nature of an agreement with General Franco as between equals would be difficult to defend in Parliament, and from this point of view it was thought better to notify General Franco of our intention to advise British ships bound for Bilbao to proceed to the port of Santander and that we assumed there would be no interference with them.

While it was recognised that British ships could not be compelled to desist from proceeding on their voyage, whether to Bilbao or Santander, it was felt that if they were warned against such voyages they were not entitled to protection and should be given to understand that they undertook the voyage at their risk. In the case of Bilbao the British ships should be warned that this was the case, and the Naval authorities should be instructed to withdraw protection from British merchant ships which disregarded the wishes of His Majesty's Government that they should not proceed to that area, and that British merchant ships should be so informed.

As regards Santander, no final decision was reached. It was felt that the British Naval Authorities should continue to dissuade ships from proceeding to that port, though in that case they should not withhold protection if they insisted on proceeding.

General Franco, it was recognised, might at first refuse to admit food ships to Santander, but it was pointed out that he had probably not the naval forces available to make blockade effective at both ports simultaneously.

With a view to clearing up the position as regards the entry of British ships to the Bilbao area in ballast and their loading mineral for export, it was decided that enquiry should be made, through His Majesty's Ambassador at Hendaye, as to General Franco's attitude, and it was suggested that in the meantime no further discussion should take place on the subject between the British Senior Naval Officer and the Spanish Naval Authorities pending further instructions.

The Cabinet agreed:

a.   That the Secretary of State for Foreign Affairs should transmit immediately through the appropriate channel to General Franco's Government a written communication to the following effect: 'We cannot recognise or concede belligerent rights and we cannot tolerate any interference with British shipping at sea. We are, however, advising our shipping that, in view of the conditions at present prevailing in the neighbourhood of Bilbao, they should not go into that area so long as these conditions continue.'

b.   That the above written communication should be accompanied by verbal communications to the following effect:

i.   His Majesty's Government assume that if British ships go to Santander there will be no interference with them. If this is so the owners of the ships at present awaiting orders will be told that they may send them to Santander, if they wish, and shipowners will be informed that other vessels destined for Bilbao may be diverted to Santander if desired:

ii.   To enable His Majesty's Government to answer any questions that may be asked of them by our Nationals, they desire to know what would be the attitude of General Franco towards ships entering the Bilbao area in ballast and loading mineral for export.

c.   That the Secretary of State for Foreign Affairs should transmit immediately a copy of the telegram or telegrams sent in pursuance of (a) and (b) above to the First Lord of the Admiralty so as to enable him to inform the Naval authorities of the Spanish coast of the instructions issued by the Foreign Office.

d.   That the First Lord of the Admiralty, besides notifying the Naval authorities on the Spanish coast of the instructions issued by the Foreign Office, should instruct them that all Naval protection is to be withdrawn from British merchant ships which disregard the wishes of His Majesty's Government that they should not proceed to the Bilbao area and that British merchant ships should be so informed if the occasion arises: also he should inform the Naval authorities that as regards Santander a final decision has not yet been taken and that he should continue to dissuade ships from proceeding to that port but should afford them Naval protection on the same basis as hitherto.

e.   That the President of the Board of Trade should give appropriate warning to British shipowners in accordance with the instructions issued by the Foreign Office and the Admiralty in accordance with the above decisions.

f.   That, in order to enable a final decision to be taken as regards Santander, the following steps should be taken:

i.   The Secretary of State for Foreign Affairs should request His Majesty's Ambassador at Hendaye to send information as to the conditions in or near the harbour at Santander and more especially as to whether the approaches are mined and to what extent this constitutes a danger to shipping. He should ask if Santander is subject to insurgent bombardment from land or air;

ii. The First Lord of the Admiralty should send a corresponding message to the Naval authorities on the Spanish coast.

g.   That, in the event of the matter being raised in Parliament, the Prime Minister (in the absence of the Secretary of State for Foreign Affairs who had an important engagement in the provinces) should make a statement on the lines of conclusion (a) above.

(Copies of telegrams sent in accordance with the above Conclusions are attached as Appendix II.)

APPENDIX I

Decypher, Sir H. Chilton (Hendaye),
7th April, 1937.
Dispatched 6:00 p.m., 7th April, 1937,
Received 6:44 p.m., 7th April, 1937. No. 87.

Important: Please see Senior Naval Officer's signals ending with his number 2200/6 to Admiralty regarding incident involving *Thorp Hall*. Owing probably to advice which Senior Naval Officer thinks German man-of-war may have given insurgent cruisers (but which may not always be given or taken) yesterday's affair ended successfully; but this type of emergency is likely to recur at any moment and to become increasingly dangerous.

Bilbao is now effectively blockaded by one battleship, cruiser, light cruiser and destroyer plus armed trawler, all of which operate outside territorial waters more especially as the harbour entrance is fortified. Under present instructions British vessels entering or leaving Bilbao must be protected by His Majesty's Ships from this blockade when outside three mile limit. This involves escorting them and in order to do so properly and to be prepared to meet force with force Senior Naval Officer reckons that considerable reinforcements to his present effective strength would be required. Such numbers could not, however, be accommodated on this coast. It follows therefore that policy of protection of British shipping on high seas cannot be carried on in present circumstances affecting Bilbao.

Senior Naval Officer therefore suggests and I recommend that British shipping be warned that so long as port of Bilbao is effectively closed as at present His Majesty's Ships cannot protect them whatever their cargo from consequence of trying to run the blockade. I realise that this would be tantamount to agreeing to insurgents' exercise of belligerent rights, but such rights are already being effectively used by a considerable naval force such as circumstances unluckily prevent us from meeting, and further warning to insurgents would therefore appear to be an undesirable bluff.

Cypher telegram to Sir H. Chilton
(Hendaye),
Foreign Office,
8th April 1937, 10:30 p.m. No. 106.

Your telegram No. 87.

Question was discussed yesterday by Cabinet Committee as a result of which following action has been taken.

A. Admiralty have informed Commander-in-Chief that existing naval instructions stand, namely: protection to be given to British ships on the high seas, but not in territorial waters. His Majesty's ships are not however expected to engage forces in greatly superior strength or beyond what might reasonably be expected of them in war.

B. Board of Trade are sending private warning to ship-owners that owing to military operations, the neighbourhood of the Basque coast particularly off Bilbao is especially dangerous at present for shipping.

2   Effect of the above is that we will continue to resist interference on the high seas with force if necessary provided it is physically possible. As an additional deterrent to General Franco the Admiralty have decided to send an 8" gun cruiser to the Basque coast, based on La Rochelle but maintaining close contact with the destroyers. We are further endeavouring by our notice to shipowners to prevent the case arising.

3   At the same time as regards action in territorial waters, the Committee did not feel prepared either on the one hand publicly to admit that the Navy will not interfere in Spanish waters to protect British ships approaching Bilbao, or on the other hand to convoy British shipping through Spanish waters. The first course might mean that British ships could no longer carry from Bilbao and other Basque ports cargoes of iron-ore which are urgently needed in this country. It would also be equivalent to an invitation to General Franco to capture British ships as soon as they enter the three mile limit. The second course could not be justified legally if it came to a dispute.

4   Position therefore is somewhat complicated and Committee consider that it could best be straightened out by a personal visit of one of your staff, e.g. Mr Pack, to Salamanca for purpose of endeavouring to reach *modus vivendi* with the insurgent authorities on the whole question. The line which the messenger should take is as follows:

   A.   The general attitude of His Majesty's Government towards treatment of British ships is as set out in my despatch No. 333 which should be read out to and summarised in writing for the use of the insurgent authorities. This attitude is an integral part and an inescapable result of the policy of non-intervention and of non-recognition of belligerent rights which His Majesty's government and all other European Governments have adopted since the outbreak of the war and which has resulted in at least as great advantage to the insurgent Government as to their opponents. In particular it will be recalled that at the outset of the war when the Spanish Government had control of Spanish Mediterranean waters, this policy enabled His Majesty's Government to give protection to British trade with all Spanish ports, including those under General Franco's control. Further to the fact should be noted that without any action on their part and without any risk of conflict with His Majesty's Government, the insurgents have been and are assured that arms and war material cannot reach the Spanish Government in British ships.

B.   His Majesty's Government therefore feel justified in asking the insurgent authorities to assist them in maintaining this attitude by once more reaffirming the instructions which they have already, on several occasions, issued to their warships not to interfere with British shipping to Spain. Only by this means can the risk be avoided of serious incidents between British and insurgent warships which could only have the most dangerous results on the relations between His Majesty's Government and the insurgent authorities.

C.   The situation at Bilbao is somewhat exceptional and the insurgent authorities may insist that their close investment of the town justifies them in refusing to permit supplies of any sort from reaching it by sea. They may argue that at any rate in territorial waters His Majesty's Government have no right to force British ships through. The messenger can reply that His Majesty's Government do not admit the authority of the insurgents to exercise belligerent rights – e.g. to blockade a port – either on the high seas or elsewhere, but that he has no instructions as to whether they would prevent such action by force in territorial waters. If further pressed he must repeat that he has no instructions regarding territorial waters and must refer back to his Government.

* * *

64. *British Attitude in the Event of a Blockade by Japan of Canton*[1]

Memorandum by E.A. Seal, for Head of M.[2]

[CO 323/1523/13; Secret, P.D. 06367/37]   19 August 1937

Attention is drawn to the enclosed copy of a telegram No. 295 from Japan which seems to imply that the Japanese are seriously considering the exercise of belligerent rights in some form or another. The questions which will be raised if they proceed to do so were accordingly discussed at a semi-official meeting held at the Foreign Office this morning which was attended by Mr Ords, Sir John Pratt, Mr Fitzmaurice and Mr Ronald on behalf of the Foreign Office, and by Captain Syfret, Mr Seal and Major Grover on behalf of the Admiralty.

---

[1]See also CO 323/1523/14, Memorandum on the Closure of the China Coast, 24 September 1937.
[2]'M' branch, part of the Admiralty secretariat.

2.   At the present moment, although fighting is going on, there has been no declaration of war by either side, nor has any action been taken which could be construed into an avowal of the fact that a state of war exists. The first question discussed was whether an attempt by the Japanese to exercise belligerent rights would necessarily amount to such an avowal and, if so, what the effect would be.

3.   The normal rule of international law is that belligerent rights, as the name implies, can only exist if a state of war exists. Normally therefore the exercise of belligerent rights amounts, if not to a declaration of war, at least to an open avowal that a state of war exists.

4.   In the course of the discussion, however, it appeared that there is at least the theoretical possibility that the Japanese might attempt to establish what is known as a 'pacific blockade.' The attitude which HMG have maintained at any rate in recent years with regard to such blockades is that they cannot be binding upon the shipping of third parties. There is, however, the precedent of the French blockade of Formosa, when the French notified us that a blockade had been established but stated that, in their view, a state of war did not exist. The British reply was to the effect that HMG were prepared to accept the blockade but considered that the circumstances were such that a state of war did exist. Mr Fitzmaurice thought that it would be possible to argue that a State is free to acquiesce in the exercise of blockade against its shipping, without necessarily admitting that a state of war exists. It seems, however, very difficult to believe that it would be politically practicable for the British Government to follow such a procedure in this case, especially having regard to the undoubted fact that there will be considerable feeling in the country against the Japanese as aggressors. It would also run counter to the attitude adopted by HMG in the past as explained above. The above argument only applies to blockade – not contraband.

5.   The meeting, therefore, passed on to consider the practical consequences of an act by Japan (or by ourselves) which would be tantamount to an admission that a state of war existed. Attention was drawn to Article 17 of the Covenant of the League of Nations which covers the case where one of the parties to a war (i.e. Japan) is not a member of the League. Mr Fitzmaurice's view was that it would be open to any member of the League to draw the attention of the Council to the fact that a state of war between China and Japan had been openly avowed, and to request that the Council should put the procedure of the Article into operation. The Article provides that Japan should be asked to assume the obligations of a Member; and it must be assumed that in all probability she would refuse to do so. In this event the provisions of

Article 16 (i.e. Sanctions) would automatically become applicable to Japan – which is not a very pleasant prospect.

6.   The Admiralty representatives were inclined to think that to invoke the League in this way would offer great advantages to China and that it might be difficult to prevent her doing so; they also suggested that Russia might be likely to follow the same line. The Foreign Office representatives, however, thought that the risk was comparatively remote.

7.   The meeting then passed on to consider the fore-going in relation to belligerent rights. Leaving on one side the possibility of a 'pacific blockade' (which is dealt with in paragraph 4 above), if the Japanese intend to exercise belligerent rights there are two alternative lines upon which the matter may develop, depending upon whether or not the dispute comes within the cognisance of the League of Nations.

8.   If the matter does not come before the League of Nations it would be extremely difficult for us, having regard to the fighting which is actually going on, to take the line that a state of war does not exist. The old fashioned rules of neutrality would therefore apply, under which it is not possible to deny belligerent rights to either party.

9.   If, on the other hand, Article 16 is put into force, a position is established identical with that which existed during the Italy-Abyssinian war, when sanctions had been put into force against Italy, but when she fortunately refrained from exercising belligerent rights. On that occasion there was an awkward dispute between the Admiralty and the Foreign Office, the Admiralty maintaining that apart from the specific provisions of Article 16, the ordinary rules of neutrality (including belligerent rights) apply, and the Foreign Office that the Covenant of the League creates an entirely new relationship and that a covenant breaking State cannot expect to receive the benefits of the ordinary law. It was admitted, however, that if a similar position arose in connection with the Sino-Japanese dispute, the Admiralty case would be stronger than it was in the Italo-Abyssinian war, inasmuch as Japan, not being a member of the League, cannot be a covenant breaking power.

10.   It was stated on behalf of the Admiralty that if any attempt should be made to deny belligerent rights to Japan, either on the basis of Article 16 of the Covenant of the League or on any other basis, the result would very likely be to involve us in war. It was also pointed out that any such attempt would be extremely ill-advised, since a precedent set by ourselves in a Sino-Japanese war might be used against us by USA if we became [a] belligerent. The Foreign Office representatives, however, were not prepared to admit the validity of this last argument if the withholding of belligerent rights was based upon Article 16 of the

Covenant, on the principle that Article 16 would never be put into force against this country.

11.   The meeting then passed on to consider in a somewhat summary form the practical difficulties of permitting Japan to exercise belligerent rights. It was agreed that a blockade of the Yangtse would lead to endless difficulty and trouble because Shanghai and the other treaty ports up the river would be blockaded with the rest of Chinese territory. Mr Fitzmaurice expressed the view that it would not be possible to urge that these concessions should be exempted from the blockade on the ground that they were neutral territory, since the residual sovereignty is undoubtedly Chinese.

12.   As regards a possible blockade of Canton, the practical difficulties enumerated in paragraphs 2 and 3 of D. of P's minute of the 16th August were explained.

13.   On the other hand an attempt by the Japanese to exercise contraband control would very likely mean that ships bound for any port in China, including Hong Kong and Shanghai, might be diverted for search to Japanese territory such as Formosa or the Pescadores. It would be difficult for us, who followed the practice of diversion for search in the late war, to protest. The meeting also felt that, having regard to Japanese methods, the search of ships would probably be carried out with unwarrantable severity and that endless illegalities would take place. The result would be continual piling up of protests and annoyances of a very vexatious character.

14.   Before the meeting broke up it was agreed that Mr Fitzmaurice should prepare a memorandum dealing with the pros and cons of recognising that a state of war exists in the Far East. Mr Fitzmaurice pointed out that there may be other considerations (such as internment of Chinese in Shanghai) beyond those arising from the possible application of Articles 16 and 17 which should be taken into account; and as it may well be that at some stage HM Government will be in a position to exercise influence in determining this issue, it seems just as well that the matter should be fully explored.

15.   It is clear from the above report of the meeting that if the Japanese decided to exercise belligerent rights (and they would clearly be strongly tempted to reap the benefits of sea power in this way) we may be faced with a very difficult position. On the assumption that we do not want war with Japan from the Admiralty point of view an attempt to prevent them exercising belligerent rights would probably be the worst thing that could happen, since not only would it mean virtually certain war, but it would also set a bad precedent which might be quoted by America against ourselves. On the other hand it cannot be denied that

to permit Japan to attempt to blockade the Yangtse, or to exercise contraband control in the way we exercised it in the late war, would not only inflict a great loss on legitimate shipping, but would also place a very considerable strain upon Anglo-Japanese relations.

16.   It is therefore felt that it may be desirable to suggest to the Japanese some reasonable procedure which we could accept and which would give them all they reasonably require. It is clear that the Japanese Admiralty is in a state of uncertainty about the best method of proceeding; also that the Japanese Government are anxious to avoid estranging British and American opinion. If, therefore, some scheme could be worked out under which the Japanese should be regarded as entitled to exercise belligerent rights, but would undertake not to search British liners and other important ships on the understanding that we could guarantee their innocence, it seems likely that the Japanese would accept it. It might also be possible to work out an agreement with the Japanese under which their consular Officers could have facilities for checking the loading of British ships destined for China.

17.   The difficulty about any such arrangement would be that we should be giving indirect aid to the Japanese in waging war against the Chinese and if anything were done it would presumably have to be unobtrusive for this reason. On the other hand, it is felt that the risks of any other course are so great as to provide ample justification.

18.   It is, therefore, proposed to submit for decision whether the Admiralty should not suggest that the details of some such scheme should be worked out in consultation with the Board of Trade and the Foreign Office. The matter seems to be of some urgency as no one can say when the Japanese will show their hand.

* * *

BRITISH SHIPPING IN CHINESE WATERS,
POSSIBLE EXERCISE OF BELLIGERENT RIGHTS
Board of Trade, September 1937

1.   The Admiralty, supported by the Foreign Office, have called the attention of the Board of Trade to the difficulties which may arise if the Japanese begin to exercise belligerent rights, and, in pursuance of those rights, stop and search British ships trading with China in order to see whether they are carrying contraband. Previous experience has shown that British ships which get into the hands of Japanese officials (e.g., through inadvertently entering prohibited Japanese waters) receive very

unpleasant treatment. The Admiralty fear that in the exercise of belligerent rights the Japanese would take British ships into Japanese ports
for examination, and that those ships might then not only suffer great
delay, but also be subjected to such harsh and inconsiderate treatment
as to provoke incidents of which the British Government would have to
take serious notice.

2.   It is for this and other special reasons that the Admiralty desire to
see arrangements made with the Japanese for enabling British ships to
avoid being searched for contraband, notwithstanding that in any war in
which this country was engaged the Government would presumably (as
in the Great War) claim and exercise belligerent rights on a very extensive scale and would refuse to accept any limitation.

3.   The general purpose is that British shipowners trading with China,
who decide not to carry contraband, should be enabled to obtain certificates which the Japanese would accept as exempting the ships from
search. The British shipping industry would like to have arrangements
of this kind, and it appears probable that a large number of British
shipowners trading with China would, in any case, refrain from carrying contraband so that they would be in a position to take advantage of
the arrangements if they were brought into existence.

4.   The suggestions put forward by the Admiralty envisaged the possibility of Government participation in the scheme as a means of securing
its acceptance by the Japanese. This may be found indispensable (see
paragraph 10 below) but Government participation seems open to many
serious objections, both nationally and internationally.

5.   Public opinion in this country might well criticise the Government
very strongly for participating in (or, as would be alleged, for promot-
ing) a scheme under which British shipowners undertook not to carry
contraband to China. It would be represented that this scheme conferred great advantages on the Japanese and corresponding disadvantages
on the Chinese, on such grounds as (1) that it helped to make effective
the Japanese attempt to keep munitions of war out of China, and (2)
that, by making it unnecessary for Japanese warships to search merchant ships, it set free the warships for military operations against the
Chinese.

6.   Internationally, the action of the Government might be criticised
on similar grounds, and it would not doubt be resented by China. This
last point seems very important in connection with the future relations
of this country with China for trading and other purposes. In so far as
Japan secures control of Chinese territory, it seems very unlikely that
our trade with that territory can be regarded as secure in the future.
There is, therefore, little or nothing to be gained from this point of view

by trying to propitiate Japan. On the other hand, in so far as China successfully resists Japanese aggression and remains master of its own territory, the question whether British trade with China will be satisfactorily maintained after the conclusion of hostilities may well depend on whether or not our action during the hostilities has commended itself to Chinese opinion.

7.   A recent telegram from our Embassy in China strongly emphasised the violent reaction of Chinese opinion that would follow the imposition of an embargo on the export of arms from Hong Kong to China. The same considerations would no doubt apply, though with rather less immediacy, to any action by His Majesty's Government which could be represented as impeding the shipment of arms to China. Past experience shows how strongly politics in China are liable to react on trade.

8.   From this point of view, if the only way of protecting British shipping from the unrestricted exercise of Japanese belligerent rights involved Government action which would arouse strong hostility in China, the question would arise whether, in the general interest of British trade, the scheme for the protection of shipping should be proceeded with.

9.   It is possible, though not certain, that the same objections would not apply if the shipping industry could itself work out a scheme for enabling British ships not carrying contraband to China to avoid being searched by Japanese naval officers. The Board of Trade have asked the shipping industry in the UK to consider whether a scheme for this purpose could be worked out without involving the participation of the Government. Until they have considered the matter, no definite opinion can be given; but the attached note indicates the possible lines on which a scheme might be prepared.

10.   It is, of course, quite impossible to know in advance whether the Japanese would accept any scheme under which ships trading with China could pass through without being searched for contraband. They would no doubt want to be completely satisfied that the scheme was a reliable one, and they would probably press for the participation of His Majesty's Government in the scheme. For example, they might ask for ships to be provided with a certificate from the British officials (Consular Officers or Customs Officers as the case might be) at each port of call. They might also want to have the certificates endorsed by the Japanese consuls at each port – a proposal which would probably not be agreeable to British shipping and trading interests.

11.   The shipping industry have already emphasised how important it is from their point of view that if the Japanese issue a contraband list, the list should be short and definite. It is clear that unless this condition

is complied with, a scheme of certificates for ships not carrying contraband would be very difficult, if not impossible, to work. Here again, the situation would be in pronounced contrast with the position during the Great War when this country, in its blockade of Germany, enforced a belligerent list of a very extensive character.

Ships carrying goods for Hong Kong

12.   It will be clear that one of the great difficulties which will arise in the event of the Japanese exercising belligerent rights will be the resulting interference with trade with Hong Kong. Hong Kong is at all times one of the most important ports of entry for goods destined for China; and with Shanghai practically closed to trade, and other Chinese ports becoming more restricted, goods for China will tend more and more to be landed at Hong Kong. [Illegible insert.] These goods may include arms, munitions and oil (which may well be one of the items in a Japanese contraband list) intended for use or consumption in Hong Kong itself. The Japanese would not be entitled, in pursuance of belligerent rights, to blockade Hong Kong, but they would be entitled to stop and search ships bound for Hong Kong in order to ascertain whether their cargo included any contraband ultimately destined for China. [Illegible alteration.]

13.   Whatever may be done about ships carrying goods intended for China, some arrangement would seem necessary to ensure that, in the event of the Japanese issuing a contraband list, there shall be no interference with shipments to Hong Kong, for use in that Colony, of goods falling under the categories in the list. [Illegible addition.]

* * *

MEMORANDUM ON THE CLOSURE OF THE CHINA COAST
CONFIDENTIAL, F 7977/130/10

[CO 323/1523/14]   October 15, 1937

Institution of a Peacetime 'Blockade'

On the 10th August the naval attaché was informed at the Ministry of Marine that in the event of war with China the Japanese navy would probably institute a form of blockade in order to prevent contraband from entering China. They did not wish to interfere with other legitimate trade, and would welcome the co-operation of the Powers in stopping contraband imports. The naval attaché received the impression that they had no definite plans yet, but were considering the effect of such action on other Powers (see telegram No. 280 of the 10th August). Two days later (see telegram No. 286 of the 12th August), Captain Rawlings was informed that if a blockade were instituted the Japanese would issue a list of contraband. On the 16th August (see telegram No. 295 of that date) the Ministry added that it might be necessary to address a note to the Powers to the effect that circumstances might require the establishment of a system of searching merchant ships for armaments, etc., at Canton and Shanghai, though such search would not be necessary at other ports. They hoped that the Powers would collaborate in the interest of shortening the hostilities.

2.   On the morning of the 26th August an official of the Ministry for Foreign Affairs called at this Embassy to leave a copy of a statement, which had been issued to the press, that the Japanese naval authorities had closed the China coast to Chinese vessels from 32°4' north latitude and 121°44' east longitude to 23°14' north latitude and 116°48' east longitude (*i.e.*, from the Yangtze estuary to Swatow) beginning at 6 p.m. on the 25th August, 1937. The statement added that this measure applied only to Chinese vessels and that 'peaceful commerce' carried on by other Powers would be fully respected (see telegram No. 317 of the 26th August). On the 5th September (see telegram No. 349 of that date) the Ministry for Foreign Affairs sent this Embassay a copy of a statement, which they had just issued, announcing the decision of the Japanese Government to extend the above-named length of coast line and close, from noon of the 5th September, 1937, the rest of the Chinese coast, namely, from 40° north latitude and 119°54' east longitude (Shanhaikuan, where the Great Wall meets the sea) to 21°33' north latitude and 108°3' east longitude (the boarder of Indo-China), excluding Tsingtao and the leased territories of third Powers. This statement repeated the intention of the Japanese Government to 'pay due respect to the peaceful commerce of third Powers with which they have no intention of interfering.'

Attitude of Great Britain and Other Powers

3.   In his telegram (No. 317 of the 26th August) reporting the closing of part of the China coast, Mr Dodds enquired whether he should ask what the Japanese Government meant by their reference to the 'peaceful' commerce of other Powers. On the 27th August the aide-de-camp to the Ministry of Marine informed the United States naval attaché that the Japanese would only remove troops and armament stores, but not normal cargo, from Chinese ships; that they would not confiscate Chinese registered ships; that they would not interfere in any way with

neutral ships, even if known to be carrying munitions; but that the above would apply only as long as no state of war existed (see telegram No. 321 of the 27th August). On the 28th August (see telegram No. 326 of the 29th August) the French counsellor asked the Vice-Minister for Foreign Affairs informally what was meant by the word 'peaceful.' Mr Horinouchi replied that he must have notice of that question; and to a similar enquiry made by the American counsellor answered that he must have such questions in writing.

4.   An attempt was made by the Foreign Office (see Foreign Office telegram to Washington No. 338 of the 30th August) to secure concerted action between the United States and British representatives at Tokyo with a view to eliciting from the Japanese Government a precise statement of the measures which they intended to take against shipping on the China coast. Meanwhile, the French counsellor was sent for on the 31st August (see telegram No. 333 of that date) by the Vice-Minister for Foreign Affairs, who took advantage of the former's informal enquiry of the 28th August to make an oral communication to the effect that the 'blockade' measures did not apply to arms and ammunition carried by vessels of third Powers. Chinese ships had, however, been flying foreign flags and the Japanese were forced to inspect suspects. To avoid misunderstandings the Japanese would find it convenient to have advance notice of ships of third Powers entering the prescribed area. If China received large supplies of arms and ammunition from abroad the conflict would be prolonged and intensified, and the Japanese Government accordingly hoped that third Powers would refrain as far as possible from encouraging China in that direction. Although the Japanese Government did not for the present contemplate taking action to prevent the importation of arms and ammunition into China by third Powers, future developments might compel them to devise more effective and suitable measures to stop such importation. The United States Ambassador, having telegraphed this information to his Government, was instructed (see telegram No. 335 of the 1st September) to take no action.

5.   On the 9th September instructions were sent (in Foreign Office telegram No. 297) to Sir R. Craigie to inform the Japanese Government that, while His Majesty's Government in the United Kingdom did not admit the right of the Japanese Government in this matter, they would in practice allow the verification of the nationality of vessels flying the British flag on certain conditions, but could acquiesce in no further interference. His Majesty's Government, however, reserved the right to claim compensation for damage sustained by the owners of British ships delayed or stopped under the proposed procedure, which was as follows:

His Majesty's Government would advise British shipping in the Far East that (a) in the presence of a British man-of-war, a Japanese man-of-war on suspecting that a vessel bound for the China coast was flying the British flag under false pretences would ask the British man-of-war to verify the right of the vessel to fly the British flag; and that (b) in the absence of any British man-of-war, His Majesty's Government would not stand on their rights (if there were genuine reason to suspect that the vessel was not entitled to fly the British flag) if the Japanese boarded her and examined her certificates of registry, provided that the Japanese man-of-war simultaneously made an immediate report to the British naval authorities.

6.   A memorandum in this sense was left by Sir R. Craigie with the Vice-Minister for Foreign Affairs on the 11th September. On the 20th September the press were informed by an assistant to the spokesman of the Ministry for Foreign Affairs, that His Majesty's Government had informed the Japanese Government by note that they would raise no objections to the stopping [and] searching of British ships by Japanese men-of-war seeking to verify their identity. No replies had been received from other countries, but it was understood that they would likewise co-operate with Japan. Later on the same day a reply was received from the Japanese Government to the Embassy's memorandum of the 11th September. In this reply, the substance of which was given to the Foreign Office in telegram No. 415 of the 20th September, the Japanese Government agreed that a British man-of-war, if one was present, would be asked to verify the right of a suspected vessel to fly the British flag, and requested that the result of its investigations might be communicated to the Japanese navy immediately. Should the commander of the British man-of-war request the presence of an officer from the Japanese man-of-war as a witness, consent would readily be given. It was hoped that precautions would be taken to prevent misuse by Chinese vessels of British flags in order to avoid visits of inspection by the Japanese. When a Japanese man-of-war visited a vessel flying the British flag and found it to be British, there was no objection to informing the British naval authorities by the quickest available means.

7.   The Japanese Government had a few days previously (see telegram No. 407 of the 18th September) issued a statement that they would not recognise the validity of transfers of nationality of Chinese ships subsequent to the 25th August unless the transfer was effected in accordance with the laws of the countries concerned and fully completed. Suspect ships might be detained and inspected for verification purposes. The Powers concerned were requested to beware of Chinese vessels acquir-

ing their nationality simply in order to evade measures by the Japanese navy.

British Shipping and the Hostilities

8. On the 23rd August the Commander-in-Chief, China Squadron, requested that the Chinese and Japanese Governments might be officially informed that British men-of-war stationed in Chinese waters had the Union flag on the horizontal surfaces of turrets and on awnings as an identification mark to aircraft (see Commander-in-Chief's telegram to Tokyo of the 23rd August). This information was given to the Japanese Government in a note dated the 24th August.

9. The steamship *Luchow* of the Chinese Navigation Company, on a voyage from Saigon to Dairen, was on the 23rd August signalled to stop by a Japanese aircraft carrier in the open sea north-east of the mouth of the Yangtze. After boarding and interrogation, she was permitted to proceed, but no explanation of the boarding was given (see telegram No. 324 of the 28th August). On the 28th August the steamship *Shenking* was challenged by a Japanese cruiser off (?) Savage Island, but on replying to the signal was allowed to proceed (Commander-in-Chief's telegram No. 175 of the 28th August to the Admiralty).

10. The aide-de-camp to the Ministry of Marine informed the naval attaché on the 1st September (see telegram No. 336 of that date) that the Japanese Government were concerned over the fact that Hong Kong was being used to import arms and ammunition for the Chinese. He stated that ships carrying arms had actually arrived there and that others were on their way, but could give no details. The object of Japanese air operations in the south was to interrupt the transport of these arms northwards.

11. A memorandum addressed to the British Embassy at Nanking by the Chinese Government on the 8th September stated that in view of the blockade the Chinese air force and other defensive forces must take appropriate action against all Japanese naval vessels along the coast. The ships of friendly Powers should keep well away from Japanese men-of-war and military transports, and were requested to paint on them their national colours in such a way as to be recognisable from the air (see Nanking telegram No. 189 of the 9th September to the Commander-in-Chief). The Commander-in-Chief observed in this connexion (in his telegram to Nanking No. 17 of the 9th September) that the Chinese and Japanese Governments should be reminded, whenever they made mention of identification marks, that the onus of identification rests with them; and on the 16th September the Foreign Office addressed a telegram (No. 299) to Nanking with instructions that the

Chinese Government should be informed that His Majesty's Government could not agree to instruct British merchantmen to adopt the prescribed markings and would hold the Chinese Government fully responsible for any attacks on British merchantmen, though every endeavour would be made by British ships to steer clear of Japanese men-of-war.

12.   A Domei report that the British steamship *Tishan, en route* to Canton from Hong Kong, had twice been turned back to British territorial waters by Japanese warships (see telegram No. 363 of the 7th September) proved to be inaccurate; though the *Taishan* [*sic*] did in fact turn back of her own accord on sighting a Japanese destroyer (see telegram from Commodore, Hong Kong, timed 17:49 the 7th September). Later the *Taishan*, with a cargo of arms, proceeded to Canton. On her return voyage she was stopped and boarded from a Japanese destroyer and allowed to proceed with an apology for the mistake in her identity which had been taken for Chinese (see telegram from Commodore, Hong Kong, timed 16:29 of the 8th September).

13.   On the receipt of instructions contained in Foreign Office telegram No. 292 of the 8th September, Sir R. Craigie on the 10th September addressed to the Japanese Government a note protesting strongly against the abuse of Hong Kong territorial waters by a Japanese destroyer which, on the 5th September, fired from within 3 miles of Black Point upon a Chinese maritime customs preventive motor-boat which she subsequently captured. The note reserved the rights of His Majesty's Government as regards claiming compensation and requested urgent instructions might be issued to prevent the recurrence of such illegal acts. To this protest the Japanese Government replied on the 18th September stating that action was taken by Japanese men-of-war in respect of Chinese customs surveillance vessels at two points which were defined and declared to be outside Hong Kong territorial waters, and that there was therefore no reason why a protest should be received from His Majesty's Government (see despatch No. 471 of the 21st September).

14.   In Foreign Office telegram No. 301 of the 10th September, R. Craigie was instructed to make an enquiry of the Japanese Government regarding their apparent intention to attack merchant vessels on the Yangtze from the air. This intention appeared from the oral reply given by the Japanese Government on the 23rd August when the representatives of Great Britain, France, Germany, Italy and the United States requested that a safety zone might be established at Nanking which would not be subjected to bombing by the Japanese (see paragraph 11 of the memorandum enclosed in Tokyo despatch No. 446 of the 8th

September), Sir R. Craigie first, in accordance with his instructions informed his four interested colleagues of his proposed action in case they should wish to take similar action themselves. They did not, and on the 13th September his excellency left with the Vice-Minister for Foreign Affairs a memorandum in which were expounded the arguments against attacking any merchant vessels, whether enemy or neutral, in wartime or not, from the air, and asking whether such was really the intention of the Japanese Government. The Vice-Minister for Foreign Affairs and the Vice-Minister of Marine, who was also present on another matter, both emphatically denied that the Japanese Government had any intention of attacking merchant ships from the air if they were not marked in accordance with the Japanese request, and claimed that this request was intended to diminish the risk of an accidental hit (see telegram No. 379 of the 14th September). An official reply was promised as soon as possible. It was sent on the 16th September, and stated that the request of the Japanese Government that merchant vessels of third countries should be marked with their national colours was not made as the result of a deliberate plan to bomb merchant vessels. Sir R. Craigie, in a letter to the Vice-Minister for Foreign Affairs, pointed out that this reply did not explain what *was* the purpose of the request. Mr Horinouchi telephoned on the 21st September to say that he had meant to R. Craigie in his previous conversation with him on the subject that foreign vessels should be marked with their national colours 'since Japanese aircraft would try to pay special attention to vessels so marked' (see telegram No. 427 of the 23rd September).

Sinking of a Japanese Merchant Vessel

15. A report has been received from His Majesty's consul-general at Seoul that the Japanese steamship *Kongosan Maru* was sunk off Gensan about the 20th August in calm and clear weather. It was rumoured that the cause was sabotage. No mention of this was allowed to appear in the local press.

Tokyo, September 24, 1937

* * *

65.   *Admiralty to Commander-in-Chief. Mediterranean*

[ADM 1/9948]   3 December 1937

My 1430/3. The following is repetition of telegram No. 409 dated 3rd December from Foreign Office to Sir H. Chilton, Hendaye, Begins:

Your telegrams No. 440 and No. 39 Saving.
Presumably Cape Cervera referred to in your telegram No. 440 should read Cape Cerbere, as otherwise only a small portion of coast in the south would be covered.

Note Verbale dated 24 November appears to be intended as a definite notification of a blockade of the whole of the Spanish coast now in Government hands. You should therefore address a note to Nationalist authorities stating that as belligerent rights have not been recognised to either party in the Spanish conflict, HM Government are not prepared to admit their right to declare any blockade. Whilst recognising and appreciating the desire of the Nationalist authorities as evidenced by the Note Verbale reported in your telegram No. 69 Saving, to avoid any vexatious incident, HM Government, who are animated by the same desire, must nevertheless warn them against any interference with British shipping trading with Spanish ports; such shipping will continue to be protected as hitherto.

You should draw special attention to the passage in the Note indicating that Portsmouth will be blocked with mines. Article 2 of the Eighth Hague Convention, which must be regarded as constituting the minimum requirements of international law on the subject, forbids the laying of mines off the coasts and ports of the enemy with the sole object of intercepting commercial navigation. It would appear from the context that this is the precise object with which these mines are to be laid. In these circumstances HM Government consider it necessary to enter a most emphatic protest against this measure, which would constitute a breach of international law even if belligerent rights had been recognised. Ends. 2135/3 for Head of M.

* * *

66. *Possible Abrogation of the Declaration of Paris*

Foreign Office Minutes

Registry No. A 4770/4770/45   31 May to 15 June 1938
[FO 371/21548]

'H.W.M.'   May 31, 1938
1. On December 18, 1918, a body called the 'International Law Committee,' of which Lord Cave was Chairman, made a report to the
Attorney-General on 'The Freedom of the Seas'; the report was subsequently reprinted in January 1928 as a CID paper (B.R.7), but we no
doubt received a copy of it in 1918. In paragraph 17 of that report the
Committee recommended that, if possible, the Declaration of Paris
should be abrogated, a course which had been urged by the Admiralty
in a letter to the Foreign Office of April 30th, 1918. This recommendation has never been acted on, and I should be grateful if I could have a
short note showing what happened about it.
2. Can you produce a copy, or better still, a translation of the Italian
Rules of Maritime Prize of March 1917?

F.J.W. Legg, 1938, Deputy Naval Stores Officer. June 10, 1938.
The recommendation in question was passed by the Committee on 11th
October 1918 and communicated to the Foreign Office for necessary
action about a week later, i.e., well in advance of the Committee's
report of 18th December 1918 [176416/539/1918].
    It was felt that formal withdrawal from the Declaration of Paris
might have been regarded as a retrograde step on the part of His
Majesty's Government and there was the further difficulty that the
Declaration contained no provision for denunciation, and withdrawal
could therefore only be effected with the consent of the other parties, or
at least of our Allies, France and Italy, which was unlikely to be forthcoming.
    It was therefore suggested that the best course was for His Majesty's
Government to urge that the Declaration should be determined on the
ground that belligerent rights at sea ought not to be restricted in view of
the possible break-down of the League of Nations or of some nation
refusing to join it.
    A draft memorandum on these lines was accordingly prepared for
the War Cabinet in November, but does not seem to have been submitted to that body, nor can I find any record of Cabinet discussions on the
International Law Committee's recommendation.

Sir C[ecil] Hurst took the draft memorandum with him to the Peace Conference, but returned the papers towards the end of January, 1919, because there seemed a prospect of the whole question being shelved. This, in fact turned out to be the case, as President Wilson did not press his point about the Freedom of the Seas at the Peace Conference. Furthermore the International Law Committee reached the definite conclusion in their report that discussion of questions relating to maritime belligerent rights should be postponed if possible.

The text of the Italian Rules of Maritime Prize of 25th March, 1917 will be found on page 1302 *et seq* of the attached volume [Cat. 8vo. 2764 Vol. 2, 1917]. We do not seem to have an English translation.

'H.W.M.' June 15 1938.
Many thanks; this information was most useful.

* * *

67. *Handbook of Economic Warfare*

[FO 837/3]   July 1939

INTRODUCTION

THE object of this Handbook is to set out in convenient form the nature, purpose and scope of the war-time measures which, taken as a whole, are incorrectly named 'blockade' and, more accurately, economic warfare. It is intended to serve not only as a basis for the preparation of economic warfare plans in peace-time, but also as a guide for those officials and others who would be seconded or temporarily appointed to the Ministry of Economic Warfare upon its establishment in time of war, or whose functions bring them into contact with the planning or conduct of economic warfare.

2.   It will be obvious that not all the measures described in this Handbook will be appropriate to the circumstances of every war in which this country might be engaged. Some of them may be regarded as natural consequences of a state of war and would be put into effect automatically either during the Precautionary Period or as soon as a state of war exists. Others might never be required, while others again raise questions of high policy upon which the Cabinet must pronounce before action can be taken. Nearly all of them will in any case require to be reviewed not only at intervals in peace-time but also, and especially, at any time of apprehended emergency. The responsibility for

such reviews falls mainly upon the Foreign Office, which has been designated by the Committee of Imperial Defence as 'parent' department of the Ministry which would be set up in wartime to co-ordinate and, in most cases, execute the measures described in this Handbook.

3.   The Handbook is divided into four parts. The first deals with the theory and organisation of economic warfare, the second with its weapons, and the third with the administrative machinery for its execution. The last part contains, in the form of annexes, the texts of the draft Bills, Orders, Proclamations, &c., necessary for the conduct of economic warfare, and of the instructions relating to economic warfare held by His Majesty's Diplomatic and Consular Representatives abroad and by Collectors of Customs at home.

PART I
THEORY AND ORGANISATION

Chapter I   Objects, Methods and Peace-time Organisation
Chapter II   Ministry of Economic Warfare
Chapter III   Intelligence Organisation

CHAPTER I
OBJECTS, METHODS AND PEACE-TIME ORGANISATION

I – THE AIM

THE aim of economic warfare is so to disorganise the enemy's economy as to prevent him from carrying on the war. Its effectiveness in any war in which this country may be engaged will vary inversely with the degree of self-sufficiency which the enemy has attained, and/or the facilities he has, and can maintain, for securing supplies from neighbouring neutral countries, and directly with extent to which (i) his imports must be transported across seas which can be controlled by His Majesty's ships, (ii) his industry and centres of storage, production, manufacture and distribution are vulnerable to attack[1] from the air, and (iii) opportunities arise for interfering with exports originating from his territories.

2.   Economic warfare is a military operation, comparable to the operations of the three Services in that its object is the defeat of the enemy, and complementary to them in that its function is to deprive the enemy of the material means of resistance. But, unlike the operations of the armed forces, its results are secured not only by direct attack upon the

---

[1]*This factor depends of course on the policy of His Majesty's Government in regard to bombing from the air, which in turn depend[s] on that of the enemy.

enemy but also by bringing pressure to bear upon those neutral countries from which the enemy draws his supplies. It must be distinguished from coercive measures appropriate for adoption in peace to settle international differences without recourse to war, e.g., sanctions, pacific blockade, economic reprisals, &c., since, unlike such measures, it has as its ultimate sanction the use of belligerent rights.

II – WEAPONS

3. Broadly speaking, there are three categories of weapons:
    (a) Legislative action.
    (b) Diplomatic action.
    (c) Military action (in the broadest sense).
Of these –
    (a) Controls commercial and financial activities within the belligerent's own territories.
    (b) Aims at controlling the commercial and financial activities of neutral countries which serve as sources or channels of supply to the enemy.
    (c) Attacks the enemy directly by interfering with his supplies from overseas, whether consigned direct or, indirectly, through neutral countries, by destroying them or preventing their distribution after they have reached his territories, and, so far as may be practicable, by interfering with his exports.

4. The objects and method of operation of these three weapons are set out in detail in Part II of this handbook.

III – MACHINERY AND ORGANISATION

(a) In Peace

5. In peace-time questions concerning economic warfare are the responsibility of a Sub-Committee of the Committee of Imperial Defence – the Advisory Committee on Trade Questions in Time of War (ATB Committee) – on which are represented the Treasury, Foreign Office, Board of Trade, Board of Customs and Excise, Department of Overseas Trade, Admiralty, War Office, Air Ministry, Home Office, Scottish Office, Dominions Office, Colonial Office and India Office.

6. For the preparation of specific plans for economic warfare against potential enemies, this Committee has appointed an Economic Pressure Sub-Committee, over which the Chairman of the A.T.B. Committee presides also. On this sub-Committee are represented the Treasury, Foreign Office, Board of Trade, Admiralty and Department of Overseas Trade (Industrial Intelligence Centre).

7. The Foreign Office, as the parent Department of the Ministry of Economic Warfare, is specifically responsible for the detailed preparation of economic warfare plans for submission to the Economic Pressure Sub-Committee.

(b)   In War

8. In the event of a major war a Ministry of Economic Warfare will be set up. This Ministry will be responsible both for the initiation of plans and the direction of policy in regard to economic warfare as a whole, and for the actual administration of a considerable part of the work.

(c)   Co-ordination

9. The work of the Ministry needs to be planned, both in peace and in war, in constant and unremitting touch with the Admiralty, War Office, and Air Ministry, and those civil departments whose activities may require co-ordination with those of the Ministry. Co-ordination with the Fighting Services is of paramount importance, for, however different may be the weapons used, the objective of the Ministry is identical with that of the Fighting Services, namely, the defeat of the enemy.

CHAPTER II
MINISTRY OF ECONOMIC WARFARE

I – FUNCTIONS

A Ministry of Economic Warfare will be established in any major war; it will be responsible for the initiation of plans and direction of policy in regard to economic warfare as a whole and for the administration of a considerable part of the work. Certain aspects of economic warfare will, however, remain the responsibility of existing Government Departments, with which the Ministry will, therefore, need to remain in close and constant touch.

2. The extent of the executive action to be performed by the Ministry itself will be apparent from the description in Annex I of the functions of its constituent departments; other executive action connected with economic warfare for which existing Government Departments or their war-time equivalents will remain responsible includes the following:

(i)   Control of United Kingdom imports and exports – Board of Trade and Board of Customs and Excise.

(ii)   Bunker control and chartering – Board of Trade (Ministry of Shipping) and Board of Customs and Excise.

(iii)   Control of finance – Treasury.

(iv)   Trading with the Enemy – Board of Trade, Treasury and Board of Customs and Excise.

(v)   Naval measures and Organisation of contraband control service – Admiralty.

(vi)   Examination of detained ships – Admiralty and Board of Customs and Excise.

(vii)   Disposal of detained and condemned goods – Board of Customs and Excise.

(viii)   Control of insurance – Board of Trade and Board of Trade (Ministry of Shipping).

(ix)   Co-operation of other Empire territories in the conduct of economic warfare – Dominions Office, Colonial Office, India Office and Burma Office.

3.   The Ministry, although empowered to communicate direct with His Majesty's Diplomatic Representatives and Consular Officers and with Contraband Control Bases, will not itself hold any codes or cyphers. While, therefore, en clair telegrams may be addressed to it direct (telegraphic address, WHISKERS, LONDON), code and cypher telegrams intended for it will be sent to the Foreign Office, addressed, ARFAR, CHEZ PRODROME, LONDON.

II – ESTABLISHMENT

4.   The formal establishment of the Ministry requires Cabinet approval. The Secretary of State for Foreign Affairs, in consultation with the First Lord of the Admiralty, will be responsible for raising the matter in the Cabinet. In order to facilitate the establishment of the Ministry, certain permanent officials are designated in peace-time for appointment to key positions. The Secretary of State for Foreign Affairs has authority to summon these officials before the formal establishment of the Ministry and in advance of hostilities, in order that plans may be reviewed and that such measures of economic warfare as it is practicable to take at that stage may he put in train. This nucleus staff will be housed in the Foreign Office until additional accommodation is required.

III – ORGANISATION

5.   The Ministry will be divided into seven departments, namely, the Plans Department, the Foreign Relations Department, the Prize Department, the Financial Pressure Department, the Legal Department, the Intelligence Department and the Establishment Department. Their respective functions are described in Annex I. These main Departments will be sub-divided into sections as follows:

(a)   Plans Department

Sections –

Commodities I	(food-stuffs and fodder).
Commodities II	(raw materials and petroleum products).
Commodities III	(manufactures and semi-manufactures).
Parliamentary and Press	(parliamentary questions, propaganda, &c.).
Co-ordination	(liaison with other Governments and Departments).

(b)   Foreign Relations Department

The Foreign Relations Department will be divided into a number of sections on a geographical basis, with the addition of a General Section to deal with all questions not obviously falling within the scope of the other sections.

(c)   Prize Department

The Prize Department will be divided into three or more sections to conform with the arrangements for Contraband Control Bases, with a General Section entitled 'Navicert and General.'

(d)   Financial Pressure Department

Sections –
   North America.
   South and Central America.
   Northern Europe.
   General.

(e)   Legal Department

This will consist at the outset of two lawyers, one nominated by the Procurator-General and the other by the Legal Adviser to the Foreign Office, to whom will be added as necessary a third member either from the Solicitor's Department of the Board of Trade or from the Bar.

(f)   Intelligence Department

This will be divided into two branches, Intelligence A and Intelligence B, the latter being responsible for the collection and collation of information and the former for its appraisal and dissemination. Intelligence A will be divided into the following four main sections: 'Enemy Countries,' 'Commodity Intelligence,' 'Neutral Countries,' and 'Liaison and General.' Intelligence B will be divided into four main Sections: 'Enemy Trade Intelligence,' 'Rationing Intelligence,' 'Black List,' and 'Ship's Cargo Intelligence.'

(g)   Establishment Department

The Establishment Department will be divided into two Sections, dealing respectively with Establishment and Accounts.

Registry

6.   So far as accommodation permits, there will be a central Registry under the superintendence of a Registrar and Assistant Registrar, and composed of an Opening Branch, Divisions corresponding to the Departments of the Ministry, and a Despatch Branch. The lay-out of the Registry is indicated diagrammatically in Annex II, which also describes the method of operation the Registry and the filing system to be adopted.

IV – STAFF REQUIREMENTS

7.   The staff requirements of the Ministry are set out in Annex III, which indicates also the allocation of staff by departments. In order to facilitate the rapid expansion of the nucleus staff in the event of a threat of war, the Foreign Office maintains a register of persons and organisations provisionally approved by the Treasury for employment in the Ministry.

V – COMMITTEES

8.   As stated in paragraph I above, the Ministry will need to maintain close contact with a number of Government Departments, notably, the Admiralty, War Office, Air Ministry, Board of Trade, Treasury, Foreign Office, Board of Customs and Excise and Procurator-General's Department. To a large extent this will be achieved by special liaison officers rather than by standing committees. The following Committees concerned wholly or partly with economic warfare will, however, require to be set up on, or even before, the outbreak of war:

By the Ministry.
   (i)   Contraband Committee.
   (ii)   Black List Committee.
   (iii)   Neutral Tonnage Policy Committee.
By the Board of Trade.
   (iv)   Export Licensing Committee.
(By the Board of Trade Ministry of Shipping).
   (v)   Bunker Control Committee.

In addition to these an Enemy Exports Committee will be required if action is taken against enemy exports (see Chapter VI, paragraphs 34–36).

9.   *The Contraband Committee*[1] will consist of the following:

A Chairman drawn from outside the Civil Service.

One representative each of the Admiralty and Board of Trade.

The Procurator-General's representative in the Legal Department of the Ministry.

One representative each of the Prize Department, the Intelligence Department and the Foreign Relations Department.

Its functions will be to decide whether ships or cargoes detained in United Kingdom ports or by His Majesty's ships are to be released or whether sufficient evidence of enemy ownership or, in the case of cargoes, enemy destination, is available to justify the submission to the Prize Court of a case for their condemnation. The Committee will reach its decisions on the basis of evidence submitted to it by the Prize Department; and that Department will be responsible for requesting the Procurator-General to institute proceedings in the Prize Court or, as the case may be, for conveying the order for release to the Contraband Control Base or port where the ship or cargo is detained. In either case the Admiralty will be informed of the action taken.

10.   The functions of the *Black List Committee* will be to give decisions as to firms and persons to be placed on the Black and White Lists, and to submit recommendations in regard to the Statutory List.[2] It will be presided over by an independent person of suitable standing, and will contain representatives of the following departments:

Ministry of Economic Warfare (Foreign Relations, Prize and Intelligence Departments).

Treasury.

Admiralty.

Board of Trade.

Board of Trade (Ministry of Shipping).

As a further safeguard against the black-listing of firms and persons who, despite undesirable connexions with the enemy, may be of use to other departments of His Majesty's Government (*e.g.*, as supplying some essential article of military equipment), all proposed additions to the Black or Statutory Lists will be communicated 10 days before submission to the Black List Committee to the other two service departments, the Foreign Office, the Ministry of Supply, and any other

---

[1]*For the objects and machinery of Contraband Control, see Chapter VI, below.

[2]*For Black, White and Statutory List procedure, see Chapter V, paragraph 22 *et seq.*

Departments which desire to be consulted, in order that they may, if they wish, put forward a case against the proposed addition to the lists.

11.   The functions of the *Neutral Tonnage Policy Committee* will be to advise the Ministry of Economic Warfare and the Ministry of Shipping as to the policy to be followed for the purpose of (i) denying the use of neutral shipping to the enemy,[1] and (ii) securing the services of neutral shipping for this country. The Committee will be composed of representatives of the following departments:

Ministry of Economic Warfare (Foreign Relations Department),

Board of Trade (Ministry of Shipping), and

Admiralty;

and representatives of a leading firm of charterers and of Lloyd's or some marine insurance company may be invited to serve on the Committee to advise on the technical questions which will no doubt arise. Other Government Departments (*e.g.*, Dominions Office, Colonial Office, India Office, Burma Office, and Foreign Office) will be invited to send representatives to any meeting of special concern to them.

12.   The functions of the *Export Licensing Committee*,[2] on which the Plans Department of the Ministry will be represented, will be to assist the Board of Trade in reconciling the conflicting claims of the departments responsible for the maintenance of exports, the conservation of supplies, and the use of export control as a weapon of economic warfare.

13.   The functions of the *Bunker Control Committee*[3] will be to advise the Board of Trade (Ministry of Shipping) and other Departments concerned as to the policy to be followed in regard to the supply of coal and oil for bunkers, and to deal with such applications for bunkers as cannot be dealt with by Customs Collectors or other officials at the port of shipment. Its objects will be (i) to ensure that bunkers are readily available for British and allied shipping, regard being had to the need for the conservation of supplies of oil, (ii) to employ bunker control as a means of forcing neutral ships into British service, and (iii) to employ bunker control as a means of pressure upon neutral shipowners working in the enemy's interest. It will also be used as a means of checking and amplifying intelligence received from other sources. The Ministry, which will be represented on this Committee by a member of the Intelligence Department, will be responsible for maintaining the Black Lists and

---

[1]*For the control of neutral shipping, as a weapon of economic warfare, see Chapter V, paragraph 35, below.

[2]*For the objects and machinery of export licensing, see Chapter IV, paragraph 9 *et seq*, below.

[3]*For the machinery of Bunker Control, see Chapter V, paragraph 96, below.

White Lists of neutral shipowners upon which the Committee will base its decisions.

14.   If the *Enemy Exports Committee*[1] *is* set up, its functions and constitution will be exactly parallel to those of the Contraband Committee.

VI – PROCEDURE FOR ESTABLISHMENT OF MINISTRY

15.   The following paragraphs set out in chronological order the steps which will be taken to establish the Ministry,

16.   *Stage I. – When there is a threat of war, the Secretary of State for Foreign Affairs, at his discretion, summons the nucleus staff.*

(a)   Designated officials, including the Secretary-designate, the heads of Departments, the Legal Advisers, and a nucleus clerical staff, will be informed by telephone and letter.

(b)   The nucleus staff will assemble at the Foreign Office, where limited accommodation is available. The greater part of the staff of the Industrial Intelligence Centre, which forms the nucleus of the Intelligence Department, will, however, remain temporarily in its own quarters.

(c)   All Government Departments will be notified of the summoning of the nucleus staff, and the following departments will be asked to nominate representatives on the committees indicated:

  Board of Trade
    Contraband Committee.
    Black List Committee.
  Board of Trade (Ministry of Shipping)
    Neutral Tonnage Policy Committee.
    Black List Committee.
  Admiralty
    Contraband Committee.
    Black List Committee.
    Neutral Tonnage Policy Committee.
  Treasury
    Black List Committee.

Other departments will be asked to designate liaison officers as necessary.

(d)   The Secretary-designate will nominate the Ministry's own representatives on the Export Licensing Committee and the Bunker

---

[1]For the legal considerations affecting the seizure of enemy exports, and for the machinery to be employed if such seizure proves possible, see Chapter VI, paragraph 34, below.

Control Committee, and the Board of Trade and Board of Trade (Ministry of Shipping) will be informed.

(e)   The Intelligence Department (IIC) puts into effect the arrangements made in peace-time for liaison with the Service Departments; with the Ministry of Information and Censorship Organisation; with the Dominions, India, Burma and Colonial Offices; and with the Board of Trade (Ministry of Shipping), the Board of Customs and Excise, and Lloyd's.

(f)   The Establishment Officer-designate obtains such additional staff as may be necessary from sources arranged in peace-time, and puts into effect pre-arranged scheme for acquiring additional accommodation.

17.   *Stage II – Formal establishment of the Ministry.*

(NOTE – This stage is unlikely to be reached until after the outbreak of war. Preparations for it will, however, be made in the Precautionary Period.)

(a)   The Secretary of State for Foreign Affairs, after consultation with the First Lord of the Admiralty, raises in the Cabinet the question of the establishment of the Ministry.

(b)   When Cabinet approval has been obtained, Government Departments and His Majesty's Diplomatic and Consular representatives, and, if war has already broken out, foreign representatives in London and the Press are notified.

(c)   The Secretary-designate acts as head of the Ministry until a Minister is appointed.

(d)   The Establishment Officer completes arrangements for accommodation, and obtains additional staff as it becomes available. All officers previously earmarked for service in the Ministry, including those drawn from non-official sources, are instructed to report for duty.

CHAPTER III
INTELLIGENCE ORGANISATION

I – GENERAL

Measures of economic warfare, like any other military operation, demand the provision of adequate and prompt intelligence. But, since economic warfare must necessarily be conducted indirectly by means of control over neutral trade as well as directly against the enemy, so its demands for intelligence extend beyond information as to the enemy's plans and activities, and include that relating to the plans and activities of those neutral countries from which the enemy may derive supplies or economic assistance. In peace, information may be derived from trade returns: in war, this source will largely dry up, and must therefore be replaced as far as possible by an ad hoc organisation.

An effective economic warfare intelligence organisation must therefore be almost world-wide in its scope, and must enable information to be obtained under the following three main headings:

(a)   Advance information on individual consignments of suspected contraband, on the basis of which action could be taken (chiefly through the Contraband Control Service) to obstruct the passage to the enemy of the particular consignment in question.

(b)   Statistical information to assist the Ministry in calculating the total imports of key commodities[1] into enemy countries and into those neutral countries whose communications with the enemy remain open, in order that our policy towards the countries acting as suppliers or channels of supply may be determined accordingly.

(c)   Information as to persons and firms known or suspected to be engaged in trading, or attempting to trade, directly or indirectly, with the enemy.

2.   The sources from which this information can be obtained are three fold. In non-enemy countries, His Majesty's Diplomatic Representatives and certain consular officers (the latter being known as Trade Reporting Officers) will be responsible for the collection and reporting of war trade intelligence. At home, Collectors of Customs will obtain and report such information as they may be able to obtain in regard to calling ships. Finally, the Censorship will make available to the Ministry all information bearing on economic warfare that can be derived from intercepted mails, cables and other forms of communications. In addition, of course, all Departments will make available to the Ministry any information obtained through their own channels which has a bearing on economic warfare.

II – WAR TRADE REPORTING ORGANISATION OVERSEAS

3.   His Majesty's Diplomatic Representatives and salaried Consular officers hold standing instructions regarding the institution of a War Trade Intelligence Organisation (see Annex XVII). The Mission in each country will, in most cases, act as the co-ordinating centre for war trade reporting; but in certain countries this function will for convenience be exercised by the consular post at the main commercial centre. The

---

[1]The list of commodities in regard to which information will be needed will vary according to the import requirements of the enemy. A provisional list, for review in the Precautionary Period, is attached as Annex XXII.

organisation will be set in motion in advance of hostilities in the event
of any threat of a major war; its functions at this stage will be to report
to the Foreign Office:

(i)   all recent shipments to the prospective enemy country, or to the
neutral countries adjacent thereto, of certain key commodities (see
Annex XXII), if they are likely to be still on the high seas, and

(ii)   all future shipments of such commodities.

Information under these heads is required to enable His Majesty's ships
to intercept all suspicious shipments[1] in the event of war ensuing.

4.   Upon the outbreak of war, the scope of the information required
from His Majesty's Diplomatic Representatives and Consular Officers
will be increased to include the three categories mentioned in paragraph 1 above.

5.   Information in the first category – advance information on individual consignments of suspected contraband – will normally be reported
direct to the Ministry by consular officers at ports, copies being sent (i)
to the officer's superintending mission (or other war trade centre, where
appropriate), and (ii) in certain cases to trade reporting officers at
intermediate ports of call. Any unsalaried officers who may be appointed trade reporting officers will normally furnish their reports
through their superintending consular officer.

6.   Information in the second category – statistical information as to
shipments of key commodities and abnormal shipments of other commodities – will require to be collated and examined at the war trade
reporting centre in the country concerned before despatch to the Ministry of Economic Warfare. Such information will sometimes be obtainable
by friendly arrangement with local authorities; where this is not practicable, it may be necessary to compile it from the particulars of individual
shipments (exports only in the case of *overseas* countries, imports *and*
exports in the case of countries adjacent to the enemy) supplied by
Trade Reporting Officers.

7.   Information in the third category – as to persons and firms dealing
or believed to be dealing with the enemy – will normally be reported to
the Ministry of Economic Warfare through His Majesty's Diplomatic
Representatives. It is required for the purpose of maintaining the Black
and Statutory Lists (see Chapter V, paragraphs 22 to 34), and to assist
in securing the condemnation of contraband by the Prize Court (see
Chapter VI, paragraph 21).

---

[1]Sailings of prospective enemy *vessels*, as distinct from *shipments* to the prospective
enemy, are reported direct to the appropriate naval authorities under standing instructions.

8.   The provision of war trade intelligence will make large additional demands on the staffs of His Majesty's Missions and Consulates, and at many of them additional staff will be necessary. In certain countries it will also be necessary to open new consular posts to act as war trade reporting centres or to replace local non-career consuls of foreign nationality by British subjects. Annex XVII, Appendix G, lists in column 1 the trade reporting centre for each country, in column 2 the existing consular posts which will automatically become trade reporting posts on the outbreak of war, and, in column 3, the other consular posts, or towns in which there is at present no consular officer, which it would be desirable to include, as opportunity offers, within the war trade reporting organisation.

III – WAR TRADE REPORTING BY THE CUSTOMS

9.   Customs Collectors at ports in the United Kingdom will, so far as is practicable, furnish the Ministry of Economic Warfare with telegraphic reports of all contraband goods on board vessels which call at United Kingdom ports *en route* for the enemy country or neutral countries adjacent thereto. In addition, they will, *before* the outbreak of war, report to the Foreign Office all loadings of key commodities destined for such countries and the departures of all ships carrying them.

IV – CENSORSHIP

10.   Special provision is made in the plans for the establishment of a Censorship Organisation to enable all communications passing through the Censorship to be scrutinised from the point of view of economic warfare. All relevant information derived from them will be communicated at once to the Ministry. In order to assist the Censorship to recognise and keep track of correspondence and other communications relating to enemy trade and transactions on behalf of the enemy, the Censorship authorities will be supplied with copies of the Black and Statutory Lists of traders in neutral countries, which, as described in Chapter V, paragraphs 22–34, will be maintained by the Ministry of Economic Warfare. In addition, special liaison officers will be appointed to maintain contact between the Censorship and the Ministry of Economic Warfare.

11.   Special considerations apply to the censorship of mails on board neutral vessels which are intercepted on the high seas and diverted forcibly into port for examination. According to Article I of The Hague Convention of 1907, such mails are inviolable, and a decision to subject them to censorship would require Cabinet authority. They may, however, legitimately be examined to see if they contain contraband, such as securities and remittances.

PART II
THE WEAPONS

Chapter IV   Legislative Action
Chapter V   Diplomatic Action
Chapter VI   Military Action

CHAPTER IV
LEGISLATIVE ACTION

I – DEFINITION

The measures of economic warfare falling under this head are, broadly speaking, those which consist in controlling, by legislative or administrative action, the activities of persons and firms within a belligerent's own territories or jurisdiction. Such control will, however, be exercised not merely as a means of preventing such persons and firms from assisting the enemy, but also as a means of bringing pressure to bear upon neutrals known or suspected to be assisting the enemy; and this aspect of it will be discussed more fully under the heading 'Diplomatic Action' (Chapter V). The measures in question may be listed as follows:

(1)   Trading with the Enemy Act.
(2)   Control of Exports.
(3)   Control of Imports.
(4)   Control of Shipping.

The objects of these measures, and the procedure for executing them, are set out in the following paragraphs.

II – TRADING WITH THE ENEMY ACT

2.   Trading with the enemy is an offence at common law, but, in order that the offence may be more exactly defined and appropriate penalties fixed, and in order, *inter alia,* to prohibit undesirable transactions which might not be unlawful at common law, a Trading with the Enemy Bill will be introduced as soon as possible after the outbreak of war. This will be preceded, immediately upon the outbreak of war, by the issue of a 'Notice to Traders' reminding them of their obligations at common law. The text of this Notice and of the draft Bill will be found in Annexes V and IV respectively.

3.   The principal object of the Trading with the Enemy legislation is to prohibit (save with official permission) all persons in the United Kingdom and the other countries and places to which it applies (see paragraph

7 below) from having any commercial, financial or other intercourse or dealing with, or for the benefit of, an enemy as defined in section 2 of the Act. For this purpose the term 'enemy' may be assumed to cover: –

(a)   Governmental agencies in enemy territory;

(b)   Any person or persons resident or established in enemy territory;

(c)   Any branch (in any country) controlled from a principal place of business in enemy territory; and

(d)   Any company or other body of persons constituted or incorporated under enemy law.

It does not, however, include any person by *reason only* that he is a national of an enemy country.

4.   Moreover, the Bill gives power to the Board of Trade to make Orders directing that any person or firm named in them shall, for the purposes of the Trading with the Enemy Act, be deemed to be an enemy; this power may be used to prevent commercial or other transactions with, or for the benefit of, persons who, though not resident or carrying on business in or directly controlled from enemy territory, ought, by reason of their enemy associations or of the assistance they are giving to the enemy, to be prevented from trading with this country. The list of persons named in these Orders will be known as the 'Statutory List;' the uses to which this list may be put as a means of controlling trade between neutral countries and the enemy are described in Chapter V, paragraphs 22–24, below.

5.   In order to ensure that goods of enemy origin are not admitted into the United Kingdom or the colonies &c., a system of certificates of origin and interest will be instituted as soon as possible after the outbreak of war. Consular officers in neutral countries from which enemy goods, or goods derived from enemy materials, might be re-exported, will be authorised by the Foreign Office to issue to intending exporters to this country certificates indicating:

(i)   That the goods which it is desired to export are of neutral origin, and

(ii)   That no enemy national has an interest in them exceeding x per cent. of the value of the goods.

Goods from the countries to which the system applies will be liable to seizure[1] if despatched to this country without a valid certificate. The form of the certificate[2] is shown in Annex VI.

---

[1]*Some latitude in this respect must be permitted at the outbreak of war. No action will be taken against goods which at the time of the outbreak of war were already on their way to this country, or which were shipped before a certificate of origin could be obtained.

[2]*The Foreign Office are responsible for the submission for the King's signature of

6. Similarly, to ensure that goods are not exported to enemy countries, declarations of ultimate destination will be required in respect of exports to certain neutral countries. The form of the declaration is shown in Annex VIII.

7. The provisions of the Trading with the Enemy Act may by Order-in-Council be extended to the colonies, protectorates and mandated territories, and also to foreign territories in which His Majesty has jurisdiction, *e.g.*, in parts of China and in the Persian Gulf States.

8. To facilitate the administration of the Trading with the Enemy legislation, the Board of Trade and the Treasury will set up a joint branch to be known as the Trading with the Enemy Branch, Treasury and Board of Trade.

III – CONTROL OF EXPORTS

(a)   Objects

9. The control of exports from this country in war-time will be effected in the first place by Proclamation or Order-in-Council under existing statutory powers and as soon as possible by Order under the Import, Export and Customs Powers (Defence) Act (for draft Bill, see Annex IX) which will give the Board of Trade power to prohibit or regulate the export of goods to any or all destinations. The Act, *inter alia*, empowers the Board of Trade to issue licences for approved consignments. In view of the special circumstances of the coal trade, control of coal exports will be largely carried out (through local Coal Export Officers in the principal coal shipping districts) by an Exports Branch of the Mines Department, under the general direction of the Export Licensing Department of the Board of Trade.

10. The main objects of export control are

   (1)   To conserve supplies for use in this country; and

   (2)   To prevent exports from this country reaching the enemy directly or indirectly.

Export control will also be used, *inter alia* –

   (3)   To ensure that exports are directed to the most desirable markets from the economic point of view; and

   (4)   To enable His Majesty's Government to bring pressure to bear on neutral Governments and firms.

11. It must always be borne in mind that the successful prosecution of the war depends upon the maintenance of the export trade at as high a level as possible (subject to the limitations imposed by economic war-

Orders-in-Council reducing the peace-time consular fees for these certificates to a standard level of £58. The texts are appended as Annex VII.

fare and the conservation of supplies and services) particularly with a view to safeguarding the exchange position. It is, therefore, important to ensure that any control imposed on export will not prejudice our interests or those of our allies more than the enemy's.

(b) Machinery

12.   Export control will be imposed in three stages
(i)   During the period immediately preceding the outbreak of war, the Board of Trade will, by means of a Proclamation or an Order-in-Council under the Customs and Inland Revenue Act, 1879, prohibit, except under licence, the export to all destinations of the essential commodities listed in Annex X,[1] Part I.
(ii)   On the outbreak of war, the export to all or certain destinations of the foods listed in Annex X, Part II, will be prohibited except under licence. At the outset prohibition will be effected by means of a Proclamation or an Order-in-Council under existing statutory powers, but this procedure will be superseded by that under the Import, Export and Customs Powers (Defence) Bill when that has been passed.
(iii)   As soon as possible after the outbreak of war, the list of export controlled goods will be expanded to include all the goods in Annex X, Part III.
13.   The restrictions in stage (i) will necessarily apply only to those few commodities which it is essential either to retain in this country or to prevent from reaching the enemy. Moreover, practical reasons make it impossible to subject to an export licensing system any extensive list of commodities until (a) pre-entry[2] is enforced in respect of all goods, and (b) the export licensing section of the Board of Trade is able to meet a large increase in the demand for licences. To reinforce such limited statutory restrictions as it is possible to impose before the outbreak of war, steps will be taken to approach selected exporting firms or trade associations in this country with a request in the terms of Annex XI that they will, so far as possible, restrict or delay exports to the prospective enemy country or to adjacent countries.
14.   It will be noted from Annex X that the goods referred to under (ii) and (iii) in paragraph 12 are divided into three categories: -
(i)   Export prohibited to all destinations (A).

---

[1]*The lists referred to will be subject to review in the Precautionary Stage.
[2]*Pre-entry involves the entry of goods with, and their clearance by, the Customs *before* shipment. In peace-time this is only necessary in respect of limited classes of goods; with other goods the documents need not be presented until six days after shipment. In war-time all goods will have to be pre-entered and cleared, thus enabling the Customs to exercise effective control over exports.

(ii)   Export prohibited to all destinations other than the British Empire (B).

(iii)   Export prohibited to all countries from which they could readily be exported to the enemy (C).

Goods in all these categories will be eligible for export licences, provided always that the issue of such a licence would not be incompatible with the objects of export control. Of these objects (paragraph 10 above) only No. 2 and No. 4 are of importance from the point of view of economic warfare, and the factors which would govern the grant of licences under these two heads are:

(i)   The intending exporter must satisfy himself, and the Export Licensing authority, that the goods in respect of which he is applying for a licence will not be re-exported from the country of destination to the enemy.

(ii)   No licences will be issued for the export of goods to persons or firms on the Statutory List or Black List (see Chapter V, paragraph 22 *et seq.*, below).

(iii)   Steps will be taken to ensure that the export of 'rationed' goods to a neutral country will not be in excess of the 'ration' accepted by, or imposed upon, that country as being adequate for its domestic consumption (see Chapter V, paragraph 19, below).

15.   In order to facilitate the observance of these conditions, the following steps will be taken:[1]

(i)   A competent officer of the Ministry of Economic Warfare will be appointed to the Export Licensing Department and will be responsible for examining expeditiously all applications for licences for the export of commodities to countries adjacent to the enemy, with a view to eliminating undesirable consignees. He will be in direct touch by telephone with the Black List Section of the Ministry, and will be entitled to request that consideration of applications shall be deferred while the status of the consignee is investigated.

(ii)   In respect to the export to 'adjacent neutrals' of key commodities (see Annex XXII) no licenses will at first be issued without the approval of the Ministry of Economic Warfare. But as soon as possible general conditions will be laid down which will enable the Export Licensing Department to function without referring every license to the Ministry of Economic Warfare.

(iii)   The Export Licensing Department will send the Ministry copies of all licences actually issued for the export of any commodities to 'adjacent neutrals.' As soon as possible, the Ministry of Eco-

---

[1]*Separate arrangements for dealing with coal exports are under consideration.

nomic Warfare will consider whether this condition can be dispensed with.

(iv)   Copies of all shipping bills will be sent by the Customs to the Export Licensing Department. These will be sorted on receipt and all those showing shipments to 'adjacent neutrals' will be forwarded immediately to the Ministry of Economic Warfare. They will be examined and recorded by the Ministry (Intelligence Department, Rationing Section), and then returned at once to the Export Licensing Department.

16.   The forms of licence to be used are shown in Annex XII.

IV – CONTROL OF IMPORTS

(a)   Objects

17.   The main objects of import control, which are outside the scope of economic warfare, and therefore of this Handbook, will be to ensure:

   (i)   That the financial resources of this country are spent to the best advantage.

   (ii)   That tonnage is employed in the most economical way.

18.   In certain circumstances the control of imports may also be utilised to bring pressure to bear on a neutral country or on neutral exporters. In the case of essential commodities, it can, of course, only be used for this purpose when alternative sources of supply are available. It may also be employed to direct purchases to allied countries or perhaps to a particular neutral in connexion with an aspect of economic warfare.

(b)   Machinery

19.   Imports will be controlled by means of the Import, Export and Customs Powers (Defence) Act (Annex IX), which gives the Board of Trade power to prohibit or regulate by order the importation of any goods specified in the Order. Absolute prohibition of imports will in most cases be impracticable, and provision *will* be made in the Order for licensing the importation of prohibited goods in certain circumstances. Licences will not be granted for the import of goods from persons or firms on the Statutory List, nor, as a general rule, from those on the Black List.

V – CONTROL OF SHIPPING

(a)   Objects

20.   The main object of the control of shipping, whether British or neutral, is to ensure an adequate supply of tonnage to meet the essential requirements of this country and other Empire countries, and of any

allies we may have. From this aspect, the control of shipping is largely outside the scope of economic warfare, and therefore of this Handbook. There are, nevertheless, three points of contact between it and economic warfare, viz.:

(i)   The treatment of enemy ships on the outbreak of war;

(ii)   The necessity of ensuring that British ships do not engage in trade with, or for the benefit of, the enemy; and

(iii)   The desirability of discouraging neutral shipowners from trading with, or for the benefit of, the enemy, and from chartering their ships to him.

21.   Apart from Government chartering or purchase of neutral ships, the means available for achieving the object defined in (iii) above consist in bringing pressure to bear on neutral shipowners with a view to influencing them in the use to which they put their ships; and, although that pressure is produced partly by legislative and administrative action in this country, it may be more conveniently dealt with under the heading 'Diplomatic Action' (Chapter V below).

(b)   Treatment of Enemy Shipping

22.   (i) *Before the Outbreak of War.* In the past, embargoes have sometimes been laid in advance of hostilities upon the ships of a prospective enemy country. Such a step would be taken under the Prerogative, and would not present any difficulty from the point of view of municipal law. But there is very considerable doubt whether to-day such an embargo could be justified under international law, unless, of course, it were imposed by way of retaliation for some corresponding or equivalent arbitrary action by the prospective enemy. Apart from this legal difficulty, it is doubtful whether an embargo of this nature would be of any great practical value, since experience has shown that one of the first acts of any prospective enemy during a period of strained relations is to remove its merchant shipping from all ports in which it might be liable to interference.

23.   Nevertheless, in view of the possibility of action by way of retaliation, the Foreign Office, in consultation with the Admiralty and Board of Trade (Ministry of Shipping), is charged with the duty, at any time of strained relations, of considering whether circumstances offer any justification for placing am embargo on the departure of prospective enemy merchant ships. Should such justification be found, action will be taken under an Order-in-Council; and the Board of Customs and Excise will issue instructions to Customs Collectors for the detention or seizure, as the case may be, of all merchant ships of the country concerned then, or thereafter arriving, in port.

24.   (ii) *On the Outbreak of War*. As soon as war begins, the right to seize enemy ships becomes indisputable. Seizure will be authorised by an Order-in-Council (Annex XIII), and, at ports in the United Kingdom, will be effected by Customs Collectors, acting on behalf of the Admiralty Marshal. The Order-in-Council provides, however, that enemy ships of certain classes may be released if reciprocal treatment is accorded to British ships in enemy ports. Such ships will, therefore, be detained (not seized) until the expiry of the period mentioned in the Order-in-Council or until the enemy gives notice of his intention to release British ships. If no such notice is received, the enemy ships detained are seized at the end of the stated period and put into prize.

(c)   Control of Employment of British Shipping to Prevent Trading with, or for the Benefit of, the Enemy

25.   As soon as war begins, the Board of Trade (Ministry of Shipping) [shall] obtain power to requisition all British ships other than those registered in the Dominions, India and Burma. They may also, if it is necessary, bring passenger and cargo space under control and institute a licensing scheme. These measures, combined with the control[1] of ships' bunkers, ships' stores, repair and dry-docking facilities and insurance, amount to a complete control of the employment of the British merchant marine, and will provide means of preventing ships subject to them from engaging in trade contrary to the objects of economic warfare – that is to say, from carrying goods to or from persons and firms (and, if necessary, countries) known or suspected to be engaged in contraband trade with the enemy. In addition, shipowners are, of course, subject to the provisions of the Trading with the Enemy Act, and are therefore under a statutory obligation not to engage in trade not only with the enemy country but also with persons and firms in neutral countries who may be on the Statutory List (see paragraph 4 above). Customs Collectors in United Kingdom ports will, on and after the outbreak of war, refuse clearance to British vessels bound for enemy ports.

---

[1]*For the application of these measures of control to neutral ships, see Chapter V, paragraph 35.

CHAPTER V
DIPLOMATIC ACTION

I – DEFINITION

The phrase 'diplomatic action' is used to describe all those measures of economic warfare which consist in persuading or inducing neutral Governments, firms and persons to refrain from transactions advantageous to the enemy. Its precise objects vary according to the situation of the neutral country concerned.

2. If a neutral country is separated from the enemy country by seas *under our control,* the main object of diplomatic action is to prevent that country from supplying its products to the enemy either directly or through an adjacent neutral. Countries in this group are called for convenience 'overseas neutrals.'

3. If, on the other hand, the neutral country is, by reason of its geographical position, able to maintain direct land or sea communications with the enemy, the object of diplomatic action is to prevent that country not only from supplying the enemy with its own products, but also from acting as a channel of supplies between other neutrals and the enemy. Such countries are, for convenience, called 'adjacent neutrals;' and since they are, by definition, in close proximity to the enemy, the degree of success to be attained by diplomatic action against them is conditioned not only by their political sympathies and by the relative degree of economic pressure which each belligerent can bring to bear on them, but also by the risk that, if pressed too hard, they will either throw in their lot with the enemy or expose themselves to attack, and even the occupation of their territory, by the enemy.

4. It is clear that the objects of diplomatic action can generally be more easily attained in the case of overseas neutrals than in that of adjacent neutrals; for trade between overseas neutrals and the enemy, whether direct or indirect, can, if necessary, be intercepted on the high seas, while trade between adjacent neutrals and the enemy can only be interrupted indirectly by bringing pressure to bear upon the neutral Government or its traders. The two problems of preventing or restricting exports to the enemy from adjacent neutrals and from overseas neutrals are, in short, different both in themselves and in the methods appropriate for dealing with them; and they are therefore dealt with separately below.

II – OVERSEAS NEUTRALS

(a)　Contraband Control

5.　Exports from overseas neutrals to the enemy, or to adjacent neutrals for transmission to the enemy, can, as stated above, be intercepted on the high seas; and, if they are contraband, and if sufficient evidence of their enemy destination can be produced, they can be put into the Prize Court for condemnation (see Chapter VI, paragraph 3 *et seq.* below). This, however, involves (i) the examination of all ships carrying goods to the enemy or to adjacent neutrals, (ii) the detention of such ships while the necessary enquiries are being made as to the destination of goods on board, and (iii) the production of concrete evidence of enemy destination sufficiently clear to satisfy a court of law. Apart from the difficulties attendant upon obtaining the evidence required under (iii), the disadvantages of this procedure are that it not only involves neutral traders in delays and uncertainties, but, to the extent that it achieves its purpose, results in a definite interruption of a part of their export trade, which may be only partly offset by increased exports in other directions, and thereby necessarily tends adversely to affect our relations with them. The main objects of diplomatic action in regard to overseas neutrals will therefore be to minimize, in the interests of our friendly relations with them, the losses and delays to which their traders are subject, while at the same time preventing them from trading with the enemy.

6.　Ideally, these objects could best be attained if overseas neutrals were to agree –

(i)　To prohibit all direct contraband exports to the enemy country; and

(ii)　Either to limit their exports of contraband to adjacent neutrals so that the latter had no margin for re-export to the enemy, or else to subject all contraband exports to other neutrals to the requirement of adequate guarantees that they would not be re-exported to the enemy.

Any such undertakings would, however, be likely to expose the neutral offering them to a charge of unneutral action; and such a solution is therefore unlikely to be practical politics except in the unlikely event of a particularly friendly overseas neutral being emboldened to accept it by a decision of the League of Nations.

(b)　Other Measures

7.　In these circumstances the practical steps open to us are limited to –

(i)　A general approach to neutral Governments on the outbreak of war emphasising both our determination to prevent contraband from reaching the enemy and our desire to harm neutral trade as little as possible by the exercise of our legitimate belligerent rights;

(ii)   In certain cases, offers to purchase guaranteed quantities of certain commodities to compensate for the loss of enemy markets;

(iii)   The institution of a 'Navicert system;' and

(iv)   Certain other measures, such as the control of shipping and the use of Statutory and Black or White Lists, which are equally applicable to both adjacent and overseas neutrals; these are described in section IV below.

(c)   Dormant Instructions to His Majesty's Diplomatic Representatives

8.   Of the measures described in the preceding paragraph, (i) is covered by the issue of dormant instructions to His Majesty's Representatives abroad. These instructions (see Annex XVII) will not be acted upon automatically on the outbreak of war, but only on receipt of telegraphic instructions, despatched by the Ministry after consultation with the Foreign Office and Admiralty.

(d)   Purchases

9.   As regards (ii), no hard-and-fast plans can be made in advance, since our ability to use guaranteed purchases as an inducement to neutrals will necessarily depend on the availability of foreign exchange and tonnage, and on our own import requirements. All proposals for purchases will therefore require to be worked out in close consultation with the Treasury, the Ministry of Shipping, the Board of Trade and the Ministry of Supply. Where, however, we are in any case obliged to make large purchases abroad to meet our essential requirements, it will be important that the departments of His Majesty's government responsible for making the purchases should bear in mind (i) the possibility of using them as a *quid pro quo* for some concession in regard to economic warfare and (ii) the importance of keeping the Ministry informed of their plans. Apart from purchases intended merely as inducements to neutrals, cases may arise, especially with commodities of which we already control a large part of world production, where purchases may be made solely in order to prevent the commodities in question from reaching the enemy.

(e)   Navicerts

10.   As regards (iii), the object of the 'Navicert system' is, briefly, to facilitate *bona fide* trade between overseas neutrals and adjacent neutrals by the issue of 'commercial passports,' or Navicerts, in respect of

consignments which have been approved by the appropriate British authorities *before* shipment. Goods covered by navicerts will (unless subsequent evidence of enemy destination is obtained) receive favoured treatment at the hands of the Contraband Control Service, and will escape most of the delays to which other goods will be subject.

11.   A subsidiary, but nevertheless important, object of the Navicert system will be to forestall the criticism frequently levelled against us in the earlier phases of the war of 1914–18 that we deliberately employed our rights of visit and search to hinder neutral trade and thereby to foster our own. As far as possible, therefore, the Navicert system will be so operated as to correspond to the control of exports from this country (see Chapter IV, paragraphs 9–16, above).

12.   *Machinery.* The Navicert system can only be operated when sufficient information has been accumulated to enable the Ministry of Economic Warfare to distinguish between consignments which are *bona fide* intended for neutral consumption and those which, there is reason to believe, are ultimately intended for the enemy. The information required for this purpose will be, in effect, information as to the status and activities of the consignors, consignees and shippers of each consignment for which a Navicert is sought – i.e., information which will only become available as the Black List (see paragraph 25 *et seq.* below) is built up. The system cannot, therefore, be introduced immediately on the outbreak of war. Nevertheless, in order to contribute to the object defined in paragraph 11 above, His Majesty's Representatives in certain overseas neutral countries will be authorised to announce, on the outbreak of war, that a Navicert System will be introduced, for the convenience of neutral traders desiring to export certain goods to certain overseas neutrals, as soon as the necessary machinery can be set up. The lists of goods and of countries, both overseas and adjacent, to which the system will apply (and which will, of course, vary according to the enemy with whom we are engaged) will be gradually extended as the necessary information becomes available.

13.   The methods of operation of the system are described in detail in Chapter IX below.

III – ADJACENT NEUTRALS

(a)   *General*

14.   All action designed to prevent adjacent neutrals from acting as suppliers or channels of supply to the enemy depends, in the last resort, mainly on our power to interfere with their import trade and shipping on the high seas. The greater their dependence on imported supplies,

the more effectively we shall be able to achieve our objects. Since dependence on imported supplies varies widely from country to country, no one method of pressure would be appropriate to all of them. Generally speaking, however, the following are the measures open to us:

(i)   Interruption of supplies from overseas, on the ground that they are suspected of being contraband (see also Chapter VI, paragraph 3 *et seq.* below).

(ii)   Witholding of supplies produced in, or controlled by, this country and its dependencies, or the territories of its allies.

(iii)   Offers to purchase, on conditions, guaranteed quantities of their staple products.

(iv)   Other measures (e.g., control of shipping, use of Statutory and Black or White Lists) which, as stated above, are dealt with in Section IV below as being equally applicable to both adjacent and overseas neutrals.

15.   Of the measures described in the preceding paragraph, it will be our aim to use (i) and (ii) as bargaining levers for the purpose of securing our aims by agreement with the neutral Governments concerned, rather than as weapons to be employed automatically. Our action vis-à-vis adjacent neutrals will in fact fall into two stages; in the first, attempts will be made to secure our objects by negotiation, while in the second, if negotiation fails, direct action will be employed.

(b)   Negotiation

16.   As far as possible His Majesty's Representatives in the more important of the countries which might be expected to fall into the category of adjacent neutrals are provided in peacetime with dormant instructions for the negotiation of war trade agreements. A specimen is attached as Annex XIX. These instructions will be reviewed when war appears imminent, and, if they are approved, instructions will be sent to His Majesty's Representatives, as soon as possible after the outbreak of war, to open negotiations on the lines prescribed. An important point is that, without awaiting the outcome of the negotiations, adjacent neutral Governments will be urged to control at once the export of certain commodities in which the enemy is known to be deficient, in order to restrict supplies of goods of those classes to the enemy.

17.   Negotiations with adjacent neutrals which for political, military or economic reasons are highly susceptible to pressure from the enemy, and scarcely susceptible at all to any counter-measure from us, will probably only prove possible, if at all, when the war has been in progress for some time – i.e., when the risks to which they would

expose themselves by negotiating with us can be calculated, and when our methods of pressure have convinced them that, despite the risks involved, it would be in their interest to come to terms with us. His Majesty's Representatives in such countries are, therefore, not provided with dormant instructions, and direct action (see below) will be employed from the outset if necessary.

(c)   Direct Action

18.   The extent to which direct action can be employed, when negotiations have either failed or been ruled out as unlikely to succeed will, of course, depend on political, military and economic factors which cannot be foreseen. In the extreme case, however, the following weapons will be available for use:

   (i)   Ruthless employment of belligerent rights at sea, designed to prevent the importation by adjacent neutrals of sea-borne supplies for re-export to the enemy, but actually operated so as to cause such dislocation of trade that importers and traders will either compel their Government to come to terms with us or else seek separate and private agreements with us.

   (ii)   Withholding, mainly by means of the export licensing system, of supplies of essential commodities under our own control.

   (iii)   Interference by means of the import licensing system with a neutral's export trade to this country.

   (iv)   Withholding of financial, shipping and insurance facilities.

Of these, (i), which is in effect 'forcible rationing,' is described in detail below: (ii) and (iii) need no further elucidation; while (iv) is dealt, with in Section IV below.

(d)   Forcible Rationing

19.   The dormant instructions described in paragraph 16 above provide, as will be seen from Annex XIX, for an attempt to obtain from adjacent neutral Governments undertakings that they will limit their imports of certain commodities to quantities corresponding to their normal requirements, less any exports to the enemy. Failing agreement, direct action would, in the case of a large proportion of adjacent neutrals, enable similar results to be obtained, although it could only be effectively and safely applied to a limited number of essential commodities. The procedure would be as follows.

   (i)   The adjacent neutral's normal imports of the commodity to be rationed (reckoned on a quarterly or half-yearly basis as may be most convenient) will be calculated from peace-time statistics. From these will be deducted (a) stocks, so far as they can be ascertained, and (b)

normal exports, whether in the same form or in the shape of manufactures, to the enemy. If necessary, normal exports to other adjacent
neutrals, or even to all destinations, will also be deducted unless
satisfactory guarantees against direct or indirect re-export to the
enemy can be secured. The resulting figure constitutes the 'permitted
ration,' *i.e.,* the amount which in our estimation corresponds to the
bona fide requirements of the adjacent neutral concerned.

(ii)   The adjacent neutral's actual imports, from *all* sources, of the
commodity concerned will be calculated by the Ministry from reports received from War Trade Reporting Officers (see Chapter III,
above) and other available sources. As soon as total imports are seen
to be approaching the permitted ration for the quota period selected,
imports from overseas neutrals and from sources under our control
will be interrupted, the former by means of contraband control and
the latter mainly by the refusal of export licences. (For the legal basis
for the use of contraband control for the purpose of forcible rationing, see Chapter VI, paragraphs 7 and 8.). Simultaneously, applications
for navicerts for the export of the commodity concerned to the adjacent neutral in question will be refused, general instructions to this
effect being circulated to Missions in all countries where the system
is in force. Banks, &c., will also be requested to withhold financial
facilities for any transactions involving exports of the rationed commodity to the adjacent neutral concerned, and shipowners under our
control (see paragraphs 37 below) will be warned not to carry the
commodity to the adjacent neutral.

(iii)   The measures described above will be withdrawn only (a) on
the expiry of the quota period in which the permitted ration has been
filled or (b) on such other terms, including satisfactory guarantees
against re-export, as may be considered acceptable.

20.   Before forcible rationing can be put into force, it will, of course,
be of vital importance to ensure that it will not prejudice our own
interests or those of our allies more than the enemy's, either politically
or by depriving the adjacent neutral of raw materials, &c., required for
the production of goods exported to this country and essential for our
requirements. The fullest consultation with other Government departments will therefore be necessary, and Cabinet approval must be
obtained, before forcible rationing can be employed.

IV – MEASURES APPLICABLE TO BOTH OVERSEAS AND ADJACENT NEUTRALS

(a) General

21.   The following measures will, to the extent that circumstances permit, be applied to all neutral countries, whether adjacent or overseas, whose commercial activities are or might be of assistance to the enemy:
    (1)   Black List, or White List, and Statutory List.
    (2)   Control of shipping.
    (3)   Control of finance.
    (4)   Control of insurance.
These measures are described in detail in the succeeding paragraphs.

(b)   The Statutory List: Definition and Objects

22.   The Statutory List, as an adjunct to the Trading with the Enemy Act, has been defined in Chapter, IV, paragraph 4, above. Its primary object is to inform persons and firms in this country, and in any other territory to which that Act or corresponding regulations apply, of the names of persons and firms in neutral countries with whom they are prohibited from dealing. For this purpose the following may qualify for inclusion in the list: –
    (i)   Enemy firms – that is to say, firms established in neutral territory but controlled wholly or largely from enemy territory.
    (ii)   Neutral firms in which there is an important enemy interest, or which act as agents for enemy Governments.
    (iii)   Neutral firms which are engaged mainly or largely in trade with the enemy.
    (iv)   Neutral concerns which assist the enemy financially, by credits or loans or in any other way, beyond what is legitimately incidental to their commercial dealings.

23.   Secondary objects of the Statutory List are the replacement of enemy interests in neutral countries by British, and the weakening of the prestige and standing of local residents of enemy nationality or association. For these purposes, the following will also qualify for inclusion in the list:
    (v)   Neutral persons or firms acting exclusively or mainly as agents for enemy firms.
    (vi)   Persons of enemy nationality or known enemy sympathy or association, when their influence or standing is such as to justify measures against them.

24.   There will be no 'Secondary Statutory List.' That is to say, neutral traders will not be penalised merely for continuing to trade with an-

other who has been placed on the Statutory List. The fear, which was discreetly fostered, that a secondary Statutory List might be enforced proved, however, extremely efficacious in the war of 1914–18, and there is evidence that some neutral firms on the Statutory List were virtually boycotted by other firms for fear of consequences that we had no intention of permitting.

(c)   Black List: Definition and Objects

25.   The Black List is similar to, but more elastic than, the Statutory List, in that its object is to enable the authorities to interfere by administrative, rather than by legislative, action with the commercial activities of persons or firms known or suspected to be trading with the enemy. The Statutory List is published, while the Black List is confidential; so that, whereas a firm can only be placed on the Statutory List when definite proof of enemy nationality or association can, if required, be adduced in justification, a firm may be black-listed if suspected on reasonable grounds of engaging in contraband trade or other undesirable transactions with the enemy, or if it is undesirable for political or other reasons to place it on the Statutory List.

(d)   White List

26.   In countries where evidence as to undesirable commercial activities proves especially difficult to obtain (e.g., in territories where commerce is subject to little or no regulation and where men of straw, or 'cloaks,' can readily be found to cover undesirable transactions) the White List may be employed as an alternative to the Black List and Statutory List. It is, in essence, a list of traders known to be above suspicion; consignments to or from them are subject to no interference, while all transactions involving traders not on the White List are regarded with suspicion and as far as possible hindered. White Lists are unlikely to be employed on a significant scale in the early stages of any war, and the machinery for their operation need not, therefore, be discussed in detail.

(e)   Effects of Inclusion in the Statutory or Black List

27.   Persons or firms included in the Statutory List are subjected to the following disabilities:
(i)   Persons and firms to whom the Trading with the Enemy Act applies are not permitted to have any commercial, financial or other intercourse or dealing with them or for their benefit.
(ii)   No licences will be granted for the export of goods to them from this country or from any territory to which the Import, Export

and Customs Powers (Defence) Act or corresponding enactments apply.

(iii)   Shipping facilities, e.g., bunkers, ships' stores, insurance, repair and dry docking facilities (see paragraphs 36–44 below) may be withheld from neutral shipowners who decline to give undertakings that they will not carry goods to, from or for them.

(iv)   Goods owned by them and/or consigned by them to neutral destinations, and intercepted on the high seas, will be regarded with particular suspicion, and, if it is not possible to prove that they are contraband ultimately destined for the enemy, will be subjected to every possible administrative delay (see Chapter VI, paragraph 8 below).

28.   Persons or firms included in the Black List, but not in the Statutory List, may be subjected to identical disabilities, except that, since the Trading with the Enemy Act does not render commercial dealings with them illegal, the measures described in paragraph 27 (i) above can be enforced only by administrative, instead of legislative, action – e.g., by the withholding of export licences and by warning[1] firms and banks, &c., not to deal with them. Names of firms, &c., against which there is not sufficient evidence to justify black-listing may be placed without reference to the Black List Committee on a 'Suspect List,' which will receive the same circulation as the Black List and which will serve to indicate to all authorities concerned the firms whose transactions require to be watched with particular care.

29.   Firms whose names appear in the Black or Statutory List may be removed on conditions. In the case of the former, substantial bonds or sureties for good behaviour may be demanded, while, for the latter, proof will be required that the taint of enemy association has been effectively removed. Thus, a firm domiciled in, say, Buenos Aires, and placed on the Statutory List because two of its directors were of enemy nationality, would be eligible for removal from the list if it dismissed them.

(f)   Statutory and Black Lists: Machinery

30.   In peace-time, the names of traders domiciled in potentially neutral countries but of the nationality of or associated with certain potential enemy countries are reported by His Majesty's Diplomatic and Consular Representatives and are card-indexed by the Industrial Intelligence Centre as nucleus of the Intelligence Department of the Ministry of Economic Warfare. The names thus indexed will form the basis of the first Suspect List.

---

[1]*For forms of warning, see Annex XX.

31.   On the outbreak of war, the Black List Committee (see Chapter II, paragraph 10, above) comes into being, and names regarded as suitable for inclusion in the Statutory or Black List are submitted to it for examination. It would be desirable that a Statutory List, however limited, should be issued as soon as possible, since the knowledge that we intend to use this weapon may be expected to exert a powerful deterrent effect. On the other hand, care must, of course, be taken, in the early stages at least, only to place upon the Statutory List persons or firms carrying on business in neutral countries from which no serious adverse political reactions may be expected in consequence. Moreover, in order to forestall, during the critical early stages of the war, the common but mistaken criticism that the use of the Statutory List is an infringement of neutral sovereignty, the first list to be issued will, if possible, be confined to persons and firms of indisputably enemy nationality and association. Its adoption will in any case be subject to Cabinet sanction.

32.   Similar care will have to be exercised during the early stages in regard to the Black List, since, of the traders whose names have been collected in peace time as carrying on trade with the enemy country, many of those of neutral nationality (and, indeed, some of those of enemy nationality) may of their own volition give up their trade with the enemy country. At first, therefore, the only names to be placed on the Black List will be

(i)   Names placed on the Statutory List.

(ii)   Names of persons and firms of indisputably enemy nationality and association not regarded, for political reasons, as suitable for inclusion in the first Statutory List.

The bulk of the remaining names will, pending the receipt of further evidence, stay provisionally on the Suspect List.

33.   All names on the Statutory List will be placed automatically on the Black List.

34.   As stated in Chapter II, paragraph 10, all names selected for consideration by the Black List Committee as suitable for inclusion in the Statutory and/or Black List will be referred to other Departments concerned ten days before submission to the Committee. In addition, names for inclusion in the Statutory and Black Lists will be referred by telegram to His Majesty's Representative in the country concerned, unless the recommendation originated with him and was of recent date. Names for inclusion in the Statutory List are communicated by the Ministry of Economic Warfare to the Board of Trade, who will issue the necessary Order under Section 2 of the Trading with the Enemy Act, while names for the Black List are inserted in that list by the

Ministry of Economic Warfare. All lists, and all additions to them, will be communicated regularly to the following:–

    (i)   All Government Departments concerned.

    (ii)   Admiralty, for communication to the Fleet.

    (iii)   Contraband Control Bases.

    (iv)   The Board of Customs and Excise, for communication to Customs Collectors in the United Kingdom.

    (v)   His Majesty's Diplomatic representatives and (salaried) consular officers.

    (vi)   Colonial Governments.

    (vii) Dominion Governments.

    (viii) The Governments of India and Burma.

    (ix)   Allied Governments.[1]

    (xx)   The Censorship Organisation.

(g)   Control of Employment of Neutral Shipping

    (i)   Objects

35.   As stated in Chapter IV, paragraph 20, the main object of the control of employment of shipping, whether British or neutral, is to ensure that sufficient tonnage is available for the transportation of supplies essential to this country and its allies. Its secondary object is to deprive the enemy of its use, direct or indirect. Both objects are attained by similar methods, which, so far as British shipping is concerned, have been described in Chapter IV, paragraph 25 above. The methods to be employed for the control of employment of neutral shipping are the following:

    (1)   Bunker control.

    (2)   Control of repair and dry-docking facilities.

    (3)   Control of ships' stores.

    (4)   Control of insurance.

    (5)   Purchase and chartering of neutral tonnage.

    (6)   Ships' Black List and White list.

The use of these weapons will be subject to the general control of the Neutral Tonnage Policy Committee (see Chapter II, paragraph 11).

    (ii)   Bunker Control

36.   In the war of 1914–18 bunker control was exercised almost exclusively as a means of checking contraband trade and of forcing neutral vessels into our service or that of our allies. In any future war an

---

[1]*Every effort will be made to secure parallel action by allied Governments. If necessary, they will be invited to appoint representatives on the Black List Committee.

additional object of bunker control will be to conserve our own supplies, more especially as regards oil bunkers. It consists, in essence, of requiring oil-burning vessels to bunker abroad wherever possible and of limiting the shipment of coal or oil fuel for bunker purposes to vessels which are (a) already engaged in or prepared to enter essential trades, or (b) operated by owners who have agreed to accept certain conditions which prevent their having any commercial relations with enemy firms or individuals and ensure that no cargoes are carried in their vessels to destinations whence they might reach the enemy.

37.   The necessary legislative authority for withholding or otherwise controlling ships' bunkers will be furnished in this country by orders made by the Board of Trade under the Import, Export and Customs Powers (Defence) Act (see Annex IX) and in other British territories by analogous legislation or regulations. In this country, until the Customs obtain further authority under the above-mentioned Act, they will regulate bunkers (and ships' stores) under existing powers. In neutral countries, as far as local conditions allow, bunker control will be exercised through British-controlled bunker depots, and, as regards foreign owned bunker depots, by limiting the quantity of coal allowed to be exported from the United Kingdom or by requiring adequate guarantees, in advance of the issue of any export licence, as to the use to which the coal will be put.

38.   The general administration of bunker control policy will be the responsibility of the Board of Trade (Ministry of Shipping) assisted by a Bunker Control Committee (see Chapter II, paragraph 13). This Committee meets in peace-time for the preparation of detailed plans and contains representatives of the following Departments:

> Admiralty, Foreign-Office, Dominions Office, Colonial Office, Board of Customs and Excise, India Office and, Burma Office, Mines Department, Petroleum Department.

39.   Actual control will be effected in this country at the ports through the Customs, whose War Instructions will describe the procedure to be followed. These instructions will be based on the decisions of the Board of Trade (Ministry of Shipping) in the light of the advice given to it by the Bunker Control Committee and will define the categories of ships which can be dealt with locally and which are eligible to receive bunkers, the approved voyages for which bunkers may be issued, the conditions to be imposed where necessary, and the cases which must be referred by the Customs Collectors through Headquarters to the Bunker Control Committee for consideration.

40.   In order to avoid driving neutral tonnage into the service of the enemy and to encourage neutral tonnage to remain in our trade, it is

anticipated that in the early stage of war restrictions on the issue of coal or oil-fuel for bunker purposes will not be severe except where necessary to conserve supplies. The organisation will admit of the restrictions being rapidly tightened up as necessary.

(iii)   Control of repair and dry-docking facilities

41.   Repair and dry-docking facilities in British ports will be refused to all neutral ships on the Ships' Black List (see paragraph 46 below),

(iv)   Control of ships' stores

42.   Regulations for the supply of ships' stores to neutral vessels will be issued by the Board of Trade in conjunction with the Ministry of Food. In general, ships' stores will be denied to neutral vessels on the Ships' Black List.

(v)   Purchasing and chartering of neutral tonnage

43.   The Board of Trade (Ministry of Shipping) may charter or purchase neutral ships in order to obtain full control over their employment.

(vi)   Marine Insurance (see also paragraphs 53–54 below).

44.   It maybe possible, by refusing insurance facilities to neutral ships which normally place their insurance in this country, to influence the employment of such ships and persuade their owners to accept White List conditions. (See below.) Insurance facilities will be refused to neutral ships on the Ships' Black List.

(vii)   Ships' Black List and White List

45.   Black and White Lists of neutral ships will be maintained by the Ministry of Economic Warfare through the machinery of the Black List Committee, as described in paragraphs 30–34 above. The Ships' Black List will contain the names of vessels known or suspected to be trading with enemy ports, or carrying goods to, from or on behalf of, the enemy, or belonging to owners[1] any of whose other vessels are known or suspected to be engaged in undesirable trades as defined above. The Ships' White List will contain the names of vessels whose owners have given, *in respect of all their vessels*, the undertakings set out in Annex XXI.

46.   Vessels on the Ships' Black List will be subjected to the following disabilities:–

---

[1]*The owners of black-listed ships will themselves automatically figure on the Black List proper.

(i)   Bunkers, repair and dry-docking facilities, ships' stores and insurance facilities will be denied to them at all ports in this country and in other territories where such measures can be applied.

(ii)   Their cargoes will be regarded with particular suspicion (see paragraph 27 (iv) above).

(iii)   As a rule, Navicerts will not be issued in respect of cargoes to be shipped in black-listed vessels.

47.   Vessels on the Ships' White List will be eligible for the following privileges:

(i)   So far as the necessity for conserving our supplies permits, unconditional supply of bunkers and stores for approved voyages and special consideration in the case of non-approved voyages.

(ii)   Access to repair, dry-docking and insurance facilities.

(iii)   Exemption from detention at Contraband Control Bases except where there is reason to believe that the owner is not observing his undertakings. (See Chapter X, paragraph 14.)

In addition, it may be necessary to offer special concessions to vessels whose owners undertake not to refuse to carry goods on the enemy's contraband list to British or allied ports.

(h)   Control of Finance

48.   The objective of this control is, as far as practicable, to prevent the financial resources of this country being put at the disposal of neutrals, who, though not on the Statutory List,[1] are affording assistance to the enemy beyond what is strictly incidental to the ordinary course of legitimate trade.

49.   Any information obtained by the Intelligence Department tending to show that neutral concerns are giving credit facilities to enemies, either by way of advances or discounts in cash or by selling goods on credit or in any other manner, in excess of what is in the ordinary course of trade, will be submitted to the Financial Pressure Department of the Ministry. If action is called for, the Department may either

(i)   Ask the Black List Committee to place them on the Black List or Statutory List, or

---

[1]*The Trading with the Enemy Act will render illegal financial transactions with or for the benefit of the enemy, including persons and businesses on the Statutory List. The prohibition extends to any transaction in which a neutral is acting as the agent (open or disguised) of an enemy, but not to transactions with neutrals who are separately carrying on business with the enemy, so long as they are engaged in the two sets of transactions independently and on their own account, or as agents of neutral principals.

(ii)   Warn banks, and request the Trading with the Enemy Branch to warn not to do so (see paragraph 28 and Annex XX).

50.   In the case of neutral countries assisting the enemy by loans or credits, or by allowing Clearing Accounts to accumulate large arrears, the Department will be responsible for arranging through the Bank of England that credits should not be allowed to the neutral country in question in such a way as to assist it to give credit to the enemy. (If this country had a Clearing with the neutral, the Department would ask the Board of Trade and Treasury to prevent, if possible, the neutral accumulating arrears in the Clearing and thus in effect borrowing from this country.)

51.   The Department will also keep under consideration the need for withholding banking credits from neutral countries which continue contraband trade with the enemy.

52.   Generally speaking, the Department will maintain contact with the City in order to advise as to transactions which are to be avoided as likely to benefit the enemy indirectly, and to collect and interpret information from City sources.

(i)   Control of Insurance

53.   Insurance firms subject to the Trading with the Enemy Act will automatically be prohibited from insuring or re-insuring risks for enemy firms or firms on the Statutory List. In addition, the Board of Trade, at the instance of the Ministry of Economic Warfare, will request underwriters, insurance companies, insurance brokers and agents not to insure the hulls or cargoes of vessels on the Ships' Black List. The names of such vessels will be notified to the Government Cargo War Risks Insurance Office.

54.   Re-insurance in this country by foreign insurance companies is usually effected on the basis of annual contracts, renewable as a rule on the 1st January. Such contracts, unless with enemy firms, would not be interrupted by war, and it will therefore be for consideration, before the end of the calendar year of the war, whether British firms should be asked to make the renewal of re-insurance contracts conditional upon a guarantee from the neutral firm not to undertake insurance for enemy interests or for neutrals firms and vessels on the Statutory List and/or Black List. In view, however, of the growth of foreign insurance undertakings and the increasing facilities for effecting re-insurance elsewhere than in this country, such a step might only have the effect of imperiling a valuable invisible Export; and it would, therefore, only be taken after consultation with the leading insurance interests.

CHAPTER VI
MILITARY ACTION

I – DEFINITION

Military action as a weapon of economic warfare denotes the use of the armed forces to deny to the enemy commodities required for the prosecution of the war. It may be taken at sea, on land, and by air, and may take the following forms:–

At Sea

(i)   Capture[1] of enemy ships and enemy cargoes therein.
(ii)   Contraband control, *i.e.*, control of traffic bound directly or indirectly to the enemy under a neutral flag.
(iii)   Blockade of the enemy's coast,
(iv)   Capture of enemy exports under neutral flags.
(v)   Direct attack on the enemy's ports.

On Land

(vi)   The invasion of important economic areas.

By Air

(vii)   Attack on enemy shipping on the high seas.
(viii) Attack on the terminal points of the enemy's trade routes.
(ix)   Attack on centres of storage, production, manufacture or distribution.

Of these forms of military action, the first, fifth, sixth and seventh are of indirect concern only to the Ministry of Economic Warfare, and are therefore not discussed further in this handbook.

2.   The legal and other considerations affecting the remaining forms of military action are set out in detail in the following sections. But, in order to avoid misunderstanding, it should be stated here that international law accords unconditional recognition only to the second, and, in certain circumstances, to the third and fourth. The use of the air weapon would only be regarded as legitimate on certain stringent, if at present ill-defined, conditions, as described below.

---

[1]*At the outset of war, the Customs will be responsible for the seizure of enemy ships and cargoes in port in the United Kingdom.

II – CONTRABAND CONTROL

(a) Definition

3. Contraband control may be defined as the exercise of the rights conferred upon a belligerent by the following well-established rules of law:

(i) A belligerent has the right to proclaim as contraband any commodity or article which is of use for the purpose of the prosecution of the war; and

(ii) A belligerent has the right to intercept, visit and search neutral vessels if there is reason to believe that they are carrying contraband goods destined for the enemy, and to seize, on certain conditions, any contraband on board which can be shown to the satisfaction of a Prize Court to be destined for the enemy.

(b) The Law Relating to Contraband

4. International law recognises two forms of contraband – absolute contraband and conditional contraband. In principle, absolute contraband comprises articles which are fit for purposes of war only, and certain other articles which, though fit also for the purpose of peace, are in their nature peculiarly serviceable to the enemy in war; while conditional contraband comprises articles fit for purposes of war and peace alike. Goods proclaimed as absolute contraband are liable to seizure and condemnation, even if they are consigned to a neutral, if it can be proved that they are ultimately destined for enemy territory. Goods proclaimed as conditional contraband are similarly liable only if they are destined directly or ultimately for enemy territory and intended for use for the purpose of the war. Generally speaking, this will be regarded as established if it is shown that the goods are destined for enemy State authorities or their agents, for a fortified place or base belonging to or used by the enemy, or for enemy forces or Government departments. It should be noted the so-called 'doctrine of infection' permits the seizure of non-contraband goods which belong to the same owner and are carried in the same ship as other goods which can legitimately be seized as contraband.

5. It is important to realise that every capture of ships or goods has to be followed by proceedings in the Prize Court, and that it is the Court which decides, in accordance with the prize law[1] which it administers, whether the captured articles are to be condemned or not. If the Court

---

[1]*Prize law is not municipal law, but the 'Course of Admiralty and the Law of Nations.'

decides that the captured articles are not in the circumstances liable to condemnation, it will release them, and may award damages for their seizure. It is therefore necessary to have continually in mind, both as regards general policy and in relation to particular seizures, the view which the Prize Court is likely to take of the legitimacy of the action contemplated. The procedure which it is intended to follow in future, as described in this Section, is based on such estimates as can be made of the interpretation which the Prize Court, guided by the precedents of 1914–18, is likely to place upon the principles set out in paragraphs 3 and 4 above.

(c)   Contraband Policy

6.   His Majesty's Government intend to maintain in principle the distinction between absolute and conditional contraband. They will, however, regard both conditional and absolute contraband consigned to neutral countries as liable to detention and seizure wherever there is evidence of ultimate enemy destination. The *condemnation* of absolute contraband will follow automatically where that destination is substantiated to the satisfaction of the Prize Court; while the condemnation of conditional contraband will only follow where additional evidence of the destination referred to in the last sentence of paragraph 4 can be adduced, and is accepted by the Prize Court.

7.   So far as detention and seizure are concerned, therefore, the distinction between absolute and conditional contraband will tend to disappear. As regards the subsequent condemnation of conditional contraband, it is probable that, in the conditions of modern warfare, particularly if the enemy is a totalitarian State, it should not be difficult, once destination to enemy territory has been established, to provide sufficient evidence of destination to the enemy government or its armed forces to secure condemnation. Moreover, as regards contraband, whether absolute or conditional, consigned to a neutral country, precedents from the war of 1914–18 justify the assumption that the Prize Court, though it will not condemn on statistical evidence alone *(i.e.,* evidence that the goods *sub judice* would, if allowed to reach their destination, have been in excess of the importing country's reasonable requirements), is unlikely, if the statistical evidence is convincing, to award damages against the Crown for wrongful detention.

8.   The above assumption constitutes, to a certain extent, the basis of the system of forcible rationing described in Chapter V, paragraph 19; for, if substantiated, it will enable His Majesty's Government, as soon as a ration of an adjacent neutral has been exceeded, to interrupt, for a

considerable time at any rate, sea-borne supplies of the rationed goods on their way to that neutral, without the fear of untoward consequences and with a good chance that the owner of the goods, mindful of the delays and uncertainty attendant upon litigation in the Prize Court, will prefer to sell them in this country rather than await their release. At the same time a policy of placing goods in the Prize Court simply on the ground that a ration had been exceeded, and without any other evidence of enemy destination, can, for legal, political, and administrative reasons, hardly be pursued indefinitely; and it must therefore be replaced as soon as possible, by voluntary agreements or by extending the employment of measures such as the Navicert system to the point at which we can exert effective control *at the source* over the export of key commodities to adjacent neutrals.

9.   Although there was little previous authority for it in International Law, it may now be regarded as established by the precedents of the war of 1914–18 that neutral vessels, instead of being searched for suspected contraband wherever they are intercepted, may be sent into port for examination. On the outbreak of war His Majesty's Government will therefore establish Contraband Control Bases, under Admiralty control, at which neutral vessels will be encouraged to call voluntarily, and to which those that do not call voluntarily will be sent under guard for examination.

(d)   The Contraband List

10.   In the past, His Majesty's Government have listed by name, in a Proclamation or series of Proclamations, the commodities which they intended to treat as absolute and conditional contraband respectively. The disadvantages of this procedure are:

(i)   that additional items can only be added by means of supplementary Proclamations,

(ii)   that it invites protests from neutrals as to our right to proclaim a given commodity as absolute or conditional contraband, and

(iii)   that, under conditions of modern warfare, the number of commodities capable of belligerent use which it would be necessary to list as contraband is so enormous that the list, by its very length, would probably unite all neutrals, however well disposed, in opposition to it.

11.   To avoid these disadvantages, and to secure certain other advantages, the Contraband Proclamation to be issued by His Majesty's Government on the outbreak of war will not in future list articles of absolute and conditional contraband by name, but will be a brief list in general terms similar to that embodied in the instructions issued by the

United States Government to its navy in 1917. The list and draft Proclamation are set out in Annex XIV, from which it will be seen that the four categories of absolute contraband and the one category of conditional contraband are so phrased that, if desired, the great majority of articles entering into international trade can be regarded as falling into one or other of them. Since, however, it would be unnecessary, as well as politically undesirable, to treat every article of commerce as contraband,[1] all authorities responsible for administering the Contraband List will hold a Confidential Supplement (Annex XV), consisting of a detailed catalogue of articles corresponding to the five general categories of the published list: and they will be informed, on the outbreak of war by the Foreign Office and at intervals thereafter by the Ministry of Economic Warfare, which articles mentioned in the Confidential Supplement are not to be regarded as contraband for the time being. Articles marked[†] in the Supplement will not, in any case, be regarded as contraband at the outset of the war.

12.   The Confidential Supplement will thus serve as a guide to the interpretation of the published list; and it is the intention that neutral exporters, when in doubt whether a given article of commerce is covered by the published list, should be encouraged to consult the nearest British authority, who will advise them in the light of the Confidential Supplement or, in doubtful cases, telegraph to the Ministry of Economic Warfare for instructions. British authorities, when consulted in this manner, will insist on full particulars of proposed shipments, as such information will be of value to the Ministry.

13.   The advantages of the procedure described above may be summed up as follows:

(i)   The list of goods treated as contraband may be varied without publicity.

(ii)   An extremely extensive list of goods may be treated as contraband without causing such irritation to neutrals as would be produced by the publication of the vast detailed list which would otherwise be required.

(iii)   The fact that the published list is based on a United States model should tend to disarm opposition to it in the United States of America.

(iv)   Much useful information will be obtained if, as explained above, neutral exporters seek the advice of British authorities in order to

---

[1]*There are two reasons for this. In the first place, the enemy may be expected to confine his purchases abroad to commodities which are essential to him; and in the second place, it will be unnecessary to treat as contraband goods of which the enemy is an exporter, unless (as may occur) he also imports them.

ascertain whether the goods they desire to ship are regarded as contraband or not.

(v)   If neutral exporters consult British authorities in this manner, the transition to a full Navicert system (see Chapter V, paragraph 10 above) will be comparatively easy.

(e)   The Machinery of Contraband Control

14.   The constituents of efficient contraband control are:

(i)   The Navy, to intercept and divert into Contraband Control Bases vessels suspected of carrying contraband.

(ii)   Contraband Control Bases, at which diverted vessels can be subjected to preliminary examination.

(iii)   The Customs

(a)   To arrange for the discharge and examination of cargo on ships handed over by the Contraband Control Bases for full examination;

(b)   To check over for contraband (so far as conditions permit) cargo remaining on board calling ships and transhipment and transit goods; and

(c)   To deal, as agents for the Admiralty Marshal, with ships and/or cargo seized by themselves or the Navy as contraband.

(iv)   An intelligence organisation, to obtain the evidence of enemy destination or enemy ownership which is required to secure the condemnation of detained goods and vessels respectively.

(v)   Machinery for sifting the evidence obtained under (iv), and, if it is considered adequate, for preparing a case for submission to

(vi)   The Prize Court, with whom it rests to decide whether detained goods and vessels are liable to condemnation as prize.

(vii)   The Admiralty Marshal, and Customs Collectors acting as his substitutes, to dispose of goods and ships condemned as prize.

These seven essential constituents are described in the following paragraphs.

Naval Arrangements

15.   The main function of the Navy as a weapon of economic warfare is to patrol as far as possible all the sea routes by which goods may reach the enemy and to send in for examination at a Control Base all vessels which have not made a voluntary call at such a base; or, if the strategical situation does not permit of this, to intercept and send in such vessels as, from intelligence sources, there is reason to believe have on board contraband cargo destined for the enemy. The prepara-

tion of plans to enable His Majesty's Ships to carry out these duties in any given war situation is the responsibility of the Admiralty, as is the preparation and issue in peace time of the necessary instructions to Officers Commanding His Majesty's Ships.

Contraband Control Bases

16.   Bases will be set up by the Admiralty at pre-arranged ports immediately on the outbreak of war. All vessels calling voluntarily or sent in for examination at these bases will be searched, and their manifests, and any other relevant information about them or their cargoes, will be telegraphed direct to the Ministry of Economic Warfare, in order that a decision may be reached whether or not the ship and/or cargo is to be seized.

17.   When the existence of suspected contraband cannot be verified without unloading, the authority of the Ministry will first be obtained. If (as will normally be the case at Contraband Control Bases in the United Kingdom) the vessel cannot be unloaded at the Base, the Ministry will request the Ministry of Shipping (who will consult the Admiralty and, so far as ports in the United Kingdom are concerned, the Port and Transit Committee) to select the port to which the vessel should be sent. The Ministry will at the same time inform the Board of Customs and Excise of the precise reasons for which the vessel is being sent into port. The Ministry of Shipping, having selected the port, will notify the Ministry, the Admiralty and the Board of Customs and Excise. The Admiralty will then arrange for the removal of the vessel, while the Board of Customs and Excise will warn the collector at the port to which it is being sent. On arrival the vessel will be handed over to the Customs, who will be responsible for the discharge and examination of her cargo, and will report their findings to the Ministry. All expenses incurred by the Customs in discharging such Vessels *before* seizure will be charged to the Admiralty.

Goods remaining on board. Transit and Transhipment Goods.

18.   Vessels calling at United Kingdom ports will not necessarily have passed through the contraband patrols, and their cargoes may therefore require to be subjected to contraband control by the Customs.

19.   So far as cargo remaining on board such vessels is concerned, Customs Collectors will report by telegram to the Ministry of Economic Warfare (at the same time as they report to their own Headquarters) agreed particulars of goods which are covered by the Contraband List in all cases where the vessels are subsequently bound, or suspected to be bound, for adjacent neutrals.

20.   Goods landed in the United Kingdom for transhipment (whether at the same port or, after transit through the United Kingdom, at another port) are in a different category, since an 'application to tranship' must be made and approved, whatever the nature and destination of the goods. Where the application to tranship (Form S. 24) indicates that the goods are covered by the Contraband List and are, or are suspected to be, consigned to an adjacent neutral, the actual form of application will be sent by the Customs Collector to the Ministry of Economic Warfare for consideration.

Intelligence

21.   As it is improbable that anything in a ship's papers will reveal the true destination of any cargo on board destined for the enemy, it is clear that a case for condemnation can only be made out if the necessary information is available from other sources. It will be derived in the main from the War Trade Reporting Organisation described in Chapter III, and from the Censorship; and it will be the duty of the Intelligence Department of the Ministry, on receiving particulars of a diverted or detained ship and its cargo, to ascertain from its records whether anything is known of the ship, or of the cargo and its consignors and consignees or other persons concerned with the shipment, that might justify the detention for further enquiries, or the seizure, of the ship or some or all of its cargo.

Appraisal of information regarding detained vessels or goods and decision of Contraband Committee

22.   Information in regard to a diverted or detained ship or its cargo made available to the Intelligence Department will be submitted to the Prize Department, which, after consultation with the Legal Department, will, except in clear-cut cases of innocent cargoes, submit a brief statement for consideration by the Contraband Committee (see Chapter II, paragraph 8). On the basis of the statement submitted to it by the Prize Department and of any other material which is available the Contraband Committee will decide whether the vessel and/or cargo (or part of it) is to be –
   (i)   Released,
   (ii)   Detained for further enquiries, or
   (iii) Seized.

Action following the Committee's Decision

23.   The action to be taken to give effect to the Committee's decision falls into three parts, according to whether the vessel (i) is still at the

Contraband Control Base at which it has been detained (paragraph 16 above), (ii) has been sent to a port for discharge (paragraph 17 above), or (iii) has been detained by the Customs at a port (paragraphs 18–20 above).

(i) Vessels detained at a Contraband Control Base

24.   The Committee's decision will be notified by the Ministry to the Base and the Admiralty; and, if the decision is seizure, also to the Ministry of Shipping, the Admiralty Marshal and the Procurator-General. Where a seized vessel, or a vessel whose cargo or part of it is to be seized, has to be removed to another port for unloading pending trial (as will normally be the case in the United Kingdom), the Ministry of Shipping, in consultation with the Admiralty and, so far as ports in the United Kingdom are concerned, the Port and Transit Committee, will select the port to which the vessel is to be sent and will notify the Ministry, the Admiralty and the Board of Customs and Excise. The Admiralty will be responsible for issuing the necessary instructions to the Contraband Control Base, and the Customs will warn the Collector at the port to which the vessel is to be sent. The naval authorities will be responsible for delivering the vessel to the Customs Collector at the port selected, in his capacity as Admiralty Marshal's substitute. Subsequent action is provided for in the Customs Collectors Instructions relating to Prize (Annex XVIII).

(ii) Vessels detained at a port to which they have been sent for unloading and examination

25.   The Committee's decision will be notified to the Board of Customs and Excise, and, if the decision is seizure, also to the Procurator-General and the Admiralty Marshal. The Customs Collector to whom the vessel has been handed over for discharging will be instructed by the Board of Customs and Excise either to release it, to detain it for further enquiries or to seize it (or its cargo), as the case may be. In the latter case, the Customs Collector will then act on his instructions relating to Prize (Annex XVIII). The Admiralty and Contraband Control Base concerned will subsequently be notified, for information, as to the action taken.

(iii) Calling Vessels detained at Ports by the Customs (including goods landed from such vessels for transhipment).

26.   The Committee's decision will be notified to the Admiralty for information and to the Board of Customs and Excise, who will instruct the Customs Collector at the port of detention either to release, to detain

or to seize the vessel (or its cargo), as the case may be. If the decision is seizure the Procurator-General and the Admiralty Marshal will also be notified; and the Customs Collector will act on his instructions relating to Prize. In the case of transit and transhipment goods, Form S. 24 (see paragraph 20 above) will be forwarded to the Board of Customs and Excise at the same time as they are notified of the Committee's decision.

Requisitioning and Sale

27.   As soon as the Contraband Committee has decided that vessels or goods are to be detained for further enquiries or seized, the Prize Department will circulate brief particulars to all Departments likely to desire to requisition them. If, in the case of goods, no application for requisitioning is received, the Department will consider whether it would be desirable that the goods should, if possible, be sold in order to ensure that, whatever the result of the further enquiries or of the action in the Prize Court, the goods themselves should not become available to the enemy. If it is decided that it would be desirable to requisition the vessel, or to requisition or sell the goods, and that the case is such that there is a reasonable prospect of the Prize Court being prepared to make the necessary order, the Department will inform the Admiralty Marshal and will request the Procurator-General to apply to the Court for an order for sale or requisition as the case may be. In such cases it is necessary to satisfy the Prize Court, not only that requisition or sale is desirable, but that there is sufficient *prima facie* evidence of enemy destination. Moreover, the Court is unlikely to grant an order for the sale or requisition of goods unless it can be shown that it is impossible to store them pending trial.

28.   If an order is obtained, the Admiralty Marshal will be responsible for its execution; sale will be effected at public action through brokers appointed by him, who will also undertake valuation in the case of requisitioning. The proceeds of sale or requisitioning, less expenses, will be refunded to the owners of the goods or vessels if the Crown ultimately fails in its case for condemnation.

The Prize Court

29.   On the outbreak of war, the Admiralty will be responsible for taking the necessary steps for the constitution of the High Court of Justice as a Prize Court. Corresponding action would be taken to set up Prize Courts in certain Colonies and Protectorates, and, if appropriate, in the Dominions. The question whether Prize Courts should be set up in any allied countries, such as Egypt (which would involve special legislation), may require consideration.

Disposal of Seized Vessels and Goods

30.   When diverted or calling vessels or their cargoes are seized (see paragraphs 23–26 above), they are transferred to the charge of the Admiralty Marshal, and he then becomes answerable to the Prize Court for their safe custody. (In the United Kingdom Collectors of Customs act as his substitutes for the purposes of the custody of Prize.) The subsequent procedure is as follows:

(i)   He is responsible (in consultation with the Ministry of Shipping and, so far as United Kingdom ports are concerned, the Port and Transit Committee) for the custody of the vessel and/or the warehousing of its cargo pending trial, and for effecting any necessary insurance.

(ii)   If the Court grants an order for sale or requisition (see paragraph 27), he effects the sale through his accredited brokers or arranges, also through them, for valuation for the purposes of requisitioning.

(iii)   If the Court ultimately decrees the release of a vessel or cargo disposed of under an order for sale or requisition, he refunds the proceeds, less expenses, to the owner.

(iv)   If a vessel or its cargo is not sold or requisitioned under an order of the court, but is subsequently condemned, he effects the sale of the vessel or goods through his brokers. If, on the other hand, the Court orders the release of the vessel or goods, he is responsible for restoring them to their owners, subject to the payment of such charges as may have been incurred.

III – BLOCKADE

31.   The term 'blockade,' often loosely used in the past to denote economic warfare as a whole, means in law the investment of the enemy's coast, or a part of it, by a sufficient force of ships to cut off communication by sea between the blockaded coast and the rest of the world. It is only in this sense that the term is employed in this Handbook. With a few minor exceptions, no blockades were established in 1914–1918, so that there was no such development of existing rules as occurred in the case of contraband; the matter can therefore only he dealt with, at present, on the basis of the rules as they existed before the last war. According to those rules, a blockade must

(i)   Be declared and notified, so that neutral vessels may be aware of its existence;

(ii)   Be effective – i.e., be maintained by a force sufficient really to prevent access to the blockaded coast; and

(iii)   Be applied only to the ports or coastline of the enemy.

If these conditions are fulfilled, any vessel attempting to break the blockade, either inwards or outwards, with actual or presumptive knowledge of the blockade, may be seized as lawful Prize and the ship and, generally speaking, all its cargo will be condemned in the Prize Court.

32.   Under modern conditions of warfare, it is doubtful whether a blockade which complied strictly with the above rules would prove practicable, except in unimportant cases, since the development of the submarine and air arms, and the increased range of modern coastal defence guns, render it impossible to maintain a blockading force in the immediate vicinity of the enemy coast. But the law of blockade, as described in the preceding paragraph, is, like all other rules of law, subject to development in the light of changed conditions and the possibility cannot be altogether excluded that altered conditions might be held to justify the proclamation of a long- distance blockade, maintained by forces stationed at a considerable distance from the enemy coast and applying to all vessels, whether on their way to or from enemy ports or to or from neutral ports, attempting to pass through the controlled zone and carrying goods of enemy destination or origin. Interference with neutral shipping on these lines would, however, be a formidable extension of anything previously sanctioned under international law; and the possibility of instituting such a blockade would depend on the circumstances of the moment.

33.   If a close blockade (i.e., one complying with the conditions set out in paragraph 31) of any part of the enemy's coast proves practicable, the Admiralty, after consultation with the Foreign Office and Ministry of Economic Warfare, will normally be responsible for the issue of the necessary Declaration (for draft see Annex VI). A blockade may in certain circumstances be proclaimed locally by the Commander-in-Chief of the Naval forces undertaking it.

IV – SEIZURE OF ENEMY EXPORTS

34.   If it were possible to declare a close blockade of the enemy coast, enemy exports shipped from ports in the blockaded area could legitimately be seized. But in most cases enemy exports are in any event more likely to be shipped from convenient neutral ports, and it has not been possible to find any procedure for interfering with enemy exports shipped from neutral ports in neutral bottoms which would not be open to objection on existing International Law principles. Failing some development of International Law (such as the extension of the idea of a long-distance blockade described in paragraph 32), the stoppage of enemy exports can only be effected in

retaliation for a sufficiently serious breach of International Law by the enemy, as was done in 1915.

35.   Should it prove practicable to take action against enemy exports, the procedure for their interception, seizure and condemnation would be the same as for contraband of war, as set out in paragraphs 14–30 above, except that an Enemy Exports Committee, corresponding to the Contraband Committee, would be set up to decide whether goods should be seized or released.

36.   The system of certificates of origin and interest described in Chapter IV, paragraph 5, above would require to be extended to cover all goods, *whatever their destination*, which might be of enemy origin or which might be derived from enemy products; and it would be made clear to merchants and shippers that failure to obtain certificates of origin for cargoes shipped from neutral countries adjacent to the enemy would be regarded as *prima facie* evidence of enemy origin sufficient to justify detention for investigation.

V – THE AIR WEAPON

37.   Subject to any international agreement that may be reached as to the restriction of bombing from the air, the general policy of His Majesty's Government in regard to the use of the air arm may be summarised as follows:

(i)   It is against international law to bomb civilians as such, and to make deliberate attacks upon civil populations.

(ii)   Targets aimed at from the air must be legitimate military objectives and must be capable of identification.

(iii)   Reasonable care must be taken in attacking those military objectives so that by carelessness the civil population in the neighbourhood is not bombed.

38.   The terms 'legitimate military objective' and 'civil population' present difficulties of definition under modern conditions of totalitarian war; a miner hewing coal to smelt the iron ore to produce the steel from which a gun is manufactured is, in theory, at least as essential a link in the chain which ends in the firing of the gun as is the soldier who mans it. But, whether arbitrary definitions are laid down in some international agreement or whether common-sense is to remain the criterion for judging the legitimacy or otherwise of a given attack from the air, His Majesty's Government would never initiate air attack involving heavy civilian casualties. Their policy will therefore in the last resort be determined mainly by that of the enemy, and plans must be made to enable retaliatory measures to be taken if necessary. It is on this assumption and with these qualifications that tentative plans are made in

peace time for the application of air action to the objects of economic warfare – that is to say, to the destruction or disorganisation of key-points in the enemy's economic system.

39.   These plans require no description here. It must, however, be emphasized that air action against economic objectives, if employed at all, can be most effectively employed only if carefully related to the development and effects of other forms of economic warfare. If, for instance, contraband control and agreements with neutrals fail to prevent the enemy from obtaining adequate supplies of, say, oil-seeds, the bombing of crushing-mills will achieve the same ends by rendering supplies of the imported raw material useless. Again, if an adjacent neutral is able to supply the enemy with some key commodity by rail or waterway, and proves impervious to the measures which have been described as diplomatic action, air attack on some vital point of the enemy's communication system may interrupt supplies of that commodity long enough to disorganise his industrial machine. The Ministry of Economic Warfare will, therefore, keep a close watch on the enemy's supply position and, acting on its information as to the distribution of enemy industry, centres of storage and sources of supply, and as to the key points of his transport system, will be responsible for advising the Air Ministry as to the selection of suitable economic targets.

* * *

68.   Sir Nigel Bruce Ronald, Councillor, Foreign Affairs, to Hugh Dalton, Secretary, Ministry of Economic Warfare

[BT 60/61/6, W.19227/16015/49]   15 January 1940

Sir,

I am directed by Viscount Halifax [Foreign Minister] to refer to the letter from your Department dated the 23rd December No. 1 2551 relative to the possibility of using the information at the disposal of the Minister of Economic Warfare for the benefit of British trade interests abroad, more especially with regard to the substitution of German exports now prevented by the Order-in-Council of November 27th.

2.   So far as Lord Halifax is aware, accusations regarding the misuse of the censorship for such purposes during the war of 1914–18 emanated almost entirely from United States sources, and, from the information available, it would appear that no country other than the United States protested against this alleged misuse of the censorship. In this connexion I am to transmit to you herewith, for the information of

Mr Cross, a copy of a memorandum prepared in the Foreign Office in 1936 to which is annexed Lord Robert Cecil's statement to the Press of the 25th August 1916.

3.   In these circumstances Lord Halifax sees no objection in principle to the dissemination to private traders by discreet means of information such as would enable them to supplant German exports in overseas markets, though he considers it undesirable that the source of this information should be disclosed. On the other hand it is for obvious reasons essential that no suspicion, however unfounded, that this information is being used to evict United States traders from neutral markets should be allowed to gain currency, and Lord Halifax would accordingly deem it a necessary condition of the institution of a scheme on the lines suggested that no information in regard to orders to or from [the] Unites States should be distributed.

4.   A copy of this letter is being sent to the Board of Trade.   I am, Sir
. . .

* * *

69.   Use of Censorship

Professor N.H. Hall, head of Economic Warfare Intelligence Department, Ministry of Economic Warfare to D.H. Lyal, [Industries and Industrial Enquiries Division], Department of Overseas Trade

[BT 60/61/6, I.F. 225]   22 February 1940

Dear Lyal, I have just seen a copy of Foreign Office letter to you (W.1756/14/19, dated 15th February) regarding the use of information obtained from Censorship. I may say in general I am in agreement with the contents of this letter. It seems to have been written without reference to Mr Ronald's letter to the Secretary of the Ministry of Economic Warfare (W.19227/16015/49) on the same subject.

Since we met some days ago, I have seen a telegram from Lord Halifax to Lord Lothian, FO telegram No. 260 of the 18th February, emphasising that there is no question of improper use of Censorship information to further British trade interests at the expense of American or other neutral traders, either now or after the war. The telegram goes on to say: 'I (Lord Halifax) am insisting 'that our hands shall be absolutely clean in this matter'.

It is clear to me, therefore, that we must proceed with great caution, in order to observe the undertakings given by the Foreign Secretary. I have asked Mr L.E. Jones to act as liaison officer between my Department of this Ministry and yourself, and I have called his attention to the documents referred to by me in this letter.

I have not heard whether you are yet receiving information from us. I think it desirable that we should meet with Jones in the very near future and review the situation.

Yours sincerely, . . .

* * *

70. First Monthly Report Submitted by the Minister of Economic Warfare

SECRET

[MT 59/285; W.P. (R) (40) 179]   10th June–10th July 1940

I GENERAL

1.   The events of the past three months have radically changed the conditions under which economic warfare must be waged. With Northern Europe under German control and the Mediterranean closed by Italy's entry into the war, contraband control, previously the chief weapon of the economic war, becomes relatively unimportant. Almost everywhere in Europe it must now be replaced, so far as the naval situation allows, by simple 'blockade', by the prevention of the passage of ships to Northern Europe and into the Mediterranean. But even before the defeat of France a complete naval blockade was not possible, while the fact that the Turkish Government have not closed the passage from the Black Sea inevitably reduces the pressure that could be exercised on the enemy by the complete blocking of the three exits from the Mediterranean. It was therefore clear that naval blockade must be supplemented by export control in overseas and colonial territories, which would tend to replace contraband control as the main weapon of economic warfare. There seemed to be good prospects that it would be no less effective a weapon. It was hoped that export control would rapidly be made effective throughout the four Allied Empires; that it would be powerfully supported both by export control in the USA, as the result of the Defence Bill now passed by Congress which sets up an export licensing system for key commodities, and by US purchases of raw materials for defence purposes; and that the South American countries would follow the lead of the US Government.

2.   The disaster in France and especially the collapse of the French Empire has been a severe blow for this new policy. But there is still every reason to hope that we shall be able to keep up our economic pressure on the enemy by the combined use of naval blockade, world shipping control and export control overseas. The prosecution of economic warfare will however involve this country in political problems of the greatest importance and world-wide effect. For the maintenance of the blockade of Europe will cause great suffering in all enemy and enemy-occupied territories, while in overseas countries primary producers will see the accumulation of surpluses for which, owing to the blockade, there is no market. The opportunity which this situation will provide for enemy propaganda is obvious. It might well produce a wide movement to force this country to stop the war. It will certainly result in pressure from many sides, and especially from the exiled Governments and from humanitarians in the USA, to allow relief cargoes through the blockade. The attitude of the United States Government will be of vital importance in meeting all these difficulties. Every effort is being made to enlist their understanding and support and there are good grounds for hoping that they will be forthcoming. The Administration have already taken a most important initiative in announcing that they are preparing plans for dealing with commodity surpluses in the Western Hemisphere, which are to be considered by a Pan-American Conference at Havana convened for the 21st July.

3.   To meet the new conditions, the Ministry of Economic Warfare has been re-organised. Its staff has been considerably reduced.

II   CO-OPERATION BY THE ALLIED EMPIRES IN BLOCKADE MEASURES

4.   The effect of the entrance of the Belgian and Netherlands Empires into the war against Germany at the time when France was still our ally was to give to the allied Empires a very large degree of direct control over a number of important raw materials. M.E.W. therefore evolved a policy of co-ordinated export control between the allied Empires for economic warfare purposes. An Inter-Allied Ministerial Conference, attended by the Minister of Economic Warfare and the Under-Secretaries of State for Foreign Affairs, Dominions and Colonies and the Deputy Under-Secretary of State for India and by representatives of the French, Belgian and Netherlands Governments, was held at the Ministry on June 17th. The meeting had before it a Draft Statement of Policy in the following terms:

'The representatives of the four Allies in consultation

(a)   consider that the vigorous prosecution of the economic war against the enemy constitutes an essential factor in the ultimate victory of the Allies;

(b)   resolve that, since the four Allied Empires jointly command the major part of the essential raw materials and commodities of the world, the export of these commodities and materials shall be so controlled as totally to deny the use of them to the enemy;

(c)   agree that such control cannot satisfactorily be established without the imposition in all territories of the Allied Empires of a system for licensing exports;

(d)   resolve that such systems shall, where not already in existence, be imposed and that they should be co-ordinated in scope and practice and in the policy governing their operation;

(e)   direct that a Committee of experts, representing the four Allies, shall examine how best these resolutions and this policy may be implemented;

(f)   agree to meet again from time to time as required to receive reports from the committee of experts and to undertake any necessary action.'

5.   The meeting was, of course, overshadowed by great events, but the foreign representatives all adhered in principle to the Statement of Policy. The task of the Expert Committee in implementing the Statement has been retarded by rapid political changes, but progress has been made. Thus the Netherlands Government have introduced a system of export control for blockade purposes and their expert representative is in close touch with the Ministry. In the case of the Congo, no exports whatever have taken place since May 10th, but a system is now being introduced by which all goods are subject to licence before export. No goods whatever are to be exported to territories under enemy sovereignty, protection or control. Licences are to be granted freely to the British Empire and North and South America, save that special restrictions will apply to the export of cobalt and diamonds to South America. All applications by the Congo authorities to the Belgian Embassy in London and the decision to grant or withhold a licence will rest with the Inter-Allied Expert Committee sitting in the Ministry.

6.   It is hoped when the situation in the French Empire clarifies itself further that progress will be made with an export control policy, co-ordinated between the four Allied Empires and the USA.

[Initialled] H.D.

* * *

71. Economic Pressure Through Control of Shipping[1]

*Note by E.M. Nicholson (Executive Officer) and P.SS. Ormond
(Secretary), Ministry of Shipping Departmental Committee
SECRET, E.P. (SH) 1*

[MT 59/285]   11 July 1940

The attached draft Memorandum is the outcome of a number of discussions between the Ministries of Shipping and Economic Warfare and the Admiralty. It is suggested that the proposed Memorandum should be submitted to Ministers by the Minister of Economic Warfare with the concurrence of the Ministry of Shipping. It is therefore circulated for the consideration of members of the Ministry of Shipping Departmental Committee at the first meeting of this Committee, which will be held at the Ministry of Shipping at 10:30 a.m., on Friday, 12th July, 1940 (see separate Agenda).

Harcourt's Copy

(b)   In the present phase of the war the necessity has arisen for preventing or restricting imports to virtually the whole of Europe. This extension of ~~the blockade~~ [control] changes its nature and renders less effective some of the established measures of enforcement. ✓ In particular, the extent of the waters requiring patrol places upon the Royal Navy a strain which it is important to relieve, particularly in view of the loss of the French assistance and the added burdens of convoy and coastal protection. Certain possibilities exist of relieving the Navy through extended control of the sources of supply of raw materials and extended control of shipping. The former has been rendered practicable by the association with the United Kingdom of such important raw material producing areas as the Dutch and Belgian Colonial Empires and by other recent developments, while the adherence of Norway, Holland and Belgium and the chartering of large blocks of Danish, Swedish, Greek and other tonnage have given the Ministry of Shipping increased power in relation to world shipping. The object of this memorandum is to outline the first instalment of a policy for the co-ordinated use of these resources. It will assume the need for first establishing a sound basis of effective joint action between shipping and economic warfare, and for develop-

---

[1]Deletions and annotations have been included as in the original.

ing an initial scheme capable of rapid implementation, while indicating some of the possible measures which might be adopted as opportunity arises to increase the effectiveness and extend the scope of the policy immediately proposed.

(c)   *Identification of 'Aggression-Aiding' Trade*

The first essential is that, in using various methods of persuasion and control, there should be one clearly defined and generally understood primary objective. It is proposed that this objective should be ~~formulated and given wide publicity~~ [embodied] in a statement pointing out that HM Government wish to keep the seas free for the largest possible volume of 'neighbourly' trade tending to the mutual advantage of all free peoples, while putting down those abuses of international trade which tend merely to feed aggression. This implies drawing a clear distinction between what may be called 'neighbourly' trade for purposes of useful exchange and mutual advantage between free peoples and what may be called 'aggression aiding' trade controlled or inspired by a militarist regime for the purpose of maintaining a war machine to destroy other nations' liberties. Aggression-aiding trade may be placed in three categories:

a.   Trading with the German and Italian aggressors or with countries which they are able to exploit by occupation or otherwise (i.e. Greater Germany, Italy and the Italian Colonies, Norway, Denmark, Netherlands, Belgium, France, and Poland.

b.   Sending supplies to countries adjoining the aggressor States or to the areas under their exploitation under conditions which justify an inference of enemy destination. (~~This applies particularly to~~ [Such countries might be] USSR, Finland, Sweden, Spain and Portugal, and the Balkan countries.)

c.   Unreasonably obstructing measures for identifying and restraining the above types of aggression-aiding trade.

d.   It might later be practicable and desirable to add a fourth category namely trading with particular undertaking in neutral countries which belong to or are subject to the control of the aggressor States (i.e. firms appearing on the Statutory List). As this would give rise to complications in Asia and the Americas it is proposed to postpone action under this head until conditions appear favourable.

In view of the inevitable inconvenience and suffering involved, and of the need for minimising friction, it is of the highest importance that the measures taken should be shown by effective publicity to be in the long-term interests of all free peoples and should not be allowed to be represented by German propaganda as a last effort of the pluto-democracies to strangle the peoples of Europe.

3. *Methods of Enforcement*

The next step required is to provide simple and adequate criteria by which neighbourly and aggression-aiding trade can be effectively distinguished by naval patrols and other agents of economic warfare policy. The existing Navicert System provides the basis. ~~Within the War zone~~ A ship Navicert can form the identifying mark of all ships, whether inward or outward bound, which are certified not to be engaged in aggression-aiding trade. It will be necessary to declare that any ships trading to Europe, Turkey-in-Asia, and Africa north of the Equator without such a Ship Navicert will be treated as a 'blockade-runner'. The Ship Navicert is, however, applicable only to a particular voyage ~~within the War zone~~, and there may be a case for supplementing it by a ~~more permanent and universal~~ Ship Passport to be issued only to vessels whose owners, or charterers, have bound themselves (in respect of all ships under their control) to refrain from voyages without Navicerts in areas where the Navicert System applies, and in other areas to give reasonable information about voyages and cargoes. In recognition of these undertakings, such ships should be assured of equal treatment with British ships in all British controlled ports and at sea, and should be given access on equal terms with British ships to British insurance and other facilities. Such facilities would be entirely withheld from suspected owners or charterers, and their ships, while others without a Ship Passport could be made subject to a series of inquiries and delays which would make its possession appear very desirable.

4. *Naval Patrol*

In order to make such measures effective, a strong Naval Patrol will be necessary. In the Admiralty view, lack of bases, and the shortage of patrol craft make it advisable to declare a 'war zone' adjoining North-West Africa and Western Europe within which unauthorised shipping would be liable to be sunk ~~at sight~~ or captured[,] according to the discretion of the patrol. ~~While~~ Drastic action will undoubtedly be necessary to prevent the growth of blockade-running by enemy controlled vessels, and by adventurous third parties[.] It is important that any measures decided upon should be framed, timed and announced in such a way as to avoid antagonising potential friends and prejudicing the success of the measures discussed below. Emphasis should simultaneously be laid on the contribution of the Royal Navy in keeping the seas relatively free of both surface and submarine raiders which defy international law by sinking shipping, often without warning and without making provision for the safety of the passengers and crew, and regardless of flag, cargo and position. Approved neutral vessels on approved voyages with approved cargoes should be encouraged to take advantage of British convoys. ~~in which the realised odds against sinking are about 700 to 1.~~ . . .

* * *

72. Blockade Policy

Memorandum by the Secretary of State for Foreign Affairs, Anthony Eden

[CAB 66/17; W.P. (41) 175]   19 July 1941

I wish to call the attention of my colleagues to a problem which our blockade measures are likely to raise for us in the near future.

2.   The blockade of Germany and the occupied countries of Europe has the strong support of our public: indeed, in the early stages of the war there was too great a tendency to regard it as a decisive weapon in itself. Having survived the initial period when powerful neutral opinion had to be conciliated, it has now been accepted by the remaining neutral countries abroad with varying degrees of resignation. Our blockade measures continue to be an irritant in our relations with a number of countries, and in particular with Portugal: but the only diplomatic difficulties which we have lately encountered have been certain incidents with Latin American countries over enemy exports. More serious than these are the strong appeals for food relief for the allied populations in territory now occupied by Germany. It is to these latter that I now wish to draw attention.

3.   A year ago the Ministry of Economic Warfare were able to answer such appeals by stating that there was no danger of famine in Europe during the winter of 1940–41 if food were equitably distributed. Thanks to this argument and to the general support of the United States Government, we have so far been able to maintain the food blockade intact

save for a temporary concession affecting a few shipments of wheat and dried milk for unoccupied France which we permitted at the request of the United States Government.

4. We have nevertheless been subjected to severe pressure from certain of the allied Governments and from a section of United States opinion led by Mr Hoover. The Belgian, Norwegian and Greek Governments, in particular, have been able to make out plausible cases of serious hardship, but we have been fortunate in that the allied Governments in general – admirably led by the Dutch – have declined to respond to Mr Hoover's invitation to aid him in making trouble for us in the United States of America.

5. At present, therefore, we are in as satisfactory a position as can be expected, but we must now reckon with a change in the situation.

6. The entry of the Soviet Union into the war and the damage caused by the German campaign in the Balkans may seriously affect the European food situation this winter. We may no longer be able to maintain that there is or should be no starvation. A shortage of fuel oil would still further hamper the distribution of supplies which will in any event be short. We may be sure that when the pinch comes it will be the allied peoples and not the Germans who will be made to feel it first. We shall accordingly have no answer to give the allied Governments, except that their people are suffering in the same cause as that for which our own people have endured bombardment from the air. There is reason to think that the enslaved peoples in general understand the situation and are willing to make the necessary sacrifice; but there may be limits to their endurance. We must expect some of the allied Governments, particularly the Belgian, Greek and Norwegian, to press this view strongly upon us.

7. The risks that we run in continuing too rigid an enforcement of the food blockade are:

   (a) That we may alienate United States sympathy;

   (b) That we may find ourselves in serious difficulties with crews of allied merchant vessels in our service whose families are still in the occupied countries. This applies especially to Norwegians.

   (c) That we may alienate sympathies of allied Governments and peoples.

8. As regards (a) I think that the United States Government and people are now so deeply committed to give us support in the prosecution of the war that Mr Hoover's campaign will not seriously affect the attitude of either the Administration or of public opinion. As regards (b) we must exercise great care to prevent disaffection from feeding upon this grievance. This we can only do by assiduous solicitude for the

welfare and contentment of the men. (c) Raises larger issues which require more consideration than they have yet received.

9.   In bringing this matter to my colleagues' notice I assume that they will wish to continue a strict blockade. I do not suggest that we should here and now determine upon a departure from that policy, though naturally I reserve the right to plead occasionally for flexibility in its execution where I consider this expedient. For the present all that I ask is that my colleagues should take note of what I conceive to be the probable consequences of the maintenance of that policy; and meanwhile I would propose –

1.   That the Minister of Economic Warfare should be asked to prepare as soon as possible a general forecast of what food conditions are likely to be in the various occupied countries of Europe during next winter;

2.   That a small committee of my colleagues should be appointed to consider with the Minister of Economic Warfare and myself any major questions in connexion with the blockade which may arise from time to time and to report upon them to the War Cabinet.

* * *

73.   The Food Blockade and the Occupied Territories

Memorandum by the Minister of Economic Warfare, Hugh Dalton
SECRET, W.P. (41) 176

[CAB 66/17/235]   28 July 1941

I have discussed with the Foreign Secretary his paper on Blockade Policy (W.P. (41) 175) and, as requested by him, I attach a general forecast of the food situation next winter in German-occupied Europe.

2.   The arguments against allowing food through the blockade are still, in my view, overwhelming. 'At this season of the year and for some months to come, there is the least chance of scarcity as the harvest has just been gathered in. Only agencies which can create famine in any part of Europe now and during the coming winter, will be German exactions or German failure to distribute the supplies which they command.' These words, spoken by the Prime Minister a year ago, are still true. There will be enough food in Europe next winter to meet the needs of all countries. There will be no starvation, nor even acute shortage, unless the Germans fail to distribute the supplies fairly.

3.   It is quite impossible to ensure that, if we let food through, there is no benefit to the enemy, but only to the oppressed peoples. These peoples will obtain from our charity only such crumbs as the enemy allow them and perhaps none at all.

4.   What we concede to one Ally, we must be prepared to concede to all. If, because conditions are specially bad in some areas, we send food to these, the Germans will soon arrange that conditions elsewhere become bad enough to lead us a step further. Therefore, if we let in any food, we must let in substantial quantities, and the gain to the enemy will be great.

5.   The food blockade is an essential weapon of economic warfare. If we let in food, we make possible the transfer of German man power from food production to the production of munitions or service in the armed forces; also we ease the strain on the enemy's transport system.

6.   On the other hand, I raise no objection to purchases within the blockade area which do not increase the total supplies available, but merely divert food towards the areas of greater need. We have told the Belgians that, with certain safeguards, they may buy Portuguese products. We are trying to help the Greeks to buy in Turkey.

7.   Some say that the people of the occupied territories will be more pro-British if we let food in. I do not agree. Mr Allen, the Head of the American Red Cross in France, recently reported to the Foreign Office that the French were quite prepared to pull in their belts and suffer. The French, he said 'blame the Germans for the shortage of food and they blame us for allowing supplies to go in.' Mr Allen also said that the Germans would allow no publicity to the American Relief shipments. Still less would they allow it if such shipments went to the occupied territories. Mr Allen was against allowing any supplies, except vitamins and milk concentrates for children, to enter unoccupied France. As regards the occupied territories he said that there was no possibility whatever of any adequate supervision and consequently no guarantee that anything that might be sent would reach the people for whom it was intended.

9.   Our own Parliament and public are increasingly opposed to any further relaxation of the blockade.

10.   As regards the suggestion made in paragraph 9 (2) of the Foreign Secretary's paper, I do not feel that the appointment of a Ministerial Committee to consider Blockade questions is necessary. Our two Departments keep in constant touch on these questions and will, I am sure, continue to do so. I see no advantage in adding to the machinery of consultation by setting up yet another Committee.

* * *

74.   The King's Regulations and Admiralty Instructions for the Government of His Majesty's Naval Service

[Vol. 1, London: HMSO]   1943

Chapter XXIV: PRIZE AND PRIZE MONEY, INCLUDING AWARDS FOR SALVAGE AND SPECIAL SERVICES

SECTION I – PRIZE MONEY

887.   Definition. The term Prize Money includes all awards distributable under the Naval Agency and Distribution Acts, 1864, *i.e.*, prize, prize bounty, salvage (see 896 and 903), awards for seizures under the Slave Trade, Foreign Enlistment, Pacific Islanders Protection, Customs, Merchant Shipping and Piracy Acts, or other special service in respect of which any reward is payable.

2.   **Ships' Agents.** Provision is made in the Act for the appointment of agents to act on behalf of His Majesty's ships in any of the matters referred to (*see* 675, *and* Navy List). When their services are required, they should be given instructions to take the necessary action and be provided with all the pertinent documents, but under modern conditions their employment is not called for in respect of Prize of War.

Ships' agents' commission is at the rate of 2½ per cent, calculated on the net amount distributable, except in Prize Bounty, where it is limited to 1 per cent.

888.   Legal Expenses under Naval Agency Act. Where any proceedings shall have been instituted in any court, or other action taken on instructions by, or on behalf of, any of His Majesty's ships in respect of any of the matters referred to in Article 887 (other than Prize of War) in which an award may be payable, the liability for the legal expenses incurred in such proceedings rests in the first place with the Captain of such ship. Where the Captain shall be unable himself to pay such legal expenses, or to obtain the necessary advance from or negotiate a bill for the amount on the ship's agent, he will be at liberty to demand from the Accountant Officer an advance of public money for the purpose. Such advance, which must not exceed £100, is to be debited by the Accountant Officer in the ledger against the pay of such Captain, and must be reported specially to the Admiralty.

2.   When an award is obtained, the taxed cost and expenses of the claimants (except such as may be ordered to be paid from other sources) are defrayed therefrom before its distribution.

899.   Reports. Whenever a capture shall have been made, or any services performed by a ship, for which a claim is being made or an award has been made, or for which it is expected that an award will be made, or in respect of which proceedings have been instituted, a report of the circumstances is to be made to the Admiralty.

2.   The Captain is also, except for Prize of War, to transmit to the Admiralty for the Director of Naval Accounts–

(a)   A complete list of all the officers, Naval ratings, Royal Marines and other persons actually on board on the occasion, specifying therein whether any other ship, including those of His Majesty's allies, was in sight at the time and entitled to share, the name and description of the prize, etc., and also the place and date of the capture or service; a special notation being made against the names of all supernumerary officers above the rank of Midshipman, who were doing duty by order at the time. This notation is also to be made against their names in the ledger for the period.

(b)   A complete list of all persons who were absent on duty or otherwise at the time, specifying in each case the cause of such absence.

3.   Each list is to contain the rank or rating of each person, named therein, his number on the ship's books, and, in the case of Naval ratings and Royal Marines, their official or regimental numbers as well, and is to be signed by the Captain and three of the chief officers on board, of whom the Accountant Officer is to be one.

4.   The date of the capture of the vessels or slaves is to be inserted on all vouchers for the supply of, or expenditure on, provisions, clothing or stores for the vessels or the slaves captured, or for other expenses incurred thereon after capture.

5.   Any money which may be received in His Majesty's ships as a reward for any of the special services referred to in this Chapter is to be taken on charge by the Accountant Officer in his cash account, under the head 'Naval Prize Remittances.'

890.   Distribution. All awards of prize money are distributable solely by the Director of Navy Accounts, according to the Prize Proclamation or Order-in-Council relating to such awards, or in such other manner as the Admiralty may direct.

2.   Any Captain or other person making unauthorized distribution on the spot of any such money will be held personally liable to make good the £5 per cent payable to the naval prize cash balance, and for any shares omitted or inadequately paid.

3.   The Prize Proclamation or Orders-in-Council in force, containing the scale of shares for the various ranks and ratings, are printed in the Appendix to the Navy List.

4.   Awards when ready for distribution are notified in Admiralty Fleet

Orders and the *London Gazette*. Applications for payment of shares are to be made to the Director of Navy Accounts on form S540.

5.   **Assignments.** No assignment of prize or salvage money may be made in respect of any advance or consideration.

6.   **Shares not claimed**, or to which a claim has not been proved to the satisfaction of the Admiralty, shall be deemed to be forfeited after the expiration of six years from the 1st day of April following the date when the award first became distributable, but until the relative accounts have been closed finally (ten years after the date of distribution), the Admiralty may, if good cause be shown, remit such forfeiture.

SECTION II – PRIZE OF WAR

891.   Guide for Officers. In all matters connected with naval Prize [of] War, officers are to be guided by such instructions as may be furnished by the Admiralty from time to time.

982.   Expenses of Sending in Prizes. Payments from naval funds for expenses of sending in prizes should be avoided as far as possible. Where expenses are necessarily incurred, or fuel or stores supplied, full particulars of the services and circumstances should be shown on vouchers. Claims for dues and services at the port of adjudication should be referred to the marshal of the Court in which proceedings are instituted, and a memorandum of any expenses paid from naval funds or supplies made, should be given to the Marshal.

893.   Proceeds of Prizes. Any proceeds of vessels or goods taken as Prize of War which may be received in His Majesty's ships should be remitted to the marshal of the Court dealing with the prize, or, if that is not possible, should be taken on charge by the Accountant Officer in his cash account, under the name of the prize.

894.   Right or Claim to Proceeds. The officers and crews of His Majesty's ships have no right or claim to the proceeds of Prize of War, except as may from time to time be granted by the Crown (*see* **895**, clause 4, *as to recaptures*).

2.   Special regulations will be issued when any such grant of proceeds is made.

SECTION III – CAPTURES OTHER THAN PRIZE OF WAR; SALVAGE AND SPECIAL SERVICES

895.   Claims to Awards may usually be made in respect of all seizures referred to in Article 887 (other than Prize of War) which may lead to the forfeiture of the seized vessel.

2.   A book of instructions for the guidance of Captains and Commanding Officers of HM Ships employed in the suppression of the

Slave Trade is issued to HM Ships on the Africa and East Indies Stations and in the Red Sea, and further special instructions are promulgated from time to time as necessary. Instructions in regard to the Foreign Enlistment Act are given in Article 955, and in regard to Piracy in Article 957.

3. **Prize Bounty** for the capture or destruction of enemy armed vessels may only be claimed when the Crown has declared its intention to grant this award in respect of any particular war (Naval Prize Act, 1864.S.42).

4. **Prize Salvage** for the recapture of British property in time of war is a statutory award to the actual recaptors, not affected by the withholding of a grant of prize proceeds. It cannot be claimed if the recaptured vessel has been used as a ship of war by the enemy.

In certain circumstances such salvage may be granted in respect of the recapture of neutral property, and if the ship or goods are not immediately sent to a Prize Court the recapture should obtain any security necessary to safeguard their claims before parting with the property.

8. Claims for salvage awards for services rendered to merchant vessels should be made in accordance with the instructions in Chapter XXV, Section 1.

* * *

75. Post-war Assessment of the Naval Requirements for Economic Warfare Against a European Enemy

Captain Thomas Leslie Bratt, Director of Trade Division

[ADM 1/19992; Register No. TD 0231/46
Minute Sheet No. 2]   25 February 1948

1.   After consultation with DNI's [Director Naval Intelligence] representative DTD has given further consideration to the future planning for the setting up of contraband control bases and for the general considerations of the Navy's part in economic warfare in the event of a war with a European country.

2.   The planning for contraband control for 1939/45 war was on a lavish scale. Plans were sent up for the manning of 17 contraband control bases with 207 ships attached to these bases.

3.   This lavish planning was, however, based on the assumption that the ships from the CG [Coast Guard] bases would themselves be re-

quired to find, board and subsequently escort enemy suspects into harbour.

4. In actual fact only 11 bases were established absorbing 1100 naval personnel apart from the crews of a large number of ships. Even so this is a very heavy personnel commitment which it is most desirable to avoid as far as possible.

5. The introduction of the Navicert system, merchant ship plotting, improved methods of air search and intelligence, reduced the work to an occasional interception although the actual search of a ship was in most cases necessary. The interception was normally carried out by HM ships and not by ships specially detailed for contraband control work.

6. It is considered that if the following conditions prevailing at the end of the last war can be organised and quickly put into operation.

   A.   The Navicert system,
   B.   Establishment of merchant shipping plots at all theatre head-
        quarters,
   C.   A good air reconnaissance system,
then the number of contraband control bases and the actual require-ments of personnel and ships at each base will be considerably less than those considered necessary at the beginning of the last war.

7. The introduction of the Navicert system in conjunction with the ship warrant system has the objects of:

   A.   Re-inforcing [sic] economic warfare measures,
   B.   Securing greater control over world shipping,
   C.   Obtaining more vessels on British charter.

8. It is proposed that the Navicert system for the future should be brought into force for neutral ships trading to and from continental Europe, the Mediterranean, the Persian Gulf (whose cargoes might find their way to enemy territories) and ports on the Asiatic continent in the Pacific.

9. It has been proposed by DTD that merchant shipping plots should be established in all operational theatre headquarters so that the plot will be available on the outbreak of war. Until such time, however, as an overall plan is provided the places of these theatres are not known. Instructions for the setting up and maintaining of merchant shipping plots will be worked out in Trade Division and forwarded to all Com-manders-in-Chief in due course.

10. In giving consideration to future planning it would appear that the chief commodity requirements of a European country at war with Brit-ain would be raw rubber, tin and uranium.

Details of these commodities are as follows.

Commodity	Where Found	Method of Transport
New Rubber	Brazil	Ship
	Dutch East Indies (Sumatra and Java)	Ship
Tin	Straits Settlements	Ship
Uranium	Belgian Congo	Aircraft or Ship

Note: It is presumed that the Malay States and Strait Settlements will be under our control at the commencement of hostilities.

11.   In the 1938 planning for war against the central powers there was a long and varied contraband list. It is, however, considered that in a future war against a European power, who would be doubtless much more self contained than the central powers were in 1939/45, the only important imports required would be those listed above and possibly certain manufactured articles. Even then it is a fair assumption to make that if a large country is planning war, in say, ten years then it would be possible to lay in stocks of materials so that imports of the materials would not be required during the period of hostilities in any large quantities [*sic*].

12.   The selection of suitable bases for carrying out the practical running of contraband control has been considered and it is felt that bases should be established to provide the necessary personnel and armed boarding vessels to cover the following areas.

A.   European North and West Coasts)   Bases at Kirkwall and/ or Falmouth

B.   European West Cost to North Spain)
C.   Spain and Mediterranean Area   Gibraltar or port in the vicinity.

D.   Persian Gulf and Indian Ocean   Aden or suitable port.
E.   Far East.   Commonwealth or Allied Commitment.

13.   It is not proposed at this stage to go into details of requirements of ships and personnel for the above bases but rather wait for agreement on the selection of bases.

14.   DTD wishes to establish the above broad principles and also to agree that the contraband control base will only be required to search a limited number of ships.

This is necessary to know so that some forecast of the personnel and ship requirements may be made.

15.   DTD suggests that after study of this minute it might be of value for representatives of DNI and D of P [Director of Plans] to meet to

discuss the future action necessary for the planning of the Navy's part in economic warfare.

H. du P. R./MD

C.C.B./7

Minute by Director of Trade Division, Captain Robert Jocelyn Oliver Otway-Ruthven

[ADM 1/19992; H.du P.R./DEN CCB. VII]   21 May 1948

After a meeting held between representatives of DTD, D of P and DNI, general agreement was reached on the proposals outlined in T.D.0231/ 46.

The chief points that were emphasised by the representatives were as follows:

1.   Any planning for the Contraband Control side of Naval Warfare should not be on anything like the luxurious scale that was organised prior to the 1939/45 war.

2.   When considering war against a major European country it would appear that the only commodities required in any quantity would be raw rubber, tin, uranium and certain manufactured goods. Doubtless these commodities would be built up in the country concerned, prior to the commencement of hostilities. The list of contraband goods, which filled a book before the last war, is not comparable to [i.e. for] any future war.

3.   With regard to the requirements for personnel in the Contraband Control service it is proposed that a few officers should undergo a five day course at Greenwich so that they are instructed in the naval side of Contraband Control. No other personnel, it is considered, need be earmarked for the Contraband Control service.

4.   In order to save shipping and personnel it is suggested that officers in the Contraband Control service with a few hand picked ratings, who have been trained locally, should be embarked in ships of the examination service and should carry out the necessary boarding duties from the examination vessel.

5.   In a war against a major European country, none other than total war can be envisaged. The question of ships supplying goods to neutral European countries can, therefore, hardly be imagined.

6.   It is realised that it will be difficult for a high ruling on such a point at the present time. If, however, a ruling from the Defence Ministry could be given that shipping on the high seas in a future major war is either for the use of allies or the enemy, then the question of the Navy's part in Contraband Control solves itself.

Minute by [?] for Director of Plans

1 June 1948

1. D of P cannot agree with the statement made by DTD in his para. 5 nor can he endorse DTD's para. 6; it is, in D of P's opinion quite possible that some countries in Europe would remain neutral even in a major war.

2. An EW [Economic Warfare] Sub Committee of the Defence Transition Committee has been set up with wide terms of refernce and is due to meet shortly. The Admiralty representative is D of P, who will keep in touch with DNI and DTD and ensure that

A. Admiralty policy and requirements for Contraband Control are not frustrated.

B. Relevant decisions or recommendations of the EW Sub Committee are made known to DNI and DTD.

* * *

76. *Commander-in-Chief, Far East Station, to all Ships*

[ADM 116/5713]   Information Admiralty, N.A. Nanking,
[General Message No. 219P,   A.N.A. Shanghai
24163OZ/June (Rec. 2225)]   24 June 1949

PRIORITY   The following is a guide to the action to be taken by HM Ships during the present Nationalist 'Blockade' of the Communist held coast and ports. This Blockade has not repetition not been recognised by HM Government. These instructions may also be used as background for advising shipping interests.

1. The following assumptions are made for the present

a. Both sides may be assumed to have the right to direct the movements of Merchant Ships within Territorial Waters, or when entering one of the prescribed ports, and to use force if such directions are ignored. Territorial Waters extend to the 3 mile limit and ships passing the Yangtse Light Vessel may be Assumed to be entering Shanghai.

b. Neither side has the right to seize British shipping.

c. Neither side has the right to attack British shipping with aircraft.

d. Neither side has the right to visit and search.

2. Entering Territorial Waters,

a. If it is necessary for HM Ships to go into confined waters, (such as the Whangpoo) which are Communist dominated and can be expected to be fortified, the situation is to be reported to F.O. 2 I/C F.E.S. info[rmation] C. in C. F.E.S.; unless ordered, such waters are not to be entered without Communist permission.

b. HM Ships may enter other Territorial Waters for humanitarian purposes or to prevent a British Merchant Ship being interfered with except as allowed for in para. 2 (a) above.

c. Anchorage in the Saddle Islands may be used as required.

3. Except as defined in paras. 5 and 6 below force is not to be used to prevent interference with British Shipping until permission has been obtained.

4. HM Ships may fire at aircraft either outside or in Territorial Waters in the following circumstances

a. in self defence.

b. at aircraft which are attacking or have attacked British Merchant ships when HM Ship is so close that there can be no question that the aircraft being engaged is an attacker.

5. HM Ships may fire at Chinese Warships either outside or in Territorial Waters

a. in self defence,

b. when Chinese Warships are actually firing at British Merchant Ships in circumstances other than those in para. 2 (a).

This does not forbid HM Ships using all means short of opening fire to prevent damage to a British Merchant ship in the circumstances of para. 2 (a).

Cancel my 211605 and 121455.

* * *

77. *Admiralty to Commander-in-Chief Far East Station*

TOP SECRET PRIORITY

[ADM 116/5713; 091935 A/September]   9 September 1949

Your 250016 and 250237.

Legal examination forecast in A.M. 221910 has led initially to the view that the closure by the Nationalists of Communist held ports and territorial waters is lawful, provided that Nationalists can, by force used within, repetition within, territorial waters prevent access. Please report as soon as possible

(a) whether in your opinion, and with special reference to (iii) below, Nationalist ships or aircraft could, by operating within repetition within the three mile limit, exercise any measure of control over merchant ships going to Shanghai; if so, how much and by what means?

(b) where exactly the Nationalist warships off the Yangtse are normally stationed;

(c) what risk Nationalist warships would incur from Communist shore batteries within territorial waters.

091935A
First Sea Lord.

* * *

78. Nationalist Blockade

Commander-in-Chief Far East Station to Admiralty
TOP SECRET

[ADM 116/5713; 100519 Z/September]   10 September 1949
(Recd. 0857)

PRIORITY

Your 091935. Chart 1602. Limit of Territorial Waters in North and South Channels is taken to be line joining Nanhuipsui* (Nanhuitsui) and Shaweishan. *As received.

(b) Nationalist warships are believed to be normally stationed at or above Tungshe Banks Buoy though they are rarely seen by our Patrol which is usually at the Yangtse entrance light vessel.

(c) The closure is in fact effective now and I consider that Nationalist warships at Kiutoan Spit Buoy, or even further up river, would have no difficulty in stopping traffic. In the North Channel their task is even easier. There would be no need for them to use aircraft.

(d) It is thought that the Communists have no shore batteries below Kiutoan Beacon but this is not confirmed. Recent reports from Shanghai state that Communists intend to break the closure and although their most probable method of doing this will be to capture the Chusan Islands it is possible that they will extend their batteries to seaward. Even in the latter case Nationalist warships would be in little danger.

100519Z

ANNEX II

There is no question of a 'blockade' in the ordinary sense of the term. Both HMG and US Government have informed the Chinese Nationalists that they do not admit the legality of a blockade, since there has been no admission of a state of belligerency, while the Chinese Nationalists for their part no longer claim to be imposing a blockade.

2.   What they claim is the right to close Communist held ports to trade by decree. But neither HMG nor the US Government admit the legality of this. HMG have informed the Nationalist Government that a mere decree of a lawful Government purporting to close ports occupied by insurgents, without the maintenance of a real and effective blockade, cannot be regarded as valid, inasmuch as it constitutes an attempt to secure rights of war without regard to conditions which International Law attaches to their exercise, and such a decree cannot be recognised as resulting in a blockade in the sense of International Law.

3.   HMG have also warned the Nationalist Government that they cannot accept any disclaimer by the Chinese Government of responsibility on account of damages to British interests and property ashore or afloat, arising out of action by the Chinese Government's armed forces, and at the same time they hold the Chinese Government responsible for any untoward consequences of exercise by ships of the Royal Navy or the Mercantile Marine of their inherent right of self defence or protection against hostile action.

4.   The application of the above legal arguments to the proposals now made to send escorted British ships to Shanghai, and the sequence of Action to be followed, may thus be analysed as follows:

(a)   British merchant ships have the right to enter Chinese territorial waters and to visit the ports of Shanghai.

This derives from the normal International Law and custom.

(b)   The Nationalist Government have no right to forbid this.

From the legal argument quoted above.

(c)   If British ships, exercising this right, are challenged by a Nationalist warship, they will henceforward ignore this challenge and continue the voyage.

(d) If the Nationalist warship attempt to stop British ships by any form of force, it would amount to a hostile act.

By the legal argument quoted above.

(e) Following such hostile act, any escorting British warship would have the right and duty to take any action necessary to protect the British merchant ships, and to enable them to continue their lawful journey, whether inside or outside territorial waters.

This is the 'inherent right of self defence' quoted in para. 3. This amounts to only a slight modification of the existing instructions to H.M. Ships, (as in C. in C., F.E.'s signal 241630).

5.   The essence of the matter is that from now on,

a.   British merchant ships will, if intercepted, ignore challenges by Nationalist warships, and

b.   HM Ships in escort will have to be careful not to use any force until this has first been done by a Nationalist warship or aircraft, but thereafter may use the degree of force required to protect merchant ships in continuing their voyage.

25th August 1949

First Sea Lord to Sir W. Strang
[Draft Letter]

Foreign Office
n.d.

CHINA BLOCKADE

PREAMBLE – as desired by First Sea Lord. To include a statement that letter is written with knowledge and approval of First Lord.

2.   Government policy is that the British mercantile and shipping interests should be encouraged to keep their foot in the door within Communist occupied China.

3.   The existing instructions to the Navy are to protect British Shipping at sea but not within the limit of territorial waters. H.M. Ships may only enter territorial waters (in particular the Yangtse above Entrance Light Vessel) for humanitarian purposes, and subject to the overriding rule of not getting embroiled with any Communist forces on shore.

4. The protection which the Navy may give to British shipping under the above instructions is limited to rather less than what we would traditionally have given. In any case it is completely failing to achieve our government's policy (if I have summarised it correctly).

5. This is principally due to the success of the so called blockade. The Communist naval forces have made no attempt to stop it, and in the result one or two small Nationalist warships, based on the Chusan Archipelago and the Miaotao Islands have effectively stopped all shipping, other than local craft, going into Shangai and Tientsin respectively. They are no longer trying, but if British shipping did try, the situation as regards Shanghai would be simply this: the Nationalist warship is stationed close beside the British warship at the Yangtse Light Vessel, just on the edge of territorial waters; from there it could follow up the merchant ship where the British warship is debarred from giving protection, and stop her at leisure, being still outside the range of Communist shore based batteries.

6. I believe the consequences of this situation are very serious for the British interests in Shanghai. They are, I understand, running out of materials, yet are compelled to maintain and pay their employees and therefore in turn will run out of money. In the result, our government policy will be frustrated and British interests there come to the end of their tether.

7. As you will know, we have asked the Commander-in-Chief his view as to the practicability of escorting our merchant ships, and protecting them up the Yangtse as far as is necessary against Nationalist molestation until they come under protection from the shore. However, the evidence now before me is that if this is to be done, it must be set in hand without delay. I therefore write to inform you that, in my opinion it would be quite feasible for HM Ships to protect our merchant ships, either singly or perhaps better in small convoys if necessary all the way from Hong Kong, up to the mouth of the Whangpoo. Speaking as First Sea Lord, I should add that it would be hard to justify letting British interests in Shanghai come to disaster as a direct result of failure by the Royal Navy to give that protection to our essential shipping which we are both able and willing to give.

8. The cargoes to be carried by these ships would, we assume, be confined to the material required to keep the British industries going, and to the oil and coal required for public utilities in order to prevent chaos.

9. We are, of course, aware of the alternative of letting Shanghai stew in its own juice and let the responsible Communist authorities take the odium. Chaos, indeed, may follow: lack of fuel oil will stop the power stations and the water works, and the floods may assist in producing famine. For us to exploit this chaos would presumably be in accordance with the long term policy of opposing Communism, though logically we might go further and impose economic sanctions etc. But all the evidence that has come to the Admiralty shows
    a. that the British interests in Shanghai would be the first to go under;
    b. that they could never hope to return.
10. Our view therefore is that we ought to take action as in paragraph 7 above. If it is to be done, a decision is urgent.
11. In this case it will be necessary to reach some understanding with the Communist authorities in Shanghai, as we cannot have them firing at us from the shore. Their interests are, of course, the same as ours and we might be able to take some credit and lay the foundations of stable conditions for our mercantile community in Shanghai. Above all, we would like to use this policy as a further lever to secure [the] release of *Amethyst*.
12. I appreciate that there are many other political implications e.g. the reaction of the Americans . . .

* * *

79. *Dependence upon North America – World War II*

Memorandum

[FO 371/82864]   Foreign Office
                                                         21 April 1950

1. British Empire supply of munitions from all sources:

	1944	1939–45
UK	61.2%	69.5%
Sterling Dominions	1.2%	1.6%
Canada	8.9%	7.9%
USA	28.7%	21.0%
	100%	100%

In the war as a whole, 30% of the Empire's supplies of munitions came from outside UK – at the peak of the war, nearly 40%.

2.   In 1944, UK had 5.2 million men and women in the Forces, and 5.0 million in the munitions (metal and chemical) industries. The North American munitions were equivalent to *an extra 2.9 million* workers.

3.   Without North American munitions, we should have had to divide our 10 million man-power in Forces and munitions industries, in ratio of 4 Forces : 6 munitions, rather than 5 : 5. This would have meant a completely different type of war effort.

4.   About 30% of our steel came from USA; about 20% of the new machine tools; many other materials (cotton, TNT, etc.). Not only did our Services have 2.9 million North American workers working for them; our 5 million munitions workers had North American workers working for them too.

5.   Apart from the *general* dependence upon US munitions, there was particularly critical dependence in certain items (W.P.(42)486, Revise):

40-ton tank transporters and 10-ton lorries	100%
Transport aircraft	nearly 100%
Landing Craft	88%
Auxiliary aircraft carriers	85%
Escort vessels	77%
Light bombers & GR landplanes	68%
Tanks	60%
Tank engines and track (for UK production)	40–50%
Fleet Air Arm aircraft	40%

This dependence in the most critical weapons became more marked as the war proceeded, for where a new big industrial effort was required, this was always laid on in USA.

Shipping

6.   The cargo shipping non-tanker under British control in 1943 was about 20 million deadweight tons. This included 21 million tons of foreign vessels on bareboat charter and 0.6 million tons requisitioned, both under the British flag, together with 3.3 million tons on time charter to the UK under foreign flags. Lend-Lease aid on shipping was of the order of $2 billion in the whole war.

Petroleum

7.   Petroleum transactions were very completely pooled, but US provided us with $1,850 million on Lend-Lease and we provided them

with $1,187 million on Reciprocal aid – a difference of some 24 million tons in the war. The British Empire consumption reached a peak of – million tons a year.

8. In addition, we relied heavily net on US tankers.

Food

9. Our food consumption was divided as follows:

	1944	1939–45
UK production	?	?
Imports from North America	?	?
Other imports	?	?
	100%	100%

*Table incomplete.

Finance

10. U.S. Lend-Lease aid to the British Empire was as follows:

	1944 ($billion)	1939–45 ($billion)
Munitions	6.7	18
Petroleum	0.8	2
Food	1.2	3.5
Other materials	1	3.5
Services (mainly shipping)	1.1	3
	10.8	30
Of which, to UK	–	27

11. There were US exports paid for in cash of $0.4 billion in 1944.

12. Reciprocal aid granted by the British Empire is estimated at $7.5 billion in the whole war, of which possibly $5.75 billion by UK.

13. In addition, we received assistance from Canada to a total of $3.5 billion.

14. In addition, we sold foreign investments and borrowed sterling world-wide to a tune of some £4,000 million, or $16 billion.

15. The UK war effort depended upon aid (and loss of capital) to the following rough extent:

Lend-Lease	$27 billion
Canadian assistance	$3.5 [billion]
Sale of investments	$4.5 [billion]
Growth of sterling liabilities	$11.5 [billion]
Loss of gold reserves	$0.5 [billion]
	$47 billion

Reciprocal aid	$6 [billion]
Deficit	$41 billion

16.   The peak rate of 'Deficit' in any year was probably about $12 billion. It must be remembered in considering these financial figures, that the level of dollar prices was much lower than now; $12 billion during the war might be as much as $20 billion now.

17.   The big item in this total war deficit of $41 billion, is the 'purchase' of munitions to a total of $30 billion. Another big item, of course, is the fact that we were fighting the war in Egypt, India, etc. – it so happened that we had to fight in those parts of the world where you had to pay countries to protect them.

18.   It would appear that by far the biggest element of our need for assistance in World War II was related to the way in which we fought the war – most importantly, the relationship between our fighting effort and our fabricating effort, but also the actual theatres in which we played a predominant part. Over and above this, there was a substantial degree of financial dependence, not only upon USA but also upon the Commonwealth in respect of 'non-munition' supplies. This resulted to a large extent from the destruction of our export trade – i.e. the high *level* of mobilisation of our economy, as distinct from the *nature* of the mobilisation.

19.   The actual loss of export income during the whole war may be put at $10 billion – this is the difference between the actual receipt from exports ($1,800 million) and the level of export income which would have been achieved if our pre-war volume of exports had been maintained (£4,300 million). This suggests, in fact, that we should have had no need for financial assistance at all if –

    a.   We had had a balanced fighting and fabrication effort in the British Empire so that we had not needed to buy $30 billion worth of munitions,

    b.   We had maintained our pre-war export volume – thus earning $10 billion more,

    c.   We had collected cash from the Americans instead of giving them Reciprocal Aid. ($6 billion).

20.   Of course the actual pattern which our war effort followed was absolutely inevitable and it could never have been changed, except possibly at the margin. It resulted fundamentally from the interval of two years before America came into the war. The calculation above, however, shows which the relatively important orders of magnitude were, from the point of view of future policy.

* * *

80. Korean War: Evaluation of West Coast Operation

Flag Officer, Second-in-Command, Far East Station, to Admiralty

[ADM 1/23676]   c. 19 June 1951

DISCUSSION: BLOCKADE AND PATROL

3. So far as we can tell the blockade on the west coast has been complete. The defence of the major islands has resulted in the naval forces being concentrated in the vicinity of these islands and the patrols in the YALU Gulf have been carried out less frequently. It is certain that no major vessel has entered or left the TAEDONG Estuary and junk traffic in the HAEJU, PAENGYONG DO and CHODO areas has been closely watched. It is however possible that, North of the TAEDONG, some junks have managed to move round the edge of the YALU Gulf or possibly across from SHANTUNG during the long dark winter nights. However air reconnaissance of the Continental Chinese Coastal areas has not revealed any extensive traffic. Occasional reports of junk concentrations have been received, and in every case when these have been subsequently located they have been found to be innocent fishing craft. An increase in these reports is to be expected in the next few months, and current directions to seize all those found East of Longitude 124° are in force. Some increase in patrol activity for this purpose may be necessary.

81.   Cuban Crisis: Prime Minister Harold Macmillan to President John F. Kennedy

TOP SECRET

[CAB 21/5581]   [22 October 1962]

My Dear Friend,

Ambassador Bruce called to see me this morning and gave me evidence of the Soviet build-up in Cuba. I quite understand how fiercely American public opinion will react when it knows these facts. I have this moment received through our teleprinter the text of your proposed declaration tonight. Let me say at once that we shall of course give you all the support we can in the Security Council. I hope that you will provide us immediately with the best legal case that can be made in support of the broad moral position so that our representative can weigh in effectively. Of course the international lawyers will take the point that a blockade which involves the searching of ships of all countries is difficult to defend in peace-time. Indeed quite a lot o controversy has gone on in the past about its use in wartime. However, we must rest not so much on precedent as on the unprecedented condition of the modern world in a nuclear age.

If, as I assume, the Security Council resolution is vetoed the only appeal is to the Assembly. What the result will be there no-one can tell but I doubt whether they will be in favour of any conclusive action or even if they are I do not see how they will enforce it. What I think we must now consider is Khrushchev's likely reaction. He may reply either in words or in kind or both. If he contents himself with the first he may demand the removal of all American bases in Europe. If he decides to act he may do so either in the Caribbean or elsewhere. If he reacts in the Caribbean his obvious method would be to escort his ships and force you into the position of attacking them. This fire-first dilemma has always worried us and we have always hoped to impale the Russians on this move. We doubt you have thought of this but I would be glad to know how you feel it can be handled. Alternatively, he may bring some pressure on the weaker parts of the free world defence system. This may be in South East Asia, in Iran, possibly in Turkey, but more likely in Berlin. If he reacts outside the Caribbean – as I fear he may – it will be tempting for him to answer one blockade by declaring another. We must therefore be ready. Any retaliatory action on Berlin as envisaged in the various contingency plans will lead us either to an escalation to world war or to the holding of a conference. What seems to be essential is that you and I should think over and decide in what direction we want to steer things within the Alliance and elsewhere. We should take counsel as soon as we have the Russian reaction.

While you know how deeply I sympathise with your difficulty and how much we will do to help in every way, it would only be right to tell you that there are two aspects which give me concern. Many of us in Europe have lived so long in close proximity to the enemy's nuclear weapons of the most devastating kind that we have got accustomed to it. So European opinion will need attention. The second, which is more worrying, is that if Khrushchev comes to a conference he will of course try to trade his Cuba position against his ambitions in Berlin and elsewhere. This we must avoid at all costs, as it will endanger the whole of the Alliance.

[Added in manuscript] With warm regard, H.M.

* * *

82.   President John F. Kennedy to Prime Minister Sir Harold Macmillan

TOP SECRET

[CAB 21/5581]   22 October 1962

Dear Friend,

First let me say how sorry I am that the proposed text of my state-ment has been so slow to get to you. We must use our own machine in such cases.

I am instructing our experts to confer at once with yours to provide the best possible legal case, which will rest in the first instance on the Rio Treaty. But you are certainly right about the wider issues which arise in the nuclear age, and our people feel a strong case can be built on them.

It is this whole series of wider issues that has governed my initial decision. I fully recognize the hazards which you rightly point out, but I have had to take account also of the effect of inaction in the face of so obvious and deep a Soviet challenge. This is not simply or mainly a matter of American public opinion, and as for living under a missile threat, we too have been doing that for some time. But this is so deep a breach in the conventions of the international statement that if unchal-lenged it would deeply shake confidence in the United States, especially in the light of my repeated warnings. It would persuade Krushchev and others that our determination is low, that we are unable to meet our commitments, and it would invite further and still more dangerous moves.

I recognize the particular hazard of a repost in Berlin, but in the wider sense I believe that inaction would be still more dangerous to our position in that respect.

I assure you most solemnly that this is not simply a matter of aroused public opinion or of private passion against Cuba. As I am sure you know, I have regularly resisted pressure for unreasonable or excessive action, and I am not interested in a squabble with Castro. But this is something different: the first step in a major showdown with Khrushchev, whose action in this case is so at variance with what all the Soviet experts have predicted that it is necessary to revise our whole estimate of his level of desperation, or ambition, or both.

The particular points which you raise about European public opinion are understandable and have been much in our minds. We have some thoughts about meeting them about which we must be in touch. I also agree that we must keep in the clearest touch about Berlin and that we can do this best when we have the first Soviet reaction.

Our Naval Commanders are instead instructed to use the very minimum of force, but I know of no sure escape from the problem of the first shot. Our best basic course is firmness, now. I look forward to our talk. Sincerely [Signed] John F. Kennedy.

* * *

83.   Prime Minister Harold Macmillan to Sir David Ormsby Gore, Ambassador to Washington

Personal Telegram T493/62
Cypher/UTP No. 7395, Emergency DEDIP
TOP SECRET

[CAB 21/5581]   Despeatched from Foreign Office
                                          22 October 1962 9:42 p.m.

Following Personal for Ambassador from Prime Minister.

I am having repeated to you, for your private information, my message to the President in reply to his message to me about Cuba.

(b)   I would be grateful if you could give me your thoughts upon what it is that the President is really trying to do. Is he (a) leading up to a position in which he can seize the Island as might have come off some months ago or (b) is he preparing for a conference with Khrushchev which, if it once starts, must develop into a conference of world powers?

(c)   Since it seemed impossible to stop his action I did not make the effort, although in the course of the day I was in mind to do so. I feel sure that a long period of blockade, and possibly Russian reaction in the Caribbean or elsewhere, will lead us nowhere. Therefore he must decide whether he wants a *coup de main*, which will at least put one card in his hands, or face a conference where Berlin, nuclear disarmament and many other issues will have to be discussed.

(d)   You will realize, for your personal information only, that I could not allow a situation in Europe or in the world to develop which looks like escalating into war without trying some action by calling a conference on my own, or something of the kind, to stop it. I would be grateful for your ideas and an assessment of the position in America, especially in Washington.

(e)   Please see my immediately following telegram.
       (Copies sent to the Prime Minister).

* * *

84.   Prime Minister Harold Macmillan to Foreign Secretary Sir Alec Douglas-Home

Personal Message
SECRET

[CAB 21/5581]   23 October 1962

CUBA

The position of British shipping is fairly satisfactory while the blockade is limited to weapons of a kind which they would not, in any case, be carrying.

But the President, as we know, may be forced to *widen* the scope of the blockade, to include everything (except perhaps food). In that event there will be trouble. We should be studying this possibility *now*.

I am sending a copy of this minute to the Minister of Transport.

* * *

85.   Brief for Nassau Talks

Forwarded by Richard Mercer Keene Slater, Head of American Department, to Nicholas John Alexander Cheetham, Assistant Undersecretary of State

[FO 371/168177]   Foreign Office
                                                    7 January 1963

HMG set great store by the principle of freedom of navigation. Shipping should not in their view be used as an instrument of foreign policy.

(b)   Shipping policy should be consistent with trade policy. There is an embargo on the export of arms from the UK to Cuba, but trade in other goods is unrestricted (though it has fallen to a very low level). We have appealed to British shipowners not to carry arms to Cuba, and we do not believe that arms have been or are reach-

ing Cuba in British ships. We see no reason to discourage British
ships from carrying other goods.

(c)   HMG have no powers to control the movements or cargoes of
British ships and for the reason of principle given above they do
not propose to take powers in order to divert shipping from the
Cuba run. Such action would moreover be hard to reconcile with
the maintenance of diplomatic relations with Cuba.

(d)   If, as a result of the American measures, free world shipping
withdraws from the Cuba run, the likely result is that the ships
concerned will be chartered by the Soviet Bloc for other destinations so as to release Bloc shipping for Cuba. The Soviet Bloc
have already taken measures to make themselves independent of
non-Bloc shipping for keeping Cuba supplied.

(e)   We have already made clear to the Americans that we dislike the
proposed measures, and though we have no intention of running a
publicity campaign against them, our public attitude will have to
be critical.

* * *

86.   *Edward Heath, Lord Privy Seal: Answer to Parliamentary Question*

[FO 371/168178]   11 February 1963.

During the past six months we have had several discussions with the
United States Government about the question of British ships carrying
goods to Cuba. The United States Government announced on 6th February that the shipment of United States Government financed cargoes
from the United States on vessels that had called at a Cuban port since
1st January, 1963, would be prohibited. We have made clear throughout
that Her Majesty's Government do not approve of any restriction on
freedom of navigation in times of peace.

* * *

87. *Beira Patrol*

Draft Memorandum by Foreign Secretary
Confidential

[DEFE 24/588 E49]   [1970]

I have seen copies of the Defence Secretary's minute to you of 11th January (recommending that more precise instructions should be given to HM Ships on the Beira patrol regarding the degree of force which should be used to enforce compliance with orders given to suspect tankers), and of your reply of 24th January. The following are my preliminary comments, subject to a decision on the legal point referred to in your minute.

2. I agree that the present situation puts an unfair burden on Commanding Officers. There would be much to be said for deferring a decision on this matter until we know the outcome of the review of the whole Rhodesian situation at present being carried out by the Ministerial Group, set up after the DOP Meeting on the 8th December; but I do not think it would be right to wait for this and to gamble on the chance that no suspect tanker will appear in the meantime. In my view, the course outlined in paragraph 4(b) of the Defence Secretary's minute, namely to issue specific instructions that suspect tankers which fail to comply with orders may be fired on in the last resort, is the right one. To adopt course (a) would seem to be contrary to the terms of the Security Council Resolution and would increase the criticism that we are only half-hearted in our attempts to bring down the illegal regime in Rhodesia.

3. I realise that there could be very serious political consequences if one of HM Ships had to open fire on a tanker, even though the stage-by-stage approach recommended in paragraph 5 of the Defence Secretary's minute should significantly reduce the risk. But I think that the political consequences of allowing tankers to unload without being in jeopardy of more than action on the diplomatic plane at the United Nations would be far more embarrassing.

4. If it were possible to arrest ships *after* unloading and departure from Beira, there might be a case for avoiding the use of force until guilt had been proved. But if the threat to do so failed to deter then in that case we should have left ourselves in the embarrassing position of arresting the ship after the oil had gone to Rhodesia. However, Security Council Resolution No. 221 provided for arrest in these circumstances only in the specific case of the Joanna V and I understand that, in the

absence of a further Resolution (which it would not at present be in our interest to provoke), we would have no legal justification for 'posthumous' action of this kind. . . .

* * *

88. Beira Patrol

Briefs for New Government: Strategic and Political – East of Suez

[DEFE 24/588 E 135 5/10/7/1; Brief No. 27]   June 1970

The Beira Patrol was set up in response to a United Nations resolution passed in 1966 calling upon the United Kingdom to prevent, by force if necessary, the arrival off Beira of vessels reasonably believed to be carrying oil for Rhodesia. It has attracted a good deal of interest from Members of Parliament.

Composition   At its inception the patrol was carried out by a variety of ships, with carrier borne aircraft providing air cover. Subsequently the air task was taken over by RAF Shackleton aircraft operating from Majunga in the Republic of Malagasy. The patrol forces then consisted of two frigates/destroyers and one RFA [Royal Fleet Auxiliary] tanker, together with additional RFA's providing logistic support as necessary, and three Shackleton aircraft. In 1969 the Shackleton's were reduced to two, with a third aircraft in reserve at Gan. These have been the normal force levels since then.

Effectiveness   In so far that the pipeline from Beira and the refinery at Umtali are no longer operating, it can be claimed that the patrol has been successful in closing the most direct route for petroleum products moving to Rhodesia.

Cost   Ships and aircraft concerned, if not employed on the patrol, would be deployed elsewhere. Although the total running costs per year are about £2.75m, the only meaningful costs at present are those incurred as a result of the patrol. For the RN these virtually all consist of the chartering of extra tankers to replace those supporting the patrol. As at June 1970 these costs stood at just under £0.6m. Additional costs for the RAF include operating from Majunga airfield, local expenses and additional flying time. As at June 1970 RAF extra costs were £1.3m and these will increase significantly between March 1971, and March 1972, when a special Majunga Support Squadron of 5 Shackleton aircraft will have to be formed solely for this task as Shackleton Air/Sea Warfare Squadrons are converted to Nimrods. On present plans the task will need to be taken over by the Nimrod in 1972 and costs will again increase.

Ship Availability   Naval forces on the patrol are found from ships on passage to or from the Far East, augmented as necessary by ships already on the Far East Station. Ships do a spell of about four weeks on patrol on the way out, and again on the way home. The need to provide a continuous patrol affects the operational flexibility of the Fleet, and consequently the Royal Navy's ability to meet other defence tasks and this penalty has been more marked in recent months. After the withdrawal from the Far East the naval patrol would have to be found entirely from within force levels required to meet our commitments to NATO and Priority II and III tasks.

Aircraft Availability   The Shackletons in the air patrol will, on present plans, be replaced with Nimrods in 1972. The latter will be part of our small force of 32 long-range maritime reconnaissance aircraft declared to NATO and CENTO to cover the Atlantic and Mediterranean. Their use for the Beira Patrol will inevitably be at the expense of our peace-time operations in these areas.

Sharing the Commitment   Consideration has been given to inviting other countries to participate in the patrol. However, since only the United Kingdom is empowered by the UN to intercept by force possible block-ade runners the sharing of the patrol would produce little practical advantage. It would certainly add to the operational difficulties.

* * *

LIST OF DOCUMENTS AND SOURCES

Unless otherwise indicated, all archival references are to The National Archives of Great Britain (TNA), formerly known as the Public Record Office (PRO), Ruskin Avenue, Kew, Richmond, Surrey TW9 4DU.

ADM: Admiralty Files
BT: Board of Trade Files
CAB: Cabinet Files
CO: Colonial Office Files
CP: Confidential Print
DEFE: Ministry of Defence Files
FO: Foreign Office Files
HMSO: His/Her Majesty's Stationery Office
MT: Ministry of Transport Files
PRO: Indigenous Collection at the Public Record Office

PART I

1.	Privateers and letters of marque	3 March 1854	FO 83/487
2.	Note to be addressed by British agents abroad to foreign courts	4 April 1854	FO 83/487
3.	Commercial policy towards Russia	31 October 1854	PRO 30/29/23/4/181–8
4.	Cabinet minutes respecting the Declaration of Paris	6 April 1856	FO 83/487
5.	Proposal of the US government relative to maritime law	28 July 1856	FO 83/487/968
6.	Union blockade of Confederate ports	9 March 1861–20 December 1862	PRO 30/22/35, 96 & 106
7.	Correspondence relating to the 'Trent' affair	30 November 1861	FO 881/993

8.	The Queen's regulations and the Admiralty instructions for the government of HM naval service	1862	HMSO
9.	An act for regulating naval prize of war	23 June 1864	Admiralty Statutes 27 & 28 (AD 1864, cap. XXV)
10.	Short account of *Alabama's* cruise	No date	ADM 1/8374/ 103
11.	Memorandum relative to certain statements made by Mr Sumner with regard to pacific blockades	20 May 1869	FO 881/6378, CP, 6378
12.	Franco-Prussian War	22 July 1870	FO 188/1778
13.	Treaty between her Majesty and the USA	17 June 1871	Harrison and Sons, London
14.	Memorandum on the origin of the Declaration of Paris respecting maritime law	15 February 1856	CP 2763, FO 188/2763
15.	Notification of the blockade of Formosa	24 October 1884	FO 97/570
16.	The Declaration of Paris and the proposed exemption of private property at sea from capture by a belligerent	9 February 1893	FO 881/6307, CP 6307
17.	Memorandum on blockades	September 1894	FO 97/570
18.	Discussion with Count Metternich on the nature and attributes of pacific blockade	28 November 1902	FO 881/7827; FO 97/570

PART II

19.	Progress of the naval prize bill	15 December 1903	ADM 116/1236

20.	Hague Convention XIII concerning the rights and duties of neutral powers in naval war	18 October 1907	US Department of State 8407
21.	Declaration of London concerning the laws of naval war	26 February 1909	Henry Dunant Institute for Humanitarian Dialogue, 208 Consolidated Treaty Series, 338
22.	Naval prize law committee, interim report	21 December 1909	ADM 116/1231A
23.	Prizes captured by colonial navies	April 1910	ADM 116/1231A
24.	Ratification of the Declaration of London	17 February 1911	ADM 116/1236
25.	The navy's warning against the Declaration of London	3 July 1911	ADM 116/1236
26.	Naval prize court procedure	27 November 1912	ADM 116/1231A
27.	Handbook for boarding officers and prize officers in war time	1914	ADM 186/11
28.	Wartime adjustments to the laws of contraband control	August 1914	ADM 116/1234
29.	Naval prize	3 December 1914	ADM 116/1234
30.	Repeal of the Declaration of London Order in Council	8 March 1916 & 26 March 1916	ADM 116/1234

PART III

31.	Armistice discussions, 1918	9 December 1927	CAB 16/79
32.	Memorandum on blockade	26 November 1918	ADM 116/3619
33.	The freedom of the seas	21 December 1918	CAB 21/307; CAB 16/79, parts 11/181–8, 7/231

34.	The economic blockade 1914–19	1920	ADM 186/603
35.	Trading, blockade and enemy shipping	30 May 1923	CAB 15/21
36.	Revision of the laws of war	7 February 1924	ADM 116/3619
37.	Naval enforcement of Article 16 of the League Covenant	7 September 1924	ADM 1/8671/ 215
38.	Execution and management of economic war	20 May 1926	CAB 21/319
39.	Amendment of the naval prize manual	27 September 1926	ADM 1/8700/ 132, No. 067
40.	Possibilities of exerting economic pressure on the nationalist government of South China	February 1927	CAB 21/299
41.	Shipping control in time of war	17 June 1927	CAB 21/299
42.	Enforcement of Article 16	11 June 1927	ADM 1/15037
43.	International law as affecting naval warfare	13 August 1927	ADM 116/3619
44.	Belligerent rights at sea and the relations between the US and Great Britain	26 October 1927	CAB 21/307, 157–66 CP 258 (27)
45.	A Canadian perspective	8 November 1927	ADM 116/3619
46.	Belligerent rights at sea	14 November 1927	CAB 21/307; CAB 16/79, part 9/290
47.	Private Secretary to King George V to Maurice Hankey	17 December 1927	CAB 21/310
48.	Maurice Hankey to First Sea Lord	22 December 1927	CAB 21/310; ADM 116/3619
49.	Belligerent rights at sea – American and British practices compared	14 January 1928	CAB 21/317; CAB 16/79, part 14/192–9

50. Belligerent rights at sea: 24 February 1928   CAB 16/79, part
    memorandum by Sir A.   19/362–5
    Steel-Maitland

51. Esme Howard to Austen   29 February 1928   CAB 16/79, part
    Chamberlain   23, no. 480/
                                                 321–2

52. Blockade –   April 1928   CAB 16/79/235–
    memorandum by Vice-   6; CAB 21/320
    Admiral Sir Herbert
    Richmond

53. The Havana Convention   1 May 1928   CAB 16/79/244

54. Sir Esme Howard to   17 May 1928   CAB 16/79, part
    Austen Chamberlain   35, no. 1042/425

55. Renewal of arbitration 5 October 1928   CAB 16/79/
    treaties   435–7

56. Public and private wars 31 December 1928   CAB 16/79, 57/
                                                 515–20

57. Secretary of State for the 28 January 1929   CAB 21/310
    Dominions to Maurice
    Hankey

58. Esme Howard to   26 January 1929   CAB 16/79/
    Secretary of State for   367–9
    Foreign Affairs

59. The renewal of   February 1929   CAB 16/79
    arbitration treaties: first
    report

60. Maritime belligerent   6 March 1929   CAB 16/79
    rights: second report

61. Hankey to Prime   11 October 1929   CAB 21/352/
    Minister Ramsay   212–23
    Macdonald

62. The food factor in   23 December 1929   CAB 21/328
    blockade

PART IV

63. The Spanish crisis   11 April 1937   CAB 23/88/
                                                 64–79

64. British attitude in the 19 August 1937   CO 323/1523/13
    event of a blockade by & 15 October
    Japan of Canton   1937

65.	Admiralty to Commander-in-Chief, Mediterranean	3 December 1937	ADM 1/9948
66.	Possible abrogation of the Declaration of Paris	31 May–15 June 1938	FO 371/21548
67.	Handbook of Economic Warfare	July 1939	FO 837/3
68.	Councillor, Foreign Affairs, to Secretary, Ministry of Economic Warfare	15 January 1940	BT 60/61/6, W.19227/16015/49
69.	Use of censorship	22 February 1940	BT 60/61/6, I.F. 255
70.	Report by Minister of Economic Warfare	10 June–10 July 1940	MT 59/285; W.P. (R) (40) 179
71.	Economic pressure through control of shipping	11 July 1940	MT 59/285
72.	Blockade policy	19 July 1941	CAB 66/17; W.P. (41) 175
73.	The food blockade and the occupied territories	28 July 1941	CAB 66/17/235
74.	The king's regulations and Admiralty instructions for the government of HM naval service	1943	HMSO
75.	Post-war assesment of naval requirements for economic warfare against a European enemy	25 February 1948 21 May 1948 & 1 June 1948	ADM 1/19992
76.	Commander-in-Chief, Far East Station, to all ships	24 June 1949	ADM 116/5713
77.	Admiralty to Commander-in-Chief Far East Station	9 September 1949	ADM 116/5713
78.	Nationalist blockade	10 September 1949	ADM 116/5713
79.	Dependence upon North America – World War II	21 April 1950	FO 371/82864

80.	Korean War: evaluation of west coast operation	*c.*19 June 1951	ADM 1/23676
81.	Cuban crisis: Prime Minister Macmillan to President Kennedy	22 October 1962	CAB 21/5581
82.	Kennedy to Macmillan	22 October 1962	CAB 21/5581
83.	Macmillan to ambassador to Washington	22 October 1962	CAB 21/5581
84.	Macmillan to Foreign Secretary	23 October 1962	CAB 21/5581
85.	Brief for Nassau talks	7 January 1963	FO 371/168177
86.	Lord Privy Seal: answer to parliamentary question	11 February 1963	FO 371/168178
87.	Beira Patrol: draft memorandum	[1970]	DEFE 24/588 E49
88.	Beira Patrol: briefs for new government	June 1970	DEFE 24/588 E135 5/10/7/1

GENERAL INDEX

541

SHIP INDEX

GAZETTEER

547

New York xx, xxii, xxxiii, 47, 200, 212, 406
New Zealand 160, 162, 326, 398
Nicaragua 104, 105, 343, 369
North Sea xxviii, xxix, 154, 156, 222, 225, 302, 330, 403
Norway 224–8, 501, 502
Nova Scotia xxxiii

Paengyong Do 525
Panama 105
Paraguay 99–101
Parana River 99,100, 106
Pearl Harbour xxxiii, 414, 415
Persian Gulf xxxvi, 343, 461, 512, 513
Plate, River (La Plata) 102, 105, 106, 110
Port Said 224
Portugal xxxv, 20, 21, 101, 331, 335, 502, 504, 507
Prussia viii, xvi, xxiii, 3, 14, 21, 23, 26–30, 32, 81, 91
Puerto Cabello112
Pyraeus 396

Rapidan River 205
Rhine, River 216
Rhodesia xxxv, 419, 531, 532
Rio Janeiro 69, 100, 104, 105, 107, 110, 527
Rotterdam 177, 216
Russia xvi–xx, xxiii, xxv, xxvi, xxviii, 3, 9–15, 17, 20, 21, 25–31, 39, 40, 72, 75, 76, 78–80, 88, 91, 217, 226, 242, 247, 248, 283, 287, 316, 333, 343, 393, 394, 414, 431, 534

St. Carlos 112
St. Jean de Luz 423
St. Juan d'Ulloa 79
St. Petersburg 27
Saddle Islands 516
Salonica 125
San Francisco xx, 212
San Juan 105
Santander 422–6
Sardinia 32, 91
Seven Islands, Republic of the 14
Shanghai 416, 432, 436, 437, 515
Shantung 525
Singapore 69, 401

Soo-au Bay 90
South African (Boer) xxvi, xxxv, 129, 160, 180, 181, 312, 419
South America xviii, 14, 69, 81, 91, 160, 280, 373, 498, 500, 546
Soviet Union (see Russia) xxxiv–xxxvi, 417, 505
Spain xv, xvii, xxiii, 14, 20, 21, 81, 82, 92, 102, 316, 348, 355, 411, 412, 420, 421, 429, 502, 513, 547
Sparta 396
Straits of Sunda 69, 71, 274
Straits Settlement 513
Suez xxxv, 416, 532
Sweden xxxv, 14, 21, 23, 193, 211, 225–8, 258, 261, 400, 502
Switzerland 225, 226, 355
Syria xxxvii, 99

Taedong 525
Tagus River 110
Texas 294
Tsingtao 125, 327, 427
Tokyo 438, 440–42
Tonkin 8
Turkey (Ottoman Porte) 72, 75–81, 84, 91
Tuscany 15

United States xiii, xvi, xviii, xix, xx, xxiii, xxv, xxvi, xxx–xxxvi, xxxix, 4, 6, 7, 9, 12, 14, 20, 21, 23, 32, 33, 35, 36–43, 46, 50, 52, 53, 70–75, 78, 82, 91–4, 97–101, 103, 122, 125–7, 130, 193, 197–206, 209, 210, 215, 228, 237, 241, 242, 248, 253, 266, 274, 282, 283, 287, 292–300, 305, 308, 309, 311–24, 327, 331–42, 345–56, 360, 363–83, 391, 395, 411, 414, 415–18, 437, 438, 441, 487, 496–9, 505, 527, 530
Uruguay 102, 106

Venezuela xxv, 8, 69, 92, 95, 101, 109–12
Venice 397
Versailles 290
Victoria State 149

Whangpo 520

Yalu 525
Yangtse 416, 432, 433, 515–20

NAVY RECORDS SOCIETY
(FOUNDED 1893)

The Navy Records Society was established for the purpose of printing unpublished manuscripts and rare works of naval interest. Membership of the Society is open to all who are interested in naval history, and any person wishing to become a member should apply to the Hon. Secretary, Professor A. D. Lambert, Department of War Studies, King's College London, Strand, London WC2R 2LS, United Kingdom. The annual subscription is £30, which entitles the member to receive one free copy of each work issued by the Society in that year, and to buy earlier issues at reduced prices.

A list of works, available to members only, is shown below; very few copies are left of those marked with an asterisk. Volumes out of print are indicated by **OP**. Prices for works in print are available on application to Mrs Annette Gould, 5 Goodwood Close, Midhurst, West Sussex GU29 9JG, United Kingdom, to whom all enquiries concerning works in print should be sent. Those marked 'TS', 'SP' and 'A' are published for the Society by Temple Smith, Scolar Press and Ashgate, and are available to non-members from the Ashgate Publishing Group, Gower House, Croft Road, Aldershot, Hampshire GU11 3HR. Those marked 'A & U' are published by George Allen & Unwin, and are available to non-members only through bookshops.

Vol. 1. *State papers relating to the Defeat of the Spanish Armada, Anno 1588*, Vol. I, ed. Professor J. K. Laughton. TS.

Vol. 2. *State papers relating to the Defeat of the Spanish Armada, Anno 1588*, Vol. II, ed. Professor J. K. Laughton. TS.

Vol. 3. *Letters of Lord Hood, 1781–1783*, ed. D. Hannay. **OP**.

Vol. 4. *Index to James's Naval History*, by C. G. Toogood, ed. by the Hon. T. A. Brassey. **OP**.

Vol. 5. *Life of Captain Stephen Martin, 1666–1740*, ed. Sir Clements R. Markham. **OP**.

Vol. 6. *Journal of Rear Admiral Bartholomew James, 1752–1828*, ed. Professor J. K. Laughton & Cdr. J. Y. F. Sullivan. **OP**.

Vol. 7. *Hollond's Discourses of the Navy, 1638 and 1659*, ed. J. R. Tanner. **OP**.

Vol. 8. *Naval Accounts and Inventories in the Reign of Henry VII*, ed. M. Oppenheim. **OP.**

Vol. 9. *Journal of Sir George Rooke*, ed. O. Browning. **OP.**

Vol. 10. *Letters and Papers relating to the War with France 1512–1513*, ed. M. Alfred Spont. **OP.**

Vol. 11. *Papers relating to the Spanish War 1585–1587*, ed. Julian S. Corbett. **TS.**

Vol. 12. *Journals and Letters of Admiral of the Fleet Sir Thomas Byam Martin, 1773–1854*, Vol. II (see No. 24), ed. Admiral Sir R. Vesey Hamilton. **OP.**

Vol. 13. *Papers relating to the First Dutch War, 1652–1654*, Vol. I, ed. Dr S. R. Gardiner. **OP.**

Vol. 14. *Papers relating to the Blockade of Brest, 1803–1805*, Vol. I, ed. J. Leyland. **OP.**

Vol. 15. *History of the Russian Fleet during the Reign of Peter the Great, by a Contemporary Englishman*, ed. Admiral Sir Cyprian Bridge. **OP.**

Vol. 16. *Logs of the Great Sea Fights, 1794–1805*, Vol. I, ed. Vice Admiral Sir T. Sturges Jackson. **OP.**

Vol. 17. *Papers relating to the First Dutch War, 1652–1654*, ed. Dr S. R. Gardiner. **OP.**

Vol. 18. *Logs of the Great Sea Fights*, Vol. II, ed. Vice Admiral Sir T. Sturges Jackson.

Vol. 19. *Journals and Letters of Admiral of the Fleet Sir Thomas Byam Martin*, Vol. II (see No. 24), ed. Admiral Sir R. Vesey Hamilton. **OP.**

Vol. 20. *The Naval Miscellany*, Vol. I, ed. Professor J. K. Laughton.

Vol. 21. *Papers relating to the Blockade of Brest, 1803–1805*, Vol. II, ed. J. Leyland. **OP.**

Vol. 22. *The Naval Tracts of Sir William Monson*, Vol. I, ed. M. Oppenheim. **OP.**

Vol. 23. *The Naval Tracts of Sir William Monson*, Vol. II, ed. M. Oppenheim. **OP.**

Vol. 24. *The Journals and Letters of Admiral of the Fleet Sir Thomas Byam Martin*, Vol. I, ed. Admiral Sir R. Vesey Hamilton.

Vol. 25. *Nelson and the Neapolitan Jacobins*, ed. H. C. Gutteridge. **OP.**

Vol. 26. *A Descriptive Catalogue of the Naval MSS in the Pepysian Library*, Vol. I, ed. J. R. Tanner. **OP.**

Vol. 27. *A Descriptive Catalogue of the Naval MSS in the Pepysian Library*, Vol. II, ed. J. R. Tanner. **OP.**

Vol. 28. *The Correspondence of Admiral John Markham, 1801–1807*, ed. Sir Clements R. Markham. **OP.**

Vol. 29. *Fighting Instructions, 1530–1816*, ed. Julian S. Corbett. **OP.**

Vol. 30. *Papers relating to the First Dutch War, 1652–1654*, Vol. III, ed. Dr S. R. Gardiner & C. T. Atkinson. **OP**.

Vol. 31. *The Recollections of Commander James Anthony Gardner, 1775–1814*, ed. Admiral Sir R. Vesey Hamilton & Professor J. K. Laughton.

Vol. 32. *Letters and Papers of Charles, Lord Barham, 1758–1813*, ed. Professor Sir John Laughton.

Vol. 33. *Naval Songs and Ballads*, ed. Professor C. H. Firth. **OP**.

Vol. 34. *Views of the Battles of the Third Dutch War*, ed. by Julian S. Corbett. **OP**.

Vol. 35. *Signals and Instructions, 1776–1794*, ed. Julian S. Corbett. **OP**.

Vol. 36. *A Descriptive Catalogue of the Naval MSS in the Pepysian Library*, Vol III, ed. J. R. Tanner. **OP**.

Vol. 37. *Papers relating to the First Dutch War, 1652–1654*, Vol. IV, ed. C. T. Atkinson. **OP**.

Vol. 38. *Letters and Papers of Charles, Lord Barham, 1758–1813*, Vol. II, ed. Professor Sir John Laughton. **OP**.

Vol. 39. *Letters and Papers of Charles, Lord Barham, 1758–1813*, Vol. III, ed. Professor Sir John Laughton. **OP**.

Vol. 40. *The Naval Miscellany*, Vol. II, ed. Professor Sir John Laughton.

*Vol. 41. *Papers relating to the First Dutch War, 1652–1654*, Vol. V, ed. C. T. Atkinson.

Vol. 42. *Papers relating to the Loss of Minorca in 1756*, ed. Captain H. W. Richmond, R.N. **OP**.

*Vol. 43. *The Naval Tracts of Sir William Monson*, Vol. III, ed. M. Oppenheim.

Vol. 44. *The Old Scots Navy 1689–1710*, ed. James Grant. **OP**.

Vol. 45. *The Naval Tracts of Sir William Monson*, Vol. IV, ed. M. Oppenheim.

Vol. 46. *The Private Papers of George, 2nd Earl Spencer*, Vol. I, ed. Julian S. Corbett. **OP**.

Vol. 47. *The Naval Tracts of Sir William Monson*, Vol. V, ed. M. Oppenheim.

Vol. 48. *The Private Papers of George, 2nd Earl Spencer*, Vol. II, ed. Julian S. Corbett. **OP**.

Vol. 49. *Documents relating to Law and Custom of the Sea*, Vol. I, ed. R. G. Marsden. **OP**.

*Vol. 50. *Documents relating to Law and Custom of the Sea*, Vol. II, ed. R. G. Marsden.

Vol. 51. *Autobiography of Phineas Pett*, ed. W. G. Perrin. **OP**.

Vol. 52. *The Life of Admiral Sir John Leake*, Vol. I, ed. Geoffrey Callender.

Vol. 53. *The Life of Admiral Sir John Leake*, Vol. II, ed. Geoffrey Callender.

Vol. 54. *The Life and Works of Sir Henry Mainwaring*, Vol. I, ed. G. E. Manwaring.

Vol. 55. *The Letters of Lord St Vincent, 1801–1804*, Vol. I, ed. D. B. Smith. **OP**.

Vol. 56. *The Life and Works of Sir Henry Mainwaring*, Vol. II, ed. G. E. Manwaring & W. G. Perrin. **OP**.

Vol. 57. *A Descriptive Catalogue of the Naval MSS in the Pepysian Library*, Vol. IV, ed. Dr J. R. Tanner. **OP**.

Vol. 58. *The Private Papers of George, 2nd Earl Spencer*, Vol. III, ed. Rear Admiral H. W. Richmond. **OP**.

Vol. 59. *The Private Papers of George, 2nd Earl Spencer*, Vol. IV, ed. Rear Admiral H. W. Richmond. **OP**.

Vol. 60. *Samuel Pepys's Naval Minutes*, ed. Dr J. R. Tanner.

Vol. 61. *The Letters of Lord St Vincent, 1801–1804*, Vol. II, ed. D. B. Smith. **OP**.

Vol. 62. *Letters and Papers of Admiral Viscount Keith*, Vol. I, ed. W. G. Perrin. **OP**.

Vol. 63. *The Naval Miscellany*, Vol. III, ed. W. G. Perrin. **OP**.

Vol. 64. *The Journal of the 1st Earl of Sandwich*, ed. R. C. Anderson. **OP**.

*Vol. 65. *Boteler's Dialogues*, ed. W. G. Perrin.

Vol. 66. *Papers relating to the First Dutch War, 1652–1654*, Vol. VI (with index), ed. C. T. Atkinson.

*Vol. 67. *The Byng Papers*, Vol. I, ed. W. C. B. Tunstall.

*Vol. 68. *The Byng Papers*, Vol. II, ed. W. C. B. Tunstall.

Vol. 69. *The Private Papers of John, Earl of Sandwich*, Vol. I, ed. G. R. Barnes & Lt. Cdr. J. H. Owen, R.N. Corrigenda to *Papers relating to the First Dutch War, 1652–1654, Vols I–VI*, ed. Captain A. C. Dewar, R.N. **OP**.

Vol. 70. *The Byng Papers*, Vol. III, ed. W. C. B. Tunstall.

Vol. 71. *The Private Papers of John, Earl of Sandwich*, Vol. II, ed. G. R. Barnes & Lt. Cdr. J. H. Owen, R.N. **OP**.

Vol. 72. *Piracy in the Levant, 1827–1828*, ed. Lt. Cdr. C. G. Pitcairn Jones, R.N. **OP**.

Vol. 73. *The Tangier Papers of Samuel Pepys*, ed. Edwin Chappell.

Vol. 74. *The Tomlinson Papers*, ed. J. G. Bullocke.

Vol. 75. *The Private Papers of John, Earl of Sandwich*, Vol. III, ed. G. R. Barnes & Cdr. J. H. Owen, R.N. **OP**.

Vol. 76. *The Letters of Robert Blake*, ed. the Rev. J. R. Powell. **OP**.

*Vol. 77. *Letters and Papers of Admiral the Hon. Samuel Barrington*, Vol. I, ed. D. Bonner-Smith.

Vol. 78. *The Private Papers of John, Earl of Sandwich*, Vol. IV, ed. G. R. Barnes & Cdr. J. H. Owen, R.N. **OP**.

*Vol. 79. *The Journals of Sir Thomas Allin, 1660–1678*, Vol. I *1660–1666*, ed. R. C. Anderson.

Vol. 80. *The Journals of Sir Thomas Allin, 1660–1678*, Vol. II *1667–1678*, ed. R. C. Anderson.

Vol. 81. *Letters and Papers of Admiral the Hon. Samuel Barrington*, Vol. II, ed. D. Bonner-Smith. **OP**.

Vol. 82. *Captain Boteler's Recollections, 1808–1830*, ed. D. Bonner-Smith. **OP**.

Vol. 83. *Russian War, 1854. Baltic and Black Sea: Official Correspondence*, ed. D. Bonner-Smith & Captain A. C. Dewar, R.N. **OP**.

Vol. 84. *Russian War, 1855. Baltic: Official Correspondence*, ed. D. Bonner-Smith. **OP**.

Vol. 85. *Russian War, 1855. Black Sea: Official Correspondence*, ed. Captain A.C. Dewar, R.N. **OP**.

Vol. 86. *Journals and Narratives of the Third Dutch War*, ed. R. C. Anderson. **OP**.

Vol. 87. *The Naval Brigades in the Indian Mutiny, 1857–1858*, ed. Cdr. W. B. Rowbotham, R.N. **OP**.

Vol. 88. *Patee Byng's Journal*, ed. J. L. Cranmer-Byng. **OP**.

*Vol. 89. *The Sergison Papers, 1688–1702*, ed. Cdr. R. D. Merriman, R.I.N.

Vol. 90. *The Keith Papers*, Vol. II, ed. Christopher Lloyd. **OP**.

Vol. 91. *Five Naval Journals, 1789–1817*, ed. Rear Admiral H. G. Thursfield. **OP**.

Vol. 92. *The Naval Miscellany*, Vol. IV, ed. Christopher Lloyd. **OP**.

Vol. 93. *Sir William Dillon's Narrative of Professional Adventures, 1790–1839*, Vol. I *1790–1802*, ed. Professor Michael Lewis. **OP**.

Vol. 94. *The Walker Expedition to Quebec, 1711*, ed. Professor Gerald S. Graham. **OP**.

Vol. 95. *The Second China War, 1856–1860*, ed. D. Bonner-Smith & E. W. R. Lumby. **OP**.

Vol. 96. *The Keith Papers, 1803–1815*, Vol. III, ed. Professor Christopher Lloyd.

Vol. 97. *Sir William Dillon's Narrative of Professional Adventures, 1790–1839*, Vol. II *1802–1839*, ed. Professor Michael Lewis. **OP**.

Vol. 98. *The Private Correspondence of Admiral Lord Collingwood*, ed. Professor Edward Hughes. **OP**.

Vol. 99. *The Vernon Papers, 1739–1745*, ed. B. McL. Ranft. **OP**.

Vol. 100. *Nelson's Letters to his Wife and Other Documents*, ed. Lt. Cdr. G. P. B. Naish, R.N.V.R.

Vol. 101. *A Memoir of James Trevenen, 1760–1790*, ed. Professor Christopher Lloyd & R. C. Anderson. **OP**.

Vol. 102. *The Papers of Admiral Sir John Fisher*, Vol. I, ed. Lt. Cdr. P. K. Kemp, R.N. **OP**.

Vol. 103. *Queen Anne's Navy*, ed. Cdr. R. D. Merriman, R.I.N. **OP**.

Vol. 104. *The Navy and South America, 1807–1823*, ed. Professor Gerald S. Graham & Professor R. A. Humphreys.

Vol. 105. *Documents relating to the Civil War, 1642–1648*, ed. The Rev. J. R. Powell & E. K. Timings. **OP**.

Vol. 106. *The Papers of Admiral Sir John Fisher*, Vol. II, ed. Lt. Cdr. P. K. Kemp, R.N. **OP**.

Vol. 107. *The Health of Seamen*, ed. Professor Christopher Lloyd.

Vol. 108. *The Jellicoe Papers*, Vol. I *1893–1916*, ed. A. Temple Patterson.

Vol. 109. *Documents relating to Anson's Voyage round the World, 1740–1744*, ed. Dr Glyndwr Williams. **OP**.

Vol. 110. *The Saumarez Papers: The Baltic, 1808–1812*, ed. A. N. Ryan. **OP**.

Vol. 111. *The Jellicoe Papers*, Vol. II *1916–1925*, ed. Professor A. Temple Patterson.

Vol. 112. *The Rupert and Monck Letterbook, 1666*, ed. The Rev. J. R. Powell & E. K. Timings.

Vol. 113. *Documents relating to the Royal Naval Air Service*, Vol. I (1908–1918), ed. Captain S. W. Roskill, R.N.

*Vol. 114. *The Siege and Capture of Havana, 1762*, ed. Professor David Syrett.

Vol. 115. *Policy and Operations in the Mediterranean, 1912–1914*, ed. E. W. R. Lumby. **OP**.

Vol. 116. *The Jacobean Commissions of Enquiry, 1608 and 1618*, ed. Dr A. P. McGowan.

Vol. 117. *The Keyes Papers*, Vol. I *1914–1918*, ed. Professor Paul Halpern.

Vol. 118. *The Royal Navy and North America: The Warren Papers, 1736–1752*, ed. Dr Julian Gwyn. **OP**.

Vol. 119. *The Manning of the Royal Navy: Selected Public Pamphlets, 1693–1873*, ed. Professor John Bromley.

Vol. 120. *Naval Administration, 1715–1750*, ed. Professor D. A. Baugh.

Vol. 121. *The Keyes Papers*, Vol. II *1919–1938*, ed. Professor Paul Halpern.

Vol. 122. *The Keyes Papers*, Vol. III *1939–1945*, ed. Professor Paul Halpern.

Vol. 123. *The Navy of the Lancastrian Kings: Accounts and Inventories of William Soper, Keeper of the King's Ships, 1422–1427*, ed. Dr Susan Rose.

Vol. 124. *The Pollen Papers: the Privately Circulated Printed Works of Arthur Hungerford Pollen, 1901–1916*, ed. Professor Jon T. Sumida. A. & U.

Vol. 125. *The Naval Miscellany*, Vol. V, ed. Dr N. A. M. Rodger. A & U.

Vol. 126. *The Royal Navy in the Mediterranean, 1915–1918*, ed. Professor Paul Halpern. TS.

Vol. 127. *The Expedition of Sir John Norris and Sir Francis Drake to Spain and Portugal, 1589*, ed. Professor R. B. Wernham. TS.

Vol. 128. *The Beatty Papers*, Vol. I *1902–1918*, ed. Professor B. McL. Ranft. SP.

Vol. 129. *The Hawke Papers: A Selection, 1743–1771*, ed. Dr R. F. Mackay. SP.

Vol. 130. *Anglo-American Naval Relations, 1917–1919*, ed. Michael Simpson. SP.

Vol. 131. *British Naval Documents, 1204–1960*, ed. Professor John B. Hattendorf, Dr Roger Knight, Alan Pearsall, Dr Nicholas Rodger & Professor Geoffrey Till. SP.

Vol. 132. *The Beatty Papers*, Vol. II *1916–1927*, ed. Professor B. McL. Ranft. SP

Vol. 133. *Samuel Pepys and the Second Dutch War*, transcribed by Professor William Matthews & Dr Charles Knighton; ed. Robert Latham. SP.

Vol. 134. *The Somerville Papers*, ed. Michael Simpson, with the assistance of John Somerville. SP.

Vol. 135. *The Royal Navy in the River Plate, 1806–1807*, ed. John D. Grainger. SP.

Vol. 136. *The Collective Naval Defence of the Empire, 1900–1940*, ed. Nicholas Tracy. A.

Vol. 137. *The Defeat of the Enemy Attack on Shipping, 1939–1945*, ed. Eric Grove. A.

Vol. 138. *Shipboard Life and Organisation, 1731–1815*, ed. Brian Lavery. A.

Vol. 139. *The Battle of the Atlantic and Signals Intelligence: U-boat Situations and Trends, 1941–1945*, ed. Professor David Syrett. A.

Vol. 140. *The Cunningham Papers*, Vol. I: *The Mediterranean Fleet, 1939–1942*, ed. Michael Simpson. A.

Vol. 141. *The Channel Fleet and the Blockade of Brest, 1793–1801*, ed. Roger Morriss. A.

Vol. 142. *The Submarine Service, 1900–1918*, ed. Nicholas Lambert. A.

Vol. 143. *Letters and Papers of Professor Sir John Knox Laughton (1830–1915)*, ed. Andrew Lambert. A.

Vol. 144. *The Battle of the Atlantic and Signals Intelligence: U-Boat Tracking Papers 1941–1947*, ed. Professor David Syrett. A.

Vol. 145. *The Maritime Blockade of Germany in the Great War: The Northern Patrol, 1914–1918*, ed. John D. Grainger. A.

Vol. 146. *The Naval Miscellany: Volume VI*, ed. Michael Duffy. A.

Vol. 147. *The Milne Papers*, Vol. I *1820–1859*, ed. Professor John Beeler. A.

Vol. 148. *The Rodney Papers*, Vol. I *1742–1763*, ed. Professor David Syrett. A.

Occasional Publications:

Vol. 1. *The Commissioned Sea Officers of the Royal Navy, 1660–1815*, ed. Professor David Syrett & Professor R. L. DiNardo. SP.

Vol. 2. *The Anthony Roll of Henry VIII's Navy*, ed. C. S. Knighton and D. M. Loades. A.